—COMPLETE—
PEOPLE &
PLACES

OF THE BIBLE

PAMELA L. MCQUADE

BARBOUR BOOKS
An Imprint of Barbour Publishing, Inc.

Published by Barbour Books, an imprint of Barbour Publishing, Inc., P.O. Box 719, Uhrichsville, Ohio 44683, www.barbourbooks.com.

Our mission is to publish and distribute inspirational products offering exceptional value and biblical encouragement to the masses.

 Member of the
Evangelical Christian
Publishers Association

Printed in the United States of America.

INTRODUCTION

Complete People and Places of the Bible is designed to help students of the Word understand all the specifically named characters and locales of scripture. In the pages following, you'll find information on more than 3,000 names found in the Bible—just over 2,000 people names (covering some 3,400 individuals) and approximately 1,000 place names—providing concise details on each one's contribution to the story of God's Word.

Names were very important to the people of Bible times. People's names had meanings, often assigned by a child's parents but occasionally by God Himself. Places were often named to reflect incidents that occurred there. Throughout this book, the meanings of Hebrew-based names are given; where no meaning of a name is shown, it is unknown or of foreign derivation.

In addition to meanings, the names in *Complete People and Places of the Bible* are also accompanied by

- A quick visual indicator for "people" or "place"
- The number of times mentioned; an overall figure for all people by the name, a breakdown of Old Testament and New Testament usages for place names
- The number of men or women with a particular name
- A notation indicating if a person is found in the genealogy of Jesus
- Essays describing the persons or places, with more important names receiving proportionally longer entries
- Scripture references for further study; every entry will have at least one reference (first or only), while more prominent entries will also include other key chapter-and-verse notations

Names and spellings in *Complete People and Places of the Bible* are those used in the King James Version of the Bible. This work is based on *Strong's Expanded, Exhaustive Concordance of the Bible*, a classic reference that uses the King James Version as its source. But since many readers use other Bible versions, we have sometimes provided alternative translations (for example, the Wilderness of Zin may be referred to as the Desert of Zin).

Where a person had more than one name or scripture provides us with variations of the name, alternative names or spellings are listed at the end of the biography section. For example, Jashub's biography includes the information "Same as Job (1)," referring readers to the first listing for the name Job. Please note that we have not included titles or the names of spirit beings in this dictionary.

To assist you in understanding the geography of the areas referred to in scripture, seven maps have been included beginning on page 485. Many places, especially in the Old Testament and where a name is mentioned only once, cannot be accurately identified. On some maps, a question mark indicates that scholars are not certain this is the correct site.

Because the scriptures deal with many people, places, and nations, we have provided a time line that can help you sort out the differences of empires, rulers, and times. The dates are often approximate, since accurate dating at such a distance and in various cultures is difficult. Scholars often disagree on exact dates for many of these events; and a few dates, such as those of the ministries of the prophets Obadiah and Joel, remain inconclusive. We are deeply indebted to Stephen M. Miller's book *The Complete Guide to the Bible* (Barbour Publishing) for the lists of the kings of Israel and Judah and the prophets.

For the many hundreds of people and places recorded in scripture, this book will provide the concise information you need to quickly understand their background, prominence, and contribution to history. We hope *Complete People and Places of the Bible* will spur you on to further study of scripture.

TIME LINES

Old Testament History

2100–1500 BC Age of the patriarchs (Middle Bronze Age)

c. 1950 BC The Amorites conquer Mesopotamia

1500–1200 BC The Exodus and the Promised Land conquest (Late Bronze Age)

c. 1469–c. 1211 BC Possible dates for the Exodus

1200–900 BC Establishment of Israel (Early Iron Age)

c. 1050 BC The Philistines settle in southern Palestine

Ancient Empires

Assyrian Empire 1100–609 BC

859–824 BC Reign of King Shalmaneser III

855–625 BC Assyrian influence on Palestine

783–773 BC Reign of King Shalmaneser IV

744–727 BC Reign of King Tiglath-pileser III

c. 732–612 BC Israel and Judah subject to Assyria

727–722 BC Fall of Israel to Assyria; Samaria destroyed

722 BC Reign of King Shalmaneser V

705–681 BC Reign of King Sennacherib

612 BC Fall of Nineveh to Neo-Babylonian (Chaldean) Empire

609 BC Chaldeans defeat Assyria

Neo-Babylonian (Chaldean) Empire 605–538 BC

c. 626 BC Start of Neo-Babylonian (Chaldean) Empire

586 BC Fall of Jerusalem to the Chaldeans; temple destroyed

539 BC Fall of Neo-Babylonian Empire

Persian Empire 538–331 BC

538 BC Cyrus conquers Babylon (Chaldea) and establishes Persian Empire

522–485 BC Reign of King Darius I

486–465 BC Reign of King Ahasuerus (Xerxes) of Persia

c. 479 BC Esther made queen of Persia

465–423 BC Reign of King Artaxerxes I of Persia

333 BC End of Persian control of Palestine

331 BC End of Persian Empire

Macedonian Empire 336–168 BC

336–323 BC Rule of Alexander the Great

333 BC Alexander the Great gains control of Palestine

331 BC Alexander the Great conquers Persian Empire

Seleucid rule 312–83 BC

175–163 BC Rule of Syrian king Antiochus IV (Epiphanes)

Roman Empire 27 BC–AD 476

63 BC Roman Empire takes control of Judaea

37–4 BC Reign of Herod the Great, king of Judaea

Israel/Judah

Prophets

770–750 BC Ministry of the prophet Jonah in Assyria

763–750 BC Ministry of the prophet Amos in Israel

750–722 BC Ministry of the prophet Hosea in Israel

742–687 BC Ministry of the prophet Micah in Judah

740–700 BC Ministry of the prophet Isaiah in Judah

640–621 BC Ministry of the prophet Zephaniah in Judah

627–586 BC Ministry of the prophet Jeremiah in Judah

612–588 BC Ministry of the prophet Habakkuk in Judah

c. 605–536 BC Ministry of the prophet Daniel in Babylon

593–571 BC Ministry of the prophet Ezekiel in Babylon

c. 586 BC Book of Obadiah written to Judah

520 BC Book of Haggai written to Judah

520–518 BC Ministry of the prophet Zechariah in Judah

440–430 BC Ministry of the prophet Malachi in Judah

Rulers

United Israel

1050–1010 BC Reign of King Saul of Israel

1023 BC Samuel anoints David king of Israel

1010–970 BC Reign of King David of Israel

970–930 BC Reign of King Solomon of Israel

c. 966–959 BC King Solomon builds the temple

Divided Israel

930 BC Start of Divided Kingdom (separate states of Israel and Judah)

Judah

930–913 BC Reign of King Rehoboam
913–910 BC Reign of King Abijam
910–872 BC Reign of King Asa
872–853 BC Reign of King Jehoshaphat
853–841 BC Reign of King Jehoram
841 BC Reign of King Ahaziah
841–835 BC Reign of Queen Athaliah
835–796 BC Reign of King Joash
796–792 BC Reign of King Amaziah
792–750 BC Reign of King Azariah (Uzziah)
750–735 BC Reign of King Jotham
735–715 BC Reign of King Ahaz
715–697 BC Reign of King Hezekiah
697–642 BC Reign of King Manasseh
642–640 BC Reign of King Amon
640–609 BC Reign of King Josiah
609 BC Reign of King Jehoahaz
609–598 BC Reign of King Jehoiakim
598–597 BC Reign of King Jehoiachin
597–586 BC Reign of King Zedekiah

Northern Israel

930–909 BC Reign of King Jeroboam I
909–908 BC Reign of King Nadab
908–886 BC Reign of King Baasha
886–885 BC Reign of King Elah
885–874 BC Reign of King Omri
874–853 BC Reign of King Ahab
853–852 BC Reign of King Ahaziah
852–841 BC Reign of King Joram (Jehoram)
841–814 BC Reign of King Jehu
814–798 BC Reign of King Jehoahaz
798–793 BC Reign of King Jehoash
793–753 BC Reign of King Jeroboam II
753–752 BC Reign of King Zechariah
752 BC Reign of King Shallum
752–742 BC Reign of King Menahem
742–740 BC Reign of King Pekahiah
740–732 BC Reign of King Pekah
732–722 BC Reign of King Hoshea

586 BC Babylonian Empire conquers Judah and destroys Jerusalem and Solomon's temple
538 BC The first exiles return to Jerusalem

c. 516 BC Second temple completed
457 BC Ezra returns to Judah with more exiles
c. 445 BC Nehemiah leads Jews back to Jerusalem
432 BC Nehemiah's second visit to Jerusalem
152–37 BC Rule of the Maccabees

New Testament

c. 6 BC Birth of Jesus
4 BC–AD 6 Rule of Herod Archelaus, ethnarch of Judaea, Samaria, and Idumea
4 BC–AD 39 Rule of Herod Antipas, tetrarch of Galilee and Perea
4 BC–AD 34 Rule of Herod Philip, tetrarch of Iturea and Trachonitis
AD 26 Jesus' public ministry begins
AD 30 Jesus' death and resurrection
AD 47–49 Paul's first missionary journey
AD 49 Roman emperor Claudius expels Jews from Rome; church holds Council of Jerusalem
AD 50–52 Paul's second missionary journey
c. AD 52–56 Paul's third missionary journey
AD 59 Paul's first Roman imprisonment begins
AD 67–68 Paul's final imprisonment and death in Rome
AD 70 Herod's temple destroyed

👥 AARON

\# of times mentioned: 350
\# of MEN by this name: 1

Meaning: Uncertain

The older brother of Moses, Aaron was called into God's service when Moses balked at confronting Pharaoh about his enslavement of the people of Israel. "I know that he can speak well," God said of Aaron (Exodus 4:14). He became God's spokesman and supported Moses' leadership for nearly forty years. He was the first priest of Israel and headed a familial line of priests that continued for more than a thousand years. But Aaron made three memorable mistakes: He created a golden calf idol for the people of Israel when Moses stayed long on Mount Sinai receiving God's Ten Commandments (Exodus 32)—starting a cycle of idolatry that would plague the Israelites for centuries. He and his sister, Miriam, complained about Moses' Ethiopian wife—and Miriam contracted a temporary case of leprosy as punishment (Numbers 12). And Aaron and Moses both incurred God's judgment—banishment from the Promised Land—when they disobeyed the Lord by striking, rather than speaking to, a rock to provide miraculous water for the people at Kadesh (Numbers 20). Aaron died at age 123 on Mount Hor (Numbers 33:39), with his brother at his side.

First reference: Exodus 4:14 / Last reference: Hebrews 9:4 / Key references: Exodus 4:30; 32:2–4; Leviticus 9:7

👥 ABAGTHA

\# of times mentioned: 1
\# of MEN by this name: 1

One of seven eunuchs serving the Persian king Ahasuerus in Esther's time.

Only reference: Esther 1:10

📍 ABANA

\# of times mentioned: OT 1

Meaning: Stony

A river of Damascus that the Syrian commander Naaman would have preferred to the Jordan River as a place to wash away his leprosy.

Only reference: 2 Kings 5:12

📍 ABARIM

\# of times mentioned: OT 4

Meaning: Regions beyond

On their way to conquer the Holy Land, Moses and the Israelites pitched their tents in this mountain range east of the Jordan River. From Mount Nebo, which was part of the Abarim range, God allowed Moses a view of the Holy Land just before he died.

First reference: Numbers 27:12 / Last reference: Deuteronomy 32:49

👥 ABDA

\# of times mentioned: 2
\# of MEN by this name: 2

Meaning: Work

1) Father of King Solomon's official over forced labor, Adoniram.

Only reference: 1 Kings 4:6

2) A Levite worship leader in Jerusalem after the Babylonian Exile.

Only reference: Nehemiah 11:17

👥 ABDEEL

\# of times mentioned: 1
\# of MEN by this name: 1

Meaning: Serving God

Father of Shelemiah, an official under Judah's king Jehoiakim.

Only reference: Jeremiah 36:26

👥 ABDI

\# of times mentioned: 3
\# of MEN by this name: 2

Meaning: Serviceable

1) A Levite, father of temple servant Kish of King Hezekiah's day.

First reference: 1 Chronicles 6:44 / Last reference: 2 Chronicles 29:12

2) An exiled Israelite who married a "strange" (foreign) woman.

Only reference: Ezra 10:26

👥 ABDIEL

of times mentioned: 1
# of MEN by this name: 1

Meaning: Servant of God

A descendant of Abraham through Jacob's son Gad.

Only reference: 1 Chronicles 5:15

👥 ABDON

of times mentioned: 6
# of MEN by this name: 4

Meaning: Servitude

1) The twelfth judge of Israel who led the nation for eight years. He was known for having forty sons and thirty nephews who each rode a donkey.

First reference: Judges 12:13 / Last reference: Judges 12:15

2) A descendant of Abraham through Jacob's son Benjamin.

Only reference: 1 Chronicles 8:23

3) Another descendant of Abraham through Jacob's son Benjamin.

First reference: 1 Chronicles 8:30 / Last reference: 1 Chronicles 9:36

4) One of five men sent by King Josiah to ask God's prophetess Huldah what to do about the "book of the law" recently discovered in the temple.

Only reference: 2 Chronicles 34:20

📍 ABDON

of times mentioned: OT 2

Meaning: Servitude

One of the forty-eight cities given to the Levites as God had commanded. Abdon was given to them by the tribe of Asher.

First reference: Joshua 21:30 / Last reference: 1 Chronicles 6:74

👥 ABED-NEGO

of times mentioned: 15
# of MEN by this name: 1

The Babylonian name for Azariah, one of Daniel's companions in exile. Daniel had King Nebuchadnezzar make Abed-nego a ruler in Babylon. When some Chaldeans accused Abed-nego and his fellow Jews and corulers, Shadrach and Meshach, of not worshipping the king's golden idol, the three faithful Jews were thrown into a furnace. God protected His men, who were not even singed. The king recognized the power of their God and promoted them in his service.

First reference: Daniel 1:7 / Last reference: Daniel 3:30 / Key reference: Daniel 3:16–18

👥 ABEL

of times mentioned: 12
# of MEN by this name: 1

Meaning: Emptiness or vanity

Humanity's fourth member, the second son of Adam and Eve, Abel was murdered by his jealous brother, Cain. Abel the shepherd's meat offering pleased God more than Cain's "fruit of the ground." When God asked Cain the whereabouts of his murdered brother, Cain replied, "I know not: Am I my brother's keeper?" (Genesis 4:9). Jesus called Abel "righteous" in His denunciation of the scribes and Pharisees for persecuting the prophets.

First reference: Genesis 4:2 / Last reference: Hebrews 12:24 / Key reference: Genesis 4:4

📍 ABEL

of times mentioned: OT 4

1) A stone in Joshua the Beth-shemite's field. After the Philistines stole the ark of the covenant and returned it to Israel on a cart pulled by two milk cows, the ark was set here. When God struck down seventy men for looking upon the ark, the people of Beth-shemesh asked the people of Kirjath-jearim to take it to their city.

Only reference: 1 Samuel 6:18

2) A city in the land of the tribe of Naphtali that David's battle commander Joab besieged in order to capture the rebel Sheba, who had risen up against David's rule.

First reference: 2 Samuel 20:14 / Last reference: 2 Samuel 20:18

ABEL-BETH-MAACHAH

of times mentioned: OT 2

Meaning: Meadow of Beth-maachah

One of three cities in Naphtali that was attacked by the Syrian prince Ben-hadad, at the instigation of King Asa of Judah. During the reign of Pekah, king of Israel, Abel-beth-maachah was conquered by the Assyrian king Tiglath-pileser III, who took its people into captivity in Assyria. Same as Abel-maim.

First reference: 1 Kings 15:20 / Last reference: 2 Kings 15:29

ABEL-MAIM

of times mentioned: OT 1

Meaning: Meadow of water

A city in northern Israel that was attacked by the Syrian prince Ben-hadad, at the instigation of King Asa of Judah. Same as Abel-beth-maachah.

Only reference: 2 Chronicles 16:4

ABEL-MEHOLAH

of times mentioned: OT 3

Meaning: Meadow of dancing

A city in the Jordan Valley. When Gideon's army routed them, the Midianites fled to Abel-meholah's border. Under King Solomon's governmental organization, Baana was the officer in charge of providing the king with provisions from this place. The prophet Elisha came from Abel-meholah.

First reference: Judges 7:22 / Last reference: 1 Kings 19:16

ABEL-MIZRAIM

of times mentioned: OT 1

Meaning: Meadow of Egypt

Joseph brought the body of his father, Jacob, to Abel-mizraim and buried him at this "threshing floor of Atad," east of the Jordan River. When the Canaanites saw Egyptians mourning there, they gave the place this name. Same as Atad.

Only reference: Genesis 50:11

ABEL-SHITTIM

of times mentioned: OT 1

Meaning: Meadow of acacias

A spot in the plains of Moab where the Israelites camped before entering the Promised Land.

Only reference: Numbers 33:49

ABEZ

of times mentioned: OT 1

Meaning: To gleam; conspicuous

A city that became part of the inheritance of Issachar when Joshua cast lots in Shiloh to provide territory for the seven tribes that had yet to receive their land.

Only reference: Joshua 19:20

ABI

of times mentioned: 1
# of WOMEN by this name: 1

Meaning: Fatherly

Daughter of Zachariah and mother of Judah's good king Hezekiah.

Only reference: 2 Kings 18:2

ABIA

of times mentioned: 4
# of MEN by this name: 2

Meaning: Worshipper of God

1) Grandson of King Solomon and son of King Rehoboam. He inherited the throne of Judah. Same as Abijah (3).

First reference: 1 Chronicles 3:10 / Last reference: Matthew 1:7

Genealogy of Jesus: Yes (Matthew 1:7)

2) A priest who headed a division of priests at the time of Jesus' birth.

Only reference: Luke 1:5

ABIAH

of times mentioned: 4
# of MEN by this name: 2
# of WOMEN by this name: 1

Meaning: Worshipper of God

1) The second son of the prophet Samuel. Abiah and his brother, Joel, served as judges in Beersheba, but their poor character caused Israel's leaders to ask Samuel for a king to rule over them.

First reference: 1 Samuel 8:2 / Last reference: 1 Chronicles 6:28

2) Wife of Hezron, a descendant of Abraham through Jacob's son Judah.

Only reference: 1 Chronicles 2:24

3) A descendant of Abraham through Jacob's son Benjamin.

Only reference: 1 Chronicles 7:8

ABI-ALBON

of times mentioned: 1
# of MEN by this name: 1

Meaning: Father of strength

One of King David's warriors known as the "mighty men."

Only reference: 2 Samuel 23:31

ABIASAPH

of times mentioned: 1
# of MEN by this name: 1

Meaning: Gatherer

A descendant of Abraham through Jacob's son Levi.

Only reference: Exodus 6:24

ABIATHAR

of times mentioned: 31
# of MEN by this name: 1

Meaning: Father of abundance

The only priest of Nob who escaped when King Saul killed this enclave of priests because they supported David. He became one of David's trusted counselors and the high priest of Israel. But at the end of David's life, Abiathar supported David's son Adonijah as king and drew King Solomon's displeasure down on him. He was banished to his home, though he kept the title of high priest.

First reference: 1 Samuel 22:20 / Last reference: Mark 2:26 / Key references: 1 Samuel 22:21–22; 1 Kings 1:7

ABIDA

of times mentioned: 1
# of MEN by this name: 1

Meaning: Knowing

A descendant of Abraham through his second wife, Keturah. Same as Abidah.

Only reference: 1 Chronicles 1:33

ABIDAH

of times mentioned: 1
# of MEN by this name: 1

Meaning: Knowing

A descendant of Abraham through his second wife, Keturah. Same as Abida.

Only reference: Genesis 25:4

ABIDAN

of times mentioned: 5
# of MEN by this name: 1

Meaning: Judge

A prince of Benjamin who helped Moses take a census of his tribe.

First reference: Numbers 1:11 / Last reference: Numbers 10:24

ABIEL

of times mentioned: 3
# of MEN by this name: 2

Meaning: Possessor of God

1) Grandfather of Israel's king Saul and Saul's army commander, Abner.

First reference: 1 Samuel 9:1 / Last reference: 1 Samuel 14:51

2) One of King David's valiant warriors.

Only reference: 1 Chronicles 11:32

ABIEZER

of times mentioned: 7
# of MEN by this name: 2

Meaning: Helpful

1) A descendant of Abraham through Joseph's son Manasseh.

First reference: Joshua 17:2 / Last reference: 1 Chronicles 7:18

2) A commander in King David's army, overseeing twenty-four thousand men in the ninth month of each year.

First reference: 2 Samuel 23:27 / Last reference: 1 Chronicles 27:12

ABIGAIL

of times mentioned: 17
# of WOMEN by this name: 2

Meaning: Source of joy

1) A wife of King David. She provided food for David and his men after her first husband, Nabal, refused to help these warriors who defended his land from harm while King Saul and David fought. Nabal died following his wife's telling him what she had done. Because David appreciated Abigail, he married her.

First reference: 1 Samuel 25:3 / Last reference: 1 Chronicles 3:1

2) Mother of Amasa, whom Absalom made captain of his army, and aunt of David's commander Joab.

First reference: 2 Samuel 17:25 / Last reference: 1 Chronicles 2:17

ABIHAIL

of times mentioned: 6
# of MEN by this name: 3

# of WOMEN by this name: 2

Meaning: Possessor of might

1) Forefather of a Levitical family that had responsibility for parts of the tabernacle.

Only reference: Numbers 3:35

2) Wife of Abishur, a descendant of Abraham through Jacob's son Judah.

Only reference: 1 Chronicles 2:29

3) A descendant of Abraham through Jacob's son Gad.

Only reference: 1 Chronicles 5:14

4) One of the wives of King Rehoboam of Judah.

Only reference: 2 Chronicles 11:18

5) The father of Queen Esther, who married the Persian king Ahasuerus.

First reference: Esther 2:15 / Last reference: Esther 9:29

ABIHU

of times mentioned: 12
# of MEN by this name: 1

Meaning: Worshipper of God

A son of Aaron who, along with his brother Nadab, offered strange fire before the Lord. God sent fire from His presence to consume them, and they died. He had no children.

First reference: Exodus 6:23 / Last reference: 1 Chronicles 24:2 / Key reference: Leviticus 10:1

ABIHUD

of times mentioned: 1
# of MEN by this name: 1

Meaning: Possessor of renown

A descendant of Abraham through Jacob's son Benjamin.

Only reference: 1 Chronicles 8:3

👥 ABIJAH

of times mentioned: 20
# of MEN by this name: 5
# of WOMEN by this name: 1

Meaning: Worshipper of God

1) A son of King Jeroboam of Israel who died in childhood.

Only reference: 1 Kings 14:1

2) One of twenty-four priests in David's time who was chosen by lot to serve in the tabernacle.

Only reference: 1 Chronicles 24:10

3) A son of King Rehoboam of Judah. He inherited the throne from his father and went to war against Jeroboam of Israel, claiming that God had given Israel to David and his heirs. Triumphant because his troops called on the Lord in desperation, he gained some cities from Israel and "waxed mighty" (2 Chronicles 13:21). Same as Abia (1).

First reference: 2 Chronicles 11:20 / Last reference: 2 Chronicles 14:1 / Key reference: 2 Chronicles 13:1–5

4) Mother of Judah's good king Hezekiah.

Only reference: 2 Chronicles 29:1

5) A priest who renewed the covenant under Nehemiah.

Only reference: Nehemiah 10:7

6) An exiled priest who returned to Judah under Zerubbabel.

First reference: Nehemiah 12:4 / Last reference: Nehemiah 12:17

👥 ABIJAM

of times mentioned: 5
# of MEN by this name: 1

Meaning: Seaman

Son of Rehoboam, king of Judah. He inherited his father's throne and did evil for the three years of his reign, during which he fought with King Jeroboam of Israel.

First reference: 1 Kings 14:31 / Last reference: 1 Kings 15:8

📍 ABILENE

of times mentioned: NT 1

Meaning: Grassy meadow

A Palestinian territory north of Damascus, which was ruled by the tetrarch Lysanias during Tiberius Caesar's reign.

Only reference: Luke 3:1

👥 ABIMAEL

of times mentioned: 2
# of MEN by this name: 1

Meaning: Father of Mael

A descendant of Noah through Noah's son Shem.

First reference: Genesis 10:28 / Last reference: 1 Chronicles 1:22

👥 ABIMELECH

of times mentioned: 66
# of MEN by this name: 3

Meaning: Father of the king

1) The Philistine king of Gerar who took Abraham's wife, Sarah, as his concubine because Abraham introduced her as his sister. God warned Abimelech, and the king returned Sarah to her husband. Later Abraham made a covenant with Abimelech.
   Isaac repeated his father Abraham's lie when he moved to Gerar during a famine, but the king discovered it and protected him and his wife, Rebekah. God so blessed Isaac that Abimelech asked him and his family to leave. But eventually the two made a covenant.

First reference: Genesis 20:2 / Last reference: Genesis 26:26 / Key references: Genesis 20:3–18; 26:8–11

2) A son of Gideon, by his concubine. He killed all but one of his brothers and was made king of Shechem. But three years later the Shechemites rebelled, and he destroyed the city. He moved on to attack Thebez, and there he was killed when a woman dropped part of a millstone on his head.

First reference: Judges 8:31 / Last reference: 2 Samuel 11:21 / Key references: Judges 9:5–6, 45, 50–53

3) One of the chief priests serving in the government of King David.

Only reference: 1 Chronicles 18:16

👥 ABINADAB

of times mentioned: 13
# of MEN by this name: 4

Meaning: Liberal or generous

1) A Levite who lived in Gibeah and housed the ark of the covenant for twenty years.

First reference: 1 Samuel 7:1 / Last reference: 1 Chronicles 13:7

2) The second son of Jesse and older brother of King David.

First reference: 1 Samuel 16:8 / Last reference: 1 Chronicles 2:13

3) One of three sons of Israel's king Saul. Abinadab and his brothers died with Saul in a battle against the Philistines on Mount Gilboa (1 Samuel 31:1–2). Same as Ishui.

First reference: 1 Samuel 31:2 / Last reference: 1 Chronicles 10:2

4) Father of one of King Solomon's commissary officers, who married the king's daughter Taphath.

Only reference: 1 Kings 4:11

👥 ABINOAM

of times mentioned: 4
# of MEN by this name: 1

Meaning: Gracious

Father of Barak, who led Israel's army under Deborah.

First reference: Judges 4:6 / Last reference: Judges 5:12

👥 ABIRAM

of times mentioned: 11
# of MEN by this name: 2

Meaning: Lofty

1) One of the Reubenites who, with Korah the Levite, conspired against Moses. Because they wrongly claimed that all of Israel was holy, God had the earth swallow the rebellious Reubenites.

First reference: Numbers 16:1 / Last reference: Psalm 106:17

2) The son of Hiel, who rebuilt Jericho. Abiram died as his father built the foundations of the city.

Only reference: 1 Kings 16:34

👥 ABISHAG

of times mentioned: 5
# of WOMEN by this name: 1

Meaning: Blundering

A beautiful young woman called to serve the dying King David by lying with him to keep him warm. After David died, his son Adonijah wanted to marry Abishag, but he was put to death by his half brother Solomon, who feared Adonijah was trying to usurp the kingship.

First reference: 1 Kings 1:3 / Last reference: 1 Kings 2:22

👥 ABISHAI

of times mentioned: 25
# of MEN by this name: 1

Meaning: Generous

The brother of David's commander, Joab, Abishai accompanied David to Saul's camp on a spying mission in which David chose to spare the king's life. Abishai became a military leader under his brother and supported David in his fight with Absalom. He killed the Philistine Ishbi-benob, who sought to kill David and became a respected captain of the king's troops.

First reference: 1 Samuel 26:6 / Last reference: 1 Chronicles 19:15 / Key reference: 1 Samuel 26:6–12

👥 ABISHALOM

of times mentioned: 2
# of MEN by this name: 1

Meaning: Friendly

Grandfather of King Abijam of Judah.

First reference: 1 Kings 15:2 / Last reference: 1 Kings 15:10

👥 ABISHUA

of times mentioned: 5
# of MEN by this name: 2

Meaning: Prosperous

1) A descendant of Abraham through Jacob's son Levi and a priest through the line of Aaron.

First reference: 1 Chronicles 6:4 / Last reference: Ezra 7:5

2) A descendant of Abraham through Jacob's son Benjamin.

Only reference: 1 Chronicles 8:4

👥 ABISHUR

of times mentioned: 2
# of MEN by this name: 1

Meaning: Mason

A descendant of Abraham through Jacob's son Judah.

First reference: 1 Chronicles 2:28 / Last reference: 1 Chronicles 2:29

👥 ABITAL

of times mentioned: 2
# of WOMEN by this name: 1

Meaning: Fresh

One of several wives of King David; mother of David's son Shephatiah.

First reference: 2 Samuel 3:4 / Last reference: 1 Chronicles 3:3

👥 ABITUB

of times mentioned: 1
# of MEN by this name: 1

Meaning: Good

A descendant of Abraham through Jacob's son Benjamin.

Only reference: 1 Chronicles 8:11

👥 ABIUD

of times mentioned: 2
# of MEN by this name: 1

Genealogy of Jesus: Yes (Matthew 1:13)

Meaning: My father is majesty

A descendant of Abraham through Isaac's line.

Only reference: Matthew 1:13

👥 ABNER

of times mentioned: 63
# of MEN by this name: 1

Meaning: Enlightening

The son of Ner, Abner was the uncle of King Saul of Israel and captain of his army. David confronted Abner for not protecting Saul when David crept into Israel's camp and removed Saul's spear and water jar. After Saul's death, Abner declared Saul's son Ishbosheth king of Israel. When Ishbosheth wrongly accused Abner of taking one of his father's concubines, Abner went over to David's side and began encouraging all Israel to support him as king.

David's commander, Joab, objected to David's accepting Abner as a friend, because Abner had killed the commander's brother Asahel. After Joab and his brother Abishai killed Abner, David mourned at his funeral. Solomon declared that Abner was more righteous than his killer (1 Kings 2:32).

First reference: 1 Samuel 14:50 / Last reference: 1 Chronicles 27:21 / Key reference: 2 Samuel 3:12

👥 ABRAHAM

of times mentioned: 250
# of MEN by this name: 1

Meaning: Father of a multitude

A new name for Abram, whom God called out of Ur of the Chaldees and into the Promised Land. This new name was a symbol of the covenant between God and Abraham. The Lord promised to build a nation through Abraham and his wife, Sarai (whom he renamed Sarah), though she was too old to have children. God refused to accept Ishmael, son of Abraham and Sarah's maid, Hagar, as the child of promise.

In time, God gave Sarah and Abraham a son, Isaac, who would found the nation God promised. When

God asked Abraham to sacrifice his son on an altar, Abraham took Isaac and set out toward Moriah. There he prepared the altar and laid his son on it. But the angel of the Lord intervened, and God gave Abraham a ram to sacrifice in Isaac's place. God knew the depth of Abraham's faith from his willingness to sacrifice his son. He promised to bless Abraham and his seed.

In his old age, after Sarah's death, Abraham arranged a marriage for Isaac, ensuring God's promise. Then the old man married Keturah. But her sons and the sons of his concubines were not to disturb Isaac's inheritance. Abraham gave them gifts and sent them away from his land.

Abraham lived to be 175. He was buried with Sarah in the cave of Machpelah, in Hebron. Same as Abram.

First reference: Genesis 17:5 / Last reference: 1 Peter 3:6 / Key references: Genesis 17:2–8; 22:8

👥 ABRAM

of times mentioned: 58
# of MEN by this name: 1

Meaning: High father

A man from Ur of the Chaldees, married to Sarai. God called him to the Promised Land and promised to bless him. At age seventy-five, Abram left with Sarai, his nephew Lot, and all their goods and servants. As he entered Canaan, God promised to give the land to Abram and his descendants.

God blessed Abram. When his flocks and Lot's were too large, they separated, and Lot headed for the area around Sodom. When Lot ran into trouble there, Abram rescued him and prayed for him, and God removed his family from the wicked city.

God promised Abram a son, but he and Sarai waited many years. Sarai gave him her maid, Hagar, to bear him a child, but the promised child did not come. When Abram was ninety years old, God made a covenant with him and changed his name to Abraham. Same as Abraham.

First reference: Genesis 11:26 / Last reference: Nehemiah 9:7 / Key references: Genesis 12:1–4; 17:1–5

👥 ABSALOM

of times mentioned: 102
# of MEN by this name: 1

Meaning: Friendly

King David's son by his wife Maacah. When Absalom's sister Tamar was raped by their brother Amnon, Absalom hated him and commanded his servants to kill Amnon. When this was accomplished, Absalom fled Jerusalem for three years.

Joab, the head of David's army, tried to reconcile father and son. Though David allowed Absalom to return to Jerusalem, he would not see him. But as David ignored him, Absalom won over the hearts of Israel's people. David's counselor Ahithophel went over to Absalom's side.

When David left Jerusalem, Absalom took over the city and a battle began in the wood of Ephraim. As Absalom rode under an oak tree, he was caught in it and his mule ran out from under him.

Joab heard of this, went to Absalom, and thrust three spears into his heart. Yet Absalom lived, so Joab's armor bearers killed him and threw his body into a pit. They covered his body with a pile of stones, and the battle ended.

First reference: 2 Samuel 3:3 / Last reference: 2 Chronicles 11:21 / Key references: 2 Samuel 13:22; 15:10; 18:9

📍 ACCAD

of times mentioned: OT 1

Meaning: A fortress

A city of Shinar that was part of the kingdom of Nimrod.

Only reference: Genesis 10:10–15

📍 ACCHO

of times mentioned: OT 1

Meaning: To hem in

A Canaanite seaport that was part of the inheritance of the tribe of Asher. In the Middle Ages Accho was called Acre. Same as Ptolemais.

Only reference: Judges 1:31

📍 ACELDAMA

of times mentioned: NT 1

Meaning: Field of blood

The name Jerusalem's residents gave to the field Judas bought with the money he got for betraying Jesus. In his sermon in Acts 1, Peter described the unfaithful disciple's gruesome death there: he fell headlong and "burst asunder in the midst, and all his bowels gushed out" (Acts 1:18).

Only reference: Acts 1:19

📍ACHAIA

of times mentioned: NT 11

The southern Greek province of the Roman Empire. Here the local Jews made insurrection against Paul and brought him before the proconsul Gallio for judgment. The ruler refused to hear their case and allowed the Jews to beat their synagogue ruler in front of his court.

Epaenetus and the household of Stephanas were some of the first converts in Achaia. Apollos went to Achaia with a recommendation from the Christians at Ephesus; he preached in Achaia, refuting the Jews who denied Christ. Christians of Achaia contributed to the collection of funds for the impoverished Christians in Jerusalem.

Though it bears the name of one church, Paul wrote the book of 2 Corinthians to the Achaians at large. In this epistle he comforted the suffering church of that province and encouraged them in faithfulness.

First reference: Acts 18:12 / Last reference: 1 Thessalonians 1:8 / Key references: Acts 18:12–17, 27–28; 2 Corinthians 1:1

👪ACHAICUS

of times mentioned: 1
# of MEN by this name: 1

A Corinthian Christian who visited the apostle Paul in Ephesus and "refreshed [Paul's] spirit."

Only reference: 1 Corinthians 16:17

👪ACHAN

of times mentioned: 6
# of MEN by this name: 1

Meaning: Troublesome

An Israelite who ignored Joshua's command that nothing in Jericho should live or be taken from the city. He stole a mantle, 200 shekels of silver, and 50 shekels of gold and hid them under his tent. Because of his sin, Israel could not stand at the first battle of Ai. When Joshua discovered Achan's sin, he asked, "Why hast thou troubled us?" and promised that the Lord would trouble Achan that day (Joshua 7:25). The sinner and his family were taken to the Valley of Achor and stoned.

First reference: Joshua 7:1 / Last reference: Joshua 22:20

👪ACHAR

of times mentioned: 1
# of MEN by this name: 1

Meaning: Troublesome

A variant spelling of Achan, "the troubler of Israel."

Only reference: 1 Chronicles 2:7

👪ACHAZ

of times mentioned: 2
# of MEN by this name: 1

Genealogy of Jesus: Yes (Matthew 1:9)

A descendant of Abraham through Isaac; forebear of Jesus' earthly father, Joseph. Same as Ahaz.

Only reference: Matthew 1:9

👪ACHBOR

of times mentioned: 7
# of MEN by this name: 3

1) Father of a king of Edom, "before there reigned any king over the children of Israel" (Genesis 36:31).

First reference: Genesis 36:38 / Last reference: 1 Chronicles 1:49

2) One of the men who was sent to consult Huldah the prophetess, after Josiah discovered the book of the law.

First reference: 2 Kings 22:12 / Last reference: 2 Kings 22:14

3) The father of Elnathan, who was sent by King Jehoiakim of Judah to bring the prophet Urijah back from Egypt. With the other princes of Judah, the scribe Baruch read Jeremiah's prophecies to him.

First reference: Jeremiah 26:22 / Last reference: Jeremiah 36:12

👥ACHIM

of times mentioned: 2
# of MEN by this name: 1

Genealogy of Jesus: Yes (Matthew 1:14)

A descendant of Abraham through Isaac; forebear of Jesus' earthly father, Joseph.

Only reference: Matthew 1:14

👥ACHISH

of times mentioned: 21
# of MEN by this name: 2

1) The Philistine king of Gath before whom David, who feared him, pretended madness. Later David sought refuge in Achish's land and received the town of Ziklag from him. Though Achish wanted David to fight with him against Israel, when the king's troops objected, he sent David home.

First reference: 1 Samuel 21:10 / Last reference: 1 Samuel 29:9 / Key references: 1 Samuel 21:10–15; 29:6–7

2) Another king of Gath, in the time of Solomon. Two runaway servants of Shimei came to him.

First reference: 1 Kings 2:39 / Last reference: 1 Kings 2:40

📍ACHMETHA

of times mentioned: OT 1

A city in Media. In its palace, the Persian king Darius found a record proving that, as the Jews claimed, King Cyrus had ordered Jerusalem's temple to be rebuilt.

Only reference: Ezra 6:2

📍ACHOR

of times mentioned: OT 5

Meaning: Troubled

A valley near Jericho where justice was meted out to the looter Achan, who had disobeyed God's command to destroy everything in Jericho. From the city he had taken a beautiful Babylonian robe, 200 shekels of silver, and a 50-shekel-weight wedge of gold. Knowing he was doing wrong, he buried them under his tent.

God had warned that anyone who disobeyed would trouble the camp. The trouble began when the Israelites lost a battle at Ai. Joshua inquired of God what had gone wrong, and the Lord commanded that the people sanctify themselves. Once they had done this, each tribe, then each family in that tribe, was brought before God. Achan was identified as the wrongdoer and stoned in the valley, which was named directly after this incident.

Isaiah prophesied that God would renew Achor, making it "a place for the herds to lie down in, for my people that have sought me" (Isaiah 65:10). Looking ahead, Hosea declared it would be a "door of hope" (Hosea 2:15).

First reference: Joshua 7:24 / Last reference: Hosea 2:15

👥ACHSA

of times mentioned: 1
# of WOMEN by this name: 1

Meaning: Anklet

The daughter of Caleb, descendant of Abraham through Jacob's son Judah. Same as Achsah.

Only reference: 1 Chronicles 2:49

👥ACHSAH

of times mentioned: 4
# of WOMEN by this name: 1

Meaning: Anklet

Caleb's daughter, whom he promised in marriage to the man who could capture the city of Kirjathsepher. His brother Othniel captured the city and won Achsah as his wife. Afterward Caleb gave her land that held springs, since the lands of her dowry were dry. Same as Achsa.

First reference: Joshua 15:16 / Last reference: Judges 1:13

♀ACHSHAPH

of times mentioned: OT 3

Meaning: Fascination

A Phoenician city whose king joined Jabin, king of Hazor, and other Canaanite rulers in attacking Joshua and the Israelites after they entered the Promised Land. Later, Achshaph was designated as a border landmark of the land given to the tribe of Asher when Joshua cast lots in Shiloh to provide territory for the seven tribes that had yet to receive an inheritance.

First reference: Joshua 11:1 / Last reference: Joshua 19:25

♀ACHZIB

of times mentioned: OT 4

Meaning: Deceitful

1) A city that became part of the inheritance of the tribe of Judah following the conquest of the Promised Land. Micah's prophecy played on the meaning of its name when he predicted that Achzib would be "a lie to the kings of Israel."

First reference: Joshua 15:44 / Last reference: Micah 1:14

2) A coastal city that became part of Asher's inheritance when Joshua cast lots in Shiloh to provide territory for the seven tribes that had yet to receive their land. The tribe of Asher did not drive the Canaanites out of Achzib as God had commanded them to do.

First reference: Joshua 19:29 / Last reference: Judges 1:31

♀ADADAH

of times mentioned: OT 1

Meaning: Festival

A southern city that became part of the inheritance of the tribe of Judah following the conquest of the Promised Land.

Only reference: Joshua 15:22

👥ADAH

of times mentioned: 8
# of WOMEN by this name: 2

Meaning: Ornament

1) A wife of Lamech, the first man in scripture to have two wives. Her son was named Jabal.

First reference: Genesis 4:19 / Last reference: Genesis 4:23

2) A wife of Esau, "of the daughters of Canaan." Same as Bashemath (2).

First reference: Genesis 36:2 / Last reference: Genesis 36:16

👥ADAIAH

of times mentioned: 9
# of MEN by this name: 9

Meaning: God has adorned

1) Grandfather of King Josiah of Judah, on his mother's side.

Only reference: 2 Kings 22:1

2) A descendant of Abraham through Jacob's son Levi.

Only reference: 1 Chronicles 6:41

3) A descendant of Abraham through Jacob's son Benjamin.

Only reference: 1 Chronicles 8:21

4) A Levite who returned to Jerusalem following the Babylonian captivity.

Only reference: 1 Chronicles 9:12

5) Forefather of Maaseiah, captain of hundreds for the priest Jehoiada, who crowned Joash king of Judah.

Only reference: 2 Chronicles 23:1

6) An exiled Israelite who married a "strange" (foreign) woman.

Only reference: Ezra 10:29

7) Another exiled Israelite who married a "strange" (foreign) woman.

Only reference: Ezra 10:39

8) Ancestor of a man of the tribe of Judah who was chosen by lot to resettle Jerusalem after returning from the Babylonian Exile.

Only reference: Nehemiah 11:5

9) A Levite who settled in Jerusalem following the Babylonian Exile and worked in the temple.

Only reference: Nehemiah 11:12

👥 ADALIA

of times mentioned: 1
# of MEN by this name: 1

One of ten sons of Haman, who was the villain of the story of Esther.

Only reference: Esther 9:8

👥 ADAM

of times mentioned: 30
# of MEN by this name: 1

Meaning: Ruddy

The first man, who was created by God to have dominion over the earth. Adam's first act was to name the animals; then God created Adam's wife, Eve, as "a help meet for him" (Genesis 2:18). God gave this couple the beautiful Garden of Eden to care for. There Satan, in the form of a serpent, tempted Eve. Though God had banned them from eating the fruit of the knowledge of good and evil, under Satan's influence Eve picked it, ate it, and offered it to Adam, who also ate. Aware of their sin, they attempted to avoid God. He banned them from the garden and cursed the earth's ground so Adam would have to work hard to grow food. As a result of their sin, they would die. Following their banishment, the couple had two children, Cain and Abel. When Cain killed his brother, God gave Adam another son, Seth. Adam lived to be 930.

First reference: Genesis 2:19 / Last reference: Jude 1:14 / Key references: Genesis 2:7, 21–23; 3:6

📍 ADAM

of times mentioned: OT 1

Meaning: Ruddy

When Joshua led the Israelites across the Jordan River, the river's water rose up in a heap by this city east of the river.

Only reference: Joshua 3:16

📍 ADAMAH

of times mentioned: OT 1

Meaning: Soil (probably red in color)

A fortified or walled city that became part of the inheritance of Naphtali when Joshua cast lots in Shiloh to provide territory for the seven tribes that had yet to receive their land.

Only reference: Joshua 19:36

📍 ADAMI

of times mentioned: OT 1

Meaning: Earthy

A city that became part of the inheritance of Naphtali when Joshua cast lots in Shiloh to provide territory for the seven tribes that had yet to receive their land.

Only reference: Joshua 19:33

👥 ADBEEL

of times mentioned: 2
# of MEN by this name: 1

Meaning: Disciplined of God

A descendant of Abraham through Ishmael, who was Abraham's son with his surrogate wife, Hagar.

First reference: Genesis 25:13 / Last reference: 1 Chronicles 1:29

📍 ADAR

of times mentioned: OT 1

Meaning: Ample

A city that became part of the inheritance of the tribe of Judah following the conquest of the Promised Land.

Only reference: Joshua 15:3

ADDAN

of times mentioned: OT 1

Meaning: Firm

A Babylonian city where some Jews lived during the Babylonian Exile. At the end of the exile, these people could not prove they were Israelites. Same as Addon.

Only reference: Ezra 2:59

ADDAR

of times mentioned: 1
# of MEN by this name: 1

Meaning: Ample

A descendant of Abraham through Jacob's son Benjamin.

Only reference: 1 Chronicles 8:3

ADDI

of times mentioned: 1
# of MEN by this name: 1

Genealogy of Jesus: Yes (Luke 3:28)

A descendant of Abraham through Isaac; forebear of Jesus' earthly father, Joseph.

Only reference: Luke 3:28

ADDON

of times mentioned: OT 1

Meaning: Powerful

A Babylonian city where some Jews lived during the Babylonian Exile. At the end of the exile, these people could not prove they were Israelites. Same as Addan.

Only reference: Nehemiah 7:61

ADER

of times mentioned: 1
# of MEN by this name: 1

Meaning: An arrangement

A descendant of Abraham through Jacob's son Benjamin.

Only reference: 1 Chronicles 8:15

ADIEL

of times mentioned: 3
# of MEN by this name: 3

Meaning: Ornament of God

1) A descendant of Abraham through Jacob's son Simeon.

Only reference: 1 Chronicles 4:36

2) Forefather of a Babylonian exile from the tribe of Levi who resettled Jerusalem.

Only reference: 1 Chronicles 9:12

3) Father of King David's treasurer Azmaveth.

Only reference: 1 Chronicles 27:25

ADIN

of times mentioned: 4
# of MEN by this name: 3

Meaning: Voluptuous

1) Forefather of an exiled family that returned to Judah under Zerubbabel.

First reference: Ezra 2:15 / Last reference: Nehemiah 7:20

2) A Jewish leader who renewed the covenant under Nehemiah.

Only reference: Nehemiah 10:16

3) Forefather of a Jewish exile who returned from Babylon to Judah under Ezra.

Only reference: Ezra 8:6

ADINA

of times mentioned: 1
# of MEN by this name: 1

Meaning: Effeminacy

One of King David's valiant warriors.

Only reference: 1 Chronicles 11:42

👥ADINO

of times mentioned: 1
# of MEN by this name: 1

Meaning: Slender

One of King David's warriors known as the "mighty men."

Only reference: 2 Samuel 23:8

📍ADITHAIM

of times mentioned: OT 1

Meaning: Double prey

A city that became part of the inheritance of the tribe of Judah following the conquest of the Promised Land.

Only reference: Joshua 15:36

👥ADLAI

of times mentioned: 1
# of MEN by this name: 1

Father of King David's chief shepherd over herds in the valleys.

Only reference: 1 Chronicles 27:29

📍ADMAH

of times mentioned: OT 5

Meaning: Earthy

One of five Canaanite "cities of the plain" at the southern end of the Dead Sea. Admah's king, Shinab, took part in a war coalition with Sodom and Gomorrah and the other cities of the plain against Chedorlaomer, king of Elam, and his Mesopotamian allies. After serving Chedorlaomer for twelve years, the Canaanites rebelled against him. Following their battle against Elam's king and his allies, Abram's nephew, Lot, was captured in Sodom, and Abram had to rescue him. When Sodom and Gomorrah were destroyed by God, Admah also was ruined.

First reference: Genesis 10:19 / Last reference: Hosea 11:8

👥ADMATHA

of times mentioned: 1
# of MEN by this name: 1

One of seven Persian princes serving under King Ahasuerus.

Only reference: Esther 1:14

👥ADNA

of times mentioned: 2
# of MEN by this name: 2

Meaning: Pleasure

1) An exiled Israelite who married a "strange" (foreign) woman.

Only reference: Ezra 10:30

2) Forefather of a priest who returned to Jerusalem under Zerubbabel.

Only reference: Nehemiah 12:15

👥ADNAH

of times mentioned: 2
# of MEN by this name: 2

Meaning: Pleasure

1) A captain in David's army.

Only reference: 1 Chronicles 12:20

2) A commander in King Jehoshaphat's army.

Only reference: 2 Chronicles 17:14

👥ADONI-BEZEK

of times mentioned: 3
# of MEN by this name: 1

Meaning: Lord of Bezek

The ruler of a Canaanite city who ran from the army of Judah during its cleansing of the Promised Land. When soldiers caught Adoni-bezek, they cut off his thumbs and big toes, as he had previously done to seventy kings he had conquered. He died in captivity in Jerusalem.

First reference: Judges 1:5 / Last reference: Judges 1:7

ADONIJAH

of times mentioned: 26
# of MEN by this name: 3

Meaning: Worshipper of God

1) A son of King David, born in Hebron. When David was old, Adonijah attempted to take the throne, though David had promised it to Solomon. Nathan the prophet and Bath-sheba, Solomon's mother, reported this to David, who immediately had Solomon anointed king. When Adonijah heard this, he went to the temple and grasped the horns of the altar, in fear of his life. Solomon promised he would not be killed if he showed himself a worthy man. But when Adonijah wanted David's concubine Abishag as his wife, Solomon saw it as another threat to his throne and had Adonijah executed.

First reference: 2 Samuel 3:4 / Last reference: 1 Chronicles 3:2 / Key references: 1 Kings 1:5, 50

2) A Levite sent by King Jehoshaphat to teach the law of the Lord throughout the nation of Judah.

Only reference: 2 Chronicles 17:8

3) A Jewish leader who renewed the covenant under Nehemiah.

Only reference: Nehemiah 10:16

ADONIKAM

of times mentioned: 3
# of MEN by this name: 1

Meaning: High

Forefather of a Jewish exile who returned from Babylon to Judah under Zerubbabel.

First reference: Ezra 2:13 / Last reference: Nehemiah 7:18

ADONIRAM

of times mentioned: 2
# of MEN by this name: 1

Meaning: Lord of height

King Solomon's official over forced labor for building the temple.

First reference: 1 Kings 4:6 / Last reference: 1 Kings 5:14

ADONI-ZEDEC

of times mentioned: 2
# of MEN by this name: 1

Meaning: Lord of justice

A pagan king of Jerusalem during Joshua's conquest of the Promised Land, Adoni-zedec allied with four other rulers to attack Gibeon, which had deceptively made a peace treaty with the Israelites. Joshua's soldiers defeated the five armies, and Joshua executed the allied kings.

First reference: Joshua 10:1 / Last reference: Joshua 10:3

ADORAIM

of times mentioned: OT 1

Meaning: Double mound

A city that King Rehoboam built for Judah's defense.

Only reference: Chronicles 11:9

ADORAM

of times mentioned: 2
# of MEN by this name: 2

Meaning: Lord of height

1) King David's official over forced labor.

Only reference: Samuel 20:24

2) An official over forced labor under Judah's king Rehoboam (son of Solomon). Adoram was stoned to death by rebellious Israelites, who seceded to form their own northern kingdom.

Only reference: 1 Kings 12:18

ADRAMMELECH

of times mentioned: 2
# of MEN by this name: 1

Meaning: Splendor of the king

Son of the Assyrian king Sennacherib, who, with his brother Sharezer, killed his father with a sword. After the assassination, Adrammelech fled to Armenia.

First reference: 2 Kings 19:37 / Last reference: Isaiah 37:38

ADRAMYTTIUM

of times mentioned: NT 1

An Asian seaport northeast of the island of Lesbos. This was a home port of the ship Paul sailed on when he headed for Rome.

Only reference: Acts 27:2

ADRIA

of times mentioned: NT 1

Another name for the Adriatic Sea, which lies west of Greece. Before Paul and his companion Luke suffered shipwreck, the Gospel writer records that they were "driven up and down in Adria" by the wind.

Only reference: Acts 27:27

ADRIEL

of times mentioned: 2
# of MEN by this name: 1

Meaning: Flock of God

The man who married Saul's daughter Merab, who had been promised to David.

First reference: 1 Samuel 18:19 / Last reference: 2 Samuel 21:8

ADULLAM

of times mentioned: OT 8

1) A city that became part of the inheritance of the tribe of Judah. King Rehoboam fortified Adullam for Judah's defense. It was one of the cities resettled following the Jews' return from the Babylonian Exile.

First reference: Joshua 12:15 / Last reference: Micah 1:15

2) A cave near the city of Adullam. Here David's family met him after he fled from King Saul. David gathered four hundred discontented men at Adullam and became their captain.

First reference: 1 Samuel 22:1 / Last reference: 1 Chronicles 11:15

ADUMMIM

of times mentioned: OT 2

Meaning: Red spots

A pass between Jericho and Jerusalem that formed part of the border of the tribe of Judah's territory. Jesus probably had it in mind as the setting for the parable of the Good Samaritan.

First reference: Joshua 15:7 / Last reference: Joshua 18:17–19

AENEAS

of times mentioned: 2
# of MEN by this name: 1

A lame man of Lydda healed by the apostle Peter after spending eight years in his sickbed. His healing turned many people to the Lord.

First reference: Acts 9:33 / Last reference: Acts 9:34

AENON

of times mentioned: NT 1

Meaning: Place of springs

A spot near Salim where there was "much water." Here John the Baptist baptized believers shortly before he was imprisoned.

Only reference: John 3:23

AGABUS

of times mentioned: 2
# of MEN by this name: 1

Meaning: Locust

An early Christian prophet from Jerusalem who made two recorded predictions: that a famine would affect the region of Judea and that the apostle Paul would be bound and delivered "into the hands of the Gentiles" (Acts 21:11).

First reference: Acts 11:28 / Last reference: Acts 21:10

AGAG

of times mentioned: 8
# of MEN by this name: 2

Meaning: Flame

1) A king mentioned by Balaam in his prophecy concerning God's blessing on Israel.

Only reference: Numbers 24:7

2) A king of the Amalekites whom King Saul of Israel spared in defiance of God's command. Obeying God, the prophet Samuel killed Agag.

First reference: 1 Samuel 15:8 / Last reference: 1 Samuel 15:33

AGAR

of times mentioned: 2
# of WOMEN by this name: 1

Greek form of the name Hagar, used in the New Testament.

First reference: Galatians 4:24 / Last reference: Galatians 4:25

AGEE

of times mentioned: 1
# of MEN by this name: 1

Father of one of King David's "mighty men," Shammah.

Only reference: 2 Samuel 23:11

AGRIPPA

of times mentioned: 12
# of MEN by this name: 1

Meaning: Wild horse tamer

Herod Agrippa II, great-grandson of Herod the Great. He became king of the tetrarchy of Philip and Lysanias. Porcius Festus asked for his advice on Paul's legal case, so he heard Paul's testimony, which almost persuaded him to become a Christian. Same as Herod (4).

First reference: Acts 25:13 / Last reference: Acts 26:32 / Key reference: Acts 26:28

AGUR

of times mentioned: 1
# of MEN by this name: 1

Meaning: Gathered

A little-known biblical writer who penned the thirtieth chapter of Proverbs.

Only reference: Proverbs 30:1

AHAB

of times mentioned: 94
# of MEN by this name: 2

Meaning: Friend of his father

1) A king of Israel, Ahab did great evil. He married Jezebel, daughter of the king of Zidon, and fell into Baal worship. God sent Israel a drought that only the prophet Elijah could break. The nation suffered for three years, until Elijah returned and challenged Israel to follow God. He proved that God was Lord in a showdown with the prophets of Baal, before killing them and ending the drought.

Ahab coveted the vineyard of his subject Naboth, who refused to sell his inheritance to him. While the king sulked, Jezebel plotted to kill Naboth and get the land. Because Ahab humbled himself before God, the Lord promised to bring evil in his son's life instead of visiting it on Ahab. He was killed in a battle with Syria.

First reference: 1 Kings 16:28 / Last reference: Micah 6:16 / Key reference: 1 Kings 16:29–30

2) A false prophet who claimed God would not deliver Judah into King Nebuchadnezzar's hand.

First reference: Jeremiah 29:21 / Last reference: Jeremiah 29:22

AHARAH

of times mentioned: 1
# of MEN by this name: 1

Meaning: After his brother

A descendant of Abraham through Jacob's son Benjamin. Aharah was Benjamin's third son.

Only reference: 1 Chronicles 8:1

AHARHEL

of times mentioned: 1
# of MEN by this name: 1

Meaning: Safe

A descendant of Abraham through Jacob's son Judah.

Only reference: 1 Chronicles 4:8

AHASAI

of times mentioned: 1
# of MEN by this name: 1

Meaning: Seizer

Forefather of an exiled Israelite family.

Only reference: Nehemiah 11:13

AHASBAI

of times mentioned: 1
# of MEN by this name: 1

Father of one of King David's "mighty men," Eliphelet.

Only reference: 2 Samuel 23:34

AHASUERUS

of times mentioned: 31
# of MEN by this name: 3

1) A Persian king who received accusations against the inhabitants of Judah and Jerusalem.

Only reference: Ezra 4:6

2) A king of Media and the father of Darius the Mede, who would become king of the Chaldeans.

Only reference: Daniel 9:1

3) A Persian king who reigned over an empire that ran from India to Ethiopia. When his queen Vashti displeased him, Ahasuerus ordered the beautiful women of his kingdom to be gathered at the palace so he could choose a new wife. In this way he met the Jewess Esther, loved her, and made her his queen.

Not knowing that Esther was Jewish, Ahasuerus listened to his counselor, wicked Haman, who wanted to destroy the Jews. Hearing only Haman's false information, the king gave Haman permission to eradicate what he saw as a dangerous people. When Esther heard this, she came before the king and invited both men to a banquet. That night Ahasuerus discovered the faithfulness of Esther's cousin, Mordecai, who had reported a plot against the king. Ahasuerus commanded Haman to honor this Jew whom the counselor hated and had planned to kill.

On the second day of her banquet, Esther divulged Haman's plot to harm her people. Angered, the king had Haman hanged on the gallows he had built for Mordecai. Esther gave Mordecai Haman's household, and the king made Mordecai a royal advisor. Since his original law could not be changed, Ahasuerus had Mordecai write a new law that allowed the Jews to protect themselves from the attack Haman planned.

First reference: Esther 1:1 / Last reference: Esther 10:3 / Key references: Esther 1:1; 7:5–10

AHAVA

of times mentioned: OT 3

Beside this Babylonian river Ezra gathered his people for three days while he sent a messenger to Iddo, the chief of Casiphia, to get some Levites to accompany them to Jerusalem. After they had gathered the Levites, Ezra proclaimed a fast and made preparations for the journey.

First reference: Ezra 8:15 / Last reference: Ezra 8:31

AHAZ

of times mentioned: 42
# of MEN by this name: 2

Meaning: Possessor

1) A king of Judah who became deeply involved in paganism. God sent the kings of Syria and Israel against Judah, in punishment, and Ahaz was unsuccessful in fighting off his enemies. Many people of Judah were captured and carried off. Ahaz sent to Tiglath-pileser, king of Assyria, for help, offering the temple silver and gold and the treasures of his own household to the pagan king as a gift. The Assyrian army responded by attacking Damascus, but was not otherwise helpful. When Ahaz joined the Assyrian king in Damascus, he saw and admired a pagan altar. He had it copied. When he returned

to Jerusalem, he had the altars of the Lord moved and commanded Urijah the priest to use this pagan altar for worship.

Isaiah had prophesied the sign of Immanuel, "God with us," but because God did not rescue him, Ahaz became increasingly involved in paganism. He destroyed the temple vessels and closed the building to worship. Instead he built pagan temples throughout Jerusalem and established altars on high places near other cities. When he died, he was not buried with the other kings of Israel.

First reference: 2 Kings 15:38 / Last reference: Micah 1:1 / Key references: 2 Chronicles 28:1–5; Isaiah 7:11–14

2) A descendant of Abraham through Jacob's son Benjamin, through the line of King Saul and his son Jonathan.

First reference: 1 Chronicles 8:35 / Last reference: 1 Chronicles 9:42

AHAZIAH

of times mentioned: 37
# of MEN by this name: 2

Meaning: God has seized

1) A king of Israel and the son of Ahab. He reigned for two years and walked in the pagan ways of his parents. When he fell through a lattice in his chamber and was badly hurt, he sought help from the pagan god Baalzebub. God sent Elijah to the king's messenger, asking if there was no God in Israel. Twice Ahaziah sent soldiers to Elijah to demand that he come to the king. Twice Elijah called fire down on them. When a third captain came more humbly, Elijah went to the king and prophesied that he would die.

First reference: 1 Kings 22:40 / Last reference: 2 Chronicles 20:37 / Key reference: 1 Kings 22:40–51

2) A king of Judah, son of Joram and Athaliah. Following the advice of bad counselors, he joined with Joram, king of Israel, to fight against the Syrians. When Joram was wounded, Israel's king went to Jezreel, where the king of Judah visited him. There Jehu killed Joram and sent his men on to Samaria, after Ahaziah. Ahaziah died of his wounds in Megiddo.

First reference: 2 Kings 8:24 / Last reference: 2 Chronicles 22:11 / Key reference: 2 Chronicles 22:2–4

AHBAN

of times mentioned: 1
# of MEN by this name: 1

Meaning: Possessor of understanding

A descendant of Abraham through Jacob's son Judah.

Only reference: 1 Chronicles 2:29

AHER

of times mentioned: 1
# of MEN by this name: 1

Meaning: Hinder

A descendant of Abraham through Jacob's son Benjamin.

Only reference: 1 Chronicles 7:12

AHI

of times mentioned: 2
# of MEN by this name: 2

Meaning: Brotherly

1) A descendant of Abraham through Jacob's son Gad.

Only reference: 1 Chronicles 5:15

2) A descendant of Abraham through Jacob's son Asher.

Only reference: 1 Chronicles 7:34

AHIAH

of times mentioned: 4
# of MEN by this name: 3

Meaning: Worshipper of God

1) "The Lord's priest in Shiloh" who was with King Saul at Gibeah when Jonathan and his armorbearer together conquered the Philistines.

First reference: 1 Samuel 14:3 / Last reference: 1 Samuel 14:18

2) A scribe serving under King Solomon.

Only reference: 1 Kings 4:3

3) A son of Ehud who moved to Manahath.

Only reference: 1 Chronicles 8:7

AHIAM

of times mentioned: 2
# of MEN by this name: 1

Meaning: Uncle

One of King David's valiant warriors.

First reference: 2 Samuel 23:33 / Last reference:
1 Chronicles 11:35

AHIAN

of times mentioned: 1
# of MEN by this name: 1

Meaning: Brotherly

A descendant of Abraham through Joseph's son
Manasseh.

Only reference: 1 Chronicles 7:19

AHIEZER

of times mentioned: 6
# of MEN by this name: 2

Meaning: Brother of help

1) A man of the tribe of Dan who helped Aaron number the Israelites. God made him captain of his tribe.

First reference: Numbers 1:12 / Last reference:
Numbers 10:25

2) A "mighty man" who supported the future king
David during his conflict with Saul.

Only reference: 1 Chronicles 12:3

AHIHUD

of times mentioned: 2
# of MEN by this name: 2

Meaning: Possessor of renown, mysterious

1) A prince of the tribe of Asher when the Israelites
entered the Promised Land.

Only reference: Numbers 34:27

2) A descendant of Abraham through Jacob's son
Benjamin.

Only reference: 1 Chronicles 8:7

AHIJAH

of times mentioned: 20
# of MEN by this name: 6

Meaning: Worshipper of God

1) A prophet who prophesied the division of Israel
into the countries of Israel and Judah. He promised
Jeroboam that he would rule Israel. After the king
disobeyed God, Ahijah prophesied the death of
Jeroboam's son and Jeroboam's destruction.

First reference: 1 Kings 11:29 / Last reference:
2 Chronicles 10:15

2) A descendant of Issachar. His son Baasha conspired against King Nadab of Israel.

First reference: 1 Kings 15:27 / Last reference:
2 Kings 9:9

3) A descendant of Abraham through Jacob's son
Judah.

Only reference: 1 Chronicles 2:25

4) One of King David's valiant warriors.

Only reference: 1 Chronicles 11:36

5) A Levite assigned to the treasury during King
David's reign.

Only reference: 1 Chronicles 26:20

6) A Jewish leader who renewed the covenant under
Nehemiah.

Only reference: Nehemiah 10:26

AHIKAM

of times mentioned: 20
# of MEN by this name: 1

Meaning: High

One of the men who was sent to consult Huldah
the prophetess after King Josiah rediscovered
the book of the law. Ahikam supported Jeremiah,
protecting him from death, when his prophecies
became unpopular. When Jeremiah was released

from prison, he was given into the care of Ahikam's son, Gedaliah.

First reference: 2 Kings 22:12 / Last reference: Jeremiah 43:6 / Key reference: 2 Kings 22:12–14

👥 AHILUD

of times mentioned: 5
# of MEN by this name: 1

Meaning: Brother of one born

The father of Jehoshaphat. His son served as King David's recorder.

First reference: 2 Samuel 8:16 / Last reference: 1 Chronicles 18:15

👥 AHIMAAZ

of times mentioned: 15
# of MEN by this name: 3

Meaning: Brother of anger

1) Father of King Saul's wife Ahinoam.

Only reference: 1 Samuel 14:50

2) Son of the priest Zadok. When Absalom forced David from his throne, Ahimaaz carried messages to David from his spy, Hushai the Archite. He also brought King David the news of his troops' victory over Absalom.

First reference: 2 Samuel 15:27 / Last reference: 1 Chronicles 6:53

3) One of King Solomon's twelve officials over provisions. Ahimaaz married Solomon's daughter Basmath.

Only reference: 1 Kings 4:15

👥 AHIMAN

of times mentioned: 4
# of MEN by this name: 2

Meaning: Gift

1) One of the gigantic children of Anak who was killed after Joshua's death, as Judah battled against the Canaanites.

First reference: Numbers 13:22 / Last reference: Judges 1:10

2) A Jewish exile from the tribe of Levi who resettled Jerusalem.

Only reference: 1 Chronicles 9:17

👥 AHIMELECH

of times mentioned: 16
# of MEN by this name: 2

Meaning: Brother of the king

1) The priest of Nob who gave David the hallowed bread to feed his men, when David was fleeing from Saul. When King Saul discovered this, he had all the men in Ahimelech's priestly enclave killed, except the priest's son Abiathar, who escaped.

First reference: 1 Samuel 21:1 / Last reference: Psalm 52 (title) / Key reference: 1 Samuel 21:1, 6

2) A Hittite warrior who served King David.

Only reference: 1 Samuel 26:6

👥 AHIMOTH

of times mentioned: 1
# of MEN by this name: 1

Meaning: Brother of death

A descendant of Levi through the family of Kohath.

Only reference: 1 Chronicles 6:25

👥 AHINADAB

of times mentioned: 1
# of MEN by this name: 1

Meaning: Brother of liberality

One of King Solomon's twelve officials over provisions.

Only reference: 1 Kings 4:14

👥 AHINOAM

of times mentioned: 7
# of WOMEN by this name: 2

Meaning: Brother of pleasantness

1) The wife of Saul, Israel's first king.

Only reference: 1 Samuel 14:50

2) A woman from Jezreel who became David's wife.

First reference: 1 Samuel 25:43 / Last reference: 1 Chronicles 3:1

AHIO

of times mentioned: 6
# of MEN by this name: 3

Meaning: Brotherly

1) A son of Abinadab, he went before the ark of the covenant then transported it into Jerusalem.

First reference: Samuel 6:3 / Last reference: 1 Chronicles 13:7

2) A descendant of Abraham through Jacob's son Benjamin. A son of Elpaal.

Only reference: 1 Chronicles 8:14

3) Another descendant of Abraham through Jacob's son Benjamin. His father was Jehiel.

First reference: 1 Chronicles 8:31 / Last reference: 1 Chronicles 9:37

AHIRA

of times mentioned: 5
# of MEN by this name: 1

Meaning: Brother of wrong

A prince of the tribe of Napthali, after the Exodus.

First reference: Numbers 1:15 / Last reference: Numbers 10:27

AHIRAM

of times mentioned: 1
# of MEN by this name: 1

Meaning: High

A descendant of Abraham through Jacob's son Benjamin.

Only reference: Numbers 26:38

AHISAMACH

of times mentioned: 3
# of MEN by this name: 1

Meaning: Brother of support

A descendant of Dan and father of Aholiab, a workman on the temple.

First reference: Exodus 31:6 / Last reference: Exodus 38:23

AHISHAHAR

of times mentioned: 1
# of MEN by this name: 1

Meaning: Brother of the dawn

A descendant of Abraham through Jacob's son Benjamin.

Only reference: 1 Chronicles 7:10

AHISHAR

of times mentioned: 1
# of MEN by this name: 1

Meaning: Brother of the singer

King Solomon's official over his household.

Only reference: 1 Kings 4:6

AHITHOPHEL

of times mentioned: 20
# of MEN by this name: 1

Meaning: Brother of folly

King David's counselor who conspired with David's son Absalom to overthrow the throne. Ahithophel advised Absalom to defile his father's concubines. "And the counsel of Ahithophel. . .was as if a man had enquired at the oracle of God" (2 Samuel 16:23). When Absalom did not follow his counselor's advice about attacking David and it became clear that Absalom was unlikely to win, Ahithophel hanged himself.

First reference: 2 Samuel 15:12 / Last reference: 1 Chronicles 27:34 / Key reference: 2 Samuel 16:23

AHITUB

of times mentioned: 15
# of MEN by this name: 4

Meaning: Brother of goodness

1) Son of Phineas and father of Ahiah and Ahimelech the priest of Nob.

First reference: 2 Samuel 14:3 / Last reference: 1 Samuel 22:20

2) A descendant of Abraham through Jacob's son Levi and a priest through the line of Aaron. Ahitub was the father of Zadok, the priest during King David's reign.

First reference: 2 Samuel 8:17 / Last reference: Ezra 7:2

3) Another descendant of Abraham through Jacob's son Levi and a priest through the line of Aaron.

First reference: 1 Chronicles 6:11 / Last reference: 1 Chronicles 6:12

4) A priest described as "the ruler of the house of God" (Nehemiah 11:11).

First reference: 1 Chronicles 9:11 / Last reference: Nehemiah 11:11

AHLAB

of times mentioned: OT 1

Meaning: Fatness

A city inherited by the tribe of Asher. These Jews did not drive out the Canaanites who lived in Ahlab, as God had commanded.

Only reference: Judges 1:31

AHLAI

of times mentioned: 2
# of MEN by this name: 1
# of WOMEN by this name: 1

Meaning: Wishful

1) A descendant of Abraham through Jacob's son Judah.

Only reference: 1 Chronicles 2:31

2) Father of one of King David's valiant warriors.

Only reference: 1 Chronicles 11:41

AHOAH

of times mentioned: 1
# of MEN by this name: 1

Meaning: Brotherly

A descendant of Abraham through Jacob's son Benjamin.

Only reference: 1 Chronicles 8:4

AHOLAH

of times mentioned: OT 5

Meaning: Her tent (signifying idolatry)

A name God uses for Samaria in a parable Ezekiel tells about both Israel's and Judah's unholiness.

First reference: Ezekiel 23:4 / Last reference: Ezekiel 23:44

AHOLIAB

of times mentioned: 5
# of MEN by this name: 1

Meaning: Tent of his father

An engraver and embroiderer given special ability by God to work on the tabernacle, Israel's portable worship center begun in the time of Moses. Aholiab was "a cunning workman" and a teacher of other craftsmen.

First reference: Exodus 31:6 / Last reference: Exodus 38:23

AHOLIBAH

of times mentioned: OT 6

Meaning: My tent is in her

A name God uses for Jerusalem and Judah in a parable Ezekiel tells about both Israel's and Samaria's unholiness.

First reference: Ezekiel 23:4 / Last reference: Ezekiel 23:44

👥AHOLIBAMAH

of times mentioned: 8
# of MEN by this name: 1
# of WOMEN by this name: 1

Meaning: Tent of the height

1) A wife of Esau, "of the daughters of Canaan."

First reference: Genesis 36:2 / Last reference: Genesis 36:25

2) A "duke of Edom" and a leader in the family line of Esau.

First reference: Genesis 36:41 / Last reference: 1 Chronicles 1:52

👥AHUMAI

of times mentioned: 1
# of MEN by this name: 1

Meaning: Neighbor of water

A descendant of Abraham through Jacob's son Judah.

Only reference: 1 Chronicles 4:2

👥AHUZAM

of times mentioned: 1
# of MEN by this name: 1

Meaning: Seizure

A descendant of Abraham through Jacob's son Judah.

Only reference: 1 Chronicles 4:6

👥AHUZZATH

of times mentioned: 1
# of MEN by this name: 1

Meaning: Possession

A friend of Abimelech, king of Gerar.

Only reference: Genesis 26:26

📍AI

of times mentioned: OT 36

A city east of Bethel that Joshua's spies reported did not have many inhabitants. Joshua sent three thousand men to conquer the city, but his soldiers fled before its warriors. When Joshua prayed about the defeat, God told him Israel had sinned. Once Joshua identified the sinner, Achan, and had him stoned, God commanded the Israelites to again attack the city, which He would give into their hands.

Joshua set a trap for Ai, drawing the people out of the city. Then a smaller unit of soldiers ambushed Ai, took it, and set it on fire. Israel killed all the city's inhabitants and hanged the king. When they heard of the destruction of Ai and the other cities the Israelites had taken, five Amorite kings attacked Gibeon, which had made peace with Israel.

At the time of the captivity, Jews from Ai and its vicinity were transported to Babylon. Same as Aiath, Aija, and Hai.

First reference: Joshua 7:2 / Last reference: Jeremiah 49:3 / Key references: Joshua 7:4–5; 8:1, 16–29

👥AIAH

of times mentioned: 5
# of MEN by this name: 2

Meaning: Hawk

1) A descendant of Seir, who lived in Esau's "land of Edom."

Only reference: 1 Chronicles 1:40

2) Father of Rizpah, who was a concubine of King Saul.

First reference: Samuel 3:7 / Last reference: Samuel 21:11

📍AIATH

of times mentioned: OT 1

Another form of the name Ai, used by Isaiah in his description of God's removal of the yoke of Assyria from His people. Same as Ai.

Only reference: Isaiah 10:28

📍AIJA

of times mentioned: OT 1

Another form of the name Ai, used by Nehemiah in his description of the Benjaminite resettlement there following the Babylonian Exile. Same as Ai.

Only reference: Nehemiah 11:31

AIJALON

of times mentioned: OT 7

Meaning: Deer field

1) One of the forty-eight cities given to the Levites as God had commanded. Aijalon was given to them by the tribe of Dan. Later Aijalon was taken over by the Amorites.

First reference: Joshua 21:24 / Last reference: Judges 1:35

2) A city belonging to the tribe of Zebulun. Here Elon the Zebulonite, a judge of Israel, was buried.

Only reference: Judges 12:12

3) A Benjaminite city whose Israelite inhabitants displaced the people of Gath. During one of Saul's battles with the Philistines, it became part of the battle area. King Rehoboam fortified the city for Judah's defense.

First reference: 1 Samuel 14:31 / Last reference: 2 Chronicles 11:10

4) One of the six cities of refuge established in Israel for those who had committed accidental murder. Aijalon was given to the Levites by the tribe of Judah.

Only reference: 1 Chronicles 6:69

AIN

of times mentioned: OT 5

Meaning: Fountain

1) A place that God used to identify the borders of Israel when He first gave the land to His people. Ain lay on the northeast border of Israel, somewhere between Riblah and the Sea of Chinnereth.

Only reference: Numbers 34:11

2) A city originally allotted to the tribe of Judah as part of its inheritance following the conquest of the Promised Land. It became part of the inheritance of Simeon when Joshua cast lots in Shiloh to provide territory for the seven tribes that had yet to receive their land. Later Ain became one of the six Levitical cities of refuge for accidental murderers.

First reference: Joshua 15:32 / Last reference: 1 Chronicles 4:32

AJAH

of times mentioned: 1
# of MEN by this name: 1

Meaning: Hawk

A descendant of Seir, who lived in Esau's "land of Edom."

Only reference: Genesis 36:24

AJALON

of times mentioned: OT 3

Meaning: Deer field

1) A valley in which Joshua asked God to make the moon remain still while the Israelites avenged themselves on the Amorites. For a whole day, the sun remained in the heavens so the Israelites could finish their battle. "And there was no day like that before it or after it, that the LORD hearkened unto the voice of a man: for the LORD fought for Israel" (Joshua 10:14).

Only reference: Joshua 10:12

2) A city that became part of the inheritance of Dan when Joshua cast lots in Shiloh to provide territory for the seven tribes that had yet to receive their land.

Only reference: Joshua 19:42

3) During the reign of King Ahaz, Ajalon was one of the cities of the southern low country of Judah that was invaded and occupied by the Philistines.

Only reference: 2 Chronicles 28:18

AKAN

of times mentioned: 1
# of MEN by this name: 1

Meaning: Tortuous

A descendant of Seir, who lived in Esau's "land of Edom." Same as Jaakan and Jakan.

Only reference: Genesis 36:27

AKKUB

of times mentioned: 8
# of MEN by this name: 5

Meaning: Insidious

1) A descendant of Abraham through Jacob's son Judah, in the line of the nation of Judah's third-to-last king, Jeconiah (also known as Jehoiachin).

Only reference: 1 Chronicles 3:24

2) A Jewish exile from the tribe of Levi who resettled Jerusalem.

First reference: 1 Chronicles 9:17 / Last reference: Nehemiah 12:25

3) Forefather of an exiled family that returned to Judah under Zerubbabel.

First reference: Ezra 2:42 / Last reference: Nehemiah 7:45

4) Forefather of an exiled family that returned to Judah under Zerubbabel.

Only reference: Ezra 2:45

5) A Levite who helped Ezra to explain the law to exiles returned to Jerusalem.

Only reference: Nehemiah 8:7

AKRABBIM

of times mentioned: OT 2

Meaning: Scorpion or scourge

A hill that God used to identify the southern borders of Israel when He first gave it to His people. In the time of the judges, it was a border with the Amorites.

First reference: Numbers 34:4 / Last reference: Judges 1:36

ALAMETH

of times mentioned: 1
# of MEN by this name: 1

Meaning: A covering

A descendant of Abraham through Jacob's son Benjamin.

Only reference: 1 Chronicles 7:8

ALAMMELECH

of times mentioned: OT 1

Meaning: Oak of the king

A city that became part of the inheritance of Asher when Joshua cast lots in Shiloh to provide territory for the seven tribes that had yet to receive their land.

Only reference: Joshua 19:26

ALEMETH

of times mentioned: 2
# of MEN by this name: 1

Meaning: A covering

A descendant of Abraham through Jacob's son Benjamin, through the line of King Saul and his son Jonathan.

First reference: 1 Chronicles 8:36 / Last reference: 1 Chronicles 9:42

ALEMETH

of times mentioned: OT 1

Meaning: A covering

One of the forty-eight cities given to the Levites as God had commanded. Alemeth was given to them by the tribe of Benjamin.

Only reference: 1 Chronicles 6:60

ALEXANDER

of times mentioned: 6
# of MEN by this name: 4

Meaning: Man-defender

1) One of two sons of Simon, a man from Cyrene forced by Roman soldiers to carry Jesus' cross to Golgotha, the crucifixion site.

Only reference: Mark 15:21

2) A relative of the high priest Annas, who was present when Jewish leaders questioned Peter and John about healing a lame beggar.

Only reference: Acts 4:6

3) A Jewish participant in a riot in Ephesus, instigated by idol makers against the apostle Paul's teaching.

Only reference: Acts 19:33

4) A blasphemous coppersmith who opposed the apostle Paul, doing him "much evil."

First reference: 1 Timothy 1:20 / Last reference: 2 Timothy 4:14

♀ALEXANDRIA

of times mentioned: NT 3

This Egyptian city on the western edge of the Nile Delta was the birthplace of the preacher Apollos. He came to Ephesus and was taught the complete Gospel message by Priscilla and Aquila. When Paul sailed to Rome, he did so in two ships that identified Alexandria as their home port.

First reference: Acts 18:24 / Last reference: Acts 28:11

👥ALIAH

of times mentioned: 1
# of MEN by this name: 1

Meaning: Perverseness

A "duke of Edom" and a leader in the family line of Esau. Same as Alvah.

Only reference: 1 Chronicles 1:51

👥ALIAN

of times mentioned: 1
# of MEN by this name: 1

Meaning: Lofty

A descendant of Seir, who lived in Esau's "land of Edom." Same as Alvan.

Only reference: 1 Chronicles 1:40

👥ALLON

of times mentioned: 1
# of MEN by this name: 1

Meaning: Oak

A descendant of Abraham through Jacob's son Simeon.

Only reference: 1 Chronicles 4:37

♀ALLON

of times mentioned: OT1

A city that became part of the inheritance of Naphtali when Joshua cast lots in Shiloh to provide territory for the seven tribes that had yet to receive their land.

Only reference: Joshua 19:33

♀ALLON-BACHUTH

of times mentioned: OT 1

Meaning: Oak of weeping

The place where Deborah, Rebekah's nurse, was buried.

Only reference: Genesis 35:8

👥ALMODAD

of times mentioned: 2
# of MEN by this name: 1

A descendant of Noah through Noah's son Shem.

First reference: Genesis 10:26 / Last reference: 1 Chronicles 1:20

♀ALMON

of times mentioned: OT 1

Meaning: Hidden

One of the forty-eight cities given to the Levites as God had commanded. Almon was given to them by the tribe of Benjamin.

Only reference: Joshua 21:18

♀ALMON-DIBLATHAIM

of times mentioned: OT 2

Meaning: Almon toward Diblathaim

A place where the Israelites camped on their way to the Promised Land.

First reference: Numbers 33:46 / Last reference: Numbers 33:47

⚐ALOTH

of times mentioned: OT 1

Meaning: Mistresses

Under King Solomon's governmental organization, a region responsible for supplying provisions for the king.

Only reference: 1 Kings 4:16

👥ALPHAEUS

of times mentioned: 5
# of MEN by this name: 2

1) Father of one of two apostles named James. The phrase "James the son of Alphaeus" distinguishes this James from the brother of John and the "sons of Zebedee."

First reference: Matthew 10:3 / Last reference: Acts 1:13

2) Father of the apostle Levi, also known as Matthew.

Only reference: Mark 2:14

⚐ALUSH

of times mentioned: OT 2

A place on the Exodus route where the Israelites camped after they left Egypt.

First reference: Numbers 33:13 / Last reference: Numbers 33:14

👥ALVAH

of times mentioned: 1
# of MEN by this name: 1

Meaning: Perverseness

A "duke of Edom" and a leader in the family line of Esau. Same as Aliah.

Only reference: Genesis 36:40

👥ALVAN

of times mentioned: 1
# of MEN by this name: 1

Meaning: Lofty

A descendant of Seir, who lived in Esau's "land of Edom." Same as Alian.

Only reference: Genesis 36:23

⚐AMAD

of times mentioned: OT 1

Meaning: People of time

A city that became part of the inheritance of Asher when Joshua cast lots in Shiloh to provide territory for the seven tribes that had yet to receive their land.

Only reference: Joshua 19:26

👥AMAL

of times mentioned: 1
# of MEN by this name: 1

Meaning: Worry

A descendant of Abraham through Jacob's son Asher.

Only reference: 1 Chronicles 7:35

👥AMALEK

of times mentioned: 3
# of MEN by this name: 1

A descendant of Abraham's grandson Esau, whose blessing as older brother was taken by the scheming Jacob. Amalek's descendants, the Amalekites, were longtime enemies of Israel, earning God's contempt: "The LORD hath sworn that the LORD will have war with Amalek from generation to generation" (Exodus 17:16).

First reference: Genesis 36:12 / Last reference: 1 Chronicles 1:36

⚐AMAM

of times mentioned: OT 1

Meaning: Gathering spot

A city that became part of the inheritance of the tribe of Judah following the conquest of the Promised Land. It lay between Hazor and Shema.

Only reference: Joshua 15:26

♀AMANA

of times mentioned: OT 1

Meaning: Something fixed (like a covenant or allowance)

A mountain of Lebanon that may have been near the source of the Abana River. Solomon uses it poetically in his wooing of the Shulammite.

Only reference: Song of Solomon 4:8

👥AMARIAH

of times mentioned: 16
# of MEN by this name: 9

Meaning: God has promised

1) A descendant of Abraham through Jacob's son Levi and a priest through the line of Aaron.

First reference: 1 Chronicles 6:7 / Last reference: Ezra 7:3

2) Another descendant of Abraham through Jacob's son Levi and a priest through the line of Aaron.

Only reference: 1 Chronicles 6:11

3) A Levite who served at the time of King Solomon.

First reference: 1 Chronicles 23:19 / Last reference: 1 Chronicles 24:23

4) The chief priest in the time of King Jehoshaphat of Judah.

Only reference: 2 Chronicles 19:11

5) A priest in the time of King Hezekiah, he helped to distribute the people's freewill offerings to his fellow priests.

Only reference: 2 Chronicles 31:15

6) An exiled Israelite who married a "strange" (foreign) woman.

Only reference: Ezra 10:42

7) A priest who renewed the covenant under Nehemiah.

First reference: Nehemiah 10:3 / Last reference: Nehemiah 12:13

8) Ancestor of a man of the tribe of Judah who was chosen by lot to resettle Jerusalem after returning from the Babylonian Exile.

Only reference: Nehemiah 11:4

9) An ancestor of the prophet Zephaniah.

Only reference: Zephaniah 1:1

👥AMASA

of times mentioned: 16
# of MEN by this name: 2

Meaning: Burden

1) King David's nephew who became Absalom's commander during Absalom's rebellion against his father. When David regained the throne, he made Amasa commander of his army, in Joab's place. When the king sent his new commander to gather the men of Judah, Joab followed Amasa, attacked him, and killed him.

First reference: 2 Samuel 17:25 / Last reference: 1 Chronicles 2:17 / Key reference: 2 Samuel 19:13

2) A man of the tribe of Ephraim who counseled Israel against enslaving fellow Jews from Judah who were captured in a civil war. Amasa helped to feed and clothe the prisoners before sending them home.

Only reference: 2 Chronicles 28:12

👥AMASAI

of times mentioned: 5
# of MEN by this name: 3

Meaning: Burdensome

1) A descendant of Abraham through Jacob's son Levi and the father of a Levite who cleansed the Jerusalem temple during the revival of King Hezekiah's day.

First reference: 1 Chronicles 6:25 / Last reference: 2 Chronicles 29:12

2) A chief captain in David's army.

Only reference: 1 Chronicles 12:18

3) A Levite who blew a trumpet before the ark of the covenant when David brought it to Jerusalem.

Only reference: 1 Chronicles 15:24

AMASHAI

of times mentioned: 1
# of MEN by this name: 1

Meaning: Burdensome

A Jewish exile from the tribe of Levi who resettled Jerusalem.

Only reference: Nehemiah 11:13

AMASIAH

of times mentioned: 1
# of MEN by this name: 1

Meaning: God has loaded

A warrior who raised 200,000 brave men for King Jehoshaphat of Judah.

Only reference: 2 Chronicles 17:16

AMAZIAH

of times mentioned: 40
# of MEN by this name: 4

Meaning: Strength of God

1) Son and successor of King Joash of Judah. Though he did right, the new king did not remove the pagan altars from the land. He killed the servants who had murdered his father in his bed but did not kill their children. After raising an army in his country, he hired 100,000 men from Israel. But a man of God convinced the king to rely on God, not a hired army, so Amaziah sent the Israelites home. With his own men he went to war with Edom and won; meanwhile the scorned Israelite army attacked Judah, killed 3,000, and carried away spoils. Amaziah brought back idols from Edom and began to worship them. When God sent a prophet to correct him, he would not listen, and the prophet predicted Amaziah's downfall. Amaziah confronted Jehoash, king of Israel, who tried to make peace. Judah's king refused, but when he waged war on Israel, all his men fled. Jehoash broke down Jerusalem's wall and took the precious vessels from the temple and the treasures of the king's house. Later a conspiracy grew up against Amaziah, so he fled to Lachish, where he was killed.

First reference: 2 Kings 12:21 / Last reference: 2 Chronicles 26:4 / Key references: 2 Chronicles 25:1–2, 14–16

2) A descendant of Abraham through Jacob's son Simeon.

Only reference: 1 Chronicles 4:34

3) A descendant of Abraham through Jacob's son Levi.

Only reference: 1 Chronicles 6:45

4) A false priest of Bethel who accused the prophet Amos of conspiring against King Jeroboam of Israel.

First reference: Amos 7:10 / Last reference: Amos 7:14

AMI

of times mentioned: 1
# of MEN by this name: 1

Meaning: Skilled

Forefather of an exiled Israelite family.

Only reference: Ezra 2:57

AMINADAB

of times mentioned: 3
# of MEN by this name: 1

Genealogy of Jesus: Yes (Matthew 1:4; Luke 3:33)

Meaning: People of liberality

An ancestor of Jesus, the great-grandfather of David's great-grandfather Boaz.

First reference: Matthew 1:4 / Last reference: Luke 3:33

AMITTAI

of times mentioned: 2
# of MEN by this name: 1

Meaning: Truthful

Father of the prophet Jonah, who preached in Nineveh.

First reference: 2 Kings 14:25 / Last reference: Jonah 1:1

◉AMMAH

of times mentioned: OT 1

Meaning: A unit of measure

A hill to which David's commander Joab and Joab's brother Abishai pursued Abner, the commander of Saul's army, after Abner killed their brother. The Benjaminites supported Abner, and Joab backed down.

Only reference: 2 Samuel 2:24

👥AMMIEL

of times mentioned: 6
# of MEN by this name: 4

Meaning: People of God

1) One of the twelve spies sent by Moses to spy out the land of Canaan.

Only reference: Numbers 13:12

2) A man who housed Saul's crippled son, Mephibosheth, after the king's death. Ammiel's son Machir later brought food and supplies to King David and his soldiers as they fled from the army of David's son Absalom, who had staged a coup.

First reference: 2 Samuel 9:4 / Last reference: 2 Samuel 17:27

3) Father of King David's wife Bath-sheba and the grandfather of Solomon.

Only reference: 1 Chronicles 3:5

4) A Levite "porter" (doorkeeper) in the house of the Lord.

Only reference: 1 Chronicles 26:5

👥AMMIHUD

of times mentioned: 10
# of MEN by this name: 5

Meaning: People of splendor

1) A descendant of Abraham through Joseph's son Ephraim and an ancestor of Joshua.

First reference: Numbers 1:10 / Last reference: 1 Chronicles 7:26

2) Forefather of Shemuel, prince of the tribe of Simeon when the Israelites entered the Promised Land.

Only reference: Numbers 34:20

3) Forefather of Pedahel, prince of the tribe of Naphtali when the Israelites entered the Promised Land.

Only reference: Numbers 34:28

4) Father of the king of Geshur, to whom Absalom fled after he killed Amnon.

Only reference: 2 Samuel 13:37

5) A descendant of Judah and father of Uthai.

Only reference: 1 Chronicles 9:4

👥AMMINADAB

of times mentioned: 13
# of MEN by this name: 4

Meaning: People of liberality

1) Father-in-law of Aaron.

Only reference: Exodus 6:23

2) A descendant of Judah. His son, Nahshon, became the prince of his tribe.

First reference: Numbers 1:7 / Last reference: 1 Chronicles 2:10

3) A descendant of Abraham through Jacob's son Levi.

Only reference: 1 Chronicles 6:22

4) A descendant of Abraham through Jacob's son Levi. Amminadab was among a group of Levites appointed by King David to bring the ark of the covenant from the house of Obed-edom to Jerusalem.

First reference: 1 Chronicles 15:10 / Last reference: 1 Chronicles 15:11

👥AMMISHADDAI

of times mentioned: 5
# of MEN by this name: 1

Meaning: People of the Almighty

A descendant of Dan. His son, Ahiezer, became the prince of his tribe.

First reference: Numbers 1:12 / Last reference: Numbers 10:25

👪 AMMIZABAD

of times mentioned: 1
# of MEN by this name: 1

Meaning: People of endowment

Son of Benaiah and an army officer of David.

Only reference: 1 Chronicles 27:6

📍 AMMON

of times mentioned: OT 91

Meaning: Tribal (meaning inbred)

The land of the people of Ben-Ammi, who was the son of Lot born of his incest with his younger daughter. When Israel invaded the Promised Land, God told His people they would not be given the land of Ammon, which was northeast of the Dead Sea, for it belonged to Lot's children. But Israel did take some land that had once belonged to the Ammonites and had subsequently been conquered by the Amorites.

The Ammonites did not follow the ways of the Lord and varied between rising up against Israel and paying homage to Israel's greater power. The Israelite captain Jephthah first led the people of Gilead in battle against Ammon and subdued it.

An attack of the Ammonites caused Israel to fear and beg Samuel for a king. Saul proved his leadership abilities when King Nahash of Ammon besieged Jabesh-gilead and would not make peace with that city. Saul rallied the people of Israel and Judah against Ammon and led them to victory in battle. King David had a peaceful relationship with Nahash of Ammon, but Nahash's son Hanun offended David's friendly overtures. Aware of his offense and David's contempt for him, King Hanun renewed warfare with Israel, hiring Syrian warriors to fight alongside his own troops. Together Joab and David defeated the joined armies, and David dedicated the silver and gold he captured from that nation to God.

In the spring, Joab besieged Ammon's capital, Rabbah, but David stayed behind in Jerusalem and became involved with Bathsheba. Bathsheba's husband, Uriah, died in battle against Rabbah.

But these victories did not end warfare between the countries. The Ammonites attacked Judah during King Jehoshaphat's reign. King Jotham fought and prevailed against Ammon, which paid tribute to him. Later, Ammon joined Judah's king Jehoiakim in his rebellion against the Babylonian king Nebuchadnezzar.

Nehemiah took the Jews to task for intermarrying with the Ammonites, for their children could not even speak Hebrew. The last mention of Ammon in scripture is in Zephaniah, where the prophet foretells the nation's destruction.

First reference: Genesis 19:38 / Last reference: Zephaniah 2:9 / Key references: Deuteronomy 2:19; Judges 11:32–33; 1 Samuel 12:12; 2 Chronicles 27:5

👪 AMNON

of times mentioned: 28
# of MEN by this name: 2

Meaning: Faithful

1) David's firstborn son, born in Hebron to his wife Ahinoam. Amnon fell in love with his half sister Tamar. Pretending to be sick, he asked his father to send Tamar to him with food. When she came, he raped her. His love turned to hate, and he threw her out of his house. When Tamar's full brother, Absalom, heard of this, he hated Amnon and eventually had him killed.

First reference: 2 Samuel 3:2 / Last reference: 1 Chronicles 3:1 / Key reference: 2 Samuel 13:1–2

2) A descendant of Abraham through Jacob's son Judah.

Only reference: 1 Chronicles 4:20

👪 AMOK

of times mentioned: 2
# of MEN by this name: 1

Meaning: Deep

An exiled priest who returned to Judah under Zerubbabel.

First reference: Nehemiah 12:7 / Last reference: Nehemiah 12:20

AMON

of times mentioned: 19
# of MEN by this name: 3

Meaning: Skilled

1) A governor of Samaria. When the prophet Micaiah did not please King Ahab, he sent the prophet to Amon.

First reference: 1 Kings 22:26 / Last reference: Chronicles 18:25

2) An evil king of Judah who reigned for two years. He worshipped idols and "trespassed more and more" (2 Chronicles 33:23). His servants conspired against him and killed him in his own house.

First reference: 2 Kings 21:18 / Last reference: Matthew 1:10 / Key references: 2 Kings 21:19–20; 2 Chronicles 33:23

Genealogy of Jesus: Yes (Matthew 1:10)

3) Forefather of an exiled family—former servants of Solomon—that returned to Judah under Zerubbabel.

Only reference: Nehemiah 7:59

AMOS

of times mentioned: 8
# of MEN by this name: 2

Meaning: Burdensome

1) A Judean prophet during the reigns of King Uzziah of Judah and King Jeroboam of Israel. He came from a rural setting in which he was a herdsman and fruit gatherer. When God called him as a prophet, he spoke to both Judah and Israel, condemning idolatry and disobedience.

First reference: Amos 1:1 / Last reference: Amos 8:2

2) A descendant of Abraham through Isaac; forebear of Jesus' earthly father, Joseph.

Only reference: Luke 3:25

Genealogy of Jesus: Yes (Luke 3:25)

AMOZ

of times mentioned: 13
# of MEN by this name: 1

Meaning: Strong

Father of the prophet Isaiah.

First reference: 2 Kings 19:2 / Last reference: Isaiah 38:1

AMPHIPOLIS

of times mentioned: NT 1

Meaning: A city surrounded by a river

A northeastern Macedonian city that Paul and Silas passed through on their way to Thessalonica.

Only reference: Acts 17:1

AMPLIAS

of times mentioned: 1
# of MEN by this name: 1

Meaning: Enlarged

A Roman Christian described as "my beloved in the Lord" by the apostle Paul.

Only reference: Romans 16:8

AMRAM

of times mentioned: 14
# of MEN by this name: 3

Meaning: High people

1) The father of Moses, Aaron, and Miriam.

First reference: Exodus 6:18 / Last reference: 1 Chronicles 24:20

2) An exiled Israelite who married a "strange" (foreign) woman.

Only reference: Ezra 10:34

3) A descendant of Seir the Horite, whose family married into Esau's family.

First reference: 1 Chronicles 1:41

AMRAPHEL

of times mentioned: 2
# of MEN by this name: 1

The king of Shinar in the days of Abram. Amraphel was part of a victorious battle alliance that kidnapped Abram's nephew Lot.

First reference: Genesis 14:1 / Last reference: Genesis 14:9

AMZI

of times mentioned: 2
# of MEN by this name: 2

Meaning: Strong

1) A descendant of Levi and forefather of Hashabiah, who stood to the left of Heman the choir leader of the temple.

Only reference: 1 Chronicles 6:46

2) Forefather of a Jewish exile from the tribe of Levi who resettled Jerusalem.

Only reference: Nehemiah 11:12

ANAB

of times mentioned: OT 2

Meaning: Fruit

A Canaanite city in what became part of Judah's hill country following the conquest of the Promised Land. Joshua conquered Anab and its inhabitants, the Anakim.

First reference: Joshua 11:21 / Last reference: Joshua 15:50

ANAH

of times mentioned: 12
# of MEN by this name: 2
# of WOMEN by this name: 1

Meaning: Answer

1) Mother of Aholibamah and mother-in-law of Esau.

First reference: Genesis 36:2 / Last reference: Genesis 36:25

2) A descendant of Seir, who lived in Esau's "land of Edom."

First reference: Genesis 36:20 / Last reference: 1 Chronicles 1:38

3) Another descendant of Seir, who lived in Esau's "land of Edom." Anah discovered "mules in the wilderness" as he fed his father's donkeys.

First reference: Genesis 36:24 / Last reference: 1 Chronicles 1:41

ANAHARATH

of times mentioned: OT 1

Meaning: A gorge

A city that became part of the inheritance of Issachar when Joshua cast lots in Shiloh to provide territory for the seven tribes that had yet to receive their land.

Only reference: Joshua 19:19

ANAIAH

of times mentioned: 2
# of MEN by this name: 2

Meaning: God has answered

1) A priest who assisted Ezra in reading the book of the law to the people of Jerusalem.

Only reference: Nehemiah 8:4

2) A Jewish leader who renewed the covenant under Nehemiah.

Only reference: Nehemiah 10:22

ANAK

of times mentioned: 9
# of MEN by this name: 1

Meaning: Strangling

Founder of a tribe in Hebron. His gigantic sons lived there when Joshua's spies searched the land.

First reference: Numbers 13:22 / Last reference: Judges 1:20

ANAN

of times mentioned: 1
# of MEN by this name: 1

Meaning: Cloud

A Jewish leader who renewed the covenant under Nehemiah.

Only reference: Nehemiah 10:26

ANANI

of times mentioned: 1
# of MEN by this name: 1

Meaning: Cloudy

A descendant of Abraham through Jacob's son Judah, in the line of the nation of Judah's third-to-last king, Jeconiah (also known as Jehoiachin).

Only reference: 1 Chronicles 3:24

ANANIAH

of times mentioned: 1
# of MEN by this name: 1

Meaning: God has covered

Forefather of a man who repaired Jerusalem's walls under Nehemiah.

Only reference: Nehemiah 3:23

ANANIAH

of times mentioned: OT 1

Meaning: God has covered

A Benjaminite city resettled by the Jews after the Babylonian Exile.

Only reference: Nehemiah 11:32

ANANIAS

of times mentioned: 11
# of MEN by this name: 3

Meaning: God has favored

1) A Christian who lied to the apostle Peter, saying that he and his wife, Sapphira, had donated the full price of a land sale to the church. Peter confronted Ananias, asking why he had lied to God. Ananias died immediately.

First reference: Acts 5:1 / Last reference: Acts 5:5

2) A Christian of Damascus whom God called to speak to Paul shortly after the apostle-to-be's conversion. When Ananias doubted the wisdom of meeting with Paul, God told him Paul would bear the Gospel to the Gentiles.

First reference: Acts 9:10 / Last reference: Acts 22:12

3) The high priest who accused and even hit Paul during interrogation, after the apostle was wrongly arrested for profaning the temple. Five days later Ananias appeared before Governor Felix, supporting charges of sedition against Paul.

First reference: Acts 23:2 / Last reference: Acts 24:1

ANATH

of times mentioned: 2
# of MEN by this name: 1

Meaning: Answer

Father of Israel's third judge, Shamgar.

First reference: Judges 3:31 / Last reference: Judges 5:6

ANATHOTH

of times mentioned: 2
# of MEN by this name: 2

Meaning: Answers

1) A descendant of Abraham through Jacob's son Benjamin.

Only reference: 1 Chronicles 7:8

2) A Jewish leader who renewed the covenant under Nehemiah.

Only reference: Nehemiah 10:19

ANATHOTH

of times mentioned: OT 14

Meaning: Answers

One of the forty-eight cities given to the Levites as God had commanded. Anathoth was given to them by the tribe of Benjamin. King Solomon banished Abiathar the priest to Anathoth after he supported Adonijah as heir to David's throne. Jeremiah was a priest of Anathoth, but men of that city sought his life, and God promised to punish them for their wickedness. When Babylon besieged Jerusalem, as a sign of hope for the future, God commanded Jeremiah to buy his cousin's field in his hometown of Anathoth. When Nebuchadnezzar captured Judah, 128 men from Anathoth were carried off to Babylon. Following the exile, the Benjaminites resettled the city.

First reference: Joshua 21:18 / Last reference: Jeremiah 32:9 / Key references: 1 Kings 2:26; Jeremiah 11:21–23; 32:7–9

ANDREW

\# of times mentioned: 13
\# of MEN by this name: 1

Meaning: Manly

Brother of Peter and one of Jesus' disciples and apostles. He met Jesus first and then told Peter he had found the Messiah. Jesus called both of these fishermen to leave their boat and become fishers of men. At the feeding of the five thousand, Andrew brought the boy with loaves and fish to Jesus' attention. With Philip, he brought some Greeks to meet Jesus. He was also one of the intimate group of disciples who questioned Jesus about the end times.

First reference: Matthew 4:18 / Last reference: Acts 1:13 / Key references: Matthew 4:18–19; John 6:8–9

ANDRONICUS

\# of times mentioned: 1
\# of MEN by this name: 1

Meaning: Man of victory

A Roman Christian who spent time in jail with the apostle Paul and who may have been related to Paul.

Only reference: Romans 16:7

ANEM

\# of times mentioned: OT 1

Meaning: Two fountains

One of the forty-eight cities given to the Levites as God had commanded. Anem was given to them by the tribe of Issachar.

Only reference: 1 Chronicles 6:73

ANER

\# of times mentioned: 2
\# of MEN by this name: 1

Meaning: Boy

An Amorite confederate of Abram who was part of a victorious battle alliance that kidnapped Abram's nephew Lot.

First reference: Genesis 14:13 / Last reference: Genesis 14:24

ANER

\# of times mentioned: OT 1

One of the forty-eight cities given to the Levites as God had commanded. Aner was given to them by the tribe of Manasseh.

Only reference: 1 Chronicles 6:70

ANIAM

\# of times mentioned: 1
\# of MEN by this name: 1

Meaning: Groaning of the people

A descendant of Abraham through Joseph's son Manasseh.

Only reference: 1 Chronicles 7:19

ANIM

\# of times mentioned: OT 1

Meaning: Fountains

A city that became part of the inheritance of the tribe of Judah following the conquest of the Promised Land.

Only reference: Joshua 15:50

👥ANNA

of times mentioned: 1
# of WOMEN by this name: 1

Meaning: Favored

A widowed prophetess who lived in the temple and recognized Jesus as the Messiah when He was first brought to the temple.

Only reference: Luke 2:36

👥ANNAS

of times mentioned: 4
# of MEN by this name: 1

Meaning: God has favored

High priest during Jesus' ministry. Though the Romans deposed him in favor of his son-in-law Caiaphas, many Jews still considered him the high priest. Jesus was first brought to him after Judas's betrayal. Annas was also one of the council that sought to keep Peter from preaching.

First reference: Luke 3:2 / Last reference: Acts 4:6

📍ANTIOCH

of times mentioned: NT 19

1) The capital of Syria, where Stephen preached to the Jews. Cypriot Jews who had heard the message had shared it with Greeks. The church in Jerusalem sent Barnabas to Antioch when they heard that Gentiles were hearing the Word. Barnabas went to Tarsus to get Saul's assistance in his mission. They joined Stephen in Antioch. In this city, believers first received the name Christians.

Paul and Barnabas received their missionary calling in Antioch. Later in this city, Paul confronted Peter with his refusal to eat with Gentiles. Following the Council of Jerusalem, Paul, Barnabas, Judas Barsabas, and Silas returned to Antioch to declare the council's decision about circumcision, the law, and Gentiles.

First reference: Acts 6:5 / Last reference: Galatians 2:11 / Key references: Acts 11:19, 26; 13:1; Galatians 2:11

2) Called Antioch in Pisidia, this city in the Roman province of Phrygia, in Asia Minor, received the Good News through Paul's ministry. Angered, some Jews of the city stoned Paul, who returned to the city then left the next day.

First reference: Acts 13:14 / Last reference: 2 Timothy 3:11–26

👥ANTIPAS

of times mentioned: 1
# of MEN by this name: 1

Meaning: Instead of father

A Christian martyr of Pergamos commended by Jesus.

Only reference: Revelation 2:13

📍ANTIPATRIS

of times mentioned: NT 1

A city between Caesarea and Lydda. Here Claudius Lysias's soldiers protected Paul after the Jews of Jerusalem threatened his life.

Only reference: Acts 23:31

👥ANTOTHIJAH

of times mentioned: 1
# of MEN by this name: 1

Meaning: Answers of God

A descendant of Abraham through Jacob's son Benjamin.

Only reference: 1 Chronicles 8:24

👥ANUB

of times mentioned: 1
# of MEN by this name: 1

Meaning: Borne

A descendant of Abraham through Jacob's son Judah.

Only reference: 1 Chronicles 4:8

👥APELLES

of times mentioned: 1
# of MEN by this name: 1

A Christian acquaintance of the apostle Paul in Rome.

Only reference: Romans 16:10

♀APHEK

of times mentioned: OT 8

Meaning: Fortress (implying strength)

1) A Canaanite city in which the Philistines camped before the battle in which they captured the ark of the covenant. The Philistines again gathered here under King Achish to fight King Saul. But Achish's troops refused to fight as long as David and his warriors were on their side, because David had been their enemy when he served Saul.

First reference: Joshua 12:18 / Last reference: 1 Samuel 29:1

2) A city that had not yet fully fallen under Israel's sway when Joshua was old. It became part of the inheritance of Asher when Joshua cast lots in Shiloh to provide territory for the seven tribes that had yet to receive their land. Same as Aphik.

First reference: Joshua 13:4 / Last reference: Joshua 19:30

3) A city where King Ahab of Israel and King Benhadad of Syria fought. Israel routed its enemies and captured the king.

First reference: 1 Kings 20:26 / Last reference: 2 Kings 13:17

♀APHEKAH

of times mentioned: OT 1

Meaning: Fortress

A city that became part of the inheritance of the tribe of Judah following the conquest of the Promised Land.

Only reference: Joshua 15:53

👥APHIAH

of times mentioned: 1
# of MEN by this name: 1

Meaning: Breeze

A descendant of Benjamin and forefather of King Saul.

Only reference: Samuel 9:1

♀APHIK

of times mentioned: OT 1

Meaning: Fortress (implying strength)

A city that became part of the inheritance of the tribe of Asher. The tribe of Asher did not drive the Canaanites out of Aphik as God had commanded them to do. Same as Aphek (2).

Only reference: Judges 1:31

♀APHRAH

of times mentioned: OT 1

A Philistine city cited by the prophet Micah as rolling in the dust in mourning at the judgment of the Lord.

Only reference: Micah 1:10–27

👥APHSES

of times mentioned: 1
# of MEN by this name: 1

Meaning: Sever

One of twenty-four priests in David's time who was chosen by lot to serve in the tabernacle.

Only reference: 1 Chronicles 24:15

♀APOLLONIA

of times mentioned: NT 1

Meaning: Named for the Greek god Apollo

A Macedonian city that Paul and his companions passed through on their way to Thessalonica.

Only reference: Acts 17:1

👥APOLLOS

of times mentioned: 10
# of MEN by this name: 1

Meaning: The sun

A Jewish preacher from Alexandria who had been baptized into John's baptism and knew nothing of the Holy Spirit. Aquila and Priscilla "expounded unto him the way of God more perfectly" (Acts 18:26). He went to preach in Corinth. When a dispute arose in Corinth between church members who followed Paul and those who followed Apollos, Paul called them to recognize that they all followed Jesus.

First reference: Acts 18:24 / Last reference: Titus 3:13 / Key references: Acts 18:24; 1 Corinthians 3:5

👥APPAIM

of times mentioned: 2
# of MEN by this name: 1

Meaning: Two nostrils

A descendant of Abraham through Jacob's son Judah.

First reference: 1 Chronicles 2:30 / Last reference: 1 Chronicles 2:31

👥APPHIA

of times mentioned: 1
# of WOMEN by this name: 1

A Christian woman of Colosse called "beloved" by the apostle Paul.

Only reference: Philemon 1:2

📍APPII

of times mentioned: NT 1

Meaning: Appius (Appii is its possessive case)

A town outside of Rome. Here some Roman Christians met Paul as he headed toward that city.

Only reference: Acts 28:15

👥AQUILA

of times mentioned: 6
# of MEN by this name: 1

Meaning: Eagle

A tent-making Christian who lived in Corinth and

met Paul there. Paul joined Aquila and his wife, Priscilla, in their craft. The couple became helpers in Paul's ministry and founded a house church in their home.

First reference: Acts 18:2 / Last reference: 2 Timothy 4:19

AR

of times mentioned: OT 6

A city of Moab that God gave to Lot's heirs. God would not let the Israelites fight Ar when they returned to the wilderness following their refusal to enter the Promised Land. The prophet Isaiah foretold that Ar would be destroyed.

First reference: Numbers 21:15 / Last reference: Isaiah 15:1

👥ARA

of times mentioned: 1
# of MEN by this name: 1

Meaning: Lion

A descendant of Abraham through Jacob's son Asher.

Only reference: 1 Chronicles 7:38

📍ARAB

of times mentioned: OT 1

Meaning: Ambush

A city that became part of the inheritance of the tribe of Judah following the conquest of the Promised Land.

Only reference: Joshua 15:52

📍ARABAH

of times mentioned: OT 1

Meaning: A desert (in the sense of sterility)

Another name for the Jordan Valley, in which the Jordan River lies. It was part of the inheritance of the tribe of Benjamin.

Only reference: Joshua 18:18

⦿ARABIA

of times mentioned: OT 6 / NT 2

Meaning: Sterile

A large peninsula in southwest Asia where many nomadic people lived. The children of Abraham and Keturah largely settled the northern part of Arabia, while Ishmael's descendants settled the northwestern part of the peninsula. Ishmaelites bought Joseph from his brothers (Genesis 37:25). The kings of Arabia brought gold and silver to King Solomon. Ophir, which traded gold, almug trees, and precious stones with King Solomon, may have been in Arabia. Jeremiah prophesied God's judgment of Arabia, along with many other peoples. Ezekiel described Arabia as selling "lambs, and rams, and goats" to Tyre (Ezekiel 27:21).

Following his conversion, Paul visited Arabia. He described it as the site of Mount Sinai and compared Arabia to Hagar ["Agar" in the KJV].

First reference: 1 Kings 10:15 / Last reference: Galatians 4:25–28

👥ARAD

of times mentioned: 3
# of MEN by this name: 2

Meaning: Fugitive

1) A Canaanite king who fought the Israelites as they entered the Promised Land.

First reference: Numbers 21:1 / Last reference: Numbers 33:40

2) A descendant of Abraham through Jacob's son Benjamin.

Only reference: 1 Chronicles 8:15

⦿ARAD

of times mentioned: OT 2

Meaning: Fugitive

A Canaanite kingdom west of the Jordan River. King Arad fought the Israelites when they came to the Promised Land. He captured some Israelites, and so the nation vowed to destroy the king's cities. Joshua and his army conquered Arad. The descendants of Moses' father-in-law, Jethro, moved into the "wilderness of Judah, which lieth in the south of Arad" (Judges 1:16).

First reference: Joshua 12:14 / Last reference: Judges 1:16

👥ARAH

of times mentioned: 4
# of MEN by this name: 3

Meaning: Wayfaring

1) A descendant of Abraham through Jacob's son Asher.

Only reference: 1 Chronicles 7:39

2) Forefather of an exiled family that returned to Judah under Zerubbabel.

First reference: Ezra 2:5 / Last reference: Nehemiah 7:10

3) Father of Tobiah, who opposed the rebuilding of Jerusalem's wall.

Only reference: Nehemiah 6:18

👥ARAM

of times mentioned: 8
# of MEN by this name: 3

Meaning: The highland

1) A descendant of Noah through Noah's son Shem.

First reference: Genesis 10:22 / Last reference: 1 Chronicles 1:17

2) A descendant of Abraham's brother Nahor.

Only reference: Genesis 22:21

3) A descendant of Abraham through Isaac; forebear of Jesus' earthly father, Joseph.

First reference: 1 Chronicles 7:34 / Last reference: Luke 3:33

Genealogy of Jesus: Yes (Luke 3:33)

⦿ARAM

of times mentioned: OT 2

Meaning: The highland

1) An early name for Syria, used during the time of Balaam. Aram covered more territory than modern Syria, extending to the Euphrates River. Balaam came from Aram to curse Israel. See also Syria.

Only reference: Numbers 23:7

2) A city taken by Jair, a descendant of Judah.

Only reference: 1 Chronicles 2:23

♀ARAM-NAHARAIM

of times mentioned: OT 1

Meaning: Aram of the two rivers

A name for northwest Mesopotamia. King David fought this nation and Aram-zobah.

Only reference: Psalm 60 (title)

♀ARAM-ZOBAH

of times mentioned: OT 1

Meaning: Aram of Tsoba

A name for central Syria. King David fought this nation, killing twenty-two thousand men (2 Samuel 8:5).

Only reference: Psalm 60 (title)

👥ARAN

of times mentioned: 2
# of MEN by this name: 1

Meaning: Shrill

A descendant of Seir, who lived in Esau's "land of Edom."

First reference: Genesis 36:28 / Last reference: 1 Chronicles 1:42

♀ARARAT

of times mentioned: OT 2

A name for the Assyrian province of Uratu. Noah's ark rested on its mountains when the flood subsided. Jeremiah foretold that this nation would rise up against Babylon. See also Armenia.

First reference: Genesis 8:4 / Last reference: Jeremiah 51:27

👥ARAUNAH

of times mentioned: 9
# of MEN by this name: 1

Meaning: Strong

A Jebusite who sold his threshing floor to King David, so the king could build an altar and make a sacrifice there. Same as Ornan.

First reference: 2 Samuel 24:16 / Last reference: 2 Samuel 24:24

👥ARBA

of times mentioned: 3
# of MEN by this name: 1

Meaning: Four

The father of Anak. His city was given to the Levites when the land was divided among the tribes.

First reference: Joshua 15:13 / Last reference: Joshua 21:11

♀ARBAH

of times mentioned: OT 1

Another name for Hebron. Abraham and Isaac lived here, and Jacob visited his father in Arbah.

Only reference: Genesis 35:27

👥ARCHELAUS

of times mentioned: 1
# of MEN by this name: 1

Meaning: People-ruling

Son of Herod the Great who ruled over Judea when Joseph planned to return there with Mary and Jesus. Because Joseph feared Archelaus, he took his family to Galilee instead.

Only reference: Matthew 2:22

⊙ARCHI

of times mentioned: OT 1

Part of the inheritance of Joseph's descendants through his son Ephraim.

Only reference: Joshua 16:2–9

⚏ARCHIPPUS

of times mentioned: 2
# of MEN by this name: 1

Meaning: Horse-ruler

A Colossian Christian whom Paul encouraged in faithful ministry.

First reference: Colossians 4:17 / Last reference: Philemon 1:2

⚏ARD

of times mentioned: 3
# of MEN by this name: 2

Meaning: Fugitive

1) A descendant of Abraham through Jacob's son Benjamin.

Only reference: Genesis 46:21

2) Another descendant of Abraham through Jacob's son Benjamin. His father was Bela.

Only reference: Numbers 26:40

⚏ARDON

of times mentioned: 1
# of MEN by this name: 1

Meaning: Roaming

A descendant of Abraham through Jacob's son Judah.

Only reference: 1 Chronicles 2:18

⚏ARELI

of times mentioned: 2
# of MEN by this name: 1

Meaning: Heroic

A descendant of Abraham through Jacob's son Gad.

First reference: Genesis 46:16 / Last reference: Numbers 26:17

⊙AREOPAGUS

of times mentioned: NT 1

Meaning: Rock of Ares (a Greek god)

At this hill Athens's original court and council had met. In Paul's day the council was in charge of religious matters in the city. The philosophers of the city, who had been debating with him, brought Paul to a meeting of the council and asked him about his teaching. The apostle took the opportunity to speak to them about Christ, and a few people came to the Lord as a result of his message. Others mocked his message of the resurrection of the dead. Same as Mars' Hill.

Only reference: Acts 17:19

⚏ARETAS

of times mentioned: 1
# of MEN by this name: 1

An Arabian king who ruled over Syria.

Only reference: 2 Corinthians 11:32

⚏ARGOB

of times mentioned: 1
# of MEN by this name: 1

Meaning: Stony

An Israelite official assassinated along with King Pekahiah.

Only reference: 2 Kings 15:25

⚲ARGOB

of times mentioned: OT 4

Meaning: Stony

A region of Og that the Israelites conquered after they turned back from entering the Promised Land. This territory became part of the inheritance of the tribe of Manasseh. Jair, Manasseh's son, named it Bashan-havoth-jair.

First reference: Deuteronomy 3:4 / Last reference: 1 Kings 4:13

👥ARIDAI

of times mentioned: 1
# of MEN by this name: 1

One of ten sons of Haman, the villain of the story of Esther.

Only reference: Esther 9:9

👥ARIDATHA

of times mentioned: 1
# of MEN by this name: 1

One of ten sons of Haman, the villain of the story of Esther.

Only reference: Esther 9:8

👥ARIEH

of times mentioned: 1
# of MEN by this name: 1

Meaning: Lion

An Israelite official assassinated along with King Pekahiah.

Only reference: 2 Kings 15:25

👥ARIEL

of times mentioned: 1
# of MEN by this name: 1

Meaning: Lion of God

A Jewish exile charged with finding Levites and temple servants to travel to Jerusalem with Ezra.

Only reference: Ezra 8:16

⚲ARIEL

of times mentioned: OT 4

Meaning: Lion of God; heroic

A name Isaiah used to describe the city of Jerusalem. He foresaw sorrow in the city, as it would be besieged by enemies. But when the Lord returns, it "shall be as a dream of a night vision."

First reference: Isaiah 29:1 / Last reference: Isaiah 29:7

⚲ARIMATHAEA

of times mentioned: NT 4

Home of Joseph, a rich man and member of the ruling Jewish council called the Sanhedrin. Secretly Jesus' disciple, Joseph claimed the body of Jesus after His death and placed it in his own tomb.

First reference: Matthew 27:57 / Last reference: John 19:38

👥ARIOCH

of times mentioned: 7
# of MEN by this name: 2

1) The king of Ellasar in the days of Abram. Arioch was part of a victorious battle alliance that kidnapped Abram's nephew Lot.

First reference: Genesis 14:1 / Last reference: Genesis 14:9

2) Captain of King Nebuchadnezzar's guard. When none of Nebuchadnezzar's wise men could interpret the king's dream, Arioch was to kill all the wise men. Instead he brought Daniel to the king.

First reference: Daniel 2:14 / Last reference: Daniel 2:25

👥ARISAI

of times mentioned: 1
# of MEN by this name: 1

One of ten sons of Haman, the villain of the story of Esther.

Only reference: Esther 9:9

👥 ARISTARCHUS

of times mentioned: 5
# of MEN by this name: 1

Meaning: Best ruling

One of Paul's companions at Ephesus who was captured by a crowd that objected to the Christians' teaching. He accompanied Paul on various travels, including his trip to Rome.

First reference: Acts 19:29 / Last reference: Philemon 1:24

👥 ARISTOBULUS

of times mentioned: 1
# of MEN by this name: 1

Meaning: Best counseling

A Christian acquaintance the apostle Paul greeted in Paul's letter to the Romans.

Only reference: Romans 16:10

📍 ARMAGEDDON

of times mentioned: NT 1

A symbolic name for the place of the last great battle on earth, fought between the Antichrist and Jesus, as revealed to the apostle John in the Revelation.

Only reference: Revelation 16:16

📍 ARMENIA

of times mentioned: OT 2

A name translated "Ararat" in some Bible versions. This country between the Caspian Sea and the Black Sea included the province of Ararat. Here two sons of the Assyrian king Sennacherib fled after they murdered their father. See also Ararat.

First reference: 2 Kings 19:37 / Last reference: Isaiah 37:38

👥 ARMONI

of times mentioned: 1
# of MEN by this name: 1

Meaning: Palatial

A son of the late King Saul, delivered by King David to the Gibeonites. They hanged him in vengeance for Saul's mistreatment of their people.

Only reference: 2 Samuel 21:8

👥 ARNAN

of times mentioned: 1
# of MEN by this name: 1

Meaning: Noisy

A descendant of Abraham through Jacob's son Judah, in the line of the nation of Judah's third-to-last king, Jeconiah (also known as Jehoiachin).

Only reference: 1 Chronicles 3:21

📍 ARNON

of times mentioned: OT 25

Meaning: A brawling stream

A river that formed the boundary between the lands of the Amorites and the Moabites. The territory was taken by the Israelites under Moses' leadership. Reuben's tribe inherited the land near the city of Aroer, on the bank of the Arnon. The Ammonites asked Israel's captain Jephthah to return their land, but he refused. See also Aroer (2).

First reference: Numbers 21:13 / Last reference: Jeremiah 48:20 / Key references: Deuteronomy 3:8; Joshua 13:16

👥 AROD

of times mentioned: 1
# of MEN by this name: 1

Meaning: Fugitive

A descendant of Abraham through Jacob's son Gad.

Only reference: Numbers 26:17

📍 AROER

of times mentioned: OT 16

Meaning: Nudity

1) A city built by the tribe of Gad. Joab and his captains camped here when they went to number the

Israelites for King David. Isaiah foretold that Aroer would be forsaken and only flocks would live there.

First reference: Numbers 32:34 / Last reference: Isaiah 17:2

2) An Amorite city near the Arnon River that was the capital city under King Sihon. Following Israel's conquest of the Promised Land, Aroer became part of the Reubenite inheritance. This city was part of the land the Ammonites asked Israel's captain Jephthah to return to them. He refused and fought them at Aroer instead. King Hazael of Syria conquered this city during the rule of King Jehu of Israel.

First reference: Deuteronomy 2:36 / Last reference: Jeremiah 48:19

3) A city of Judah to which David sent some of the spoils from his warfare with the Amalekites.

Only reference: 1 Samuel 30:28

⊙ARPAD

of times mentioned: OT 4

Meaning: Spread out

A Syrian city, always mentioned with Hamath, that was conquered by Assyria. To intimidate Judah, Sennacherib's messengers to Jerusalem used it as an example of a city that could not stand before their king's might. Isaiah referred to Arpad and Hamath as he spoke of God's punishment of Assyria. Jeremiah also spoke of Syria's destruction. Same as Arphad.

First reference: 2 Kings 18:34 / Last reference: Jeremiah 49:23

⊙ARPHAD

of times mentioned: OT 2

Meaning: Spread out

A name that Isaiah used for a Syrian city conquered by King Sennacherib. The Assyrian ruler's messengers used Arphad as an example of a city that could not stand before their king's might. Same as Arpad.

First reference: Isaiah 36:19 / Last reference: Isaiah 37:13

ARPHAXAD

of times mentioned: 10
# of MEN by this name: 1

Genealogy of Jesus: Yes (Luke 3:36)

A descendant of Noah through his son Shem.

First reference: Genesis 10:22 / Last reference: Luke 3:36 / Key reference: Genesis 11:11–13

⚎ARTAXERXES

of times mentioned: 15
# of MEN by this name: 3

1) Persian king who received letters objecting to the rebuilding of Jerusalem from those who opposed the Jews. Also called Longimanus.

First reference: Ezra 4:7 / Last reference: Ezra 4:11

2) One of three Persian kings who commanded that the Jews rebuild Jerusalem. Also called Cambyses.

Only reference: Ezra 6:14

3) Another name for King Darius of Persia.

First reference: Ezra 7:1 / Last reference: Nehemiah 13:6

⚎ARTEMAS

of times mentioned: 1
# of MEN by this name: 1

Meaning: Gift of Artemis

An acquaintance of the apostle Paul, whom Paul considered sending as a messenger to Titus.

Only reference: Titus 3:12

⊙ARUBOTH

of times mentioned: OT 1

Meaning: Lattices, windows, dovecots, chimneys, or sluices

Under King Solomon's governmental organization, a district responsible for supplying provisions for the king.

Only reference: 1 Kings 4:10

◊ARUMAH

of times mentioned: OT 1

Meaning: Height

Hometown of Abimelech, Gideon's son by his concubine.

Only reference: Judges 9:41

◊ARVAD

of times mentioned: OT 2

Meaning: A refuge for the roving

An island off the coast of Phoenicia, north of Sidon. Its mariners rowed and piloted Tyre's ships, and its warriors manned Tyre's walls.

First reference: Ezekiel 27:8 / Last reference: Ezekiel 27:11

👥ARZA

of times mentioned: 1
# of MEN by this name: 1

Meaning: Earthiness

Palace steward of Israel's king Elah. A drunken Elah was assassinated in Arza's house.

Only reference: 1 Kings 16:9

👥ASA

of times mentioned: 60
# of MEN by this name: 2

1) King of Judah, son of King Abijam. Asa reigned forty-one years and removed many idols from Judah. While the country was peaceful, he built fortified cities and established his army. When an Ethiopian army attacked, he called on the Lord and was victorious. When Azariah prophetically encouraged the king to seek the Lord, Asa led his people in making a covenant to seek God. He even removed his mother from her position as queen because she worshipped idols. But he did not remove the idols from the high places.

In the thirty-sixth year of his reign, Asa took the silver and gold from the temple and his own treasury and gave it to King Ben-hadad of Syria to convince him to end his alliance with Baasha,

king of Israel, and support Judah instead. Through Hanani the prophet, God declared that Asa was not depending on Him and would end his reign in wars. The angry king imprisoned Hanani and oppressed his people. Though he suffered an illness of his feet, Asa would not turn to the Lord.

First reference: 1 Kings 15:8 / Last reference: Matthew 1:8 / Key references: 2 Chronicles 14:2–4; 16:7–10 / Only reference: Ezra 10:15

Genealogy of Jesus: Yes (Matthew 1:8)

2) A Jewish Exile from the tribe of Levi who resettled Jerusalem.

👥ASAHIAH

of times mentioned: 2
# of MEN by this name: 1

Meaning: God has made

A servant of King Josiah who was part of a delegation sent to the prophetess Huldah after the "book of the law" was discovered in the temple. Same as Asaiah (5).

First reference: 2 Kings 22:12 / Last reference: 2 Kings 22:14

👥ASAIAH

of times mentioned: 6
# of MEN by this name: 5

Meaning: God has made

1) A descendant of Abraham through Jacob's son Simeon.

Only reference: 1 Chronicles 4:36

2) A descendant of Abraham through Jacob's son Levi.

Only reference: 1 Chronicles 6:30

3) A Jewish exile from the tribe of Judah who resettled Jerusalem.

Only reference: 1 Chronicles 9:5

4) A descendant of Abraham through Jacob's son Levi. Asaiah was among a group of Levites appointed by King David to bring the ark of the covenant from the house of Obed-edom to Jerusalem.

First reference: 1 Chronicles 15:6 / Last reference: 1 Chronicles 15:11

5) One of five men sent by King Josiah to ask God's prophetess, Huldah, what to do about the "book of the law" recently discovered in the temple. Same as Asahiah.

Only reference: 2 Chronicles 34:20

ASAPH

of times mentioned: 45
# of MEN by this name: 5

Meaning: Collector

1) Father of Joah, who represented King Hezekiah in a meeting with the Assyrian deputies of King Shalmaneser.

First reference: 2 Kings 18:18 / Last reference: Isaiah 36:22

2) A descendant of Abraham through Jacob's son Levi. Asaph was one of the key musicians serving in the Jerusalem temple. King David appointed Asaph's descendants to "prophesy with harps, with psalteries, and with cymbals" (1 Chronicles 25:1).

First reference: 1 Chronicles 6:39 / Last reference: Psalm 83 (title)

3) Forefather of a Jewish exile from the tribe of Levi who resettled Jerusalem.

Only reference: 1 Chronicles 9:15

4) Forefather of a Levite "porter" (doorkeeper) in the house of the Lord.

Only reference: 1 Chronicles 26:1

5) Keeper of the king's forest for King Artaxerxes of Persia.

Only reference: Nehemiah 2:8

ASAREEL

of times mentioned: 1
# of MEN by this name: 1

Meaning: Right of God

A descendant of Abraham through Jacob's son Judah.

Only reference: 1 Chronicles 4:16

ASARELAH

of times mentioned: 1
# of MEN by this name: 1

Meaning: Right toward God

A son of King David's musician Asaph, "which prophesied according to the order of the king" (1 Chronicles 25:2).

Only reference: 1 Chronicles 25:2

ASENATH

of times mentioned: 3
# of WOMEN by this name: 1

Daughter of an Egyptian priest and given as a wife to Joseph by the pharaoh. Asenath bore two sons to Joseph: Manasseh and Ephraim.

First reference: Genesis 41:45 / Last reference: Genesis 46:20

ASER

of times mentioned: 2
# of MEN by this name: 1

Meaning: Happy

Greek form of the Hebrew Asher, one of the twelve tribes of Israel.

First reference: Luke 2:36 / Last reference: Revelation 7:6

ASHAN

of times mentioned: OT 4

Meaning: Smoke; vapor; dust; anger

A city that became part of the inheritance of the tribe of Judah following the conquest of the Promised Land. Later it became a Levitical city. When Joshua further divided the land, it became part of the land given to the tribe of Simeon.

First reference: Joshua 15:42 / Last reference: 1 Chronicles 6:59

ASHBEA

of times mentioned: 1
# of MEN by this name: 1

Meaning: Adjurer

A descendant of Abraham through Jacob's son Judah. Ashbea's family was known for producing fine linen.

Only reference: 1 Chronicles 4:21

ASHBEL

of times mentioned: 3
# of MEN by this name: 1

Meaning: Flowing

A descendant of Abraham through Jacob's son Benjamin. Ashbel was Benjamin's second son.

First reference: Genesis 46:21 / Last reference: 1 Chronicles 8:1

ASHCHENAZ

of times mentioned: 1
# of MEN by this name: 1

A descendant of Noah through his son Japheth. Same as Ashkenaz.

Only reference: 1 Chronicles 1:6

ASHCHENAZ

of times mentioned: OT 1

A kingdom, along with Ararat and Minni, in Armenia. The prophet Jeremiah spoke of these nations being called into battle against Babylon during God's judgment of the Chaldeans.

Only reference: Jeremiah 51:27

ASHDOD

of times mentioned: OT 21

Meaning: Ravager

One of the few cities in which the Anakims were left after the Israelites conquered the Promised Land. Though it theoretically became part of the inheritance of the tribe of Judah, that tribe never conquered it. Instead Ashdod became one of the five most important Philistine cities. When the Philistines captured the ark of the covenant, they brought it to Ashdod. The people of the city suffered under God's judgment for taking the ark, so they asked that it be removed to Gath.

Judah's king Uzziah broke down Ashdod's walls and built cities around it. Nehemiah confronted the Jews who had married the people of this pagan city. During Isaiah's ministry, Ashdod was taken by the Assyrians. Various prophets speak of the punishment God meted out to Ashdod.

First reference: Joshua 11:22 / Last reference: Zechariah 9:6 / Key references: 1 Samuel 5:1–7; Nehemiah 13:23–24

ASHDOTH-PISGAH

of times mentioned: OT 3

Meaning: Ravines of the Pisgah (elsewhere translated "the slopes of Pisgah")

Mount Pisgah's eastern slope, which belonged to the Amorite king Sihon until Israel conquered the Promised Land. The land became part of the inheritance of the tribe of Reuben.

First reference: Deuteronomy 3:17 / Last reference: Joshua 13:20

ASHER

of times mentioned: 9
# of MEN by this name: 1

Meaning: Happy

A son of Jacob and Zilpah. He founded the tribe of Asher.

First reference: Genesis 30:13 / Last reference: 1 Chronicles 7:40

ASHER

of times mentioned: OT 4

Meaning: Happy

Under King Solomon's governmental organization, a district responsible for supplying provisions for the king.

First reference: Joshua 17:7 / Last reference: Kings 4:16

♀ASHKELON

of times mentioned: OT 9

Meaning: Weighing place

An ancient city north of Gaza, Ashkelon was one of five major Philistine cities. Here Samson killed thirty men after his wife gave them the solution to a riddle he had posed to them. The prophets condemned this pagan city. Jeremiah spoke of its punishment by God; Amos prophesied the destruction of its ruler; and Zephaniah and Zechariah foretold that Ashkelon would be desolated. Same as Askelon.

First reference: Judges 14:19 / Last reference: Zechariah 9:5

👥ASHKENAZ

of times mentioned: 1
# of MEN by this name: 1

A descendant of Noah through his son Japheth. Same as Ashchenaz.

Only reference: Genesis 10:3

♀ASHNAH

of times mentioned: OT 2

1) A city that became part of the inheritance of the tribe of Judah following the conquest of the Promised Land.

Only reference: Joshua 15:33

2) Another city that became part of the inheritance of the tribe of Judah following the conquest of the Promised Land.

Only reference: Joshua 15:43

👥ASHPENAZ

of times mentioned: 1
# of MEN by this name: 1

Chief eunuch of the Babylonian king Nebuchadnezzar. Ashpenaz selected Daniel for the ruler's service.

Only reference: Daniel 1:3

👥ASHRIEL

of times mentioned: 1
# of MEN by this name: 1

Meaning: Right of God

A descendant of Abraham through Joseph's son Manasseh.

Only reference: 1 Chronicles 7:14

♀ASHTAROTH

of times mentioned: OT 5

Meaning: Name of a Sidonian god

1) A city of Bashan on the eastern shore of the Jordan River. King Og reigned in Ashtaroth, and the book of Joshua reports that giants lived there. Manasseh's son Machir inherited the city. Same as Astaroth.

First reference: Joshua 9:10 / Last reference: Joshua 13:31

2) One of the forty-eight cities given to the Levites as God had commanded. Ashtaroth was given to them by the tribe of Manasseh.

Only reference: 1 Chronicles 6:71

♀ASHTEROTH KARNAIM

of times mentioned: OT 1

Meaning: Ashteroth of the double horns

A city of the Rephaims that was attacked by King Chedorlaomer of Elam.

Only reference: Genesis 14:5

👥ASHUR

of times mentioned: 2
# of MEN by this name: 1

Meaning: Successful

A descendant of Abraham through Jacob's son Judah.

First reference: 1 Chronicles 2:24 / Last reference: 1 Chronicles 4:5

👥ASHVATH

of times mentioned: 1
# of MEN by this name: 1

Meaning: Bright

A descendant of Abraham through Jacob's son Asher.

Only reference: 1 Chronicles 7:33

📍ASIA

of times mentioned: NT 21

A Roman province in the western part of the peninsula of Asia Minor, whose capital was Ephesus. For a time, the Holy Spirit prohibited Paul from preaching in Asia, but Paul came to Ephesus on his second missionary journey and remained there two years, spreading the Gospel to the whole province. When Demetrius the silversmith started a riot over Paul's preaching, the apostle moved on to Macedonia.

Though the apostle left, Asia was not forgotten. Paul lamented to Timothy, "All they which are in Asia be turned away from me" (2 Timothy 1:15). Peter wrote his first epistle in part to the believers of Asia, and John addressed his Revelation to "the seven churches which are in Asia" (Revelation 1:4): Ephesus, Smyrna, Pergamos, Thyatira, Sardis, Philadelphia, and Laodicea.

First reference: Acts 2:9 / Last reference: Revelation 1:11 / Key references: Acts 16:6–8; 19:10, 22, 26, 27, 31; 1 Peter 1:1

👥ASIEL

of times mentioned: 1
# of MEN by this name: 1

Meaning: Made of God

A descendant of Abraham through Jacob's son Simeon.

Only reference: 1 Chronicles 4:35

📍ASKELON

of times mentioned: OT 3

Meaning: Weighing place

The book of Judges reports that Judah conquered Askelon, taking it from the Canaanites, but the tribe did not maintain control of the city, which later became an important Philistine city. After the Philistines captured the ark of the covenant, it caused trouble in whatever city it was sent to. So the Philistines returned the troublesome object to Israel, along with a guilt offering of five golden tumors ("emerods") and five golden mice, one for each of the major cities of that nation, including Askelon.

When David lamented Saul and Jonathan's deaths, he warned that the news of their demise should not be published in Askelon, because its people would rejoice. Same as Ashkelon.

First reference: Judges 1:18 / Last reference: 2 Samuel 1:20–34

👥ASNAH

of times mentioned: 1
# of MEN by this name: 1

Forefather of an exiled family that returned to Judah under Zerubbabel.

Only reference: Ezra 2:50

👥ASNAPPER

of times mentioned: 1
# of MEN by this name: 1

An Assyrian king who resettled Samaria with other people, after the Israelites were captured.

Only reference: Ezra 4:10

👥ASPATHA

of times mentioned: 1
# of MEN by this name: 1

One of ten sons of Haman, the villain of the story of Esther.

Only reference: Esther 9:7

👥ASRIEL

of times mentioned: 2
# of MEN by this name: 1

Meaning: Right of God

A descendant of Joseph through his son Manasseh.

First reference: Numbers 26:31 / Last reference: Joshua 17:2

ASSHUR

of times mentioned: 3
# of MEN by this name: 2

Meaning: Successful

1) A descendant of Noah who built the cities of Nineveh, Rehoboth, and Calah.

Only reference: Genesis 10:11

2) A descendant of Noah through Noah's son Shem.

First reference: Genesis 10:22 / Last reference: 1 Chronicles 1:17

⦿ASSHUR

of times mentioned: OT 5

Meaning: To be straight (in the sense of being successful)

Another term for Assyria, Asshur was named for the grandson of Noah, who built the Assyrian cities of Nineveh, Rehoboth, and Calah. Balaam prophesied that Asshur would carry away the Kenites but be afflicted by ships from the coast of Chittim. Ezekiel spoke of Asshur as merchants for Tyre ("Tyrus" in the kjv) and used it as an example of a fallen nation, testified to only by graves. The prophet Hosea pointed out the inability of this nation to save Israel. Same as Assur. See also Assyria.

First reference: Numbers 24:22 / Last reference: Hosea 14:3

⦿ASSIR

of times mentioned: 5
# of MEN by this name: 3

Meaning: Prisoner

1) A descendant of Abraham through Jacob's son Levi.

First reference: Exodus 6:24 / Last reference: 1 Chronicles 6:22

2) Another descendant of Abraham through Jacob's son Levi.

First reference: 1 Chronicles 6:23 / Last reference: 1 Chronicles 6:37

3) A descendant of Abraham through Jacob's son Judah, in the line of the nation of Judah's third-to-last king, Jeconiah (also known as Jehoiachin).

Only reference: 1 Chronicles 3:17

⦿ASSOS

of times mentioned: NT 2

A port city in Asia Minor. Paul's companions met him here after they left Troas. Paul traveled on foot from Troas to Assos, while his companions went by ship.

First reference: Acts 20:13 / Last reference: Acts 20:14

⦿ASSUR

of times mentioned: OT 2

Meaning: To be straight (in the sense of being successful)

Another name for Assyria. When Israel's enemies wanted to help rebuild Jerusalem's temple, they claimed they had sacrificed to the Lord since the time of Esar-haddon, king of Assur. Psalm 83 speaks of Assur as an enemy joined with the children of Lot. Same as Asshur.

First reference: Ezra 4:2 / Last reference: Psalm 83:8

⦿ASYNCRITUS

of times mentioned: 1
# of MEN by this name: 1

Meaning: Incomparable

A Christian acquaintance whom the apostle Paul greeted in his letter to the Romans.

Only reference: Romans 16:14

⦿ASSYRIA

of times mentioned: OT 118

Meaning: To be straight (in the sense of being successful)

An empire that spread from its original nation in the upper plain of Mesopotamia to incorporate a wide arc of land that swept from Egypt north through Syria and Palestine to eastern Asia Minor, and east to Babylonia and the Persian Gulf.

For 1,000 talents of silver, King Pul (Tiglath-pileser III) of Assyria supported Israel's wicked king Menahem's claim to the throne. During the reign of King Pekah of Israel, Tiglath-pileser attacked the nation and transported captives back to his homeland.

Shalmaneser, king of Assyria, attacked Hoshea, king of Israel, who became his vassal and gave him gifts, but when Shalmaneser discovered Israel's king had conspired against him with Egypt, he besieged Hoshea's land for three years. Assyria conquered the nation, and Israel's people went into captivity. Then Assyria's king repopulated the land with pagan peoples and commanded that a priest teach these new Samaritans about the Lord.

King Ahaz of Judah called on the Assyrian king Tiglath-pileser to save him from Syria, at the price of the silver and gold in the Lord's house and his own palace. Though Tiglath-pileser did not attack Judah, neither did he provide Ahaz with the help Judah's king had hoped for. Ahaz's successor, King Hezekiah of Judah, rebelled against the Assyrians, and in the fourteenth year of his reign, Sennacherib took the fortified cities of Judah. Hezekiah submitted and paid tribute to rid his land of the Assyrians, and the temple gold and silver were given to Assyria.

Sennacherib sent messengers to Judah to undermine Hezekiah and encourage his nation's warriors to fight for Assyria. When the warriors of Judah refused, the messengers threatened them with conquest. Through the prophet Isaiah, God described Assyria as "the rod of mine anger, and the staff in their hand is mine indignation" (Isaiah 10:5), and Assyria brought God's punishment to a hypocritical nation. But the prophet also foretold the fall of Sennacherib (Isaiah 37:21–29) and Assyria (2 Kings 19:20–28). God promised the faithful Hezekiah that Assyria would not enter Jerusalem (Isaiah 37:33). In the night, the angel of the Lord killed 185,000 Assyrian soldiers in their camp. Those who were not killed arose to find the bodies around them. Sennacherib left Judah and returned to his capital at Nineveh, where he was killed by two of his sons (Isaiah 37:36–38).

During the reign of Hezekiah's son Manasseh, Assyria again attacked Judah, captured the king, and carried him to Babylon, along with many of his people. When Manasseh humbled himself before God, he was returned to his position in Jerusalem.

Through Isaiah, God promised that Assyria would be punished and a remnant of Judah would return to the Lord (Isaiah 10:12, 21). Hosea repeatedly uses Assyria as an example of unfaithfulness. Micah uses this nation's name as a symbol for Israel's enemies. Even out of Assyria, Zechariah prophesies, God will gather His people in the time of the latter rain. See also Asshur and Assur.

First reference: Genesis 2:14 / Last reference: Zechariah 10:11 / Key references: 2 Kings 15:29; 18:13–14; 19:36; 2 Chronicles 33:11; Isaiah 37:37

👥ATARAH

of times mentioned: 1
# of WOMEN by this name: 1

Meaning: Crown

A wife of Jerahmeel, a descendant of Abraham through Jacob's son Judah.

Only reference: 1 Chronicles 2:26

📍ASTAROTH

of times mentioned: OT 1

Meaning: Name of a Sidonian god

A city of Bashan where King Og lived. Same as Ashtaroth (1).

Only reference: Deuteronomy 1:4

📍ATAD

of times mentioned: OT 2

Meaning: To pierce or to make fast

A threshing floor beyond the Jordan River where Joseph and his family mourned the death of Jacob. Same as Abel-mizraim.

First reference: Genesis 50:10 / Last reference: Genesis 50:11

📍ATAROTH

of times mentioned: OT 5

Meaning: Crowns

1) A city with good lands for cattle that the tribe of Gad requested Moses to give them as they came to the Promised Land.

First reference: Numbers 32:3 / Last reference: Numbers 32:34

2) A city that was part of the inheritance of Ephraim after Israel conquered the Promised Land.

First reference: Joshua 16:2 / Last reference: Joshua 16:7

3) A place in Judah where the family of Joab lived.

Only reference: 1 Chronicles 2:54

♀ ATAROTH-ADAR

of times mentioned: OT 1

Meaning: Crowns of Addar

A city on the border of the territory of the tribes of Benjamin and Ephraim. Same as Ataroth-addar.

Only reference: Joshua 18:13

♀ ATAROTH-ADDAR

of times mentioned: OT 1

Meaning: Crowns of Addar

A city on the border of the territory of the tribes of Benjamin and Ephraim. Same as Ataroth-adar.

Only reference: Joshua 16:5

👥 ATER

of times mentioned: 5
# of MEN by this name: 3

Meaning: Maimed

1) Forefather of a Jewish exile who returned to Judah under Zerubbabel.

First reference: Ezra 2:16 / Last reference: Nehemiah 7:21

2) Forefather of an exiled family that returned to Judah under Zerubbabel.

First reference: Ezra 2:42 / Last reference: Nehemiah 7:45

3) A Jewish leader who renewed the covenant under Nehemiah.

Only reference: Nehemiah 10:17

♀ ATHACH

of times mentioned: OT 1

Meaning: To sojourn; lodging

A city of Judah to which David sent some of the spoils from his warfare with the Amalekites.

Only reference: 1 Samuel 30:30

👥 ATHAIAH

of times mentioned: 1
# of MEN by this name: 1

Meaning: God has helped

A Jewish exile from the tribe of Judah who resettled Jerusalem.

Only reference: Nehemiah 11:4

👥 ATHALIAH

of times mentioned: 17
# of MEN by this name: 2
# of WOMEN by this name: 1

Meaning: God has constrained

1) Wife of Jehoram and mother of Ahaziah, two kings of Judah. When her son was killed by Jehu, she destroyed all possible heirs to the throne, missing only Joash, who was saved by his aunt Jehosheba. Wicked, idolatrous Athaliah ruled Judah for six years. In the seventh year of her reign, the priest Jehoiada crowned Joash king while in the temple. When Athaliah saw this, she declared it treason. Jehoiada commanded his warriors to take her outside the temple and kill her. Judah did not mourn her death.

First reference: 2 Kings 8:26 / Last reference: 2 Chronicles 24:7 / Key references: 2 Kings 11:1; 2 Chronicles 22:3

2) A descendant of Abraham through Jacob's son Benjamin.

Only reference: 1 Chronicles 8:26

3) Forefather of a Jewish exile who returned to Judah under Ezra.

Only reference: Ezra 8:7

👥 ATHLAI

of times mentioned: 1
# of MEN by this name: 1

Meaning: Constricted

An exiled Israelite who married a "strange" (foreign) woman.

Only reference: Ezra 10:28

📍 ATHENS

of times mentioned: NT 7

Meaning: Named after the Greek goddess Athena

An influential Greek city on the peninsula of Attica, Athens was famed for its culture and philosophy. Paul traveled there from Berea, after the Jews of Thessalonica had stirred up trouble for him. Distressed by Athens's idolatry, which he would have seen at every turn at the Acropolis, which held many temples, the apostle preached the Gospel in the synagogue. Then at the invitation of the Athenian philosophers, who had disputed with him about the message he had been preaching in the marketplace, he spoke at Mars' Hill (the Areopagus) to those philosophers and the members of the council of the Areopagus, who were responsible for the religious life of the city. Paul pointed out their altar to an unknown god and sought to tell them about the God they did not know. A few Athenians came to faith in Christ.

First reference: Acts 17:15 / Last reference: 1 Thessalonians 3:1

📍 ATROTH

of times mentioned: OT 1

Meaning: Crowns

A fortified city built up by the children of Gad, who kept their flocks there.

Only reference: Numbers 32:35

👥 ATTAI

of times mentioned: 4
# of MEN by this name: 3

Meaning: Timely

1) A descendant of Abraham through Jacob's son Judah. Attai descended from the line of an unnamed Israelite woman and her Egyptian husband, Jarha.

First reference: 1 Chronicles 2:35 / Last reference: 1 Chronicles 2:36

2) One of several warriors from the tribe of Gad who left Saul to join David during his conflict with the king. Attai and his companions were "men of might. . .whose faces were like the faces of lions" (1 Chronicles 12:8).

Only reference: 1 Chronicles 12:11

3) A son of Judah's king Rehoboam; grandson of Solomon.

Only reference: 2 Chronicles 11:20

📍 ATTALIA

of times mentioned: NT 1

A city of Pamphylia, on the southern coast of Asia Minor, that Paul visited on his first missionary journey, between his visits to Perga and Antioch.

Only reference: Acts 14:25

👥 AUGUSTUS

of times mentioned: 4
# of MEN by this name: 1

Meaning: August

The Roman emperor who called for the census that brought Mary and Joseph to Bethlehem. He was still ruling when Paul appealed to Caesar during his imprisonment in Jerusalem. Also called Caesar Augustus.

First reference: Luke 2:1 / Last reference: Acts 27:1

📍 AVA

of times mentioned: OT 1

A city in the Assyrian Empire from which King Shalmaneser repopulated Judah after he took the Jews captive and carried them to Babylon.

Only reference: 2 Kings 17:24

AVEN

of times mentioned: OT 3

Meaning: Idolatry

1) A name for the Egyptian city of Heliopolis. The Jewish prophets foretold its destruction. Same as On.

Only reference: Ezekiel 30:17

2) A shortened form of the name Beth-aven, which means "house of vanity." This name for Bethel emphasized the religious failings of the city. Same as Beth-aven.

Only reference: Hosea 10:8

3) A plain (translated "valley" in some versions) in Syria, near Damascus, which was probably a pagan place of worship.

Only reference: Amos 1:5

AVIM

of times mentioned: OT 1

A city that became part of the inheritance of Benjamin when Joshua cast lots in Shiloh to provide territory for the seven tribes that had yet to receive their land.

Only reference: Joshua 18:23

AVITH

of times mentioned: OT 2

Meaning: Ruin

A city of Edom that was ruled by Hadad, son of Bedad, before Israel had any kings.

First reference: Genesis 36:35 / Last reference: 1 Chronicles 1:46

AZAL

of times mentioned: OT 1

Meaning: Noble

The prophet Zechariah predicted that in the day of the Lord the Mount of Olives will split, creating a great valley that will reach to this place near Jerusalem.

Only reference: Zechariah 14:5

AZALIAH

of times mentioned: 2
# of MEN by this name: 1

Meaning: God has reserved

Father of a temple scribe who served in the time of King Joash of Judah.

First reference: 2 Kings 22:3 / Last reference: 2 Chronicles 34:8

AZANIAH

of times mentioned: 1
# of MEN by this name: 1

Meaning: Heard by God

A Levite who renewed the covenant under Nehemiah.

Only reference: Nehemiah 10:9

AZARAEL

of times mentioned: 1
# of MEN by this name: 1

Meaning: God has helped

A priest who helped to dedicate the rebuilt walls of Jerusalem by playing a musical instrument.

Only reference: Nehemiah 12:36

AZAREEL

of times mentioned: 5
# of MEN by this name: 5

Meaning: God has helped

1) A "mighty man" who supported the future king David during his conflict with Saul.

Only reference: 1 Chronicles 12:6

2) One of twenty-four Levite musicians who was chosen by lot to serve in the house of the Lord.

Only reference: 1 Chronicles 25:18

3) Leader of the tribe of Dan in the days of King David.

Only reference: 1 Chronicles 27:22

4) An exiled Israelite who married a "strange" (foreign) woman.

Only reference: Ezra 10:41

5) Ancestor of a Jewish exile from the tribe of Levi who resettled Jerusalem.

Only reference: Nehemiah 11:13

👪AZARIAH

of times mentioned: 49
# of MEN by this name: 28

Meaning: God has helped

1) An officer in Solomon's army. His father was Zadok the priest.

Only reference: 1 Kings 4:2

2) Another prince under King Solomon. His father was Nathan.

Only reference: 1 Kings 4:5

3) King of Judah who was obedient to God but did not remove the idolatrous altars from the high places. Though he ruled for fifty-two years, God made Azariah a leper, and his son judged the people in his place. Same as Uzziah (1).

First reference: 2 Kings 14:21 / Last reference: 1 Chronicles 3:12

4) A descendant of Abraham through Jacob's son Judah.

Only reference: 1 Chronicles 2:8

5) Another descendant of Abraham through Jacob's son Judah. Azariah descended from the line of an unnamed Israelite woman and her Egyptian husband, Jarha.

First reference: 1 Chronicles 2:38 / Last reference: 1 Chronicles 2:39

6) A descendant of Abraham through Jacob's son Levi and a priest through the line of Aaron.

Only reference: 1 Chronicles 6:9

7) Another descendant of Abraham through Jacob's son Levi and a priest through the line of Aaron. Azariah served in Solomon's temple in Jerusalem.

First reference: 1 Chronicles 6:10 / Last reference: 1 Chronicles 6:11

8) Another descendant of Abraham through Jacob's son Levi and a priest through the line of Aaron.

First reference: 1 Chronicles 6:13 / Last reference: Ezra 7:1

9) Ancestor of Heman, a singer who ministered in the tabernacle.

Only reference: 1 Chronicles 6:36

10) A prophet who encouraged King Asa of Judah to follow the Lord.

Only reference: 2 Chronicles 15:1

11) A son of Judah's king Jehoshaphat who was given "great gifts of silver, and of gold, and of precious things" by his father (2 2 Chronicles 21:3).

Only reference: 2 Chronicles 21:2

12) Another son of Judah's king Jehoshaphat who was given "great gifts of silver, and of gold, and of precious things" by his father (2 2 Chronicles 21:3).

Only reference: 2 Chronicles 21:2

13) Son of Jehoram, king of Judah.

Only reference: 2 Chronicles 22:6

14) A captain over hundreds for the priest Jehoiada, who crowned Joash king of Judah. His father was Jeroham.

Only reference: 2 Chronicles 23:1

15) Another captain over hundreds for the priest Jehoiada, who crowned Joash king of Judah. His father was Obed.

Only reference: 2 Chronicles 23:1

16) The chief priest who stood up to King Uzziah of Judah when he tried to burn incense on the temple altar.

First reference: 2 Chronicles 26:17 / Last reference: 2 Chronicles 26:20

17) A man of the tribe of Ephraim who counseled Israel against enslaving fellow Jews from Judah who were captured in a civil war. Azariah helped to feed and clothe the prisoners before sending them home.

Only reference: 2 Chronicles 28:12

18) A descendant of Abraham through Jacob's son Levi and father of a Levite who cleansed the Jerusalem temple during the revival of King Hezekiah's day.

Only reference: 2 Chronicles 29:12

19) Another descendant of Abraham through Jacob's son Levi and father of a Levite who cleansed the Jerusalem temple during the revival of King Hezekiah's day.

Only reference: 2 Chronicles 29:12

20) "The ruler of the house of God" and chief priest during the reign of King Hezekiah of Judah (2 Chronicles 31:13).

First reference: 2 Chronicles 31:10 / Last reference: 2 Chronicles 31:13

21) Ancestor of Ezra, the scribe who led Israelites into Jerusalem after the Babylonian Exile.

Only reference: Ezra 7:3

22) A man who repaired Jerusalem's walls under Nehemiah.

First reference: Nehemiah 3:23 / Last reference: Nehemiah 3:24

23) A Jewish exile who returned to Judah under Zerubbabel.

Only reference: Nehemiah 7:7

24) A Levite who helped Ezra to explain the law to exiles returned to Jerusalem.

Only reference: Nehemiah 8:7

25) A priest who renewed the covenant under Nehemiah.

Only reference: Nehemiah 10:2

26) A prince of Judah who joined in the dedication of Jerusalem's rebuilt walls.

Only reference: Nehemiah 12:33

27) A rebellious Israelite who refused to believe Jeremiah's warning to Israel's remnant, which was not to escape into Egypt.

Only reference: Jeremiah 43:2

28) The Hebrew name for Abed-nego, one of Daniel's companions in exile.

First reference: Daniel 1:6 / Last reference: Daniel 2:17

👥 AZAZ

of times mentioned: 1
# of MEN by this name: 1

Meaning: Strong

A descendant of Abraham through Jacob's son Reuben.

Only reference: 1 Chronicles 5:8

👥 AZAZIAH

of times mentioned: 3
# of MEN by this name: 3

Meaning: God has strengthened

1) A Levite musician who performed in celebration when King David brought the ark of the covenant to Jerusalem.

Only reference: 1 Chronicles 15:21

2) Father of Hoshea, a man of Ephraim who ruled over his tribe during King David's reign.

Only reference: 1 Chronicles 27:20

3) A temple overseer during the reign of King Hezekiah of Judah.

Only reference: 2 Chronicles 31:13

👥 AZBUK

of times mentioned: 1
# of MEN by this name: 1

Meaning: Stern depopulator

Father of a man who repaired Jerusalem's walls under Nehemiah.

Only reference: Nehemiah 3:16

📍 AZEKAH

of times mentioned: OT 7

Meaning: Tilled

When Joshua fought the five Amorite kings who attacked Gibeon, he fought their army up to this town. During the battle, the Lord cast down hailstones on the Amorites. Azekah became part of the inheritance of Judah. During King Saul's reign, when the Philistines attacked Israel and wanted a man to fight Goliath, they camped near Azekah. King Rehoboam fortified the city. Azekah was one of the last fortified cities to fall when the Chaldeans (Babylonians) attacked Israel. After the Babylonian Exile, members of the tribe of Judah resettled here.

First reference: Joshua 10:10 / Last reference: Jeremiah 34:7

AZEL

of times mentioned: 6
# of MEN by this name: 1

Meaning: Noble

A descendant of Abraham through Jacob's son Benjamin, through the line of King Saul and his son Jonathan.

First reference: 1 Chronicles 8:37 / Last reference: 1 Chronicles 9:44

AZEM

of times mentioned: OT 2

Meaning: Bone

A city that became part of the inheritance of the tribe of Judah following the conquest of the Promised Land. It was given to Simeon when Joshua cast lots in Shiloh to provide territory for the seven tribes that had yet to receive their land.

First reference: Joshua 15:29 / Last reference: Joshua 19:3

AZGAD

of times mentioned: 4
# of MEN by this name: 3

Meaning: Stern troop

1) Forefather of an exiled family that returned to Judah under Zerubbabel.

First reference: Ezra 2:12 / Last reference: Nehemiah 7:17

2) Forefather of a Jewish exile who returned from Babylon to Judah under Ezra.

Only reference: Ezra 8:12

3) A Jewish leader who renewed the covenant under Nehemiah.

Only reference: Nehemiah 10:15

AZIEL

of times mentioned: 1
# of MEN by this name: 1

Meaning: Strengthened of God

A Levite musician who performed in celebration when King David brought the ark of the covenant to Jerusalem. Same as Jaaziel.

Only reference: 1 Chronicles 15:20

AZIZA

of times mentioned: 1
# of MEN by this name: 1

Meaning: Strengthfulness

An exiled Israelite who married a "strange" (foreign) woman.

Only reference: Ezra 10:27

AZMAVETH

of times mentioned: 6
# of MEN by this name: 4

Meaning: Strong one of death

1) One of King David's valiant warriors.

First reference: 2 Samuel 23:31 / Last reference: 1 Chronicles 11:33

2) A descendant of Abraham through Jacob's son Benjamin, through the line of King Saul and his son Jonathan.

First reference: 1 Chronicles 8:36 / Last reference: 1 Chronicles 9:42

3) Father of David's "mighty men" Jeziel and Pelet, who supported the future king during his conflict with Saul.

Only reference: 1 Chronicles 12:3

4) A treasurer who served under King David.

Only reference: 1 Chronicles 27:25

⚲AZMAVETH

of times mentioned: OT 2

Meaning: Strong one of death

A city in Judah to which captives returned after the Babylonian Exile.

First reference: Ezra 2:24 / Last reference: Nehemiah 12:29

⚲AZMON

of times mentioned: OT 3

Meaning: Bonelike

A spot in southern Canaan that God gave Moses as a marker of the boundary of Israel. Azmon also formed part of the border of the tribe of Judah's territory.

First reference: Numbers 34:4 / Last reference: Joshua 15:4

⚲AZNOTH-TABOR

of times mentioned: OT 1

Meaning: Flats (or tops) of Tabor

These hills marked the western border of the inheritance of Naphtali when Joshua cast lots in Shiloh to provide territory for the seven tribes that had yet to receive their land.

Only reference: Joshua 19:34–39

👥AZOR

of times mentioned: 2
# of MEN by this name: 1

Genealogy of Jesus: Yes (Matthew 1:13–14)

Meaning: Helpful

A descendant of Abraham through Isaac; forebear of Jesus' earthly father, Joseph.

First reference: Matthew 1:13 / Last reference: Matthew 1:14

⚲AZOTUS

of times mentioned: NT 1

Meaning: Greek form of Ashdod

To this city the apostle Philip was caught away by the Holy Spirit after he baptized the Ethiopian eunuch near the road between Jerusalem and Gaza.

Only reference: Acts 8:40

👥AZRIEL

of times mentioned: 3
# of MEN by this name: 3

Meaning: Help of God

1) One of the "mighty men of valour, famous men" who led the half tribe of Manasseh.

Only reference: 1 Chronicles 5:24

2) Forefather of Ishmaiah, whom David made ruler over the Zebulunites.

Only reference: 1 Chronicles 27:19

3) Father of Seraiah, whom Jehoiakim, king of Judah, commanded to seize the prophet Jeremiah and his scribe.

Only reference: Jeremiah 36:26

👥AZRIKAM

of times mentioned: 6
# of MEN by this name: 4

Meaning: Help of an enemy

1) A descendant of Abraham through Jacob's son Judah, in the line of the nation of Judah's third-to-last king, Jeconiah (also known as Jehoiachin).

Only reference: 1 Chronicles 3:23

2) A descendant of Abraham through Jacob's son Benjamin, through the line of King Saul and his son Jonathan.

First reference: 1 Chronicles 8:38 / Last reference: 1 Chronicles 9:44

3) Forefather of a Jewish exile from the tribe of Levi who resettled Jerusalem.

First reference: 1 Chronicles 9:14 / Last reference: Nehemiah 11:15

4) Official in charge of the palace of King Ahaz of Judah.

Only reference: 2 Chronicles 28:7

AZUBAH

of times mentioned: 4
# of WOMEN by this name: 2

Meaning: Desertion

1) Mother of King Jehoshaphat of Judah and daughter of Shilhi.

First reference: 1 Kings 22:42 / Last reference: 2 Chronicles 20:31

2) Wife of Caleb (2).

First reference: 1 Chronicles 2:18 / Last reference: 1 Chronicles 2:19

AZUR

of times mentioned: 2
# of MEN by this name: 2

Meaning: Helpful

1) A prophet whose son, Hanani, spoke prophetically to the prophet Jeremiah.

Only reference: Jeremiah 28:1

2) A wicked counselor in Jerusalem following the Babylonian Exile.

Only reference: Ezekiel 11:1

AZZAH

of times mentioned: OT 3

Meaning: Strong

A city of the Avim tribe, it later became the Philistine city of Gaza. King Solomon had dominion over Azzah and its king.

First reference: Deuteronomy 2:23 / Last reference: Jeremiah 25:20

AZZAN

of times mentioned: 1
# of MEN by this name: 1

Meaning: Strong one

Forefather of Paltiel, prince of the tribe of Issachar when the Israelites entered the Promised Land.

Only reference: Numbers 34:26

AZZUR

of times mentioned: 1
# of MEN by this name: 1

Meaning: Helpful

A Jewish leader who renewed the covenant under Nehemiah.

Only reference: Nehemiah 10:17

BAAL

of times mentioned: 3
# of MEN by this name: 2

Meaning: Master

1) A descendant of Abraham through Jacob's son Reuben.

Only reference: 1 Chronicles 5:5

2) The fourth son of the Benjaminite Jeiel, who founded the city of Gibeon.

First reference: 1 Chronicles 8:30 / Last reference: 1 Chronicles 9:36

BAAL

of times mentioned: OT 1

Meaning: Name of a Phoenician god

A city that became part of the inheritance of the tribe of Simeon.

Only reference: 1 Chronicles 4:33

♀BAALAH

of times mentioned: OT 5

Meaning: A mistress

1) A city that formed part of the border of the tribe of Judah's territory. Here the ark of the covenant rested from the time the Philistines returned it to Judah until King David brought it to Jerusalem. Same as Baale of Judah and Kirjath-jearim.

First reference: Joshua 15:9 / Last reference: 1 Chronicles 13:6

2) A mountain that formed part of the border of the tribe of Judah's territory.

Only reference: Joshua 15:11

♀BAALATH

of times mentioned: OT 3

Meaning: Mistresship

A border city that became part of the inheritance of Dan when Joshua cast lots in Shiloh to provide territory for the seven tribes that had yet to receive their land. King Solomon fortified Baalath.

First reference: Joshua 19:44 / Last reference: 2 Chronicles 8:6

♀BAALATH-BEER

of times mentioned: OT 1

Meaning: Mistress of a well

A city that became part of the inheritance of Simeon when Joshua cast lots in Shiloh to provide territory for the seven tribes that had yet to receive their land.

Only reference: Joshua 19:8

♀BAALE OF JUDAH

of times mentioned: OT 1

Meaning: Masters of Judah

A place where the ark of the covenant was placed after the Philistines stole it then returned it to Judah. David went there to bring the ark into Jerusalem. Same as Baalah (1), Kirjath-baal, and Kirjath-jearim.

Only reference: 2 Samuel 6:2

♀BAAL-GAD

of times mentioned: OT 3

Meaning: Baal of fortune

A Canaanite city in the valley of Lebanon that was conquered by Joshua, who killed its king. When Joshua was old, the Israelites had not subdued Baal-gad.

First reference: Joshua 11:17 / Last reference: Joshua 13:5

♀BAAL-HAMON

of times mentioned: OT 1

Meaning: Possessor of a multitude

A place where King Solomon owned a profitable vineyard. Its exact location is unknown.

Only reference: Song of Solomon 8:11

👥BAAL-HANAN

of times mentioned: 5
# of MEN by this name: 2

Meaning: Possessor of grace

1) A king of Edom, "before there reigned any king over the children of Israel" (Genesis 36:31).

First reference: Genesis 36:38 / Last reference: 1 Chronicles 1:50

2) A Gederite who had charge of King David's olive and sycamore trees in the low plains.

Only reference: 1 Chronicles 27:28

♀BAAL-HAZOR

of times mentioned: OT 1

Meaning: Possessor of a village

A place near Ephraim where King David's son Absalom had sheepshearers.

Only reference: 2 Samuel 13:23

⚲BAAL-HERMON

of times mentioned: OT 2

Meaning: Possessor of Hermon

A Philistine city that became part of the land of the half tribe of Manasseh. It lay near Mount Hermon.

First reference: Judges 3:3 / Last reference: 1 Chronicles 5:23

⚲BAALIS

of times mentioned: 1
# of MEN by this name: 1

Meaning: In exultation

An Ammonite king who sent an assassin against Gedaliah, the Babylonian-appointed governor of Judah.

Only reference: Jeremiah 40:14

⚲BAAL-MEON

of times mentioned: OT 3

Meaning: Baal of the habitation

A town in the Transjordan area that the tribe of Reuben rebuilt after the conquest of the Promised Land. Though the Reubenites occupied the lane to Nebo and Baal-meon, they evidently did not hold on to it. Ezekiel spoke of it as being Moabite in his prophecy against Moab and Seir. The prophet called Baal-meon "the glory of that land" (NIV) but spoke of its punishment by God, because Moab believed the house of Judah was just like other nations.

First reference: Numbers 32:38 / Last reference: Ezekiel 25:9

⚲BAAL-PERAZIM

of times mentioned: OT 4

Meaning: Possessor of breaches

A place where David attacked the Philistines after they heard that he had been anointed king over Israel. The Lord broke forth "as the breach of waters" (2 Samuel 5:20), giving David victory.

First reference: 2 Samuel 5:20 / Last reference: 1 Chronicles 14:11

⚲BAAL-SHALISHA

of times mentioned: OT 1

Meaning: Baal of Shalisha

Hometown of a man who brought Elisha bread as a firstfruits offering. Elisha gave it to the men whose deadly stew he had purified.

Only reference: 2 Kings 4:42

⚲BAAL-TAMAR

of times mentioned: OT 1

Meaning: Possessor of the palm tree

Site of a battle between Israel and the tribe of Benjamin. After members of the tribe of Benjamin abused a Levite's concubine until she died, Israel took up arms against the tribe to punish this evil act.

Only reference: Judges 20:33

⚲BAAL-ZEPHON

of times mentioned: OT 3

Meaning: Baal of winter (in the sense of cold)

A place by the Red Sea where the Israelites camped at the beginning of the Exodus.

First reference: Exodus 14:2 / Last reference: Numbers 33:7

⚲BAANA

of times mentioned: 2
# of MEN by this name: 2

Meaning: In affliction

1) One of King Solomon's twelve officials over provisions.

Only reference: 1 Kings 4:12

2) Father of a man who repaired Jerusalem's walls under Nehemiah.

Only reference: Nehemiah 3:4

👥BAANAH

\# of times mentioned: 10
\# of MEN by this name: 4

Meaning: In affliction

1) A leader of the raiding bands of Ish-bosheth, one of Saul's sons. Baanah and his brother, Rechab, killed Ish-bosheth. In turn, David had the brothers killed.

First reference: 2 Samuel 4:2 / Last reference: 2 Samuel 4:9

2) Father of one of King David's valiant warriors.

First reference: 2 Samuel 22:39 / Last reference: 1 Chronicles 11:30

3) One of King Solomon's twelve officials over provisions.

Only reference: 1 Kings 4:16

4) A Jewish leader who renewed the covenant under Nehemiah.

First reference: Ezra 2:2 / Last reference: Nehemiah 10:27

👥BAARA

\# of times mentioned: 1
\# of WOMEN by this name: 1

Meaning: Brutish

One of two wives of a Benjamite named Shaharaim. He divorced her in favor of other wives in Moab.

Only reference: 1 Chronicles 8:8

👥BAASEIAH

\# of times mentioned: 1
\# of MEN by this name: 1

Meaning: In the work of God

Forefather of Asaph, the Levite singer.

Only reference: 1 Chronicles 6:40

👥BAASHA

\# of times mentioned: 28
\# of MEN by this name: 1

Meaning: Offensiveness

The idolatrous king of Israel who fought with Asa, king of Judah. After conspiring against and killing King Nadab, he took Israel's throne. Baasha attempted to fortify Ramah, to limit access to Judah. But Asa bribed Ben-hadad, king of Syria, who had a covenant with both nations, to support him instead of Baasha. Asa's army tore down the unfinished fortifications at Ramah and carried the stones away. Baasha and Asa fought for the rest of their reigns. Jehu, son of Hanani, prophesied the destruction of Baasha's household. This occurred when Baasha's son Elah was killed by Zimri.

First reference: 1 Kings 15:16 / Last reference: Jeremiah 41:9 / Key references: 1 Kings 15:16, 33; 16:1–4

📍BABEL

\# of times mentioned: OT 2

Meaning: Confusion

Nimrod's kingdom, in Mesopotamia, where the Lord confused the language of the people and scattered them across the earth.

First reference: Genesis 10:10 / Last reference: Genesis 11:9

📍BABYLON

\# of times mentioned: OT 274 / NT 12

Meaning: Confusion

An ancient Mesopotamian city on the Euphrates River. Babylon's location made it an important city of trade. Genesis 10:10 describes Babel (some versions translate this "Babylon") as the start of Nimrod's kingdom. During the Old Babylonian Empire and King Hammurabi's reign, the city reached a peak it would not match until the Neo-Babylonian Empire. The Kassite Nebuchadnezzar I made it his capital. Under the Assyrians Babylon was destroyed by Sennacherib then rebuilt by Ashurbanipal.

After conquering Israel during the reign of King Hoshea, Shalmaneser V, king of Assyria, took people from this, his capital city, and moved them to the cities of Samaria to replace the Israelites his conquering army had captured and carried to Babylon. Through the Babylonian settlers, pagan worship combined with Jewish religious practices became standard in Samaria, causing New Testament–era Jews to despise the people who lived there.

When King Hezekiah of Judah showed his precious objects to the emissaries of the Assyrian king, Isaiah prophesied that all these goods and the children of Judah would be carried to Babylon. The next king of Judah, Hezekiah's son Manasseh, was captured by the Assyrians and carried to Babylon. He remained there until he humbled himself before God.

The Chaldean King Nebuchadnezzar II fulfilled Isaiah's prophecy of goods and people being carried off to Babylon when he attacked Jerusalem and captured King Jehoiakim, his people, and his valuables. Nebuchadnezzar conquered the last three kings of Judah: Jehoiakim, his son Jehoiachin, and Jehoiachin's uncle Zedekiah. He took them all to Babylon. Along with Zedekiah, the people of Judah went into exile in 586 BC.

The Chaldean (Babylonian) Empire fell to Persia in 539 BC. In the same year, King Cyrus of Persia declared that Jerusalem's temple should be rebuilt. From Babylon, Ezra led the first Israelites back to Judah to carry out this command.

Repeatedly, scripture speaks of the destruction of Babylon. Isaiah compares its fall to Lucifer's and castigates Babylon as an oppressor. Jeremiah predicted the fall of Zedekiah and the destruction of Jerusalem, but through him God also promised the exile would last only seventy years. Even before Jerusalem fell to Nebuchadnezzar, the prophet promised that another nation would come from the north and vanquish Babylon, destroying it completely.

The prophet Ezekiel spoke of the empire of Babylon almost as a weapon in God's hand as it fought against Tyre ("Tyrus" in the KJV) and Egypt.

When Judah fell to Nebuchadnezzar, the prophet Daniel was carried to Babylon, along with other young men from his nation. Daniel became one of Babylon's wise men and served Nebuchadnezzar and his son Belshazzar. When Darius the Mede ("Median" in the KJV) took the throne, Daniel became a high official of the nation.

In the New Testament, Peter refers to a church at Babylon, which may be a reference to the congregation at Rome. In the book of Revelation, Babylon takes on a symbolic meaning as a fallen, sinful city. Numerous scholars have also equated this with Rome.

First reference: 2 Kings 17:24 / Last reference: Revelation 18:21 / Key references: 2 Kings 20:17; 24:10–12; 2 Chronicles 36:10; Revelation 14:8; 17:5

◉BACA

of times mentioned: OT 1

Meaning: Weeping

A valley poetically described by the sons of Korah as becoming a place of springs when believers go through it.

Only reference: Psalm 84:6

◉BAHURIM

of times mentioned: OT 5

Meaning: Young men

After King David insisted that his wife Michal be returned to him, Abner carried her back to Jerusalem. When they reached this village outside Jerusalem, Abner ordered Michal's grieving second husband, Paltiel, to turn back from following her. Here Shimei cursed King David as he fled from Absalom, then changed his mind and supported David with a thousand men. David's messengers, Jonathan and Ahimaaz, hid from Absalom in a well at Bahurim.

First reference: 2 Samuel 3:16 / Last reference: 1 Kings 2:8

◉BAJITH

of times mentioned: OT 1

Meaning: A house; family

One of Moab's "high places" where pagan worship occurred. Here Isaiah prophesied the Moabites would grieve after their nation was destroyed.

Only reference: Isaiah 15:2

👥BAKBAKKAR

of times mentioned: 1
# of MEN by this name: 1

Meaning: Searcher

A Jewish exile from the tribe of Levi who resettled Jerusalem.

Only reference: 1 Chronicles 9:15

👥BAKBUK

of times mentioned: 2
# of MEN by this name: 1

Meaning: Bottle

Forefather of an exiled family that returned to Judah under Zerubbabel.

First reference: Ezra 2:51 / Last reference: Nehemiah 7:53

👥BAKBUKIAH

of times mentioned: 3
# of MEN by this name: 1

Meaning: Emptying of God

An exiled Levite who resettled Jerusalem under Nehemiah.

First reference: Nehemiah 11:17 / Last reference: Nehemiah 12:25

👥BALAAM

of times mentioned: 63
# of MEN by this name: 1

Meaning: Foreigner

A Mesopotamian prophet, sent for by Balak, king of Moab, to curse the Israelites who were invading nearby nations and would soon come to his. Balak called for Balaam twice and offered the prophet great honor if he would come, so God allowed him to go to Moab. But the prophet had something perverse in mind. During his trip, his donkey first refused to follow the road then lay down upon it. Suffering a beating because of the prophet's anger, the beast spoke. Suddenly the angel of the Lord that had barred the donkey's way appeared before Balaam and reminded him that God had called for his obedience. Balaam continued on his way and would not curse Israel, no matter how the king pressed him; instead he prophesied blessings on Israel. But he gave the king an idea: distract Israel from its faith by leading its people into idolatry (Revelation 2:14–15).

First reference: Numbers 22:5 / Last reference: Revelation 2:14 / Key references: Numbers 22:18; 23:12; Revelation 2:14–15

👥BALAC

of times mentioned: 1
# of MEN by this name: 1

Meaning: Waster

Greek form of the name Balak, a king of Moab.

Only reference: Revelation 2:14

👥BALADAN

of times mentioned: 2
# of MEN by this name: 1

Meaning: Bel is his lord

Father of the Babylonian king Berodach-baladan, who sent well wishes to Judah's ill king Hezekiah.

First reference: 2 Kings 20:12 / Last reference: Isaiah 39:1

📍BALAH

of times mentioned: OT 1

Meaning: Failure

A city that became part of the inheritance of Simeon when Joshua cast lots in Shiloh to provide territory for the seven tribes that had yet to receive their land.

Only reference: Joshua 19:3

👥BALAK

of times mentioned: 43
# of MEN by this name: 1

Meaning: Waster

The king of Moab who saw the Israelites heading toward his country and sent for the Mesopotamian prophet Balaam to curse the intruders. At first, Balaam would not come to Moab. When he did come, Balak was angered by his unwillingness to curse Israel. Though Balak brought the prophet to numerous idolatrous high places and made many offerings, he could not sway the prophet's mind because God had told Balaam that Israel was blessed. But in the end Balak did suggest that the king might influence Israel by leading the people into idolatry—and the idea was successful (Numbers 25:1–2).

First reference: Numbers 22:2 / Last reference: Micah 6:5 / Key reference: Numbers 22:5–6

⊙BAMAH

of times mentioned: OT 1

Meaning: High place

A high place where idols were worshipped in Israel. Through the prophet Ezekiel, God confronted the nation about its idolatry here and called them to return to Him.

Only reference: Ezekiel 20:29–44

⊙BAMOTH

of times mentioned: OT 2

Meaning: Heights

A place in Moab where the Israelites camped on their way to the Promised Land. Perhaps the same as Bamoth-baal.

First reference: Numbers 21:19 / Last reference: Numbers 21:20

⊙BAMOTH-BAAL

of times mentioned: OT 1

Meaning: Heights of Baal

A city east of the Jordan River that became part of the inheritance of the tribe of Reuben. Perhaps the same as Bamoth.

Only reference: Joshua 13:17

👥BANI

of times mentioned: 15
# of MEN by this name: 10

Meaning: Built

1) One in the group of King David's warriors known as the "mighty men."

Only reference: 2 Samuel 23:36

2) Ancestor of the sons of Merari, who ministered in the tabernacle.

Only reference: 1 Chronicles 6:46

3) One of a group of Levites who led a revival among the Israelites in the time of Nehemiah.

Only reference: 1 Chronicles 9:4

4) Forefather of exiled Israelites who returned to Judah under Zerubbabel.

First reference: Ezra 2:10 / Last reference: Ezra 10:29

5) Father of exiled Israelites who married a "strange" (foreign) woman.

Only reference: Ezra 10:34

6) An exiled Israelite who married a "strange" (foreign) woman.

Only reference: Ezra 10:38

7) A priest who helped Ezra to explain the law to exiles returned to Jerusalem; father of a rebuilder of the city walls.

First reference: Nehemiah 3:17 / Last reference: Nehemiah 9:5

8) One of a group of Levites who led a revival among the Israelites in the time of Nehemiah.

First reference: Nehemiah 9:4 / Last reference: Nehemiah 10:13

9) A Jewish leader who renewed the covenant under Nehemiah.

Only reference: Nehemiah 10:14

10) Forefather of a Jewish exile from the tribe of Levi who resettled Jerusalem.

Only reference: Nehemiah 11:22

👥BARABBAS

of times mentioned: 11
# of MEN by this name: 1

Meaning: Son of Abba

A man variously described by the Gospel writers as a murderer, a robber, and one accused of sedition. Barabbas was in prison when Jesus came to trial, and Pilate offered the Jewish people a choice concerning which of the two men he should release for the Passover. At the instigation of the chief priests, the people chose Barabbas. He was released, and Jesus died on the cross instead.

First reference: Matthew 27:16 / Last reference: John 18:40 / Key references: Matthew 27:17, 21–22

👥BARACHEL

of times mentioned: 2
# of MEN by this name: 1

Meaning: God has blessed

Father of Job's young friend (and accuser) Elihu.

First reference: Job 32:2 / Last reference: Job 32:6

👥BARACHIAS

of times mentioned: 1
# of MEN by this name: 1

Meaning: Blessing of God

Father of Zacharias, who was killed between the temple and altar.

Only reference: Matthew 23:35

👥BARAK

of times mentioned: 14
# of MEN by this name: 1

Meaning: Lightning

The judge Deborah's battle captain, who refused to enter battle without her support. With Deborah, he went to Kadesh and joined battle against the Canaanite king Jabin's captain Sisera. Barak successfully routed the troops, but Sisera was killed by a woman—Jael, wife of Heber the Kenite.

First reference: Judges 4:6 / Last reference: Hebrews 11:32 / Key references: Judges 4:8, 15–16

👥BARIAH

of times mentioned: 1
# of MEN by this name: 1

Meaning: Fugitive

A descendant of Abraham through Jacob's son Judah, in the line of the nation of Judah's third-to-last king, Jeconiah (also known as Jehoiachin).

Only reference: 1 Chronicles 3:22

👥BAR-JESUS

of times mentioned: 1
# of MEN by this name: 1

Meaning: Son of Jesus

A Jewish sorcerer, also called Elymas, who was miraculously blinded for opposing the apostle Paul's preaching of the Gospel in Paphos. Same as Elymas.

Only reference: Acts 13:6

👥BARJONA

of times mentioned: 1
# of MEN by this name: 1

Meaning: Son of Jonas

Another name for the apostle Peter, used by Jesus Christ.

Only reference: Matthew 16:17

👥BARKOS

of times mentioned: 2
# of MEN by this name: 1

Forefather of an exiled family that returned to Judah under Zerubbabel.

First reference: Ezra 2:53 / Last reference: Nehemiah 7:55

👥BARNABAS

of times mentioned: 29
# of MEN by this name: 1

Meaning: Son of prophecy

A Cypriot Christian who sold some land and gave the profits to the church. After Saul's conversion, Barnabas introduced this previous persecutor of the church to the apostles and spoke up for him. When the Jerusalem church heard that Gentiles of Antioch had been converted, they sent Barnabas, who became one of the "prophets and teachers" at that church. Saul and Barnabas were sent on a missionary journey. In Lycaonia, the people wrongly proclaimed them gods. Together the two taught against the Judaizers, who wanted Gentiles to be circumcised. But these missionaries disagreed over the addition of John Mark to their ministry and separated. Barnabas and Mark went to Cyprus. Same as Joses (3).

First reference: Acts 4:36 / Last reference: Colossians 4:10 / Key references: Acts 9:26–27; 11:22–24

👥BARSABAS

of times mentioned: 2
# of MEN by this name: 2

Meaning: Son of Sabas

1) Also called Joseph Justus, a potential apostolic replacement for Judas Iscariot. He lost by lot to the other candidate, Matthias. Same as Joseph (11) and Justus (1).

Only reference: Acts 1:23

2) Surname of a Christian named Judas, who was sent by the Jerusalem Council to Antioch with Paul and Barnabas.

Only reference: Acts 15:22

👥BARTHOLOMEW

of times mentioned: 4
# of MEN by this name: 1

Meaning: Son of Tolmai

One of Jesus' disciples. Probably the same as Nathanael.

First reference: Matthew 10:3 / Last reference: Acts 1:13

👥BARTIMAEUS

of times mentioned: 1
# of MEN by this name: 1

Meaning: Son of Timaeus

A blind beggar of Jericho who shouted for Jesus' attention, disturbing the crowds that had gathered to see the Lord. Jesus called for Bartimaeus and asked what he wanted. When the man said he wanted his sight, Jesus healed him, saying, "Thy faith hath made thee whole" (Mark 10:52).

Only reference: Mark 10:46

👥BARUCH

of times mentioned: 26
# of MEN by this name: 3

Meaning: Blessed

1) A rebuilder of the walls of Jerusalem and a priest who renewed the covenant under Nehemiah.

First reference: Nehemiah 3:20 / Last reference: Nehemiah 10:6

2) Forefather of a Jewish exile from the tribe of Judah who resettled Jerusalem.

Only reference: Nehemiah 11:5

3) A scribe who wrote down all the words the prophet Jeremiah received from God. He went to the temple and read these prophecies to the people. When he read them to the princes of the land, they warned him and Jeremiah to hide while they told Jehoiakim, king of Judah. After the king destroyed the first copy of the prophecies, Baruch rewrote it at Jeremiah's dictation.

The proud men who opposed Jeremiah falsely accused Baruch of setting Jeremiah against Judah and trying to deliver the nation into the hands of the Chaldeans.

First reference: Jeremiah 32:12 / Last reference: Jeremiah 45:2 / Key reference: Jeremiah 36:4

👥BARZILLAI

of times mentioned: 12
# of MEN by this name: 2

Meaning: Iron-hearted

1) An elderly man who brought food and supplies to King David and his soldiers as they fled from the army of David's son Absalom. When David returned to Jerusalem, Barzallai conducted him over the Jordan River. David invited him to Jerusalem, but he sent Chimham, who was probably his son, in his place.

First reference: 2 Samuel 17:27 / Last reference: Nehemiah 7:63

2) Father of Adriel, who was husband of Merab, Saul's daughter.

Only reference: 2 Samuel 21:8

♀BASHAN

of times mentioned: OT 59

The nation of the Amorite king Og and home of the remnant of the giants that area was famous for. Bashan lay to the east and north of the Sea of Galilee, above Gilead. Israel fought Og at Edrei and conquered Bashan. Later it became part of the inheritance of the tribe of Manasseh. Machir, Manasseh's son, a man of war, inherited Bashan. King Hazael of Syria attacked and conquered this land. The prophets speak of the oaks of Bashan, which will be subdued by the Lord.

First reference: Numbers 21:33 / Last reference: Zechariah 11:2 / Key references: Deuteronomy 3:1, 13

♀BASHAN-HAVOTH-JAIR

of times mentioned: OT 1

Meaning: Bashan hamlets of Jair

A region of Og that the Israelites conquered after they refused to enter the Promised Land. Moses gave this territory to the tribe of Manasseh. Jair, Manasseh's son, inherited and named it. Same as Argob.

Only reference: Deuteronomy 3:14

👥BASHEMATH

of times mentioned: 6
# of WOMEN by this name: 2

Meaning: Fragrance

1) The Hittite wife of Esau. Same as Adah (2).

Only reference: Genesis 26:34

2) Ishmael's daughter and another wife of Esau. Mother of Reuel, Nahath, Zerah, Shammah, and Mizzah. Possibly the same as Bashemath (1).

First reference: Genesis 36:3 / Last reference: Genesis 36:17

👥BASMATH

of times mentioned: 1
# of WOMEN by this name: 1

Meaning: Fragrance

A daughter of King Solomon who married Ahimaaz, a royal official over the king's provisions.

Only reference: Kings 4:15

♀BATH-RABBIM

of times mentioned: OT 1

Meaning: The daughter (or city) of Rabbah

A gate in Heshbon that Solomon used to describe the beauty of his beloved.

Only reference: Song of Solomon 7:4

👥BATH-SHEBA

of times mentioned: 11
# of WOMEN by this name: 1

Genealogy of Jesus: Yes (Matthew 1:6)

Meaning: Daughter of an oath

The beautiful wife of the warrior Uriah the Hittite, whom King David saw bathing on her rooftop. The king desired her and committed adultery with her, and she became pregnant. To solve his problem, he arranged for Uriah to die in battle and then married Bath-sheba. But God was displeased and the child died. After David repented, God gave them a son, Solomon, who became heir to David's throne. When David's son Adonijah tried to take the throne just before the king's death, Bath-sheba intervened, asking David to remember his promise. Later she intervened with Solomon when Adonijah sought to marry Abishag, David's concubine.

First reference: 2 Samuel 11:3 / Last reference: Psalm 51 (title) / Key references: 2 Samuel 11:3–4; 1 Kings 1:11

👥BATH-SHUA

of times mentioned: 1
# of WOMEN by this name: 1

Genealogy of Jesus: Yes (Matthew 1:6)

Meaning: Daughter of wealth

A form of the name Bath-sheba, a wife of King David.

Only reference: 1 Chronicles 3:5

👥 BAVAI

of times mentioned: 1
# of MEN by this name: 1

A man who repaired Jerusalem's walls under Nehemiah.

Only reference: Nehemiah 3:18

👥 BAZLITH

of times mentioned: 1
# of MEN by this name: 1

Meaning: Peeling

Forefather of an exiled family that returned to Judah under Zerubbabel. Same as Bazluth.

Only reference: Nehemiah 7:54

👥 BAZLUTH

of times mentioned: 1
# of MEN by this name: 1

Meaning: Peeling

Forefather of an exiled family that returned to Judah under Zerubbabel. Same as Bazlith.

Only reference: Ezra 2:52

👥 BEALIAH

of times mentioned: 1
# of MEN by this name: 1

Meaning: God is master

A "mighty man" who supported the future king David during his conflict with Saul.

Only reference: 1 Chronicles 12:5

📍 BEALOTH

of times mentioned: OT 1

Meaning: Mistresses

A city that became part of the inheritance of the tribe of Judah following the conquest of the Promised Land.

Only reference: Joshua 15:24–45

👥 BEBAI

of times mentioned: 6
# of MEN by this name: 3

1) Forefather of an exiled family that returned to Judah under Zerubbabel.

First reference: Ezra 2:11 / Last reference: Nehemiah 7:16

2) Forefather of an exiled family that returned to Judah under Ezra.

First reference: Ezra 8:11 / Last reference: Ezra 10:28

3) A Jewish leader who renewed the covenant under Nehemiah.

Only reference: Nehemiah 10:15

👥 BECHER

of times mentioned: 5
# of MEN by this name: 2

Meaning: Young camel

1) A descendant of Abraham through Jacob's son Benjamin.

First reference: Genesis 46:21 / Last reference: 1 Chronicles 7:8

2) A descendant of Joseph through his son Ephraim.

Only reference: Numbers 26:35

👥 BECHORATH

of times mentioned: 1
# of MEN by this name: 1

Meaning: Firstborn

A man of the tribe of Benjamin, ancestor of Israel's king Saul.

Only reference: 1 Samuel 9:1

BEDAD

of times mentioned: 2
# of MEN by this name: 1

Meaning: Solitary

Father of a king of Edom, "before there reigned any king over the children of Israel" (Genesis 36:31).

First reference: Genesis 36:35 / Last reference: 1 Chronicles 1:46

BEDAN

of times mentioned: 2
# of MEN by this name: 2

Meaning: Servile

1) A judge of Israel who delivered the nation from its enemies.

Only reference: 1 Samuel 12:11

2) A descendant of Abraham through Joseph's son Manasseh.

Only reference: 1 Chronicles 7:17

BEDEIAH

of times mentioned: 1
# of MEN by this name: 1

Meaning: Servant of Jehovah

An exiled Israelite who married a "strange" (foreign) woman.

Only reference: Ezra 10:35

BEELIADA

of times mentioned: 1
# of MEN by this name: 1

Meaning: Baal has known

A son of King David, born in Jerusalem.

Only reference: 1 Chronicles 14:7

BEER

of times mentioned: OT 2

1) The site of a well to which God brought Moses and the Israelites when they needed water as they wandered in the wilderness. Probably the same as Beer-elim.

Only reference: Numbers 21:16

2) A town Jotham fled to when his brother Abimelech became king of Shechem.

Only reference: Judges 9:21

BEERA

of times mentioned: 1
# of MEN by this name: 1

Meaning: A well

A descendant of Abraham through Jacob's son Asher.

Only reference: 1 Chronicles 7:37

BEERAH

of times mentioned: 1
# of MEN by this name: 1

Meaning: A well

A descendant of Abraham through Jacob's son Reuben. Beerah, a leader of the tribe of Reuben, was taken captive by the Assyrian king Tiglath-pileser.

Only reference: 1 Chronicles 5:6

BEER-ELIM

of times mentioned: OT 1

Meaning: Well of heroes

A well in Moab. Isaiah uses it to describe the grief of Moab at her destruction. Probably the same as Beer (1).

Only reference: Isaiah 15:8

BEERI

of times mentioned: 2
# of MEN by this name: 2

Meaning: Fountained

1) The Hittite father of Judith, a wife of Esau.

Only reference: Genesis 26:34

2) Father of the prophet Hosea.

Only reference: Hosea 1:1

BEER-LAHAI-ROI

of times mentioned: OT 1

Meaning: Well of a living (One), my seer

A wilderness well situated between Kadesh and Bered. The angel of the Lord met the pregnant Hagar here after she fled from Sarai, who treated her harshly after she conceived. Same as Lahai-roi.

Only reference: Genesis 16:14

BEEROTH

of times mentioned: OT 6

Meaning: Wells

1) An Israel campsite around the time Moses received the Ten Commandments. From here God's nation traveled to Moserah.

Only reference: Deuteronomy 10:6

2) A city of the Gibeonites, who tricked Joshua into making peace with them. Beeroth became part of the inheritance of the tribe of Benjamin and was the hometown of Rechab, captain over the men of Saul's son Ish-bosheth. When Judah returned from the Babylonian captivity, Beeroth was resettled.

First reference: Joshua 9:17 / Last reference: Nehemiah 7:29

BEER-SHEBA

of times mentioned: OT 34

Meaning: Well of an oath

A wilderness in which Hagar and Ishmael wandered after they were sent out of Abraham's camp. Beer-sheba was the site of a covenant between Abraham and Abimelech, king of Gerar. Subsequently Abraham planted a grove and worshipped the Lord there. After Abraham pleased God by his willingness to sacrifice his son Isaac, he lived in Beer-sheba. Here God promised to bless Abraham and renewed His covenant with Isaac.

Initially Beer-sheba was part of the inheritance of the tribe of Judah. But it became part of the inheritance of Simeon when Joshua cast lots in Shiloh to provide territory for the seven tribes that had yet to receive their land.

When scripture says "from Dan even to Beersheba," it indicates everything from the northernmost to the southernmost part of Israel.

First reference: Genesis 21:14 / Last reference: Amos 8:14 / Key references: Genesis 21:31–33; 26:23–24; Joshua 19:2

BEESH-TERAH

of times mentioned: OT 1

Meaning: With Ashteroth

One of the forty-eight cities given to the Levites as God had commanded. Beesh-terah was given to them by the tribe of Manasseh.

Only reference: Joshua 21:27

BELA

of times mentioned: 11
# of MEN by this name: 3

Meaning: A gulp

1) A king of Edom, "before there reigned any king over the children of Israel" (Genesis 36:31).

First reference: Genesis 36:32 / Last reference: 1 Chronicles 1:44

2) A descendant of Abraham through Jacob's son Benjamin. Bela was Benjamin's firstborn son.

First reference: Numbers 26:38 / Last reference: 1 Chronicles 8:3

3) A descendant of Abraham through Jacob's son Reuben.

Only reference: 1 Chronicles 5:8

BELA

of times mentioned: OT 2

Meaning: A gulp (implying destruction)

A Canaanite city of the plain that joined in the Canaanite war against King Chedorlaomer of Elam and his Mesopotamian allies. Same as Zoar.

First reference: Genesis 14:2 / Last reference: Genesis 14:8

👥 BELAH

of times mentioned: 1
# of MEN by this name: 1

Meaning: A gulp

Another form of the name Bela, a son of Benjamin.

Only reference: Genesis 46:21

👥 BELSHAZZAR

of times mentioned: 8
# of MEN by this name: 1

A Babylonian king who saw handwriting on the wall and sought to have it interpreted. When his own soothsayers could not do so, the prophet Daniel read it to him. That night, Belshazzar was killed and Darius the Mede took his throne.

First reference: Daniel 5:1 / Last reference: Daniel 8:1

👥 BELTESHAZZAR

of times mentioned: 10
# of MEN by this name: 1

A Babylonian name given to the exiled Israelite Daniel upon entering King Nebuchadnezzar's service.

First reference: Daniel 1:7 / Last reference: Daniel 10:1

👥 BEN

of times mentioned: 1
# of MEN by this name: 1

Meaning: Son

A Levite musician who performed in celebration when King David brought the ark of the covenant to Jerusalem.

Only reference: 1 Chronicles 15:18

👥 BENAIAH

of times mentioned: 42
# of MEN by this name: 12

Meaning: God has built

1) One of David's three mighty men and a commander in King David's army, who oversaw the Cherethites and Pelethites. King Solomon commanded him to kill his brother Adonijah and his battle leader Joab. Solomon rewarded Benaiah by giving him Joab's command.

First reference: 2 Samuel 8:18 / Last reference: 1 Chronicles 27:6 / Key references: 1 Kings 2:22–25; 29–34; 1 Chronicles 11:24

2) A commander in King David's army who oversaw twenty-four thousand men in the eleventh month of each year.

First reference: 2 Samuel 23:30 / Last reference: 1 Chronicles 27:14

3) A descendant of Abraham through Jacob's son Simeon.

Only reference: 1 Chronicles 4:36

4) A Levite musician who performed in celebration when King David brought the ark of the covenant to Jerusalem.

First reference: 1 Chronicles 15:18 / Last reference: 1 Chronicles 16:6

5) Son of the chief priest Jehoiada, he was military captain during the third month for King David.

Only reference: 1 Chronicles 27:34

6) Forefather of Jahaziel, a Levite worship leader who prophesied before King Jehoshaphat of Judah when Edom attacked.

Only reference: 2 Chronicles 20:14

7) A temple overseer during the reign of Hezekiah, king of Judah.

Only reference: 2 Chronicles 31:13

8) An exiled Israelite who married a "strange" (foreign) woman.

Only reference: Ezra 10:25

9) Another exiled Israelite who married a "strange" (foreign) woman.

Only reference: Ezra 10:30

10) Another exiled Israelite who married a "strange" (foreign) woman.

Only reference: Ezra 10:35

11) Another exiled Israelite who married a "strange" (foreign) woman.

Only reference: Ezra 10:43

12) Father of Pelatiah, a prince of Judah.

First reference: Ezekiel 11:1 / Last reference: Ezekiel 11:13

👪BENAMMI

\# of times mentioned: 1
\# of MEN by this name: 1

Meaning: Son of my people

Forefather of the Ammonites and a son of Lot by an incestuous relationship with his younger daughter. After the destruction of Sodom and Gomorrah, Lot's two daughters devised a plan to continue their family line by making their father drunk and then lying with him.

Only reference: Genesis 19:38

📍BENE-BERAK

\# of times mentioned: OT 1

Meaning: Sons of lightning

A city that became part of the inheritance of Dan when Joshua cast lots in Shiloh to provide territory for the seven tribes that had yet to receive their land.

Only reference: Joshua 19:45

📍BENE-JAAKAN

\# of times mentioned: OT 2

Meaning: Sons of Yaakan

An encampment of the Israelites during the Exodus.

First reference: Numbers 33:31 / Last reference: Numbers 33:32

👪BEN-HADAD

\# of times mentioned: 26
\# of MEN by this name: 3

Meaning: Son of Hadad

1) King of Syria who supported Asa, king of Judah, against Israel.

First reference: 1 Kings 15:18 / Last reference: 2 Chronicles 16:4

2) Another king of Syria who fought against King Ahab of Israel. When his army lost, Ben-hadad fled. Again Syria fought Israel, lost, and Ben-hadad fled to Aphek. He asked for mercy, and Ahab made a covenant with him. Elisha came to Damascus at a time when Ben-hadad was ill, and the king asked the prophet if he would live. Though Elisha told his messenger he would recover, he also prophesied his death. Ben-hadad was murdered by Hazael, who took over his throne.

First reference: 1 Kings 20:1 / Last reference: 2 Kings 8:9

3) Another Syrian king, son of Hazael. Amos prophesied the burning of his palaces.

First reference: 2 Kings 13:3 / Last reference: Amos 1:4

👪BEN-HAIL

\# of times mentioned: 1
\# of MEN by this name: 1

Meaning: Son of might

A prince of Judah sent by King Jehoshaphat to teach the law of the Lord throughout the nation.

Only reference: 2 Chronicles 17:7

👪BEN-HANAN

\# of times mentioned: 1
\# of MEN by this name: 1

Meaning: Son of Chanan

A descendant of Abraham through Jacob's son Judah.

Only reference: 1 Chronicles 4:20

👪BENINU

\# of times mentioned: 1
\# of MEN by this name: 1

Meaning: Our son

A Levite who renewed the covenant under Nehemiah.

Only reference: Nehemiah 10:13

👪BENJAMIN

\# of times mentioned: 20
\# of MEN by this name: 5

Meaning: Son of the right hand

1) Jacob's youngest son and the only full brother of Joseph. Their mother, Rachel, died when he was born. Benjamin became Jacob's favorite after Joseph was sold into slavery by his brothers. During a famine, Jacob sent his other sons to Egypt to get food but fearfully kept Benjamin home. Joseph, then prime minister of Egypt, imprisoned Simeon and insisted that his half brothers bring Benjamin to him. When they returned, Joseph gave his brothers more food but ordered that a silver cup be hidden in Benjamin's sack. When their half brothers came to Benjamin's defense, Joseph knew they had experienced a change of heart.

First reference: Genesis 35:18 / Last reference: 1 Chronicles 8:1

2) A descendant of Abraham through Jacob's son Benjamin.

Only reference: 1 Chronicles 7:10

3) An exiled Israelite who married a "strange" (foreign) woman.

Only reference: Ezra 10:32

4) A rebuilder of the walls of Jerusalem under Nehemiah.

Only reference: Nehemiah 3:23

5) A prince of Judah who joined in the dedication of Jerusalem's rebuilt walls.

Only reference: Nehemiah 12:34

📍BENJAMIN

\# of times mentioned: OT 3

Meaning: Son of the right hand

A gate in Jerusalem that was near the temple. Here Irijah accused the prophet Jeremiah of traitorously going over to the Chaldeans.

First reference: Jeremiah 20:2 / Last reference: Zechariah 14:10

👪BENO

\# of times mentioned: 2
\# of MEN by this name: 1

Meaning: Son

A descendant of Abraham through Jacob's son Levi.

First reference: 1 Chronicles 24:26 / Last reference: 1 Chronicles 24:27

👪BEN-ONI

\# of times mentioned: 1
\# of MEN by this name: 1

Meaning: Son of my sorrow

Name given by Rachel to her second son as she was dying in childbirth. The boy's father, Jacob, called him Benjamin.

Only reference: Genesis 35:18

👪BEN-ZOHETH

\# of times mentioned: 1
\# of MEN by this name: 1

Meaning: Son of Zoheth

A descendant of Abraham through Jacob's son Judah.

Only reference: 1 Chronicles 4:20

📍BEON

\# of times mentioned: OT 1

A place east of the Jordan River that the children of Gad and Reuben requested to have as their inheritance before Israel had finished conquering the Promised Land. Moses made them agree to aid in the conquest of the land before they would gain their inheritance.

Only reference: Numbers 32:3

👥BEOR

of times mentioned: 10
# of MEN by this name: 2

Meaning: A lamp

1) Father of Bela, an Edomite king.

First reference: Genesis 36:32 / Last reference: 1 Chronicles 1:43

2) Father of the false prophet Balaam. Same as Bosor.

First reference: Numbers 22:5 / Last reference: Micah 6:5

👥BERA

of times mentioned: 1
# of MEN by this name: 1

The king of Sodom in the days of Abram. He was killed in battle near the slime pits of Siddim.

Only reference: Genesis 14:2

👥BERACHAH

of times mentioned: 1
# of MEN by this name: 1

Meaning: Benediction

A "mighty man" who supported the future king David during his conflict with Saul.

Only reference: 1 Chronicles 12:3

📍BERACHAH

of times mentioned: OT 2

Meaning: Benediction

A valley where King Jehoshaphat of Judah and his people praised God for saving them from the Moabites and Amonites.

Only reference: 2 Chronicles 20:26

👥BERACHIAH

of times mentioned: 1
# of MEN by this name: 1

Meaning: Blessing of God

Father of Asaph, musician for King David and King Solomon of Israel. Same as Berechiah.

Only reference: 1 Chronicles 6:39

👥BERAIAH

of times mentioned: 1
# of MEN by this name: 1

Meaning: God has created

A descendant of Abraham through Jacob's son Benjamin.

Only reference: 1 Chronicles 8:21

📍BEREA

of times mentioned: NT 3

Meaning: Region beyond the coastline

Paul and Silas fled to this Macedonian city after the Jews of Thessalonica caused them trouble. The Bereans accepted the two men's message, checking it against scripture, until the Thessalonians again stirred up trouble.

First reference: Acts 17:10 / Last reference: Acts 20:4

👥BERECHIAH

of times mentioned: 10
# of MEN by this name: 7

Meaning: Blessing of God

1) A descendant of Abraham through Jacob's son Judah, in the line of the nation of Judah's third-to-last king, Jeconiah (also known as Jehoiachin).

Only reference: 1 Chronicles 3:20

2) Father of Asaph, musician for King David and King Solomon of Israel. Same as Berachiah.

Only reference: 1 Chronicles 15:17

3) A Jewish exile from the tribe of Levi who resettled Jerusalem.

Only reference: 1 Chronicles 9:16

4) A doorkeeper for the ark of the covenant when David brought it to Jerusalem.

Only reference: 1 Chronicles 15:23

5) A man of the tribe of Ephraim who counseled his nation of Israel against enslaving fellow Jews from Judah who were captured in a civil war. Berechiah helped to feed and clothe the prisoners before sending them home.

Only reference: 2 Chronicles 28:12

6) Father of a man who repaired Jerusalem's walls under Nehemiah.

First reference: Nehemiah 3:4 / Last reference: Nehemiah 6:18

7) Father of the prophet Zechariah.

First reference: Zechariah 1:1 / Last reference: Zechariah 1:7

BERED

of times mentioned: 1
# of MEN by this name: 1

Meaning: Hail

A descendant of Abraham through Joseph's son Ephraim.

Only reference: 1 Chronicles 7:20

BERED

of times mentioned: OT 1

Meaning: Hail

A southern Palestinian town near Beer-lahai-roi.

Only reference: Genesis 16:14

BERI

of times mentioned: 1
# of MEN by this name: 1

Meaning: Fountained

A descendant of Abraham through Jacob's son Asher.

Only reference: 1 Chronicles 7:36

BERIAH

of times mentioned: 11
# of MEN by this name: 4

Meaning: In trouble

1) A descendant of Abraham through Jacob's son Asher.

First reference: Genesis 46:17 / Last reference: 1 Chronicles 7:31

2) A descendant of Abraham through Joseph's son Ephraim.

Only reference: 1 Chronicles 7:23

3) A descendant of Abraham through Jacob's son Benjamin. Beriah drove the original inhabitants out of the town of Gath.

First reference: 1 Chronicles 8:13 / Last reference: 1 Chronicles 8:16

4) A Levite (worship leader) when Solomon was made king of Israel.

First reference: 1 Chronicles 23:10 / Last reference: 1 Chronicles 23:11

BERNICE

of times mentioned: 3
# of WOMEN by this name: 1

Meaning: Victorious

Daughter of Herod Agrippa and sister of Agrippa II. With her brother, she heard Paul's testimony before Festus.

First reference: Acts 25:13 / Last reference: Acts 26:30

BERODACH-BALADAN

of times mentioned: 1
# of MEN by this name: 1

A Babylonian king who sent wishes for recovery to Judah's ill king Hezekiah.

Only reference: 2 Kings 20:12

⚲BEROTHAH

of times mentioned: OT 1

Meaning: Cypress or cypresslike

In a prophetic view of the restoration of Jerusalem, Ezekiel saw this city, lying between Damascus and Hamath, as a northern boundary of the land of the tribes of Israel.

Only reference: Ezekiel 47:16

⚲BEROTHAI

of times mentioned: OT 1

Meaning: Cypress or cypresslike

A city of Hadadezer, king of Zobah, which King David conquered and plundered of its brass.

Only reference: 2 Samuel 8:8

👥BESAI

of times mentioned: 2
# of MEN by this name: 1

Meaning: Domineering

Forefather of an exiled family that returned to Judah under Zerubbabel.

First reference: Ezra 2:49 / Last reference: Nehemiah 7:52

👥BESODEIAH

of times mentioned: 1
# of MEN by this name: 1

Meaning: In the counsel of Jehovah

Father of a man who repaired Jerusalem's walls under Nehemiah.

Only reference: Nehemiah 3:6

⚲BESOR

of times mentioned: OT 3

Meaning: Cheerful

A brook where David left his tired troops as the rest of his army followed the Amalekites who had invaded his city of Ziklag and taken its women and children captive.

First reference: 1 Samuel 30:9 / Last reference: 1 Samuel 30:21

⚲BETAH

of times mentioned: OT 1

Meaning: A place of refuge; safety

A city of Hadadezer, king of Zobah. King David conquered the city as he reestablished his border at the Euphrates River. He took large quantities of brass from Betah and Berothai. Betah appears as "Tebah" in the NIV.

Only reference: 2 Samuel 8:8

⚲BETEN

of times mentioned: OT 1

Meaning: To babble (implying to vociferate loudly)

A border town that became part of the inheritance of Issachar when Joshua cast lots in Shiloh to provide territory for the seven tribes that had yet to receive their land.

Only reference: Joshua 19:25

⚲BETHABARA

of times mentioned: NT 1

Meaning: Ferry house

A place east of the Jordan River where John the Baptist baptized believers.

Only reference: John 1:28

⚲BETH-ANATH

of times mentioned: OT 3

Meaning: House of replies

A fortified or walled city that became part of the inheritance of Naphtali when Joshua cast lots in Shiloh to provide territory for the seven tribes that had yet to receive their land. Naphtali did not drive the Canaanites from this city.

First reference: Joshua 19:38 / Last reference: Judges 1:33

BETH-ANOTH

of times mentioned: OT 1

Meaning: House of replies

A city that became part of the inheritance of the tribe of Judah following the conquest of the Promised Land.

Only reference: Joshua 15:59

BETHANY

of times mentioned: NT 11

Meaning: Date house

A village about two miles outside of Jerusalem. Bethany is best known as the home of Jesus' friends Lazarus, Martha, and Mary. When Lazarus became ill, Jesus did not come to the village until he had died. When He did arrive, Martha and Mary mourned that He had not been there to prevent their brother's death. Jesus brought His friend back to life, causing trouble with the chief priests, who wanted to kill Him. For a time Jesus went to the town of Ephraim. Six days before the Last Supper, He returned and went to dinner at the home of Simon the Leper, in Bethany. There Mary of Bethany anointed him with oil. When the disciples objected to her wasting it, Jesus told them she was preparing Him for burial and that she would be remembered for her deed wherever the Gospel was told.

Near Bethany Jesus had the disciples get a donkey for him to ride into Jerusalem. After His triumphal entry into Jerusalem, He stayed at Bethany. He cursed a fig tree near this village. From Bethany after His resurrection, He ascended into heaven.

First reference: Matthew 21:17 / Last reference: John 12:1

BETH-ARABAH

of times mentioned: OT 3

Meaning: House of the desert

A border city of the tribe of Judah's territory, Beth-arabah became part of the inheritance of Benjamin when Joshua cast lots in Shiloh to provide territory for the seven tribes that had yet to receive their land.

First reference: Joshua 15:6 / Last reference: Joshua 18:22

BETH-ARAM

of times mentioned: OT 1

Meaning: House of the height

A city that was part of the inheritance of Gad when Moses gave the first inheritances to Israel.

Only reference: Joshua 13:27

BETH-ARBEL

of times mentioned: OT 1

Meaning: House of God's ambush

Hosea used the destruction of this fortress as a warning to sinful Israel.

Only reference: Hosea 10:14

BETH-AVEN

of times mentioned: OT 7

Meaning: House of vanity

A place near Ai and west of Michmash. The book of Joshua speaks of "the wilderness of Beth-aven" (Joshua 18:12). In a running battle with the Philistines, Saul's troops went as far as Beth-aven. Hosea uses this name for the city of Bethel, a place of worship that had been turned into a place of idolatry. Same as Aven (2).

First reference: Joshua 7:2 / Last reference: Hosea 10:5

BETH-AZMAVETH

of times mentioned: OT 1

Meaning: House of Azmaveth

A town of Judah to which Jews returned after the Babylonian Exile.

Only reference: Nehemiah 7:28

BETH-BAAL-MEON

of times mentioned: OT 1

Meaning: House or habitation of Baal

A Moabite town that Moses gave to the tribe of Reuben as part of its inheritance. Same as Beth-meon.

Only reference: Joshua 13:17

BETH-BARAH

of times mentioned: OT 1

Meaning: House of the ford

A place near the Jordan River. Gideon called the people of Mount Ephraim to fight the Midianites up to this place.

Only reference: Judges 7:24

BETH-BIREI

of times mentioned: OT 1

Meaning: House of a creative one

A city of the tribe of Simeon.

Only reference: 1 Chronicles 4:31

BETH-CAR

of times mentioned: OT 1

Meaning: House of pasture

When the Philistines attacked Israel at Mizpeh, the Israelites pursued them to this spot.

Only reference: Samuel 7:11

BETH-DAGON

of times mentioned: OT 2

Meaning: House of Dagon

1) A city that became part of the inheritance of the tribe of Judah following the conquest of the Promised Land.

Only reference: Joshua 15:41

2) A city that became part of the inheritance of Asher when Joshua cast lots in Shiloh to provide territory for the seven tribes that had yet to receive their land.

Only reference: Joshua 19:27

BETH-DIBLATHAIM

of times mentioned: OT 1

Meaning: House of the two fig cakes

A town in Moab that the prophet Jeremiah foresaw would be spoiled when God sent wanderers who would destroy Moab and make it wander, too.

Only reference: Jeremiah 48:22

BETHEL

of times mentioned: OT 66

Meaning: House of God

A Canaanite town, originally called Luz, where Abram and Jacob built altars and worshipped God. Here God renewed His covenant with Jacob, who renamed the town "Bethel." Deborah, Rebekah's nurse, was buried here under an oak tree, at a site named Allon-bachuth.

Joshua fought the king of Bethel as Israel took control of the Promised Land. Following the conquest, the city became part of the inheritance of the tribe of Benjamin. In the time of the judges, the ark of the covenant was housed at Bethel, and people came there to inquire of God. The Israelites did this before they fought the tribe of Benjamin and when they had to make a decision about finding wives for the remaining men of the tribe.

The prophet Samuel regularly held his circuit court in Bethel. Mount Bethel (or "the hill country of Bethel" [NIV]), a hilly area near the city, is mentioned in Joshua 16:1, when Joseph's sons inherited it, and in 1 Samuel 13:2, in connection with Saul's army.

Following the division of the kingdom, King Jeroboam of Israel made two calf idols and placed one in Bethel to encourage the people to fall away from the Lord. Amos prophesied the destruction of Bethel's altars and used the city as a picture of idolatry. After Israel fell to Assyria, the Assyrian king ordered that a captured priest of Israel direct the foreigners who had been moved to Israel in worship of the Lord. The priest who was chosen lived in Bethel.

Abijah, king of Judah, warred with King Jeroboam and won Bethel and other cities from him (2 Chronicles 13:19).

Elijah and Elisha visited Bethel just before Elijah was taken up into heaven in a fiery chariot. There "the company of the prophets" (2 Kings 2:5 NIV) asked Elisha if he knew God would take his master that day.

An unnamed prophet came to Bethel to foretell King Josiah's birth and his destruction of idolatry in the land. When he took power, Josiah destroyed the altar and high places of idolatry in Israel.

Benjaminites from Geba resettled Bethel following their return from Babylon. Same as El-bethel and Luz (1).

First reference: Genesis 12:8 / Last reference: Amos 7:13 / Key references: Genesis 28:19; 35:1; 2 Kings 23:15

BETH-EMEK

of times mentioned: OT 1

Meaning: House of the valley

A city that became part of the inheritance of Asher when Joshua cast lots in Shiloh to provide territory for the seven tribes that had yet to receive their land.

Only reference: Joshua 19:27

BETHER

of times mentioned: OT 1

Meaning: A section

Mountains that King Solomon used as part of his description comparing his beloved to a deer on the heights.

Only reference: Song of Solomon 2:17

BETHESDA

of times mentioned: NT 1

Meaning: House of kindness

This pool near Jerusalem's sheep market was surrounded by five porches where those who were blind, ill, or paralyzed waited. They believed that after an angel moved the water of the pool, the first person in the water would be healed of disease. Here Jesus came to a man who had been an invalid

for thirty-eight years and asked if he wanted to get well. After the man explained his inability to reach the pool, Jesus told him to pick up his mat and walk, and the man was immediately cured.

Only reference: John 5:25

BETH-EZEL

of times mentioned: OT 1

Meaning: House of the side

A city of Judah that Micah mentions as he prophetically mourns over Judah's unfaithfulness.

Only reference: Micah 1:11

BETH-GAMUL

of times mentioned: OT 1

Meaning: House of the weaned

A Moabite city, in that nation's plain country, that the prophet Jeremiah foretold would be judged by God.

Only reference: Jeremiah 48:23

BETH-HACCEREM

of times mentioned: OT 2

Meaning: House of the vineyard

A town of Judah that was ruled in part by Malchiah during Nehemiah's era. Jeremiah referred to it as a place from which a warning signal should be given as disaster fell on Judah.

First reference: Nehemiah 3:14 / Last reference: Jeremiah 6:1

BETH-HARAN

of times mentioned: OT 1

A fortified or walled city that became part of the inheritance of the tribe of Gad.

Only reference: Numbers 32:36

♀BETH-HOGLA

of times mentioned: OT 1

Meaning: House of a partridge

A place that formed part of the tribe of Judah's northern border. Same as Beth-hoglah.

Only reference: Joshua 15:6

♀BETH-HOGLAH

of times mentioned: OT 2

Meaning: House of a partridge

A city that became part of the inheritance of Benjamin when Joshua cast lots in Shiloh to provide territory for the seven tribes that had yet to receive their land. Same as Beth-hogla.

First reference: Joshua 18:19 / Last reference: Joshua 18:21

♀BETH-HORON

of times mentioned: OT 14

Meaning: House of hollowness

After five Amorite kings fought Joshua and his troops at Gibeon, Joshua chased these rulers and their men as far as the city of Beth-horon. Then the Lord cast great hailstones on them, defeating the army.

Beth-horon became part of the inheritance of the children of Joseph (the tribes of Manasseh and Ephraim). It became part of the inheritance of Benjamin when Joshua cast lots in Shiloh to provide territory for the seven tribes that had yet to receive their land. Later it became a Levitical city.

During Saul's kingdom, Beth-horon was attacked by the Philistines. King Solomon fortified its upper and lower cities. King Amaziah of Judah hired an army of Ephraimites to fight in his battle with the children of Seir. But when the Lord declared they should not fight, he sent them home. Instead they attacked Beth-horon and ransacked the city.

First reference: Joshua 10:10 / Last reference: 2 Chronicles 25:13 / Key references: Joshua 10:11; 2 Chronicles 8:5

♀BETH-JESHIMOTH

of times mentioned: OT 3

Meaning: House of the deserts

This frontier town of Moab, at the northeastern corner of the Dead Sea, was ruled by King Sihon before Joshua and his army conquered the Promised Land. Following the conquest, Beth-jeshimoth became part of the inheritance of the tribe of Reuben. When Ezekiel spoke of the judgment of Moab, he called this city "the glory of the country" (Ezekiel 25:9). Same as Beth-jesimoth.

First reference: Joshua 12:3 / Last reference: Ezekiel 25:9

♀BETH-JESIMOTH

of times mentioned: OT 1

Meaning: House of the deserts

A campsite for the Israelites before the conquest of Canaan. Same as Beth-jeshimoth.

Only reference: Numbers 33:49

♀BETH-LEBAOTH

of times mentioned: OT 1

Meaning: House of lionesses

A city that became part of the inheritance of Simeon when Joshua cast lots in Shiloh to provide territory for the seven tribes that had yet to receive their land.

Only reference: Joshua 19:6

👥BETHLEHEM

of times mentioned: 3
# of MEN by this name: 1

Meaning: Native of Bethlehem

A descendant of Abraham through Jacob's son Judah and a forefather of David.

First reference: 1 Chronicles 2:51 / Last reference: 1 Chronicles 4:4

BETH-LEHEM

of times mentioned: OT 24

Meaning: House of bread

1) Near this ancient town, also called Ephrath, Rachel was buried. Later it was the home of Naomi and Ruth, following the deaths of their husbands and their return to Naomi's homeland. In Bethlehem's town gate, Boaz redeemed the land of Naomi's husband, Elimelech, along with the responsibility to care for Naomi and Ruth. Most of the book of Ruth takes place here.

David and his family lived in Beth-lehem, and there Samuel anointed him king after seeing and rejecting all his brothers. When a garrison of Philistines held Beth-lehem, at his glancing mention of his desire for water from its well, three of King David's mighty men broke into the city to get him a drink. David's grandson King Rehoboam fortified the city. Micah called the city Beth-lehem Ephratah and prophesied that though she was small, the Messiah would come from her. Same as Bethlehem, Beth-lehem-judah, Ephratah, and probably Ephrath.

First reference: Genesis 35:19 / Last reference: Micah 5:2 / Key references: 1 Samuel 16:4; 1 Chronicles 11:16–18; Micah 5:2

2) A city that became part of the inheritance of Zebulun when Joshua cast lots in Shiloh to provide territory for the seven tribes that had yet to receive their land.

Only reference: Joshua 19:15

3) Home of Ibzan, who judged Israel for seven years and was buried here.

First reference: Judges 12:8 / Last reference: Judges 12:10

BETHLEHEM

of times mentioned: NT 8

Meaning: House of bread

Also called Bethlehem of Judaea, to distinguish it from another Bethlehem northwest of Nazareth, this town south of Jerusalem was the birthplace of Jesus, as foretold by the prophet Micah, who called it Bethlehem Ephratah. The wise men visited the baby Jesus here and offered Him gifts of gold, frankincense, and myrrh. God warned them in a dream not to report back to Herod, who had told them where to find the child. Then God warned Joseph to take his family into Egypt to avoid Herod's anger. The wrathful king killed all the children under age two who lived in Bethlehem. Same as Beth-lehem (1), Beth-lehem-judah, Ephratah, and probably Ephrath.

First reference: Matthew 2:1 / Last reference: John 7:42

BETH-LEHEM-JUDAH

of times mentioned: OT 10

Meaning: House of bread

Hometown of a Levite who became a priest for Micah of Mount Ephraim. It was also the home of a Levite's unnamed concubine whom the men of Gibeah abused. The next day her "husband" cut up her body and "sent her into all the coasts of Israel" (Judges 19:29). Elimelech, Naomi's husband, also came from Beth-lehem-judah, as did King David's father, Jesse. Same as Beth-lehem, Bethlehem, Ephratah, and probably Ephrath.

First reference: Judges 17:7 / Last reference: 1 Samuel 17:12

BETH-MAACHAH

of times mentioned: OT 2

Meaning: House of Maachah

Sheba, the son of Bichri, fled to this city east of Tyre when King David's battle commander Joab put down the rebellion Sheba had started. Joab followed him there and demanded that the city hand him over. The people of Beth-maachah cut off the rebel's head and threw it over the wall to Joab.

First reference: Samuel 20:14 / Last reference: Samuel 20:15

BETH-MARCABOTH

of times mentioned: OT 2

Meaning: Place of the chariots

A city that became part of the inheritance of Simeon when Joshua cast lots in Shiloh to provide territory for the seven tribes that had yet to receive their land.

First reference: Joshua 19:5 / Last reference:
1 Chronicles 4:31

BETH-MEON

of times mentioned: OT 1

Meaning: House or habitation of [Baal]

A city of Moab that Jeremiah foresaw would be judged by God. Same as Beth-baal-meon.

Only reference: Jeremiah 48:23

BETH-NIMRAH

of times mentioned: OT 2

Meaning: House of the leopard

A fortified or walled city built up by the tribe of Gad.

First reference: Numbers 32:36 / Last reference:
Joshua 13:27

BETH-PALET

of times mentioned: OT 1

Meaning: House of escape

A city that became part of the inheritance of the tribe of Judah following the conquest of the Promised Land. Same as Beth-phelet.

Only reference: Joshua 15:27

BETH-PAZZEZ

of times mentioned: OT 1

Meaning: House of dispersion

A city that became part of the inheritance of Issachar when Joshua cast lots in Shiloh to provide territory for the seven tribes that had yet to receive their land.

Only reference: Joshua 19:21

BETH-PEOR

of times mentioned: OT 4

Meaning: House of Peor

In a valley near this place in Moab, Moses and the Israelites encamped while God had Moses review His laws. God buried Moses near Beth-peor, though no one knew exactly where. When Joshua was old, this land east of the Jordan River was given to the tribe of Reuben.

First reference: Deuteronomy 3:29 / Last reference:
Joshua 13:20

BETHPHAGE

of times mentioned: NT 3

Meaning: Fig house

A village close to Jerusalem and Bethany, on the Mount of Olives. Here Jesus asked the disciples to bring Him a colt on which He would ride into Jerusalem on Palm Sunday.

First reference: Matthew 21:1 / Last reference:
Luke 19:29

BETH-PHELET

of times mentioned: OT 1

Meaning: House of escape

A city of Judah resettled by the Jews after the Babylonian exile. Same as Beth-palet.

Only reference: Nehemiah 11:26

BETH-RAPHA

of times mentioned: 1
# of MEN by this name: 1

Meaning: House of the giant

A descendant of Abraham through Jacob's son Judah.

Only reference: 1 Chronicles 4:12

⦿BETH-REHOB

of times mentioned: OT 2

Meaning: House of the street

A city near Dan. The Ammonites hired Syrian soldiers from Beth-rehob when they planned to attack Israel. They made these plans after their new king, Hanun, insulted the men David had sent to comfort him following his father's death.

First reference: Judges 18:28 / Last reference: 2 Samuel 10:6

⦿BETHSAIDA

of times mentioned: NT 7

Meaning: Fishing house

1) A city in Galilee. Jesus did many "mighty works" here and reproached its people for their lack of repentance, telling them that if the Gentile cities of Tyre and Sidon had heard His message, they would have repented. Philip, Andrew, and Peter came from Bethsaida. Perhaps the same as Bethsaida (2).

First reference: Matthew 11:21 / Last reference: John 12:21

2) A town northeast of the sea of Galilee where Jesus healed a blind man. In a desert place belonging to the city, Jesus preached to a crowd then fed a crowd of five thousand from the loaves and fish of a boy's lunch. After feeding the people, Jesus sent His disciples on to Bethsaida in a boat then came to them on the water.

Some scholars believe that Bethsaida may have been at the spot where the Jordan River flows into the Sea of Galilee, and portions of the town may have been on each side of the river. If that is true, this is the same as Bethsaida (1).

First reference: Mark 8:22 / Last reference: Luke 9:10

⦿BETH-SHAN

of times mentioned: OT 3

Meaning: House of ease

Though it was within the territory of Issachar, the tribe of Manasseh inherited this city. Manasseh could not drive the Canaanites out of the city, but at the height of their power turned them into forced labor.

The Philistines fastened the bodies of King Saul and his sons to the wall of this city after they died in battle. The men of Jabesh-gilead recovered the bodies and buried them in their town. Same as Beth-shean.

First reference: 1 Samuel 31:10 / Last reference: 2 Samuel 21:12

⦿BETH-SHEAN

of times mentioned: OT 6

Meaning: House of ease

A city that became part of the inheritance of Manasseh. The tribe never drove out the Canaanites. Under King Solomon's governmental organization, Beth-shean was responsible for supplying provisions for the king. Same as Beth-shan.

First reference: Joshua 17:11 / Last reference: 1 Chronicles 7:29

⦿BETH-SHEMESH

of times mentioned: OT 21

Meaning: House of the sun

1) A town that formed part of the border of the territory inherited by the tribe of Judah. The tribe gave Beth-shemesh to the Levites as God had commanded.

When their cities were afflicted by the Lord because they had stolen the ark of the covenant, the Philistines put it on a cart pulled by two milk cows. If the cart headed toward Beth-shemesh, they would know the Lord had sent their afflictions. As they returned the ark to Israel, the oxen that bore it went straight to Beth-shemesh, to the field of Joshua of Beth-shemesh, and stopped by a large rock. Here the people chopped up the cart and sacrificed the cows as a burnt offering to God. But because seventy men of Beth-shemesh looked into the ark, God killed them. So the grieving people of the town sent the ark to Kirjath-jearim, where it remained for twenty years.

Kings Jehoash of Israel and Amaziah of Judah met in battle at Beth-shemesh. Judah's army fled, and Jehoash captured Amaziah and attacked Jerusalem, breaking down 600 feet of its wall and plundering the city.

During the reign of King Ahaz of Judah, Beth-shemesh was one of the cities of the southern low country of Judah invaded by the Philistines. Scripture states that God used this method to punish Ahaz for his sin.

First reference: Joshua 15:10 / Last reference: 2 Chronicles 28:18 / Key references: 1 Samuel 6; 2 Kings 14:8–14

2) A city that became part of the inheritance of Issachar when Joshua cast lots in Shiloh to provide territory for the seven tribes that had yet to receive their land.

Only reference: Joshua 19:22

3) A fortified or walled city that became part of the inheritance of Naphtali when Joshua cast lots in Shiloh to provide territory for the seven tribes that had yet to receive their land. The tribe never drove the Canaanites out of this city.

First reference: Joshua 19:38 / Last reference: Judges 1:33

4) A place of idolatry, perhaps a temple, in Egypt. The prophet Jeremiah spoke of the images of Beth-shemesh being destroyed.

Only reference: Jeremiah 43:13

BETH-SHITTAH

of times mentioned: OT 1

Meaning: House of the acacia

When Gideon went to fight against the Midianites with the three hundred men God had chosen for him by the way they drank water, the Midianite army fled to Beth-shittah.

Only reference: Judges 7:22

BETH-TAPPUAH

of times mentioned: OT 1

Meaning: House of the apple

A city that became part of the inheritance of the tribe of Judah following the conquest of the Promised Land.

Only reference: Joshua 15:53

BETHUEL

of times mentioned: 9
# of MEN by this name: 1

Meaning: Destroyed of God

Son of Abraham's brother Nahor. Seeing God's hand in Jacob's request, Bethuel gave his daughter Rebekah in marriage to Isaac. He sent Rebekah off with a generous dowry.

First reference: Genesis 22:22 / Last reference: Genesis 28:5

BETHUEL

of times mentioned: OT 1

Meaning: Destroyed of God

Shimei, a man of the tribe of Simeon, who had sixteen sons and six daughters, lived with his family in this town. Same as Bethul.

Only reference: 1 Chronicles 4:30

BETHUL

of times mentioned: OT 1

Meaning: Destroyed of God

A city that became part of the inheritance of Simeon when Joshua cast lots in Shiloh to provide territory for the seven tribes that had yet to receive their land. Same as Bethuel.

Only reference: Joshua 19:4

BETH-ZUR

of times mentioned: 1
# of MEN by this name: 1

Meaning: House of the rock

A descendant of Abraham through Jacob's son Judah.

Only reference: 1 Chronicles 2:45

⚲ BETH-ZUR

of times mentioned: OT 3

Meaning: House of the rock

A city that became part of the inheritance of the tribe of Judah following the conquest of the Promised Land. King Rehoboam of Judah fortified Beth-zur. Following the return from the Babylonian Exile, Nehemiah the son of Azbuk ruled half of the city.

First reference: Joshua 15:58 / Last reference: Nehemiah 3:16

⚲ BETONIM

of times mentioned: OT 1

Meaning: Hollows

A city east of the Jordan River that Moses made part of the inheritance of Gad.

Only reference: Joshua 13:26

⚲ BEULAH

of times mentioned: OT 1

Meaning: To marry

A prophetic name for the land of Israel, picturing its restoration to God's favor.

Only reference: Isaiah 62:4

👥 BEZAI

of times mentioned: 3
# of MEN by this name: 2

Meaning: Domineering

1) Forefather of an exiled family that returned to Judah under Zerubbabel.

First reference: Ezra 2:17 / Last reference: Nehemiah 7:23

2) A Jewish leader who renewed the covenant under Nehemiah.

Only reference: Nehemiah 10:18

👥 BEZALEEL

of times mentioned: 9
# of MEN by this name: 2

Meaning: In the shadow of God

1) A craftsman given special ability by God to work on the tabernacle, Israel's portable worship center begun in the time of Moses. Bezaleel was skilled in "cunning works" in gold, silver, brass, precious stones, and wood, along with teaching other craftsmen.

First reference: Exodus 31:2 / Last reference: 2 Chronicles 1:5

2) An exiled Israelite who married a "strange" (foreign) woman.

Only reference: Ezra 10:30

⚲ BEZEK

of times mentioned: OT 3

Meaning: Lightning

A place where Judah fought and defeated the Canaanites and Perizzites after Joshua died. At Bezek Saul also gathered and numbered his three hundred thousand men of Israel and thirty thousand of Judah before he set out to rescue the city of Jabesh.

First reference: Judges 1:4 / Last reference: 1 Samuel 11:8

👥 BEZER

of times mentioned: 1
# of MEN by this name: 1

Meaning: Inaccessible

A descendant of Abraham through Jacob's son Asher.

Only reference: 1 Chronicles 7:37

⚲ BEZER

of times mentioned: OT 4

Meaning: An inaccessible spot

One of the six cities of refuge established in Israel for those who had committed accidental murder.

Bezer was given to the Levites by the tribe of Reuben.

First reference: Deuteronomy 4:43 / Last reference: 1 Chronicles 6:78

👥 BICHRI

of times mentioned: 8
# of MEN by this name: 1

Meaning: Youthful

Father of an Israelite who rebelled against King David.

First reference: 2 Samuel 20:1 / Last reference: 2 Samuel 20:22

👥 BIDKAR

of times mentioned: 1
# of MEN by this name: 1

Meaning: Assassin

An army captain serving Israel's king Jehu. Bidkar was ordered to dispose of the body of the assassinated former king, Joram.

Only reference: 2 Kings 9:25

👥 BIGTHA

of times mentioned: 1
# of MEN by this name: 1

A eunuch serving the Persian king Ahasuerus in Esther's time.

Only reference: Esther 1:10

👥 BIGTHAN

of times mentioned: 1
# of MEN by this name: 1

One of two palace doorkeepers who conspired to kill their king, Ahasuerus of Persia. Their plot was uncovered by Mordecai, and both doorkeepers were hanged. Same as Bigthana.

Only reference: Esther 2:21

👥 BIGTHANA

of times mentioned: 1
# of MEN by this name: 1

One of two palace doorkeepers who conspired to kill their king, Ahasuerus of Persia. Their plot was uncovered by Mordecai, and both doorkeepers were hanged. Same as Bigthan.

Only reference: Esther 6:2

👥 BIGVAI

of times mentioned: 6
# of MEN by this name: 4

1) A Jewish exile who returned to Judah under Zerubbabel.

First reference: Ezra 2:2 / Last reference: Nehemiah 7:7

2) Forefather of an exiled family that returned to Judah under Zerubbabel.

First reference: Ezra 2:14 / Last reference: Nehemiah 7:19

3) Forefather of a Jewish exile who returned to Judah under Ezra.

Only reference: Ezra 8:14

4) A Jewish leader who renewed the covenant under Nehemiah.

Only reference: Nehemiah 10:16

👥 BILDAD

of times mentioned: 5
# of MEN by this name: 1

One of three friends of Job who mourned his losses for a week then accused him of wrongdoing. God ultimately chastised the three for their criticism of Job, commanding them to sacrifice burnt offerings while Job prayed for them.

First reference: Job 2:11 / Last reference: Job 42:9

📍 BILEAM

of times mentioned: OT 1

Meaning: Not of the people; foreigner

One of the forty-eight cities given to the Levites as God had commanded. Bileam was given to them by the tribe of Manasseh.

Only reference: 1 Chronicles 6:70

👥BILGAH

of times mentioned: 3
# of MEN by this name: 2

Meaning: Stopping

1) One of twenty-four priests in David's time who was chosen by lot to serve in the tabernacle.

Only reference: 1 Chronicles 24:14

2) An exiled priest who returned to Judah under Zerubbabel.

First reference: Nehemiah 12:5 / Last reference: Nehemiah 12:18

👥BILGAI

of times mentioned: 1
# of MEN by this name: 1

Meaning: Stoppable

A priest who renewed the covenant under Nehemiah.

Only reference: Nehemiah 10:8

👥BILHAH

of times mentioned: 10
# of WOMEN by this name: 1

Meaning: Timid

Rachel's handmaid, whom she gave to Jacob to bear children for her. As Jacob's concubine, Bilhah had two sons, Dan and Naphtali. Jacob's son Reuben also slept with her.

First reference: Genesis 29:29 / Last reference: 1 Chronicles 7:13

📍BILHAH

of times mentioned: OT 1

Meaning: Timid

A city that became part of the inheritance of the tribe of Simeon.

Only reference: 1 Chronicles 4:29

👥BILHAN

of times mentioned: 4
# of MEN by this name: 2

Meaning: Timid

1) A descendant of Seir, who lived in Esau's "land of Edom."

First reference: Genesis 36:27 / Last reference: 1 Chronicles 1:42

2) A descendant of Abraham through Jacob's son Benjamin.

Only reference: 1 Chronicles 7:10

👥BILSHAN

of times mentioned: 2
# of MEN by this name: 1

A Jewish exile who returned to Judah under Zerubbabel.

First reference: Ezra 2:2 / Last reference: Nehemiah 7:7

👥BIMHAL

of times mentioned: 1
# of MEN by this name: 1

Meaning: With pruning

A descendant of Abraham through Jacob's son Asher.

Only reference: 1 Chronicles 7:33

👥BINEA

of times mentioned: 2
# of MEN by this name: 1

A descendant of Abraham through Jacob's son Benjamin, through the line of King Saul and his son Jonathan.

First reference: 1 Chronicles 8:37 / Last reference: 1 Chronicles 9:43

👥 BINNUI

of times mentioned: 7
# of MEN by this name: 6

Meaning: Built up

1) Father of a Levite who weighed the temple vessels after the Babylonian Exile.

Only reference: Ezra 8:33

2) An exiled Israelite who married a "strange" (foreign) woman.

Only reference: Ezra 10:30

3) Another exiled Israelite who married a "strange" (foreign) woman.

Only reference: Ezra 10:38

4) A Levite who repaired the walls of Jerusalem and renewed the covenant under Nehemiah.

First reference: Nehemiah 3:24 / Last reference: Nehemiah 10:9

5) Forefather of an exiled family that returned to Judah under Zerubbabel.

Only reference: Nehemiah 7:15

6) An exiled Israelite who returned to Judah under Zerubbabel.

Only reference: Nehemiah 12:8

👥 BIRSHA

of times mentioned: 1
# of MEN by this name: 1

Meaning: With wickedness

The king of Gomorrah in the days of Abram. He was killed in battle near the slime pits of Siddim.

Only reference: Genesis 14:2

👥 BIRZAVITH

of times mentioned: 1
# of MEN by this name: 1

Meaning: Holes

A descendant of Abraham through Jacob's son Asher.

Only reference: 1 Chronicles 7:31

👥 BISHLAM

of times mentioned: 1
# of MEN by this name: 1

A man who tried to stop the rebuilding of Jerusalem's wall.

Only reference: Ezra 4:7

👥 BITHIAH

of times mentioned: 1
# of WOMEN by this name: 1

Meaning: Daughter of God

A daughter of an Egyptian pharaoh and the wife of Mered, a descendant of Judah.

Only reference: 1 Chronicles 4:18

📍 BITHRON

of times mentioned: OT 1

Meaning: The craggy spot

An area of the eastern part of the Jordan River valley. Saul's battle commander Abner and his men escaped from David's commander Joab by walking all night and passing through Bithron.

Only reference: 2 Samuel 2:29

📍 BITHYNIA

of times mentioned: NT 2

A Roman province in northern Asia Minor that Paul and his companions sought to visit, but were kept from doing so by the Holy Spirit. Peter wrote his first epistle to the Bithynians and other people of this area. Chalcedon and Nicea were in this province.

First reference: Acts 16:7 / Last reference: 1 Peter 1:1

⦿BIZJOTHJAH

of times mentioned: OT 1

Meaning: Contempts of God

A city that became part of the inheritance of the tribe of Judah following the conquest of the Promised Land.

Only reference: Joshua 15:28

👥BIZTHA

of times mentioned: 1
# of MEN by this name: 1

A eunuch serving the Persian king Ahasuerus in Esther's time.

Only reference: Esther 1:10

👥BLASTUS

of times mentioned: 1
# of MEN by this name: 1

Meaning: To germinate

A eunuch serving Herod Agrippa I who helped the people of Tyre and Sidon gain an audience with the king.

Only reference: Acts 12:20

👥BOANERGES

of times mentioned: 1
# of MEN by this name: 2

Meaning: Sons of commotion

A nickname given to the disciples James and John, the sons of Zebedee, by Jesus.

Only reference: Mark 3:17

👥BOAZ

of times mentioned: 22
# of MEN by this name: 1

Genealogy of Jesus: Yes (Matthew 1:5; Luke 3:32)

A relative of Naomi's who acted as kinsman-redeemer for her and her daughter-in-law Ruth when they returned to Israel after their husbands' deaths. Ruth worked in Boaz's field, and he looked after her, having heard of her faithfulness to Naomi. At Naomi's urging, Ruth offered herself in marriage to Boaz. He accepted the responsibility of kinsman-redeemer. He bought back Naomi's husband's inherited land and promised that his first child would perpetuate Ruth's first husband's name. The couple married and had a son, Obed, who became the grandfather of King David. Same as Booz.

First reference: Ruth 2:1 / Last reference: Chronicles 2:12 / Key references: Ruth 2:8–16; 4:9–11

⦿BOAZ

of times mentioned: OT 2

The left pillar on the porch of Jerusalem's temple.

First reference: 1 Kings 7:21 / Last reference: 2 Chronicles 3:17

👥BOCHERU

of times mentioned: 2
# of MEN by this name: 1

Meaning: Firstborn

A descendant of Abraham through Jacob's son Benjamin, through the line of King Saul and his son Jonathan.

First reference: 1 Chronicles 8:38 / Last reference: 1 Chronicles 9:44

⦿BOCHIM

of times mentioned: OT 2

Meaning: The weepers

A place near Gilgal. Here, before the Israelite tribes went to their newly inherited lands, the angel of the Lord spoke to them, reminding them of God's covenant with them.

First reference: Judges 2:1 / Last reference: Judges 2:5

BOHAN

of times mentioned: OT 2

Meaning: Thumb

A stone that formed part of the border of the tribe of Judah's territory. Bohan was named after one of Reuben's sons.

First reference: Joshua 15:6 / Last reference: Joshua 18:17

BOOZ

of times mentioned: 3
# of MEN by this name: 1

Genealogy of Jesus: Yes (Matthew 1:5; Luke 3:32)

Greek form of the name Boaz, the hero of the story of Ruth.

First reference: Matthew 1:5 / Last reference: Luke 3:32

BOSCATH

of times mentioned: OT 1

Meaning: A swell of ground

Hometown of Jedidah, mother of King Josiah of Judah.

Only reference: 2 Kings 22:1

BOSOR

of times mentioned: 1
# of MEN by this name: 1

Meaning: A lamp

Father of the false prophet Balaam. Same as Beor.

Only reference: 2 Peter 2:15

BOZEZ

of times mentioned: OT 1

Meaning: Shining

A cliff on one side of a pass that Jonathan and his armor bearer had to cross to get to the Philistines' garrison before their heated battle at Michmash.

Only reference: 1 Samuel 14:4

BOZKATH

of times mentioned: OT 1

Meaning: A swell of ground

A city that became part of the inheritance of the tribe of Judah following the conquest of the Promised Land.

Only reference: Joshua 15:39

BOZRAH

of times mentioned: OT 9

1) A city of Edom and hometown of King Jobab, son of Zerah. Isaiah refers to a sacrifice (probably meaning a battle) in this city. The prophet Jeremiah foresaw its destruction, and Amos foretold the destruction of Bozrah's palaces.

First reference: Genesis 36:33 / Last reference: Micah 2:12

2) A Moabite city that Jeremiah foretold would be destroyed.

Only reference: Jeremiah 48:24

BUKKI

of times mentioned: 5
# of MEN by this name: 2

Meaning: Wasteful

1) A descendant of Abraham through Jacob's son Levi and a priest through the line of Aaron.

First reference: 1 Chronicles 6:5 / Last reference: Ezra 7:4

2) Prince of the tribe of Dan when the Israelites entered the Promised Land.

Only reference: Numbers 34:22

BUKKIAH

of times mentioned: 2
# of MEN by this name: 1

Meaning: Wasting of God

A son of King David's musician Heman, who was "under the hands of [his] father for song in the house of the Lord" (1 Chronicles 25:6).

First reference: 1 Chronicles 25:4 / Last reference: 1 Chronicles 25:13

BUNAH

of times mentioned: 1
# of MEN by this name: 1

Meaning: Discretion

A descendant of Abraham through Jacob's son Judah.

Only reference: 1 Chronicles 2:25

BUNNI

of times mentioned: 3
# of MEN by this name: 3

Meaning: Built

1) One of a group of Levites (worship leaders) who led a revival among the Israelites in the time of Nehemiah.

Only reference: Nehemiah 9:4

2) Forefather of a Jewish exile from the tribe of Levi who resettled Jerusalem.

Only reference: Nehemiah 11:15

3) A Jewish leader who renewed the covenant under Nehemiah.

Only reference: Nehemiah 10:15

BUZ

of times mentioned: 2
# of MEN by this name: 2

Meaning: Disrespect

1) A son of Nahor and a nephew of Abraham.

Only reference: Genesis 22:21

2) A descendant of Abraham through Jacob's son Gad.

Only reference: 1 Chronicles 5:14

BUZI

of times mentioned: 1
# of MEN by this name: 1

Meaning: Disrespect

Father of the prophet Ezekiel.

Only reference: Ezekiel 1:3

CABBON

of times mentioned: OT 1

Meaning: To heap up; hilly

A city that became part of the inheritance of the tribe of Judah following the conquest of the Promised Land.

Only reference: Joshua 15:40

CABUL

of times mentioned: OT 2

Meaning: Limitation; sterile

1) A city that became part of the inheritance of Asher when Joshua cast lots in Shiloh to provide territory for the seven tribes that had yet to receive their land.

Only reference: Joshua 19:27

2) An area in northern Israel with twenty towns that King Solomon gave to King Hiram of Tyre, who had helped build Jerusalem's temple and Solomon's palace. Unimpressed by the gift, Hiram named it appropriately. Same as Galilee.

Only reference: 1 Kings 9:13

CAESAREA

of times mentioned: NT 17

1) Known as Caesarea Philippi, to differentiate it from the Caesarea built by Herod the Great. Here

Jesus asked His disciples, "Whom do men say that I the Son of man am?" (Matthew 16:13). Same as Philippi (1).

First reference: Matthew 16:13 / Last reference: Mark 8:27

2) Hometown of Philip the evangelist, this seaport of Judea was built by Herod the Great, who lived there. When Herod Agrippa delivered a speech from his throne in Caesarea, the people acclaimed him as a god. Herod did not correct them, so an angel of the Lord struck him down and he died. The God-fearing centurion Cornelius was stationed in Caesarea when God gave both him and Peter visions that indicated that God accepted faithful Gentiles. Here Claudius Lysias and Festus judged the Jews' case against the apostle Paul. This Caesarea was also called Caesarea Maritima or Caesarea Augusta.

First reference: Acts 8:40 / Last reference: Acts 25:13 / Key references: Acts 10:1; 21:8; 23:33; 25:6

⚲CAIN

of times mentioned: OT 1

Meaning: Fixity; a lance (as in striking fast)

A city that became part of the inheritance of the tribe of Judah following the conquest of the Promised Land.

Only reference: Joshua 15:57

👥CAIAPHAS

of times mentioned: 9
# of MEN by this name: 1

Meaning: The dell

The Jewish high priest who judged Jesus at His trial. Caiaphas, who feared Roman authority, felt it was expedient to kill one man to protect his people and so accepted false testimony against Jesus. Since he could not kill anyone, he sent Jesus to Pilate for a death sentence. Following the resurrection of Jesus, Caiaphas tried to stop Peter from preaching.

First reference: Matthew 26:3 / Last reference: Acts 4:6

👥CAIN

of times mentioned: 19
# of MEN by this name: 1

Meaning: Lance

Adam and Eve's first son who became jealous of his brother, Abel, when God refused Cain's unrighteous offering but accepted Abel's offering. Cain killed Abel and did not admit it when God asked where his brother was. For his sin, God made him a "fugitive and a vagabond" (Genesis 4:12). Cain moved to the land of Nod, had children, and built the city of Enoch.

First reference: Genesis 4:1 / Last reference: Jude 1:11 / Key references: Genesis 4:9; Hebrews 11:4

👥CAINAN

of times mentioned: 7
# of MEN by this name: 1

Genealogy of Jesus: Yes (Luke 3:37)

Meaning: Fixed

Grandson of Seth and great-grandson of Adam and Eve. He lived for 910 years.

First reference: Genesis 5:9 / Last reference: Luke 3:37

⚲CALAH

of times mentioned: OT 2

Meaning: To be complete; maturity

An Assyrian city built by Asshur.

First reference: Genesis 10:11 / Last reference: Genesis 10:12

👥CALCOL

of times mentioned: 1
# of MEN by this name: 1

Meaning: Sustenance

A descendant of Abraham through Jacob's son Judah.

Only reference: 1 Chronicles 2:6

CALEB

\# of times mentioned: 36
\# of MEN by this name: 3

Meaning: Forcible

1) Jephunneh's son, sent by Moses to spy out Canaan before the Israelites entered the Promised Land. When ten other spies warned they could not win the land, Caleb believed Israel could do it. God blessed Caleb and Joshua, the only spies who believed the land could be taken. Of the twelve, only they entered the Promised Land. For his faithfulness, Caleb received Hebron as an inheritance. Caleb promised his daughter Achsah to the man who could conquer Kirjath-sepher. After his brother Othniel took it, Caleb kept his promise and the couple married.

First reference: Numbers 13:6 / Last reference: 1 Chronicles 6:56 / Key references: Numbers 13:30; 32:11–12; Joshua 14:13

2) A descendant of Abraham through Jacob's son Judah. Brother of Jerahmeel. Same as Chelubai.

First reference: 1 Chronicles 2:18 / Last reference: 1 Chronicles 2:42

3) A descendant of Abraham through Jacob's son Judah and Hur. Grandson of Caleb (2).

Only reference: 1 Chronicles 2:50

⚲ CALEB-EPHRATAH

\# of times mentioned: OT 1

Meaning: Forcible fruitfulness

The place where Heron, a descendant of Judah, died before his son Ashur was born.

Only reference: 1 Chronicles 2:24

⚲ CALNEH

\# of times mentioned: OT 2

Part of the early kingdom of Nimrod, in Shinar. Amos mentions a city by this name in connection with the Syrian city of Hamath and the Philistine city of Gath, so it is possible that these two references speak of two different cities. Same as Calno and Canneh.

First reference: Genesis 10:10 / Last reference: Amos 6:2

⚲ CALNO

\# of times mentioned: OT 1

A city of Assyria. Same as Calneh and Canneh.

Only reference: Isaiah 10:9

⚲ CALVARY

\# of times mentioned: NT 1

Meaning: Skull (a translation of the Greek word *kranion*)

The place lying not far outside of Jerusalem where Jesus was crucified. The Latin word *Calvary* is used a single time in scripture, in the book of Luke, and is often simply translated as "the Skull" (NIV). This place was also called by the Aramaic name Golgotha, the term used by the other Gospel writers. Same as Golgotha.

Only reference: Luke 23:33

CAMON

\# of times mentioned: OT 1

Meaning: An elevation

The burial place of the judge Jair. Camon may have been in Gilead.

Only reference: Judges 10:5

⚲ CANA

\# of times mentioned: NT 4

A Galilean village where Jesus and His disciples attended a wedding and the Lord performed His first miracle, turning water into wine. The family who was holding the wedding ran out of wine, so Mary, Jesus' mother, came to Him with the news. He told the servants to fill six large water jars with twenty to thirty gallons of water. When they drew the liquid out again, it was a good wine. In Cana, a royal official from Capernaum came to Jesus, asking Him to heal his dying son. Before the wonder-seeking Galileans, Jesus simply told the man his son would live. On his way home, the official's servants met him with the news that his son was alive.

Jesus' disciple Nathanael came from Cana.

First reference: John 2:1 / Last reference: John 21:2

👥 CANAAN

of times mentioned: 9
# of MEN by this name: 1

Meaning: Humiliated

Son of Ham and grandson of Noah. Noah cursed Canaan because his father did not cover Noah when he became drunk and fell asleep, naked, in his tent. Canaan became the ancestor of the Phoenicians and other peoples living between the Phoenician cities of Sidon and Gaza.

First reference: Genesis 9:18 / Last reference: 1 Chronicles 1:13

📍 CANAAN

of times mentioned: OT 81 / NT 1

Meaning: Humiliated

The land east of the Mediterranean Sea as far as the Jordan River, and from the Taurus Mountains, going south beyond Gaza. Canaan included the areas later called Phoenicia, Palestine, and Syria. Its inhabitants were the descendants of Noah's grandson Canaan, including his firstborn child, Sidon, the Hittites, Jebusites, Amorites, Girgasites, Hivites, Arkites, Sinites, Arvadites, Zemarites, and Hamathites (Genesis 10:15–18).

God brought Abram and his family from Ur of the Chaldees to the land of Canaan. Promising they would become a great nation there, the Lord covenanted with Abram that his descendants would own the land and that He would be their God.

Though Abram's grandson Isaac fled from Canaan, he returned and continued the covenant. As famine covered the land, Isaac's son Jacob sent his sons to Egypt to buy food. They discovered that Joseph, the brother they had sold into slavery, was now prime minister of that land. Jacob moved to Egypt with his entire family. But when Jacob died, Joseph buried him in Canaan.

Before Israel's return to the Promised Land, Moses sent twelve spies into Canaan to see what they were up against. The men described the people and their territory: "The Canaanites dwell by the sea, and by the coast of Jordan" (Numbers 13:29).

All but two of the spies decided these people were too powerful for Israel to attack. For this faithlessness, God caused the Israelites to wander in the wilderness for forty years. Before they finally entered the Promised Land, God commanded Moses to climb Mount Nebo and look out toward Canaan. Moses and all those of his generation, who had accepted the report of the ten spies, died before Israel claimed the land.

When the Israelites returned to Canaan, those pagan inhabitants would become their enemies. God commanded His people not to follow in the Canaanites' ways. Before Israel entered the land, God renewed His promise to give them Canaan.

Following the Promised Land's conquest, at God's command, Israel's leaders cast lots to divide the property among the tribes. However, scripture often states that the tribes did not fully eradicate the Canaanites. Where they were too powerful, Israel coexisted with its enemies. So the pagan peoples, whose gods were brutal and connected with cult prostitution, influenced the Israelites to fall into pagan worship practices. It took many years for Israel to subdue the Canaanites. Yet when Joshua was very old, God promised that He would enable His people to complete the unfinished task.

During the rule of the prophet Deborah, the Israelites contended with the Canaanites, who ruled over them. God commanded Barak to lead Israel to victory against Jabin, king of Canaan, and his battle commander Sisera. Because Barak would not go into battle without Deborah, God gave Sisera's death to a woman, Jael, wife of Heber the Kenite. But all Sisera's troops were killed by Barak's soldiers. Jabin was subdued, and eventually, as its power expanded, Israel destroyed him.

David fought the Philistine giant Goliath and later, as king of Israel, conquered Philistia. After bringing the ark of the covenant to Jerusalem, King David rejoiced in God's promise, "Unto thee will I give the land of Canaan, the lot of your inheritance" (Psalm 105:11). But the Israelites slipped ever more deeply into sin, worshipping the gods of the land they conquered. Ezekiel used the land of Canaan as a picture of Jerusalem's unfaithfulness (Ezekiel 16:3). And Zephaniah spoke of the destruction of Canaan, land of the Philistines (Zephaniah 2:5).

The only New Testament reference to Canaan is in Matthew 15:22, in the story of the woman of Canaan whose daughter was demon-possessed. Same as Chanaan.

First reference: Genesis 11:31 / Last reference: Matthew 15:22 / Key references: Genesis 12:5; 17:8; Leviticus 18:3

👥 CANDACE

of times mentioned: 1
# of WOMEN by this name: 1

Queen of Ethiopia whose treasurer was converted to Christianity by Philip the evangelist.

Only reference: Acts 8:27

📍 CANNEH

of times mentioned: OT 1

An Assyrian city that the prophet Ezekiel called "the merchants of Sheba." Same as Calneh and Calno.

Only reference: Ezekiel 27:23

📍 CAPERNAUM

of times mentioned: NT 16

Meaning: Comfortable village

A village on the Sea of Galilee's north shore, Capernaum was chosen by Jesus as His ministry headquarters. He left Nazareth for Capernaum when Herod imprisoned John the Baptist. Thus He fulfilled the prophecy of Isaiah that Zebulun (which was the tribe of Nazareth) and Naphtali (which was the tribe of Capernaum) would see a great light. Jesus taught in Capernaum's synagogue. From here, He called several disciples—fishermen Peter, Andrew, James, and John, and the tax collector Matthew—and He performed many miracles. While He ministered in Cana, Jesus healed a royal official's son who was ill in Capernaum. On the way back home, the official met his servants, who gave him the news that his son lived.

Before a crowd of people, Jesus healed a man sick with palsy who had been lowered through the roof to Him because his bearers could not get through the crowd that surrounded the place. Jesus forgave the man's sin, and when the people around him became offended, He commanded him to walk. A Roman centurion came to Capernaum asking Jesus to heal his servant. When the Lord prepared to visit his home, the man asked that He simply say the words to heal the servant, since he was a man accustomed to such authority. Jesus publicly commended his faith.

Yet despite the miracles they viewed and their astonishment at Jesus' doctrine, the people of this city did not believe in Him. Jesus took them to task for their desire for miracles and lack of faith, warning: "Thou, Capernaum, which art exalted unto heaven, shalt be brought down to hell: for if the mighty works, which have been done in thee, had been done in Sodom, it would have remained until this day. But I say unto you, That it shall be more tolerable for the land of Sodom in the day of judgment, than for thee" (Matthew 11:23–24).

In Capernaum Peter rashly promised the tax collectors that Jesus would pay the temple tax. Therefore Jesus ordered Peter to catch a fish. The fish had money in its mouth to pay the tax for both of them.

First reference: Matthew 4:13 / Last reference: John 6:59 / Key references: Matthew 4:12–17; 8:5–13; 17:24–27; Mark 2:1–12; John 6:16–24

📍 CAPHTOR

of times mentioned: OT 3

Meaning: A wreath-shaped island

The original Philistine homeland, before the Philistines conquered Palestine. Some scholars believe it was Crete, but a certain identification of Caphtor cannot be made.

First reference: Deuteronomy 2:23 / Last reference: Amos 9:7

📍 CAPPADOCIA

of times mentioned: NT 2

A Roman province in Asia Minor, north of Cilicia and east of Galatia. People from this area were in Jerusalem and heard their language spoken at Pentecost. Peter wrote his first epistle to the Christians of Cappadocia, as well as others in central and northern Asia Minor.

First reference: Acts 2:9 / Last reference: 1 Peter 1:1

👥 CARCAS

of times mentioned: 1
# of MEN by this name: 1

A eunuch serving the Persian king Ahasuerus in Esther's time.

Only reference: Esther 1:10

♀ CARCHEMISH

of times mentioned: OT 2

A city on the upper Euphrates River where Egypt's pharaoh Necho met Nebuchadrezzar (also called Nebuchadnezzar), king of Babylon, in battle. Though Necho warned the king of Judah not to take part in the battle, Josiah disguised himself and went to the plain of Megiddo to fight. Josiah was shot by archers. His men brought him to Jerusalem, where he died of his wounds.

Nebuchadrezzar captured Carchemish and established his nation as rulers of the Near East. Same as Charchemish.

First reference: Isaiah 10:9 / Last reference: Jeremiah 46:2

👥 CAREAH

of times mentioned: 1
# of MEN by this name: 1

Meaning: Bald

Father of Johanan, a Jewish leader when the Chaldeans captured Jerusalem.

Only reference: 2 Kings 25:23

♀ CARMEL

of times mentioned: OT 26

Meaning: A planted field

1) A Palestinian mountain range that became part of the inheritance of the tribe of Asher. On Mount Carmel, Elijah confronted Ahab, king of Israel, and the priests of Baal. He suggested that both he and the Baal's priests prepare a sacrifice. Both would call on their gods, and Israel would worship the one who lit the sacrifice with fire. Though the 450 prophets of Baal called on Baal for half the day, there was no response. Elijah mocked them, and they continued their efforts until evening with no response.

Then Elijah called the people to him and repaired the altar of the Lord. Three times he had them pour four large jars of water on the altar and the sacrifice. The prophet stepped forward and prayed. God sent down fire that consumed the altar, the water, and the wood beneath the sacrifice. At this dramatic event, Israel's faith turned to the Lord. Elijah ordered that the prophets of Baal be killed, so

the people of Israel captured them, brought them to the Kishon Valley, and executed them there.

A Shunammite woman whom Elisha had promised a child came to him at Carmel when her son died. Under King Uzziah of Judah, vineyards flourished on Carmel.

Isaiah prophesied that Carmel would "see the glory of the LORD" (Isaiah 35:2); Amos predicted that when the Lord roars from Zion, "the top of Carmel shall wither" (Amos 1:2), and those who hide there He will "take. . .out thence" (Amos 9:3).

First reference: Joshua 12:22 / Last reference: Nahum 1:4 / Key reference: 1 Kings 18:19–42

2) A town that became part of the inheritance of the tribe of Judah following the conquest of the Promised Land. Nabal held property in Carmel. Though David protected the wealthy Nabal's property, at sheep-shearing time the foolish man refused to share his bounty with David and his men. David was about to attack Nabal when his wife, Abigail, heard what her husband had done and stepped in, bringing David bread, wine, sheep, grain, and fruit. On her way to David, she met him and his men as they were ready to attack. She fell before David, apologized for her husband, and gave him the food. After Abigail stepped in to help David, her husband died, and David sent to Carmel to ask her to marry him.

First reference: Joshua 15:55 / Last reference: 1 Samuel 25:40

👥 CARMI

of times mentioned: 8
# of MEN by this name: 2

Meaning: Gardener

1) A descendant of Abraham through Jacob's son Judah.

First reference: Joshua 7:1 / Last reference: 1 Chronicles 4:1

2) A descendant of Abraham through Jacob's son Reuben.

First reference: Genesis 46:9 / Last reference: 1 Chronicles 5:3

👥 CARPUS

of times mentioned: 1
# of MEN by this name: 1

Meaning: Fruit

A friend of Paul in Troas—one with whom the apostle once left a cloak.

Only reference: 2 Timothy 4:13

👥 CARSHENA

of times mentioned: 1
# of MEN by this name: 1

One of seven Persian princes serving under King Ahasuerus.

Only reference: Esther 1:14

📍 CASIPHIA

of times mentioned: OT 1

Meaning: Silvery

Home of the chief Iddo, Casiphia lay somewhere near the route that Ezra and the returning Babylonian exiles traveled on their way home to Jerusalem. While he and the exiles waited at the Ahava canal, Ezra sent messengers to Casiphia, asking Iddo to send him ministers for the house of the Lord. Three days later the Levites and temple servants whom Iddo sent Ezra arrived at the canal.

Only reference: Ezra 8:17

📍 CEDRON

of times mentioned: NT 1

A brook near Jerusalem. Jesus crossed the Cedron Valley on His way to the Garden of Gethsemane, where He prayed before Judas betrayed Him. Same as Kidron.

Only reference: John 18:1

📍 CENCHREA

of times mentioned: NT 3

Meaning: Probably from the Greek word meaning "millet"

Corinth's port city, where Paul shaved his head for a vow. Paul described Phoebe, who carried his letter to the Romans from Greece, as a "servant of the church which is at Cenchrea" (Romans 16:1).

First reference: Acts 18:18 / Last reference: Romans 16:1

👥 CEPHAS

of times mentioned: 6
# of MEN by this name: 1

Meaning: The rock

A name Jesus gave the apostle Peter. It is used most often in the book of 1 Corinthians. Same as Peter.

First reference: John 1:42 / Last reference: Galatians 2:9

👥 CHALCOL

of times mentioned: 1
# of MEN by this name: 1

Meaning: Sustenance

A wise man, the son of Mahol, mentioned in comparison to Solomon's wisdom.

Only reference: 1 Kings 4:31

📍 CHALDEA

of times mentioned: OT 7

Though in its early use, Chaldea meant the southern part of Babylonia, near the Persian Gulf, in scripture this name is also sometimes used to describe the Neo-Babylonian (or Chaldean) Empire.

Abraham originally came from the Chaldean city of Ur (Genesis 11:28).

Twice the Chaldeans attempted to take power from Assyria, conquering Babylon, but their conquests were not successful for long. One of these rebels, Merodach-Baladan, took over Babylon for a time and sent to King Hezekiah, seeking his support against Assyria. Hezekiah showed Merodach-Baladan's representatives his treasures—his storehouses, armory, and palace. The prophet Isaiah foretold that everything the men had seen and some of Hezekiah's descendants would be carried off to Babylon (2 Kings 20:12–19).

Around 626 BC Nabopolassar rebelled, conquered the Assyrian capital, Nineveh, and successfully established the Neo-Babylonian (or Chaldean) Empire. Scripture uses "Babylonians" to describe this nation, not the Old Babylonian Empire that had preceded Assyria in power.

God prospered Chaldea for a while as He brought Nabopolassar's son Nebuchadnezzar and his troops against the land of Judah. Under King Nebuchadnezzar's power, King Jehoiakim of Judah became a Chaldean vassal and then rebelled against his overlord. His son Jehoiachin surrendered to the Chaldeans within three months, and Zedekiah was made king. But Zedekiah also rebelled, and Jerusalem was taken by Chaldea. Many of Judah's people were taken into exile.

Jeremiah promised that God would destroy this nation that opposed Judah and repay the evil that had been done against His people. The prophet Ezekiel told a parable in which Jerusalem played the harlot with the Chaldeans. For her involvement with these pagan nations, God promised to bring His wrath against Jerusalem.

First reference: Jeremiah 50:10 / Last reference: Ezekiel 23:16

♀ CHANAAN

of times mentioned: NT 2

Meaning: Greek form of Canaan

This is the Greek word Paul and Stephen used to describe the land of Canaan and its history. Same as Canaan.

First reference: Acts 7:11 / Last reference: Acts 13:19

♀ CHARASHIM

of times mentioned: OT 1

Meaning: Mechanics

A valley settled by a descendant of Judah, a craftsman named Joab.

Only reference: 1 Chronicles 4:14

♀ CHARCHEMISH

of times mentioned: OT 1

A city on the west bank of the Euphrates River that became the site of a battle between Necho, pharaoh of Egypt, and King Nebuchadnezzar of Babylon. Same as Carchemish.

Only reference: 2 Chronicles 35:20

♀ CHARRAN

of times mentioned: NT 2

Meaning: Greek form of Haran

A Greek form of the name Haran that Stephen used when he preached in the synagogue before he was stoned to death. Same as Haran.

First reference: Acts 7:2 / Last reference: Acts 7:4

♀ CHEBAR

of times mentioned: OT 8

Meaning: Length

The prophet Ezekiel was near this Mesopotamian river, with other exiles to Babylon, when he saw a prophetic vision of God and His cherubim. Some of the captives from Judah lived near this river, which was probably a canal south of Babylon and near the city of Nippur. Chebar may have been a place of prayer for the Jews.

First reference: Ezekiel 1:1 / Last reference: Ezekiel 43:3

👥 CHEDORLAOMER

of times mentioned: 5
# of MEN by this name: 1

The king of Elam in the days of Abram. Chedorlaomer was part of a victorious battle alliance that kidnapped Abram's nephew Lot.

First reference: Genesis 14:1 / Last reference: Genesis 14:17

👥 CHELAL

of times mentioned: 1
# of MEN by this name: 1

Meaning: Complete

An exiled Israelite who married a "strange" (foreign) woman.

Only reference: Ezra 10:30

👥 CHELLUH

of times mentioned: 1
# of MEN by this name: 1

Meaning: Completed

An exiled Israelite who married a "strange" (foreign) woman.

Only reference: Ezra 10:35

👥 CHELUB

of times mentioned: 2
# of MEN by this name: 2

Meaning: Basket

1) A descendant of Abraham through Jacob's son Judah.

Only reference: 1 Chronicles 4:11

2) Father of Ezri, the overseer of King David's servants who tilled the soil.

Only reference: 1 Chronicles 27:26

👥 CHELUBAI

of times mentioned: 1
# of MEN by this name: 1

Meaning: Forcible

A descendant of Abraham through Jacob's son Judah. Same as Caleb (2).

Only reference: 1 Chronicles 2:9

👥 CHENAANAH

of times mentioned: 5
# of MEN by this name: 2

Meaning: Humiliated

1) A false prophet who told King Ahab to fight against Ramoth-gilead.

First reference: 1 Kings 22:11 / Last reference: 2 Chronicles 18:23

2) A descendant of Abraham through Jacob's son Benjamin.

Only reference: 1 Chronicles 7:10

👥 CHENANI

of times mentioned: 1
# of MEN by this name: 1

Meaning: Planted

One of a group of Levites who led a revival among the Israelites in the time of Nehemiah.

Only reference: Nehemiah 9:4

👥 CHENANIAH

of times mentioned: 3
# of MEN by this name: 2

Meaning: God has planted

1) A Levite musician, "the master of the song," who led singers in celebration when King David brought the ark of the covenant to Jerusalem.

First reference: 1 Chronicles 15:22 / Last reference: 1 Chronicles 15:27

2) Head of a family appointed as officers and judges under King David.

Only reference: 1 Chronicles 26:29

📍 CHEPHAR-HAAMMONAI

of times mentioned: OT 1

Meaning: Village of the Ammonite

A city that became part of the inheritance of Benjamin when Joshua cast lots in Shiloh to provide territory for the seven tribes that had yet to receive their land.

Only reference: Joshua 18:24

📍 CHEPHIRAH

of times mentioned: OT 4

Meaning: The village

A city of the Gibeonites that became part of the inheritance of Benjamin when Joshua cast lots in Shiloh to provide territory for the seven tribes that had yet to receive their land. It was resettled by the Jews after the Babylonian Exile.

First reference: Joshua 9:17 / Last reference: Nehemiah 7:29

CHERAN

of times mentioned: 2
# of MEN by this name: 1

A descendant of Seir, who lived in Esau's "land of Edom."

First reference: Genesis 36:26 / Last reference: 1 Chronicles 1:41

CHERITH

of times mentioned: OT 2

Meaning: A cut

A ravine east of the Jordan River, in Gilead. After the prophet Elijah foretold a drought that would last for a few years, God sent him to Cherith, where he could hide from King Ahab of Israel. Here Elijah was fed by ravens and drank from the brook in the ravine.

First reference: 1 Kings 17:3 / Last reference: 1 Kings 17:5

CHERUB

of times mentioned: 2
# of MEN by this name: 1

An exile of unclear ancestry who returned to Judah under Zerubbabel.

First reference: Ezra 2:59 / Last reference: Nehemiah 7:61

CHESALON

of times mentioned: OT 1

Meaning: Fertile

A mountain that formed part of the northern border of the tribe of Judah's territory. In some translations it is spelled "Kesalon." Same as Jearim.

Only reference: Joshua 15:10

CHESED

of times mentioned: 1
# of MEN by this name: 1

A son of Nahor and a nephew of Abraham.

Only reference: Genesis 22:22

CHESIL

of times mentioned: OT 1

A city that became part of the inheritance of the tribe of Judah following the conquest of the Promised Land.

Only reference: Joshua 15:30

CHESULLOTH

of times mentioned: OT 1

Meaning: Fattened

A city that became part of the inheritance of Issachar when Joshua cast lots in Shiloh to provide territory for the seven tribes that had yet to receive their land.

Only reference: Joshua 19:18

CHEZIB

of times mentioned: OT 1

The village where Judah's son Shelah was born.

Only reference: Genesis 38:5

CHIDON

of times mentioned: OT 1

Meaning: Probably related to striking with a dart

A threshing floor where Uzza died because he put out his hand to keep the ark of the covenant from falling as the oxen that drew it stumbled. God killed him for disrespecting His holiness, which was symbolized by the ark.

Only reference: 1 Chronicles 13:9

👥 CHILEAB

of times mentioned: 1
# of MEN by this name: 1

Meaning: Restraint of his father

A son of David, born to his wife Abigail in Hebron.

Only reference: 2 Samuel 3:3

👥 CHILION

of times mentioned: 3
# of MEN by this name: 1

Meaning: Pining

One of Elimelech and Naomi's sons, he died in Moab.

First reference: Ruth 1:2 / Last reference: Ruth 4:9

📍 CHILMAD

of times mentioned: OT 1

An unknown place that, along with Sheba and Asshur, traded with Tyre.

Only reference: Ezekiel 27:23

👥 CHIMHAM

of times mentioned: 4
# of MEN by this name: 1

Meaning: Pining

Possibly a son of Barzillai, who offered him to King David to serve in his place. David probably gave him a land grant near Bethlehem (Jeremiah 41:17).

First reference: 2 Samuel 19:37 / Last reference: Jeremiah 41:17

📍 CHINNERETH

of times mentioned: OT 4

Meaning: Harp-shaped

An Old Testament name for the Sea of Galilee and the area around it. Joshua 19:35 mentions a fortified or walled city by this name that became part of the inheritance of Naphtali when Joshua cast lots in Shiloh to provide territory for the seven tribes that had yet to receive their land. Same as Chinneroth and Cinneroth.

First reference: Numbers 34:11 / Last reference: Joshua 19:35

📍 CHINNEROTH

of times mentioned: OT 2

Meaning: Harp-shaped

A variant spelling of Chinnereth. Same as Chinnereth and Cinneroth.

First reference: Joshua 11:2 / Last reference: Joshua 12:3

📍 CHIOS

of times mentioned: NT 1

An island in the Aegean Sea, west of Smyrna. Paul sailed near Chios on his voyage from Troas to Jerusalem.

Only reference: Acts 20:15

👥 CHISLON

of times mentioned: 1
# of MEN by this name: 1

Meaning: Hopeful

Forefather of Elidad, prince of the tribe of Benjamin when the Israelites entered the Promised Land.

Only reference: Numbers 34:21

📍 CHISLOTH-TABOR

of times mentioned: OT 1

Meaning: Flanks of Tabor

A city that became part of the inheritance of Zebulun when Joshua cast lots in Shiloh to provide territory for the seven tribes that had yet to receive their land.

Only reference: Joshua 19:12

CHLOE

of times mentioned: 1
# of WOMEN by this name: 1

Meaning: Green

A Corinthian Christian and acquaintance of Paul. Her family informed the apostle of divisions within the church.

Only reference: 1 Corinthians 1:11

⚲ CHOR-ASHAN

of times mentioned: OT 1

Meaning: Furnace of smoke

A city of Judah to which David sent some of the spoils from his warfare with the Amalekites.

Only reference: 1 Samuel 30:30

⚲ CHORAZIN

of times mentioned: NT 2

A city in which Jesus did many "mighty works." When the people did not repent, He reproved them, remarking that the Syrian cities of Tyre and Sidon would have repented had they seen these works.

First reference: Matthew 11:21 / Last reference: Luke 10:13

⚲ CHOZEBA

of times mentioned: OT 1

Meaning: Fallacious

A city of Judah that was settled by the sons of Shelah.

Only reference: 1 Chronicles 4:22

⚲ CHUN

of times mentioned: OT 1

Meaning: Established

A city ruled by King Hadarezer of Zobah, whom Israel's king David conquered. Following the con-quest, David brought much brass from Chun, which his son Solomon used to create some of the temple implements. In some Bible versions it is spelled "Cun."

Only reference: 1 Chronicles 18:8

👥 CHUSHAN-RISHATHAIM

of times mentioned: 4
# of MEN by this name: 1

Meaning: Cushan of double wickedness

A Mesopotamian king into whose hands God gave the disobedient Israelites. When they repented, He raised up Othniel, Caleb's younger brother, to deliver the nation. Same as Cushan.

First reference: Judges 3:8 / Last reference: Judges 3:10

👥 CHUZA

of times mentioned: 1
# of MEN by this name: 1

King Herod's household manager whose wife, Joanna, financially supported the ministry of Jesus.

Only reference: Luke 8:3

⚲ CILICIA

of times mentioned: NT 8

A Roman province in southeastern Asia Minor that included Paul's hometown, Tarsus. The Council of Jerusalem wrote to the Gentile Christians of Cilicia, encouraging them in their faith and not requiring them to be circumcised. Paul and Silas ministered to the churches there. On Paul's way to Rome, he sailed along the coast of this province.

First reference: Acts 6:9 / Last reference: Galatians 1:21

⚲ CINNEROTH

of times mentioned: OT 1

Meaning: Harp-shaped

An Old Testament name for the Sea of Galilee and the area around it. Here Ben-hadad fought in support of King Asa of Judah against Baasha, king of Israel, conquering the area. Same as Chinnereth and Chinneroth.

Only reference: 1 Kings 15:20

CIS

of times mentioned: 1
# of MEN by this name: 1

Meaning: A bow

Father of Israel's first king, Saul. Same as Kish (1).

Only reference: Acts 13:21

CLAUDA

of times mentioned: NT 1

An island near Crete. A ship that Paul took to Rome met with a storm and was driven past Clauda.

Only reference: Acts 27:16

CLAUDIA

of times mentioned: 1
# of WOMEN by this name: 1

A Roman Christian who sent greetings to Timothy in Paul's second letter to his "dearly beloved son."

Only reference: 2 Timothy 4:21

CLAUDIUS

of times mentioned: 3
# of MEN by this name: 2

1) A Roman emperor who ruled when a famine affected the empire and the Antioch church took up a collection for the church in Judea. Claudius also commanded the Jews to leave Rome, causing Priscilla and Aquila to move to Corinth.

First reference: Acts 11:28 / Last reference: Acts 18:2

2) A Roman military officer to whom Paul's nephew reported a plot against Paul's life. Also called Lysias.

Only reference: Acts 23:26

CLEMENT

of times mentioned: 1
# of MEN by this name: 1

Meaning: Merciful

A Philippian Christian and coworker of the apostle Paul.

Only reference: Philippians 4:3

CLEOPAS

of times mentioned: 1
# of MEN by this name: 1

Meaning: Renowned father

A Christian who met Jesus on the road to Emmaus. Not recognizing Jesus, Cleopas described the events of the crucifixion and resurrection to Jesus. As they walked, Jesus interpreted the scriptures about Himself to Cleopas and his traveling companion. They shared dinner, Jesus blessed the bread, and they recognized Him.

Only reference: Luke 24:18

CLEOPHAS

of times mentioned: 1
# of MEN by this name: 1

Husband of Mary, one of the women who stood at the cross when Jesus was crucified.

Only reference: John 19:25

CNIDUS

of times mentioned: NT 1

A city of southwest Asia Minor that Paul's ship sailed past on its way to Rome.

Only reference: Acts 27:7

COL-HOZEH

of times mentioned: 2
# of MEN by this name: 1

Meaning: Every seer

Forefather of a Jewish exile from the tribe of Judah who resettled Jerusalem.

First reference: Nehemiah 3:15 / Last reference: Nehemiah 11:5

♀ COLOSSE

of times mentioned: NT 1

Meaning: Colossal

A city in the Roman province of Phrygia, in Asia Minor. The apostle Paul wrote the book of Colossians to the Christians in Colosse. He probably ministered in Colosse when he visited Phrygia.

Only reference: Colossians 1:2

👥 CONANIAH

of times mentioned: 1
# of MEN by this name: 1

Meaning: God has sustained

A descendant of Abraham through Jacob's son Levi. Conaniah was among those who distributed sacrificial animals to fellow Levites preparing to celebrate the Passover under King Josiah.

Only reference: 2 Chronicles 35:9

👥 CONIAH

of times mentioned: 3
# of MEN by this name: 1

Meaning: God will establish

An alternative name for Judah's king Jehoiachin. Same as Jeconiah.

First reference: Jeremiah 22:24 / Last reference: Jeremiah 37:1

👥 CONONIAH

of times mentioned: 2
# of MEN by this name: 1

Meaning: God has sustained

A Levite (worship leader) in charge of tithes and offerings during King Hezekiah's reign.

First reference: 2 Chronicles 31:12 / Last reference: 2 Chronicles 31:13

♀ COOS

of times mentioned: NT 1

An island where Paul stopped on his voyage to Jerusalem. He visited here after he sailed from Ephesus and before he reached Rhodes.

Only reference: Acts 21:1

👥 CORE

of times mentioned: 1
# of MEN by this name: 1

Meaning: Ice

Greek form of Korah, a man who led a rebellion against Moses.

Only reference: Jude 1:11

♀ CORINTH

of times mentioned: NT 6

A Greek city, a trading center, and capital of the Roman province of Achaia. Paul visited Corinth during his second missionary journey, after he ministered in Athens. In Corinth Paul met fellow tentmakers Aquila and Priscilla, who became friends and co-laborers with him. Paul preached in the Corinthian synagogue until the Jews there strongly opposed him. But Crispus, the chief ruler of the synagogue, and his household were converted and baptized. Paul stayed for a year and a half, teaching among the Gentiles, until the Jews brought him up on charges before Gallio, deputy of Achaia. Gallio refused to hear the case and allowed Crispus to be beaten before his court. Shortly thereafter Paul left the city.

Paul wrote two epistles (1 and 2 Corinthians) to the troubled church at Corinth. A letter of rebuke, written between the two letters that appear in scripture, seems to have been lost.

First reference: Acts 18:1 / Last reference: 2 Timothy 4:20

👥 CORNELIUS

of times mentioned: 10
# of MEN by this name: 1

A God-fearing centurion of the Italian band. In a vision, an angel told him to call for Peter. Peter traveled to see Cornelius and preached to him and his companions. The Holy Spirit fell on them. They were the first Gentiles to be baptized by Peter.

First reference: Acts 10:1 / Last reference: Acts 10:31

👥 COSAM

of times mentioned: 1
# of MEN by this name: 1

Genealogy of Jesus: Yes (Luke 3:28)

Meaning: Divination

A descendant of Abraham through Isaac; forebear of Jesus' earthly father, Joseph.

Only reference: Luke 3:28

👥 COZ

of times mentioned: 1
# of MEN by this name: 1

Meaning: Thorn

A descendant of Abraham through Jacob's son Judah.

Only reference: 1 Chronicles 4:8

👥 COZBI

of times mentioned: 2
# of WOMEN by this name: 1

Meaning: False

Daughter of a Midian prince, she was killed for consorting with an Israelite.

First reference: Numbers 25:15 / Last reference: Numbers 25:18

👥 CRESCENS

of times mentioned: 1
# of MEN by this name: 1

Meaning: Growing

A coworker of Paul who left the apostle in Rome before preaching in Galatia.

Only reference: 2 Timothy 4:10

📍 CRETE

of times mentioned: NT 5

An island south of Greece that Paul passed on his way to Rome. Though Paul advised the centurion in whose care he was traveling that they should stop at Crete, his advice was not heeded and their ship was wrecked. Paul's student Titus ministered on Crete, appointing elders for the church.

First reference: Acts 27:7 / Last reference: Titus 1:5

👥 CRISPUS

of times mentioned: 2
# of MEN by this name: 1

Meaning: Crisp

A head of the Corinthian synagogue who, along with his household, believed in Jesus. He was baptized by Paul.

First reference: Acts 18:8 / Last reference: 1 Corinthians 1:14

👥 CUSH

of times mentioned: 7
# of MEN by this name: 2

1) A grandson of Noah, through his son Ham.

First reference: Genesis 10:6 / Last reference: 1 Chronicles 1:10

2) Author of Psalm 7, which David put to music.

Only reference: Psalm 7 (title)

♀ CUSH

of times mentioned: OT 1

The exact location of Cush is unclear in scripture, and scholars have varying opinions of its location. Ezekiel 29:10 seems to indicate that it was south of Egypt, but other verses seem to imply that it also included Arabia (Isaiah 11:11; 45:14). The word translated "Cush" in modern versions often appears as "Ethiopia" in the King James Version of the Bible. Isaiah prophesied that God would recover a remnant of His people from Cush. See Ethiopia.

Only reference: Isaiah 11:11

👥 CUSHAN

of times mentioned: 1
# of MEN by this name: 1

Mesopotamian king into whose hands God gave the disobedient Israelites. Same as Chushan-rishathaim.

Only reference: Habakkuk 3:7

👥 CUSHI

of times mentioned: 10
# of MEN by this name: 3

Meaning: A Cushite

1) The messenger who brought David the news that his son Absalom was dead.

First reference: 2 Samuel 18:21 / Last reference: 2 Samuel 18:32

2) A messenger for the princes of Judah who called Jeremiah's scribe to read his prophecies to them.

Only reference: Jeremiah 36:14

3) Father of the prophet Zephaniah.

Only reference: Zephaniah 1:1

♀ CUTH

of times mentioned: OT 1

A city northeast of Babylon from which people were brought to resettle Samaria after its people were taken away as captives by the Assyrians. The people of Cuth worshipped a pagan god named Nergal. Same as Cuthah.

Only reference: 2 Kings 17:30

♀ CUTHAH

of times mentioned: OT 1

A city northeast of Babylon from which people were brought to resettle Samaria after its people were taken away as captives by the Assyrians. Same as Cuth.

Only reference: 2 Kings 17:24

♀ CYPRUS

of times mentioned: NT 8

An island south of Asia Minor's Roman province of Cilicia and west of Syria that was the disciple Barnabas's homeland. During the persecution following Stephen's death, Jewish believers traveled to Cyprus and preached only to the Jews. But the believers of Cyprus passed the Good News on to Antioch, preaching to the Greeks there. Barnabas and Saul visited Cyprus early in their missionary efforts. After they went their separate ways, Barnabas returned with Mark. Paul only passed by Cyprus on his way to Jerusalem and again on his way to Rome.

First reference: Acts 4:36 / Last reference: Acts 27:4

♀ CYRENE

of times mentioned: NT 4

A Greek city of Libya and hometown of Simon, the man whom the Romans chose to bear Jesus' cross. People from Cyrene were present at Pentecost. Jews from Cyrene argued with Stephen and persuaded others to charge him with blasphemy. With the Cypriots, some men of Cyrene helped spread the Gospel to the Greeks in Antioch.

First reference: Matthew 27:32 / Last reference: Acts 13:1

👥 CYRENIUS

of times mentioned: 1
# of MEN by this name: 1

Roman governor of Syria at the time when Jesus was born.

Only reference: Luke 2:2

👥 CYRUS

of times mentioned: 23
# of MEN by this name: 1

The king of Persia who commanded that the temple in Jerusalem be rebuilt. He ordered all his people to give donations to help the Jews, and he returned the temple vessels that Nebuchadnezzar of Babylon had taken. When opposers objected to the work, the Jews reminded them of Cyrus's command, and the work went forward again. The prophet Daniel also lived and prospered during the early part of Cyrus's reign.

First reference: 2 Chronicles 36:22 / Last reference: Daniel 10:1 / Key references: 2 Chronicles 36:23; Ezra 5:13–15

📍 DABAREH

of times mentioned: OT 1

Meaning: A word

A Levitical city of the tribe of Issachar. Same as Daberath.

Only reference: Joshua 21:28

📍 DABBASHETH

of times mentioned: OT 1

Meaning: Sticky mass (meaning the hump of a camel)

A city that became part of the inheritance of Zebulun when Joshua cast lots in Shiloh to provide territory for the seven tribes that had yet to receive their land.

Only reference: Joshua 19:11

📍 DABERATH

of times mentioned: OT 2

Meaning: A word

A city that became part of the inheritance of Issachar when Joshua cast lots in Shiloh to provide territory for the seven tribes that had yet to receive their land. Same as Dabareh.

First reference: Joshua 19:12 / Last reference: 1 Chronicles 6:72

👥 DALAIAH

of times mentioned: 1
# of MEN by this name: 1

Meaning: God has delivered

A descendant of Abraham through Jacob's son Judah, in the line of the nation of Judah's third-to-last king, Jeconiah (also known as Jehoiachin).

Only reference: 1 Chronicles 3:24

📍 DALMANUTHA

of times mentioned: NT 1

A place on the western shore of the Sea of Galilee. Jesus and His disciples left for Dalmanutha after the feeding of the four thousand.

Only reference: Mark 8:10

📍 DALMATIA

of times mentioned: NT 1

An area on the eastern coast of the Adriatic Sea. Paul sent Titus to minister here.

Only reference: 2 Timothy 4:10

👥 DALPHON

of times mentioned: 1
# of MEN by this name: 1

Meaning: Dripping

One of ten sons of Haman, the villain of the story of Esther.

Only reference: Esther 9:7

👥 DAMARIS

of times mentioned: 1
# of WOMEN by this name: 1

Meaning: Gentle

A woman of Athens converted under the ministry of the apostle Paul.

Only reference: Acts 17:34

♀ DAMASCUS

of times mentioned: OT 45 / NT 15

An ancient Syrian city, northeast of Tyre, that King David conquered when the Syrians supported Hadadezer, king of Zobah, in battle. Following David's conquest, Damascus paid Israel tribute. But by the time of King Asa, Judah was paying tribute to King Ben-hadad of Damascus and attempting to gain the support of the city against Baasha, king of Israel.

After he lost a battle and was captured, the Syrian king Ben-hadad II promised King Ahab of Israel that he would return the cities his father had taken from Israel and allow Israel to trade in Damascus's lucrative markets, if Ahab would spare his life. When King Ahaz of Judah met Assyria's king Tiglath-pileser in Damascus, he saw a pagan altar there and had it copied so he could use it in pagan worship in the temple in Jerusalem.

The prophets Isaiah, Jeremiah, and Amos foretold the destruction of Damascus by the Assyrians.

Near Damascus Saul was confronted by Christ. Temporarily blinded, he had to be led into the city, where he was healed when Ananias laid hands on him. Converted, Saul quickly began preaching Christ in the synagogues of Damascus. Same as Syria-Damascus.

First reference: Genesis 14:15 / Last reference: Galatians 1:17 / Key references: 2 Samuel 8:6; 1 Kings 20:26–34; 2 Kings 16:10–14; Isaiah 17:1; Acts 9:3

👥 DAN

of times mentioned: 10
# of MEN by this name: 1

Meaning: Judge

Son of Jacob and Bilhah, Rachel's maid. Before his death, Jacob prophesied that Dan would judge his people and be as a "serpent by the way, an adder in the path" (Genesis 49:17).

First reference: Genesis 30:6 / Last reference: 1 Chronicles 2:2

♀ DAN

of times mentioned: OT 23

Meaning: Judge

The name of both a city and the area inherited by the tribe of Dan.

The city of Dan was originally named Laish (or Leshem). Before the tribe received its inheritance in the west, they attacked this city and renamed it after their forefather. The city lay in the northernmost part of Israel, leading to the expression "from Dan even to Beer-sheba," which indicated the two farthest points of the nation (Judges 20:1).

After Jeroboam became king of Israel, he feared his people would return to the rule of David's descendants. So he drew them into idolatry by setting up a golden calf god in the city of Dan.

The tribal area of Dan lay in the west, between Ephraim and Judah. When Ezekiel prophesied about the coming Messiah and the division of the land, Dan was given land in the northernmost part of Israel. He also foresaw that there would be a gate of Dan in the New Jerusalem.

First reference: Genesis 14:14 / Last reference: Amos 8:14 / Key references: Judges 18:29; 2 Kings 10:29; Ezekiel 48:1

👥 DANIEL

of times mentioned: 83
# of MEN by this name: 3

Meaning: Judge of God

1) A son of David, born to his wife Abigail in Hebron.

Only reference: 1 Chronicles 3:1

2) A priest who renewed the covenant under Nehemiah.

First reference: Ezra 8:2 / Last reference: Nehemiah 10:6

3) An Old Testament major prophet. As a child Daniel was taken into exile in Babylon. Because he refused to defile himself with meat and wine from the king's table, God blessed him with knowledge and wisdom.

Daniel described and interpreted a dream about an image of various metals and clay for King Nebuchadnezzar, and the king made him ruler over the province of Babylon. Daniel revealed the meaning of a second dream to Nebuchadnezzar, predicting his downfall until he worshipped the Lord.

During King Belshazzar's reign, Daniel interpreted the meaning of the mysterious handwriting on the wall. For this he was made third ruler in the kingdom, but Belshazzar died that night.

Darius the Mede took over the kingdom of Babylonia and planned to make Daniel head of the whole kingdom. Other leaders plotted against Daniel. Knowing he would not worship anyone but the Lord, they convinced the king to punish any person who worshipped anyone but the king for thirty days. For disobeying this law, Daniel was thrown into the lions' den. But God closed the beasts' mouths. When his favored man came out safely, Darius honored the Lord. Daniel prospered in the reigns of Darius and Cyrus the Persian. Same as Belteshazzar.

First reference: Ezekiel 14:14 / Last reference: Mark 13:14 / Key references: Daniel 1:8, 17; 2:31–45; 6:22–23

📍 DAN-JAAN

of times mentioned: OT 1

Meaning: Judge of purpose

A place where Joab, the commander of David's army, brought the captains of his host when they counted the people of Israel.

Only reference: 2 Samuel 24:6

📍 DANNAH

of times mentioned: OT 1

A city that became part of the inheritance of the tribe of Judah following the conquest of the Promised Land.

Only reference: Joshua 15:49

👥 DARA

of times mentioned: 1
# of MEN by this name: 1

Meaning: Pearl of knowledge

A descendant of Abraham through Jacob's son Judah.

Only reference: 1 Chronicles 2:6

👥 DARDA

of times mentioned: 1
# of MEN by this name: 1

Meaning: Pearl of knowledge

A wise man, the son of Mahol, whose wisdom is compared to Solomon's.

Only reference: 1 Kings 4:31

👥 DARIUS

of times mentioned: 25
# of MEN by this name: 3

1) Son of Hystaspes and king of Persia. He followed in the footsteps of King Cyrus and supported the Jews in their efforts to rebuild Jerusalem. When those who opposed the rebuilding wrote to Darius, he looked into the question and then ordered the opposition to allow the building to continue.

First reference: Ezra 4:5 / Last reference: Zechariah 7:1

2) Darius the Persian. He was either Darius the II or Darius the III.

Only reference: Nehemiah 12:22

3) Darius the Mede, king of Persia during part of the prophet Daniel's life. Darius wanted to promote Daniel, but Daniel's enemies plotted against him. When Daniel refused to worship the king, Daniel was thrown into the lions' den despite Darius's efforts to save him. God protected his servant, and Darius glorified God.

First reference: Daniel 5:31 / Last reference: Daniel 11:1

👥 DARKON

of times mentioned: 2
# of MEN by this name: 1

Forefather of an exiled family—former servants of Solomon—that returned to Judah under Zerubbabel.

First reference: Ezra 2:56 / Last reference: Nehemiah 7:58

👥 DATHAN

of times mentioned: 10
# of MEN by this name: 1

With Korah and Abiram, Dathan conspired against

Moses, declaring that all the people of Israel were holy. Dathan stayed in his tent when Moses called them before God, so Moses came to him. The ground broke open at Dathan's feet and swallowed him, his family, and his possessions.

First reference: Numbers 16:1 / Last reference: Psalm 106:17

DAVID

of times mentioned: 1,139
# of MEN by this name: 1

Genealogy of Jesus: Yes (Matthew 1:1; Luke 3:31)

Meaning: Loving

Popular king of Israel. As a young shepherd and musician, David was anointed king by the prophet Samuel in the place of disobedient King Saul. David vanquished the Philistine giant Goliath and Saul brought young David to his court, where the king's son Jonathan befriended him. Because the new hero became popular with the people, Saul became jealous and first sent David to war then sought to kill him. With Jonathan's help, David fled.

David escaped to Nob, where he received help from the priests, who were then killed by Saul. So began a period of war between the two men. Though David twice had opportunities to kill Saul, he would not touch the Lord's anointed.

Fearing Saul, David eventually fled into Philistine territory but would not fight against his own people. He concealed from Achish, king of Gath, the fact that his troops never attacked Israel. When Achish prepared for battle against Israel, the king's troops refused to have David's men in their ranks. David never fought against Saul for the Philistines.

Following the battle with the Philistines and the deaths of Saul and his sons, David was anointed king of Judah. Saul's remaining son, Ish-bosheth, was made king of Israel, but following Ish-bosheth's murder, these northern tribes made David their king.

David defeated the Philistines and brought the ark of the covenant to Jerusalem. But God would not let him build a temple. The king continued to defeat his foreign enemies, until he fell into sin with Bath-sheba and killed her husband, Uriah. Though David repented, this began a period of family troubles. David's son Amnon raped his half sister Tamar, and in retaliation her brother Absalom killed Amnon then attempted to take the throne.

Though David's troops overcame Absalom's army, David grieved at the death of his rebellious son.

Before David's death, when Adonijah tried to usurp his throne, David quickly had Solomon anointed king.

David wrote many of the psalms and sang a song of praise about the victories God brought him (2 Samuel 22). Despite his failings, scripture refers to David as a man after God's own heart (Acts 13:22).

First reference: Ruth 4:17 / Last reference: Revelation 22:16 / Key references: 1 Samuel 16:13; 18:6–9; 24:6–7; 2 Samuel 12:13; 22

DEBIR

of times mentioned: 1
# of MEN by this name: 1

Meaning: Shrine

A pagan king of Eglon during Joshua's conquest of the Promised Land, Debir allied with four other rulers to attack Gibeon, which had deceptively made a peace treaty with the Israelites. Joshua's soldiers defeated the five armies, and Joshua executed the allied kings.

Only reference: Joshua 10:3

♀ DEBIR

of times mentioned: OT 13

Meaning: Shrine or oracle

1) A city of the Anakim that Joshua and his troops attacked, captured, and destroyed. Debir became part of the inheritance of the tribe of Judah following the conquest of the Promised Land and later became a Levitical city. Same as Kirjath-sannah and Kirjath-sepher.

First reference: Joshua 10:38 / Last reference: 1 Chronicles 6:58 / Key references: Joshua 10:38–39; 15:15; Judges 1:11

2) Part of the border of the territory given to the tribe of Gad.

Only reference: Joshua 13:26

DEBORAH

of times mentioned: 10
# of WOMEN by this name: 2

Meaning: Bee

1) A nurse who accompanied Rebekah when she married Isaac (Genesis 24:59). This treasured servant's burial place, under an oak near Bethel, is recorded in Genesis 35:8.

Only reference: Genesis 35:8

2) Israel's only female judge and prophetess, she held court under a palm tree. Deborah called Barak to lead warriors into battle against the Canaanite army commander, Sisera. But Barak would fight only if Deborah went with him. For this, she prophesied that God would hand Sisera over to a woman.

Deborah supported Barak as he gathered his troops on Mount Tabor, and she advised him to go into battle. With him she sang a song of victory that praised the Lord.

First reference: Judges 4:4 / Last reference: Judges 5:15

📍 DECAPOLIS

of times mentioned: NT 3

Meaning: Ten-city region

A territory defined by a confederation of ten cities settled by the Greeks, Decapolis was largely southeast of the Sea of Galilee, with an area west of the Jordan River around Scythopolis (Beth-shan). People from this area were among the crowd that followed Jesus early in His ministry. Around the Decapolis, a Gadarene whom Jesus released from a legion of evil spirits testified to his healing.

First reference: Matthew 4:25 / Last reference: Mark 7:31

👥 DEDAN

of times mentioned: 5
# of MEN by this name: 2

1) A descendant of Noah through his son Ham.

First reference: Genesis 10:7 / Last reference: 1 Chronicles 1:9

2) A descendant of Abraham through his second wife, Keturah.

First reference: Genesis 25:3 / Last reference: 1 Chronicles 1:32

📍 DEDAN

of times mentioned: OT 6

An area near Edom that the prophet Jeremiah described as drinking of God's wrath. When the prophet Ezekiel prophesied against Edom, he foretold its desolation to Dedan. He also spoke multiple times of Dedan's people as being merchants to Tyre.

First reference: Jeremiah 25:23 / Last reference: Ezekiel 38:13

👥 DEKAR

of times mentioned: 1
# of MEN by this name: 1

Meaning: Stab

Father of one of King Solomon's royal officials over provisions.

Only reference: 1 Kings 4:9

👥 DELAIAH

of times mentioned: 6
# of MEN by this name: 4

Meaning: God has delivered

1) One of twenty-four priests in David's time who was chosen by lot to serve in the tabernacle.

Only reference: 1 Chronicles 24:18

2) An exile of unclear ancestry who returned to Judah under Zerubbabel.

First reference: Ezra 2:60 / Last reference: Nehemiah 7:62

3) A man who tried to terrify Nehemiah with threats on his life.

Only reference: Nehemiah 6:10

4) A prince of Judah who heard Jeremiah's prophecies.

First reference: Jeremiah 36:12 / Last reference: Jeremiah 36:25

👥 DELILAH

\# of times mentioned: 6
\# of WOMEN by this name: 1

Meaning: Languishing

A woman Samson fell in love with. Delilah was bribed by the Philistines to discover the source of her lover's strength. She nagged Samson until he told her that if his head was shaved, he would become weak. When this was done, Samson became weak and the Philistines overpowered him.

First reference: Judges 16:4 / Last reference: Judges 16:18

👥 DEMAS

\# of times mentioned: 3
\# of MEN by this name: 1

A Christian worker who was with Paul at Corinth. He became attracted by worldly things and left Paul to go to Thessalonica.

First reference: Colossians 4:14 / Last reference: Philemon 1:24

👥 DEMETRIUS

\# of times mentioned: 3
\# of MEN by this name: 2

1) A silversmith of Ephesus who opposed Paul and his teachings because they tended to destroy his business of making pagan shrines.

First reference: Acts 19:24 / Last reference: Acts 19:38

2) A man to whose character the apostle John testified.

Only reference: John 1:12

📍 DERBE

\# of times mentioned: NT 4

A city of Asia Minor's Roman province of Lycaonia. Paul and Barnabas fled to Derbe after Paul was stoned at Lystra. Paul's companion Gaius was from Derbe.

First reference: Acts 14:6 / Last reference: Acts 20:4

👥 DEUEL

\# of times mentioned: 4
\# of MEN by this name: 1

Meaning: Known of God

Father of Eliasaph, who was a prince of the tribe of Gad.

First reference: Numbers 1:14 / Last reference: Numbers 10:20

👥 DIBLAIM

\# of times mentioned: 1
\# of MEN by this name: 1

Meaning: Two cakes

Father of Gomer, the wife of the prophet Hosea.

Only reference: Hosea 1:3

📍 DIBLATH

\# of times mentioned: OT 1

The prophet Ezekiel described Diblath, a place in northern Canaan, as being desolate. Same as Riblah.

Only reference: Ezekiel 6:14

📍 DIBON

\# of times mentioned: OT 9

Meaning: Pining

1) A Moabite city that the tribe of Gad asked to have as their inheritance and turned into a fortified city. But Joshua 13:17 counts it as part of the inheritance of Reuben. The prophet Isaiah saw Moab weeping in Dibon, and the prophet Jeremiah foresaw the city's judgment by God. Same as Dimon and Dimonah.

First reference: Numbers 21:30 / Last reference: Jeremiah 48:22

2) A city of Judah resettled by the Jews after the Babylonian Exile.

Only reference: Nehemiah 11:25

DIBON-GAD

of times mentioned: OT 2

Meaning: Pining Gad

A campsite of the Israelites on their way to the Promised Land.

First reference: Numbers 33:45 / Last reference: Numbers 33:46

DIBRI

of times mentioned: 1
# of MEN by this name: 1

Meaning: Wordy

Father of Shelomith, whose son blasphemed the Lord.

Only reference: Leviticus 24:11

DIDYMUS

of times mentioned: 3
# of MEN by this name: 1

Meaning: Twin

An alternate name for Thomas, one of the twelve disciples of Jesus.

First reference: John 11:16 / Last reference: John 21:2

DIKLAH

of times mentioned: 2
# of MEN by this name: 1

A descendant of Noah through his son Shem.

First reference: Genesis 10:27 / Last reference: 1 Chronicles 1:21

DILEAN

of times mentioned: OT 1

A city that became part of the inheritance of the tribe of Judah following the conquest of the Promised Land.

Only reference: Joshua 15:38

DIMNAH

of times mentioned: OT 1

Meaning: A dung heap

A Levitical city of the tribe of Zebulun.

Only reference: Joshua 21:35

DIMON

of times mentioned: OT 1

Meaning: Pining

A Moabite city. The prophet Isaiah described its waters as being full of blood. Same as Dibon (1) and Dimonah.

Only reference: Isaiah 15:9

DIMONAH

of times mentioned: OT 1

Meaning: Pining

A city that became part of the inheritance of the tribe of Judah following the conquest of the Promised Land. Same as Dibon (1) and Dimon.

Only reference: Joshua 15:22

DINAH

of times mentioned: 8
# of WOMEN by this name: 1

Meaning: Justice

Daughter of Jacob and Leah, who was sexually assaulted by the prince Shechem. Her brothers retaliated, killing the men of his city.

First reference: Genesis 30:21 / Last reference: Genesis 46:15

DINHABAH

of times mentioned: OT 2

The capital city of King Bela of Edom.

First reference: Genesis 36:32 / Last reference: 1 Chronicles 1:43

👥 DIONYSIUS

of times mentioned: 1
# of MEN by this name: 1

Meaning: Reveler

A man of Athens converted under the ministry of the apostle Paul.

Only reference: Acts 17:34

👥 DIOTREPHES

of times mentioned: 1
# of MEN by this name: 1

Meaning: Jove-nourished

An arrogant church member condemned by the apostle John. Diotrephes spoke out against the apostles and refused to welcome Christian visitors.

Only reference: 3 John 1:9

👥 DISHAN

of times mentioned: 5
# of MEN by this name: 1

Meaning: Antelope

A descendant of Seir, who lived in Esau's "land of Edom."

First reference: Genesis 36:21 / Last reference: 1 Chronicles 1:42

👥 DISHON

of times mentioned: 7
# of MEN by this name: 2

Meaning: Antelope

1) A descendant of Seir, who lived in Esau's "land of Edom."

First reference: Genesis 36:21 / Last reference: 1 Chronicles 1:38

2) Another descendant of Seir, who lived in Esau's "land of Edom."

First reference: Genesis 36:25 / Last reference: 1 Chronicles 1:41

📍 DIZAHAB

of times mentioned: OT 1

Meaning: Of gold

A spot in the Sinai Desert near which Moses spoke to the Israelites. His speeches are preserved in the book of Deuteronomy.

Only reference: Deuteronomy 1:1

👥 DODAI

of times mentioned: 1
# of MEN by this name: 1

Meaning: Sick

A commander in King David's army, overseeing twenty-four thousand men in the second month of each year.

Only reference: 1 Chronicles 27:4

👥 DODAVAH

of times mentioned: 1
# of MEN by this name: 1

Meaning: Love of God

Father of the prophet Eliezer, who prophesied against Jehoshapat.

Only reference: 2 Chronicles 20:37

👥 DODO

of times mentioned: 5
# of MEN by this name: 3

Meaning: Loving

1) Grandfather of Israel's seventh judge, Tola.

Only reference: Judges 10:1

2) Father of Eleazar, one of David's three mighty men.

First reference: 2 Samuel 23:9 / Last reference: 1 Chronicles 11:12

3) Father of Elhanan, one of David's thirty mighty men.

First reference: 2 Samuel 23:24 / Last reference: 1 Chronicles 11:26

👥 DOEG

of times mentioned: 6
# of MEN by this name: 1

Meaning: Anxious

King Saul's chief herdsman, who told the king that David had visited Nob. Doeg slaughtered the priests of Nob at Saul's command.

First reference: 1 Samuel 21:7 / Last reference: Psalm 52 (title)

📍 DOPHKAH

of times mentioned: OT 2

Meaning: A knock

A campsite of the Israelites on their way to the Promised Land.

First reference: Numbers 33:12 / Last reference: Numbers 33:13

📍 DOR

of times mentioned: OT 6

Meaning: Dwelling

A Canaanite city and its surrounding area that Joshua and his troops conquered. It became part of the inheritance of Manasseh, but the tribe did not drive out the original inhabitants of the area. Under King Solomon's governmental organization, Dor was responsible for supplying provisions for the king.

First reference: Joshua 11:2 / Last reference: 1 Chronicles 7:29

👥 DORCAS

of times mentioned: 2
# of WOMEN by this name: 1

Meaning: Gazelle

A Christian of Joppa who did many good works. When she died, her friends called Peter, who raised her back to life. Same as Tabitha.

First reference: Acts 9:36 / Last reference: Acts 9:39

📍 DOTHAN

of times mentioned: OT 3

A place where Joseph's brothers pastured their sheep and sold him into slavery. Later Dothan became the prophet Elisha's home.

First reference: Genesis 37:17 / Last reference: 2 Kings 6:13

👥 DRUSILLA

of times mentioned: 1
# of WOMEN by this name: 1

Wife of Felix, the Roman governor of Judea in Paul's time.

Only reference: Acts 24:24

👥 DUMAH

of times mentioned: 2
# of MEN by this name: 1

Meaning: Silence

A descendant of Abraham through Ishmael, Abraham's son with his surrogate wife, Hagar.

First reference: Genesis 25:14 / Last reference: 1 Chronicles 1:30

📍 DUMAH

of times mentioned: OT 2

Meaning: To be dumb; silence; death (figuratively)

1) A city that became part of the inheritance of the tribe of Judah following the conquest of the Promised Land.

Only reference: Joshua 15:52

2) An oasis in Edom. In the prophet Isaiah's oracle about Dumah, a watchman is asked, "What is left of the night?" (NIV) as Edom seeks to hope for the morning.

Only reference: Isaiah 21:11

📍 DURA

of times mentioned: OT 1

Meaning: Circle or dwelling

A plain in Babylon where King Nebuchadnezzar set up a golden statue and demanded that his subjects bow before it. Shadrach, Meshach, and Abednego refused and were thrown into the fiery furnace.

Only reference: Daniel 3:1

👥 EBAL

of times mentioned: 3
# of MEN by this name: 2

Meaning: Bare

1) A descendant of Seir, who lived in Esau's "land of Edom."

First reference: Genesis 36:23 / Last reference: 1 Chronicles 1:40

2) A descendant of Noah through Noah's son Shem.

Only reference: 1 Chronicles 1:22

👥 EBED

of times mentioned: 6
# of MEN by this name: 2

Meaning: Servant

1) Father of Gaal, who incited the men of Shechem against King Abimelech.

First reference: Judges 9:26 / Last reference: Judges 9:35

2) A Jewish exile who returned from Babylon to Judah under Ezra.

Only reference: Ezra 8:6

👥 EBED-MELECH

of times mentioned: 6
# of MEN by this name: 1

Meaning: Servant of a king

An Ethiopian eunuch who rescued Jeremiah from a dungeon by reporting his situation to King Zedekiah. Jeremiah prophesied that God would deliver the faithful eunuch.

First reference: Jeremiah 38:7 / Last reference: Jeremiah 39:16

📍 EBEN-EZER

of times mentioned: OT 3

Meaning: Stone of the help

1) The site of Israel's camp when, during the time of the judge Samuel, they went into battle against the Philistines encamped at Aphek. Israel brought the ark of the covenant from Shiloh to their campsite at Eben-ezer, hoping the ark would save them. Instead Israel fled before the Philistines, who captured the ark, and the priest Eli's sons were slain.

First reference: 1 Samuel 4:1 / Last reference: 1 Samuel 5:1

2) A stone that Samuel set up between Mizpeh and Shen that commemorated Israel's victory over the Philistines at Mizpeh.

Only reference: 1 Samuel 7:12

👥 EBER

of times mentioned: 12
# of MEN by this name: 3

Meaning: Other side

1) Great-grandson of Shem and descendant of Noah.

First reference: Genesis 10:21 / Last reference: 1 Chronicles 1:25

2) A descendant of Abraham through Jacob's son Benjamin.

Only reference: 1 Chronicles 8:12

3) Forefather of a priest who returned to Jerusalem under Zerubbabel.

Only reference: Nehemiah 12:20

# EBIASAPH

# of times mentioned: 3
# of MEN by this name: 1

Meaning: Gatherer

A descendant of Abraham through Jacob's son Levi.

First reference: 1 Chronicles 6:23 / Last reference: 1 Chronicles 9:19

EBRONAH

of times mentioned: OT 2

Meaning: Transitional

A campsite of the Israelites on their way to the Promised Land.

First reference: Numbers 33:34 / Last reference: Numbers 33:35

ED

of times mentioned: OT 1

The name of an altar built by the Reubenites and Gadites as a witness that, though they lived across the Jordan River, they shared in the western tribes' worship of the Lord.

Only reference: Joshua 22:34

EDAR

of times mentioned: OT 1

Meaning: An arrangement (that is, a muster of animals)

A tower that Israel camped by after Rachel died and was buried near Beth-lehem.

Only reference: Genesis 35:21

EDEN

of times mentioned: 2
# of MEN by this name: 2

Meaning: Pleasure

1) A descendant of Abraham through Jacob's son Levi. Eden was among the Levites who cleansed the Jerusalem temple during the revival of King Hezekiah's day.

Only reference: 2 Chronicles 29:12

2) A priest in the time of King Hezekiah who helped to distribute the people's freewill offerings to his fellow priests.

Only reference: 2 Chronicles 31:15

EDEN

of times mentioned: OT 18

Meaning: Pleasure

1) A garden that God planted for Adam and Eve to live in just after their creation. Eden was filled with pleasant trees and plants for food. God made the animals and had Adam name them. The couple were to care for Eden but were commanded not to eat of "the tree of the knowledge of good and evil." When they listened to the serpent and disobeyed God's command, God sent the couple out of the garden so they could not eat of the tree of life and live forever in their sin.

The prophets Isaiah and Ezekiel promised that if God's people sought righteousness, God would make their desolate land like the Garden of Eden.

First reference: Genesis 2:8 / Last reference: Joel 2:3 / Key references: Genesis 2:8–3:24; Isaiah 51:3; Ezekiel 36:35

2) The Assyrians conquered this area that traded with Tyre. According to the book of Amos, its people went into exile in Kir.

First reference: 2 Kings 19:12 / Last reference: Amos 1:5

EDER

of times mentioned: 2
# of MEN by this name: 1

Meaning: Arrangement

A descendant of Abraham through Jacob's son Levi.

First reference: 1 Chronicles 23:23 / Last reference: 1 Chronicles 24:30

EDER

of times mentioned: OT 1

Meaning: An arrangement (that is, a muster of animals)

A city that became part of the inheritance of the tribe of Judah following the conquest of the Promised Land.

Only reference: Joshua 15:21

EDOM

of times mentioned: 3
# of MEN by this name: 1

Meaning: Red

A name given to Esau when he sold his birthright to his brother, Jacob, for a meal of red lentil stew. Because he was given this name, his descendants were called Edomites. Same as Esau.

First reference: Genesis 25:30 / Last reference: Genesis 36:8

EDOM

of times mentioned: OT 7

Meaning: Red

The land of Esau (who was also called Edom), which was inhabited by his descendants and lay south of Moab and southeast of the Dead Sea, south of Zered Brook. The prophet Jeremiah described the inhabitants of this mountainous nation as living "in the clefts of the rock, that holdest the height of the hill" (Jeremiah 49:16). Edom was ruled by kings well before Israel established a kingly line. Refused permission to cross Edom on the King's Highway, the Israelites traveled just beyond the edge of that nation on their way to the Promised Land.

King Saul fought Edom, along with the other nations that surrounded Israel. When David conquered the nation, putting garrisons throughout it, he fulfilled Balaam's prophecy that Israel would possess it, including its highest point, Mount Seir (2 Samuel 8:14; Numbers 24:18). For six months after this conquest, David's battle commander Joab remained in Edom "until he had cut off every male in Edom" (1 Kings 11:16).

Solomon used the Edomite ports of Elath and Ezion-geber for the ships sent to him by Hiram of Tyre. During King Jehoram of Judah's reign, Edom successfully rebelled, freeing itself from Jewish rule (2 Kings 8:22). King Amaziah of Judah went to war with Edom, killed ten thousand of its warriors, and took its capital, Selah. Amaziah's son, King Azariah, regained Elath for Judah, but the nation did not hold it. Under King Ahaz, it was taken by Rezin, king of Syria.

Edom did not forget its history of warfare with Judah. When Jerusalem was attacked by the Chaldeans, the Edomites delighted in its destruction (Psalm 137:7). But Jeremiah continued his prophecy with the promise that though the nation made its nest "as high as the eagle," God would bring it down (Jeremiah 49:16). The prophet Ezekiel foretold that because Edom took vengeance on Israel, its land would be made desolate by God (Ezekiel 25:13–14).

Eventually, under the Maccabees, the Edomites were incorporated into the Jewish people. Same as Idumaea and Idumea.

First reference: Genesis 36:21 / Last reference: 2 Chronicles 8:17

EDREI

of times mentioned: OT 8

Meaning: Mighty

1) A city of Bashan and site of a battle between Og, king of Bashan, and the Israelites. It became part of the inheritance of the tribe of Manasseh following Israel's conquest of the Promised Land.

First reference: Numbers 21:33 / Last reference: Joshua 13:31

2) A fortified or walled city that became part of the inheritance of Naphtali when Joshua cast lots in Shiloh to provide territory for the seven tribes that had yet to receive their land.

Only reference: Joshua 19:37

EGLAH

of times mentioned: 2
# of WOMEN by this name: 1

Meaning: Calf

One of several wives of King David and mother of David's son Ithream.

First reference: 2 Samuel 3:5 / Last reference:
1 Chronicles 3:3

📍 EGLAIM

of times mentioned: OT 1

Meaning: A double pond

A Moabite city that Isaiah prophesied would grieve at the destruction of its nation.

Only reference: Isaiah 15:8

👥 EGLON

of times mentioned: 5
# of MEN by this name: 1

Meaning: Calf-like

A king of Moab who attacked Israel. Eglon subjugated the Israelites for eighteen years but was killed by the Israelite judge Ehud.

First reference: Judges 3:12 / Last reference: Judges 3:17

📍 EGLON

of times mentioned: OT 8

Meaning: Vituline (having to do with calves or veal)

An Amorite city, ruled by King Debir, that opposed Joshua and the Israelites when they invaded the Promised Land. Joshua killed Debir and his battle allies. Then Israel besieged Eglon, conquered it, and killed all its people. The city became part of the inheritance of the tribe of Judah following the conquest of the Promised Land.

First reference: Joshua 10:3 / Last reference: Joshua 15:39

📍 EGYPT

of times mentioned: OT 587 / NT 24

An often-powerful nation southwest of Israel, in the northeastern corner of Africa, Egypt first appears in scripture when famine affected Canaan and Abram and Sarai attempted to find sanctuary in that country. Because of her beauty, Pharaoh took Sarai into his household and gave her brother Abram many gifts. When Pharaoh discovered that Abram was also her husband, he sent the couple out of his country.

God promised in His covenant with Abram that his ancestors would own the land "from the river of Egypt," a stream marking Judah's southwestern border, to the Euphrates (Genesis 15:18).

Sold into slavery by his jealous brothers, Jacob's son Joseph ended up ruling Egypt, second in power only to Pharaoh. As the famine Joseph foretold spread to Canaan, his brothers traveled to Egypt for some of the food their brother had stockpiled to provide for the lean years. After Joseph revealed himself to them, Jacob and his family moved to Egypt, to the land of Goshen, where they prospered and multiplied.

A new king ruled Egypt and, fearing the Israelites, made them slaves. Attempting to limit their numbers, he ordered the midwives to kill all male newborns. So when Moses was born, his mother hid him then set him adrift in a small basket. An Egyptian princess found and raised the infant. As an adult, Moses attempted to defend his fellow Israelites, killed an Egyptian, and fled to Midian. But God returned him to Egypt with a message of judgment for Pharaoh and one of hope for Israel.

When Pharaoh refused to let Israel leave his country, God poured out increasing judgments, in the form of plagues, on the ruler and his nation. Though God turned the Nile to blood; overwhelmed the land with frogs, gnats, and flies; struck the cattle with a plague and the people with boils; sent hail and locusts down on the land; and darkened the sun, Pharaoh remained adamant. Only after all the firstborn of both humans and animals died did he let Israel go.

Still unable to give them up, the ruler gathered his soldiers and followed God's people. Therefore God destroyed Egypt's troops in the Red Sea as He led His people to safety on dry ground. This salvation of His people became an ongoing theme in scripture, and there are numerous references to this event in the Bible.

King Solomon married one of Pharaoh's daughters and traded with that land. But his son Rehoboam, king of Judah, saw Jerusalem attacked and plundered by Shishak, king of Egypt. Hoshea, king of Israel, conspired with So, king of Egypt, and brought down on himself the wrath of the king of Assyria. As a result, the northern kingdom was made captive by the Assyrians. When Egypt's pharaoh Necho opposed the king of Assyria, King Josiah of Judah supported Assyria and was killed in battle. Josiah's son Jehoahaz was captured by Necho, who made Jehoiakim king in his place.

After Nebuchadnezzar conquered Judah, the remaining leaders of Judah did not believe Jeremiah's prophecy when he told them to remain in that land. Instead they led all the Jews who had not been deported to Babylon, including Jeremiah and his scribe Baruch, to Egypt. As the prophet had warned, Nebuchadnezzar attacked Egypt, so the people of Judah did not avoid the empire they so feared. In the Prophets, Egypt is commonly associated with paganism and the Jews' unfaithfulness to God.

Following the birth of Jesus, God commanded Joseph to take Mary and Jesus into Egypt to escape Herod the Great's rage. After Herod's death, God called the family back to Israel.

First reference: Genesis 12:10 / Last reference: Revelation 11:8 / Key references: Genesis 41:41; Exodus 6:11; 20:2; 2 Kings 25:26; Matthew 2:14

👥 EHI

of times mentioned: 1
# of MEN by this name: 1

Meaning: Brotherly

A son of Benjamin who went to Egypt with Jacob.

Only reference: Genesis 46:21

👥 EHUD

of times mentioned: 10
# of MEN by this name: 2

Meaning: United

1) The second judge of Israel who subdued the oppressing Moabites. A left-handed man, Ehud killed Eglon, the obese king of Moab, with a hidden dagger while pretending to be on a peace mission.

First reference: Judges 3:15 / Last reference: Judges 4:1

2) A descendant of Abraham through Jacob's son Benjamin.

First reference: 1 Chronicles 7:10 / Last reference: 1 Chronicles 8:6

👥 EKER

of times mentioned: 1
# of MEN by this name: 1

Meaning: A transplanted person

A descendant of Abraham through Jacob's son Judah.

Only reference: 1 Chronicles 2:27

📍 EKRON

of times mentioned: OT 22

Meaning: Eradication

One of the five major Philistine cities, Ekron remained unconquered when Joshua was old. Originally part of the inheritance of the tribe of Judah, it became part of the inheritance of Dan when Joshua cast lots in Shiloh to provide territory for the seven tribes that had yet to receive their land. Judges 1:18 tells of Judah's capture of Ekron and its territory, but obviously the land fell back into Philistine hands, since Ekron again belonged to the Philistines when the ark of the covenant was captured. After the Philistines captured the ark, the people of Ekron refused to have it in their city because they had heard of the destruction it caused in Ashdod and Gath.

King Ahaziah of Israel looked to Baal-zebub, the god of Ekron, when he wanted to know if he would recover from a fall. God sent Elijah to confront the king with his faithlessness. The prophets foretold the destruction of this pagan city. Jeremiah described it as one of the places upon which God's wrath will be poured, and Zephaniah foresaw that it will be uprooted (Jeremiah 25:20; Zephaniah 2:4).

First reference: Joshua 13:3 / Last reference: Zechariah 9:7 / Key references: 1 Samuel 5:10; 2 Kings 1:2

👥 ELADAH

of times mentioned: 1
# of MEN by this name: 1

Meaning: God has decked

A descendant of Abraham through Joseph's son Ephraim.

Only reference: 1 Chronicles 7:20

👥 ELAH

of times mentioned: 14
# of MEN by this name: 6

Meaning: Oak

1) A "duke of Edom," a leader in the family line of Esau.

First reference: Genesis 36:41 / Last reference: 1 Chronicles 1:52

2) Father of Shimei, an officer under King Solomon.

Only reference: 1 Kings 4:18

3) King of Israel, a contemporary of Asa, who was the king of Judah. Elah was killed by Zimri, who usurped his throne.

First reference: 1 Kings 16:6 / Last reference: 1 Kings 16:14

4) Father of Hoshea, who killed King Pekah of Israel and usurped his throne.

First reference: 2 Kings 15:30 / Last reference: 2 Kings 18:9

5) A descendant of Abraham through Jacob's son Judah.

Only reference: 1 Chronicles 4:15

6) A Jewish exile from the tribe of Benjamin who resettled Jerusalem.

Only reference: 1 Chronicles 9:8

📍 ELAH

of times mentioned: OT 3

Meaning: An oak (or other strong tree)

The valley where King Saul and his men camped when they confronted Goliath and the Philistines. None of the soldiers in Saul's army was willing to fight the giant. David came to visit his brothers, fought with the Philistine champion, and killed Goliath here.

First reference: 1 Samuel 17:2 / Last reference: 1 Samuel 21:9

👥 ELAM

of times mentioned: 13
# of MEN by this name: 9

Meaning: Distant

1) A descendant of Noah through his son Shem.

First reference: Genesis 10:22 / Last reference: 1 Chronicles 1:17

2) A descendant of Abraham through Jacob's son Benjamin.

Only reference: 1 Chronicles 8:24

3) A Levite "porter" (doorkeeper) in the house of the Lord.

Only reference: 1 Chronicles 26:3

4) Forefather of an exiled family that returned to Judah under Zerubbabel.

First reference: Ezra 2:7 / Last reference: Nehemiah 7:12

5) Forefather of an exiled family that returned to Judah under Zerubbabel.

First reference: Ezra 2:31 / Last reference: Nehemiah 7:34

6) Forefather of a Jewish exile who returned from Babylon to Judah under Ezra.

Only reference: Ezra 8:7

7) An Israelite whose descendants married "strange" (foreign) women.

First reference: Ezra 10:2 / Last reference: Ezra 10:26

8) A Jewish leader who renewed the covenant under Nehemiah.

Only reference: Nehemiah 10:14

9) A priest who helped to dedicate the rebuilt wall of Jerusalem by giving thanks.

Only reference: Nehemiah 12:42

⚲ ELAM

of times mentioned: OT 15

Meaning: Hidden (that is, distant)

A nation east of Babylonia, north of the Persian Gulf. Elam's king Chedorlaomer led the force that attacked Sodom and captured Abram's nephew Lot.

The prophet Isaiah foretold a time when God would recall His people from Elam, a nation that had allied itself with Assyria and attacked Jerusalem. Jeremiah prophesied that the Lord would judge Elam, and Ezekiel foresaw a slain multitude of its soldiers.

First reference: Genesis 14:1 / Last reference: Daniel 8:2 / Key references: Jeremiah 49:34; Ezekiel 32:24

⚎ ELASAH

of times mentioned: 2
# of MEN by this name: 2

Meaning: God has made

1) An exiled Israelite priest who married a "strange" (foreign) woman.

Only reference: Ezra 10:22

2) An ambassador of Judah's king Zedekiah sent to King Nebuchadnezzar of Babylon.

Only reference: Jeremiah 29:3

⚲ ELATH

of times mentioned: OT 5

Meaning: Trees or a grove of palms

A port on the Gulf of Aqabah that is mentioned as Israel bypassed Edom during the Exodus. Azariah (also called Uzziah), king of Judah, rebuilt Elath. During King Ahaz of Judah's reign, Rezin, king of Syria, recovered the city. Same as Eloth.

First reference: Deuteronomy 2:8 / Last reference: 2 Kings 16:6

⚲ EL-BETHEL

of times mentioned: OT 1

Meaning: The God of Bethel

A place where Jacob built an altar because God had appeared there before him as he fled from his brother, Esau. Same as Bethel and Luz (1).

Only reference: Genesis 35:7

⚎ ELDAAH

of times mentioned: 2
# of MEN by this name: 1

Meaning: God of knowledge

A descendant of Abraham through his second wife, Keturah.

First reference: Genesis 25:4 / Last reference: 1 Chronicles 1:33

⚎ ELDAD

of times mentioned: 2
# of MEN by this name: 1

Meaning: God has loved

A man who prophesied in the camp after God sent the Israelites quail to eat in the wilderness.

First reference: Numbers 11:26 / Last reference: Numbers 11:27

⚎ ELEAD

of times mentioned: 1
# of MEN by this name: 1

Meaning: God has testified

A descendant of Abraham through Joseph's son Ephraim. He was killed by men of Gath in a dispute over livestock.

Only reference: 1 Chronicles 7:21

📍 ELEALEH

of times mentioned: OT 5

Meaning: God is going up

A town the tribe of Reuben requested as part of its inheritance before Israel crossed the Jordan River. In his oracle about the destruction of Moab, Isaiah saw Elealeh crying out and weeping in grief.

First reference: Numbers 32:3 / Last reference: Jeremiah 48:34

👥 ELEASAH

of times mentioned: 4
# of MEN by this name: 2

Meaning: God has made

1) A descendant of Abraham through Jacob's son Judah. Eleasah descended from the line of an unnamed Israelite woman and her Egyptian husband, Jarha.

First reference: 1 Chronicles 2:39 / Last reference: 1 Chronicles 2:40

2) A descendant of Abraham through Jacob's son Benjamin, through the line of King Saul and his son Jonathan.

First reference: 1 Chronicles 8:37 / Last reference: 1 Chronicles 9:43

👥 ELEAZAR

of times mentioned: 74
# of MEN by this name: 8

Meaning: God is helper

1) Aaron's third son. His older brothers Nadab and Abihu were killed by God for illicit worship practices, so Eleazar became the chief over the Levites. He oversaw the temple worship, including the use of the temple vessels, meat offerings, and anointing oil, and was in charge of the tabernacle.
   When Aaron died, Eleazar became high priest. With Moses, God commanded him to count the Israelites. After Israel came to the Promised Land, Eleazar and Joshua divided the territory among Israel's tribes. He died and was buried on a hill belonging to his son Phinehas.

First reference: Exodus 6:23 / Last reference: Ezra 7:5 / Key references: Numbers 4:16; 26:1–2; Deuteronomy 10:6

2) Son of Abinadab (1), who was consecrated to guard the ark of the covenant.

Only reference: 1 Samuel 7:1

3) One of David's three mighty men.

First reference: 2 Samuel 23:9 / Last reference: 1 Chronicles 11:12

4) A descendant of Abraham through Jacob's son Levi.

First reference: 1 Chronicles 23:21 / Last reference: 1 Chronicles 24:28

5) One of the men who weighed the temple vessels after the Babylonian Exile.

Only reference: Ezra 8:33

6) An exiled Israelite who married a "strange" (foreign) woman.

Only reference: Ezra 10:25

7) A priest who helped to dedicate the rebuilt wall of Jerusalem by giving thanks.

Only reference: Nehemiah 12:42

8) A descendant of Abraham through Isaac; forebear of Jesus' earthly father, Joseph.

Only reference: Matthew 1:15

Genealogy of Jesus: Yes (Matthew 1:5)

📍 EL-ELOHE-ISRAEL

of times mentioned: OT 1

Meaning: The mighty God of Israel

An altar that Jacob erected at Shalem after his reconciliation with his brother, Esau.

Only reference: Genesis 33:20

📍 ELEPH

of times mentioned: OT 1

Meaning: A family (as in yoking or taming an ox or cow)

A city that became part of the inheritance of Benjamin when Joshua cast lots in Shiloh to provide territory for the seven tribes that had yet to receive their land.

Only reference: Joshua 18:28

ELHANAN

of times mentioned: 4
# of MEN by this name: 2

Meaning: God is gracious

1) A man from Bethlehem who killed Goliath's brother.

First reference: 2 Samuel 21:19 / Last reference: 1 Chronicles 20:5

2) One of King David's valiant warriors.

First reference: 2 Samuel 23:24 / Last reference: 1 Chronicles 11:26

ELI

of times mentioned: 33
# of MEN by this name: 1

Meaning: Lofty

The high priest in Shiloh, where the ark of the covenant rested for a time. He rebuked Hannah for being drunk (though she wasn't) as she prayed for God to give her a child. When her son Samuel was born, she brought him to Eli and dedicated him to God. Eli acted as Samuel's foster father and trained him in the priesthood. Eli's own sons, Hophni and Phinehas, did not know the Lord and sinned greatly. Because Eli honored them above God, the priest had done little to restrain them. Yet God promised to raise up a faithful priest in their place.

Samuel began to hear the Word of God, and Eli encouraged him to listen. Though his own sons were spiritual failures, Eli did much better with his foster son. Samuel went on to be a powerful prophet of the Lord.

The Lord had told Eli that his sons would die on the same day, and they did—in a battle with the Philistines, who stole the ark. When Eli heard the news of his sons' deaths, he fell backward in his chair and broke his neck.

First reference: 1 Samuel 1:3 / Last reference: 1 Kings 2:27 / Key references: 1 Samuel 1:13–14; 2:29; 3:8–9

ELIAB

of times mentioned: 21
# of MEN by this name: 6

Meaning: God of his father

1) A prince of Zebulun who assisted Moses in taking the census of his tribe.

First reference: Numbers 1:9 / Last reference: Numbers 10:16

2) Father of Dathan and Abiram, who rebelled against Moses.

First reference: Numbers 16:1 / Last reference: Deuteronomy 11:6

3) The first son of Jesse and the older brother of King David. The prophet Samuel, sent by God to anoint the successor to King Saul, thought the tall and good-looking Eliab would be the Lord's choice—but God said, "The Lord seeth not as man seeth; for man looketh on the outward appearance, but the Lord looketh on the heart" (1 Samuel 16:7). A warrior in Saul's army, Eliab criticized his youngest brother when David questioned Israelite soldiers about their fear of Goliath.

First reference: 1 Samuel 16:6 / Last reference: 2 Chronicles 11:18

4) A descendant of Abraham through Jacob's son Levi.

Only reference: 1 Chronicles 6:27

5) One of several warriors from the tribe of Gad who left Saul to join David during his conflict with the king. Eliab and his companions were "men of might. . .whose faces were like the faces of lions" (1 Chronicles 12:8).

Only reference: 1 Chronicles 12:9

6) A Levite musician who performed in celebration when King David brought the ark of the covenant to Jerusalem.

First reference: 1 Chronicles 15:18 / Last reference: 1 Chronicles 16:5

ELIADA

of times mentioned: 3
# of MEN by this name: 2

Meaning: God is knowing

1) A son of King David, born at Jerusalem.

First reference: 2 Samuel 5:16 / Last reference: 1 Chronicles 3:8

2) A Benjaminite "mighty man of valour" who fought for King Jehoshaphat of Judah.

Only reference: 2 Chronicles 17:17

👥 ELIADAH

of times mentioned: 1
# of MEN by this name: 1

Meaning: God is knowing

Father of Rezon, an opponent of Israel's king Solomon.

Only reference: 1 Kings 11:23

👥 ELIAH

of times mentioned: 2
# of MEN by this name: 1

Meaning: God of Jehovah

A descendant of Abraham through Jacob's son Benjamin. Eliah married a "strange" (foreign) woman in exile.

First reference: 1 Chronicles 8:27 / Last reference: Ezra 10:26

👥 ELIAHBA

of times mentioned: 2
# of MEN by this name: 1

Meaning: God will hide

One of King David's valiant warriors.

First reference: 2 Samuel 23:32 / Last reference: 1 Chronicles 11:33

👥 ELIAKIM

of times mentioned: 15
# of MEN by this name: 4

Meaning: God of raising

1) Palace administrator for King Hezekiah of Judah. He confronted the king of Assyria's messengers who tried to convince Hezekiah and his people to submit to Assyria.

First reference: 2 Kings 18:18 / Last reference: Isaiah 37:2

2) Son of King Josiah of Judah. Pharaoh Necho of Egypt put him in power and changed his name to Jehoiakim. Same as Jehoiakim.

First reference: 2 Kings 23:34 / Last reference: 2 Chronicles 36:4

3) A priest who helped to dedicate the rebuilt wall of Jerusalem by giving thanks.

Only reference: Nehemiah 12:41

4) A descendant of Abraham through Isaac; forebear of Jesus' earthly father, Joseph.

First reference: Matthew 1:13 / Last reference: Luke 3:30

Genealogy of Jesus: Yes (Matthew 1:13)

👥 ELIAM

of times mentioned: 2
# of MEN by this name: 2

Meaning: God of the people

1) Father of Bath-sheba, the beautiful woman whom King David took as a wife.

Only reference: 2 Samuel 11:3

2) One of King David's warriors known as the "mighty men."

Only reference: 2 Samuel 23:34

👥 ELIAS

of times mentioned: 30
# of MEN by this name: 1

Meaning: God of Jehovah

Greek form of the name Elijah, used in six New Testament books.

First reference: Matthew 11:14 / Last reference: James 5:17

ELIASAPH

of times mentioned: 6
# of MEN by this name: 2

Meaning: God is gatherer

1) A prince of Gad who helped Moses take a census of his tribe.

First reference: Numbers 1:14 / Last reference: Numbers 10:20

2) The leader of the Gershonites, under Moses.

Only reference: Numbers 3:24

ELIASHIB

of times mentioned: 17
# of MEN by this name: 7

Meaning: God will restore

1) A descendant of Abraham through Jacob's son Judah, in the line of the nation of Judah's third-to-last king, Jeconiah (also known as Jehoiachin).

Only reference: 1 Chronicles 3:24

2) One of twenty-four priests in David's time who was chosen by lot to serve in the tabernacle.

Only reference: 1 Chronicles 24:12

3) A Levite worship leader, son of Jehoiakim and grandson of Jeshua, who returned from Babylon.

First reference: Ezra 10:6 / Last reference: Nehemiah 12:23

4) An exiled Levite who married a "strange" (foreign) woman.

Only reference: Ezra 10:24

5) Another exiled Israelite who married a "strange" (foreign) woman.

Only reference: Ezra 10:27

6) Another exiled Israelite who married a "strange" (foreign) woman.

Only reference: Ezra 10:36

7) High priest during the rebuilding of Jerusalem's walls. He defiled the temple by assigning Tobiah the Ammonite a room there.

First reference: Nehemiah 3:1 / Last reference: Nehemiah 13:28

ELIATHAH

of times mentioned: 2
# of MEN by this name: 1

Meaning: God of his consent

A son of King David's musician Heman, who was "under the hands of [his] father for song in the house of the LORD" (1 Chronicles 25:6).

First reference: 1 Chronicles 25:4 / Last reference: 1 Chronicles 25:27

ELIDAD

of times mentioned: 1
# of MEN by this name: 1

Meaning: God of his love

Prince of the tribe of Benjamin when the Israelites entered the Promised Land.

Only reference: Numbers 34:21

ELIEL

of times mentioned: 10
# of MEN by this name: 10

Meaning: God of his God

1) One of the "mighty men of valour, famous men" leading the half tribe of Manasseh.

Only reference: 1 Chronicles 5:24

2) An ancestor of the prophet Samuel. Same as Elihu (1).

Only reference: 1 Chronicles 6:34

3) A descendant of Abraham through Jacob's son Benjamin.

Only reference: 1 Chronicles 8:20

4) Another descendant of Abraham through Jacob's son Benjamin.

Only reference: 1 Chronicles 8:22

5) One of King David's valiant warriors.

Only reference: 1 Chronicles 11:46

6) Another of King David's valiant warriors.

Only reference: 1 Chronicles 11:47

7) One of several warriors from the tribe of Gad who left Saul to join David during his conflict with the king. Eliel and his companions were "men of might. . .whose faces were like the faces of lions" (1 Chronicles 12:8).

Only reference: 1 Chronicles 12:11

8) A descendant of Hebron who helped to bring the ark of the covenant to Jerusalem.

Only reference: 1 Chronicles 15:9

9) A descendant of Abraham through Jacob's son Levi. Eliel was among a group of Levites appointed by King David to bring the ark of the covenant from the house of Obed-edom to Jerusalem.

Only reference: 1 Chronicles 15:11

10) A supervisor of temple donations under King Hezekiah of Judah.

Only reference: 2 Chronicles 31:13

🗣 ELIENAI

of times mentioned: 1
# of MEN by this name: 1

Meaning: Toward Jehovah are my eyes

A descendant of Abraham through Jacob's son Benjamin.

Only reference: 1 Chronicles 8:20

🗣 ELIEZER

of times mentioned: 15
# of MEN by this name: 11

Meaning: God of help

1) The steward of Abraham's house and Abraham's presumed heir before the miraculous birth of Isaac.

Only reference: Genesis 15:2

2) A son of Moses by his wife, Zipporah.

First reference: Exodus 18:4

Last reference: 1 Chronicles 26:25

3) A priest who blew a trumpet before the ark of the covenant when David brought it to Jerusalem.

Only reference: 1 Chronicles 15:24

4) Leader of the tribe of Reuben in the days of King David.

Only reference: 1 Chronicles 27:16

5) A prophet who predicted trouble for the ships of Judah's king Jehoshaphat, who had entered into a trading alliance with Ahaziah, king of Israel.

Only reference: 2 Chronicles 20:37

6) A Jewish exile charged with finding Levites and temple servants to travel to Jerusalem with Ezra.

Only reference: Ezra 8:16

7) An exiled Israelite priest who married a "strange" (foreign) woman.

Only reference: Ezra 10:18

8) An exiled Levite who married a "strange" (foreign) woman.

Only reference: Ezra 10:23

9) An exiled Israelite who married a "strange" (foreign) woman.

Only reference: Ezra 10:31

10) An ancestor of Jesus Christ according to Luke's genealogy.

Only reference: Luke 3:29

Genealogy of Jesus: Yes (Luke 3:29)

🗣 ELIHOENAI

of times mentioned: 1
# of MEN by this name: 1

Meaning: Toward Jehovah are my eyes

Forefather of a Jewish exile who returned from Babylon to Judah under Ezra.

Only reference: Ezra 8:4

👥 ELIHOREPH

of times mentioned: 1
# of MEN by this name: 1

Meaning: God of autumn

A scribe serving Israel's king Solomon.

Only reference: 1 Kings 4:3

👥 ELIHU

of times mentioned: 11
# of MEN by this name: 5

Meaning: God of him

1) An ancestor of the prophet Samuel. Same as Eliel (2).

Only reference: 1 Samuel 1:1

2) A warrior who defected to David at Ziklag and became an army commander.

Only reference: 1 Chronicles 12:20

3) A Levite "porter" (doorkeeper) in the house of the Lord.

Only reference: 1 Chronicles 26:7

4) Leader of the tribe of Judah in the days of King David.

Only reference: 1 Chronicles 27:18

5) A young man who becomes a mediator in the discussion between Job and his comforters. Unlike the comforters, God did not accuse Elihu of any wrong.

First reference: Job 32:2 / Last reference: Job 36:1

👥 ELIJAH

of times mentioned: 69
# of MEN by this name: 2

Meaning: God of Jehovah

1) One of the Old Testament's major prophets, Elijah came from Tishbe, in Gilead. His prophecy that no rain would fall in Israel except at his command angered wicked King Ahab, and Elijah had to flee across the Jordan River and on to Zarephath.

God hid him for three years and sent him to Mount Carmel. At Carmel he had a showdown with the priests of Baal that proved the Lord was God. Baal could not ignite the offering made by the pagans, but God sent fire from heaven that lit a water-soaked offering made by Elijah. The people of Israel worshipped God, and rain fell.

Angry that Elijah had all the priests of Baal killed, Queen Jezebel threatened his life, and the discouraged prophet fled to Horeb. God gave Elijah the prophet Elisha as a disciple. Elijah returned to Ahab to prophesy the ruling couple's end, and Ahab repented.

Following Ahab's death, Elijah prophesied the death of King Ahaziah, who consulted the god of Ekron when he was ill.

Knowing God would take Elijah to heaven, his disciple Elisha asked to receive a double portion of his spirit. Elijah said that if Elisha saw his ascension into heaven, he would have it. Suddenly a chariot with horses of fire appeared before the two men, and Elijah went up into heaven in a whirlwind. Same as Elias.

First reference: 1 Kings 17:1 / Last reference: Malachi 4:5 / Key references: 1 Kings 17:1–6; 1 Kings 18:21–40; 2 Kings 2:11

2) An exiled Israelite priest who married a "strange" (foreign) woman.

Only reference: Ezra 10:21

👥 ELIKA

of times mentioned: 1
# of MEN by this name: 1

Meaning: God of rejection

One of King David's mightiest warriors known as "the thirty."

Only reference: 2 Samuel 23:25

📍 ELIM

of times mentioned: OT 6

Meaning: Palm trees

An encampment of the Israelites during the Exodus. Elim had twelve wells and seventy palm trees.

First reference: Exodus 15:27 / Last reference: Numbers 33:10

 ELIMELECH

of times mentioned: 6
# of MEN by this name: 1

Meaning: God of the king

Naomi's husband. He died in Moab, where the family had moved from Bethlehem to escape a famine.

First reference: Ruth 1:2 / Last reference: Ruth 4:9

ELIOENAI

of times mentioned: 8
# of MEN by this name: 7

Meaning: Toward Jehovah are my eyes

1) A descendant of Abraham through Jacob's son Judah, in the line of the nation of Judah's third-to-last king, Jeconiah (also known as Jehoiachin).

First reference: 1 Chronicles 3:23 / Last reference: 1 Chronicles 3:24

2) A descendant of Abraham through Jacob's son Simeon.

Only reference: 1 Chronicles 4:36

3) A descendant of Abraham through Jacob's son Benjamin.

Only reference: 1 Chronicles 7:8

4) A Levite "porter" (doorkeeper) in the house of the Lord.

Only reference: 1 Chronicles 26:3

5) An exiled Israelite priest who married a "strange" (foreign) woman.

Only reference: Ezra 10:22

6) An exiled Israelite who married a "strange" (foreign) woman.

Only reference: Ezra 10:27

7) A priest who helped to dedicate the rebuilt wall of Jerusalem by giving thanks.

Only reference: Nehemiah 12:41

ELIPHAL

of times mentioned: 1
# of MEN by this name: 1

Meaning: God of judgment

One of King David's valiant warriors.

Only reference: 1 Chronicles 11:35

ELIPHALET

of times mentioned: 2
# of MEN by this name: 1

Meaning: God of deliverance

A son of King David, born to him in Jerusalem.

First reference: 2 Samuel 5:16 / Last reference: 1 Chronicles 14:7

ELIPHAZ

of times mentioned: 15
# of MEN by this name: 2

Meaning: God of gold

1) A son of Esau. Esau's blessing as the older brother was taken by the scheming Jacob.

First reference: Genesis 36:4 / Last reference: 1 Chronicles 1:36

2) One of three friends of Job who mourned his losses for a week then accused him of wrongdoing. God ultimately chastised the three for their criticism of Job, commanding them to sacrifice burnt offerings while Job prayed for them.

First reference: Job 2:11 / Last reference: Job 42:9

ELIPHELEH

of times mentioned: 2
# of MEN by this name: 1

Meaning: God of his distinction

A Levite musician who performed in celebration when King David brought the ark of the covenant to Jerusalem.

First reference: 1 Chronicles 15:18 / Last reference: 1 Chronicles 15:21

👥 ELIPHELET

of times mentioned: 6
# of MEN by this name: 6

Meaning: God of deliverance

1) One of King David's warriors known as the "mighty men."

Only reference: 2 Samuel 23:34

2) A son of King David, born in Jerusalem.

Only reference: 1 Chronicles 3:6

3) Another son of King David, born in Jerusalem.

Only reference: 1 Chronicles 3:8

4) A descendant of Abraham through Jacob's son Benjamin, through the line of King Saul and his son Jonathan. Eliphelet was a courageous archer.

Only reference: 1 Chronicles 8:39

5) A Jewish exile who returned to Judah under Ezra.

Only reference: Ezra 8:13

6) An exiled Israelite who married a "strange" (foreign) woman.

Only reference: Ezra 10:33

👥 ELISABETH

of times mentioned: 9
# of WOMEN by this name: 1

Meaning: God of the oath

Wife of Zacharias and mother of John the Baptist. For many years Elisabeth had been barren, but her husband received a vision promising she would conceive. When Elisabeth heard, she rejoiced at God's favor. Her cousin Mary visited her for three months when Mary learned that she herself would bear the Messiah.

First reference: Luke 1:5 / Last reference: Luke 1:57

👥 ELISEUS

of times mentioned: 1
# of MEN by this name: 1

Meaning: God of supplication

Greek form of the Old Testament name Elisha.

Only reference: Luke 4:27

📍 ELISHA

of times mentioned: 58
# of MEN by this name: 1

Meaning: God of supplication

The prophet Elijah's successor and disciple, Elisha saw Elijah carried up to heaven on a whirlwind of fire and received a double portion of his spirit. Taking over the role of prophet, Elisha performed many miracles for individuals—he healed a polluted water source for the people of Jericho, provided oil for a widow, and caused a "great woman" of Shunem to have a child then brought him back to life after he died. He fed one hundred people from twenty loaves of bread, prefiguring Christ's feeding of the five thousand and the three thousand. At Elisha's command, Naaman, captain of the Syrian king, bathed in the Jordan and was healed of leprosy.

At Elisha's request, God blinded a host of Syrian warriors. Elisha led them to Samaria then persuaded the king of Israel to send them home. This ended the incursion of Syria's raiding bands on Israel. The prophet prophesied the recovery and then the death of King Ben-hadad of Syria and told King Jeroboam of Israel that he would strike Syria three times but not fully defeat that nation.

After Elisha died, some men put a body into his tomb for safekeeping. The man's body touched the prophet's bones and was revived. Same as Eliseus.

First reference: 1 Kings 19:16 / Last reference: 2 Kings 13:21 / Key references: 2 Kings 2:9; 2 Kings 4:8–37; 5:8–19

👥 ELISHAH

of times mentioned: 3
# of MEN by this name: 1

A descendant of Noah, through his son Japheth.

First reference: Genesis 10:4 / Last reference: Ezekiel 27:7

👥 ELISHAMA

of times mentioned: 17
# of MEN by this name: 7

Meaning: God of hearing

1) A descendant of Abraham through Joseph's son Ephraim and an ancestor of Joshua.

First reference: Numbers 1:10 / Last reference: 1 Chronicles 7:26

2) A son of King David, born in Jerusalem. Same as Elishua.

First reference: 2 Samuel 5:16 / Last reference: 1 Chronicles 14:7

3) Forefather of Ishmael, who was the assassin of Gedaliah, governor of Israel.

Only reference: Jeremiah 41:1

4) A descendant of Abraham through Jacob's son Judah. Elishama descended from the line of an unnamed Israelite woman and her Egyptian husband, Jarha.

Only reference: 1 Chronicles 2:41

5) A priest sent by King Jehoshaphat to teach the law of the Lord throughout the nation of Judah.

Only reference: 2 Chronicles 17:8

6) Forefather of Ishmael, who killed Gedaliah, governor of Jerusalem.

Only reference: 2 Kings 25:25

7) Secretary to King Jehoiakim of Judah; he heard the prophecies of Jeremiah.

First reference: Jeremiah 36:12 / Last reference: Jeremiah 36:21

👥 ELISHAPHAT

of times mentioned: 1
# of MEN by this name: 1

Meaning: God of judgment

A commander who entered into a covenant with the priest Jehoiada, young King Joash's protector.

Only reference: 2 Chronicles 23:1

👥 ELISHEBA

of times mentioned: 1
# of WOMEN by this name: 1

Meaning: God of the oath

Aaron's wife, who bore him four sons.

Only reference: Exodus 6:23

👥 ELISHUA

of times mentioned: 2
# of MEN by this name: 1

Meaning: God of supplication

A son of King David, born in Jerusalem. Same as Elishama (2).

First reference: 2 Samuel 5:15 / Last reference: 1 Chronicles 14:5

👥 ELIUD

of times mentioned: 2
# of MEN by this name: 1

Genealogy of Jesus: Yes (Matthew 1:14–15)

Meaning: God of majesty

The great-great-great-grandfather of Jesus' earthly father, Joseph, according to Matthew's genealogy of Jesus.

First reference: Matthew 1:14 / Last reference: Matthew 1:15

👥 ELIZAPHAN

of times mentioned: 3
# of MEN by this name: 2

Meaning: God of treasure

1) The leader of the Kohathite clans during the Exodus. Same as Elzaphan.

First reference: Numbers 3:30 / Last reference: 2 Chronicles 29:13

2) Prince of the tribe of Zebulun when the Israelites entered the Promised Land.

Only reference: Numbers 34:25

👥 ELIZUR

of times mentioned: 5
# of MEN by this name: 1

Meaning: God of the rock

A prince of Reuben who helped Moses take a census of his tribe and led the tribe out of Sinai.

First reference: Numbers 1:5 / Last reference: Numbers 10:18

👥 ELKANAH

of times mentioned: 20
# of MEN by this name: 8

Meaning: God has obtained

1) A descendant of Abraham through Jacob's son Levi.

First reference: Exodus 6:24 / Last reference: 1 Chronicles 6:23

2) Father of the prophet Samuel. Elkanah's wife Hannah was barren and prayed to have a child. When God gave her Samuel, Elkanah agreed with her that their son should become a priest under the high priest Eli.

First reference: 1 Samuel 1:1 / Last reference: 1 Chronicles 6:34

3) Another descendant of Abraham through Jacob's son Levi.

First reference: 1 Chronicles 6:25 / Last reference: 1 Chronicles 6:36

4) Another descendant of Abraham through Jacob's son Levi.

First reference: 1 Chronicles 6:26 / Last reference: 1 Chronicles 6:35

5) A Jewish exile from the tribe of Levi who resettled Jerusalem.

Only reference: 1 Chronicles 9:16

6) A "mighty man" who supported the future king David during his conflict with Saul.

Only reference: 1 Chronicles 12:6

7) A doorkeeper for the ark of the covenant when David brought it to Jerusalem.

Only reference: 1 Chronicles 15:23

8) One of King Ahaz's officers, his second in command.

Only reference: 2 Chronicles 28:7

📍 ELLASAR

of times mentioned: OT 2

A nation that joined King Chedorlaomer of Elam in an attack on Sodom, during which Abram's nephew Lot was captured. Ellasar's king was named Arioch.

First reference: Genesis 14:1 / Last reference: Genesis 14:9

👥 ELMODAM

of times mentioned: 1
# of MEN by this name: 1

Genealogy of Jesus: Yes (Luke 3:28)

A descendant of Abraham through Isaac; forebear of Jesus' earthly father, Joseph.

Only reference: Luke 3:28

👥 ELNAAM

of times mentioned: 1
# of MEN by this name: 1

Meaning: God is his delight

Father of two of King David's valiant warriors.

Only reference: 1 Chronicles 11:46

👥 ELNATHAN

of times mentioned: 7
# of MEN by this name: 4

Meaning: God is the giver

1) Grandfather of King Jehoiachin of Judah.

First reference: 2 Kings 24:8 / Last reference: Jeremiah 36:25

2) A Jewish exile charged with finding Levites and temple servants to travel to Jerusalem with Ezra.

Only reference: Ezra 8:16

3) Another Jewish exile charged with finding Levites and temple servants to travel to Jerusalem with Ezra.

Only reference: Ezra 8:16

4) Yet another Jewish exile charged with finding Levites and temple servants to travel to Jerusalem with Ezra.

Only reference: Ezra 8:16

👥 ELON

of times mentioned: 6
# of MEN by this name: 3

Meaning: Oak grove

1) Father of Esau's wife Bashemath (or Adah).

First reference: Genesis 26:34 / Last reference: Genesis 36:2

2) A son of Zebulun, founder of the tribe of the Elonites.

First reference: Genesis 46:14 / Last reference: Numbers 26:26

3) The eleventh judge of Israel, who led the nation for ten years.

First reference: Judges 12:11 / Last reference: Judges 12:12

📍 ELON

of times mentioned: OT 1

Meaning: Oak grove

A city that became part of the inheritance of Dan when Joshua cast lots in Shiloh to provide territory for the seven tribes that had yet to receive their land.

Only reference: Joshua 19:43

📍 ELON-BETH-HANAN

of times mentioned: OT 1

Meaning: Oak grove of the house of favor

Under King Solomon's governmental organization, a town responsible for supplying provisions for the king.

Only reference: 1 Kings 4:9

📍 ELOTH

of times mentioned: OT 3

Meaning: Trees or a grove (of palms)

An Edomite port on the Red Sea where King Solomon started a navy. King Uzziah (also called Azariah) of Judah built up the port and regained it as part of Judah's territory. Same as Elath.

First reference: 1 Kings 9:26 / Last reference: 2 Chronicles 26:2

👥 ELPAAL

of times mentioned: 3
# of MEN by this name: 1

Meaning: God act

A descendant of Abraham through Jacob's son Benjamin.

First reference: 1 Chronicles 8:11 / Last reference: 1 Chronicles 8:18

👥 ELPALET

of times mentioned: 1
# of MEN by this name: 1

Meaning: Meaning

A son of King David, born to him in Jerusalem.

Only reference: 1 Chronicles 14:5

📍 EL-PARAN

of times mentioned: OT 1

Meaning: Oak of Paran

A place near Canaan's wilderness. King Chedor-laomer of Elam and the other kings who rose up against Sodom fought a battle up to this place.

Only reference: Genesis 14:6

📍 ELTEKEH

of times mentioned: OT 2

A city that became part of the inheritance of Dan when Joshua cast lots in Shiloh to provide territory for the seven tribes that had yet to receive their land. Eltekeh became one of the six cities of refuge established in Israel for those who had committed accidental murder.

First reference: Joshua 19:44 / Last reference: Joshua 21:23

📍 ELTEKON

of times mentioned: OT 1

Meaning: God is straight

A city that became part of the inheritance of the tribe of Judah following the conquest of the Promised Land.

Only reference: Joshua 15:59

📍 ELTOLAD

of times mentioned: OT 2

Meaning: God is generator

A city that became part of the inheritance of the tribe of Judah following the conquest of the Promised Land. Later Eltolad became part of the inheritance of Simeon when Joshua cast lots in Shiloh to provide territory for the seven tribes that had yet to receive their land.

First reference: Joshua 15:30 / Last reference: Joshua 19:4

👥 ELUZAI

of times mentioned: 1
# of MEN by this name: 1

Meaning: God is defensive

A "mighty man" who supported the future king David during his conflict with Saul.

Only reference: 1 Chronicles 12:5

👥 ELYMAS

of times mentioned: 1
# of MEN by this name: 1

A Jewish sorcerer who was miraculously blinded for opposing the apostle Paul's preaching of the Gospel in Paphos. Same as Bar-jesus.

Only reference: Acts 13:8

👥 ELZABAD

of times mentioned: 2
# of MEN by this name: 2

Meaning: God has bestowed

1) One of several warriors from the tribe of Gad who left Saul to join David during his conflict with the king. Elzabad and his companions were "men of might. . .whose faces were like the faces of lions" (1 Chronicles 12:8).

Only reference: 1 Chronicles 12:12

2) A Levite "porter" (doorkeeper) in the house of the Lord.

Only reference: 1 Chronicles 26:7

👥 ELZAPHAN

of times mentioned: 2
# of MEN by this name: 1

Meaning: God of treasure

A descendant of Levi and son of Uzziel who was part of the Exodus. Same as Elizaphan (1).

First reference: Exodus 6:22 / Last reference: Leviticus 10:4

👥 EMMANUEL

of times mentioned: 1
# of MEN by this name: 1

Meaning: God with us

A prophetic name for Jesus, given by the angel of the Lord to Joseph, husband of Mary.

Only reference: Matthew 1:23

📍 EMMAUS

of times mentioned: NT 1

A village about seven miles from Jerusalem. As Cleopas and another disciple were traveling to Emmaus after the Crucifixion, they met the resurrected Jesus but did not recognize Him. They discussed the events surrounding His crucifixion, and Jesus interpreted the scriptures about Himself. The two disciples recognized Him as He broke bread with them in Emmaus.

Only reference: Luke 24:13

👥 EMMOR

of times mentioned: 1
# of MEN by this name: 1

Meaning: Ass

A prince of Shechem whose sons sold Abraham a tomb.

Only reference: Acts 7:16

📍 ENAM

of times mentioned: OT 1

Meaning: Double fountain

A city that became part of the inheritance of the tribe of Judah following the conquest of the Promised Land.

Only reference: Joshua 15:34

👥 ENAN

of times mentioned: 5
# of MEN by this name: 1

Meaning: Having eyes

Forefather of a prince of Naphtali who helped Moses take a census of his tribe.

First reference: Numbers 1:15 / Last reference: Numbers 10:27

📍 ENDOR

of times mentioned: OT 3

Meaning: Fountain of dwelling

A town that became part of the inheritance of Manasseh, though it fell within Issachar's boundaries. When God did not respond to Saul's inquiry about the threat of the Philistine troops at Gilboa, Saul went to Endor to consult a medium. Saul asked the medium to bring up Samuel for him. The spirit told Saul that both Israel and Saul would be given into the hands of the Philistines. When Saul went into battle, Israel lost, and Saul and his sons were killed.

First reference: Joshua 17:11 / Last reference: Psalm 83:10

📍 EN-EGLAIM

of times mentioned: OT 1

Meaning: Fountain of two calves

A place in the Red Sea that Ezekiel foretold would be filled with fish when Jerusalem is finally restored.

Only reference: Ezekiel 47:10

📍 EN-GANNIM

of times mentioned: OT 3

Meaning: Fountain of gardens

1) A city that became part of the inheritance of the tribe of Judah following the conquest of the Promised Land.

Only reference: Joshua 15:34

2) A city that became part of the inheritance of Issachar when Joshua cast lots in Shiloh to provide territory for the seven tribes that had yet to receive their land. Later it became a Levitical city.

First reference: Joshua 19:21 / Last reference: Joshua 21:29

📍 EN-GEDI

of times mentioned: OT 6

Meaning: Fountain of a kid

A city on the Dead Sea that became part of the inheritance of the tribe of Judah following the conquest of the Promised Land. David lived here for a time when Saul sought his life. Ezekiel foresaw it as a place whose waters would be teeming with fish when Jerusalem is finally restored. Same as Hazazon-tamar and Hazezon-tamar.

First reference: Joshua 15:62 / Last reference: Ezekiel 47:10

📍 EN-HADDAH

of times mentioned: OT 1

Meaning: Fountain of sharpness

A city that became part of the inheritance of Issachar when Joshua cast lots in Shiloh to provide territory for the seven tribes that had yet to receive their land.

Only reference: Joshua 19:21

📍 EN-HAKKORE

of times mentioned: OT 1

A spring in Lehi that God created for the thirsty Samson after he killed a thousand men with the jawbone of a donkey.

Only reference: Judges 15:19

📍 EN-HAZOR

of times mentioned: OT 1

Meaning: Fountain of a village

A fortified or walled city that became part of the inheritance of Naphtali when Joshua cast lots in Shiloh to provide territory for the seven tribes that had yet to receive their land.

Only reference: Joshua 19:37

📍 EN-MISHPAT

of times mentioned: OT 1

Meaning: Fountain of judgment

A city or its surrounding area that King Chedor-laomer of Elam and his Mesopotamian allies attacked as they battled against the Amalekites and the Amorites. Same as Kadesh, Kadesh-barnea, and Kedesh (4).

Only reference: Genesis 14:7

👥 ENOCH

of times mentioned: 11
# of MEN by this name: 2

Meaning: Initiated

1) Cain's eldest son, after whom he named a city.

First reference: Genesis 4:17 / Last reference: Genesis 4:18

2) A descendant of Seth, son of Adam. "Enoch walked with God: and he was not; for God took him" (Genesis 5:24). He was immediately translated into eternity. Same as Henoch (1).

First reference: Genesis 5:18 / Last reference: Jude 1:14

Genealogy of Jesus: Yes (Luke 3:37)

📍 ENOCH

of times mentioned: OT 1

Meaning: Initiated

A city that Cain built and named after his son.

Only reference: Genesis 4:17

👥 ENOS

of times mentioned: 7
# of MEN by this name: 1

Genealogy of Jesus: Yes (Luke 3:38)

Meaning: Mortal

Son of Seth, Adam's son, and forebear of Jesus' earthly father, Joseph. Same as Enosh.

First reference: Genesis 4:26 / Last reference: Luke 3:38

👥 ENOSH

of times mentioned: 1
# of MEN by this name: 1

Meaning: Mortal

An alternative form of the name Enos, son of Seth.

Only reference: 1 Chronicles 1:1

📍 EN-RIMMON

of times mentioned: OT 1

Meaning: Fountain of a pomegranate

A place in Judah resettled by the Jews after the Babylonian Exile.

Only reference: Nehemiah 11:29

📍 EN-ROGEL

of times mentioned: OT 4

Meaning: Fountain of a traveler

A spring that identified part of the border between the tribes of Judah and Benjamin. When King David's son Adonijah attempted to take the throne, he held a feast here.

First reference: Joshua 15:7 / Last reference: 1 Kings 1:9

📍 EN-SHEMESH

of times mentioned: OT 2

Meaning: Fountain of the sun

A spring that identified part of the border between the tribes of Judah and Benjamin.

First reference: Joshua 15:7 / Last reference: Joshua 18:17

📍 EN-TAPPUAH

of times mentioned: OT 1

Meaning: Fountain of an apple tree

A town that identified part of the border of the tribe of Manasseh.

Only reference: Joshua 17:7

👥 EPAENETUS

of times mentioned: 1
# of MEN by this name: 1

Meaning: Praised

A Christian acquaintance of the apostle Paul in Rome and the first Christian convert from Achaia.

Only reference: Romans 16:5

👥 EPAPHRAS

of times mentioned: 3
# of MEN by this name: 1

Meaning: Devoted

A fellow servant, with Paul, to the Colossian church. Epaphras was a native of Colossae.

First reference: Colossians 1:7 / Last reference: Philemon 1:23

👥 EPAPHRODITUS

of times mentioned: 2
# of MEN by this name: 1

Meaning: Devoted

A fellow laborer, with Paul, whom the apostle sent to the church at Philippi. Epaphroditus also brought Paul some gifts from that church.

First reference: Philippians 2:25 / Last reference: Philippians 4:18

👥 EPHAH

of times mentioned: 5
# of MEN by this name: 2
# of WOMEN by this name: 1

Meaning: Obscurity

1) A grandson of Abraham and Keturah through their son Midian.

First reference: Genesis 25:4 / Last reference: Isaiah 60:6

2) Concubine of Caleb (2).

Only reference: 1 Chronicles 2:46

3) A descendant of Abraham through Jacob's son Judah.

Only reference: 1 Chronicles 2:47

👥 EPHAI

of times mentioned: 1
# of MEN by this name: 1

Meaning: Birdlike

Forefather of an Israelite family that stayed in Judah during the Babylonian captivity.

Only reference: Jeremiah 40:8

👥 EPHER

of times mentioned: 4
# of MEN by this name: 3

Meaning: Gazelle

1) A descendant of Abraham through his second wife, Keturah.

First reference: Genesis 25:4 / Last reference: 1 Chronicles 1:33

2) A descendant of Abraham through Jacob's son Judah.

Only reference: 1 Chronicles 4:17

3) One of the "mighty men of valour, famous men" leading the half tribe of Manasseh.

Only reference: 1 Chronicles 5:24

📍 EPHES-DAMMIM

of times mentioned: OT 1

Meaning: Boundary of blood drops

A place where the Philistine army established a camp. From here Goliath challenged the Israelites to battle.

Only reference: 1 Samuel 17:1

📍 EPHESUS

of times mentioned: NT 17

Capital of the Roman province of Asia, in the western part of Asia Minor. On his way to Jerusalem, Paul stopped in Ephesus and spoke to the Jews in its synagogue. Apollos preached in the city, knowing only the baptism of John the Baptist, but when Priscilla and Aquila heard his preaching, they taught him the full way of God.

The idol maker Demetrius stirred up a riot against Paul in Ephesus, because the apostle's preaching hurt his business. He made his case against Paul with his fellow silversmiths, who became so angered they took to the streets. A crowd formed, caught up two of Paul's companions, and headed for the theater. For two hours they cried out, "Great is Diana of the Ephesians." Finally the town clerk calmed them and encouraged them to make use of the law instead of continuing this unlawful gathering.

From prison in Rome, Paul wrote an epistle to the Ephesian church focusing on the need for unity in the body of Christ.

In the book of Revelation, John relays Jesus' message to the church in Ephesus. Christ praises them for their good deeds but warns that they have lost their first love.

First reference: Acts 18:19 / Last reference: Revelation 2:1 / Key references: Acts 18:24–26; 19:21–41; Revelation 2:1–7

👥 EPHLAL

of times mentioned: 2
# of MEN by this name: 1

Meaning: Judge

A descendant of Abraham through Jacob's son Judah. Ephlal descended from the line of an unnamed Israelite woman and her Egyptian husband, Jarha.

Only reference: 1 Chronicles 2:37

👥 EPHOD

of times mentioned: 1
# of MEN by this name: 1

Meaning: Girdle

Forefather of Hanniel, prince of the tribe of Manasseh when the Israelites entered the Promised Land.

Only reference: Numbers 34:23

👥 EPHRAIM

of times mentioned: 11
# of MEN by this name: 1

Meaning: Double fruit

Joseph and his wife Asenath's second son. Ephraim and his brother, Manasseh, were adopted and blessed by Jacob. But Ephraim received the greater blessing, for Jacob insisted he would be the greater brother. Eventually the brothers superseded Jacob's oldest sons, Reuben and Simeon.

First reference: Genesis 41:52 / Last reference: 1 Chronicles 7:22 / Key references: Genesis 48:5, 17–19

📍 EPHRAIM

of times mentioned: OT 38 / NT 1

Meaning: Double fruit

1) A mountainous area that was part of the inheritance of the tribes of Ephraim and Manasseh. Joshua, son of Nun, received the city of Timnath-serah in Mount Ephraim, where he lived and was buried.

Mount Ephraim was also the home of a man named Micah, who established a "house of gods" and asked a Levite to become his priest. The Danites took Micah's priest and his idols from him and used them to fall into their own idolatry. King Jehoshaphat of Judah brought Mount Ephraim back to the Lord.

Though Jeremiah saw the people of Mount Ephraim being afflicted by God for their sinfulness, in the end he foretold their satisfaction of the soul.

First reference: Joshua 17:15 / Last reference: Jeremiah 50:19 / Key references: Joshua 24:30; Judges 7:24

2) A town near Baal-hazor, where Absalom had sheepshearers.

Only reference: 2 Samuel 13:23

3) A forest where King David's troops fought the troops of his son Absalom. During the battle

Absalom's hair became caught in the thick boughs of an oak tree. When David's battle commander Joab heard of this, he went to the tree and killed Absalom, against the king's command.

Only reference: 2 Samuel 18:6

4) A gate in the wall of Jerusalem. The city's walls were broken down between this gate and the corner gate when, after capturing King Amaziah of Judah, Jehoash, king of Israel, attacked the city.

First reference: 2 Kings 14:13 / Last reference: Nehemiah 12:39

5) A city near Israel's wilderness where Jesus went after He raised Lazarus from the dead and the Jewish leaders sought to kill Him.

Only reference: John 11:54

📍 EPHRAIN

of times mentioned: OT 1

Meaning: Fawnlike

A city taken from King Jeroboam of Israel by Abijah, king of Judah.

Only reference: 2 Chronicles 13:19

👥 EPHRATAH

of times mentioned: 2
# of WOMEN by this name: 1

Meaning: Fruitfulness

Wife of Hur; mother of Caleb, the son of Hur. Same as Ephrath.

First reference: 1 Chronicles 2:50 / Last reference: 1 Chronicles 4:4

📍 EPHRATAH

of times mentioned: OT 3

Meaning: Fruitfulness

Hometown of Boaz and Ruth. The prophet Micah foretold that the Messiah would come from here. Same as Beth-lehem, Bethlehem, Beth-lehem-judah, and probably Ephrath.

First reference: Ruth 4:11 / Last reference: Micah 5:2

👥 EPHRATH

of times mentioned: 1
# of WOMEN by this name: 1

Meaning: Fruitfulness

An alternative form of the name Ephratah.

Only reference: 1 Chronicles 2:19

📍 EPHRATH

of times mentioned: OT 4

Meaning: Fruitfulness

Rachel was buried near this town. Probably the same as Beth-lehem, Bethlehem, Beth-lehem-judah, and Ephratah.

First reference: Genesis 35:16 / Last reference: Genesis 48:7

👥 EPHRON

of times mentioned: 12
# of MEN by this name: 1

Meaning: Fawnlike

The Hittite from whom Abraham bought the cave of Machpelah, where he buried Sarah. Though Ephron wanted to give Abraham the land, Abraham insisted on buying it.

First reference: Genesis 23:8 / Last reference: Genesis 50:13 / Key reference: Genesis 23:10–11

📍 EPHRON

of times mentioned: OT 1

Meaning: Fawnlike

A mountain that formed part of the border of the tribe of Judah.

Only reference: Joshua 15:9

👥 ER

of times mentioned: 11
# of MEN by this name: 3

Meaning: Watchful

1) Judah's firstborn son, who was wicked. "The Lord. . .slew him" (Genesis 38:10). Both he and his brother Onan died in Canaan.

First reference: Genesis 38:3 / Last reference: 1 Chronicles 2:3

2) A son of Judah's son Shelah.

Only reference: 1 Chronicles 4:21

3) A descendant of Abraham through Isaac; forebear of Jesus' earthly father, Joseph.

Only reference: Luke 3:28

Genealogy of Jesus: Yes (Luke 3:28)

👥 ERAN

of times mentioned: 1
# of MEN by this name: 1

Meaning: Watchful

A descendant of Abraham through Jacob's son Ephraim.

Only reference: Numbers 26:36

👥 ERASTUS

of times mentioned: 3
# of MEN by this name: 2

Meaning: Beloved

1) A companion of Timothy on a mission to Macedonia. Erastus then went to Corinth.

First reference: Acts 19:22 / Last reference: 2 Timothy 4:20

2) The chamberlain (treasurer) of Corinth, who greeted the Roman Christians through Paul when the apostle wrote that church.

Only reference: Romans 16:23

📍 ERECH

of times mentioned: OT 1

Meaning: Length

A city in the kingdom of Nimrod, who ruled the land of Shinar.

Only reference: Genesis 10:10

 # ERI

# of times mentioned: 2
# of MEN by this name: 1

Meaning: Watchful

A descendant of Abraham through Jacob's son Gad.

First reference: Genesis 46:16 / Last reference: Numbers 26:16

ESAIAS

of times mentioned: 21
# of MEN by this name: 1

Meaning: God has saved

Greek form of the name Isaiah, used in the New Testament.

First reference: Matthew 3:3 / Last reference: Romans 15:12 / Key reference: Luke 4:14–21

ESAR-HADDON

of times mentioned: 3
# of MEN by this name: 1

The son of Sennacherib who inherited the throne of Assyria. As king, following the exile, Esar-haddon resettled people of other nations in Israel.

First reference: 2 Kings 19:37 / Last reference: Isaiah 37:38

ESAU

of times mentioned: 82
# of MEN by this name: 1

Meaning: Rough

A son of Isaac and Rebekah and the twin brother of Jacob. Esau was a good hunter and the favorite of his father, but he sold his birthright to Jacob for some lentil stew. Then he disturbed his parents by marrying two Hittite women.

Rebekah and Jacob plotted to trick Isaac into giving Jacob the elder son's blessing, and they succeeded, creating bad feelings between the brothers. Because the elder brother, Esau, received a lesser blessing, he plotted to kill Jacob, who had to flee.

Years later, before Jacob returned to his homeland, he sent word to his brother. Fearing Esau's anger, he sent a peace offering of cattle before him. But Esau's rage had cooled, and he greeted him joyfully, refusing the gift Jacob offered.

When the brothers' cattle became too many for them to live on the same land, Esau moved to Mount Seir. His descendants became the Edomites, called after Esau's nickname, which came from the red stew for which he sold his birthright. Edom means "red." Same as Edom.

First reference: Genesis 25:25 / Last reference: Hebrews 12:16 / Key references: Genesis 25:30–33; 27:41; 36:6–8

ESAU

of times mentioned: OT 4

Meaning: Handling; rough (that is, sensibly felt)

A mountain in Edom (another name for Esau). The book of Obadiah speaks of God's judgment falling on the Mount of Esau as it loses its understanding and its people are killed. In the end, God will rule Edom.

First reference: Obadiah 1:8 / Last reference: Obadiah 1:21

ESEK

of times mentioned: OT 1

Meaning: Strife

A well dug by Isaac's servants. When the herdsmen of Gerar found out about it, they tried to claim this well.

Only reference: Genesis 26:20

ESH-BAAL

of times mentioned: 2
# of MEN by this name: 1

Meaning: Man of Baal

A son of Saul, who was Israel's first king.

First reference: 1 Chronicles 8:33 / Last reference: 1 Chronicles 9:39

👥 ESHBAN

\# of times mentioned: 2
\# of MEN by this name: 1

Meaning: Vigorous

A descendant of Seir, who lived in Esau's "land of Edom."

First reference: Genesis 36:26 / Last reference: 1 Chronicles 1:41

👥 ESHCOL

\# of times mentioned: 2
\# of MEN by this name: 1

Meaning: Bunch of grapes

An Amorite confederate of Abram who went with him to recover Abram's nephew Lot from the king of Sodom.

First reference: Genesis 14:13 / Last reference: Genesis 14:24

📍 ESHCOL

\# of times mentioned: OT 4

A brook in a valley of the same name where the spies whom Moses sent into Canaan cut down a large cluster of grapes and other fruit to show the bounty of the land.

First reference: Numbers 13:23 / Last reference: Deuteronomy 1:24

📍 ESHEAN

\# of times mentioned: OT 1

Meaning: Support

A city that became part of the inheritance of the tribe of Judah following the conquest of the Promised Land.

Only reference: Joshua 15:52

👥 ESHEK

\# of times mentioned: 1
\# of MEN by this name: 1

Meaning: Oppression

A descendant of Abraham through Jacob's son Benjamin, through the line of King Saul and his son Jonathan.

Only reference: 1 Chronicles 8:39

📍 ESHTAOL

\# of times mentioned: OT 7

Meaning: Entreaty

A city that became part of the inheritance of the tribe of Judah following the conquest of the Promised Land. Later it became part of the inheritance of Dan when Joshua cast lots in Shiloh to provide territory for the seven tribes that had yet to receive their land.

First reference: Joshua 15:33 / Last reference: Judges 18:11

👥 ESHTEMOA

\# of times mentioned: 2
\# of MEN by this name: 1

Meaning: Obedience

A descendant of Abraham through Jacob's son Judah.

First reference: 1 Chronicles 4:17 / Last reference: 1 Chronicles 4:19

📍 ESHTEMOA

\# of times mentioned: OT 3

Meaning: To hear intelligently (with the sense of obedience)

A Levitical city of the tribe of Judah. David sent some of the spoils from his warfare with the Amalekites to Eshtemoa. Same as Eshtemoh.

First reference: Joshua 21:14 / Last reference: 1 Chronicles 6:57

⚲ ESHTEMOH

of times mentioned: OT 1

A city that became part of the inheritance of the tribe of Judah following the conquest of the Promised Land. See Eshtemoa.

Only reference: Joshua 15:50

👥 ESHTON

of times mentioned: 2
# of MEN by this name: 1

Meaning: Restful

A descendant of Abraham through Jacob's son Judah.

First reference: 1 Chronicles 4:11 / Last reference: 1 Chronicles 4:12

👥 ESLI

of times mentioned: 1
# of MEN by this name: 1

Genealogy of Jesus: Yes (Luke 3:25)

Meaning: Toward Jehovah are my eyes

A descendant of Abraham through Isaac; forebear of Jesus' earthly father, Joseph.

Only reference: Luke 3:25

👥 ESROM

of times mentioned: 3
# of MEN by this name: 1

Genealogy of Jesus: Yes (Matthew 1:3; Luke 3:33)

Meaning: Courtyard

A descendant of Abraham through Isaac; forebear of Jesus' earthly father, Joseph.

First reference: Matthew 1:3 / Last reference: Luke 3:33

👥 ESTHER

of times mentioned: 56
# of WOMEN by this name: 1

The Jewish wife of the Persian king Ahasuerus. Angered by his first wife, Vashti, the king sought a new bride from among the most beautiful women of his kingdom. As a result of this search, he found Esther, fell in love with her, married her, and made her his queen.

Ahasuerus's favorite counselor, Haman, lied to the king and plotted to kill the Jewish people. Esther's cousin Mordecai, who had raised her, convinced the new queen to confront her husband. When she expressed her doubts, he told her: "For if thou altogether holdest thy peace at this time, then shall there enlargement and deliverance arise to the Jews from another place; but thou and thy father's house shall be destroyed: and who knoweth whether thou art come to the kingdom for such a time as this?" (Esther 4:14).

The queen boldly went to the king, though it could have meant her death to appear before him unrequested. She asked that he and Haman come to a banquet. On the second day of the banquet, Esther told the king of Haman's plan to kill her people. Angered, Ahasuerus had Haman killed, and Esther and her people were saved. Same as Hadassah.

First reference: Esther 2:7 / Last reference: Esther 9:32 / Key reference: Esther 4:14–16

👥 ETAM

of times mentioned: 1
# of MEN by this name: 1

Meaning: Hawk ground

A descendant of Abraham through Jacob's son Judah.

Only reference: 1 Chronicles 4:3

⚲ ETAM

of times mentioned: OT 4

Meaning: Hawk ground

1) A rock where Samson lived after he attacked the Philistines for giving his wife to another man. The men of Judah came there and bound him, planning

to hand him over to their Philistine overlords. But when they reached Lehi, the ropes that bound Samson loosened, and he attacked his enemies with the jawbone of a donkey.

First reference: Judges 15:8 / Last reference: Judges 15:11

2) A village that became part of the inheritance of the tribe of Simeon.

Only reference: 1 Chronicles 4:32

3) A city that King Rehoboam fortified to defend Judah.

Only reference: 2 Chronicles 11:6

⦿ ETHAM

of times mentioned: OT 4

A campsite of the Israelites on their way to the Promised Land.

First reference: Exodus 13:20 / Last reference: Numbers 33:8

👥 ETHAN

of times mentioned: 8
# of MEN by this name: 4

Meaning: Permanent

1) The wise man who wrote Psalm 89. His wisdom was surpassed by Solomon's.

First reference: 1 Kings 4:31 / Last reference: Psalm 89 (title)

2) A descendant of Abraham through Jacob's son Judah.

First reference: 1 Chronicles 2:6 / Last reference: 1 Chronicles 2:8

3) A forefather of Asaph, a chief singer in the temple.

Only reference: 1 Chronicles 6:42

4) Another forefather of Asaph, a chief singer in the temple.

First reference: 1 Chronicles 6:44 / Last reference: 1 Chronicles 15:19

👥 ETHBAAL

of times mentioned: 1
# of MEN by this name: 1

Meaning: With Baal

King of the Zidonians and father of Jezebel, the evil queen of Israel's king Ahab.

Only reference: 1 Kings 16:31

⦿ ETHER

of times mentioned: OT 2

Meaning: Abundance

A city that became part of the inheritance of the tribe of Judah following the conquest of the Promised Land. Later it became part of the inheritance of Simeon when Joshua cast lots in Shiloh to provide territory for the seven tribes that had yet to receive their land.

First reference: Joshua 15:42 / Last reference: Joshua 19:7

⦿ ETHIOPIA

of times mentioned: OT 8 / NT 1

A nation south of Egypt, stretching along the Nile River from Aswan to Khartoum. Esther's husband, the Persian king Ahasuerus (also called Xerxes), ruled over Ethiopia, which formed a border of his domain. The eunuch whom the apostle Philip met and baptized on his journey from Jerusalem to Gaza came from Ethiopia and served Candace, the queen of that nation. The word translated "Cush" in modern Bible versions often appears as "Ethiopia" in the King James Version of the Bible. Same as Cush.

First reference: Genesis 2:13 / Last reference: Acts 8:27

👥 ETHNAN

of times mentioned: 1
# of MEN by this name: 1

Meaning: Gift

A descendant of Abraham through Jacob's son Judah.

Only reference: 1 Chronicles 4:7

ETHNI

of times mentioned: 1
# of MEN by this name: 1

Meaning: Munificence

A forefather of Asaph, a chief singer in the temple.

Only reference: 1 Chronicles 6:41

EUBULUS

of times mentioned: 1
# of MEN by this name: 1

Meaning: Good-willer

A Roman Christian who sent greetings to Timothy in Paul's second letter to his "dearly beloved son."

Only reference: 2 Timothy 4:21

EUNICE

of times mentioned:
# of WOMEN by this name: 1

Meaning: Victorious

The Jewish mother of the apostle Paul's protégé Timothy. She was married to a Greek man (Acts 16:1), but Paul described Eunice as a person of "unfeigned faith" (2 Timothy 1:5).

Only reference: 2 Timothy 1:5

EUODIAS

of times mentioned: 1
# of WOMEN by this name: 1

Meaning: Fine traveling

A Christian woman of Philippi who had "laboured with me [Paul] in the gospel" (Philippians 4:3) but who had conflict with another church member, Syntyche. Paul begged them to "be of the same mind in the Lord" (Philippians 4:2).

Only reference: Philippians 4:2

EUPHRATES

of times mentioned: OT 19 / NT 2

Meaning: To break forth; rushing

A river that Genesis 2:14 describes as flowing out of Eden's river. The Euphrates River flows from Turkey to the Persian Gulf and is one of the rivers enclosing Mesopotamia.

God covenanted with Abram that the land from the river of Egypt, on Judah's southwestern border, to the Euphrates would be given to his descendants. The Lord renewed the promise with Joshua as Israel entered the Promised Land.

King Solomon's kingdom stretched as far as the Euphrates River in the north, and King Josiah of Judah fought near the Euphrates with Pharaoh Necho of Egypt.

In the book of Revelation, John describes the vial of wrath that will be poured out on the Euphrates, drying it up.

First reference: Genesis 2:14 / Last reference: Revelation 16:12 / Key references: Genesis 15:18; Joshua 1:4; 1 Chronicles 18:3

EUTYCHUS

of times mentioned: 1
# of MEN by this name: 1

Meaning: Fortunate

A young man of Troas who drifted off to sleep during a late-night sermon of the apostle Paul. Eutychus fell from his window seat three floors to his death. Paul brought him back to life, and the Christians were "not a little comforted" (Acts 20:12).

Only reference: Acts 20:9

EVE

of times mentioned: 4
# of WOMEN by this name: 1

Meaning: Life-giver

Adam's wife, "the mother of all living." Tempted by the snake, Eve ate the fruit of the tree of the knowledge of good and evil and offered it to her husband, who also ate. Suddenly fearful of God because of their sin, they hid from Him. God placed a curse on Adam and Eve. For her part, Eve would suffer greatly during childbirth, desire her husband, and be ruled over by him. God removed the couple from the Garden of Eden.

Eve and Adam had two children named in the Bible—Cain and Abel. After Cain murdered Abel, God gave them another child, Seth.

First reference: Genesis 3:20 / Last reference: 1 Timothy 2:13

EVI

of times mentioned: 2
# of MEN by this name: 1

Meaning: Desirous

A Midianite king killed by the Israelites at God's command.

First reference: Numbers 31:8 / Last reference: Joshua 13:21

EVIL-MERODACH

of times mentioned: 2
# of MEN by this name: 1

Meaning: Soldier of Merodach

Successor to the Babylonian king Nebuchadnezzar. Evil-merodach showed kindness to Judah's second-to-last king, Jehoiachin, who had been imprisoned in the first deportation of Jews to Babylon. Evil-merodach "spoke kindly" to Jehoiachin, "changed his prison garments," and allowed him to eat at the king's table for the rest of his life.

First reference: 2 Kings 25:27 / Last reference: Jeremiah 52:31

EZAR

of times mentioned: 1
# of MEN by this name: 1

Meaning: Treasure

A descendant of Seir, who lived in Esau's "land of Edom."

Only reference: 1 Chronicles 1:38

EZBAI

of times mentioned: 1
# of MEN by this name: 1

Meaning: Hyssop-like

Father of one of King David's valiant warriors.

Only reference: 1 Chronicles 11:37

EZBON

of times mentioned: 2
# of MEN by this name: 2

1) A son of Gad and a grandson of Jacob.

Only reference: Genesis 46:16

2) A descendant of Abraham through Jacob's son Benjamin.

Only reference: 1 Chronicles 7:7

EZEKIAS

of times mentioned: 2
# of MEN by this name: 1

Genealogy of Jesus: Yes (Matthew 1:9–10)

Meaning: Strengthened of God

Greek form of the name Hezekiah, used in the New Testament.

First reference: Matthew 1:9 / Last reference: Matthew 1:10

EZEKIEL

of times mentioned: 2
# of MEN by this name: 1

Meaning: God will strengthen

A priest, the son of Buzi, who was taken into exile at about age twenty-five when Nebuchadnezzar, king of Babylon, carried off most of Jerusalem. When Ezekiel was thirty and still in exile, God came to him in a vision and sent him to the rebellious Israelites as a prophet. The little we know about Ezekiel comes from his prophetic book. A contemporary of Daniel and Jeremiah, he was married, and his wife died before the Babylonians destroyed

Jerusalem. His prophecies focus on judgment for both Israel and the other nations and God's grace and mercy for Israel. He is probably best known for his prophetic vision of the dry bones that came to life.

First reference: Ezekiel 1:3 / Last reference: Ezekiel 24:24

📍 EZEL

of times mentioned: OT 1

Meaning: Departure

A stone where Jonathan met David to warn him to flee from Saul.

Only reference: 1 Samuel 20:19

📍 EZEM

of times mentioned: OT 1

Meaning: Bone

A city that became part of the inheritance of the tribe of Simeon.

Only reference: 1 Chronicles 4:29

👥 EZER

of times mentioned: 9
# of MEN by this name: 6

Meaning: Treasure, help

1) A descendant of Seir, who lived in Esau's "land of Edom."

First reference: Genesis 36:21 / Last reference: 1 Chronicles 1:42

2) A descendant of Abraham through Jacob's son Judah.

Only reference: 1 Chronicles 4:4

3) A descendant of Abraham through Joseph's son Ephraim. He was killed by men of Gath in a dispute over livestock.

Only reference: 1 Chronicles 7:21

4) One of several warriors from the tribe of Gad who left Saul to join David during his conflict with

the king. Ezer and his companions were "men of might. . .whose faces were like the faces of lions" (1 Chronicles 12:8).

Only reference: 1 Chronicles 12:9

5) A man who repaired Jerusalem's walls under Nehemiah.

Only reference: Nehemiah 3:19

6) A priest who helped to dedicate the rebuilt wall of Jerusalem by giving thanks.

Only reference: Nehemiah 12:42

📍 EZION-GABER

of times mentioned: OT 4

Meaning: Backbone of a man

An Edomite seaport that the Israelites used as a campsite on their way to the Promised Land. Jehoshaphat, king of Judah, joined with Ahaziah, king of Israel, to build a fleet in Ezion-gaber, intending the ships to sail for Tarshish. But the ships were broken by the Lord. Same as Ezion-geber.

First reference: Numbers 33:35 / Last reference: 2 Chronicles 20:36

📍 EZION-GEBER

of times mentioned: OT 3

Meaning: Backbone of a man

An Edomite seaport at which King Solomon developed a navy for Israel. King Jehoshaphat of Judah made ships he intended to send to Ophir for gold, but they were broken at Ezion-geber. Same as Ezion-gaber.

First reference: 1 Kings 9:26 / Last reference: 2 Chronicles 8:17

👥 EZRA

of times mentioned: 26
# of MEN by this name: 3

Meaning: Aid

1) A descendant of Abraham through Jacob's son Judah.

Only reference: 1 Chronicles 4:17

2) An Israelite scribe and teacher of the law who returned from the Babylonian Exile along with some priests, Levites, temple servants, and other Israelites. Ezra had received the backing of King Artaxerxes of Persia and returned with money and the temple vessels. Ezra also had the right to appoint magistrates and judges in Israel. When they reached Jerusalem, the officials told Ezra that many men of Israel had intermarried with the people around them and followed their ways. Ezra prayed for the people, read them the law, and called them to confess their sin. All Israel repented and put away their foreign spouses.

First reference: Ezra 7:1 / Last reference: Nehemiah 12:36 / Key reference: Ezra 7:6

3) A priest who returned to Jerusalem under Zerubbabel.

Only reference: Nehemiah 12:1

EZRI

of times mentioned: 1
# of MEN by this name: 1

Meaning: Helpful

A superintendent of agriculture who served under King David.

Only reference: 1 Chronicles 27:26

📍 FAIR HAVENS

of times mentioned: NT 1

An anchorage on Crete, near Lasea, where Paul and his companions stopped on their way to Rome. Though Paul warned against putting to sea again, Fair Havens was not a good place to stay for the winter. The vessel set off again and was shipwrecked.

Only reference: Acts 27:8

📍 FELIX

of times mentioned: 9
# of MEN by this name: 1

Meaning: Happy

Governor of Judea before whom Paul appeared after the Roman guard rescued him from his appearance at the Jewish council. Felix, hoping for a bribe and wanting to please the Jews, delayed in making a decision in Paul's case. When his successor, Porcius Festus, came, they heard his case together and sent Paul to Caesar in Rome.

First reference: Acts 23:24 / Last reference: Acts 25:14 / Key reference: Acts 24:24–26

👥 FESTUS

of times mentioned: 13
# of MEN by this name: 1

Meaning: Festal

The governor of Judea who replaced Felix. He heard Paul's case and determined to send Paul to Rome, since the apostle had appealed to Caesar. When Festus brought the case before King Agrippa, Agrippa agreed. Also called Porcius Festus.

First reference: Acts 24:27 / Last reference: Acts 26:32 / Key reference: Acts 25:24–25

👥 FORTUNATUS

of times mentioned: 1
# of MEN by this name: 1

Meaning: Fortunate

A Corinthian Christian who visited the apostle Paul in Ephesus and "refreshed [Paul's] spirit" (1 Corinthians 16:18).

Only reference: 1 Corinthians 16:17

👥 GAAL

of times mentioned: 9
# of MEN by this name: 1

Meaning: Loathing

A would-be ruler who got the men of Shechem drunk and convinced them to rise up against their king, Abimelech. Zebul, the ruler of the city, warned the king of their planned ambush. Abimelech stealthily returned to his city, fought, and won. Gaal and his relatives were banished from Shechem.

First reference: Judges 9:26 / Last reference: Judges 9:41

◉ GAASH

of times mentioned: OT 4

Meaning: A quaking

Joshua was buried on the north side of this hill in Mount Ephraim. One of David's valiant warriors was Hurai of the brooks of Gaash.

First reference: Joshua 24:30 / Last reference: 1 Chronicles 11:32

◉ GABA

of times mentioned: OT 3

Meaning: A hillock

A city that became part of the inheritance of Benjamin when Joshua cast lots in Shiloh to provide territory for the seven tribes that had yet to receive their land. Exiles returned here from Babylon. Same as Geba.

First reference: Joshua 18:24 / Last reference: Nehemiah 7:30

👥 GABBAI

of times mentioned: 1
# of MEN by this name: 1

Meaning: Collective

A Jewish exile from the tribe of Benjamin who resettled Jerusalem.

Only reference: Nehemiah 11:8

◉ GABBATHA

of times mentioned: NT 1

Meaning: The knoll

Also called the Pavement, Gabbatha was the place where Pilate judged cases. Here he heard the Jews' complaints against Jesus and gave Him over to be crucified.

Only reference: John 19:13

👥 GAD

of times mentioned: 19
# of MEN by this name: 2

Meaning: Attack

1) A son of Jacob and Leah's handmaid Zilpah. At Gad's birth Leah said, "A troop cometh," so she gave him a name meaning "attack." Jacob prophesied that a troop would overcome Gad but that he would at last overcome.

First reference: Genesis 30:11 / Last reference: 1 Chronicles 5:11

2) A prophet who warned David, when he ran from Saul, to leave Moab and return to Judea. When King David sinned by taking a census of the people, Gad came to him with God's choices for punishment and a way to end it.

First reference: 1 Samuel 22:5 / Last reference: 2 Chronicles 29:25 / Key references: 1 Samuel 22:5; 1 Chronicles 21:9–14

◉ GADARA

of times mentioned: NT 3

The land of the Gadarenes. The name Gadara never actually appears in scripture, only the name of its people. Here Jesus healed the man with a legion of unclean spirits who lived among the tombs. Despite this amazing miracle, the Gadarenes requested that Jesus and His disciples leave their land.

First reference: Mark 5:1 / Last reference: Luke 8:37

👥 GADDI

of times mentioned: 1
# of MEN by this name: 1

Meaning: Fortunate

One of twelve spies sent by Moses to spy out the land of Canaan.

Only reference: Numbers 13:11

◉ GADDIEL

of times mentioned: 1

# of MEN by this name: 1
Meaning: Fortune of God

One of twelve spies sent by Moses to spy out the land of Canaan.

Only reference: Numbers 13:10

GADI

of times mentioned: 2
# of MEN by this name: 1

Meaning: Fortunate

Father of Menahem, who killed King Shallum of Israel and reigned in his place.

First reference: 2 Kings 15:14 / Last reference: 2 Kings 15:17

 GAHAM

of times mentioned: 1
# of MEN by this name: 1

Meaning: Flame

A nephew of Abraham, born to his brother Nahor's concubine, Reumah.

Only reference: Genesis 22:24

GAHAR

of times mentioned: 2
# of MEN by this name: 1

Meaning: Lurker

Forefather of an exiled family that returned to Judah under Zerubbabel.

First reference: Ezra 2:47 / Last reference: Nehemiah 7:49

GAIUS

of times mentioned: 5
# of MEN by this name: 4

1) A man from Macedonia and a traveling companion of the apostle Paul. Gaius was caught in a riot started against Paul by Ephesian idol makers.

Only reference: Acts 19:29

2) A man from Derbe and a traveling companion of the apostle Paul.

Only reference: Acts 20:4

3) A Corinthian Christian who hosted the apostle Paul when he wrote the letter to the Romans. Gaius was one of a handful of believers whom Paul personally baptized.

First reference: Romans 16:23 / Last reference: 1 Corinthians 1:14

4) The "wellbeloved" of John, addressee of John's third letter.

Only reference: 3 John 1:1

GALAL

of times mentioned: 3
# of MEN by this name: 2

Meaning: Great

1) A Jewish exile from the tribe of Levi who resettled Jerusalem.

Only reference: 1 Chronicles 9:15

2) Forefather of a Jewish exile who was chosen by lot to resettle Jerusalem.

First reference: 1 Chronicles 9:16 / Last reference: Nehemiah 11:17

GALATIA

of times mentioned: NT 6

A Roman province in the center of Asia Minor. For a time, the Holy Spirit forbade Paul and Silas to preach here. But later, on his third missionary journey, Paul strengthened the disciples in the provinces of Galatia and Phrygia. The apostle reminded the church of Galatia that he first preached to them because of an illness he suffered (Galatians 4:13).

Paul wrote an epistle to the Galatians to establish the authority for his apostleship, to counter the influence of the law-bound Judaizers who had swayed some Galatians away from the Gospel, and to encourage these Christians to believe in salvation by grace.

First reference: Acts 16:6 / Last reference: 1 Peter 1:1

♀ GALEED

of times mentioned: OT 2

Meaning: Heap of testimony

Jacob's name for the memorial mound that commemorated his covenant with his father-in-law, Laban. Laban called it Jegar-sahadutha. Same as Jegar-sahadutha and Mizpah (1).

First reference: Genesis 31:47 / Last reference: Genesis 31:48

♀ GALILEE

of times mentioned: OT 6 / NT 66

Meaning: A circle

An area in the north of Israel that may originally have been part of the inheritance of the tribe of Naphtali. Israel did not overpower the people who inhabited the area, so it became a racially mixed area, earning it the name "Galilee of the Gentiles."

When King Solomon gave twenty Galilean towns to Hiram, king of Tyre, the area also included the tribe of Asher's land. Same as Cabul (2).

Following the Jews' return from exile, this name referred to a much larger territory that included the northernmost of the three provinces of Palestine.

King Tiglath-pileser of Assyria overthrew Pekah, king of Israel; the victor captured Galilee and transported captives to his own land.

In Nazareth, a city of Galilee, Mary received the news that she would bear the Messiah. Following Jesus' birth and the family's flight into Egypt, Joseph received an angelic message that he was to return to Israel. He brought his family to Galilee to avoid the rule of Archelaeus, a son of Herod the Great. Jesus grew up in Nazareth but moved to another Galilean town, Capernaum, at the beginning of His ministry, to fulfill Isaiah's prophecy that the lands of Zebulun (the tribe of Nazareth) and Naphtali (the tribe of Capernaum) would see a great light.

At the Sea of Galilee, Jesus called the disciples Simon, Andrew, James, John, and Philip. He preached to the people of Galilee, drawing crowds to Himself. In Cana of Galilee, He performed the first miracle, followed by healings. When the Jews sought His life, at the time of the Feast of Tabernacles, Jesus remained for a while in Galilee. When He finally went to Jerusalem, many questioned whether a prophet would come from Galilee. At the Last Supper, Jesus promised that after His resurrection He would go before His disciples to Galilee.

When the Jews wanted to kill Jesus, Pilate, discovering that Jesus was from Galilee, sent Him to its tetrarch, Herod Antipas, to be judged. But Herod, unwilling to take on this hot issue, sent Jesus back to Pilate for judgment.

When the women who had followed Jesus from Galilee discovered that His body was missing from the tomb, both an angel and the Lord gave them a message that the disciples should return to Galilee, where they would see Him again. When they obeyed, they were reunited with the Master.

First reference: Joshua 20:7 / Last reference: Acts 13:31 / Key references: 1 Kings 9:10–13; 2 Kings 15:29; Matthew 4:12–16

♀ GALLIM

of times mentioned: OT 2

Meaning: Springs

Hometown of Mical's second husband, Phalti. Isaiah foretold that this Benjaminite city would rejoice at the Assyrians' destruction.

First reference: 1 Samuel 25:44 / Last reference: Isaiah 10:30

♣ GALLIO

of times mentioned: 3
# of MEN by this name: 1

Deputy (proconsul) of Achaia who refused to hear the case when the Jews accused Paul of breaking the law.

First reference: Acts 18:12 / Last reference: Acts 18:17

♣ GAMALIEL

of times mentioned: 7
# of MEN by this name: 2

Meaning: Reward of God

1) Leader of the tribe of Manasseh under Moses during the Exodus.

First reference: Numbers 1:10 / Last reference: Numbers 10:23

2) A Pharisee and doctor of the law who warned the Jews to leave the apostles alone. He was Paul's teacher.

First reference: Acts 5:34 / Last reference: Acts 22:3

GAMUL

of times mentioned: 1
# of MEN by this name: 1

Meaning: Rewarded

One of twenty-four priests in David's time who was chosen by lot to serve in the tabernacle.

Only reference: 1 Chronicles 24:17

GAREB

of times mentioned: 2
# of MEN by this name: 1

Meaning: Scabby

One of King David's valiant warriors.

First reference: 2 Samuel 23:38 / Last reference: 1 Chronicles 11:40

● GAREB

of times mentioned: OT 1

Meaning: Scabby

A hill that Jeremiah foretold will be used as a measurement for the final rebuilding of Jerusalem when the city is restored.

Only reference: Jeremiah 31:39

GASHMU

of times mentioned: 1
# of MEN by this name: 1

Meaning: A shower

A man who falsely reported to Sanballat that Nehemiah and his men meant to rebel.

Only reference: Nehemiah 6:6

GATAM

of times mentioned: 3
# of MEN by this name: 1

A descendant of Abraham's grandson Esau, whose blessing as older brother was taken by the scheming Jacob.

First reference: Genesis 36:11 / Last reference: 1 Chronicles 1:36

● GATH

of times mentioned: OT 33

Meaning: Treading out grapes; a winepress

One of the few Anakite cities in which Joshua did not entirely eradicate that people. But Gath did not remain under Israel's control, instead becoming one of Philistia's five most important cities. During the time of the judge Samuel, the Philistines captured the ark of the covenant and it was moved to Gath. After the people of that city were afflicted with tumors for their possession of the ark, they sent it to Ekron. During Samuel's rule, Gath was returned to Israel (1 Samuel 7:14).

Goliath came from this city. After David killed the giant, Israel's troops chased the Philistines as far as Gath. But when Saul sought to kill David, Israel's popular warrior fled to Gath and pretended he was mad. King Achish objected to having him there, so David escaped to the cave of Adullam. Eventually David and his troops returned to Gath and served the Philistine king.

Shimei, who had cursed King David and been forgiven, was required by King Solomon to stay in Jerusalem, because David had warned his son against the man. When Shimei traveled to Gath to recover an escaped slave, Solomon had Shimei executed.

Ownership of Gath went back and forth between Judah and its enemies. King Rehoboam of Judah built up the defenses of the city to defend his country, but Hazael, king of Aram, captured it. King Uzziah of Judah conquered Gath again and broke down the city walls.

First reference: Joshua 11:22 / Last reference: Micah 1:10 / Key references: 1 Samuel 21:10; 27:2; 1 Chronicles 18:1

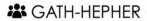 GATH-HEPHER

of times mentioned: OT 1

Meaning: Winepress of the well

Hometown of the prophet Jonah.

Only reference: 2 Kings 14:25

GATH-RIMMON

of times mentioned: OT 4

Meaning: Winepress of the pomegranate

1) A city that became part of the inheritance of Dan when Joshua cast lots in Shiloh to provide territory for the seven tribes that had yet to receive their land. It was later one of the forty-eight cities given to the Levites as God had commanded.

First reference: Joshua 19:45 / Last reference: Joshua 21:24

2) One of the forty-eight cities given to the Levites as God had commanded. Gath-rimmon was given to them by the tribe of Manasseh.

First reference: Joshua 21:25 / Last reference: 1 Chronicles 6:69

GAZA

of times mentioned: OT 18 / NT 1

Meaning: Strong

1) An ancient Canaanite city that was conquered by the Philistines and became one of their most important cities. Joshua subdued Gaza, and it became part of the inheritance of Judah, but some Canaanites remained in the city.

Samson tore loose Gaza's city gates, where his enemies lay in wait to attack him. After the Philistines finally captured him and made him their slave, they took him to Gaza. As his hair grew, Samson regained his strength and pulled down the pillars of the temple of Dagon, killing himself and the worshippers.

King Hezekiah of Judah defeated the Philistines as far as Gaza. The prophets foresaw God's judgment of the Philistines and Gaza's destruction.

On the road to Gaza, Philip met the Ethiopian eunuch and led him to the Lord.

First reference: Genesis 10:19 / Last reference: Acts 8:26 / Key references: Judges 16:1, 21

2) A city of the tribe of Ephraim. At the time of Gideon, the Midianites destroyed the land of Israel up to Gaza.

First reference: Judges 6:4 / Last reference: 1 Chronicles 7:28

GAZER

of times mentioned: OT 2

Meaning: Something cut off; a portion

God commanded David to fight the Philistines from Gibeon to this city. Same as Gezer.

First reference: 2 Samuel 5:25 / Last reference: 1 Chronicles 14:16

GAZEZ

of times mentioned: 2
# of MEN by this name: 2

Meaning: Shearer

1) A descendant of Abraham through Jacob's son Judah.

Only reference: 1 Chronicles 2:46

2) Another descendant of Abraham through Jacob's son Judah.

Only reference: 1 Chronicles 2:46

GAZZAM

of times mentioned: 2
# of MEN by this name: 1

Meaning: Devourer

Forefather of an exiled family that returned to Judah under Zerubbabel.

First reference: Ezra 2:48 / Last reference: Nehemiah 7:51

GEBA

of times mentioned: OT 12

Meaning: A hillock

One of the forty-eight cities given to the Levites as God had commanded. Geba was given to them by the tribe of Benjamin. When the city was in Philistine hands, Jonathan attacked this garrison, and David fought the Philistines up to Geba. King Josiah of Judah defiled Geba, which had become a place of pagan worship. After the return from exile, the people of this city lived at Michmash, Aija, and Bethel. Same as Gaba.

First reference: Joshua 21:17 / Last reference: Zechariah 14:10

GEBAL

of times mentioned: OT 2

Meaning: Chain of hills; mountain

1) A nation near the Dead Sea that joined other persistent enemies of Israel in opposing God's people.

Only reference: Psalm 83:7

2) Another name for the Phoenician city of Byblos, which traded extensively in papyrus scrolls.

Only reference: Ezekiel 27:9

GEBER

of times mentioned: 2
# of MEN by this name: 2

Meaning: Warrior

1) Father of one of King Solomon's twelve officials over provisions.

Only reference: 1 Kings 4:13

2) One of King Solomon's twelve officials over provisions.

Only reference: 1 Kings 4:19

GEBIM

of times mentioned: OT 1

Meaning: Cisterns

A village above Jerusalem. Isaiah foresaw Gebim attempting to hide from God's wrath.

Only reference: Isaiah 10:31

GEDALIAH

of times mentioned: 32
# of MEN by this name: 5

Meaning: God has become great

1) The ruler appointed by Nebuchadnezzar over the remnant of Jews left behind in Judah at the time of the Babylonian Exile. When the prophet Jeremiah was freed from prison, he chose to stay with Gedaliah and the people of Judah instead of heading for Babylon. Gedaliah persuaded the captains of Judah not to worry about serving the Chaldeans. Though one of his captains warned about a plot against him, Gedaliah refused to believe it. Ishmael, the son of Nethaniah, another captain, killed Gedaliah and all his men with him at Mizpah.

First reference: 2 Kings 25:22 / Last reference: Jeremiah 43:6 / Key references: Jeremiah 40:6–9, 16; 41:2

2) A son of King David's musician Jeduthun, "who prophesied with a harp, to give thanks and to praise the LORD" (1 Chronicles 25:3).

First reference: 1 Chronicles 25:3 / Last reference: 1 Chronicles 25:9

3) An exiled Israelite priest who married a "strange" (foreign) woman.

Only reference: Ezra 10:18

4) Grandfather of the prophet Zephaniah.

Only reference: Zephaniah 1:1

5) A prince of Judah who sought to have King Zedekiah kill Jeremiah because of his negative prophecy.

Only reference: Jeremiah 38:1

GEDEON

of times mentioned: 1
# of MEN by this name: 1

Meaning: Warrior

Greek form of the name Gideon, used in the New Testament.

Only reference: Hebrews 11:32

📍 GEDER

of times mentioned: OT 1

Meaning: A circumvallation or siege wall

A Canaanite city on the western side of the Jordan River that Joshua and his men overthrew.

Only reference: Joshua 12:13

📍 GEDERAH

of times mentioned: OT 1

Meaning: Enclosure (especially for flocks)

A city that became part of the inheritance of the tribe of Judah following the conquest of the Promised Land.

Only reference: Joshua 15:36

📍 GEDEROTH

of times mentioned: OT 2

Meaning: Enclosures (especially for flocks)

A city that became part of the inheritance of the tribe of Judah following the conquest of the Promised Land. During the reign of King Ahaz of Judah, it was one of the cities of the southern low country of Judah that was invaded and occupied by the Philistines.

First reference: Joshua 15:41 / Last reference: 2 Chronicles 28:18

📍 GEDEROTHAIM

of times mentioned: OT 1

Meaning: Double wall

A city that became part of the inheritance of the tribe of Judah following the conquest of the Promised Land.

Only reference: Joshua 15:36

GEDOR

of times mentioned: 4
# of MEN by this name: 2

Meaning: Enclosure

1) A leader of the tribe of Benjamin who lived in Jerusalem.

First reference: 1 Chronicles 8:31 / Last reference: 1 Chronicles 9:37

2) A descendant of Abraham through Jacob's son Judah.

First reference: 1 Chronicles 4:4 / Last reference: 1 Chronicles 4:18

📍 GEDOR

of times mentioned: OT 3

Meaning: Enclosure

1) A city that became part of the inheritance of the tribe of Judah following the conquest of the Promised Land.

Only reference: Joshua 15:58

2) Hometown of Jehoram, whose sons Joelah and Zebadiah joined David's mighty men at Ziklag.

Only reference: 1 Chronicles 12:7

3) A valley that the descendants of Simeon conquered, displacing the Hamites and Meunites, so they would have pastures for their flocks.

Only reference: 1 Chronicles 4:39

👥 GEHAZI

of times mentioned: 12
# of MEN by this name: 1

Meaning: Valley of a visionary

The prophet Elisha's servant, who pointed out to Elisha that the Shunnamite woman had no son. Elisha promised her one in a year. Gehazi later laid Elisha's staff on her son in an attempt to bring him back to life. After Elisha healed the Syrian captain Naaman of leprosy and refused gifts, Gehazi followed him to elicit money and clothing from him. For this, Gehazi was made leprous.

First reference: 2 Kings 4:12 / Last reference:
2 Kings 8:5 / Key references: 2 Kings 4:14; 5:25–27

📍 GELILOTH

of times mentioned: OT 1

Meaning: Circles

A place on the border of the tribe of Benjamin's
territory.

Only reference: Joshua 18:17

👥 GEMALLI

of times mentioned: 1
# of MEN by this name: 1

Meaning: Camel driver

Father of one of the twelve spies sent by Moses to
spy out the land of Canaan.

Only reference: Numbers 13:12

👥 GEMARIAH

of times mentioned: 5
# of MEN by this name: 2

Meaning: God has perfected

1) A scribe and prince of Judah in whose room
Baruch read the prophecies of Jeremiah. Son of
Shaphan.

First reference: Jeremiah 36:10 / Last reference:
Jeremiah 36:25

2) A messenger who took Jeremiah's letter to the
exiles in Babylon. Son of Hilkiah.

Only reference: Jeremiah 29:3

📍 GENNESARET

of times mentioned: NT 3

A plain along the northwest border of the Sea of
Galilee. The Lake of Gennesaret is another name
for the Sea of Galilee.

First reference: Matthew 14:34 / Last reference:
Luke 5:1

👥 GENUBATH

of times mentioned: 2
# of MEN by this name: 1

Meaning: Theft

Son of Hadad the Edomite, Solomon's adversary
and leader of a marauding band.

Only reference: 1 Kings 11:20

👥 GERA

of times mentioned: 9
# of MEN by this name: 4

Meaning: Grain

1) A son of Benjamin. He was a left-handed man.

Only reference: Genesis 46:21

2) Father of Ehud, a left-handed man who became
Israel's deliverer.

Only reference: Judges 3:15

3) Father of Shimei. Shimei cursed David but later
recognized him as king.

First reference: 2 Samuel 16:5 / Last reference:
1 Kings 2:8

4) A son of Bela, Benjamin's oldest son.

First reference: 1 Chronicles 8:3 / Last reference:
1 Chronicles 8:7

📍 GERAR

of times mentioned: OT 10

Meaning: A rolling country

A Canaanite city where Abraham and Sarah lived.
Because the couple had said they were brother and
sister, Abimelech, king of Gerar, took Sarah as one
of his women. When God revealed their marriage
to Abimelech, he gave Abraham and Sarah many
gifts and told them to live wherever they wanted
in his land.

Isaac lived in Gerar at God's command. When
Abimelech's people became jealous over Abraham's
wells, the king of Gerar told Isaac to leave. The patriarch settled in the valley of Gerar, but the herdsmen there demanded the wells Isaac's servants had

dug, so Isaac moved again.

King Asa of Judah conquered the cities around Gerar.

First reference: Genesis 10:19 / Last reference: 2 Chronicles 14:14

📍 GERIZIM

of times mentioned: OT 4

Meaning: Cut up

A mountain in Samaria, near Shechem, where the Israelite leaders were to bless the people after they entered the Promised Land. From this mountain Jotham also spoke to the men of Shechem about making Abimelech their king.

First reference: Deuteronomy 11:29 / Last reference: Judges 9:7

👥 GERSHOM

of times mentioned: 14
# of MEN by this name: 4

Meaning: Refugee

1) Moses and Zipporah's firstborn son.

First reference: Exodus 2:22 / Last reference: 1 Chronicles 26:24

2) Firstborn son of Levi. Same as Gershon.

First reference: 1 Chronicles 6:16 / Last reference: 1 Chronicles 15:7

3) A Jewish exile who returned to Judah from Babylon under Ezra.

Only reference: Ezra 8:2

4) Father of Jonathan. Jonathan was a priest to the tribe of Dan when they worshipped graven images.

Only reference: Judges 18:30

👥 GERSHON

of times mentioned: 18
# of MEN by this name: 1

Meaning: Refugee

Firstborn son of Levi. From his line came the Libnites and Shimites. His clan carried the curtains of the tabernacle, its cords, and the equipment. Same as Gershom (2).

First reference: Genesis 46:11 / Last reference: 1 Chronicles 23:6 / Key reference: Genesis 46:11

👥 GESHAM

of times mentioned: 1
# of MEN by this name: 1

Meaning: Lumpish

A descendant of Abraham through Jacob's son Judah.

Only reference: 1 Chronicles 2:47

👥 GESHEM

of times mentioned: 3
# of MEN by this name: 1

Meaning: A shower

An Arabian who opposed Nehemiah's rebuilding of the walls of Jerusalem.

First reference: Nehemiah 2:19 / Last reference: Nehemiah 6:2

📍 GESHUR

of times mentioned: OT 8

Meaning: Bridge

Maacah, daughter of the Syrian king of Geshur, married David and bore him a son, Absalom. After killing his half brother Amnon, Absalom fled to Geshur for three years. When King David commanded that his son return to Jerusalem, Joab traveled to Geshur and brought Absalom back.

First reference: 2 Samuel 3:3 / Last reference: 1 Chronicles 3:2

👥 GETHER

of times mentioned: 2
# of MEN by this name: 1

A descendant of Noah through his son Shem.

First reference: Genesis 10:23 / Last reference: 1 Chronicles 1:17

📍 GETHSEMANE

of times mentioned: NT 2

Meaning: Oil press

A garden across the Kidron Valley from Jerusalem, on the Mount of Olives. Jesus brought His disciples to Gethsemane, where He prayed, asking the Father to take the cup of crucifixion from Him. Despite His deep sorrow, Jesus accepted His Father's will, while His nearby disciples, Peter, James, and John, fell asleep. An armed crowd came to Gethsemane, and Jesus was arrested after Judas betrayed Him with a kiss. The disciples fled as their Master was led away to face the Sanhedrin.

First reference: Matthew 26:36 / Last reference: Mark 14:32

👥 GEUEL

of times mentioned: 1
# of MEN by this name: 1

Meaning: Majesty of God

A man from the tribe of Gad sent by Moses to spy out the land of Canaan.

Only reference: Numbers 13:15

📍 GEZER

of times mentioned: OT 13

Meaning: Something cut off; a portion

A Canaanite city on the west side of the Jordan River whose king, Horam, fought against Joshua and his people at Lachish. Israel killed all of Horam's troops and conquered the city. Gezer fell to the lot of Ephraim, but that tribe did not drive out the Canaanites, only made them do forced labor for Israel. Ephraim gave Gezer to the Levites as a city of refuge as God had commanded. During King David's reign, war erupted with the Philistines at Gezer, and these enemies of Israel were conquered.

The pharaoh of Egypt, King Solomon's father-in-law, conquered Gezer, taking it from the Canaanites

and burning the city. Then he gave it as a present or dowry to his daughter. Solomon rebuilt and fortified the city. Same as Gazer.

First reference: Joshua 10:33 / Last reference: 1 Chronicles 20:4 / Key reference: 1 Kings 9:15–17

📍 GIAH

of times mentioned: OT 1

Meaning: A fountain

A place near the wilderness of Gibeon where Abner attempted to make peace between his tribe (the tribe of Benjamin) and Joab, commander of King David's troops.

Only reference: 2 Samuel 2:24

👥 GIBBAR

of times mentioned: 1
# of MEN by this name: 1

Meaning: Warrior

Forefather of an exiled family that returned to Judah under Zerubbabel.

Only reference: Ezra 2:20

📍 GIBBETHON

of times mentioned: OT 6

Meaning: A hilly spot

A city that became part of the inheritance of Dan when Joshua cast lots in Shiloh to provide territory for the seven tribes that had yet to receive their land. One of the forty-eight cities given to the Levites as God had commanded, Gibbethon was given to them by the tribe of Dan.

The Philistines controlled Gibbethon when Baasha killed King Nadab of Israel, who was besieging the city, then took his throne. Later, Zimri murdered Baasha's son, King Elah, in an attempt to make himself king. Omri, Israel's battle commander, withdrew from Gibbethon and laid siege to Zimri's capital of Tirzah.

First reference: Joshua 19:44 / Last reference: 1 Kings 16:17

GIBEA

of times mentioned: 1
# of MEN by this name: 1

Meaning: A hill

A descendant of Abraham through Jacob's son Judah.

Only reference: 1 Chronicles 2:49

◉ GIBEAH

of times mentioned: OT 48

Meaning: A hillock

A city that became part of the inheritance of the tribe of Judah following the conquest of the Promised Land. Scripture implies that it became part of the inheritance of Benjamin when Joshua cast lots in Shiloh to provide territory for the seven tribes that had yet to receive their land.

The wickedness of the men of Gibeah was indicated by their attempt to abuse a Levite, a visitor to their city. When his host would not allow it, the Levite sent his concubine out to them. They sexually abused and killed her. That Levite roused Israel against Gibeah. After a three-day battle, the Israelites withdrew to Baal-tamar, drawing the Benjaminites out of Gibeah. Then the Israelites entered the city and conquered it. The Israelites outside the city surrounded their enemies as they fled, and Israel won the battle.

Gibeah was Saul's home, and the book of 1 Samuel often places him there. Hosea several times refers to the sinfulness of the incident in Judges. Same as Gibeath.

First reference: Joshua 15:57 / Last reference: Hosea 10:9 / Key reference: Judges 19:1–20:48

◉ GIBEATH

of times mentioned: OT 1

Meaning: Hilliness

A city that became part of the inheritance of Benjamin when Joshua cast lots in Shiloh to provide territory for the seven tribes that had yet to receive their land. Same as Gibeah.

Only reference: Joshua 18:28

◉ GIBEON

of times mentioned: OT 35

Meaning: Hilly

This Hivite city's wily leaders saw that the invading Israelites were a danger and sent representatives to Joshua, who tricked him into believing they came from a distant country that wanted to make peace with Israel. After Joshua made an agreement with them, he discoverd they were near neighbors.

The Gibeonites called on Joshua to defend them against five Amorite kings who besieged their city because they had made peace with Israel. Joshua kept his agreement and supported Gibeon in battle. When Joshua asked God to make the sun stand still so the battle could continue, it remained in the sky until they had avenged their allies. Gibeon was the only city that made peace with Israel as the Israelites conquered the Promised Land.

Gibeon became part of the inheritance of Benjamin when Joshua cast lots in Shiloh to provide territory for the seven tribes that had yet to receive their land. It later became one of the forty-eight cities given to the Levites as God had commanded.

At Gibeon, Joab, David's battle commander, fought and overcame Abner, commander of Saul's host. But Abner killed Joab's brother Asahel, beginning a feud that brought about Abner's death. Later, on a stone at Gibeon, Joab killed Amasa, commander of Daid's army.

Before the Jerusalem temple was built, sacrifices were made to the Lord at Gibeon. Solomon sacrificed here after he became king.

First reference: Joshua 9:3 / Last reference: Jeremiah 41:16 / Key reference: 1 Kings 3:4–5

GIDDALTI

of times mentioned: 2
# of MEN by this name: 1

Meaning: I have made great

A son of King David's musician Heman, who was "under the hands of [his] father for song in the house of the LORD" (1 Chronicles 25:6).

First reference: 1 Chronicles 25:4 / Last reference: 1 Chronicles 25:29

👥 GIDDEL

of times mentioned: 4
# of MEN by this name: 2

Meaning: Stout

1) Forefather of an exiled family that returned to Judah under Zerubbabel.

First reference: Ezra 2:47 / Last reference: Nehemiah 7:49

2) Forefather of an exiled family—former servants of Solomon—that returned to Judah under Zerubbabel.

First reference: Ezra 2:56 / Last reference: Nehemiah 7:58

👥 GIDEON

of times mentioned: 39
# of MEN by this name: 1

Meaning: Warrior

The fifth judge of Israel, whom God raised up to lead his nation against the Midianites. The angel of the Lord appeared to Gideon when he was hiding his threshing from the enemy, told him God was with him, and called him a "mighty man of valour." Gideon's many doubts did not keep him from obeying God. He made an offering then tore down the altar to Baal and cut down its grove, for which the men of his town wanted to kill him.

The Spirit of God came upon Gideon, and he sent to the tribes of Manasseh, Asher, Zebulun, and Naphtali, who came to him. Doubtful that God would save Israel, several times Gideon sought proof by placing a fleece on the ground and asking God to make either the fleece or ground wet; every time God answered his request. When Israel gathered against Midian, God reduced Gideon's forces, cutting out the fearful and identifying the rest by the way they drank water. Gideon attacked Midian with only three hundred men. Holding trumpets and pitchers filled with lamps, the men drew near the Midianite camp. They blew the trumpets and broke the pitchers, and their enemy fled. Gideon and his troops followed, capturing two princes and two kings and killing them. Same as Gedeon, Jerubbaal, and Jerubbesheth.

First reference: Judges 6:11 / Last reference: Judges 8:35 / Key references: Judges 6:11; 7:6–7, 20–22

👥 GIDEONI

of times mentioned: 5
# of MEN by this name: 1

Meaning: Warlike

Father of Abidan, a captain of the Benjaminites who helped Moses take a census and lead his people toward the Promised Land.

First reference: Numbers 1:11 / Last reference: Numbers 10:24

📍 GIDOM

of times mentioned: OT 1

Meaning: A cutting (that is, desolation)

After the men of Gibeah abused and killed a visiting Levite's concubine, the Israelites rose up against the tribe of Benjamin, chased them, and fought them as far as Gidom, killing two thousand men.

Only reference: Judges 20:45

📍 GIHON

of times mentioned: OT 6

Meaning: Stream

1) An Ethiopian river that was one of the four fed by Eden's river.

Only reference: Genesis 2:13

2) A spring near Jerusalem where Solomon was anointed king by Zadok the priest at King David's command. King Hezekiah, threatened by war with Babylon, cut a shaft that redirected the water of this spring directly into Jerusalem.

First reference: 1 Kings 1:33 / Last reference: 2 Chronicles 33:14

👥 GILALAI

of times mentioned: 1
# of MEN by this name: 1

Meaning: Dungy

A priest who helped to dedicate the rebuilt walls of Jerusalem by playing a musical instrument.

Only reference: Nehemiah 12:36

♀ GILBOA

of times mentioned: OT 8

Meaning: Fountain of ebullition

A mountain southeast of the city of Jezreel (2). On Mount Gilboa, the Philistines fought and killed the Israelites in their last battle with King Saul. King Saul's sons died in battle. When the king realized he would lose the battle, he killed himself there.

First reference: 1 Samuel 28:4 / Last reference: 1 Chronicles 10:8

👥 GILEAD

of times mentioned: 13
# of MEN by this name: 3

Meaning: Heap of testimony

1) A descendant of Abraham through Joseph's son Manasseh.

First reference: Numbers 26:29 / Last reference: 1 Chronicles 7:17

2) Father of Israel's ninth judge, Jephthah, by a relationship with a prostitute.

First reference: Judges 11:1 / Last reference: Judges 11:2

3) A descendant of Abraham through Jacob's son Gad.

Only reference: 1 Chronicles 5:14

♀ GILEAD

of times mentioned: OT 87

Meaning: Probably derived from "heap of testimony"

1) From this mountainous area east of the Jordan River, sometimes called Mount Gilead, came the Ishmaelite spice merchants who took Joseph to Egypt as a slave. Gilead was well known for its trade in spices and medicinal herbs. In perhaps the best-known reference to this, Jeremiah ironically asked, "Is there no balm in Gilead?" (Jeremiah 8:22).

Here Jacob fled when he left his father-in-law, Laban.

Before the Israelites entered the Promised Land, Gilead was ruled by Og, king of Bashan, and Sihon, king of the Amorites. Before they entered the Promised Land, Reuben and Gad requested that Moses allot them the rich pasturelands of Gilead as their inheritance, since these tribes owned many cattle. Manasseh inherited the northernmost area of Gilead and dispossessed the Amorites who lived there.

In the time of the judges, the Ammonites camped in Gilead while the Israelites gathered at Mizpeh. The Israelites called on the outcast Jephthah to command them, and he led their troops to victory in battle. Later he led the men of Gilead in battle against Ephraim.

Abner, commander of Saul's army, made Saul's son Ish-bosheth king of Gilead after his father's death. But Ish-bosheth ruled only two years before David was made king. The Syrian king Hazael conquered Gilead, taking it from Jehu, king of Israel.

The prophet Hosea denounced Gilead for its wickedness. But Zechariah promised that God would bring so many of His scattered people back to the land that they would not all fit there.

First reference: Genesis 31:21 / Last reference: Zechariah 10:10 / Key references: Numbers 32:1; Judges 10:17–11:33; 2 Samuel 2:8–9; Jeremiah 8:22

2) A mountain range from which Gideon sent the fearful portion of his troops home.

Only reference: Judges 7:3

3) A city of Gilead, possibly Ramoth-gilead. Or it may be the Gilead referred to in Judges 10:17. See Gilead (1).

Only reference: Hosea 6:8

♀ GILGAL

of times mentioned: OT 41

Meaning: A wheel

1) The first Israelite encampment in the Promised Land, "in the east border of Jericho." Here Joshua made a memorial of the twelve stones the Israelites took out of the Jordan River after they crossed it. Joshua circumcised the Israelites at Gilgal, and God removed the reproach of Egypt from them there.

Samuel judged Israel at Gilgal in a kind of circuit court. And here he made Saul king, with public sacrifices. Later, when Saul and his people faced war with the Philistines, and Samuel did not come to Gilgal, Saul wrongly took the prophet's place and sacrificed a burnt offering. At Gilgal Samuel confronted Saul for another disobedience, his failure to obey God's command to kill all the Amalekites' cattle following Israel's victorious battle over that nation. The men of Judah met King David at Gilgal after he had fled from Jerusalem and his traitorous son, Absalom, and put down the rebellion. From Gilgal, the men escorted the rightful king back over the Jordan River.

The prophets repeatedly condemned Israel's sin at Gilgal, which had become a site of pagan worship.

First reference: Deuteronomy 11:30 / Last reference: Micah 6:5 / Key references: Joshua 4:19; 5:9–10; 2 Samuel 19:12–15

2) A city between Dor and Tirzah. Gilgal was conquered by Joshua and the Israelites.

Only reference: Joshua 12:23

3) A place Elijah and Elisha passed through before God took Elijah up in a whirlwind. Elisha returned there during a famine and performed a miracle when Gilgal's prophets had eaten a poisonous stew. Elisha put meal or flour in the pot, and it was no longer harmful.

First reference: 2 Kings 2:1 / Last reference: 2 Kings 4:38

📍 GILOH

of times mentioned: OT 2

Meaning: Open

A city that became part of the inheritance of the tribe of Judah following the conquest of the Promised Land. It was the home of Ahithophel, King David's counselor who traitorously supported the claim of David's son Absalom to the throne.

First reference: Joshua 15:51 / Last reference: 2 Samuel 15:12

📍 GIMZO

of times mentioned: OT 1

A city of the southern low country of Judah that the Philistines invaded and occupied during the reign of King Ahaz.

Only reference: 2 Chronicles 28:18

👥 GINATH

of times mentioned: 2
# of MEN by this name: 1

Father of Tibni. Half of Israel sought to make Tibni king after Zimri's death.

First reference: 1 Kings 16:21 / Last reference: 1 Kings 16:22

👥 GINNETHO

of times mentioned: 1
# of MEN by this name: 1

Meaning: Gardener

An exiled priest who returned to Judah under Zerubbabel.

Only reference: Nehemiah 12:4

👥 GINNETHON

of times mentioned: 2
# of MEN by this name: 1

Meaning: Gardener

A priest who renewed the covenant under Nehemiah.

First reference: Nehemiah 10:6 / Last reference: Nehemiah 12:16

👥 GISPA

of times mentioned: 1
# of MEN by this name: 1

A Jewish exile of the Nethinims who resettled in Ophel.

Only reference: Nehemiah 11:21

📍 GITTAH-HEPHER

of times mentioned: OT 1

Meaning: Winepress of the well

A city that became part of the inheritance of Zebulun when Joshua cast lots in Shiloh to provide territory for the seven tribes that had yet to receive their land.

Only reference: Joshua 19:13

📍 GITTAIM

of times mentioned: OT 2

Meaning: Double winepress

1) A city, possibly of Benjamin, that the non-Jewish Beerothites fled to and made their home.

Only reference: Samuel 4:3

2) A town of Benjamin resettled by the Jews after the Babylonian Exile.

Only reference: Nehemiah 11:33

📍 GOATH

of times mentioned: OT 1

Meaning: Lowing

A place near Jerusalem that Jeremiah foretold would be encompassed by the restored Jerusalem as it was finally "built to the Lord" (Jeremiah 31:38).

Only reference: Jeremiah 31:39

📍 GOB

of times mentioned: OT 2

Meaning: Pit

During King David's reign, Israel twice fought the Philistines here, and his mighty men killed some Philistine giants.

First reference: 2 Samuel 21:18 / Last reference: 2 Samuel 21:19

👥 GOG

of times mentioned: 11
# of MEN by this name: 2

1) A descendant of Abraham through Jacob's son Reuben.

Only reference: 1 Chronicles 5:4

2) A prince of Magog, a place perhaps in Scythia but certainly from the "north parts" (Ezekiel 39:2), against whom Ezekiel prophesied. God spoke of Gog's destruction and graves in Israel. In the book of Revelation, "Gog and Magog" refers to the Lord's last enemies.

First reference: Ezekiel 38:2 / Last reference: Revelation 20:8

📍 GOLAN

of times mentioned: OT 4

Meaning: Captive

A city of refuge established by Moses on the east bank of the Jordan River, before Israel entered the Promised Land. It became part of the inheritance of the tribe of Manasseh.

First reference: Deuteronomy 4:43 / Last reference: 1 Chronicles 6:71

📍 GOLGOTHA

of times mentioned: NT 3

Meaning: The skull

The place near Jerusalem where Jesus was crucified. Golgotha is mentioned by all the Gospel writers except Luke, who calls it by the Latin name, Calvary. Scripture tells us Golgotha was beyond the walls of the city: "Jesus also suffered outside the city gate" (Hebrews 13:12 NIV). John adds that there was a garden there, as well as an unused tomb in which He was buried (John 19:41–42). Same as Calvary.

First reference: Matthew 27:33 / Last reference: John 19:17

👥 GOLIATH

of times mentioned: 6
# of MEN by this name: 1

Meaning: Exile

A nine-foot, nine-inch-tall Philistine champion who was well armored and carried a spear that had a shaft like a weaver's beam. He challenged any Israelite to a fight; the losing nation would become the winner's servants. David fought Goliath with a slingshot and killed him and then cut off his head.

First reference: 1 Samuel 17:4 / Last reference: 1 Chronicles 20:5

GOMER

of times mentioned: 5
# of MEN by this name: 1
# of WOMEN by this name: 1

Meaning: Completion

1) Firstborn son of Japheth, Noah's son.

First reference: Genesis 10:2 / Last reference:
1 Chronicles 1:6

2) The unfaithful wife of the prophet Hosea. She represented the unfaithfulness of God's people. God told Hosea to redeem her from her lover and live with her again.

Only reference: Hosea 1:3

GOMORRAH

of times mentioned: OT 19 / NT 1

Meaning: A ruined heap

One of five Canaanite "cities of the plain" at the southern end of the Dead Sea. In scripture Gomorrah is most often connected with its sister city of the plain, Sodom. Both lay in the well-watered plain of the Jordan River, where Lot decided to settle. When the cities of the plain were attacked by the king of Shinar and his allies, Lot was taken captive.

Because of their sinfulness, God destroyed these cities by raining down fire and brimstone upon them until the smoke went up as if they were furnaces. In the Prophets, Sodom and Gomorrah's names became bywords for God's judgment of sin. Same as Gomorrha.

First reference: Genesis 10:19 / Last reference:
Peter 2:6 / Key references: Genesis 13:10; 19:24, 28

GOMORRHA

of times mentioned: NT 4

This Greek form of the name Gomorrah refers to the Canaanite city destroyed by God. Same as Gomorrah.

First reference: Matthew 10:15 / Last reference:
Jude 1:7

GOSHEN

of times mentioned: OT 15

1) A section east of the Nile River delta that the Israelites settled in after Joseph brought them to Egypt. Here Joseph first met his father after many years of separation. In Goshen the Jews lived separately from the Egyptians because foreign shepherds were not held in high esteem. Yet Pharaoh approved of their resettlement in his land. When God sent the plagues against Egypt, they did not affect His people in Goshen.

First reference: Genesis 45:10 / Last reference:
Exodus 9:26 / Key references: Genesis 46:29, 34;
Exodus 8:22

2) An area in the southern part of what would later become Judah. Joshua and the Israelites conquered Goshen, along with the rest of the south country.

First reference: Joshua 10:41 / Last reference:
Joshua 11:16

3) A city that became part of the inheritance of the tribe of Judah following the conquest of the Promised Land.

Only reference: Joshua 15:51

GOZAN

of times mentioned: OT 5

Meaning: A quarry

An Assyrian river and probably the area around it to which the Samaritans were transported after Shalmaneser, king of Assyria, conquered Israel.

First reference: 2 Kings 17:6 / Last reference:
Isaiah 37:12

GRECIA

of times mentioned: OT 3

Meaning: Latin form of Greece

This variation of the name Greece is used only in the book of Daniel, describing the prophet's vision about the empires of Media, Persia, and Greece.

First reference: Daniel 8:21 / Last reference:
Daniel 11:2

📍 GREECE

of times mentioned: OT 1 / NT 1

Though Greece was a mighty ancient European empire, it is infrequently mentioned in scripture. Zechariah spoke of Greece as an enemy of God's people. The book of Acts only once uses the nation's name to describe Paul's mission there. More often, scripture speaks of the individual Greek cities or provinces that were stops on the apostle's second and third missionary journeys.

First reference: Zechariah 9:13 / Last reference: Acts 20:2

📍 GUDGODAH

of times mentioned: OT 1

Meaning: Cleft

An encampment of the Israelites after God gave Moses the second tablets of the law and after Aaron's death.

Only reference: Deuteronomy 10:7

👥 GUNI

of times mentioned: 4
# of MEN by this name: 2

Meaning: Protected

1) A descendant of Abraham through Jacob's son Naphtali.

First reference: Genesis 46:24 / Last reference: 1 Chronicles 7:13

2) A descendant of Abraham through Jacob's son Gad.

Only reference: 1 Chronicles 5:15

📍 GUR

of times mentioned: OT 1

A place near Ibleam where Ahaziah, king of Judah, was attacked by the soldiers of Israel's king Jehu.

Only reference: 2 Kings 9:27

📍 GUR-BAAL

of times mentioned: OT 1

An area in Arabia conquered by King Uzziah of Judah.

Only reference: 2 Chronicles 26:7

👥 HAAHASHTARI

of times mentioned: 1
# of MEN by this name: 1

Meaning: Courier

A descendant of Abraham through Jacob's son Judah.

Only reference: 1 Chronicles 4:6

👥 HABAIAH

of times mentioned: 2
# of MEN by this name: 1

Meaning: God has hidden

Forefather of an exile who returned to Jerusalem with Zerubbabel but lost his role as priest when his genealogical record could not be found.

First reference: Ezra 2:61 / Last reference: Nehemiah 7:63

👥 HABAKKUK

of times mentioned: 2
# of MEN by this name: 1

Meaning: Embrace

An Old Testament minor prophet who served during the reign of King Josiah of Judah. He asked God why He was not delivering Israel and why the wicked seemed to win over the righteous. God replied that He would raise the Chaldeans against His sinful people and showed Habakkuk the profitlessness of the deeds of the wicked. Habakkuk accepted God's judgment and glorified Him.

First reference: Habakkuk 1:1 / Last reference: Habakkuk 3:1

👥 HABAZINIAH

of times mentioned: 1
# of MEN by this name: 1

Forefather of Jaazeniah, an obedient Rechabite whom God used as an example to Judah.

Only reference: Jeremiah 35:3

📍 HABOR

of times mentioned: OT 3

Meaning: United

A district of Assyria to which King Shalmaneser of Assyria transported the Israelites after he conquered Samaria.

First reference: 2 Kings 17:6 / Last reference: 1 Chronicles 5:26

👥 HACHALIAH

of times mentioned: 2
# of MEN by this name: 1

Meaning: Darkness of God

Father of the rebuilder of Jerusalem's walls, Nehemiah.

First reference: Nehemiah 1:1 / Last reference: Nehemiah 10:1

📍 HACHILAH

of times mentioned: OT 3

Meaning: Dark

While King Saul was pursuing David, twice the Ziphites reported to him that David was hiding in this wooded hill south of Jeshimon. When Saul went to capture David, the first time he received a report that the Philistines were attacking Israel, and he had to leave. The second time, David's spies warned their leader. David entered Saul's camp at night and took a spear and water jar to prove he had been there. The next day, he confronted Saul and proved he did not want to harm the king.

First reference: 1 Samuel 23:19 / Last reference: 1 Samuel 26:3

👥 HACHMONI

of times mentioned: 1
# of MEN by this name: 1

Meaning: Skillful

Forefather of Jehiel, who was a tutor to King David's sons.

Only reference: 1 Chronicles 27:32

👥 HADAD

of times mentioned: 14
# of MEN by this name: 4

1) A king of Edom, "before there reigned any king over the children of Israel" (Genesis 36:31).

First reference: Genesis 36:35 / Last reference: 1 Chronicles 1:47

2) Israel's Edomite adversary who arose after Solomon turned from the Lord. Hadad formed a marauding band that attacked Israel for the rest of Solomon's reign.

First reference: 1 Kings 11:14 / Last reference: 1 Kings 11:25

3) A descendant of Abraham through Ishmael, Abraham's son with his surrogate wife, Hagar.

Only reference: 1 Chronicles 1:30

4) A king of Edom, "before there reigned any king over the children of Israel" (Genesis 36:31).

First reference: 1 Chronicles 1:50 / Last reference: 1 Chronicles 1:51

👥 HADADEZER

of times mentioned: 9
# of MEN by this name: 1

Meaning: Hadad is his help

Syrian king of Zobah whose troops David defeated along with the Syrians of Damascus who supported Hadadezer. Same as Hadarezer.

First reference: 2 Samuel 8:3 / Last reference: 1 Kings 11:23

HADADRIMMON

of times mentioned: OT 1

A place in the valley of Megiddo that the prophet Zechariah spoke of as suffering deep mourning.

Only reference: Zechariah 12:11

HADAR

of times mentioned: 2
# of MEN by this name: 2

Meaning: Magnificence

1) The eighth son of Ishmael.

Only reference: Genesis 25:15

2) A king of Edom, "before there reigned any king over the children of Israel" (Genesis 36:31).

Only reference: Genesis 36:39

HADAREZER

of times mentioned: 12
# of MEN by this name: 1

Meaning: Hadad is his help

Syrian king of Zobar whom David defeated along with the Syrians of Damascus who supported him. Later, Hadarezer hired out his men to fight King David for the Ammonites. After they lost, Hadarezer made peace with Israel. Same as Hadadezer.

First reference: 2 Samuel 10:16 / Last reference: 1 Chronicles 19:19 / Key references: 1 Chronicles 18:3–5; 19:6, 16

HADASHAH

of times mentioned: OT 1

Meaning: New

A city that became part of the inheritance of the tribe of Judah following the conquest of the Promised Land.

Only reference: Joshua 15:37

HADASSAH

of times mentioned: 1
# of WOMEN by this name: 1

Meaning: Myrtle

An alternative name for Esther, the Jewish woman who became queen of Persia.

Only reference: Esther 2:7

HADATTAH

of times mentioned: OT 1

A city that became part of the inheritance of the tribe of Judah following the conquest of the Promised Land.

Only reference: Joshua 15:25

HADID

of times mentioned: OT 3

A place in Benjamin resettled by the Jews after the Babylonian Exile.

First reference: Ezra 2:33 / Last reference: Nehemiah 11:34

HADLAI

of times mentioned: 1
# of MEN by this name: 1

Meaning: Idle

A man of the tribe of Ephraim whose son Amasa counseled his nation of Israel against enslaving fellow Jews from Judah who were captured in a civil war.

Only reference: 2 Chronicles 28:12

HADORAM

of times mentioned: 4
# of MEN by this name: 3

1) A descendant of Noah through Noah's son Shem.

First reference: Genesis 10:27 / Last reference: 1 Chronicles 1:21

2) Son of Tou, king of Hamath, who sent Hadoram to congratulate King David on his victory over King Hadarezer.

Only reference: 1 Chronicles 18:10

3) Taskmaster over forced labor for King Rehoboam of Israel. Hadoram was stoned to death by the Israelites.

Only reference: 2 Chronicles 10:18

HADRACH

of times mentioned: OT 1

A part of Syria that is mentioned nowhere else in scripture. The prophet Zechariah proclaimed that the word of the Lord was against this land by the Orontes River.

Only reference: Zechariah 9:1

HAGAB

of times mentioned: 1
# of MEN by this name: 1

Meaning: Locust

Forefather of an exiled family that returned to Judah under Zerubbabel. Same as Hagaba and Hagabah.

Only reference: Ezra 2:46

HAGABA

of times mentioned: 1
# of MEN by this name: 1

Meaning: Locust

Forefather of an exiled family that returned to Judah under Zerubbabel. Same as Hagab and Hagabah.

Only reference: Nehemiah 7:48

HAGABAH

of times mentioned: 1
# of MEN by this name: 1

Meaning: Locust

Forefather of an exiled family that returned to Judah under Zerubbabel. Same as Hagab and Hagaba.

Only reference: Ezra 2:45

HAGAR

of times mentioned: 12
# of WOMEN by this name: 1

Sarai's Egyptian maid who became a surrogate wife to Abram so he and Sarai could have a child. When Hagar conceived, she despised Sarai and fled from her. The angel of the Lord told Hagar to return and submit to Sarai. After Sarai's own child, Isaac, was born, Sarai threw Hagar and her son, Ishmael, out of the camp. God provided Hagar with water in the wilderness and promised to make Ishmael into a great nation.

First reference: Genesis 16:1 / Last reference: Genesis 25:12 / Key references: Genesis 16:1–2, 15; 21:10

HAGGAI

of times mentioned: 11
# of MEN by this name: 1

Meaning: Festive

A prophet of Judah who wrote the book that bears his name. With the prophet Zechariah, he encouraged the disheartened Jews to continue in their efforts to rebuild the temple. During the era of Haggai's prophecies and the temple building project, the Jews prospered. God promised this second temple would be greater than the original temple that Solomon had built.

First reference: Ezra 5:1 / Last reference: Haggai 2:20 / Key references: Ezra 6:14; Haggai 2:9–10

HAGGERI

of times mentioned: 1
# of MEN by this name: 1

Father of one of King David's valiant warriors.

Only reference: 1 Chronicles 11:38

HAGGI

of times mentioned: 2
# of MEN by this name: 1

Meaning: Festive

A descendant of Abraham through Jacob's son Gad.

First reference: Genesis 46:16 / Last reference:
Numbers 26:15

👥 HAGGIAH

of times mentioned: 1
# of MEN by this name: 1

Meaning: Festival of God

A descendant of Abraham through Jacob's son Levi.

Only reference: 1 Chronicles 6:30

👥 HAGGITH

of times mentioned: 5
# of WOMEN by this name: 1

Meaning: Festive

One of several wives of King David and mother of
David's son Adonijah.

First reference: 2 Samuel 3:4 / Last reference:
1 Chronicles 3:2

📍 HAI

of times mentioned: OT 2

Abram camped at this city, building an altar near
Hai, when he first entered the Promised Land.
Same as Ai.

First reference: Genesis 12:8 / Last reference:
Genesis 13:3

👥 HAKKATAN

of times mentioned: 1
# of MEN by this name: 1

Meaning: Small

Forefather of a Jewish exile who returned from
Babylon to Judah under Ezra.

Only reference: Ezra 8:12

👥 HAKKOZ

of times mentioned: 1
# of MEN by this name: 1

Meaning: Thorn

One of twenty-four priests in David's time who was
chosen by lot to serve in the tabernacle.

Only reference: 1 Chronicles 24:10

👥 HAKUPHA

of times mentioned: 2
# of MEN by this name: 1

Meaning: Crooked

Forefather of an exiled family that returned to
Judah under Zerubbabel.

First reference: Ezra 2:51 / Last reference:
Nehemiah 7:53

📍 HALAH

of times mentioned: OT 3

A district in Assyria to which King Shalmaneser
transported the Israelites after he conquered
Samaria.

First reference: 2 Kings 17:6 / Last reference:
1 Chronicles 5:26

📍 HALAK

of times mentioned: OT 2

Meaning: Bare

A mountain in southern Canaan that Joshua and
his warriors conquered.

First reference: Joshua 11:17 / Last reference:
Joshua 12:7

📍 HALHUL

of times mentioned: OT 1

Meaning: Contorted

A city that became part of the inheritance of the tribe of Judah following the conquest of the Promised Land.

Only reference: Joshua 15:58

HALI

of times mentioned: OT 1

Meaning: A trinket (as polished)

A city that became part of the inheritance of Asher when Joshua cast lots in Shiloh to provide territory for the seven tribes that had yet to receive their land.

Only reference: Joshua 19:25

 HALLOHESH

of times mentioned: 1
# of MEN by this name: 1

Meaning: Enchanter

Father of a man who repaired Jerusalem's walls under Nehemiah. Same as Halohesh.

Only reference: Nehemiah 10:24

HALOHESH

of times mentioned: 1
# of MEN by this name: 1

Meaning: Enchanter

Father of a man who repaired Jerusalem's walls under Nehemiah. Same as Hallohesh.

Only reference: Nehemiah 3:12

HAM

of times mentioned: 12
# of MEN by this name: 1

Meaning: Hot

The youngest of Noah's three sons. After the flood, when Noah became drunk and lay naked in his tent, Ham looked on and reported it to his brothers. For this, Noah cursed Ham's youngest son and blessed the brothers who covered him without looking. Ham fathered four sons from whom come many of Israel's worst enemies.

First reference: Genesis 5:32 / Last reference: 1 Chronicles 1:8 / Key references: Genesis 9:22–25; 10:6

HAMAN

of times mentioned: 53
# of MEN by this name: 1

King Ahasuerus's wicked counselor, who plotted to eradicate the Jews from the Persian kingdom. When Mordecai, the cousin of Ahasuerus's wife, Queen Esther, refused to bow before the king, Haman decided to destroy all the Jews. The counselor extracted permission from the king to create a law to that end. But Mordecai heard of his plan and reported it to the queen.

When Haman came to the court one day, the king asked what should be done to honor a man in whom the king delighted. Thinking the king meant himself, Haman suggested that the man be dressed in the king's clothes, placed on a horse, and his good deeds proclaimed as he was led throughout the streets. To the counselor's horror, the king commanded him to do this for Haman's enemy, Mordecai.

Queen Esther invited Haman and the king to a banquet. The proud counselor was honored until the second day of the feast, when the queen revealed the truth of his plans to the king. Ahasuerus, angry at the deceit of his counselor, had him hanged on the gallows that Haman had erected to destroy Mordecai.

First reference: Esther 3:1 / Last reference: Esther 9:24 / Key reference: Esther 3:5–11

HAMATH

of times mentioned: OT 34

Meaning: Walled

Capital of a kingdom, called by the same name, in northern Syria, held by the Hivites. When God used the Philistines, Canaanites, Sidonians, and Hivites to teach the children of Israel war as they conquered the Promised Land, it was in the area from Baal-hermon "unto the entering in of Hamath" (Judges 3:3; translated "Lebo Hamath" in some Bible versions). Later, when King David conquered Hadadezer, king of Zobah, King Toi (or Tou) of Hamath sent his son to David "to salute him, and to bless him" and bring him gifts (2 Samuel 8:9–10; 1 Chronicles 18:9–10).

At least part of the area of Hamath eventually belonged to Israel. When King Solomon dedicated the temple, all Israel from Hamath to the river of Egypt joined in the celebration. Solomon also made Hamath a store city that housed provisions for his nation. Though it once belonged to Judah, Hamath came into Israel's grasp when King Jeroboam recovered both it and Damascus.

After the king of Assyria conquered Samaria, he repeopled it with pagan men from Hamath. When Rabshakeh tried to win Jerusalem without a fight, he warned the people in that holy city of his master's power, pointing out that the gods of Hamath had not protected its people during the Assyrian conquest.

After being conquered by Pharaoh Necho, King Jehoahaz of Judah was imprisoned in the land of Hamath. Here also Nebuchadnezzar killed Israel's chief priests, King Zedekiah's sons, and all the princes of Judah after the fall of Jerusalem.

Isaiah prophesied that when the Messiah established His kingdom, God's people from Hamath would be recovered. But Isaiah also asked where the gods of that land were, to point out their total lack of power and complete destruction. The prophet Ezekiel foretold a day when Hamath would be a border of the restored Israel.

First reference: Numbers 13:21 / Last reference: Zechariah 9:2 / Key references: 1 Kings 8:65; 2 Kings 14:28; 2 Chronicles 8:4

📍 HAMATH-ZOBAH

of times mentioned: OT 1

Meaning: Walled station

A city conquered by King Solomon. Scholars disagree on whether this is the same city as Hamath.

Only reference: 2 Chronicles 8:3

📍 HAMMATH

of times mentioned: OT 1

Meaning: Hot springs

A fortified or walled city that became part of the inheritance of Naphtali when Joshua cast lots in Shiloh to provide territory for the seven tribes that had yet to receive their land.

Only reference: Joshua 19:35

👥 HAMMEDATHA

of times mentioned: 5
# of MEN by this name: 1

Father of Haman, the villain of the story of Esther.

First reference: Esther 3:1 / Last reference: Esther 9:24

👥 HAMMELECH

of times mentioned: 2
# of MEN by this name: 1

Meaning: King

Father of Jerameel and Malchiah. His sons imprisoned the prophet Jeremiah.

First reference: Jeremiah 36:26 / Last reference: Jeremiah 38:6

👥 HAMMOLEKETH

of times mentioned: 1
# of WOMEN by this name: 1

Meaning: Queen

Sister of Gilead and a descendant of Abraham through Joseph's son Manasseh.

Only reference: 1 Chronicles 7:18

📍 HAMMON

of times mentioned: OT 2

Meaning: Warm spring

1) A city that became part of the inheritance of Asher when Joshua cast lots in Shiloh to provide territory for the seven tribes that had yet to receive their land.

Only reference: Joshua 19:28

2) One of the forty-eight cities given to the Levites as God had commanded. Hammon was given to them by the tribe of Naphtali. Same as Hammoth-dor.

Only reference: 1 Chronicles 6:76

📍 HAMMOTH-DOR

of times mentioned: OT 1

Meaning: Hot springs of Dor

One of the forty-eight cities given to the Levites as God had commanded. Hammoth-dor was given to them by the tribe of Naphtali. Same as Hammon (2).

Only reference: Joshua 21:32

📍 HAMONAH

of times mentioned: OT 1

Meaning: Multitude

A town in the valley of Hamon-gog that the prophet Ezekiel foretold would become a graveyard.

Only reference: Ezekiel 39:16

📍 HAMON-GOG

of times mentioned: OT 2

Meaning: The multitude of Gog

Following God's destruction of Israel's enemy Gog, Ezekiel foresaw that Gog's dead troops would be buried in this valley. It would take seven months to bury all the dead there.

First reference: Ezekiel 39:11 / Last reference: Ezekiel 39:15

👥 HAMOR

of times mentioned: 13
# of MEN by this name: 1

Meaning: Ass

A prince of Shechem whose son raped Dinah, Jacob's daughter. Hamor arranged a marriage, but Dinah's brothers, angered at the situation, killed all the men in the city.

First reference: Genesis 33:19 / Last reference: Judges 9:28 / Key references: Genesis 34:2, 8–10, 24–26

👥 HAMUEL

of times mentioned: 1
# of MEN by this name: 1

Meaning: Anger of God

A descendant of Abraham through Jacob's son Simeon.

Only reference: 1 Chronicles 4:26

👥 HAMUL

of times mentioned: 3
# of MEN by this name: 1

Meaning: Pitied

Descendant of Abraham through Jacob's son Judah. Hamul founded the tribe of the Hamulites.

First reference: Genesis 46:12 / Last reference: 1 Chronicles 2:5

👥 HAMUTAL

of times mentioned: 3
# of WOMEN by this name: 1

Meaning: Father-in-law of dew

Mother of kings Jehoahaz and Zedekiah of Judah.

First reference: 2 Kings 23:31 / Last reference: Jeremiah 52:1

👥 HANAMEEL

of times mentioned: 4
# of MEN by this name: 1

Meaning: God has favored

The prophet Jeremiah's cousin, from whom he bought land as a sign from God.

First reference: Jeremiah 32:7 / Last reference: Jeremiah 32:12

👥 HANAN

of times mentioned: 12
# of MEN by this name: 9

Meaning: Favor

1) A descendant of Abraham through Jacob's son Benjamin.

Only reference: 1 Chronicles 8:23

2) A descendant of Abraham through Jacob's son Benjamin, through the line of King Saul and his son Jonathan.

First reference: 1 Chronicles 8:38 / Last reference: 1 Chronicles 9:44

3) One of King David's valiant warriors.

Only reference: 1 Chronicles 11:43

4) Forefather of an exiled family that returned to Judah under Zerubbabel.

First reference: Ezra 2:46 / Last reference: Nehemiah 7:49

5) A Levite who helped Ezra to explain the law to exiles returned to Jerusalem.

Only reference: Nehemiah 8:7

6) A Levite who renewed the covenant under Nehemiah and became a temple treasurer.

First reference: Nehemiah 10:10 / Last reference: Nehemiah 13:13

7) A Jewish leader who renewed the covenant under Nehemiah.

Only reference: Nehemiah 10:22

8) Another Jewish leader who renewed the covenant under Nehemiah.

Only reference: Nehemiah 10:26

9) A man of God in whose sons' chamber Jeremiah tested the obedience of the Rechabites.

Only reference: Jeremiah 35:4

♀ HANANEEL

of times mentioned: OT 4

Meaning: God has favored

One of Jerusalem's towers, Hananeel was sanctified by the high priest Eliashib after Nehemiah rebuilt the walls. Jeremiah foretold that this tower will be part of the eternal Jerusalem of God's kingdom.

First reference: Nehemiah 3:1 / Last reference: Zechariah 14:10

👥 HANANI

of times mentioned: 11
# of MEN by this name: 6

Meaning: Gracious

1) A son of King David's musician Heman, who was "under the hands of [his] father for song in the house of the LORD" (1 Chronicles 25:6).

First reference: 1 Chronicles 25:4 / Last reference: 1 Chronicles 25:25

2) A prophet who confronted Judah's king Asa for trusting his alliance with Syria more than trusting God. "The eyes of the LORD run to and fro throughout the whole earth, to shew himself strong in the behalf of them whose heart is perfect toward him," Hanani warned (2 Chronicles 16:9). Asa, furious, imprisoned Hanani.

Only reference: 2 Chronicles 16:7

3) Father of King Jehu of Israel.

First reference: 1 Kings 16:1 / Last reference: 2 Chronicles 20:34

4) An exiled Israelite priest who married a "strange" (foreign) woman.

Only reference: Ezra 10:20

5) A brother of the rebuilder of Jerusalem's walls, Nehemiah.

First reference: Nehemiah 1:2 / Last reference: Nehemiah 7:2

6) A priest who helped to dedicate the rebuilt walls of Jerusalem by playing a musical instrument.

Only reference: Nehemiah 12:36

👥 HANANIAH

of times mentioned: 29
# of MEN by this name: 14

Meaning: God has favored

1) A son of King David's musician Heman, who was "under the hands of [his] father for song in the house of the LORD" (1 Chronicles 25:6).

First reference: 1 Chronicles 25:4 / Last reference: 1 Chronicles 25:23

2) A commander under King Uzziah of Judah.

Only reference: 2 Chronicles 26:11

3) Father of Zedekiah, one of the officials of King Jehoiakim of Judah.

Only reference: Jeremiah 36:12

4) A false prophet who told King Zedekiah of Judah that the king of Babylon's yoke had been broken. He claimed that within two years, the temple vessels and King Jehoiakim's exiled son Jeconiah would be returned.

Jeremiah was not convinced. God gave him a prophecy that denied Hananiah's and promised to take the false prophet's life within a year. Hananiah died in the seventh month.

First reference: Jeremiah 28:1 / Last reference: Jeremiah 28:17

5) Forefather of a sentry who accused Jeremiah of deserting to the Chaldeans.

Only reference: Jeremiah 37:13

6) A descendant of Abraham through Jacob's son Benjamin.

Only reference: 1 Chronicles 8:24

7) The Hebrew name of Daniel's friend better known as Shadrach.

First reference: Daniel 1:6 / Last reference: Daniel 2:17

8) A descendant of Abraham through Jacob's son Judah, in the line of the nation of Judah's third-to-last king, Jeconiah (also known as Jehoiachin).

First reference: 1 Chronicles 3:19 / Last reference: 1 Chronicles 3:21

9) An exiled Israelite who married a "strange" (foreign) woman.

Only reference: Ezra 10:28

10) Son of a perfume maker, Hananiah was a repairer of Jerusalem's walls under Nehemiah.

Only reference: Nehemiah 3:8

11) Another repairer of Jerusalem's walls under Nehemiah.

Only reference: Nehemiah 3:30

12) The overseer of Nehemiah's palace in Jerusalem, a "faithful man" given charge over the city's gates.

Only reference: Nehemiah 7:2

13) A Jewish leader who renewed the covenant under Nehemiah.

Only reference: Nehemiah 10:23

14) A priest who helped to dedicate the rebuilt wall of Jerusalem by giving thanks.

Only reference: Nehemiah 12:41

⊙ HANES

of times mentioned: OT 1

Isaiah warned God's people against trusting in Egypt and its power. Egypt's ambassadors, he said, would come to this place, which was probably in Egypt.

Only reference: Isaiah 30:4

👥 HANIEL

of times mentioned: 1
# of MEN by this name: 1

Meaning: Favor of God

A descendant of Abraham through Jacob's son Asher.

Only reference: 1 Chronicles 7:39

👥 HANNAH

of times mentioned: 13
# of WOMEN by this name: 1

Meaning: Favored

Hannah could not bear a child, but her husband, Elkanah, loved her, though his second wife abused her. Distraught, Hannah went to the temple to pray and promised God that if He gave her a child, she would give the boy to Him for his whole life. As she fervently prayed in the temple, Eli the priest mistook her praying for drunkenness; then he discovered how wrong he had been. In time, Hannah conceived and bore Samuel. When he was weaned, the couple brought the boy to Eli to foster. Samuel became a powerful prophet of Israel who crowned Saul and David king.

First reference: 1 Samuel 1:2 / Last reference: 1 Samuel 2:21 / Key references: 1 Samuel 1:11, 15–16

📍 HANNATHON

of times mentioned: OT 1

Meaning: Favored

A city on the border of the tribe of Zebulun's territory.

Only reference: Joshua 19:14

👥 HANNIEL

of times mentioned: 1
# of MEN by this name: 1

Meaning: Favor of God

Prince of the tribe of Manasseh when the Israelites entered the Promised Land.

Only reference: Numbers 34:23

👥 HANOCH

of times mentioned: 5
# of MEN by this name: 2

Meaning: Initiated, favor of God

1) A descendant of Abraham through his second wife, Keturah. Same as Henoch (2).

Only reference: Genesis 25:4

2) A descendant of Abraham through Jacob's son Reuben.

First reference: Genesis 46:9 / Last reference: 1 Chronicles 5:3

👥 HANUN

of times mentioned: 11
# of MEN by this name: 3

Meaning: Favored

1) An Ammonite king to whom David sent comforters after his father died. The princes of Ammon convinced Hanun these men were spies. So the new king shaved half their beards off, cut off half their clothing, and sent them home. Then Hanun hired Syrian warriors and unsuccessfully attacked Israel.

First reference: 2 Samuel 10:1 / Last reference: 1 Chronicles 19:6

2) A man who repaired Jerusalem's walls under Nehemiah.

Only reference: Nehemiah 3:30

3) Another man who repaired Jerusalem's walls under Nehemiah. Hanun repaired the Valley Gate and "a thousand cubits" of the wall.

Only reference: Nehemiah 3:13

📍 HAPHRAIM

of times mentioned: OT 1

Meaning: Double pit

A city that became part of the inheritance of Issachar when Joshua cast lots in Shiloh to provide territory for the seven tribes that had yet to receive their land.

Only reference: Joshua 19:19

📍 HARA

of times mentioned: OT 1

Meaning: Mountainousness

Because of the idolatry of the tribes of Reuben, Gad, and Manasseh, God stirred up the Assyrians, who conquered these tribes and carried them to this Assyrian province.

Only reference: 1 Chronicles 5:26

📍 HARADAH

of times mentioned: OT 2

Meaning: Fear; anxiety

A campsite of the Israelites on their way to the Promised Land.

First reference: Numbers 33:24 / Last reference: Numbers 33:25

👥 HARAN

\# of times mentioned: 9
\# of MEN by this name: 3

Meaning: Rest; mountaineer; parched

1) Brother of Abram. He died while they were still in Ur of the Chaldees. His son Lot traveled to Canaan with Abram and Sarai.

First reference: Genesis 11:26 / Last reference: Genesis 11:31

2) A head Levite who was part of King David's religious leadership reorganization.

Only reference: 1 Chronicles 23:9

3) A descendant of Abraham through Jacob's son Judah.

Only reference: 1 Chronicles 2:46

📍 HARAN

\# of times mentioned: OT 10

Meaning: Parched

A Mesopotamian city where Terah and his family settled after they left Ur of the Chaldees. Terah died in Haran, but God sent Terah's son Abram and his family on to the Promised Land.

When Jacob was threatened by his brother, Esau, Rebekah sent her favorite son to her brother, Laban, who lived in Haran.

Rabshakeh's message to King Hezekiah of Judah uses Haran as an example of a city destroyed by Assyria's troops, and Isaiah spoke of its destruction by that nation. Same as Charran.

First reference: Genesis 11:31 / Last reference: Ezekiel 27:23

👥 HARBONA

\# of times mentioned: 1
\# of MEN by this name: 1

A eunuch serving the Persian king Ahasuerus in Esther's time. Same as Harbonah.

Only reference: Esther 1:10

👥 HARBONAH

\# of times mentioned: 1
\# of MEN by this name: 1

A eunuch serving the Persian king Ahasuerus in Esther's time. He informed the king of the gallows Haman had built for hanging Mordecai, gallows on which Haman himself was executed. Same as Harbona.

Only reference: Esther 7:9

👥 HAREPH

\# of times mentioned: 1
\# of MEN by this name: 1

Meaning: Reproachful

A descendant of Abraham through Jacob's son Judah.

Only reference: 1 Chronicles 2:51

📍 HARETH

\# of times mentioned: OT 1

Meaning: Forest

A forest in Judah where David hid from King Saul.

Only reference: 1 Samuel 22:5

👥 HARHAIAH

\# of times mentioned: 1
\# of MEN by this name: 1

Meaning: Fearing God

Father of a man who repaired Jerusalem's walls under Nehemiah.

Only reference: Nehemiah 3:8

👥 HARHAS

\# of times mentioned: 1
\# of MEN by this name: 1

Meaning: Shining
Grandfather of Shallum, husband of the prophetess

Huldah in the days of King Josiah. Same as Hasrah.

Only reference: 2 Kings 22:14

👥 HARHUR

of times mentioned: 2
# of MEN by this name: 1

Meaning: Inflammation

Forefather of an exiled family that returned to Judah under Zerubbabel.

First reference: Ezra 2:51 / Last reference: Nehemiah 7:53

👥 HARIM

of times mentioned: 11
# of MEN by this name: 5

Meaning: Snub-nosed

1) One of twenty-four priests in David's time who was chosen by lot to serve in the tabernacle. Harim was also forefather of a man who repaired Jerusalem's walls under Nehemiah.

First reference: 1 Chronicles 24:8 / Last reference: Nehemiah 12:15

2) Forefather of an exiled family that returned to Judah under Zerubbabel.

First reference: Ezra 2:32 / Last reference: Nehemiah 7:35

3) Forefather of exiled Israelites who married "strange" (foreign) women.

Only reference: Ezra 10:31

4) A priest who renewed the covenant under Nehemiah.

Only reference: Nehemiah 10:5

5) A Jewish leader who renewed the covenant under Nehemiah.

Only reference: Nehemiah 10:27

👥 HARIPH

of times mentioned: 2
# of MEN by this name: 2

Meaning: Autumnal

1) Forefather of an exiled family that returned to Judah under Zerubbabel.

Only reference: Nehemiah 7:24

2) A Jewish leader who renewed the covenant under Nehemiah.

Only reference: Nehemiah 10:19

👥 HARNEPHER

of times mentioned: 1
# of MEN by this name: 1

A descendant of Abraham through Jacob's son Asher.

Only reference: 1 Chronicles 7:36

📍 HAROD

of times mentioned: OT 1

Meaning: To shudder with terror; to fear; to hasten with anxiety

A spring that Gideon and his men camped by before God had Gideon send home the fearful warriors. God used the way the warriors drank water to whittle down the number that would battle against Midian.

Only reference: Judges 7:1

👥 HAROEH

of times mentioned: 1
# of MEN by this name: 1

Meaning: Prophet

A descendant of Abraham through Jacob's son Judah.

Only reference: 1 Chronicles 2:52

⚲ HAROSHETH

of times mentioned: OT 3

Meaning: Mechanical work

Home of Sisera, commander of the army of Jabin, king of Canaan. After God gave His people the victory, Israel's battle commander Barak pursued the Canaanites to this city, where all Sisera's troops were killed.

First reference: Judges 4:2 / Last reference: Judges 4:16

👥 HARSHA

of times mentioned: 2
# of MEN by this name: 1

Meaning: Magician

Forefather of an exiled family that returned to Judah under Zerubbabel.

First reference: Ezra 2:52 / Last reference: Nehemiah 7:54

👥 HARUM

of times mentioned: 1
# of MEN by this name: 1

Meaning: High

A descendant of Abraham through Jacob's son Judah.

Only reference: 1 Chronicles 4:8

👥 HARUMAPH

of times mentioned: 1
# of MEN by this name: 1

Meaning: Snub-nosed

Father of a man who repaired Jerusalem's walls under Nehemiah.

Only reference: Nehemiah 3:10

👥 HARUZ

of times mentioned: 1
# of MEN by this name: 1

Meaning: Earnest

Grandfather of King Amon of Judah.

Only reference: 2 Kings 21:19

👥 HASADIAH

of times mentioned: 1
# of MEN by this name: 1

Meaning: God has favored

A descendant of Abraham through Jacob's son Judah, in the line of the nation of Judah's third-to-last king, Jeconiah (also known as Jehoiachin).

Only reference: 1 Chronicles 3:20

👥 HASENUAH

of times mentioned: 1
# of MEN by this name: 1

Meaning: Pointed

Forefather of a Jewish exile from the tribe of Benjamin who resettled Jerusalem.

Only reference: 1 Chronicles 9:7

👥 HASHABIAH

of times mentioned: 15
# of MEN by this name: 14

Meaning: God has regarded

1) A descendant of Levi who stood next to Heman, the choir leader, in the temple.

Only reference: 1 Chronicles 6:45

2) Forefather of a Jewish exile from the tribe of Levi who resettled Jerusalem.

Only reference: 1 Chronicles 9:14

3) A son of King David's musician Jeduthun, "who prophesied with a harp, to give thanks and to praise the LORD" (1 Chronicles 25:3).

First reference: 1 Chronicles 25:3 / Last reference: 1 Chronicles 25:19

4) A Hebronite who controlled Israel west of the Jordan River under King David's reorganization.

Only reference: 1 Chronicles 26:30

5) Leader of the tribe of Levi in the days of King David.

Only reference: 1 Chronicles 27:17

6) A descendant of Abraham through Jacob's son Levi. Hashabiah was among those who distributed sacrificial animals to fellow Levites preparing to celebrate the Passover under King Josiah.

Only reference: 2 Chronicles 35:9

7) A Levite whom Ezra called to serve in the temple upon his return to Jerusalem.

Only reference: Ezra 8:19

8) A priest trusted by Ezra to carry money and temple vessels to Israel.

Only reference: Ezra 8:24

9) A rebuilder of the walls of Jerusalem under Nehemiah.

Only reference: Nehemiah 3:17

10) A Levite who renewed the covenant under Nehemiah.

Only reference: Nehemiah 10:11

11) Forefather of a Levite who returned to Jerusalem.

Only reference: Nehemiah 11:15

12) Forefather of a Levite overseer in Jerusalem after the Babylonian Exile.

Only reference: Nehemiah 11:22

13) Forefather of a priest who returned to Jerusalem under Zerubbabel.

Only reference: Nehemiah 12:21

14) A chief of the Levites in the time of Nehemiah.

Only reference: Nehemiah 12:24

📍 HASHABNAH

of times mentioned: 1
# of MEN by this name: 1

Meaning: Inventiveness

One of a group of Levites who led a revival among the Israelites in the time of Nehemiah.

Only reference: Nehemiah 10:25

👥 HASHABNIAH

of times mentioned: 2
# of MEN by this name: 2

Meaning: Thought of God

1) Father of a man who repaired Jerusalem's walls under Nehemiah.

Only reference: Nehemiah 3:10

2) A Levite worship leader when the Israelites confessed their sins following the Babylonian Exile.

Only reference: Nehemiah 9:5

👥 HASHBADANA

of times mentioned: 1
# of MEN by this name: 1

Meaning: Considerate judge

A priest who assisted Ezra in reading the book of the law to the people of Jerusalem.

Only reference: Nehemiah 8:4

👥 HASHEM

of times mentioned: 1
# of MEN by this name: 1

Meaning: Wealthy

Father of several of King David's valiant warriors.

Only reference: 1 Chronicles 11:34

📍 HASHMONAH

of times mentioned: OT 2

Meaning: Fertile

A campsite of the Israelites on their way to the Promised Land.

First reference: Numbers 33:29 / Last reference: Numbers 33:30

HASHUB

of times mentioned: 4
# of MEN by this name: 4

Meaning: Intelligent

1) Forefather of a Levite who oversaw the outside work of the rebuilt temple.

Only reference: Nehemiah 11:15

2) A man who repaired Jerusalem's walls under Nehemiah. Hashub helped to rebuild "the tower of the furnaces."

Only reference: Nehemiah 3:11

3) Another man who repaired Jerusalem's walls under Nehemiah.

Only reference: Nehemiah 3:23

4) A Jewish leader who renewed the covenant under Nehemiah.

Only reference: Nehemiah 10:23

HASHUBAH

of times mentioned: 1
# of MEN by this name: 1

Meaning: Estimation

A descendant of Abraham through Jacob's son Judah, in the line of the nation of Judah's third-to-last king, Jeconiah (also known as Jehoiachin).

Only reference: 1 Chronicles 3:20

HASHUM

of times mentioned: 5
# of MEN by this name: 3

Meaning: Enriched

1) Forefather of an exiled family that returned to Judah under Zerubbabel.

First reference: Ezra 2:19 / Last reference: Nehemiah 7:22

2) A priest who assisted Ezra in reading the book of the law to the people of Jerusalem.

Only reference: Nehemiah 8:4

3) A Jewish leader who renewed the covenant under Nehemiah.

Only reference: Nehemiah 10:18

HASHUPHA

of times mentioned: 1
# of MEN by this name: 1

Meaning: Nakedness

Forefather of an exiled family that returned to Judah under Zerubbabel.

Only reference: Nehemiah 7:46

HASRAH

of times mentioned: 1
# of MEN by this name: 1

Meaning: Want

Grandfather of Shallum, husband of the prophetess Huldah in the days of King Josiah. Same as Harhas.

Only reference: 2 Chronicles 34:22

HASSENAAH

of times mentioned: 1
# of MEN by this name: 1

Meaning: Thorny

Father of several men who repaired Jerusalem's walls under Nehemiah.

Only reference: Nehemiah 3:3

HASSHUB

of times mentioned: 1
# of MEN by this name: 1

Meaning: Intelligent

Forefather of a Levite exile to Babylon who resettled Jersualem.

Only reference: 1 Chronicles 9:14

👥 HASUPHA

\# of times mentioned: 1
\# of MEN by this name: 1

Meaning: Nakedness

Forefather of an exiled family that returned to Judah under Zerubbabel.

Only reference: Ezra 2:43

👥 HATACH

\# of times mentioned: 4
\# of MEN by this name: 1

One of King Ahasuerus's eunuchs, who attended Queen Esther. He acted as a messenger between her and Mordecai when Mordecai discovered Haman's plot.

First reference: Esther 4:5 / Last reference: Esther 4:10

👥 HATHATH

\# of times mentioned: 1
\# of MEN by this name: 1

Meaning: Dismay

A descendant of Abraham through Jacob's son Judah.

Only reference: 1 Chronicles 4:13

👥 HATIPHA

\# of times mentioned: 2
\# of MEN by this name: 1

Meaning: Robber

Forefather of an exiled family that returned to Judah under Zerubbabel.

First reference: Ezra 2:54 / Last reference: Nehemiah 7:56

👥 HATITA

\# of times mentioned: 2
\# of MEN by this name: 1

Meaning: Explorer

Forefather of an exiled family that returned to Judah under Zerubbabel.

First reference: Ezra 2:42 / Last reference: Nehemiah 7:45

👥 HATTIL

\# of times mentioned: 2
\# of MEN by this name: 1

Meaning: Fluctuating

Forefather of an exiled family—former servants of Solomon—that returned to Judah under Zerubbabel.

First reference: Ezra 2:57 / Last reference: Nehemiah 7:59

👥 HATTUSH

\# of times mentioned: 5
\# of MEN by this name: 5

1) A descendant of Abraham through Jacob's son Judah, in the line of the nation's third-to-last king, Jeconiah (also known as Jehoiachin).

Only reference: 1 Chronicles 3:22

2) An exiled priest who returned to Judah under Zerubbabel.

Only reference: Ezra 8:2

3) A priest who returned to Israel with Zerrubbabel.

Only reference: Nehemiah 12:12

4) A rebuilder of the walls of Jerusalem under Nehemiah.

Only reference: Nehemiah 3:10

5) A priest who renewed the covenant under Nehemiah.

Only reference: Nehemiah 10:4

📍 HAURAN

\# of times mentioned: OT 2

Meaning: Cavernous

A province southeast of Damascus and east of the Sea of Galilee and the Jordan River. The prophet Ezekiel describes it as part of the border of the land of the twelve tribes when Jerusalem is finally restored.

First reference: Ezekiel 47:16 / Last reference: Ezekiel 47:18

👥 HAVILAH

of times mentioned: 4
# of MEN by this name: 2

Meaning: Circular

1) A descendant of Noah through his son Ham.

First reference: Genesis 10:7 / Last reference: 1 Chronicles 1:9

2) A descendant of Noah through his son Shem.

First reference: Genesis 10:29 / Last reference: 1 Chronicles 1:23

📍 HAVILAH

of times mentioned: OT 3

Meaning: Circular

1) An area fed by the Pison River, which flowed from the river of the Garden of Eden. Havilah was a land that had gold.

Only reference: Genesis 2:11

2) An area whose name the Bible always connects with the Shur Desert. It was described as being "before Egypt, as thou goest toward Assyria," and it belonged to the Ishmaelites.

First reference: Genesis 25:18 / Last reference: 1 Samuel 15:7

📍 HAVOTH-JAIR

of times mentioned: OT 2

Meaning: Hamlets of Jair

Some small towns of Gilead that were part of the land of Manasseh. They belonged to the thirty sons of Jair, a judge of Israel.

First reference: Numbers 32:41 / Last reference: Judges 10:4

👥 HAZAEL

of times mentioned: 23
# of MEN by this name: 1

Meaning: God has seen

A king of Syria anointed to his position by Elijah. While Hazael served the Syrian king Ben-hadad, he was sent to Elisha to ask if the king would recover from an illness. Elisha replied that he would recover but told Hazael he would die. Hazael suffocated Ben-hadad and took his throne. Throughout his reign Hazael fought Israel and Judah. King Jehoash of Judah bribed him not to attack Jerusalem. Because Jehoash did not obey God, he continually fought Hazael and his son, Ben-hadad. Hazael oppressed Israel through King Jehoahaz's reign.

First reference: 1 Kings 19:15 / Last reference: Amos 1:4 / Key references: 1 Kings 19:15; 2 Kings 8:8–10; 12:18; 13:22

👥 HAZAIAH

of times mentioned: 1
# of MEN by this name: 1

Meaning: God has seen

A Jewish exile from the tribe of Judah who resettled Jerusalem.

Only reference: Nehemiah 11:5

📍 HAZAR-ADDAR

of times mentioned: OT 1

Meaning: Village of Addar

A place that God used to identify the southern border of Israel when He first gave it to His people.

Only reference: Numbers 34:4

📍 HAZAR-ENAN

of times mentioned: OT 4

Meaning: Village of springs

A place that God used to identify the northern border of Israel when He first gave it to His people. Ezekiel foretold it will be part of the border of the land of the twelve tribes when Jerusalem is finally restored.

First reference: Numbers 34:9 / Last reference: Ezekiel 48:1

HAZAR-GADDAH

of times mentioned: OT 1

Meaning: Village of fortune

A city that became part of the inheritance of the tribe of Judah when Joshua cast lots in Shiloh to provide territory for the seven tribes that had yet to receive their land.

Only reference: Joshua 15:27

HAZAR-HATTICON

of times mentioned: OT 1

Meaning: Village of the middle

Part of the border of the land of the twelve tribes when Jerusalem is finally restored. Hazar-hatticon lay by the coast of Hauran.

Only reference: Ezekiel 47:16

HAZARMAVETH

of times mentioned: 2
# of MEN by this name: 1

Meaning: Village of death

A descendant of Noah through his son Shem.

First reference: Genesis 10:26 / Last reference: 1 Chronicles 1:20

HAZAR-SHUAL

of times mentioned: OT 4

Meaning: Village of the fox

A city that became part of the inheritance of the tribe of Judah following the conquest of the Promised Land. It became part of the inheritance of Simeon when Joshua cast lots in Shiloh to provide territory for the seven tribes that had yet to receive their land. After the Babylonian Exile, Hazar-shual was resettled by the Jews.

First reference: Joshua 15:28 / Last reference: Nehemiah 11:27

HAZAR-SUSAH

of times mentioned: OT 1

Meaning: Village of cavalry

A city that became part of the inheritance of Simeon when Joshua cast lots in Shiloh to provide territory for the seven tribes that had yet to receive their land. Same as Hazar-susim.

Only reference: Joshua 19:5

HAZAR-SUSIM

of times mentioned: OT 1

Meaning: Village of horses

A city that became part of the inheritance of the tribe of Simeon. Same as Hazar-susah.

Only reference: 1 Chronicles 4:31

HAZAZON-TAMAR

of times mentioned: OT 1

Meaning: Division of the palm tree

Those who warned Jehoshaphat, king of Judah, used this name to describe the location of the encampment of the Moabites, Ammonites, and other enemies of Judah who were poised to attack Judah. Same as En-gedi and Hazezon-tamar.

Only reference: 2 Chronicles 20:2

HAZELELPONI

of times mentioned: 1
# of WOMEN by this name: 1

Meaning: Shade-facing

A descendant of Abraham through Jacob's son Judah.

Only reference: 1 Chronicles 4:3

📍 HAZERIM

of times mentioned: OT 1

Meaning: Yards

The territory belonging to a people who were displaced by the Philistines (Caphtorim) who came from Caphtor and settled in Palestine.

Only reference: Deuteronomy 2:23

📍 HAZEROTH

of times mentioned: OT 6

Meaning: Yards

A campsite of the Israelites on their way to the Promised Land.

First reference: Numbers 11:35 / Last reference: Deuteronomy 1:1

📍 HAZEZON-TAMAR

of times mentioned: OT 1

Another name for En-gedi. It was called by this name when Chedor-laomer, king of Elam, and his allies attacked the kings of Sodom, Gommorah, Admah, Zeboiim, and Zoar. Same as En-gedi and Hazazon-tamar.

Only reference: Genesis 14:7

👥 HAZIEL

of times mentioned: 1
# of MEN by this name: 1

Meaning: Seen of God

A chief Levite who was part of King David's religious leadership reorganization.

Only reference: 1 Chronicles 23:9

👥 HAZO

of times mentioned: 1
# of MEN by this name: 1

Meaning: Seer

A son of Nahor, Abraham's brother.

Only reference: Genesis 22:22

📍 HAZOR

of times mentioned: OT 19

Meaning: Village

1) Joshua fought and killed King Jabin of Hazor, destroyed all the people in his city, and burned it. Later Hazor became part of the inheritance of the tribe of Naphtali. When Israel disobeyed the Lord, He "sold them into the hand of [another] Jabin king of Canaan, that reigned in Hazor" (Judges 4:2). King Solomon raised a levy to fortify Hazor. When King Tiglath-pileser captured Israel, Hazor's people were taken captive to Assyria.

First reference: Joshua 11:1 / Last reference: 1 Kings 9:15 / Key references: Joshua 19:32–36; Judges 4:2; 2 Kings 15:29

2) A city that became part of the inheritance of the tribe of Judah following the conquest of the Promised Land.

Only reference: Joshua 15:23

3) Another city that became part of the inheritance of the tribe of Judah following the conquest of the Promised Land.

Only reference: Joshua 15:25

4) A place resettled by the tribe of Benjamin after the Babylonian Exile.

Only reference: Nehemiah 11:33

5) A district in Arabia captured by King Nebuchadnezzar of Babylon.

First reference: Jeremiah 49:28 / Last reference: Jeremiah 49:33

👥 HEBER

of times mentioned: 14
# of MEN by this name: 6

Meaning: Community, across

1) A descendant of Abraham through Jacob's son Asher.

First reference: Genesis 46:17 / Last reference: Luke 3:35

Genealogy of Jesus: Yes (Luke 3:35)

2) Called Heber the Kenite, he was the husband of Jael, the woman who killed the Canaanite commander Sisera.

First reference: Judges 4:11 / Last reference: Judges 5:24

3) A descendant of Abraham through Jacob's son Judah.

Only reference: 1 Chronicles 4:18

4) A descendant of Abraham through Jacob's son Benjamin.

Only reference: 1 Chronicles 8:17

5) A descendant of Abraham through Jacob's son Gad.

Only reference: 1 Chronicles 5:13

6) Another descendant of Abraham through Jacob's son Benjamin.

Only reference: 1 Chronicles 8:22

👥 HEBRON

of times mentioned: 10
# of MEN by this name: 2

Meaning: Association

1) A descendant of Abraham through Jacob's son Levi.

First reference: Exodus 6:18 / Last reference: 1 Chronicles 24:23

2) A descendant of Abraham through Jacob and Caleb the brother of Jerahmeel.

First reference: 1 Chronicles 2:42 / Last reference: 1 Chronicles 15:9

📍 HEBRON

of times mentioned: OT 63

Meaning: Seat of association

1) A city that became part of the inheritance of

Asher when Joshua cast lots in Shiloh to provide territory for the seven tribes that had yet to receive their land.

Only reference: Joshua 19:28

2) A place in Palestine where Abram lived and built an altar to the Lord. Sarah died and was buried here. Abraham (Abram) and Isaac lived in the city of Hebron.

During Israel's conquest of the Promised Land, Hoham, king of Hebron, joined an alliance to attack Gibeon, because that city had made peace with Joshua. Joshua came to Gibeon's aid and won the battle, killing Hebron's king and his allies. Then Israel attacked the city, destroying all the people within.

Hebron was one of the forty-eight cities given to the Levites by the tribe of Judah as God had commanded. But the fields and villages became the inheritance of Caleb, as Moses and Joshua had promised. Caleb expelled the three sons of Anak from Hebron.

David sent some of the spoils from his warfare with the Amalekites to Hebron. Here David lived and was anointed king of Judah, and he ruled in Hebron for seven and a half years. After the Israelites came to Hebron to make David their king, he, too moved to Jerusalem. David's son Absalom had himself declared king in Hebron after telling his father he wanted to go there to fulfill a vow.

Under King Rehoboam of Judah, Hebron became a fortified or walled city. Same as Arbah and Kirjath-arba.

First reference: Genesis 13:18 / Last reference: 2 Chronicles 11:10 / Key references: Joshua 10:23–39; 14:13–14; 21:11–13

👥 HEGAI

of times mentioned: 3
# of MEN by this name: 1

The keeper of the harem for King Ahasuerus of Persia. He treated Esther preferentially, and she took his advice on what to take when she went to the king. Same as Hege.

First reference: Esther 2:8 / Last reference: Esther 2:15

HEGE

of times mentioned: 1
# of MEN by this name: 1

An alternative name for Hegai, servant of the Persian king Ahasuerus.

Only reference: Esther 2:3

HELAH

of times mentioned: 2
# of WOMEN by this name: 1

Meaning: Rust

Wife of Ashur, a descendant of Abraham through Jacob's son Judah.

First reference: 1 Chronicles 4:5 / Last reference: 1 Chronicles 4:7

HELAM

of times mentioned: OT 2

Meaning: Fortress

A place where King David conquered King Hadarezer of Zobah, who led the Syrians against Israel. After this loss, the Syrians were afraid to continue helping the Ammonites.

First reference: 2 Samuel 10:16 / Last reference: 2 Samuel 10:17

HELBAH

of times mentioned: OT 1

Meaning: Fertility

A town that became part of the inheritance of the tribe of Asher. The tribe did not drive the original inhabitants from this place.

Only reference: Judges 1:31

HELBON

of times mentioned: OT 1

Meaning: Fruitful

A city near Damascus that produced wine and traded with Tyre.

Only reference: Ezekiel 27:18

HELDAI

of times mentioned: 2
# of MEN by this name: 2

Meaning: Worldliness

1) A commander in King David's army, overseeing twenty-four thousand men in the twelfth month of each year.

Only reference: 1 Chronicles 27:15

2) Forefather of a family of Jewish exiles in Babylon who participated in a symbolic crowning of the future Messiah by the prophet Zechariah. Same as Helem (2).

Only reference: Zechariah 6:10

HELEB

of times mentioned: 1
# of MEN by this name: 1

Meaning: Fatness

One of King David's valiant warriors. Same as Heled.

Only reference: 2 Samuel 23:29

HELED

of times mentioned: 1
# of MEN by this name: 1

Meaning: To glide

One of King David's valiant warriors. Same as Heleb.

Only reference: 1 Chronicles 11:30

HELEK

of times mentioned: 2
# of MEN by this name: 1

Meaning: Portion

A descendant of Abraham through Jacob's son Joseph.

First reference: Numbers 26:30 / Last reference: Joshua 17:2

👥 HELEM

of times mentioned: 2
# of MEN by this name: 2

Meaning: Dream

1) A descendant of Abraham through Jacob's son Asher.

Only reference: 1 Chronicles 7:35

2) Forefather of a family of Jewish exiles who participated in a symbolic crowning of the future Messiah by the prophet Zechariah. Same as Heldai (2).

Only reference: Zechariah 6:14

📍 HELEPH

of times mentioned: OT 1

Meaning: Change

A city that became part of the inheritance of Naphtali when Joshua cast lots in Shiloh to provide territory for the seven tribes that had yet to receive their land.

Only reference: Joshua 19:33

👥 HELEZ

of times mentioned: 5
# of MEN by this name: 2

Meaning: Strength

1) A commander in King David's army, overseeing twenty-four thousand men in the seventh month of each year.

First reference: Samuel 23:26 / Last reference: 1 Chronicles 27:10

2) A descendant of Abraham through Jacob's son Judah. Helez descended from the line of an unnamed Israelite woman and her Egyptian husband, Jarha.

Only reference: 1 Chronicles 2:39

👥 HELI

of times mentioned: 1
# of MEN by this name: 1

Genealogy of Jesus: Yes (Luke 3:23)

Meaning: Lofty

The father of Jesus' earthly father, Joseph.

Only reference: Luke 3:23

👥 HELKAI

of times mentioned: 1
# of MEN by this name: 1

Meaning: Apportioned

Forefather of a priest who returned to Jerusalem under Zerubbabel.

Only reference: Nehemiah 12:15

📍 HELKATH

of times mentioned: OT 2

Meaning: Smoothness

A city that became part of the inheritance of Asher when Joshua cast lots in Shiloh to provide territory for the seven tribes that had yet to receive their land. Helkath became one of the forty-eight cities given to the Levites as God had commanded.

First reference: Joshua 19:25 / Last reference: Joshua 21:31

📍 HELKATH-HAZZURIM

of times mentioned: OT 1

Meaning: Smoothness of the rocks

A place near the pool of Gibeon where selected warriors of David and Ish-bosheth competed with and killed each other. In the ensuing battle, David's troops won.

Only reference: 2 Samuel 2:16

HELON

\# of times mentioned: 5
\# of MEN by this name: 1

Meaning: Strong

Father of a prince of Zebulun who helped Moses take a census of his tribe.

First reference: Numbers 1:9 / Last reference: Numbers 10:16

HEMAM

\# of times mentioned: 1
\# of MEN by this name: 1

Meaning: Raging

A descendant of Seir, who lived in Esau's "land of Edom."

Only reference: Genesis 36:22

HEMAN

\# of times mentioned: 16
\# of MEN by this name: 2

Meaning: Faithful

1) A wise man, the son of Mahol, mentioned in comparison to Solomon's wisdom.

First reference: 1 Kings 4:31 / Last reference: 1 Chronicles 2:6

2) A descendant of Abraham through Jacob's son Levi. Heman was one of the key musicians serving in the Jerusalem temple. King David appointed Heman's descendants to "prophesy with harps, with psalteries, and with cymbals" (1 Chronicles 25:1).

First reference: 1 Chronicles 6:33 / Last reference: Psalm 88 (title)

HEMATH

\# of times mentioned: 1
\# of MEN by this name: 1

Meaning: Walled

A descendant of Abraham through Jacob's son Judah.

Only reference: 1 Chronicles 2:55

HEMDAN

\# of times mentioned: 1
\# of MEN by this name: 1

Meaning: Pleasant

A descendant of Seir, who lived in Esau's "land of Edom."

Only reference: Genesis 36:26

HEN

\# of times mentioned: 1
\# of MEN by this name: 1

Meaning: Grace

A son of Zephaniah who received a memorial crown in the temple.

Only reference: Zechariah 6:14

HENA

\# of times mentioned: OT 2

A city conquered by Assyria. Rabshakeh used its destruction as an example of why Jerusalem should side with his nation.

First reference: 2 Kings 18:34 / Last reference: Isaiah 37:13

HENADAD

\# of times mentioned: 4
\# of MEN by this name: 1

Meaning: Favor of Hadad

Father of a man who repaired Jerusalem's walls and led a revival under Nehemiah.

First reference: Ezra 3:9 / Last reference: Nehemiah 10:9

HENOCH

\# of times mentioned: 2
\# of MEN by this name: 2

Meaning: Initiated

1) A descendant of Seth, son of Adam. "Enoch walked with God: and he was not; for God took him" (Genesis 5:24). He was immediately translated into eternity. Same as Enoch (2).

Only reference: 1 Chronicles 1:3

2) A descendant of Abraham through his second wife, Keturah. Same as Hanoch (1).

Only reference: 1 Chronicles 1:33

👥 HEPHER

of times mentioned: 7
# of MEN by this name: 3

Meaning: Shame

1) A descendant of Abraham through Jacob's son Joseph.

First reference: Numbers 26:32 / Last reference: Joshua 17:3

2) A descendant of Abraham through Jacob's son Judah.

Only reference: 1 Chronicles 4:6

3) One of King David's valiant warriors.

Only reference: 1 Chronicles 11:36

📍 HEPHER

of times mentioned: OT 2

Meaning: A pit or shame

A kingdom east of the Jordan River conquered by Joshua and his army. Under King Solomon's governmental organization, this region was responsible for supplying provisions for the king.

First reference: Joshua 12:17 / Last reference: 1 Kings 4:10

👥 HEPHZIBAH

of times mentioned: 1
# of WOMEN by this name: 1

Meaning: My delight is in her

Wife of Judah's good king Hezekiah and the mother of the evil king Manasseh.

Only reference: 2 Kings 21:1

📍 HEPHZI-BAH

of times mentioned: OT 1

Meaning: My delight is in her

A symbolic name that Isaiah used for Jerusalem. It showed God's love for her.

Only reference: Isaiah 62:4

📍 HERES

of times mentioned: OT 1

Meaning: Shining

An Amorite mountain in Aijalon that was subject to the tribe of Ephraim.

Only reference: Judges 1:35

👥 HERESH

of times mentioned: 1
# of MEN by this name: 1

Meaning: Magical craft

A Jewish exile from the tribe of Levi who resettled Jerusalem.

Only reference: 1 Chronicles 9:15

👥 HERMAS

of times mentioned: 1
# of MEN by this name: 1

Meaning: To utter

A Christian acquaintance of the apostle Paul, greeted in Paul's letter to the Romans.

Only reference: Romans 16:14

👥 HERMES

of times mentioned: 1
# of MEN by this name: 1

Meaning: To utter

A Christian acquaintance of the apostle Paul, greeted in Paul's letter to the Romans.

Only reference: Romans 16:14

👥 HERMOGENES

of times mentioned: 1
# of MEN by this name: 1

Meaning: Born of Hermes

An Asian Christian who turned away from Paul.

Only reference: 2 Timothy 1:15

📍 HERMON

of times mentioned: OT 13

Meaning: Abrupt

A mountain north and slightly east of the Sea of Galilee. Og, king of Bashan, ruled this land before he was defeated by Joshua and his army. Joshua conquered "unto Baal-gad in the valley of Lebanon under mount Hermon" (Joshua 11:17). The psalms speak of Hermon in terms of blessing. Same as Senir, Shenir, Sion (1), and Sirion.

First reference: Deuteronomy 3:8 / Last reference: Song of Solomon 4:8 / Key references: Joshua 12:4–5; 13:5, 11

👥 HEROD

of times mentioned: 44
# of MEN by this name: 4

Meaning: Heroic

1) Known as Herod the Great, this evil king of Judea killed several of his own sons and completed many building projects, including improvements on the temple. He was much hated by those he ruled. When the wise men from the East appeared, looking for the king of the Jews, Herod feared for his throne and killed all the male toddlers and infants in Bethlehem. But Joseph and his family had escaped into Egypt. Upon Herod's death, Joseph, Mary, and Jesus returned from Egypt but, fearing to live in the land ruled by his son, moved to Nazareth.

First reference: Matthew 2:1 / Last reference: Acts 23:35

2) Herod Antipas, son of Herod the Great, ruled as tetrarch of Galilee and Perea. John the Baptist opposed Antipas's marriage to Herodias, Antipas's brother's wife, saying that their union was unlawful. When the ruler's stepdaughter danced publicly and pleased him, Herod offered her whatever she wanted. He sorrowfully fulfilled her request—John the Baptist's head on a plate. Hearing of Jesus' miracles, he believed John had returned from the dead.

When Pilate learned that Jesus was from Galilee, he passed him on to Herod to judge. Herod mocked Him and dressed Him in fine clothing. The two rulers became friends that day.

First reference: Matthew 14:1 / Last reference: Acts 12:21

3) The grandson of Herod the Great who ruled over the tetrarchy of Philip and Lysanias, Herod Agrippa I had the apostle James killed and arrested. Seeing that this pleased the Jewish leaders, he also imprisoned Peter. Herod Agrippa died suddenly and horribly when the people of Tyre and Sidon declared him a god and he did not correct them.

First reference: Acts 12:1 / Last reference: Acts 13:1

4) Son of Herod Agrippa I, he ruled over the tetrarchy of Philip and Lysanias. This Herod (Herod Agrippa II) had an incestuous relationship with his sister Bernice, with whom he heard Paul's case with Porcius Festus. Paul almost convinced him to become a Christian. Same as Agrippa.

First reference: Acts 25:13 / Last reference: Acts 26:28

👥 HERODIAS

of times mentioned: 6
# of WOMEN by this name: 1

Meaning: Heroic

Granddaughter of Herod the Great whose second marriage was opposed by John the Baptist. When Herodias's daughter asked what she should request from Herod Antipas, she pushed her to ask for John the Baptist's head on a plate.

First reference: Matthew 14:3 / Last reference: Luke 3:19

👥 HERODION

of times mentioned: 1
# of MEN by this name: 1

Meaning: Heroic

A relative of the apostle Paul, whom Paul greeted in his letter to the Romans.

Only reference: Romans 16:11

HESED

of times mentioned: 1
# of MEN by this name: 1

Meaning: Favor

Father of one of King Solomon's twelve officials over provisions.

Only reference: 1 Kings 4:10

◉ HESHBON

of times mentioned: OT 38

Meaning: Contrivance (implying intelligence)

Capital city of King Sihon of the Amorites. It was conquered by the Israelites after Sihon refused to let Moses and his people pass through on the King's Highway on their way to the Promised Land. Before entering the Promised Land, the tribes of Gad and Reuben requested that Moses make this rich cattle land their inheritance. The prophets Isaiah and Jeremiah speak repeatedly of Heshbon's destruction.

First reference: Numbers 21:25 / Last reference: Jeremiah 49:3 / Key reference: Numbers 21:21–26

◉ HESHMON

of times mentioned: OT 1

Meaning: Opulent

A city that became part of the inheritance of the tribe of Judah following the conquest of the Promised Land.

Only reference: Joshua 15:27

HETH

of times mentioned: 14
# of MEN by this name: 1

Meaning: Terror

A descendant of Noah through his son Ham. Abraham bought a burial site for his wife, Sarah, from the descendants of Heth.

First reference: Genesis 10:15 / Last reference: 1 Chronicles 1:13

◉ HETHLON

of times mentioned: OT 2

Meaning: Enswathed

A landmark on the border of the land of the twelve tribes when Jerusalem is finally restored.

First reference: Ezekiel 47:15 / Last reference: Ezekiel 48:1

HEZEKI

of times mentioned: 1
# of MEN by this name: 1

Meaning: Strong

A descendant of Abraham through Jacob's son Benjamin.

Only reference: 1 Chronicles 8:17

HEZEKIAH

of times mentioned: 128
# of MEN by this name: 3

Meaning: Strengthened of God

1) King of Judah, son of Ahaz, who did right in God's eyes. Hezekiah removed pagan worship from the kingdom and kept God's commandments. Under his command, the Levites cleansed the temple and worship was restored. When the Assyrian king Sennacherib attacked his nation, Hezekiah gave him a large tribute. Sennacherib sent officials to confer with Hezekiah's aides and try to convince his people to side with Sennacherib against their king and God. As Assyria threatened, Isaiah brought the king a comforting prophecy. Sennacherib sent a message to Hezekiah that belittled God and threatened Judah. Hezekiah brought the letter before God and asked Him to save Judah. Again, Isaiah prophesied the Assyrians' fall.

Hezekiah became ill to the point of death, and Isaiah told him he would not recover. After weeping and praying, the king received a message from the prophet that God had extended his life by fifteen years and would deliver and defend Jerusalem from its enemies. Isaiah confirmed this with the sign of a shadow moving back ten steps.

After Hezekiah showed the emissaries of the king of Babylon all that was in his house, Isaiah told him everything in his house would be carried away to that land. His sons would also be taken away and made eunuchs to the Babylonian king. Same as Ezekias.

First reference: 2 Kings 16:20 / Last reference: Micah 1:1 / Key references: 2 Kings 18:1–7; 19:4–7; 20:9–11

2) A descendant of Abraham through Jacob's son Judah, in the line of the nation of Judah's third-to-last king, Jeconiah (also known as Jehoiachin).

Only reference: 1 Chronicles 3:23

3) Forefather of an exiled family that returned to Judah under Zerubbabel.

First reference: Ezra 2:16 / Last reference: Nehemiah 7:21

HEZION

of times mentioned: 1
# of MEN by this name: 1

Meaning: Vision

Grandfather of Ben-hadad, the king of Syria in the days of Judah's king Asa.

Only reference: 1 Kings 15:18

HEZIR

of times mentioned: 2
# of MEN by this name: 2

Meaning: Protected

1) One of twenty-four priests in David's time who was chosen by lot to serve in the tabernacle.

Only reference: 1 Chronicles 24:15

2) A Jewish leader who renewed the covenant under Nehemiah.

Only reference: Nehemiah 10:20

HEZRAI

of times mentioned: 1
# of MEN by this name: 1

Meaning: Enclosure

One of King David's valiant warriors. Same as Hezro.

Only reference: 2 Samuel 23:35

HEZRO

of times mentioned: 1
# of MEN by this name: 1

Meaning: Enclosure

One of King David's valiant warriors. Same as Hezrai.

Only reference: 1 Chronicles 11:37

HEZRON

of times mentioned: 16
# of MEN by this name: 2

Meaning: Courtyard

1) A descendant of Abraham through Jacob's son Judah.

First reference: Genesis 46:12 / Last reference: 1 Chronicles 4:1

2) A descendant of Abraham through Jacob's son Reuben.

First reference: Genesis 46:9 / Last reference: 1 Chronicles 5:3

HEZRON

of times mentioned: OT 2

Meaning: Courtyard

A town that formed part of the border of the tribe of Judah's territory following the conquest of the Promised Land.

First reference: Joshua 15:3 / Last reference: Joshua 15:25

HIDDAI

\# of times mentioned: 1
\# of MEN by this name: 1

One of King David's warriors known as the "mighty men."

Only reference: 2 Samuel 23:30

HIDDEKEL

\# of times mentioned: OT 2

One of the rivers that flowed out of Eden's river. The Hiddekel River flowed into Assyria. It was identified in the Septuagint as the Tigris River.

First reference: Genesis 2:14 / Last reference: Daniel 10:4

HIEL

\# of times mentioned: 1
\# of MEN by this name: 1

Meaning: Living of God

The rebuilder of Jericho. Joshua's prophecy was fulfilled (Joshua 6:26) as Hiel rebuilt the city at the cost of two of his sons' lives.

Only reference: 1 Kings 16:34

HIERAPOLIS

\# of times mentioned: NT 1

Meaning: Holy city

A Phrygian city with a church that was served and possibly founded by Epaphras.

Only reference: Colossians 4:13

HILEN

\# of times mentioned: OT 1

Meaning: Fortress

One of the forty-eight cities given to the Levites as God had commanded. Hilen was given to them by the tribe of Judah.

Only reference: 1 Chronicles 6:58

HILKIAH

\# of times mentioned: 34
\# of MEN by this name: 6

Meaning: Portion of God

1) A priest and father of Eliakim. His son met King Sennacherib's messengers for King Hezekiah of Judah.

First reference: 2 Kings 18:18 / Last reference: Isaiah 36:22

2) High priest during the reign of King Josiah of Judah. He oversaw the counting of the money collected for the work of restoring the temple, discovered the book of the law, and consulted the prophetess Huldah about the discovery.

First reference: 2 Kings 22:4 / Last reference: Jeremiah 29:3 / Key reference: 2 Kings 22:8

3) A forefather of Asaph, a chief singer in the temple.

Only reference: 1 Chronicles 6:45

4) A Levite "porter" (doorkeeper) in the house of the Lord.

Only reference: 1 Chronicles 26:11

5) A priest who assisted Ezra in reading the book of the law to the people of Jerusalem.

First reference: Nehemiah 8:4 / Last reference: Nehemiah 12:7

6) Father of the prophet Jeremiah.

Only reference: Jeremiah 1:1

HILLEL

\# of times mentioned: 2
\# of MEN by this name: 1

Meaning: Praising

Father of Israel's twelfth judge, Abdon.

First reference: Judges 12:13 / Last reference: Judges 12:15

HINNOM

\# of times mentioned: OT 13

A valley southwest of Jerusalem that identifies the borders of the inheritance of the tribes of Judah and Benjamin. Here Kings Ahaz and Manasseh led Judah into idolatry, worshipping Baal in its high places. When good King Josiah of Judah put down idolatry in his land, he defiled Topheth, a site in the valley where the previous kings had sacrificed their children to the pagan god Moloch.

The prophet Jeremiah foresaw that Hinnom would become known as "the valley of slaughter" and would become a graveyard (Jeremiah 7:32). Also called "the valley of the son of Hinnom."

First reference: Joshua 15:8 / Last reference: Jeremiah 32:35 / Key references: 2 Kings 23:10; 2 Chronicles 28:3; 33:6

HIRAH

of times mentioned: 2
# of MEN by this name: 1

Meaning: Splendor

A man from Adullam who became Judah's friend.

First reference: Genesis 38:1 / Last reference: Genesis 38:12

HIRAM

of times mentioned: 23
# of MEN by this name: 2

Meaning: Milk

1) A king of Tyre who provided cedar trees and workmen for building in Israel. "Hiram was ever a lover of David" (1 Kings 5:1) and offered David cedar trees and workmen to build a home. As he prepared to build the temple, Solomon ordered cedar and cypress from Hiram. The two men made a treaty, and Solomon gave Hiram twenty cities in Galilee. When Solomon built a fleet of ships, Hiram provided experienced seamen to aid Solomon's sailors. Hiram's own fleet brought back almug wood, which was used to make supports for the temple.

First reference: 2 Samuel 5:11 / Last reference: 1 Chronicles 14:1 / Key references: 1 Kings 5:1, 8

2) A skilled craftsman who was especially gifted in working brass. He came from Tyre to help build Solomon's house and make utensils for the temple.

First reference: 1 Kings 7:13 / Last reference: 1 Kings 7:45

HIZKIAH

of times mentioned: 1
# of MEN by this name: 1

Meaning: Strengthened of God

An ancestor of the prophet Zephaniah.

Only reference: Zephaniah 1:1

HIZKIJAH

of times mentioned: 1
# of MEN by this name: 1

Meaning: Strengthened of God

A Jewish leader who renewed the covenant under Nehemiah.

Only reference: Nehemiah 10:17

HOBAB

of times mentioned: 2
# of MEN by this name: 1

Meaning: Cherished

Father-in-law of Moses. Same as Jethro.

First reference: Numbers 10:29 / Last reference: Judges 4:11

HOBAH

of times mentioned: OT 1

Meaning: Hiding place

Chedorlaomer, king of Elam, and his Mesopotamian allies captured Abram's nephew Lot in Sodom. When Abram discovered this, he attacked the allies and pursued them to Hobah, near Damascus, to rescue Lot.

Only reference: Genesis 14:15

HOD

of times mentioned: 1
# of MEN by this name: 1

Meaning: How?

A descendant of Abraham through Jacob's son Asher.

Only reference: 1 Chronicles 7:37

👥 HODAIAH

of times mentioned: 1
# of MEN by this name: 1

Meaning: Majesty of God

A descendant of Abraham through Jacob's son Judah, in the line of the nation of Judah's third-to-last king, Jeconiah (also known as Jehoiachin).

Only reference: 1 Chronicles 3:24

👥 HODAVIAH

of times mentioned: 3
# of MEN by this name: 3

Meaning: Majesty of God

1) One of the "mighty men of valour, famous men" leading the half tribe of Manasseh.

Only reference: 1 Chronicles 5:24

2) A descendant of Abraham through Jacob's son Benjamin.

Only reference: 1 Chronicles 9:7

3) Forefather of an exiled family that returned to Judah under Zerubbabel.

Only reference: Ezra 2:40

👥 HODESH

of times mentioned: 1
# of WOMEN by this name: 1

Meaning: A month

Third wife of Shaharaim, with whom she had children in Moab.

Only reference: 1 Chronicles 8:9

👥 HODEVAH

of times mentioned: 1
# of MEN by this name: 1

Meaning: Majesty of God

Forefather of an exiled family that returned to Judah under Zerubbabel.

Only reference: Nehemiah 7:43

👥 HODIAH

of times mentioned: 1
# of WOMEN by this name: 1

Meaning: Celebrated

Wife of Mered, a descendant of Abraham through Jacob's son Judah.

Only reference: 1 Chronicles 4:19

👥 HODIJAH

of times mentioned: 5
# of MEN by this name: 2

Meaning: Celebrated

1) A Levite who helped Ezra to explain the law to exiles returned to Jerusalem. Hodijah was among a group of Levites who led a revival among the Israelites in the time of Nehemiah.

First reference: Nehemiah 8:7 / Last reference: Nehemiah 10:13

2) A Jewish leader who renewed the covenant under Nehemiah.

Only reference: Nehemiah 10:18

👥 HOGLAH

of times mentioned: 4
# of WOMEN by this name: 1

Meaning: Partridge

One of five daughters of Zelophehad, an Israelite who died during the wilderness wanderings. The women asked Moses if they could inherit their father's property in the Promised Land (a right normally reserved for sons), and God ruled that they should.

First reference: Numbers 26:33 / Last reference: Joshua 17:3

HOHAM

of times mentioned: 1
# of MEN by this name: 1

A pagan king of Hebron during Joshua's conquest of the Promised Land, Hoham allied with four other rulers to attack Gibeon, which had deceptively made a peace treaty with the Israelites. Joshua's soldiers defeated the five armies, and Joshua executed the allied kings.

Only reference: Joshua 10:3

HOLON

of times mentioned: OT 3

Meaning: Sandy

1) A city that became part of the inheritance of the tribe of Judah following the conquest of the Promised Land. It became one of the forty-eight cities given to the Levites as God had commanded.

First reference: Joshua 15:51 / Last reference: Joshua 21:15

2) A Moabite city that the prophet Jeremiah foresaw would be judged by God.

Only reference: Jeremiah 48:21

HOMAM

of times mentioned: 1
# of MEN by this name: 1

Meaning: Raging

A descendant of Seir, who lived in Esau's "land of Edom."

Only reference: 1 Chronicles 1:39

HOPHNI

of times mentioned: 5
# of MEN by this name: 1

Meaning: Pugilist

Son of the high priest Eli, who had honored Hophni and his brother Phinehas more than the Lord. The brothers did not know the Lord, misused their priestly office, and disobeyed the law. A man of God prophesied that they would die on the same day. When the Philistines attacked and took the ark of the covenant, both Hophni and Phinehas were killed.

First reference: 1 Samuel 1:3 / Last reference: 1 Samuel 4:17

HOR

of times mentioned: OT 12

Meaning; Mountain

1) A mountain in Edom to which the Israelites came after traveling to Kadesh and being refused passage through Edom by its king. At the age of 123, Aaron died at Mount Hor. His son Eleazar was made high priest in his place.

First reference: Numbers 20:22 / Last reference: Deuteronomy 32:50 / Key reference: Numbers 20:22–28

2) A mountain that God used to mark the northern border of Canaan when He gave it to His people.

First reference: Numbers 34:7 / Last reference: Numbers 34:8

HORAM

of times mentioned: 1
# of MEN by this name: 1

Meaning: High

A king of Gezer who was killed, along with all of his people, by Joshua's army during the conquest of the Promised Land.

Only reference: Joshua 10:33

HOREB

of times mentioned: OT 17

Meaning: Desolate

On this mountain range Moses grazed the sheep belonging to his father-in-law, Jethro, before he brought God's message to Israel. Scholars have debated whether Horeb is another name for Mount Sinai or is simply in the range of mountains in which Mount Sinai lay.

Here Moses struck the rock, at God's command, to provide water for the Israelites during the Exodus. After the Israelites rebelled by worshipping the golden calf, God met Moses at Horeb. But He could not show the prophet His face. Instead He put Moses in a cleft of the rock and let him see His back.

The last chapters of the book of Exodus and Numbers 1–11 take place at Horeb. Here God made a covenant with His people and provided them with a second set of the tablets of the Ten Commandments, since Moses had destroyed the originals in his anger at their idolatry. Then God sent the Israelites to the land of the Amorites and on into the land of Canaan.

At Horeb, the prophet Elijah met God after fleeing from Queen Jezebel. God encouraged and strengthened the prophet, telling him that he was not alone in faithful service to the Lord.

First reference: Exodus 3:1 / Last reference: Malachi 4:4 / Key references: Exodus 34:6–23; Deuteronomy 1:6–8

📍 HOREM

of times mentioned: OT 1

Meaning: Devoted

A fortified or walled city that became part of the inheritance of Naphtali when Joshua cast lots in Shiloh to provide territory for the seven tribes that had yet to receive their land.

Only reference: Joshua 19:38

📍 HOR-HAGIDGAD

of times mentioned: OT 2

Meaning: Hole in the cleft

A campsite of the Israelites on their way to the Promised Land.

First reference: Numbers 33:32 / Last reference: Numbers 33:33

👥 HORI

of times mentioned: 4
# of MEN by this name: 2

Meaning: Cave dweller

1) A descendant of Seir, who lived in Esau's "land

of Edom."

First reference: Genesis 36:22 / Last reference: 1 Chronicles 1:39

2) Father of one of the twelve spies sent by Moses to spy out the land of Canaan.

Only reference: Numbers 13:5

📍 HORMAH

of times mentioned: OT 9

Meaning: Devoted

A city the Canaanites called Zephath, which the Israelites promised God they would destroy if God gave it into their hand. Joshua and his men won the battle and destroyed the city. Hormah became part of the inheritance of the tribe of Judah and then became part of the inheritance of Simeon. This occurred when Joshua cast lots in Shiloh to provide territory for the seven tribes that had yet to receive their land.

Following their conquest of Canaan, the Israelites renamed the city and rebuilt it. David sent some of the spoils from his warfare with the Amalekites to Hormah. Same as Zephath.

First reference: Numbers 14:45 / Last reference: 1 Chronicles 4:30

📍 HORONAIM

of times mentioned: OT 4

Meaning: Double cave town

A city of Moab. Isaiah and Ezekiel described its judgment by God.

First reference: Isaiah 15:5 / Last reference: Jeremiah 48:34

👥 HOSAH

of times mentioned: 4
# of MEN by this name: 1

Meaning: Hopeful

A Levite who was chosen by lot to guard the west side of the house of the Lord.

First reference: 1 Chronicles 16:38 / Last reference: 1 Chronicles 26:16

📍 HOSAH

of times mentioned: OT 1

Meaning: Hopeful

A city that became part of the inheritance of Asher when Joshua cast lots in Shiloh to provide territory for the seven tribes that had yet to receive their land.

Only reference: Joshua 19:29

👥 HOSEA

of times mentioned: 3
# of MEN by this name: 1

Meaning: Deliverer

A minor prophet told by God to marry a prostitute named Gomer. She took a lover and ran from him. God told Hosea to go to her and win her back. The prophet's tumultuous family life paralleled the unfaithfulness of the people of Israel, who had abandoned their covenant with God. The three children born during Hosea's marriage had symbolic names that pointed out Israel's sin. In the Old Testament book that bears his name, Hosea called God's people away from idolatry and back into an intimate relationship with Him.

First reference: Hosea 1:1 / Last reference: Hosea 1:2

👥 HOSHAIAH

of times mentioned: 3
# of MEN by this name: 2

Meaning: God has saved

1) A prince of Judah who participated in the dedication of Jerusalem's rebuilt walls.

Only reference: Nehemiah 12:32

2) Captain of the Israelite forces and father of Azariah (27) who refused to believe Jeremiah's warning not to escape into Egypt.

First reference: Jeremiah 42:1 / Last reference: Jeremiah 43:2

👥 HOSHAMA

of times mentioned: 1
# of MEN by this name: 1

Meaning: Jehovah has heard

A descendant of Abraham through Jacob's son Judah, in the line of the nation of Judah's third-to-last king, Jeconiah (also known as Jehoiachin).

Only reference: 1 Chronicles 3:18

👥 HOSHEA

of times mentioned: 11
# of MEN by this name: 4

Meaning: Deliverer

1) Another name of Joshua, successor to Moses as leader of Israel.

Only reference: Deuteronomy 32:44

2) Leader of the tribe of Ephraim in the days of King David.

Only reference: 1 Chronicles 27:20

3) The Israelite who conspired against King Pekah, killed him, and took his throne. He became a vassal to King Shalmaneser of Assyria but sent messengers to the king of Egypt. Shalmaneser imprisoned Hoshea, captured Samaria, and carried the Israelites off to Assyria.

First reference: 2 Kings 15:30 / Last reference: 2 Kings 18:10

4) A Jewish leader who renewed the covenant under Nehemiah.

Only reference: Nehemiah 10:23

👥 HOTHAM

of times mentioned: 1
# of MEN by this name: 1

Meaning: Seal

A descendant of Abraham through Jacob's son Asher.

Only reference: 1 Chronicles 7:32

HOTHAN

of times mentioned: 1
# of MEN by this name: 1

Meaning: Seal

Father of one of King David's valiant warriors.

Only reference: 1 Chronicles 11:44

HOTHIR

of times mentioned: 2
# of MEN by this name: 1

Meaning: He has caused to remain

A son of King David's musician Heman, who was "under the hands of [his] father for song in the house of the LORD" (1 Chronicles 25:6).

First reference: 1 Chronicles 25:4 / Last reference: 1 Chronicles 25:28

HUKKOK

of times mentioned: OT 1

Meaning: Appointed

A city that became part of the inheritance of Naphtali when Joshua cast lots in Shiloh to provide territory for the seven tribes that had yet to receive their land.

Only reference: Joshua 19:34

HUKOK

of times mentioned: OT 1

Meaning: Appointed

One of the forty-eight cities given to the Levites as God had commanded. Hukok was given to them by the tribe of Asher.

Only reference: 1 Chronicles 6:75

HUL

of times mentioned: 2
# of MEN by this name: 1

Meaning: Circle

A descendant of Noah through his son Shem.

First reference: Genesis 10:23 / Last reference: 1 Chronicles 1:17

HULDAH

of times mentioned: 2
# of WOMEN by this name: 1

Meaning: Weasel

A prophetess who spoke to King Josiah's messengers about a coming judgment of God on Judah. Because King Josiah had heard the book of the law and responded to it, she told him God would defer judgment until after his death.

First reference: 2 Kings 22:14 / Last reference: 2 Chronicles 34:22

HUMTAH

of times mentioned: OT 1

Meaning: Low

A city that became part of the inheritance of the tribe of Judah following the conquest of the Promised Land.

Only reference: Joshua 15:54

HUPHAM

of times mentioned: 1
# of MEN by this name: 1

Meaning: Protection

A descendant of Abraham through Jacob's son Benjamin.

Only reference: Numbers 26:39

HUPPAH

of times mentioned: 1
# of MEN by this name: 1

Meaning: Canopy

One of twenty-four priests in David's time who was chosen by lot to serve in the tabernacle.

Only reference: 1 Chronicles 24:13

HUPPIM

of times mentioned: 3
# of MEN by this name: 1

Meaning: Canopies

A descendant of Abraham through Jacob's son Benjamin.

First reference: Genesis 46:21 / Last reference: 1 Chronicles 7:15

HUR

of times mentioned: 16
# of MEN by this name: 7

Meaning: White

1) An Israelite who held up Moses' hand as the battle against the Amalekites raged so Israel could win. With Aaron, he ruled Israel while Moses was on Mount Sinai.

First reference: Exodus 17:10 / Last reference: Exodus 24:14

2) Father of a craftsman who devised metals and stone designs for the tabernacle.

First reference: Exodus 31:2 / Last reference: 2 Chronicles 1:5

3) A Midianite king killed by the Israelites at God's command to Moses.

First reference: Numbers 31:8 / Last reference: Joshua 13:21

4) Father of one of King Solomon's twelve officials over provisions.

Only reference: 1 Kings 4:8

5) Father of Caleb (1), who spied out the land of Canaan.

First reference: 1 Chronicles 2:50 / Last reference: 1 Chronicles 4:4

6) A descendant of Abraham through Jacob's son Judah.

Only reference: 1 Chronicles 4:1

7) Father of a man who repaired Jerusalem's walls under Nehemiah.

Only reference: Nehemiah 3:9

HURAI

of times mentioned: 1
# of MEN by this name: 1

Meaning: Linen worker

One of King David's valiant warriors.

Only reference: 1 Chronicles 11:32

HURAM

of times mentioned: 12
# of MEN by this name: 3

Meaning: Whiteness

1) A descendant of Abraham through Jacob's son Benjamin.

Only reference: 1 Chronicles 8:5

2) Variation of the name Hiram. Same as Hiram (1).

First reference: 2 Chronicles 2:3 / Last reference: 2 Chronicles 9:21

3) Variation of the name Hiram. Same as Hiram (2).

First reference: 2 Chronicles 4:11 / Last reference: 2 Chronicles 4:16

HURI

of times mentioned: 1
# of MEN by this name: 1

Meaning: Linen worker

A descendant of Abraham through Jacob's son Gad.

Only reference: 1 Chronicles 5:14

HUSHAH

of times mentioned: 1
# of MEN by this name: 1

Meaning: Haste

A descendant of Abraham through Jacob's son Judah.

Only reference: 1 Chronicles 4:4

👥 HUSHAI

of times mentioned: 14
# of MEN by this name: 1

Meaning: Hasty

David's friend, Hushai the Archite, remained in Jerusalem when Absalom ousted the king from the city. At David's request, Hushai became Absalom's advisor, with the intent of protecting David. When Ahithophel wanted to attack his father quickly, Hushai advised against it; then he sent a warning to David to escape.

First reference: 2 Samuel 15:32 / Last reference: 1 Chronicles 27:33 / Key references: 2 Samuel 15:32–34; 16:18

👥 HUSHAM

of times mentioned: 4
# of MEN by this name: 1

Meaning: Hastily

A king of Edom, "before there reigned any king over the children of Israel" (Genesis 36:31).

First reference: Genesis 36:34 / Last reference: 1 Chronicles 1:46

👥 HUSHIM

of times mentioned: 4
# of MEN by this name: 2
# of WOMEN by this name: 1

Meaning: Hasters

1) A descendant of Abraham through Jacob's son Dan.

Only reference: Genesis 46:23

2) A descendant of Abraham through Jacob's son Benjamin.

Only reference: 1 Chronicles 7:12

3) One of two wives of a Benjamite named Shaharaim. He divorced her in favor of other wives in Moab.

First reference: 1 Chronicles 8:8 / Last reference: 1 Chronicles 8:11

👥 HUZ

of times mentioned: 1
# of MEN by this name: 1

Meaning: Consultation

Firstborn son of Nahor, Abraham's brother.

Only reference: Genesis 22:21

📍 HUZZAB

of times mentioned: OT 1

Scholars disagree on the meaning of this name, used poetically only in Nahum 2:7. Some think it describes a queen of Assyria, while others think it is a personification of the nation of Assyria or a region within it.

Only reference: Nahum 2:7

👥 HYMENAEUS

of times mentioned: 2
# of MEN by this name: 1

Meaning: Nuptial

A man who made wrecked his faith and whom Paul accused of blasphemy. Second Timothy 2:18 indicates he had fallen into the Gnostic heresy.

First reference: 1 Timothy 1:20 / Last reference: 2 Timothy 2:17

👥 IBHAR

of times mentioned: 3
# of MEN by this name: 1

Meaning: Choice

A son of King David, born in Jerusalem.

First reference: 2 Samuel 5:15 / Last reference: 1 Chronicles 14:5

📍 IBLEAM

of times mentioned: OT 3

Meaning: Devouring people

A city that became part of the inheritance of the tribe of Manasseh, though it seems to have been in Issachar or Asher's territory. The original inhabitants were not driven out of Ibleam after Israel's conquest of the land. Near here Ahaziah, king of Judah, was killed at Jehu's orders.

First reference: Joshua 17:11 / Last reference: 2 Kings 9:27

IBNEIAH

of times mentioned: 1
# of MEN by this name: 1

Meaning: Built of God

A Jewish exile from the tribe of Benjamin who re-settled Jerusalem.

Only reference: 1 Chronicles 9:8

IBNIJAH

of times mentioned: 1
# of MEN by this name: 1

Meaning: Building of God

Forefather of a Jewish exile from the tribe of Benjamin who resettled Jerusalem.

Only reference: 1 Chronicles 9:8

IBRI

of times mentioned: 1
# of MEN by this name: 1

Meaning: Eberite (Hebrew)

A Levite worship leader during David's reign. Lots were cast to determine his duties.

Only reference: 1 Chronicles 24:27

IBZAN

of times mentioned: 2
# of MEN by this name: 1

Meaning: Splendid

The tenth judge of Israel, who led the nation for seven years. He was known for having thirty sons and thirty daughters. Ibzan sent his daughters abroad and brought in thirty foreign women as wives for his sons.

First reference: Judges 12:8 / Last reference: Judges 12:10

👥 I-CHABOD

of times mentioned: 2
# of MEN by this name: 1

Meaning: There is no glory

Grandson of the high priest Eli, born just after Eli's death.

First reference: 1 Samuel 4:21 / Last reference: 1 Samuel 14:3

📍 ICONIUM

of times mentioned: NT 6

Meaning: Imagelike

Paul and Barnabas first came to this city of Asia Minor after the Jews in Antioch of Pisidia incited the leading people of their city against the apostles. The two men spoke to the Iconian Jews first, but many Greeks of the city were also converted. The city became split, some supporting Paul and Barnabas, others supporting the unbelieving Jews who stirred up trouble for them.

When the Jews sought to stone them, Paul and Barnabas fled to Lystra. But their enemies from Antioch and Iconium followed, and Paul was stoned in Lystra. After moving on to Derbe and preaching there, Paul and Barnabas returned to Iconium and the other cities where they had encountered trouble. They strengthened the churches there, appointing elders to lead them.

When Paul considered adding Timothy to his ministry, the Christians at Iconium recommended the young disciple.

First reference: Acts 13:51 / Last reference: 2 Timothy 3:11

📍 IDALAH

of times mentioned: OT 1

A city that became part of the inheritance of the tribe of Zebulun when Joshua cast lots in Shiloh to provide territory for the seven tribes that had yet to receive their land.

Only reference: Joshua 19:15

👥 IDBASH

of times mentioned: 1
# of MEN by this name: 1

Meaning: Honeyed

A descendant of Abraham through Jacob's son Judah.

Only reference: 1 Chronicles 4:3

👥 IDDO

of times mentioned: 14
# of MEN by this name: 7

Meaning: Timely, appointed

1) Father of one of David's officers who provided food for King Solomon's household.

Only reference: 1 Kings 4:14

2) A descendant of Abraham through Jacob's son Levi.

Only reference: 1 Chronicles 6:21

3) Leader of half the tribe of Manasseh in the days of King David.

Only reference: 1 Chronicles 27:21

4) A prophet who recorded the acts of Kings Solomon, Rehoboam, and Abijah.

First reference: 2 Chronicles 9:29 / Last reference: 2 Chronicles 13:22

5) Father of the prophet Zechariah.

First reference: Ezra 5:1 / Last reference: Zechariah 1:7

6) The leading man of Casiphia, whom Ezra asked for ministers for the temple.

Only reference: Ezra 8:17

7) An exiled priest who returned to Judah under Zerubbabel.

First reference: Nehemiah 12:4 / Last reference: Nehemiah 12:16

📍 IDUMAEA

of times mentioned: NT 1

A Greek name for Edom. Some people from this area, southeast of Judah, were part of the crowd that followed Jesus to the Sea of Galilee. So many people surrounded Him that He had to preach from a boat. Same as Edom and Idumea.

Only reference: Mark 3:8

📍 IDUMEA

of times mentioned: OT 4

Meaning: Edom; red

Another name for Edom, used by the prophets Isaiah and Ezekiel. Isaiah foretold the judgment of this land and a great slaughter there. Ezekiel foresaw that the land would be desolate. Same as Edom and Idumaea.

First reference: Isaiah 34:5 / Last reference: Ezekiel 36:5

👥 IGAL

of times mentioned: 2
# of MEN by this name: 2

Meaning: Avenger

1) One of twelve spies sent by Moses to spy out the land of Canaan.

Only reference: Numbers 13:7

2) One of King David's warriors known as the "mighty men."

Only reference: 2 Samuel 23:36

👥 IGDALIAH

of times mentioned: 1
# of MEN by this name: 1

Meaning: Magnified of God

Father of Hanan, whose chambers Jeremiah borrowed when he tested the Rechabites' obedience.

Only reference: Jeremiah 35:4

IGEAL

\# of times mentioned: 1
\# of MEN by this name: 1

Meaning: Avenger

A descendant of Abraham through Jacob's son Judah, in the line of the nation of Judah's third-to-last king, Jeconiah (also known as Jehoiachin).

Only reference: 1 Chronicles 3:22

 # IIM

\# of times mentioned: OT 2

Meaning: Ruins

1) A campsite of the Israelites on their way to the Promised Land. Same as Ije-abarim.

Only reference: Numbers 33:45

2) A city that became part of the inheritance of the tribe of Judah following the conquest of the Promised Land.

Only reference: Joshua 15:29

IJE-ABARIM

\# of times mentioned: OT 2

Meaning: Ruins of the passers

A campsite of the Israelites on their way to the Promised Land. It lay in the wilderness before Moab. Same as Iim (1).

First reference: Numbers 21:11 / Last reference: Numbers 33:44

IJON

\# of times mentioned: OT 3

Meaning: Ruin

A town of Naphtali that the Syrian prince Ben-hadad conquered at the instigation of King Ada of Judah. During the reign of Pekah, king of Israel, the Assyrian king Tiglath-pileser conquered Ijon and carried away all the people to his own land.

First reference: 1 Kings 15:20 / Last reference: 2 Chronicles 16:4

IKKESH

\# of times mentioned: 3
\# of MEN by this name: 1

Meaning: Perverse

Father of one of King David's valiant warriors.

First reference: 2 Samuel 23:36 / Last reference: 1 Chronicles 27:9

ILAI

\# of times mentioned: 1
\# of MEN by this name: 1

Meaning: Elevated

One of King David's valiant warriors.

Only reference: 1 Chronicles 11:29

ILLYRICUM

\# of times mentioned: NT 1

A Roman province that lay on the northwest border of Macedonia. When he wrote the book of Romans, Paul said he had preached the Gospel from Jerusalem to this area.

Only reference: Romans 15:19

IMLA

\# of times mentioned: 2
\# of MEN by this name: 1

Meaning: Full

Father of Micaiah, a prophet in the time of Israel's king Ahab. Same as Imlah.

First reference: 2 Chronicles 18:7 / Last reference: 2 Chronicles 18:8

IMLAH

\# of times mentioned: 2
\# of MEN by this name: 1

Meaning: Full

Father of Micaiah, a prophet in the time of Israel's king Ahab. Same as Imla.

First reference: 1 Kings 22:8 / Last reference: 1 Kings 22:9

👥 IMMANUEL

of times mentioned: 2
# of MEN by this name: 1

Meaning: With us is God

A prophetic name for a child promised to King Ahaz of Judah. Various Old Testament–era children have been identified as the fulfillment, but this most clearly prophesies the coming of Jesus.

First reference: Isaiah 7:14 / Last reference: Isaiah 8:8

👥 IMMER

of times mentioned: 10
# of MEN by this name: 5

Meaning: Talkative

1) Forefather of a Levite who returned to Jerusalem following the Babylonian captivity.

First reference: 1 Chronicles 9:12 / Last reference: Nehemiah 11:13

2) One of twenty-four priests in David's time who was chosen by lot to serve in the tabernacle.

Only reference: 1 Chronicles 24:14

3) An exile of unclear ancestry who returned to Judah under Zerubbabel.

First reference: Ezra 2:59 / Last reference: Nehemiah 7:61

4) Father of a man who repaired Jerusalem's walls under Nehemiah.

Only reference: Nehemiah 3:29

5) Father of Pashur, a senior priest in the temple who put Jeremiah in the stocks.

Only reference: Jeremiah 20:1

👥 IMNA

of times mentioned: 1
# of MEN by this name: 1

Meaning: He will restrain

A descendant of Abraham through Jacob's son Asher.

Only reference: 1 Chronicles 7:35

👥 IMNAH

of times mentioned: 2
# of MEN by this name: 2

Meaning: Prosperity

1) A descendant of Abraham through Jacob's son Asher.

Only reference: 1 Chronicles 7:30

2) A Levite worship leader whose son Kore had charge of freewill offerings under King Hezekiah.

Only reference: 2 Chronicles 31:14

👥 IMRAH

of times mentioned: 1
# of MEN by this name: 1

Meaning: Interchange

A descendant of Abraham through Jacob's son Asher.

Only reference: 1 Chronicles 7:36

👥 IMRI

of times mentioned: 2
# of MEN by this name: 2

Meaning: Force

1) Forefather of a Jewish exile who returned to Jerusalem.

Only reference: 1 Chronicles 9:4

2) Father of a man who repaired Jerusalem's walls under Nehemiah.

Only reference: Nehemiah 3:2

📍 INDIA

of times mentioned: OT 2

An eastern border of the empire ruled by King Ahasuerus. His Jewish bride, Esther, was queen over this huge territory.

First reference: Esther 1:1 / Last reference: Esther 8:9

IPHEDEIAH

of times mentioned: 1
# of MEN by this name: 1

Meaning: God will liberate

A descendant of Abraham through Jacob's son Benjamin.

Only reference: 1 Chronicles 8:25

IR

of times mentioned: 1
# of MEN by this name: 1

Meaning: City

A descendant of Abraham through Jacob's son Benjamin.

Only reference: 1 Chronicles 7:12

IRA

of times mentioned: 6
# of MEN by this name: 3

Meaning: Wakefulness

1) A royal official serving under Israel's king David.

Only reference: 2 Samuel 20:26

2) A commander in King David's army, overseeing twenty-four thousand men in the sixth month of each year.

First reference: 2 Samuel 23:26 / Last reference: 1 Chronicles 27:9

3) Another of King David's valiant warriors.

First reference: 2 Samuel 23:28 / Last reference: 1 Chronicles 11:40

IRAD

of times mentioned: 2
# of MEN by this name: 1

Meaning: Fugitive

A grandson of Cain and son of Enoch.

Only reference: Genesis 4:18

IRAM

of times mentioned: 2
# of MEN by this name: 1

Meaning: City-wise

A "duke of Edom," a leader in the family line of Esau.

First reference: Genesis 36:43 / Last reference: 1 Chronicles 1:54

IRI

of times mentioned: 1
# of MEN by this name: 1

Meaning: Urbane

A descendant of Abraham through Jacob's son Benjamin.

Only reference: 1 Chronicles 7:7

IRIJAH

of times mentioned: 2
# of MEN by this name: 1

Meaning: Fearful of God

A sentry who seized the prophet Jeremiah, accusing him of deserting to the Chaldeans.

First reference: Jeremiah 37:13 / Last reference: Jeremiah 37:14

IRNAHASH

of times mentioned: 1
# of MEN by this name: 1

Meaning: City of a serpent

A descendant of Abraham through Jacob's son Judah.

Only reference: 1 Chronicles 4:12

IRON

of times mentioned: OT 1

A city that became part of the inheritance of Naphtali when Joshua cast lots in Shiloh to provide territory for the seven tribes that had yet to receive their land.

Only reference: Joshua 19:38

IRPEEL

of times mentioned: OT 1

Meaning: God will heal

A city that became part of the inheritance of Benjamin when Joshua cast lots in Shiloh to provide territory for the seven tribes that had yet to receive their land.

Only reference: Joshua 18:27

IR-SHEMESH

of times mentioned: OT 1

Meaning: City of the sun

A city that became part of the inheritance of Dan when Joshua cast lots in Shiloh to provide territory for the seven tribes that had yet to receive their land.

Only reference: Joshua 19:41

IRU

of times mentioned: 1
# of MEN by this name: 1

Meaning: City-wise

A descendant of Abraham through Jacob's son Judah.

Only reference: 1 Chronicles 4:15

ISAAC

of times mentioned: 132
# of MEN by this name: 1

Meaning: Laughter

The son of Abraham and Sarah whom God promised to the long-barren couple. After Sarah gave Abraham her servant Hagar to bear him a son, Ishmael, Sarah bore Isaac. God tested Abraham by asking him to sacrifice Isaac at Moriah. When Isaac commented on the lack of a lamb to sacrifice, Abraham replied that God would provide it. At the site of sacrifice, Abraham built an altar and placed his son atop it. But the angel of the Lord stopped the sacrifice, and God provided a ram instead.

Abraham sent a servant to his brother Nahor's household to find a wife for Isaac. The man returned with Nahor's daughter Rebekah; Isaac married her and loved her. Rebekah had trouble conceiving, so Isaac prayed for a child. She bore two sons, Esau and Jacob. Esau was Isaac's favorite, but Jacob fooled his elderly, blind father into giving him the blessing of the firstborn child. Isaac had to give Esau a lesser blessing, which caused Esau to hate his brother and required Jacob to leave for a time.

Isaac lived to be 180 years old, and his sons buried him.

First reference: Genesis 17:19 / Last reference: James 2:21 / Key references: Genesis 22:7–9; 24:3–4; 25:19–34

ISAIAH

of times mentioned: 32
# of MEN by this name: 1

Meaning: God has saved

A prophet of Jerusalem who served during the last year of the reign of King Uzziah and through the reigns of Jotham, Ahaz, and Hezekiah. This aristocratic prophet was married to a prophetess and had at least two children.

Isaiah warned Ahaz of an attack by Syria. He supported Ahaz and Hezekiah as the Assyrians became aggressive and sought to expand their empire. But the prophet warned against making treaties with foreign nations.

When Sennacherib, king of Assyria, attacked Judah and encouraged the people of Judah not to fight against him, Isaiah counseled Hezekiah to pray and prophesied that a spirit would enter the Assyrian king and he would return to his own land. Later he promised that God would not let Assyria enter Jerusalem. It happened as Isaiah had foretold.

Hezekiah became sick, and Isaiah prophesied that he would die. Yet when the king prayed, God promised him fifteen more years of life. Isaiah proved it to the king by causing a shadow to go backward on the steps of Ahaz. But after Hezekiah showed his wealth to messengers from the king of Babylon, Isaiah foretold that everything in his house, including his sons, would be captured by Babylon. Same as Esaias.

First reference: 2 Kings 19:2 / Last reference: Isaiah 39:8 / Key references: 2 Kings 19:20–24; 20; Isaiah 1:1

ISCAH

of times mentioned: 1
# of WOMEN by this name: 1

Meaning: Observant

Brother of Abram's sister-in-law Milcah.

Only reference: Genesis 11:29

ISCARIOT

of times mentioned: 11
# of MEN by this name: 1

Meaning: Inhabitant of Kerioth

A name identifying Judas, the disciple who betrayed Jesus. Same as Judas (1).

First reference: Matthew 10:4 / Last reference: John 14:22 / Key references: Mark 14:10; John 13:2, 26

ISHBAH

of times mentioned: 1
# of MEN by this name: 1

Meaning: He will praise

A descendant of Abraham through Jacob's son Judah.

Only reference: 1 Chronicles 4:17

ISHBAK

of times mentioned: 2
# of MEN by this name: 1

Meaning: He will leave

A son of Abraham by his second wife, Keturah.
First reference: Genesis 25:2 / Last reference: 1 Chronicles 1:32

ISHBI-BENOB

of times mentioned: 1
# of MEN by this name: 1

Meaning: His dwelling is in Nob

A Philistine giant who planned to kill a weary King David in battle, but he was felled by David's soldier Abishai. Ishbi-benob carried a spear weighing more than seven pounds.

Only reference: 2 Samuel 21:16

ISH-BOSHETH

of times mentioned: 12
# of MEN by this name: 1

Meaning: Man of shame

King Saul's son who was made king over Israel by Abner, the captain of Saul's army. Ish-bosheth offended Abner by claiming that the captain had slept with Saul's concubine. So Abner turned to David, who sent word to Ish-bosheth and demanded that he return David's wife Michal. Ish-bosheth took her from her second husband and sent her to David. Baanah and Rechab killed Ish-bosheth. The murderers took his head to David, who had them killed and buried the dead king's head in Abner's tomb.

First reference: 2 Samuel 2:8 / Last reference: 2 Samuel 4:12 / Key references: 2 Samuel 3:7; 4:5–8

ISHI

of times mentioned: 5
# of MEN by this name: 4

Meaning: Saving

1) A descendant of Abraham through Jacob's son Judah.

Only reference: 1 Chronicles 2:31

2) Another descendant of Abraham through Jacob's son Judah.

Only reference: 1 Chronicles 4:20

3) The father of four sons who were captains over the sons of Simeon for King Hezekiah of Judah.

Only reference: 1 Chronicles 4:42

4) One of the "mighty men of valour, famous men" leading the half tribe of Manasseh.

Only reference: 1 Chronicles 5:24

👥 ISHIAH

of times mentioned: 1
# of MEN by this name: 1

Meaning: God will lend

A descendant of Abraham through Jacob's son Issachar.

Only reference: 1 Chronicles 7:3

👥 ISHIJAH

of times mentioned: 1
# of MEN by this name: 1

Meaning: God will lend

An exiled Israelite who married a "strange" (foreign) woman.

Only reference: Ezra 10:31

👥 ISHMA

of times mentioned: 1
# of MEN by this name: 1

Meaning: Desolate

A descendant of Abraham through Jacob's son Judah.

Only reference: 1 Chronicles 4:3

👥 ISHMAEL

of times mentioned: 48
# of MEN by this name: 6

Meaning: God will hear

1) Son of Hagar the Egyptian and Abram. He was born after Abram's barren wife, Sarai (later called Sarah), encouraged her husband to have a child with her maid. God rejected Ishmael, who was not the son of His covenant promise. But He promised to bless Ishmael and make him fruitful, so he would found a great nation. Because Ishmael mocked Isaac, Sarah's son, Sarah insisted that Hagar and Ishmael be cast out of the camp. But God watched over them, and they made a home in the wilderness of Paran.

First reference: Genesis 16:11 / Last reference: 1 Chronicles 1:31 / Key references: Genesis 17:18, 20; 21:9–12

2) An official who ruled over the household of Judah's king Jehoshaphat.

Only reference: 2 Chronicles 19:11

3) A descendant of Abraham through Jacob's son Benjamin and the line of King Saul by his son Jonathan.

First reference: 1 Chronicles 8:38 / Last reference: 1 Chronicles 9:44

4) A captain of hundreds under the priest Jehoiada, the regent for King Joash of Judah.

Only reference: 2 Chronicles 23:1

5) An exiled Israelite priest who married a "strange" (foreign) woman.

Only reference: Ezra 10:22

6) An army captain of Judah under Gedaliah, the governor of Judah who was appointed by King Nebuchadnezzar of Babylon. Under the influence of the Ammonite king Baalis, Ishmael killed the governor and his men and fled with the people of Judah toward Egypt. When the captain Johanan came to him, the people followed Johanan, and Ishmael escaped to the Ammorites.

First reference: 2 Kings 25:23 / Last reference: Jeremiah 41:18 / Key references: Jeremiah 40:13–16; 41:2–3, 15

👥 ISHMAIAH

of times mentioned: 1
# of MEN by this name: 1

Meaning: God will hear

Leader of the tribe of Zebulun in the days of King David.

Only reference: 1 Chronicles 27:19

 ISHMERAI

of times mentioned: 1
# of MEN by this name: 1

Meaning: Preservative

A descendant of Abraham through Jacob's son Benjamin.

Only reference: 1 Chronicles 8:18

ISHOD

of times mentioned: 1
# of MEN by this name: 1

Meaning: Man of renown

A descendant of Abraham through Joseph's son Manasseh.

Only reference: 1 Chronicles 7:18

ISHPAN

of times mentioned: 1
# of MEN by this name: 1

Meaning: He will hide

A descendant of Abraham through Jacob's son Benjamin.

Only reference: 1 Chronicles 8:22

ISH-TOB

of times mentioned: OT 2

Meaning: Man of Tob

A small Palestinian kingdom, possibly in Syria, that provided the Ammonites with twelve thousand troops to fight against King David.

First reference: 2 Samuel 10:6 / Last reference: 2 Samuel 10:8

ISHUAH

of times mentioned: 1
# of MEN by this name: 1

Meaning: He will level

A descendant of Abraham through Jacob and his son Asher.

Only reference: Genesis 46:17

ISHUAI

of times mentioned: 1
# of MEN by this name: 1

Meaning: Level

A descendant of Abraham through Jacob's son Asher.

Only reference: 1 Chronicles 7:30

ISHUI

of times mentioned: 1
# of MEN by this name: 1

Meaning: Level

One of three sons of Israel's king Saul. Ishui and his brothers died with Saul in a battle against the Philistines on Mount Gilboa (1 Samuel 31:1–2). Same as Abinadab (3).

Only reference: 1 Samuel 14:49

ISMACHIAH

of times mentioned: 1
# of MEN by this name: 1

Meaning: God will sustain

A temple overseer of offerings during the reign of King Hezekiah of Judah.

Only reference: 2 Chronicles 31:13

ISMAIAH

of times mentioned: 1
# of MEN by this name: 1

Meaning: God will hear

One of King David's warriors known as the "mighty men." Ismaiah was part of an elite group called "the thirty."

Only reference: 1 Chronicles 12:4

👥 ISPAH

of times mentioned: 1
# of MEN by this name: 1

Meaning: He will scratch

A descendant of Abraham through Jacob's son Benjamin.

Only reference: 1 Chronicles 8:16

👥 ISRAEL

of times mentioned: 55
# of MEN by this name: 1

Meaning: He will rule as God

The name given to Jacob by God when he wrestled with Him at Peniel. After renaming him, God again appeared to Jacob, confirmed His covenant promises, and blessed him.

Of his twelve sons, Israel loved Joseph more than the others, gave him a coat of many colors to show his preferred status, and put him in a position of authority. For this, Israel's other sons hated Joseph. They sold him into slavery and convinced their father that Joseph was dead.

When famine came to the land, Israel sent all his sons except Benjamin to Egypt for food. Joseph had risen to second in command of the kingdom there, but his brothers did not recognize him. Joseph demanded that they leave Simeon with him and bring Benjamin to Egypt. Israel reluctantly agreed to send Benjamin. When his sons returned again, telling him Egypt's second in command was Joseph, Israel could hardly believe it. At God's command he traveled to Egypt with all his family and flocks. Joseph met them in Goshen and was reunited with his father. With Pharaoh's approval, Joseph gave his family land in Goshen to settle on.

Israel blessed Joseph's sons, Ephraim and Manasseh, taking them as his own sons. But he gave the younger, Ephraim, the greater blessing, saying he would be the greater one. Then he blessed all his sons and asked that he should be buried in the field at Machpelah with his forefathers. When Israel died, Joseph had him embalmed and buried him as he requested. Same as Jacob (1).

First reference: Genesis 32:28 / Last reference: Ezra 8:18 / Key references: Genesis 35:10–12; 42:1–2; 48:1–5

📍 ISRAEL

of times mentioned: OT 2,511

Meaning: He will rule as God

The nation of God's chosen people, named with the covenant name He gave to Jacob. The Lord originally covenanted with Abraham, calling him to Canaan from Ur of the Chaldees and promising him that he would become a great nation and God would bless him (Genesis 12:1–3). Though Abraham was old, God gave Abraham his son Isaac as the child of promise through whom the blessing would come true. God renewed His covenant with Isaac's son Jacob, promising He would make a nation from his descendants and give them the Promised Land. The nation of Israel was established from Jacob's line and consisted of the twelve tribes named for his sons.

When famine struck, Jacob's sons traveled to Egypt to buy food and discovered that their brother Joseph, whom they had sold into slavery, was second in command of that land and in charge of the food supplies. Joseph invited his family to move to Egypt's land of Goshen, where they could thrive during the famine. The people of Israel stayed in Egypt for four hundred years (Genesis 15:13) and were enslaved by a new pharaoh, who feared their numbers.

Finally, under the leadership of Moses and Aaron, all Israel left Egypt in a huge exodus. But at the doorstep of the Promised Land, the fearful people refused to enter. So this faithless generation lived in the wilderness until they all died. Under the leadership of Joshua, the next generation of Israelites conquered many nations around the Promised Land, as God again led them toward their new country. After conquering the nations of Canaan, they took possession of the land to which God had brought them forty years before.

Unlike the nations around them, Israel was ruled by judges until the people asked the prophet-judge Samuel for a king. Saul became Israel's first king, followed by David, one of Israel's greatest kings. David's line ruled the nation, and God promised to continue his kingly line if his descendants would follow Him. But his son Solomon fell into idolatry, and under David's grandson Rehoboam, the nation split. Only the tribes of Judah and Benjamin followed Rehoboam, who was then crowned king of Judah. The rest of the tribes made Jeroboam king of the nation then called Israel or later Samaria (after the newly established capital).

Many of the kings of both nations turned away

from the Lord. During the rule of Israel's king Hoshea, Assyria conquered Israel, or the northern kingdom. Finding Hoshea unfaithful, Assyria imprisoned him, invaded his land, and eventually captured Samaria. The Israelites were sent to Assyria as captives.

Judah was captured by the Chaldean (Babylonian) Empire, which succeeded Assyria as the major Mesopotamian power. In turn, the Persian king Cyrus conquered Assyria and sent many Jews back to their homeland. Following the Jews' return from exile, the name Israel was again used to refer to the whole nation.

In the intertestamental period, Israel was ruled by various foreign empires, existed a short time as an independent nation, then was conquered by Rome. During the New Testament era, this pagan empire continued to rule the often rebellious nation.

First reference: Genesis 32:32 / Last reference: Malachi 2:11 / Key references: 1 Kings 9:4–5; 12:16–24; 2 Kings 17:1–6

👥 ISSACHAR

of times mentioned: 8
# of MEN by this name: 2

Meaning: He will bring a reward

1) Leah and Jacob's fifth son and Jacob's ninth son. His mother saw him as God's payment to her because she gave her servant, Zilpah, to Jacob. Issachar had four sons.

First reference: Genesis 30:18 / Last reference: 1 Chronicles 7:1

2) A Levite "porter" (doorkeeper) in the house of the Lord.

Only reference: 1 Chronicles 26:5

👥 ISSHIAH

of times mentioned: 3
# of MEN by this name: 2

Meaning: God will lend

1) A Levite worship leader during David's reign. Lots were cast to determine his duties.

Only reference: 1 Chronicles 24:21

2) Another Levite worship leader during David's reign. Lots were cast to determine his duties.

Only reference: 1 Chronicles 24:25

👥 ISUAH

of times mentioned: 1
# of MEN by this name: 1

Meaning: Level

A descendant of Abraham through Jacob's son Asher.

Only reference: 1 Chronicles 7:30

👥 ISUI

of times mentioned: 1
# of MEN by this name: 1

Meaning: Level

A descendant of Abraham through Jacob's son Asher.

Only reference: Genesis 46:17

📍 ITALY

of times mentioned: NT 4

A peninsula south of the Alps whose major city was Rome, capital of the Roman Empire.

Aquila, a Jew who aided Paul in his ministry, had to leave Italy with his wife, Priscilla, because Emperor Claudius expelled the Jews from Rome. Paul sailed for Italy when Herod Agrippa II decided to send him to Rome to be judged by the emperor.

First reference: Acts 18:2 / Last reference: Hebrews 13:24

👥 ITHAI

of times mentioned: 1
# of MEN by this name: 1

Meaning: Near

Father of one of King David's valiant warriors.

Only reference: 1 Chronicles 11:31

👥 ITHAMAR

of times mentioned: 21
# of MEN by this name: 1

Meaning: Coast of the palm tree

A son of Aaron and his wife, Elisheba. With his father and brothers, Ithamar served as a priest. Moses became angry at Ithamar and his brother Eleazar because they would not eat the sin offering in the tabernacle. Ithamar oversaw the Gershonites and the duties of the sons of Merari in the tabernacle.

First reference: Exodus 6:23 / Last reference: Ezra 8:2 / Key references: Numbers 3:4; 4:28, 33

👥 ITHIEL

of times mentioned: 3
# of MEN by this name: 2

Meaning: God has arrived

1) Ancestor of a Benjamite who was chosen by lot to resettle Jerusalem after returning from the Babylonian Exile.

Only reference: Nehemiah 11:7

2) A man to whom Agur spoke the words of Proverbs 30.

Only reference: Proverbs 30:1

👥 ITHMAH

of times mentioned: 1
# of MEN by this name: 1

Meaning: Orphanage

One of King David's valiant warriors.

Only reference: 1 Chronicles 11:46

📍 ITHNAN

of times mentioned: OT 1

Meaning: Extensive

A city that became part of the inheritance of the tribe of Judah following the conquest of the Promised Land.

Only reference: Joshua 15:23

👥 ITHRA

of times mentioned: 1
# of MEN by this name: 1

Meaning: Excellence

An Ishmaelite whose son, Amasa, replaced Joab as David's commander.

Only reference: 2 Samuel 17:25

👥 ITHRAN

of times mentioned: 3
# of MEN by this name: 2

Meaning: Excellent

1) A descendant of Seir, who lived in Esau's "land of Edom."

First reference: Genesis 36:26 / Last reference: 1 Chronicles 1:41

2) A descendant of Abraham through Jacob's son Asher.

Only reference: 1 Chronicles 7:37

👥 ITHREAM

of times mentioned: 2
# of MEN by this name: 1

Meaning: Excellence of people

The sixth son of David, born to his wife Eglah in Hebron.

First reference: 2 Samuel 3:5 / Last reference: 1 Chronicles 3:3

📍 ITTAH-KAZIN

of times mentioned: OT 1

Meaning: Time of a judge

A city that became part of the inheritance of Zebulun when Joshua cast lots in Shiloh to provide territory for the seven tribes that had yet to receive their land.

Only reference: Joshua 19:13

ITTAI

of times mentioned: 8
# of MEN by this name: 2

Meaning: Near

1) A Gittite who remained faithful to David when Absalom tried to overthrow the king. David set Ittai over a third of the people who followed him out of Jerusalem.

First reference: 2 Samuel 15:19 / Last reference: 2 Samuel 18:12

2) One of King David's warriors known as the "mighty men."

Only reference: 2 Samuel 23:29

ITURAEA

of times mentioned: NT 1

A tetrarchy in the northwest part of Palestine, near Mount Hermon. Herod Antipas's brother Philip ruled over Ituraea.

Only reference: Luke 3:1

IVAH

of times mentioned: OT 3

A city conquered by Assyria. Rabshakeh used its destruction as an example to Judah of why Jerusalem should side with his nation.

First reference: 2 Kings 18:34 / Last reference: Isaiah 37:13

IZEHAR

of times mentioned: 1
# of MEN by this name: 1

Meaning: Anointing

A descendant of Levi through his son Kohath.

Only reference: Numbers 3:19

IZHAR

of times mentioned: 8
# of MEN by this name: 1

Meaning: Anointing

A descendant of Abraham through Jacob's son Levi.

First reference: Exodus 6:18 / Last reference: 1 Chronicles 23:18

IZRAHIAH

of times mentioned: 2
# of MEN by this name: 1

Meaning: God will shine

A descendant of Abraham through Jacob's son Issachar.

Only reference: 1 Chronicles 7:3

IZRI

of times mentioned: 1
# of MEN by this name: 1

Meaning: Trough

One of twenty-four Levite musicians who was chosen by lot to serve in the house of the Lord.

Only reference: 1 Chronicles 25:11

JAAKAN

of times mentioned: 1
# of MEN by this name: 1

Meaning: To twist

A descendant of Seir the Horite who lived in the land of Edom; founder of the Jaakanite tribe. Same as Akan and Jakan.

Only reference: Deuteronomy 10:6

JAAKOBAH

of times mentioned: 1
# of MEN by this name: 1

Meaning: Heel catcher

A descendant of Abraham through Jacob's son Simeon.

Only reference: 1 Chronicles 4:36

JAALA

of times mentioned: 1
# of MEN by this name: 1

Meaning: Roe

Forefather of an exiled family—former servants of Solomon—that returned to Judah under Zerubbabel. Same as Jaalah.

Only reference: Nehemiah 7:58

JAALAH

of times mentioned: 1
# of MEN by this name: 1

Meaning: Roe

Forefather of an exiled family—former servants of Solomon—that returned to Judah under Zerubbabel. Same as Jaala.

Only reference: Ezra 2:56

JAALAM

of times mentioned: 4
# of MEN by this name: 1

Meaning: Occult

A son of Esau, whose blessing as older brother was taken by the scheming Jacob.

First reference: Genesis 36:5 / Last reference: 1 Chronicles 1:35

JAANAI

of times mentioned: 1
# of MEN by this name: 1

Meaning: Responsive

A descendant of Abraham through Jacob's son Gad.

Only reference: 1 Chronicles 5:12

JAARE-OREGIM

of times mentioned: 1
# of MEN by this name: 1

Meaning: Woods of weavers

Father of Elhanan. Same as Jair (4).

Only reference: 2 Samuel 21:19

JAASAU

of times mentioned: 1
# of MEN by this name: 1

Meaning: They will do

An exiled Israelite who married a "strange" (foreign) woman.

Only reference: Ezra 10:37

JAASIEL

of times mentioned: 1
# of MEN by this name: 1

Meaning: Made of God

Leader of the tribe of Benjamin in the days of King David.

Only reference: 1 Chronicles 27:21

JAAZANIAH

of times mentioned: 4
# of MEN by this name: 4

Meaning: Heard of God

1) A captain of the army of Judah under Nebuchadnezzar's governor, Gedaliah. Also called Jezaniah.

Only reference: 2 Kings 25:23

2) One of the Rechabites who refused to drink the wine Jeremiah offered them.

Only reference: Jeremiah 35:3

3) A wicked counselor in Jerusalem after the Babylonian Exile.

Only reference: Ezekiel 8:11

4) A prince of Judah whom God described as devising mischief and giving wicked counsel.

Only reference: Ezekiel 11:1

📍 JAAZER

of times mentioned: OT 2

Meaning: Helpful

Moses sent spies to this Amorite city. Israel attacked and took the villages around it, driving out the Amorites who lived there. It became part of the inheritance of the tribe of Gad, which turned it into a fortified city.

First reference: Numbers 21:32 / Last reference: Numbers 32:35

👥 JAAZIAH

of times mentioned: 2
# of MEN by this name: 1

Meaning: Emboldened of God

A Levite worship leader during David's reign. Lots were cast to determine his duties.

First reference: 1 Chronicles 24:26 / Last reference: 1 Chronicles 24:27

👥 JAAZIEL

of times mentioned: 1
# of MEN by this name: 1

Meaning: Emboldened of God

A Levite musician who performed in celebration when King David brought the ark of the covenant to Jerusalem. Same as Aziel.

Only reference: 1 Chronicles 15:18

👥 JABAL

of times mentioned: 1
# of MEN by this name: 1

Meaning: Stream

A descendant of Cain through Lamech and his wife Adah. Jabal was "the father of such as dwell in tents, and of such as have cattle."

Only reference: Genesis 4:20

📍 JABBOK

of times mentioned: OT 7

Meaning: Pouring forth

This river flows from the mountains of Gilead into the Jordan River. Jacob met the Lord near here, at Peniel, after he sent his family across the ford of Jabbok. When the Amorite king Sihon refused to let the Israelites pass through his land on their way to the Promised Land, Israel conquered his land, north to the Jabbok. The Amorite territory east of the Jordan became the inheritance of the tribes of Reuben and Gad. Later the Ammonites demanded that Israel return the land south of the Jabbok to them, but Israel refused their claim.

First reference: Genesis 32:22 / Last reference: Judges 11:22

👥 JABESH

of times mentioned: 3
# of MEN by this name: 1

Meaning: Dry

Forefather of Shallum, who killed King Azariah of Judah and ruled in his place.

First reference: 2 Kings 15:10 / Last reference: 2 Kings 15:14

📍 JABESH

of times mentioned: OT 9

Meaning: Dry

A city of Gad that tried to make peace with Nahash the Ammonite. Nahash declared he would only make peace if the city would let him put out their right eyes. When Saul heard of Jabesh's situation, he rallied all Israel to come to the aid of the city. The tribes gathered and defeated Nahash and his troops. The people were so impressed with Saul's leadership that they confirmed Saul as king of Israel.

After Saul and his sons were killed in battle with the Philistines, the inhabitants of Jabesh, perhaps remembering Saul's defense of their city, recovered the royal family's bodies and burned them. Their bones were buried at Jabesh. Same as Jabesh-gilead.

First reference: 1 Samuel 11:1 / Last reference: 1 Chronicles 10:12

📍 JABESH-GILEAD

of times mentioned: OT 12

Meaning: Dry Gilead

When Israel attacked the Benjaminites for disregarding the rules of hospitality toward a Levite and his concubine and abusing the concubine until she died, the town of Jabesh-gilead did not come to battle. So the Israelites attacked Jabesh-gilead and killed everyone in the city except four hundred young virgins, whom they gave to the remaining Benjaminites as wives.

After Saul and his sons were killed in battle with the Philistines, the inhabitants of Jabesh-gilead recovered their bodies and burned them. Their bones were buried at Jabesh-gilead. Same as Jabesh.

First reference: Judges 21:8 / Last reference: 1 Chronicles 10:11 / Key reference: Judges 21:8–14

👥 JABEZ

of times mentioned: 3
# of MEN by this name: 1

Meaning: To grieve

A pious man of the line of Judah who prayed for God's blessing, that He would enlarge his border, and that God's hand would be with him and keep him from harm.

First reference: 1 Chronicles 4:9 / Last reference: 1 Chronicles 4:10

📍 JABEZ

of times mentioned: OT 1

Meaning: Sorrowful

A city of Judah where Kenite scribes lived.

Only reference: 1 Chronicles 2:55

👥 JABIN

of times mentioned: 8
# of MEN by this name: 2

Meaning: Intelligent

1) The king of Hazor who raised armies against Joshua and his invading troops.

Only reference: Joshua 11:1

2) The king of Canaan who had Sisera as the captain of his army. Since there was peace between Jabin and Heber the Kenite, Sisera fled to Heber's tents, where Heber's wife, Jael, killed him. God used this event to subdue Jabin.

First reference: Judges 4:2 / Last reference: Psalm 83:9

📍 JABNEEL

of times mentioned: OT 2

Meaning: Built of God

1) A city that formed part of the border of the tribe of Judah's territory.

Only reference: Joshua 15:11

2) A city that became part of the inheritance of Naphtali when Joshua cast lots in Shiloh to provide territory for the seven tribes that had yet to receive their land.

Only reference: Joshua 19:33

📍 JABNEH

of times mentioned: OT 1

Meaning: A building

A city of the Philistines that was conquered by Judah's king Uzziah.

Only reference: 2 Chronicles 26:6

👥 JACHAN

of times mentioned: 1
# of MEN by this name: 1

Meaning: Troublesome

A descendant of Abraham through Jacob's son Gad.

Only reference: 1 Chronicles 5:13

👥 JACHIN

of times mentioned: 6
# of MEN by this name: 3

Meaning: He will establish

1) A descendant of Abraham through Jacob's son Simeon.

First reference: Genesis 46:10 / Last reference: Numbers 26:12

2) A Jewish exile and priest who resettled Jerusalem.

First reference: 1 Chronicles 9:10 / Last reference: Nehemiah 11:10

3) One of twenty-four priests in David's time who was chosen by lot to serve in the tabernacle.

Only reference: 1 Chronicles 24:17

⚑ JACHIN

of times mentioned: OT 2

Meaning: He will establish

The right pillar on the porch of Solomon's temple.

First reference: 1 Kings 7:21 / Last reference: 2 Chronicles 3:17

👥 JACOB

of times mentioned: 280
# of MEN by this name: 2

Genealogy of Jesus: Yes (Matthew 1:2)

Meaning: Supplanter

1) Isaac and Rebekah's son who was born clinging to the heel of his twin brother, Esau. When the exhausted hunter, Esau, came home and asked Jacob for his lentil stew, Jacob offered to sell it to him for his birthright. Esau accepted.

When Isaac was old and blind, he asked Esau to hunt game for him and promised his blessing. Rebekah overheard and warned Jacob. Together they plotted to gain the blessing for Jacob. Jacob covered himself with goatskins so he would seem as hairy as his brother, fed his father goat stew, and received the firstborn's greater blessing. Esau had to make do with a lesser one. To evade Esau's anger, Jacob fled to his uncle Laban's household. During his trip there, God promised to bring Jacob many descendants and bless the earth through them.

Tricked by Laban, Jacob married both his daughters, Leah and Jacob's beloved Rachel. From them and their handmaids, Bilhah and Zilpah, Jacob had twelve sons, who became the founders of Israel's twelve tribes. After deceiving his father-in-law, Jacob fled toward home. He met God, wrestled with Him, was renamed Israel, and began to understand God's deliverance. When he met Esau, Jacob discovered that his fears were groundless. Esau was no longer angry. See also Israel. Same as Israel.

First reference: Genesis 25:26 / Last reference: Hebrews 11:21 / Key references: Genesis 27:27–29, 39–40; 32:28–30

2) A descendant of Abraham through Isaac; forebear of Jesus' earthly father, Joseph.

First reference: Matthew 1:15 / Last reference: Matthew 1:16

Genealogy of Jesus: Yes (Matthew 1:15–16)

👥 JADA

of times mentioned: 2
# of MEN by this name: 1

Meaning: Knowing

A descendant of Abraham through Jacob's son Judah.

First reference: 1 Chronicles 2:28 / Last reference: 1 Chronicles 2:32

👥 JADAU

of times mentioned: 1
# of MEN by this name: 1

Meaning: Praised

An exiled Israelite who married a "strange" (foreign) woman.

Only reference: Ezra 10:43

👥 JADDUA

of times mentioned: 3
# of MEN by this name: 2

Meaning: Knowing

1) A Jewish leader who renewed the covenant under Nehemiah.

Only reference: Nehemiah 10:21

2) A Levite worship leader who returned to Jerusalem with Zerubbabel.

First reference: Nehemiah 12:11 / Last reference: Nehemiah 12:22

JADON

of times mentioned: 1
# of MEN by this name: 1

Meaning: Thankful

A man who repaired Jerusalem's walls under Nehemiah.

Only reference: Nehemiah 3:7

JAEL

of times mentioned: 6
# of WOMEN by this name: 1

Meaning: Ibex

The wife of Heber the Kenite who killed the Canaanite commander Sisera when he fled to her tent following his defeat by the Israelites. She invited him in and then took a tent peg and drove it through his temple. This death fulfilled the Israelite judge Deborah's prophecy.

First reference: Judges 4:17 / Last reference: Judges 5:24

JAGUR

of times mentioned: OT 1

Meaning: A lodging

A city that became part of the inheritance of the tribe of Judah following the conquest of the Promised Land.

Only reference: Joshua 15:21

JAHATH

of times mentioned: 8
# of MEN by this name: 5

Meaning: Unity

1) A descendant of Abraham through Jacob's son Judah.

Only reference: 1 Chronicles 4:2

2) A descendant of Abraham through Jacob's son Levi.

First reference: 1 Chronicles 6:20 / Last reference: 1 Chronicles 6:43

3) A Levite worship leader who was part of King David's reorganization of the Levites.

First reference: 1 Chronicles 23:10 / Last reference: 1 Chronicles 23:11

4) A Levite worship leader during David's reign. Lots were cast to determine his duties.

Only reference: 1 Chronicles 24:22

5) A Levite worship leader who oversaw the repair of the temple under King Josiah.

Only reference: 2 Chronicles 34:12

JAHAZ

of times mentioned: OT 5

Meaning: Threshing floor

A city where the Amorite king Sihon fought and lost to Israel after he would not let the Israelites travel through his land on their way to the Promised Land. Same as Jahaza, Jahazah, and Jahzah.

First reference: Numbers 21:23 / Last reference: Jeremiah 48:34

JAHAZA

of times mentioned: OT 1

Meaning: Threshing floor

A city east of the Dead Sea that became part of the inheritance of Reuben. Same as Jahaz, Jahazah, and Jahzah.

Only reference: Joshua 13:18

JAHAZAH

of times mentioned: OT 2

Meaning: Threshing floor

One of the forty-eight cities given to the Levites as God had commanded. Jahazah was given to them by the tribe of Reuben. Jeremiah foresaw its judgment by God. Same as Jahaz, Jahaza, and Jahzah.

First reference: Joshua 21:36 / Last reference: Jeremiah 48:21

👥 JAHAZIAH

of times mentioned: 1
# of MEN by this name: 1

Meaning: God will behold

A man who oversaw the Israelites who needed to put away "strange" (foreign) wives under Ezra.

Only reference: Ezra 10:15

👥 JAHAZIEL

of times mentioned: 6
# of MEN by this name: 5

Meaning: Beheld of God

1) A "mighty man" who supported the future king David during his conflict with Saul.

Only reference: 1 Chronicles 12:4

2) A priest who blew a trumpet when David brought the ark of the Lord to Jerusalem.

Only reference: 1 Chronicles 16:6

3) A Levite worship leader who was part of David's reorganization of the Levites.

First reference: 1 Chronicles 23:19 / Last reference: 1 Chronicles 24:23

4) A Levite worship leader who prophesied before King Jehoshaphat of Judah when Edom attacked.

Only reference: 2 Chronicles 20:14

5) Forefather of a Jewish exile who returned from Babylon to Judah under Ezra.

Only reference: Ezra 8:5

👥 JAHDAI

of times mentioned: 1
# of MEN by this name: 1

Meaning: Jehovah fired

A descendant of Abraham through Jacob's son Judah.

Only reference: 1 Chronicles 2:47

👥 JAHDIEL

of times mentioned: 1
# of MEN by this name: 1

Meaning: Unity of God

One of the "mighty men of valour, famous men" leading the half tribe of Manasseh.

Only reference: 1 Chronicles 5:24

👥 JAHDO

of times mentioned: 1
# of MEN by this name: 1

Meaning: His unity; together

A descendant of Abraham through Jacob's son Gad.

Only reference: 1 Chronicles 5:14

👥 JAHLEEL

of times mentioned: 2
# of MEN by this name: 1

Meaning: Wait for God

A descendant of Abraham through Jacob's son Zebulun.

First reference: Genesis 46:14 / Last reference: Numbers 26:26

👥 JAHMAI

of times mentioned: 1
# of MEN by this name: 1

Meaning: Hot

A descendant of Abraham through Jacob's son Issachar.

Only reference: 1 Chronicles 7:2

♀ JAHZAH

of times mentioned: OT 1

Meaning: Threshing floor

One of the forty-eight cities given to the Levites as God had commanded. Jahzah was given to them by the tribe of Reuben. Same as Jahaz, Jahaza, and Jahazah.

Only reference: 1 Chronicles 6:78

👥 JAHZEEL

of times mentioned: 2
# of MEN by this name: 1

Meaning: God will allot

A descendant of Abraham through Jacob's son Naphtali. Same as Jahziel.

First reference: Genesis 46:24 / Last reference: Numbers 26:48

👥 JAHZERAH

of times mentioned: 1
# of MEN by this name: 1

Meaning: Protection

Forefather of a Levite who returned to Jerusalem after the Babylonian captivity.

Only reference: 1 Chronicles 9:12

👥 JAHZIEL

of times mentioned: 1
# of MEN by this name: 1

Meaning: Allotted of God

A descendant of Abraham through Jacob's son Naphtali. Same as Jahzeel.

Only reference: 1 Chronicles 7:13

👥 JAIR

of times mentioned: 9
# of MEN by this name: 4

Meaning: Enlightener

1) A descendant of Manasseh who captured twenty-three cities of Bashan and named them Havvoth-jair.

First reference: Numbers 32:41 / Last reference: 1 Chronicles 2:22

2) The eighth judge of Israel, who led the nation for twenty-two years. He was known for having thirty sons who rode thirty donkeys.

First reference: Judges 10:3 / Last reference: Judges 10:5

3) The father of Mordecai, Queen Esther's cousin.

Only reference: Esther 2:5

4) Father of Elhanan, who killed Goliath's brother. Same as Jaare-oregim.

Only reference: 1 Chronicles 20:5

♀ JAIR

of times mentioned: OT 2

Meaning: Enlightener

An area of Bashan that became part of the inheritance of the tribe of Manasseh.

First reference: Joshua 13:30 / Last reference: 1 Chronicles 2:23

👥 JAIRUS

of times mentioned: 2
# of MEN by this name: 1

Meaning: Enlightener

A synagogue ruler who asked Jesus to come and heal his daughter. She died before they could reach her, but Jesus brought her back to life.

First reference: Mark 5:22 / Last reference: Luke 8:41

👥 JAKAN

of times mentioned: 1
# of MEN by this name: 1

Meaning: Tortuous

A descendant of Seir the Horite who lived in the land of Edom. Same as Akan or Jaakan.

Only reference: 1 Chronicles 1:42

JAKEH

of times mentioned: 1
# of MEN by this name: 1

Meaning: Obedient

Father of the little-known biblical writer who wrote the thirtieth chapter of Proverbs.

Only reference: Proverbs 30:1

JAKIM

of times mentioned: 2
# of MEN by this name: 2

Meaning: He will raise

1) A descendant of Abraham through Jacob's son Benjamin.

Only reference: 1 Chronicles 8:19

2) One of twenty-four priests in David's time who was chosen by lot to serve in the tabernacle.

Only reference: 1 Chronicles 24:12

JALON

of times mentioned: 1
# of MEN by this name: 1

Meaning: Lodging

A descendant of Abraham through Jacob's son Judah.

Only reference: 1 Chronicles 4:17

JAMBRES

of times mentioned: 1
# of MEN by this name: 1

An opponent of Moses mentioned by the apostle Paul as an example of apostasy.

Only reference: 2 Timothy 3:8

JAMES

of times mentioned: 42
# of MEN by this name: 3

1) Zebedee's son and John's brother. With John, this fisherman was called by Jesus to become a fisher of men as one of His disciples. He was part of the intimate group of disciples who witnessed the healing of Simon's mother-in-law, the raising of Jairus's daughter, and the transfiguration of Jesus. With his brother, he boldly sought to call down fire on an unbelieving village and asked to sit at Jesus' right or left hand in glory. He was among the disciples who asked when the temple would fall and who spent the night in Gethsemane with Jesus.

Following Jesus' death, James remained with the disciples in the upper room in prayer. He was executed by Herod Agrippa I.

First reference: Matthew 4:21 / Last reference: Acts 12:2 / Key references: Mark 1:17–20; 5:37; 9:2–3; Acts 12:1–2

2) Son of Alphaeus and disciple of Jesus. Scripture only mentions him in lists of the disciples. He was one of those in the upper room, praying, following Jesus' death.

First reference: Matthew 10:3 / Last reference: Acts 1:13

3) Jesus' brother, called James the less (younger). When the people of the synagogue were astonished at Jesus' teachings, they asked if this was not the brother of James.

James became a leader in the Jerusalem church. Paul visited him after returning from Arabia. When he saw that Paul had received God's grace, James and some other disciples accepted him for ministry. Freed from prison, Peter requested that James be informed, and James spoke for the disciples during the Jerusalem Council, which had convened to address the subject of Gentile circumcision. Paul again consulted James on this subject when he returned to Jerusalem.

This James is believed by many to be the writer of the book of James in the New Testament.

First reference: Matthew 13:55 / Last reference: Jude 1:1 / Key references: Mark 6:3; 15:40; 1 Corinthians 15:7; Galatians 2:9

👥 JAMIN

of times mentioned: 6
# of MEN by this name: 3

Meaning: Right hand

1) A descendant of Abraham through Jacob's son Simeon.

First reference: Genesis 46:10 / Last reference: 1 Chronicles 4:24

2) A descendant of Abraham through Jacob's son Judah.

Only reference: 1 Chronicles 2:27

3) A Levite who helped Ezra to explain the law to exiles who returned to Jerusalem.

Only reference: Nehemiah 8:7

👥 JAMLECH

of times mentioned: 1
# of MEN by this name: 1

Meaning: He will make king

A descendant of Abraham through Jacob's son Simeon.

Only reference: 1 Chronicles 4:34

👥 JANNA

of times mentioned: 1
# of MEN by this name: 1

Genealogy of Jesus: Yes (Luke 3:24)

Meaning: Oppressor

A descendant of Abraham through Isaac; forebear of Jesus' earthly father, Joseph.

Only reference: Luke 3:24

👥 JANNES

of times mentioned: 1
# of MEN by this name: 1

Meaning: To cure

An opponent of Moses mentioned by the apostle Paul as an example of apostasy.

Only reference: 2 Timothy 3:8

📍 JANOAH

of times mentioned: OT 1

Meaning: Quiet

During the reign of Pekah, king of Israel, the Assyrian king Tiglath-pileser conquered this city of the tribe of Naphtali, captured its people, and carried them to his own land.

Only reference: 2 Kings 15:29

📍 JANOHAH

of times mentioned: OT 2

Meaning: Quiet

A border city of Ephraim that lay between Taanath-shiloh and Naarath.

First reference: Joshua 16:6 / Last reference: Joshua 16:7

📍 JANUM

of times mentioned: OT 1

Meaning: Asleep

A city that became part of the inheritance of the tribe of Judah following the conquest of the Promised Land.

Only reference: Joshua 15:53

👥 JAPHETH

of times mentioned: 11
# of MEN by this name: 1

Meaning: Expansion

Noah's third son, who joined his family in the ark. After leaving the ark, when Noah became drunk and lay unclothed in his tent, Japheth and his brother Shem covered their father without looking at him. For this, Noah asked that God would bless him. Japheth had seven sons and became forefather of the coastland peoples.

First reference: Genesis 5:32 / Last reference: 1 Chronicles 1:5

JAPHIA

of times mentioned: 4
# of MEN by this name: 2

Meaning: Bright

1) The king of Lachish during Joshua's conquest of the Promised Land. Japhia allied with four other rulers to attack Gibeon, which had deceptively made a peace treaty with the Israelites. Joshua's soldiers defeated the five armies, and Joshua executed the allied kings.

Only reference: Joshua 10:3

2) A son of King David, born in Jerusalem.

First reference: 2 Samuel 5:15 / Last reference: 1 Chronicles 14:6

JAPHIA

of times mentioned: OT 1

Meaning: Bright

A town that became part of the inheritance of Zebulun when Joshua cast lots in Shiloh to provide territory for the seven tribes that had yet to receive their land.

Only reference: Joshua 19:12

JAPHLET

of times mentioned: 3
# of MEN by this name: 1

Meaning: He will deliver

A descendant of Abraham through Jacob's son Asher.

First reference: 1 Chronicles 7:32 / Last reference: 1 Chronicles 7:33

JAPHLETI

of times mentioned: OT 1

Meaning: He will deliver

"The coast of Japhleti" marked the border of the inheritance of the children of Joseph (Ephraim and Manasseh).

Only reference: Joshua 16:3

JAPHO

of times mentioned: OT 1

Meaning: Beautiful

A city that became part of the inheritance of Dan when Joshua cast lots in Shiloh to provide territory for the seven tribes that had yet to receive their land.

Only reference: Joshua 19:46

JARAH

of times mentioned: 2
# of MEN by this name: 1

Meaning: Honey in the comb

A descendant of Abraham through Jacob's son Benjamin. Same as Jehoadah.

Only reference: 1 Chronicles 9:42

JAREB

of times mentioned: 2
# of MEN by this name: 1

Meaning: He will contend

An Assyrian king mentioned in the prophecies of Hosea.

First reference: Hosea 5:13 / Last reference: Hosea 10:6

JARED

of times mentioned: 6
# of MEN by this name: 1

Meaning: A descent

A descendant of Adam through Adam's son Seth. Jared was the second-longest-lived individual in the Bible at 962 years. Same as Jered.

First reference: Genesis 5:15 / Last reference: Luke 3:37

 JARESIAH

of times mentioned: 1
# of MEN by this name: 1

Meaning: Uncertain

A descendant of Abraham through Jacob's son Benjamin.

Only reference: 1 Chronicles 8:27

JARHA

of times mentioned: 2
# of MEN by this name: 1

The Egyptian servant of Sheshan, a descendant of Abraham through Jacob's son Judah. Jarha married a daughter of Sheshan.

First reference: 1 Chronicles 2:34 / Last reference: 1 Chronicles 2:35

JARIB

of times mentioned: 3
# of MEN by this name: 3

Meaning: He will contend

1) A descendant of Abraham through Jacob's son Simeon.

Only reference: 1 Chronicles 4:24

2) A Jewish exile in Babylon charged with finding Levites and temple servants to travel to Jerusalem with Ezra.

Only reference: Ezra 8:16

3) An exiled Israelite priest who married a "strange" (foreign) woman.

Only reference: Ezra 10:18

JARMUTH

of times mentioned: OT 7

Meaning: Elevation

1) An Amorite city that fought Gibeon because Gibeon made a covenant with the Israelites. After Israel joined its ally and won the battle, Joshua killed Jarmuth's king. Jarmuth became part of the inheritance of the tribe of Judah following the conquest of the Promised Land. It was resettled after the return from the Babylonian Exile.

First reference: Joshua 10:3 / Last reference: Nehemiah 11:29

2) One of the forty-eight cities given to the Levites as God had commanded. Jarmuth was given to them by the tribe of Issachar.

Only reference: Joshua 21:29

JAROAH

of times mentioned: 1
# of MEN by this name: 1

Meaning: Born at the new moon

A descendant of Abraham through Jacob's son Gad.

Only reference: 1 Chronicles 5:14

JASHEN

of times mentioned: 1
# of MEN by this name: 1

Meaning: Sleepy

Father of several of King David's warriors known as the "mighty men."

Only reference: 2 Samuel 23:32

JASHOBEAM

of times mentioned: 3
# of MEN by this name: 2

Meaning: People will return

1) A commander in King David's army, overseeing twenty-four thousand men in the first month of each year. Jashobeam was one of David's "mighty men," who once single-handedly killed three hundred enemy soldiers.

First reference: 1 Chronicles 11:11 / Last reference: 1 Chronicles 27:2

2) A "mighty man" who supported the future king David during his conflict with Saul.

Only reference: 1 Chronicles 12:6

JASHUB

of times mentioned: 3
# of MEN by this name: 2

Meaning: He will return

1) A descendant of Abraham through Jacob's son Issachar. Same as Job (1).

First reference: Numbers 26:24 / Last reference: 1 Chronicles 7:1

2) An exiled Israelite who married a "strange" (foreign) woman.

Only reference: Ezra 10:29

JASHUBI-LEHEM

of times mentioned: 1
# of MEN by this name: 1

Meaning: Returner of bread

A descendant of Abraham through Jacob and his son Judah.

Only reference: 1 Chronicles 4:22

JASIEL

of times mentioned: 1
# of MEN by this name: 1

Meaning: Made of God

One of King David's valiant warriors.

Only reference: 1 Chronicles 11:47

JASON

of times mentioned: 5
# of MEN by this name: 2

Meaning: About to cure

1) A Christian of Thessalonica whose house was attacked by jealous Jews who dragged him and other Christians before the city officials. The Jews claimed the Christians had said there was another king, Jesus. After taking money from the Christians as security, the Roman officials released them.

First reference: Acts 17:5 / Last reference: Acts 17:9

2) A relative of Paul, living in Rome, who was greeted in the apostle's letter to the Romans.

Only reference: Romans 16:21

JATHNIEL

of times mentioned: 1
# of MEN by this name: 1

Meaning: Continued of God

A Levite "porter" (doorkeeper) in the house of the Lord.

Only reference: 1 Chronicles 26:2

JATTIR

of times mentioned: OT 4

Meaning: Redundant

A city that became part of the inheritance of the tribe of Judah following the conquest of the Promised Land. It later became one of the forty-eight cities given to the Levites as God had commanded. David sent Jattir some of the spoils from his warfare with the Amalekites.

First reference: Joshua 15:48 / Last reference: 1 Chronicles 6:57

JAVAN

of times mentioned: 4
# of MEN by this name: 1

Meaning: Effervescing

A grandson of Noah through his son Japheth. Javan had four sons.

First reference: Genesis 10:2 / Last reference: 1 Chronicles 1:7

📍 JAVAN

of times mentioned: OT 2

Meaning: Dregs; mud

A city of southern Arabia that traded with Tyre, selling goods in its fairs and marketplaces.

First reference: Ezekiel 27:13 / Last reference: Ezekiel 27:19

📍 JAZER

of times mentioned: OT 11

Meaning: Helpful

An Amorite city east of the Jordan River that the tribe of Gad requested as part of its inheritance. It later became one of the forty-eight cities given to the Levites as God had commanded. The prophets Isaiah and Jeremiah speak of the city's mourning over a destroyed harvest.

First reference: Numbers 32:1 / Last reference: Jeremiah 48:32

👥 JAZIZ

of times mentioned: 1
# of MEN by this name: 1

Meaning: He will make prominent

Called Jaziz the Hagarite, he was in charge of King David's flocks.

Only reference: 1 Chronicles 27:31

📍 JEARIM

of times mentioned: OT 1

Meaning: Forests

A mountain that formed part of the border of the tribe of Judah's territory. Same as Chesalon.

Only reference: Joshua 15:10

👥 JEATERAI

of times mentioned: 1
# of MEN by this name: 1

Meaning: Stepping

A descendant of Abraham through Jacob's son Levi.

Only reference: 1 Chronicles 6:21

👥 JEBERECHIAH

of times mentioned: 1
# of MEN by this name: 1

Meaning: Blessed of God

Forefather of Zechariah (27).

Only reference: Isaiah 8:2

📍 JEBUS

of times mentioned: OT 4

Meaning: Trodden (that is, threshing place)

The name of Jerusalem when it belonged to the Jebusites. A Levite refused to stay overnight in Jebus and went on to Gibeah, where his concubine was abused and died. After David was anointed king of Israel, the Jebusites refused to have him come to the city, so David captured it. In this battle, Joab earned the position as commander of David's troops. Same as Jebusi, Jerusalem, Salem, and Zion.

First reference: Judges 19:10 / Last reference: 1 Chronicles 11:5

📍 JEBUSI

of times mentioned: OT 2

Meaning: A Jebusite

An early name for Jerusalem. When Joshua cast lots in Shiloh to provide territory for the seven tribes that had yet to receive their land, Jebusi was the name used to describe this city on the border of the tribe of Benjamin's territory. Same as Jebus, Jerusalem, Salem, and Zion.

First reference: Joshua 18:16 / Last reference: Joshua 18:28

👥 JECAMIAH

of times mentioned: 1
# of MEN by this name: 1

Meaning: God will rise

A descendant of Abraham through Jacob's son Judah, in the line of the nation of Judah's third-to-last king, Jeconiah (also known as Jehoiachin). Same as Jekamiah.

Only reference: 1 Chronicles 3:18

👪 JECHOLIAH

of times mentioned: 1
# of WOMEN by this name: 1

Meaning: Jehovah will enable

Mother of Judah's good king Azariah, also known as Uzziah. Same as Jecoliah.

Only reference: 2 Kings 15:2

👪 JECHONIAS

of times mentioned: 2
# of MEN by this name: 1

Genealogy of Jesus: Yes (Matthew 1:11–12)

Meaning: Jehovah will establish

Greek form of the name Jeconiah, used in the New Testament.

First reference: Matthew 1:11 / Last reference: Matthew 1:12

👪 JECOLIAH

of times mentioned: 1
# of WOMEN by this name: 1

Meaning: God will enable

Mother of Judah's good king Uzziah, also known as Azariah. Same as Jecholiah.

Only reference: 2 Chronicles 26:3

👪 JECONIAH

of times mentioned: 7
# of MEN by this name: 1

Meaning: God will establish

King of Judah and son of King Jehoiakim. King Nebuchadnezzar carried him and his nobles to Babylon. Hananiah prophesied that he would return to Jerusalem, but, through Jeremiah, God revealed that he would not. Same as Coniah, Jechonias, and Jehoiachin.

First reference: 1 Chronicles 3:16 / Last reference: Jeremiah 29:2

👪 JEDAIAH

of times mentioned: 13
# of MEN by this name: 5

Meaning: Praised of God

1) A descendant of Abraham through Jacob's son Simeon.

Only reference: 1 Chronicles 4:37

2) A rebuilder of the walls of Jerusalem under Nehemiah.

Only reference: Nehemiah 3:10

3) One of twenty-four priests in David's time who was chosen by lot to serve in the tabernacle.

First reference: 1 Chronicles 9:10 / Last reference: Nehemiah 7:39

4) A priest who returned from exile with Zerubbabel and lived in Jerusalem. The prophet Zechariah prophesied that there would be a memorial to him in the temple.

First reference: Nehemiah 11:10 / Last reference: Zechariah 6:14

5) An exiled priest who returned to Judah under Zerubbabel.

First reference: Nehemiah 12:7 / Last reference: Nehemiah 12:21

👪 JEDIAEL

of times mentioned: 6
# of MEN by this name: 4

Meaning: Knowing God

1) A descendant of Abraham through Jacob's son Benjamin.

First reference: 1 Chronicles 7:6 / Last reference: 1 Chronicles 7:11

2) One of King David's valiant warriors.

Only reference: 1 Chronicles 11:45

3) A captain of thousands for the tribe of Manasseh, which supported David against Saul.

Only reference: 1 Chronicles 12:20

4) A Levite "porter" (doorkeeper) in the house of the Lord.

Only reference: 1 Chronicles 26:2

👥 JEDIDAH

of times mentioned: 1
# of WOMEN by this name: 1

Meaning: Beloved

Mother of Judah's good king Josiah.

Only reference: 2 Kings 22:1

👥 JEDIDIAH

of times mentioned: 1
# of MEN by this name: 1

Meaning: Beloved of God

God's special name for Solomon, as delivered by the prophet Nathan.

Only reference: 2 Samuel 12:25

👥 JEDUTHUN

of times mentioned: 17
# of MEN by this name: 1

Meaning: Laudatory

A descendant of Abraham through Jacob's son Levi. Jeduthun was one of the key musicians serving in the Jerusalem temple. King David appointed Jeduthun's descendants to "prophesy with harps, with psalteries, and with cymbals" (1 Chronicles 25:1).

First reference: 1 Chronicles 9:16 / Last reference: Psalm 77 (title)

👥 JEEZER

of times mentioned: 1
# of MEN by this name: 1

Meaning: Helpless

A descendant of Joseph's son Manasseh and a son of Gilead.

Only reference: Numbers 26:30

📍 JEGAR-SAHADUTHA

of times mentioned: OT 1

Meaning: Heap of the testimony

A stone that Jacob set up as a pillar of testimony to the covenant he made with his father-in-law, Laban. Jegar-sahadutha was the name Laban gave to the stone, which Jacob called Galeed. Same as Galeed and Mizpah (1).

Only reference: Genesis 31:47

👥 JEHALELEEL

of times mentioned: 1
# of MEN by this name: 1

Meaning: Praising God

A descendant of Abraham through Jacob's son Judah.

Only reference: 1 Chronicles 4:16

👥 JEHALELEL

of times mentioned: 1
# of MEN by this name: 1

Meaning: Praising God

Father of a Levite who cleansed the temple under King Hezekiah of Judah.

Only reference: 2 Chronicles 29:12

👥 JEHDEIAH

of times mentioned: 2
# of MEN by this name: 2

Meaning: Unity of God

1) A descendant of Abraham through Jacob's son Levi.

Only reference: 1 Chronicles 24:20

2) An official responsible for King David's herds of donkeys.

Only reference: 1 Chronicles 27:30

👥 JEHEZEKEL

of times mentioned: 1
# of MEN by this name: 1

Meaning: God will strengthen

One of twenty-four priests in David's time who was chosen by lot to serve in the tabernacle.

Only reference: 1 Chronicles 24:16

👥 JEHIAH

of times mentioned: 1
# of MEN by this name: 1

Meaning: God will live

A doorkeeper of the ark of the covenant under King David.

Only reference: 1 Chronicles 15:24

👥 JEHIEL

of times mentioned: 16
# of MEN by this name: 13

Meaning: God will live

1) A Levite musician who performed in celebration when King David brought the ark of the covenant to Jerusalem.

First reference: 1 Chronicles 15:18 / Last reference: 1 Chronicles 16:5

2) A leader of the Gershonites who cared for the precious stones donated for Solomon's temple.

First reference: 1 Chronicles 23:8 / Last reference: 1 Chronicles 29:8

3) Tutor to King David's sons.

Only reference: 1 Chronicles 27:32

4) A son of Judah's king Jehoshaphat, given "great gifts of silver, and of gold, and of precious things" by his father (2 Chronicles 21:3).

Only reference: 2 Chronicles 21:2

5) A descendant of Abraham through Jacob's son Levi. Jehiel was among the Levites who cleansed the Jerusalem temple during the revival of King Hezekiah's day.

Only reference: 2 Chronicles 29:14

6) A temple overseer during the reign of King Hezekiah of Judah.

Only reference: 2 Chronicles 31:13

7) A chief temple officer under King Josiah of Judah.

Only reference: 2 Chronicles 35:8

8) Forefather of a Jewish exile who returned to Judah under Ezra.

Only reference: Ezra 8:9

9) Father of Shechaniah, an exiled Israelite who married a "strange" (foreign) woman but suggested to Ezra that he and his fellow offenders "make a covenant with our God to put away all the wives, and such as are born of them" (Ezra 10:3).

Only reference: Ezra 10:2

10) An exiled Israelite priest who married a "strange" (foreign) woman.

Only reference: Ezra 10:21

11) Another exiled Israelite who married a "strange" (foreign) woman.

Only reference: Ezra 10:26

12) A forefather of King Saul.

Only reference: 1 Chronicles 9:35

13) One of King David's valiant warriors.

Only reference: 1 Chronicles 11:44

👥 JEHIELI

of times mentioned: 2
# of MEN by this name: 1

Meaning: God will live

A Levite whose sons were in charge of the temple treasury.

First reference: 1 Chronicles 26:21 / Last reference: 1 Chronicles 26:22

👥 JEHIZKIAH

of times mentioned: 1
# of MEN by this name: 1

Meaning: Strengthened of God

A man of the tribe of Ephraim who counseled his nation of Israel against enslaving fellow Jews from Judah who were captured in a civil war. Jehizkiah helped to feed and clothe the prisoners before sending them home.

Only reference: 2 Chronicles 28:12

👥 JEHOADAH

of times mentioned: 2
# of MEN by this name: 1

Meaning: Jehovah adorned

A descendant of Abraham through Jacob's son Benjamin, through the line of King Saul and his son Jonathan. Same as Jarah.

Only reference: 1 Chronicles 8:36

👥 JEHOADDAN

of times mentioned: 2
# of WOMEN by this name: 1

Meaning: Jehovah pleased

Mother of Amaziah, king of Judah.

First reference: 2 Kings 14:2 / Last reference: 2 Chronicles 25:1

👥 JEHOAHAZ

of times mentioned: 23
# of MEN by this name: 3

Meaning: Jehovah seized

1) King of Israel and son of King Jehu, Jehoahaz did what was evil in God's sight. He fought and lost battles with Hazael, king of Syria. When he sought

the Lord concerning the oppression that the nation inflicted upon Israel, God provided a savior.

First reference: 2 Kings 10:35 / Last reference: 2 Chronicles 25:25 / Key reference: 2 Kings 13:4–5

2) King of Judah, son of King Josiah. This evil king reigned only three months before Pharaoh-necho of Egypt captured Jehoahaz and sent him to Egypt, where he died. Same as Shallum (1).

First reference: 2 Kings 23:30 / Last reference: 2 Chronicles 36:4

3) Son of King Jehoram of Judah. When the Philistines and Arabians attacked Judah, they carried away all of Jehoram's sons but Jehoahaz.

First reference: 2 Chronicles 21:17 / Last reference: 2 Chronicles 25:23

👥 JEHOASH

of times mentioned: 17
# of MEN by this name: 2

Meaning: Jehovah fired

1) Another name for Joash (5).

First reference: 2 Kings 11:21 / Last reference: 2 Kings 14:13

2) An evil king of Israel, son of King Jehoahaz. Jehoash regained from Hazael, king of Syria, the cities Hazael had won from Israel in battle. Jehoash fought King Amaziah of Judah, broke down Jerusalem's wall, and took gold and silver from the temple and the king. With hostages, he returned to Samaria. Same as Joash (6).

First reference: 2 Kings 13:10 / Last reference: 2 Kings 14:17

👥 JEHOHANAN

of times mentioned: 6
# of MEN by this name: 6

Meaning: Jehovah favored

1) A Levite "porter" (doorkeeper) in the house of the Lord.

Only reference: 1 Chronicles 26:3

2) A military captain of Judah who stood next to Adnah, the commander.

Only reference: 2 Chronicles 17:15

3) Father of a captain of hundreds under the priest Jehoiada of Judah.

Only reference: 2 Chronicles 23:1

4) An exiled Israelite who married a "strange" (foreign) woman.

Only reference: Ezra 10:28

5) Forefather of a priest who returned to Jerusalem under Zerubbabel.

Only reference: Nehemiah 12:13

6) A priest who helped to dedicate the rebuilt wall of Jerusalem by giving thanks.

Only reference: Nehemiah 12:42

👥 JEHOIACHIN

of times mentioned: 10
# of MEN by this name: 1

Meaning: Jehovah will establish

King of Judah and son of King Jehoiakim, this evil king reigned only three months before King Nebuchadnezzar of Babylon carried him and the best of his people to Babylon. In the thirty-seventh year of Jehoiachin's captivity, King Evil-merodach brought him out of prison and gave him preferential treatment. Same as Coniah, Jeconiah, and Jeconias.

First reference: 2 Kings 24:6 / Last reference: Jeremiah 52:31

👥 JEHOIADA

of times mentioned: 52
# of MEN by this name: 6

Meaning: Jehovah known

1) Father of Benaiah, a commander in King David's army, who also served Solomon.

First reference: 2 Samuel 8:18 / Last reference: 1 Chronicles 27:5

2) The high priest who made a covenant with the army's leaders to protect young King Joash. For six years Jehoiada protected Joash from his grandmother, Athaliah, who had usurped Judah's throne. In the seventh year, the priest anointed and crowned Joash. When Athaliah objected, he had her killed then made a covenant between Joash and his people. At the king's command, Jehoiada took up a collection for refurbishing the temple, which Athaliah had caused to be damaged. Because Jehoiada had done much good for the people, he was buried with the kings of Judah.

First reference: 2 Kings 11:4 / Last reference: 2 Chronicles 24:25 / Key references: 2 Chronicles 23:1; 24:6–7, 15–16

3) A leader descended from Aaron who joined David at Hebron to make him king over Israel.

Only reference: 1 Chronicles 12:27

4) The son of Benaiah, who succeeded Ahithophel as David's counselor.

Only reference: 1 Chronicles 27:34

5) A man who repaired Jerusalem's walls under Nehemiah.

Only reference: Nehemiah 3:6

6) A priest mentioned by Jeremiah in his prophecy against the false prophet Shemaiah.

Only reference: Jeremiah 29:26

👥 JEHOIAKIM

of times mentioned: 37
# of MEN by this name: 1

Meaning: Jehovah will raise

Originally named Eliakim, he was a son of King Josiah of Judah. After the Egyptian pharaoh Necho killed Josiah and later deposed his son Jehoahaz, the pharaoh made Eliakim king of Judah and changed his name to Jehoiakim. Following Necho's defeat by King Nebuchadnezzar, Jehoiakim served the Babylonian king. But three years later, Jehoiakim rebelled. When Jeremiah's prophetic, warning words were read to this wicked king, piece by piece he burned the scroll they were written on—so God declared that Babylon would destroy Judah. Nebuchadnezzar attacked and defeated Jerusalem, bound Jehoiakim in chains, and carried him to Babylon, along with most of the people of Judah. Following Jehoiakim's capture, a prophet told how he murdered another prophet who spoke out against him then had his body dumped in a common burial ground. Same as Eliakim (2).

First reference: 2 Kings 23:34 / Last reference:
Daniel 1:2 / Key references: 2 Kings 23:34; 24:1;
Jeremiah 26:20–23; 36:22–24

JEHOIARIB

of times mentioned: 2
# of MEN by this name: 2

Meaning: Jehovah will contend

1) A priest who returned to Jerusalem after the
Babylonian captivity.

Only reference: 1 Chronicles 9:10

2) One of twenty-four priests of David's time who
was chosen by lot to serve in the tabernacle.

Only reference: 1 Chronicles 24:7

JEHONADAB

of times mentioned: 3
# of MEN by this name: 1

Meaning: Jehovah largessed

One of the Rechabites, known for their spiritual
austerity. He met King Jehu in Samaria and saw
his destruction of the temple of Baal, with all the
worshippers in it.

First reference: 2 Kings 10:15 / Last reference:
2 Kings 10:23

JEHONATHAN

of times mentioned: 3
# of MEN by this name: 3

Meaning: Jehovah given

1) An official in charge of King David's storehouses.

Only reference: Chronicles 27:25

2) A Levite sent by King Jehoshaphat to teach the
law of the Lord throughout the nation of Judah.

Only reference: 1 Chronicles 17:8

3) Forefather of a priest who returned to Jerusalem
under Zerubbabel.

Only reference: Nehemiah 12:18

JEHORAM

of times mentioned: 23
# of MEN by this name: 3

Meaning: Jehovah raised

1) Firstborn son of King Jehoshaphat of Judah.
After Jehoram became king, he killed all his brothers. He married the daughter of King Ahab of Israel
and led his nation into idolatry. Philistines and
Arabians invaded Judah and captured Jehoram's
family. As God had warned, Jehoram died, un-
mourned, of an incurable bowel disease. He was not
buried in the kings' tombs. Same as Joram (2).

First reference: 1 Kings 22:50 / Last reference:
2 Chronicles 22:11 / Key references: 2 Chronicles
21:4–6, 11, 20

2) King of Israel, son of Ahab, and brother of
Ahaziah, from whom he inherited the throne.
Though he did not worship Baal, neither did he stop
his nation from worshipping Jeroboam's golden
calves. With Jehoshaphat, king of Judah, he went
to war against Moab. Discouraged, they consulted
the prophet Elijah, who told them how to win their
battle. Jehoram was killed by Jehu (2), who took his
throne. Same as Joram (2).

First reference: 2 Kings 1:17 / Last reference:
2 Chronicles 22:7

3) A priest sent by King Jehoshaphat to teach the
law of the Lord throughout the nation of Judah.

Only reference: 2 Chronicles 17:8

JEHOSHABEATH

of times mentioned: 2
# of WOMEN by this name: 1

Meaning: Jehovah sworn

Daughter of Judah's king Jehoram and sister of
Judah's king Ahaziah. When Ahaziah was killed,
Jehoshabeath saved her infant nephew Joash from
a family massacre engineered by Ahaziah's mother,
Athaliah, who wanted to make herself queen. Same
as Hehosheba.

Only reference: 2 Chronicles 22:11

👥 JEHOSHAPHAT

of times mentioned: 83
# of MEN by this name: 5

Meaning: Jehovah judged

1) An official in King David's court who was his recorder.

First reference: 2 Samuel 8:16 / Last reference: 1 Chronicles 18:15

2) One of King Solomon's twelve officials over provisions.

Only reference: 1 Kings 4:17

3) The king of Judah, who inherited the throne from his father, Asa. Though he had blessings and "riches and honour in abundance" (2 Chronicles 17:5; 18:1), he repeatedly allied himself with Israel. Though he followed God, Jehoshaphat became inconsistent in his obedience and did not completely end idolatry in Judah. Despite the warning of the prophet Micaiah, he joined King Ahab of Israel in a disastrous attack on Ramoth-gilead. Later, as a great army came against his own nation, Jehoshaphat sought the Lord. When King Jehoram of Israel asked Jehoshaphat to join him in attacking Moab, Judah's king suggested they consult a prophet. Elijah gave them the winning battle plan.

First reference: 1 Kings 15:24 / Last reference: 2 Chronicles 22:9 / Key references: 1 Kings 22:4–5, 43; 2 Kings 3:11–20; 2 Chronicles 18:1, 31; 20:5–12

4) Father of Jehu, king of Israel.

First reference: 2 Kings 9:2 / Last reference: 2 Kings 9:14

5) A priest who blew a trumpet as David moved the ark of the covenant.

Only reference: 1 Chronicles 15:24

📍 JEHOSHAPHAT

of times mentioned: OT 2

Meaning: Jehovah judged

A valley where God will plead with the nations for His people, Israel, and where He will judge the ungodly.

First reference: Joel 3:2 / Last reference: Joel 3:12

👥 JEHOSHEBA

of times mentioned: 1
# of WOMEN by this name: 1

Meaning: Jehovah sworn

King Joash's aunt, who protected him from his wicked grandmother, Athaliah. Same as Jehoshabeath.

Only reference: 2 Kings 11:2

👥 JEHOSHUA

of times mentioned: 1
# of MEN by this name: 1

Meaning: Jehovah saved

A variant name for Joshua, son of Nun, successor to Moses.

Only reference: Numbers 13:16

👥 JEHOSHUAH

of times mentioned: 1
# of MEN by this name: 1

Meaning: Jehovah saved

A variant name for Joshua, son of Nun, successor to Moses.

Only reference: 1 Chronicles 7:27

📍 JEHOVAH-JIREH

of times mentioned: OT 1

Meaning: Jehovah will see to it

Another name for Mount Moriah, where God stopped Abraham from sacrificing his son Isaac and instead provided a ram for the offering. Same as Moriah.

Only reference: Genesis 22:14

📍 JEHOVAH-NISSI

of times mentioned: OT 1

Meaning: Jehovah is my banner

An altar that Moses built to commemorate God's promise to save His people by fighting the Amalekites Himself, from generation to generation.

Only reference: Exodus 17:15

📍 JEHOVAH-SHALOM

of times mentioned: OT 1

Meaning: Jehovah is peace

Gideon was amazed at the visit of an angel of the Lord, who called him a mighty man of valor. This angel also told him that God would be with him as he fought the Midianites, who controlled Israel. Gideon built an altar to God in Ophrah of the Abiezrites and called it by this name.

Only reference: Judges 6:24

👥 JEHOZABAD

of times mentioned: 4
# of MEN by this name: 3

Meaning: Jehovah endowed

1) One of two royal officials who conspired to kill Judah's king Joash.

First reference: 2 Kings 12:21 / Last reference: 2 Chronicles 24:26

2) A Levite "porter" (doorkeeper) in the house of the Lord.

Only reference: 1 Chronicles 26:4

3) A commander in the army of King Jehoshaphat of Israel.

Only reference: 2 Chronicles 17:18

👥 JEHOZADAK

of times mentioned: 2
# of MEN by this name: 1

Meaning: Jehovah righted

A descendant of Abraham through Jacob's son Levi and a priest through the line of Aaron. Jehozadak served when the Babylonians overran Judah, and he was carried into captivity.

First reference: 1 Chronicles 6:14 / Last reference: 1 Chronicles 6:15

👥 JEHU

of times mentioned: 59
# of MEN by this name: 5

Meaning: Jehovah (is) He

1) A prophet who prophesied the destruction of Baasha, king of Israel, and Baasha's heirs. He also confronted King Jehoshaphat of Judah with his inconsistent faith.

First reference: 1 Kings 16:1 / Last reference: 2 Chronicles 20:34

2) A king of Israel. God commanded Elijah to anoint Jehu king to destroy King Ahab and his dynasty. Stunned, Jehu received Elijah's servant and the anointing. Jehu killed kings Joram of Israel and Ahaziah of Judah. Then he killed Jezebel by commanding servants to throw her from a window, made the Samaritans slaughter Ahab's sons, and killed forty-two of King Ahaziah's relatives. After calling the priests of Baal and the idol's worshippers together, Jehu had his men put them all to the sword. But Jehu did not walk carefully in God's ways and lost part of Israel to Syria.

First reference: 1 Kings 19:16 / Last reference: Hosea 1:4 / Key references: 2 Kings 9:6–10, 23–24, 27, 33; 10:18–27

3) A descendant of Abraham through Jacob's son Judah. Jehu descended from the line of an unnamed Israelite woman and her Egyptian husband, Jarha.

Only reference: 1 Chronicles 2:38

4) A descendant of Abraham through Jacob's son Simeon.

Only reference: 1 Chronicles 4:35

5) A "mighty man" who supported the future king David during his conflict with Saul.

Only reference: 1 Chronicles 12:3

👥 JEHUBBAH

of times mentioned: 1
# of MEN by this name: 1

Meaning: Hidden

A descendant of Abraham through Jacob's son Asher.

Only reference: 1 Chronicles 7:34

👥 JEHUCAL

of times mentioned: 1
# of MEN by this name: 1

Meaning: Potent

A man sent by King Zedekiah to ask Jeremiah to pray for Judah as Egypt attacked.

Only reference: Jeremiah 37:3

📍 JEHUD

of times mentioned: OT 1

Meaning: Judah

A city that became part of the inheritance of Dan when Joshua cast lots in Shiloh to provide territory for the seven tribes that had yet to receive their land.

Only reference: Joshua 19:45

👥 JEHUDI

of times mentioned: 4
# of MEN by this name: 1

Meaning: Descendant of Jehudah

Nethaniah's son who carried a message from King Josiah's court to Jeremiah's scribe, commanding him to read Judah's princes the word God sent through the prophet.

First reference: Jeremiah 36:14 / Last reference: Jeremiah 36:23

👥 JEHUDIJAH

of times mentioned: 1
# of WOMEN by this name: 1

Meaning: Female descendant of Jehudah

A wife of Ezra (1).

Only reference: 1 Chronicles 4:18

👥 JEHUSH

of times mentioned: 1
# of MEN by this name: 1

Meaning: Hasty

A descendant of Abraham through Jacob's son Benjamin, through the line of King Saul and his son Jonathan. Jehush was a courageous archer.

Only reference: 1 Chronicles 8:39

👥 JEIEL

of times mentioned: 11
# of MEN by this name: 8

Meaning: Carried away of God

1) A descendant of Abraham through Jacob's son Reuben.

Only reference: 1 Chronicles 5:7

2) A Levite worship leader who played a harp as the ark of the covenant was brought into Jerusalem.

First reference: 1 Chronicles 15:18 / Last reference: 1 Chronicles 16:5

3) Forefather of Jahaziel, who prophesied to King Jehoshaphat that he would not be overcome by his enemies.

Only reference: 2 Chronicles 20:14

4) A scribe who counted the men who went to battle with King Uzziah of Judah.

Only reference: 2 Chronicles 26:11

5) A descendant of Abraham through Jacob's son Levi. Jeiel was among the Levites who cleansed the Jerusalem temple during the revival of King Hezekiah's day.

Only reference: 2 Chronicles 29:13

6) A descendant of Abraham through Jacob's son Levi. Jeiel was among those who distributed sacrificial animals to fellow Levites preparing to celebrate the Passover under King Josiah.

Only reference: 2 Chronicles 35:9

7) A Jewish exile who returned from Babylon to Judah under Ezra.

Only reference: Ezra 8:13

8) An exiled Israelite who married a "strange" (foreign) woman.

Only reference: Ezra 10:43

📍 JEKABZEEL

of times mentioned: OT 1

Meaning: God will gather

A city of Judah resettled by the Jews after the Babylonian Exile.

Only reference: Nehemiah 11:25

👪 JEKAMEAM

of times mentioned: 2
# of MEN by this name: 1

Meaning: The people will rise

A descendant of Abraham through Jacob's son Levi.

First reference: 1 Chronicles 23:19 / Last reference: 1 Chronicles 24:23

👪 JEKAMIAH

of times mentioned: 2
# of MEN by this name: 1

Meaning: God will rise

A descendant of Abraham through Jacob's son Judah. Jekamiah descended from the line of an unnamed Israelite woman and her Egyptian husband, Jarha.

Only reference: 1 Chronicles 2:41

👪 JEKUTHIEL

of times mentioned: 1
# of MEN by this name: 1

Meaning: Obedience of God

A descendant of Abraham through Jacob's son Judah.

Only reference: 1 Chronicles 4:18

👪 JEMIMA

of times mentioned: 1
# of WOMEN by this name: 1

Meaning: Dove

A daughter of Job. Jemima was the oldest of three daughters born to Job after God restored his fortunes. Jemima and her two sisters, Kezia and Kerenhappuch, were said to be more beautiful than any other women "in all the land" (Job 42:15).

Only reference: Job 42:14

👪 JEMUEL

of times mentioned: 2
# of MEN by this name: 1

Meaning: Day of God

A descendant of Abraham through Jacob's son Simeon. Same as Nemuel (2).

First reference: Genesis 46:10 / Last reference: Exodus 6:15

👪 JEPHTHAE

of times mentioned: 1
# of MEN by this name: 1

Meaning: He will open

Greek form of the name Jephthah, used in the New Testament.

Only reference: Hebrews 11:32

👪 JEPHTHAH

of times mentioned: 29
# of MEN by this name: 1

Meaning: He will open

The eighth judge of Israel, Jephthah the Gileadite was Gilead's son by a prostitute. His half brothers drove him out, and he went to the land of Tob. When the Ammonites fought Israel, he became Gilead's leader. He unsuccessfully tried to make peace with these enemies. Then Jephthah promised God that he would give Him whatever greeted him when he came home, should he be victorious. After he won the battle, his daughter, his only child, came to greet him on his return. After giving his daughter a two-month reprieve, Jephthah kept his vow. For passing over Ephraim's land, he battled the Ephraimites. Jephthah judged Israel for six years. Same as Jephthae.

First reference: Judges 11:1 / Last reference: 1 Samuel 12:11 / Key references: Judges 11:5–10, 29–30

👪 JEPHUNNEH

of times mentioned: 16
# of MEN by this name: 2

Meaning: He will be prepared

1) Father of Caleb, one of two spies (along with Joshua) who argued in favor of entering the Promised Land.

First reference: Numbers 13:6 / Last reference: 1 Chronicles 6:56

2) A descendant of Abraham through Jacob's son Asher.

Only reference: 1 Chronicles 7:38

👪 JERAH

of times mentioned: 2
# of MEN by this name: 1

Meaning: Month

A descendant of Noah through his son Shem.

First reference: Genesis 10:26 / Last reference: 1 Chronicles 1:20

👪 JERAHMEEL

of times mentioned: 8
# of MEN by this name: 3

Meaning: God will be compassionate

1) A descendant of Abraham through Jacob's son Pharez.

First reference: 1 Chronicles 2:9 / Last reference: 1 Chronicles 2:42

2) A descendant of Abraham through Jacob's son Levi.

Only reference: 1 Chronicles 24:29

👪 JERED

of times mentioned: 2
# of MEN by this name: 2

Meaning: A descent

1) A descendant of Adam through his son Seth. Jered was the second-longest-lived individual in the Bible at 962 years. Same as Jared.

Only reference: 1 Chronicles 1:2

2) A descendant of Abraham through Jacob's son Judah.

Only reference: 1 Chronicles 4:18

👪 JEREMAI

of times mentioned: 1
# of MEN by this name: 1

Meaning: Elevated

An exiled Israelite who married a "strange" (foreign) woman.

Only reference: Ezra 10:33

👪 JEREMIAH

of times mentioned: 146
# of MEN by this name: 7

Meaning: God will rise

1) Grandfather of kings Jehoahaz and Zedekiah of Judah.

First reference: 2 Kings 23:31 / Last reference: Jeremiah 52:1

2) One of the "mighty men of valour, famous men" leading the half tribe of Manasseh.

Only reference: 1 Chronicles 5:24

3) One of King David's mightiest warriors known as "the thirty."

Only reference: 1 Chronicles 12:4

3) A man ordered by King Jehoiakim to imprison the prophet Jeremiah and his scribe.

Only reference: Jeremiah 36:26

4) One of several warriors from the tribe of Gad who left Saul to join David during his conflict with the king. Jeremiah and his companions were "men of might. . .whose faces were like the faces of lions" (1 Chronicles 12:8).

Only reference: 1 Chronicles 12:10

5) Another of several warriors from the tribe of Gad who left Saul to join David during his conflict with the king. Jeremiah and his companions were "men of might. . .whose faces were like the faces of lions" (1 Chronicles 12:8).

Only reference: 1 Chronicles 12:13

6) A prophet of Judah during the reigns of Kings Josiah, Jehoahaz, Jehoiakim, Jehoiachin, and Zedekiah. Following Assyria's destruction of Israel, Babylon threatened Judah. The turmoil of his age was clearly reflected in the gloomy prophecies of Jeremiah. He condemned Judah for idolatry and called the nation to repentance. God warned of Judah's destruction and mourned over it, yet Jerusalem refused to repent, and Jeremiah warned of their judgment.

When Pashur (3), chief officer of the temple, heard Jeremiah's prophecies, he put him in the stocks. Released, the prophet spoke against this false prophet, predicting the fall of Judah to Babylon. Pashur was only one of many men who became angry with the prophet, because Jeremiah contended with kings and false prophets as he spoke God's word.

Before the fall of Jerusalem, Jeremiah was imprisoned and accused of deserting to the enemy. For a while he was cast into a muddy cistern. When Jerusalem fell, Nebuchadnezzar treated him well. Jeremiah warned the remnant of people who remained in Judah not to go to Egypt. But the commanders of Judah took the people, including Jeremiah, there anyway. Jeremiah may have died in Egypt. Same as Jeremias and Jeremy.

First reference: 2 Chronicles 35:25 / Last reference: Daniel 9:2 / Key references: Jeremiah 1:1, 5; 20:1–6; 21:3–6; 35:8–17; 37:12–15; 38:6

7) A priest who renewed the covenant under Nehemiah.

First reference: Nehemiah 10:2 / Last reference: Nehemiah 12:34

👥 JEREMIAS

of times mentioned: 1
# of MEN by this name: 1

Meaning: God will rise

Greek form of the name Jeremiah, used in the New Testament. Same as Jeremiah (6).

Only reference: Matthew 16:14

👥 JEREMOTH

of times mentioned: 5
# of MEN by this name: 5

Meaning: Elevations

1) A descendant of Abraham through Jacob's son Benjamin.

Only reference: 1 Chronicles 8:14

2) An exiled Israelite who married a "strange" (foreign) woman.

Only reference: Ezra 10:26

3) Another exiled Israelite who married a "strange" (foreign) woman.

Only reference: Ezra 10:27

4) A descendant of Abraham through Jacob's son Levi. Same as Jerimoth (4).

Only reference: 1 Chronicles 23:23

5) One of twenty-four Levite musicians who was chosen by lot to serve in the house of the Lord.

Only reference: 1 Chronicles 25:22

👥 JEREMY

of times mentioned: 2
# of MEN by this name: 1

Meaning: God will rise

Latin form of the name Jeremiah, used in the New Testament. Same as Jeremiah (6).

First reference: Matthew 2:17 / Last reference: Matthew 27:9

JERIAH

\# of times mentioned: 2
\# of MEN by this name: 1

Meaning: God will throw

A descendant of Abraham through Jacob's son Levi.

First reference: 1 Chronicles 23:19 / Last reference: 1 Chronicles 24:23

JERIBAI

\# of times mentioned: 1
\# of MEN by this name: 1

Meaning: Contentious

One of King David's valiant warriors.

Only reference: 1 Chronicles 11:46

JERICHO

\# of times mentioned: OT 57 / NT 7

Meaning: Fragrant

A Moabite city next to Mount Nebo, west of the Jordan River, Jericho was also called the "city of palm trees." The Israelites entered Canaan, crossing the Jordan River near Jericho, and camped in the Jericho plain as they conquered the Midianites and for some time afterward.

From Shittim, before they crossed the Jordan River, Joshua sent two spies to Jericho. When the men were caught inside the city, Rahab hid them and then helped them escape by lowering them out a window, using a rope. In return the spies promised that she and her family would be safe when Israel conquered her city.

God gave Joshua an unusual battle plan to take Jericho: For six days Israel's soldiers were to walk once around the city; on the seventh day they were to go around the city seven times, with the priests walking before the troops, blowing their trumpets and carrying the ark of the covenant. When the priests made a long blast, the people were to shout, and Jericho would be theirs. Joshua and his troops followed these instructions, captured Jericho, and destroyed it.

Jericho became part of the inheritance of the tribe of Benjamin. But Eglon, king of Moab, captured the city and held it for eighteen years. Then Ehud killed him and led Israel into battle against the Moabites, regaining the city.

Elijah and Elisha went to Jericho on the day Elijah was carried into heaven by a chariot of fire. That city's prophets were aware of the event that was to come.

As He left Jericho, Jesus healed two blind men, one of whom was Bartimaeus. As He passed through another time, Jesus saw Zacchaeus in a tree and brought him salvation.

First reference: Numbers 22:1 / Last reference: Hebrews 11:30 / Key references: Joshua 2, 6; Luke 19:1–10

JERIEL

\# of times mentioned: 1
\# of MEN by this name: 1

Meaning: Thrown of God

A descendant of Abraham through Jacob's son Issachar.

Only reference: 1 Chronicles 7:2

JERIJAH

\# of times mentioned: 1
\# of MEN by this name: 1

Chief of the Hebronites whom King David gave authority over the Reubenites, Gadites, and half tribe of Manasseh.

Only reference: 1 Chronicles 26:31

JERIMOTH

\# of times mentioned: 8
\# of MEN by this name: 8

Meaning: Elevations

1) A descendant of Abraham through Jacob's son Benjamin.

Only reference: 1 Chronicles 7:7

2) A descendant of Abraham through Jacob's son Benjamin.

Only reference: 1 Chronicles 7:8

3) A "mighty man" who supported the future king David during his conflict with Saul.

Only reference: 1 Chronicles 12:5

4) A descendant of Abraham through Jacob's son Levi. Same as Jeremoth (4).

Only reference: 1 Chronicles 24:30

5) A son of King David's musician Heman, who was "under the hands of [his] father for song in the house of the LORD" (1 1 Chronicles 25:6).

Only reference: 1 Chronicles 25:4

6) Leader of the tribe of Naphtali in the days of King David.

Only reference: 1 Chronicles 27:19

7) The father-in-law of King Rehoboam of Judah.

Only reference: 2 Chronicles 11:18

8) A temple overseer during the reign of King Hezekiah of Judah.

Only reference: 2 Chronicles 31:13

👥 JERIOTH

of times mentioned: 1
# of WOMEN by this name: 1

Meaning: Curtains

A descendant of Abraham through Jacob's son Judah.

Only reference: 1 Chronicles 2:18

👥 JEROBOAM

of times mentioned: 104
# of MEN by this name: 2

Meaning: The people will contend

1) A servant of King Solomon who had authority over the forced labor for the tribes of Ephraim and Manasseh. The prophet Ahijah the Shilonite prophesied that Jeroboam would be king over ten tribes of Israel when Solomon died. Solomon heard this and sought to kill Jeroboam, who fled to Egypt. Israel rebelled against Solomon's son, King Rehoboam, and made Jeroboam king. Fearing that his people would return to Rehoboam if they worshipped in Jerusalem, Jeroboam established idolatrous worship in Israel. Because Jeroboam did not obey God, the prophet Abijah warned the king's wife that God would cut

off all the men of Jeroboam's household and burn his house. Jeroboam's son became ill and died.

When Jeroboam went to war with King Abijah of Judah, God routed Jeroboam. Israel never regained its power during Jeroboam's lifetime.

First reference: 1 Kings 11:26 / Last reference: 2 Chronicles 13:20 / Key references: 1 Kings 12:20, 28; 2 Chronicles 13:14–16, 20

2) King of Israel, son of King Joash, Jeroboam continued the idolatrous worship established by Jeroboam (1). God used Jeroboam to regain Israel's lost territory, and he even took the Syrian capital, Damascus. The prophet Amos predicted Jeroboam's death by the sword.

First reference: 2 Kings 13:13 / Last reference: Amos 7:11 / Key references: 2 Kings 14:25–27; Amos 7:11

👥 JEROHAM

of times mentioned: 10
# of MEN by this name: 7

Meaning: Compassionate

1) A descendant of Abraham through Jacob's son Levi. Jeroham was the grandfather of the prophet Samuel.

First reference: 1 Samuel 1:1 / Last reference: 1 Chronicles 6:34

2) A descendant of Abraham through Jacob's son Benjamin.

Only reference: 1 Chronicles 8:27

3) Forefather of a Levite who returned to Jerusalem following the Babylonian captivity.

Only reference: 1 Chronicles 9:8

4) Forefather of a priest who lived in Jerusalem following the return from exile.

First reference: 1 Chronicles 9:12 / Last reference: Nehemiah 11:12

5) Father of David's "mighty men" Joelah and Zebadiah, who supported the future king during his conflict with Saul.

Only reference: 1 Chronicles 12:7

6) A prince of the tribe of Dan, assigned to rule by King David.

Only reference: 1 Chronicles 27:22

7) Father of one of the captains of Jehoiada the priest.

Only reference: 2 Chronicles 23:1

👥 JERUBBAAL

of times mentioned: 14
# of MEN by this name: 1

Meaning: Baal will contend

A name given to Gideon by his father after he destroyed the altars to Baal.

First reference: Judges 6:32 / Last reference:
1 Samuel 12:11 / Key reference: Judges 6:32

👥 JERUBBESHETH

of times mentioned: 1
# of MEN by this name: 1

Meaning: Shame will contend

An alternative name for the judge Gideon.

Only reference: 2 Samuel 11:21

📍 JERUEL

of times mentioned: OT 1

Meaning: Founded of God

A wilderness near the place where King Jehoshaphat of Judah and his army fought the Moabites and Ammonites.

Only reference: 2 Chronicles 20:16

📍 JERUSALEM

of times mentioned: OT 669 / NT 142

Meaning: Founded peaceful

When Abraham lived in Canaan, Jerusalem (known as "Salem") was ruled by Melchizedec, "priest of the most high God" (Genesis 14:18–20). But before Israel entered the Promised Land, the Jebusite king Adoni-zedec and some neighboring kings went to war against Gibeon, which had made a covenant with the Israelites. Joshua supported Gibeon, conquered and burned Jerusalem, and killed the kings of Adoni-zedec's alliance. Though the Israelites

conquered the land and the Benjaminites held Jerusalem as part of their inheritance, they could not expel the Jebusites.

When David became king of Israel, the Jebusites refused to let him into their city, which they called Jebus, so he conquered the city and made it his capital. Israel called it "the city of David" or Jerusalem. David brought the ark of the covenant into the city.

Jerusalem became part of a power struggle between David and his son Absalom, when Absalom sought to overthrow his father. Rather than having the city destroyed, David left it for a time, until his son had been killed and the rebellion ended. After David sinned by numbering the people of Israel, God afflicted Israel with a pestilence. But instead of destroying Jerusalem, God turned back His hand. David built an altar on the threshing floor of Araunah the Jebusite, and the plague ended.

David passed his throne to his son Solomon, who in seven years built the temple in Jerusalem, with the aid of King Hiram of Tyre's skilled workmen. Solomon had the ark of the covenant brought in, and God's glory filled the temple. Because it was the center of worship, Psalm 46:4 refers to Jerusalem as "the city of God, the holy place of the tabernacles of the most high." Solomon's building projects did not end there. He also built his own palace, which took thirteen years to complete.

King Rehoboam took the throne following Solomon's death, but he alienated ten tribes of Israel, leaving Rehoboam with Judah, Simeon, and part of Benjamin. Jerusalem was the capital of the kingdom of Judah. In the fifth year of Rehoboam's reign, Shishak, king of Egypt, attacked and conquered Jerusalem and took all the treasures of the king's house and the temple. Later, Pharaoh Necho conquered Judah, killing King Josiah and taking King Jehoahaz prisoner. He made Jehoiakim king in his place and exacted tribute from Judah.

The last king of Judah, Zedekiah, reinstituted the celebration of Passover in Jerusalem and rebuilt the watercourse of Gihon so that it fed directly into the city. But when Zedekiah rebelled in 586 BC, Nebuchadnezzar, king of Babylon, besieged and defeated Jerusalem, destroying much of the city and all of the temple, and took Zedekiah captive. After killing the rest of Israel's leaders, Nebuchadnezzar took the people of Judah captive and carried them to Babylon. Yet the prophet Joel prophesied that Judah would "dwell for ever" and Jerusalem would last "from generation to generation" (Joel 3:20).

When Cyrus, king of Persia, came to power in Babylon, he commanded that the Jews rebuild their temple. He returned the temple vessels to them and sent some Jews back to Jerusalem. The temple they rebuilt was not as glorious as Solomon's. Later, after more Jews returned to their homeland, Nehemiah rebuilt the walls of the city at the command of the Persian king Artaxerxes.

During the New Testament era, Rome held sway over Israel. Herod the Great, king of Judea, began a massive building project to restore the temple, nearly doubling its size. He also rebuilt Jerusalem's walls. When Herod heard that the wise men were seeking the king of the Jews, both he and all Jerusalem were troubled. Though Herod did his best to kill the king whom the magi sought, God saved Jesus and His earthly parents.

Shortly after His birth, Jesus was brought to the temple so His parents could offer a sacrifice. Here Simeon and the prophetess Anna recognized God's salvation in Jesus. After their return to Nazareth, Joseph and Mary went to Jerusalem each year at Passover. When Jesus was twelve, they found him in the temple, talking with the teachers of the law.

In Jerusalem, Satan tempted Jesus to throw Himself down from the temple. Early in His ministry, Jesus went to the temple and cleared it of the cattle, sheep, and doves that were sold for sacrifice, declaring, "How dare you turn my Father's house into a market!" (John 2:16 NIV). Many people, including the Pharisees, came from Jerusalem to hear His preaching. But because the religious and civil leaders did not accept His message and even sought to kill Him, Jesus did not spend large amounts of time in the city. Only the feasts or major Jewish holidays seemed to draw Him to the city.

As He headed toward Jerusalem, just before His death, Jesus recognized that His death had to take place in the city. He grieved over Jerusalem's history of killing the prophets and expressed a wish to gather its people together, like a hen protecting her chicks. Jesus was arrested outside Jerusalem, tried within it, and crucified and buried just outside the city, near Golgotha.

At Pentecost in Jerusalem, the Holy Spirit filled believers and they spoke with other tongues. Here Stephen preached the Gospel with power, doing miracles. Unable to counter this powerful testimony, the leaders of a synagogue stirred up people against him. Setting false witnesses against him, they brought Stephen before the Sanhedrin. Angered by his testimony, these Jews attacked and stoned Stephen. In the persecution that followed the faithful disciple's death, many Christians left Jerusalem, preaching as they traveled.

Saul and Barnabas delivered a relief offering, collected from the other churches, to the persecuted Christians of Jerusalem.

Jerusalem remained important even as the church spread beyond Israel. When Paul and Barnabas disagreed with the Judaizers, they met with the church's council in Jerusalem, where it was decided that Gentiles need not be circumcised in order to become Christians.

When Paul again returned to Jerusalem, he reported to James, who led the church in that city, and all the elders. After Paul completed a ritual of purification at the temple, he was seized by some Jews of Asia, who accused him of bringing Greeks into the temple. As they attempted to kill Paul, the Roman guard rescued him. But it was two years before Porcius Festus came to Jerusalem, heard his case, and sent him to Rome for judgment.

In the book of Revelation, the apostle John foresaw the New Jerusalem coming down out of heaven. Here God will live with His people in a beautiful city without sin. Same as Jebus, Jebusi, Salem, and Zion.

First reference: Joshua 10:1 / Last reference: Revelation 21:10 / Key references: 2 Samuel 5:6–7; 6:12; 1 Kings 8:1–11; Luke 13:33–34; Revelation 21:2–27

👥 JERUSHA

of times mentioned: 1
# of WOMEN by this name: 1

Meaning: Possessed (married)

Mother of Jotham, king of Judah.

Only reference: 2 Kings 15:33

👥 JERUSHAH

of times mentioned: 1
# of WOMEN by this name: 1

Meaning: Possessed (married)

Another spelling for Jerusha, mother of King Jotham of Judah.

Only reference: 2 Chronicles 27:1

👥 JESAIAH

of times mentioned: 2
# of MEN by this name: 2

Meaning: God has saved

1) A descendant of Abraham through Jacob's son Judah, in the line of the nation of Judah's third-to-last king, Jeconiah (also known as Jehoiachin).

Only reference: 1 Chronicles 3:21

2) Forefather of a descendant of Benjamin who was chosen by lot to resettle Jerusalem after returning from the Babylonian Exile.

Only reference: Nehemiah 11:7

👥 JESHAIAH

of times mentioned: 5
# of MEN by this name: 4

Meaning: God has saved

1) A son of King David's musician Jeduthun, "who prophesied with a harp, to give thanks and to praise the LORD" (1 Chronicles 25:3).

First reference: 1 Chronicles 25:3 / Last reference: 1 Chronicles 25:15

2) A Levite worship leader under King David.

Only reference: 1 Chronicles 26:25

3) A Jewish exile who returned from Babylon to Judah under Ezra.

Only reference: Ezra 8:7

4) A temple minister sent to Ezra by Iddo, the chief at Casiphia.

Only reference: Ezra 8:19

📍 JESHANAH

of times mentioned: OT 1

Meaning: Old

King Abijah of Judah took this city, along with its towns, from King Jeroboam of Israel.

Only reference: 2 Chronicles 13:19

👥 JESHARELAH

of times mentioned: 1
# of MEN by this name: 1

Meaning: Right toward God

One of twenty-four Levite musicians in David's time who was chosen by lot to serve in the house of the Lord.

Only reference: 1 Chronicles 25:14

👥 JESHEBEAB

of times mentioned: 1
# of MEN by this name: 1

Meaning: People will return

One of twenty-four priests in David's time who was chosen by lot to serve in the tabernacle.

Only reference: 1 Chronicles 24:13

👥 JESHER

of times mentioned: 1
# of MEN by this name: 1

Meaning: The right

A descendant of Abraham through Jacob's son Judah.

Only reference: 1 Chronicles 2:18

📍 JESHIMON

of times mentioned: OT 6

Meaning: A desolation

1) An area visible from the Pisgah mountain range and Mount Peor.

First reference: Numbers 21:20 / Last reference: Numbers 23:28

2) A wilderness area near the hill of Hachilah where David hid from King Saul.

First reference: 1 Samuel 23:19 / Last reference: 1 Samuel 26:3

👥 JESHISHAI

of times mentioned: 1
# of MEN by this name: 1

Meaning: Aged

A descendant of Abraham through Jacob's son Gad.

Only reference: 1 Chronicles 5:14

 JESHOHAIAH

of times mentioned: 1
# of MEN by this name: 1

Meaning: God will empty

A descendant of Abraham through Jacob's son Simeon.

Only reference: 1 Chronicles 4:36

JESHUA

of times mentioned: 29
# of MEN by this name: 9

Meaning: He will save

1) Forefather of a priestly family who returned from captivity with Zerubbabel.

First reference: Ezra 2:36 / Last reference: Nehemiah 7:39

2) A priest in the time of King Hezekiah who helped to distribute the people's freewill offerings to his fellow priests.

First reference: 1 Chronicles 24:11 / Last reference: 2 Chronicles 31:15

3) High priest who returned from exile with Zerubbabel and built the temple altar with him. With the priests and Levites, Jeshua took part in a praise service when the temple foundation was laid. When Judah's adversaries wanted to help build the temple, Jeshua and other leaders refused to allow it.

First reference: Ezra 2:2 / Last reference: Nehemiah 12:26 / Key reference: Ezra 3:2

4) Father of a Levite worship leader who weighed the temple vessels after the Babylonian Exile.

Only reference: Ezra 8:33

5) Forefather of an exiled family that returned to Judah under Zerubbabel.

First reference: Ezra 2:6 / Last reference: Nehemiah 7:11

6) Father of a man who repaired Jerusalem's walls under Nehemiah.

Only reference: Nehemiah 3:19

7) A Levite who helped Ezra to explain the law to exiles returned to Jerusalem. Jeshua was among a group of Levites who led a revival among the Israelites in the time of Nehemiah.

First reference: Nehemiah 8:7 / Last reference: Nehemiah 12:24

8) Another form of the name Joshua. Same as Joshua (1).

Only reference: Nehemiah 8:17

9) A Jewish leader who renewed the covenant under Nehemiah.

Only reference: Nehemiah 10:9

📍 JESHUA

of times mentioned: OT 1

Meaning: He will save

A city of Judah resettled by the Jews after the Babylonian Exile.

Only reference: Nehemiah 11:26

JESIAH

of times mentioned: 2
# of MEN by this name: 2

Meaning: God will lend

1) A "mighty man" who supported the future king David during his conflict with Saul.

Only reference: 1 Chronicles 12:6

2) A descendant of Abraham through Jacob's son Levi.

Only reference: 1 Chronicles 23:20

JESIMIEL

of times mentioned: 1
# of MEN by this name: 1

Meaning: God will place

A descendant of Abraham through Jacob's son Simeon.

Only reference: 1 Chronicles 4:36

JESSE

of times mentioned: 47
# of MEN by this name: 1

Genealogy of Jesus: Yes (Matthew 1:5–6)

Meaning: Extant

Father of David. Jesse had seven of his sons pass before the prophet Samuel, but none was the king whom Samuel was seeking. Only when the youngest, David, was brought before Samuel did the prophet anoint him king.

Jesse allowed his youngest son to become King Saul's harpist and then his armor bearer. After David returned home, his father sent him to bring food to his brothers, who were with Saul's army, and there David fought Goliath.

The prophet Isaiah foresaw the coming of the Messiah with the words, "There shall come forth a rod out of the stem of Jesse, and a Branch shall grow out of his roots" (Isaiah 11:1). Jesus' earthly lineage comes from the line of Jesse, through David.

First reference: Ruth 4:17 / Last reference: Romans 15:12 / Key references: 1 Samuel 16:8–11; Isaiah 11:1

JESUI

of times mentioned: 1
# of MEN by this name: 1

Meaning: Level

A descendant of Abraham through Jacob's son Asher.

Only reference: Numbers 26:44

JESUS

of times mentioned: 983
# of MEN by this name: 3

Meaning: Jehovah saved

1) God's Son and humanity's Savior, Jesus existed from the beginning. Through the Holy Spirit, He became incarnated within the womb of Mary and was born in a humble Bethlehem stable. He grew up in Nazareth, learning the carpentry trade of His earthly father, Joseph. At twelve He amazed the religious leaders of Jerusalem with His understanding of spiritual things. Jesus began His ministry when He was about thirty.

Baptized by His cousin John, Jesus went into the wilderness, where He was tempted by Satan but did not fail. After announcing His new ministry in the synagogue, He called twelve disciples to leave their work and follow Him. With them, He traveled through Israel, teaching and calling people to repentance and new relationship with God. During His ministry Jesus preached about the kingdom of God and corrected the false beliefs of the Pharisees and Sadducees. Jesus taught the spiritual ruler Nicodemus that he needed to be born again. In the Sermon on the Mount, He gave the multitudes a short course in what it meant to truly love God and serve Him. With signs and miracles, He proved His own divine status and drew curious crowds to whom He preached.

Jesus healed many people of illnesses and broke through their spiritual darkness. But when He raised Lazarus from the dead, the chief priests and Pharisees began to plot to kill Him because they feared the Romans' reaction to this news. As His enemies sought to kill Him, Jesus entered Jerusalem on a donkey. The people spread garments before Him and greeted Him as the Messiah, calling out, "Hosanna." A week later, after Judas betrayed Him, the crowd agreed with the chief priests and cried, "Crucify Him!"

Following an illegal trial, Jesus, who had done no wrong, died for humanity's sin on the cross. After His resurrection, three days later, He showed Himself to Mary Magdalene and then the disciples and others. He appeared to the faithful for forty days then commissioned the apostles to spread the Good News, afterward ascending to heaven.

The book of Revelation pictures Jesus as the Lamb who is Lord of lords and King of kings. He will return to judge the world. Finally He will establish a New Jerusalem, where He will live with those who trust in Him.

First reference: Matthew 1:1 / Last reference: Revelation 22:21 / Key references: Matthew 5–7; Mark 11:7–9; Luke 4:18; 24:28–32; John 1:1, 14; 3:3–21; 20:10–22; Revelation 17:14; 19:11–16; 21:1–3

2) Another form of the name Joshua. Same as Joshua (1).

Only reference: Hebrews 4:8

3) A believing Jew and fellow worker with the apostle Paul in Rome. Paul called Jesus, also known as Justus, "a comfort unto me."

Only reference: Colossians 4:11

JETHER

of times mentioned: 8
# of MEN by this name: 5

Meaning: Superiority

1) Gideon's son who fearfully disobeyed when his father told him to kill Zebah and Zalmunna.

Only reference: Judges 8:20

2) Father of Amasa, one of David's army commanders.

First reference: 1 Kings 2:5 / Last reference: 1 Chronicles 2:17

3) A descendant of Abraham through Jacob's son Judah.

Only reference: 1 Chronicles 2:32

4) Another descendant of Abraham through Jacob's son Judah.

Only reference: 1 Chronicles 4:17

5) A descendant of Abraham through Jacob's son Asher.

Only reference: 1 Chronicles 7:38

JETHETH

of times mentioned: 2
# of MEN by this name: 1

A "duke of Edom," a leader in the family line of Esau.

First reference: Genesis 36:40 / Last reference: 1 Chronicles 1:51

JETHLAH

of times mentioned: OT 1

Meaning: It will hang (that is, be high)

A city that became part of the inheritance of Dan when Joshua cast lots in Shiloh to provide territory for the seven tribes that had yet to receive their land.

Only reference: Joshua 19:42

 # JETHRO

# of times mentioned: 10
# of MEN by this name: 1

Meaning: His excellence

Moses' father-in-law, for whom Moses kept flocks until God called him to Egypt. For a time, Moses' wife, Zipporah, along with her two sons, lived with Jethro. The four of them joined up at Mt. Sinai. There Jethro advised Moses to appoint others who could help him rule over the people. Same as Hobab.

First reference: Exodus 3:1 / Last reference: Exodus 18:12

JETUR

of times mentioned: 2
# of MEN by this name: 1

Meaning: Encircled, enclosed

A descendant of Abraham through Ishmael, Abraham's son by his surrogate wife, Hagar.

First reference: Genesis 25:15 / Last reference: 1 Chronicles 1:31

JEUEL

of times mentioned: 1
# of MEN by this name: 1

Meaning: Carried away of God

A Jewish exile from the tribe of Judah who resettled Jerusalem.

Only reference: 1 Chronicles 9:6

JEUSH

of times mentioned: 8
# of MEN by this name: 4

Meaning: Hasty

1) A son of Esau.

First reference: Genesis 36:5 / Last reference: 1 Chronicles 1:35

2) A descendant of Abraham through Jacob's son Benjamin.

Only reference: 1 Chronicles 7:10

3) A descendant of Gershon who was numbered when David counted the Levites.

First reference: 1 Chronicles 23:10 / Last reference: 1 Chronicles 23:11

4) A son of Judah's king Rehoboam and a grandson of Solomon.

Only reference: 2 Chronicles 11:19

JEUZ

\# of times mentioned: 1
\# of MEN by this name: 1

Meaning: Counselor

A descendant of Abraham through Jacob's son Benjamin.

Only reference: 1 Chronicles 8:10

JEZANIAH

\# of times mentioned: 2
\# of MEN by this name: 1

Meaning: Heard of God

A captain of Israel's forces under Nebuchadnezzar's governor, Gedaliah. Same as Jaazaniah (1).

First reference: Jeremiah 40:8 / Last reference: Jeremiah 42:1

JEZEBEL

\# of times mentioned: 22
\# of WOMEN by this name: 1

Meaning: Chaste

A Sidonian princess who married King Ahab of Israel, Jezebel killed or persecuted Israel's prophets, including Elijah, who fled from her wrath after he killed the priests of her god Baal. When Ahab coveted Naboth's vineyard, Jezebel arranged for charges of blasphemy to be brought against Naboth. After he was stoned, she commanded Ahab to take the vineyard.

God ordered Jehu to strike Jezebel down. After assassinating her son, King Joram, Jehu went to Jezreel. There he commanded Jezebel's slaves to throw her from a window. When he ordered her burial, only her skull, feet, and the palms of her hands were left, fulfilling Elijah's prophecy that dogs would eat her.

First reference: 1 Kings 16:31 / Last reference: Revelation 2:20 / Key references: 1 Kings 18:13; 19:1–3; 21:8–16; 2 Kings 9:7–10

JEZER

\# of times mentioned: 3
\# of MEN by this name: 1

Meaning: Form

A descendant of Abraham through Jacob's son Naphtali.

First reference: Genesis 46:24 / Last reference: 1 Chronicles 7:13

JEZIAH

\# of times mentioned: 1
\# of MEN by this name: 1

Meaning: Sprinkled of God

An exiled Israelite who married a "strange" (foreign) woman.

Only reference: Ezra 10:25

JEZIEL

\# of times mentioned: 1
\# of MEN by this name: 1

Meaning: Sprinkled of God

A "mighty man" who supported the future king David during his conflict with Saul.

Only reference: 1 Chronicles 12:3

JEZLIAH

\# of times mentioned: 1
\# of MEN by this name: 1

Meaning: He will draw out

A descendant of Abraham through Jacob's son Benjamin.

Only reference: 1 Chronicles 8:18

👥 JEZOAR

of times mentioned: 1
# of MEN by this name: 1

Meaning: He will shine

A descendant of Abraham through Jacob's son Judah.

Only reference: 1 Chronicles 4:7

👥 JEZRAHIAH

of times mentioned: 1
# of MEN by this name: 1

Meaning: God will shine

A priest who helped to dedicate the rebuilt wall of Jerusalem by leading the singing.

Only reference: Nehemiah 12:42

👥 JEZREEL

of times mentioned: 4
# of MEN by this name: 2

Meaning: God will sow

1) A descendant of Abraham through Jacob's son Judah.

Only reference: 1 Chronicles 4:3

2) The firstborn son of the prophet Hosea whose name signified the judgment God planned for the rebellious people of Judah.

First reference: Hosea 1:4 / Last reference: Hosea 1:11

📍 JEZREEL

of times mentioned: OT 32

Meaning: God will sow

1) A city that became part of the inheritance of the tribe of Judah following the conquest of the Promised Land. David's wife Ahinoam came from Jezreel. David and his men camped by a fountain in this city when he served King Achish and the Philistines were gathering in Aphek. As the Israelites moved to the rear of the troops, the Philistine army refused to fight with them, since David had once been associated with Saul's army.

First reference: Joshua 15:56 / Last reference: 1 Samuel 29:11

2) A city that became part of the inheritance of Issachar when Joshua cast lots in Shiloh to provide territory for the seven tribes that had yet to receive their land. King Ahab of Israel had a palace here. When he coveted a nearby vineyard belonging to Naboth, his wife, Jezebel, had Naboth killed so her husband could get it. By the walls of this city, Elijah prophesied, dogs would eat the body of the queen who had done this wicked deed. Near Jezreel, Jehu killed King Joram, Ahab's son, as God had commanded him to do. Then he ordered Jezebel killed in the manner the prophet had foretold. Finally, he ordered the rulers of Samaria to kill all Ahab's sons and send their heads to him in Jezreel.

First reference: Joshua 19:18 / Last reference: 2 Chronicles 22:6 / Key references: 1 Kings 21:1–16, 23; 2 Kings 9:30–37

3) The tribes of Ephraim and Manasseh told Joshua they feared the Canaanites in this valley because they had iron chariots. The Midianites and Amalekites camped at Jezreel before they fought Gideon and the three hundred men God chose for him according to the way they drank water. Hosea foretold that God would "break the bow of Israel, in the valley of Jezreel" (Hosea 1:5), but the valley would also become a blessing for Israel (Hosea 2:22–23).

First reference: Joshua 17:16 / Last reference: Hosea 2:22

👥 JIBSAM

of times mentioned: 1
# of MEN by this name: 1

Meaning: Fragrant

A descendant of Abraham through Jacob's son Issachar.

Only reference: 1 Chronicles 7:2

👥 JIDLAPH

of times mentioned: 1
# of MEN by this name: 1

Meaning: Tearful

A son of Nahor, Abraham's brother.

Only reference: Genesis 22:22

👥 JIMNA

of times mentioned: 1
# of MEN by this name: 1

Meaning: Prosperity

A descendant of Abraham through Jacob's son Asher. Same as Jimnah.

Only reference: Numbers 26:44

👥 JIMNAH

of times mentioned: 1
# of MEN by this name: 1

Meaning: Prosperity

Another spelling for the name Jimna, a descendant of Abraham.

Only reference: Genesis 46:17

📍 JIPHTAH

of times mentioned: OT 1

Meaning: He will open

A city that became part of the inheritance of the tribe of Judah following the conquest of the Promised Land.

Only reference: Joshua 15:43

📍 JIPHTHAH-EL

of times mentioned: OT 2

Meaning: God will open

A valley that marked the border of the inheritances of Zebulun and Asher when Joshua cast lots in Shiloh to provide territory for the seven tribes that had yet to receive their land.

First reference: Joshua 19:14 / Last reference: Joshua 19:27

👥 JOAB

of times mentioned: 146
# of MEN by this name: 5

Meaning: Jehovah fathered

1) Though he displeased David when he killed Saul's army commander, Abner, for many years Joab was commander of David's army. He fought the Ammonites for David and obeyed David's command to put Uriah the Hittite on the front lines so he would be killed.

Joab sought to bring David and his estranged son Absalom together by sending a wise woman to him with a story similar to David's own. David immediately guessed that Joab was behind her story and allowed the exiled Absalom to come home. Two years later, Joab intervened again to bring Absalom into his father's favor.

David set Amasa as commander over Joab, but he sent Joab and a third of the army into battle against Absalom, who was trying to dethrone his father. Though David asked Joab to deal gently with his son, when the commander heard that Absalom was caught in a tree, Joab killed him.

Joab killed Amasa, too, and again commanded the whole army. He obeyed David, but not God, when he took a census of Israel. At the end of David's life, Joab supported David's son Adonijah as king instead of Solomon. On his deathbed, David warned Solomon not to let Joab die peacefully. Solomon had Joab killed in the tabernacle, where he had fled.

First reference: 1 Samuel 26:6 / Last reference: Psalm 60 (title) / Key references: 2 Samuel 3:26–30; 11:14–17; 14:2–3; 18:14; 1 Kings 2:33–34

2) A descendant of Abraham through Jacob's son Judah.

Only reference: 1 Chronicles 2:54

3) Another descendant of Abraham through Jacob's son Judah.

Only reference: 1 Chronicles 4:14

4) Forefather of an exiled family that returned to Judah under Zerubbabel.

First reference: Ezra 2:6 / Last reference: Nehemiah 7:11

5) Forefather of a Jewish exile who returned from Babylon to Judah under Ezra.

Only reference: Ezra 8:9

👥 JOAH

of times mentioned: 11
# of MEN by this name: 4

Meaning: Jehovah brothered

1) An officer of King Hezekiah of Judah. With Eliakim and Shebna, he confronted the king of Assyria's messengers, who tried to convince Hezekiah and his people to submit to Assyria.

First reference: 2 Kings 18:18 / Last reference: Isaiah 36:22

2) A descendant of Abraham through Jacob's son Levi. Joah was among the Levites who cleansed the Jerusalem temple during the revival of King Hezekiah's day.

First reference: 1 Chronicles 6:21 / Last reference: 2 Chronicles 29:12

3) A Levite "porter" (doorkeeper) in the house of the Lord.

Only reference: 1 Chronicles 26:4

4) An official under King Josiah of Judah, whom the king sent to repair the temple.

Only reference: 2 Chronicles 34:8

👥 JOAHAZ

of times mentioned: 1
# of MEN by this name: 1

Meaning: Jehovah seized

Father of Joah, an official whom King Josiah of Judah sent to repair the temple.

Only reference: 2 Chronicles 34:8

👥 JOANNA

of times mentioned: 3
# of MEN by this name: 1
# of WOMEN by this name: 1

1) A woman who followed Jesus and provided for his financial needs. Joanna was the wife of one of King Herod's officials and was later one of the first to learn of and tell others about Jesus' resurrection.

First reference: Luke 8:3 / Last reference: Luke 24:10

2) A descendant of Abraham through Isaac; forebear of Jesus' earthly father, Joseph.

Genealogy of Jesus: Yes (Luke 3:27)

Only reference: Luke 3:27

👥 JOASH

of times mentioned: 49
# of MEN by this name: 8

Meaning: Jehovah hastened

1) A descendant of Abraham through Jacob's son Benjamin.

Only reference: 1 Chronicles 7:8

2) The official over stores of oil under King David.

Only reference: 1 Chronicles 27:28

3) Father of Gideon, Joash stood up for his son when their neighbors wanted to kill Gideon for destroying the altar of Baal.

First reference: Judges 6:11 / Last reference: Judges 8:32

4) A son of King Ahab of Israel.

First reference: 1 Kings 22:26 / Last reference: 2 Chronicles 18:25

5) King of Judah, son of King Ahaziah. He was hidden from his wicked grandmother Athaliah and protected by the priest Jehoiada, who instructed him. Though he followed the Lord, Joash did not remove idolatry from the nation. He ordered that money be collected to refurbish the temple. But when Hazael, king of Syria, was about to attack, Joash took the gold from the temple and his own house and sent it as tribute to Hazael. Joash was killed by his servants, who formed a conspiracy against him. Same as Jehoash (1).

First reference: 2 Kings 11:2 / Last reference: 2 Chronicles 25:25 / Key references: 2 Chronicles 22:11; 24:2, 25

6) Another name for Jehoash (2), a king of Israel.

First reference: 2 Kings 13:9 / Last reference: Amos 1:1

7) A descendant of Abraham through Jacob's son Judah. Joash was a potter.

Only reference: 1 Chronicles 4:22

8) A "mighty man" who supported the future king David during his conflict with Saul.

Only reference: 1 Chronicles 12:3

👥 JOATHAM

of times mentioned: 2
# of MEN by this name: 1

Genealogy of Jesus: Yes (Matthew 1:9)

A descendant of Abraham through Isaac; forebear of Jesus' earthly father, Joseph.

Only reference: Matthew 1:9

👥 JOB

of times mentioned: 60
# of MEN by this name: 2

Meaning: Hated, persecuted

1) A descendant of Abraham through Jacob's son Issachar. Same as Jashub (1).

Only reference: Genesis 46:13

2) A righteous man from the land of Uz whom God tested to prove to Satan that Job was not faithful to Him because he had many physical blessings. For a time, God gave Job into Satan's power. First Job lost his cattle and servants. Then a messenger came with news that all his children had been killed. Yet Job continued to worship God.

Satan then covered Job with sores, and his wife told him, "Curse God, and die" (Job 2:9). Yet he still remained faithful. Three comfortless comforters, his friends, came to share his misery. For a week they were silent. But when Job began to speak, they answered with accusations that he had done something wrong. Eliphaz, Bildad, and Zophar took turns attempting to convince him that he needed to repent. Job made his case against them. Aware that no one is completely righteous before God, Job remained at a loss to understand what he had done wrong and voiced many moving expressions of faith.

A young man, Elihu, confronted them with God's justice and power, until God intervened and made Job aware of his own lack of understanding. Job repented. God rebuked his three friends and restored all of Job's original blessings.

First reference: Job 1:1 / Last reference: James 5:11 / Key references: Job 1:21; 9:1–3; 13:12, 15; 19:25–27; 38:1–3; 40:4–5; 42:1–17

👥 JOBAB

of times mentioned: 9
# of MEN by this name: 5

Meaning: Howler

1) A descendant of Noah through his son Shem.

First reference: Genesis 10:29 / Last reference: 1 Chronicles 1:23

2) A king of Edom, "before there reigned any king over the children of Israel" (Genesis 36:31).

First reference: Genesis 36:33 / Last reference: 1 Chronicles 1:45

3) The king of Madon who joined an alliance to attack the Israelites under Joshua.

Only reference: Joshua 11:1

4) A descendant of Abraham through Jacob's son Benjamin.

Only reference: 1 Chronicles 8:9

5) Another descendant of Abraham through Jacob's son Benjamin.

Only reference: 1 Chronicles 8:18

👥 JOCHEBED

of times mentioned: 2
# of WOMEN by this name: 1

Meaning: Jehovah gloried

Wife of Amram and mother of Moses, Aaron, and Miriam. She was a daughter of Levi.

First reference: Exodus 6:20 / Last reference: Numbers 26:59

JOED

of times mentioned: 1
# of MEN by this name: 1

Meaning: Appointer

Ancestor of a Benjamite who was chosen by lot to resettle Jerusalem after returning from the Babylonian Exile.

Only reference: Nehemiah 11:7

JOEL

of times mentioned: 20
# of MEN by this name: 14

Meaning: Jehovah is his God

1) The firstborn son of the prophet Samuel. Joel and his brother, Abiah, served as judges in Beersheba, but their poor character caused Israel's leaders to ask Samuel for a king to rule over them. Joel's son Heman was a well-known singer. Same as Vashni.

First reference: 1 Samuel 8:2 / Last reference: 1 Chronicles 15:17

2) A descendant of Abraham through Jacob's son Simeon.

Only reference: 1 Chronicles 4:35

3) A descendant of Abraham through Jacob's son Reuben.

First reference: 1 Chronicles 5:4 / Last reference: 1 Chronicles 5:8

4) A descendant of Abraham through Jacob's son Gad.

Only reference: 1 Chronicles 5:12

5) Ancestor of Heman, a singer who ministered in the tabernacle.

Only reference: 1 Chronicles 6:36

6) A descendant of Abraham through Jacob's son Issachar.

Only reference: 1 Chronicles 7:3

7) One of King David's valiant warriors.

Only reference: 1 Chronicles 11:38

8) A descendant of Abraham through Jacob's son Levi. Joel was among a group of Levites appointed by King David to bring the ark of the covenant from the house of Obed-edom to Jerusalem.

First reference: 1 Chronicles 15:7 / Last reference: 1 Chronicles 23:8

9) A Levite worship leader in charge of the temple treasures during David's reign.

Only reference: 1 Chronicles 26:22

10) Leader of half the tribe of Manasseh in the days of King David.

Only reference: 1 Chronicles 27:20

11) A descendant of Abraham through Jacob's son Levi. Joel was among the Levites who cleansed the Jerusalem temple during the revival of King Hezekiah's day.

Only reference: 2 Chronicles 29:12

12) An exiled Israelite who married a "strange" (foreign) woman.

Only reference: Ezra 10:43

13) A descendant of Benjamin who was chosen by lot to resettle Jerusalem after returning from the Babylonian Exile.

Only reference: Nehemiah 11:9

14) An Old Testament minor prophet who spoke of the coming day of the Lord and prophesied that God would pour out His Spirit on all flesh in the last days.

First reference: Joel 1:1 / Last reference: Acts 2:16

JOELAH

of times mentioned: 1
# of MEN by this name: 1

Meaning: To ascend

A "mighty man" who supported the future king David during his conflict with Saul.

Only reference: 1 Chronicles 12:7

JOEZER

of times mentioned: 1
# of MEN by this name: 1

Meaning: Jehovah is his help

A "mighty man" who supported the future king David during his conflict with Saul.

Only reference: 1 Chronicles 12:6

📍 JOGBEHAH

of times mentioned: OT 2

Meaning: Hillock

A fortified or walled city built by the tribe of Gad.

First reference: Numbers 32:35 / Last reference: Judges 8:11

👥 JOGLI

of times mentioned: 1
# of MEN by this name: 1

Meaning: Exiled

Forefather of Bukki, prince of the tribe of Dan when the Israelites entered the Promised Land.

Only reference: Numbers 34:22

👥 JOHA

of times mentioned: 2
# of MEN by this name: 2

Meaning: Jehovah revived

1) A descendant of Abraham through Jacob's son Benjamin.

Only reference: 1 Chronicles 8:16

2) One of King David's valiant warriors.

Only reference: 1 Chronicles 11:45

👥 JOHANAN

of times mentioned: 27
# of MEN by this name: 11

Meaning: Jehovah favored

1) A rebellious Jewish leader. Johanan supported the new Chaldean governor, Gedaliah, after the fall of Jerusalem. Following the governor's murder, he disobeyed God and took the remaining Israelites to Egypt.

First reference: 2 Kings 25:23 / Last reference: Jeremiah 43:5 / Key reference: Jeremiah 43:2

2) A descendant of King Solomon through his son Rehoboam.

Only reference: 1 Chronicles 3:15

3) A descendant of Abraham through Jacob's son Judah, in the line of the nation of Judah's third-to-last king, Jeconiah (also known as Jehoiachin).

Only reference: 1 Chronicles 3:24

4) A descendant of Abraham through Jacob's son Levi and a priest through the line of Aaron.

First reference: 1 Chronicles 6:9 / Last reference: 1 Chronicles 6:10

5) A "mighty man" who supported the future king David during his conflict with Saul.

Only reference: 1 Chronicles 12:4

6) One of several warriors from the tribe of Gad who left Saul to join David during his conflict with the king. Johanan and his companions were "men of might. . .whose faces were like the faces of lions" (1 1 Chronicles 12:8).

Only reference: 1 Chronicles 12:12

7) A man of the tribe of Ephraim whose son Azariah counseled his nation of Israel against enslaving fellow Jews from Judah who were captured in a civil war.

Only reference: 2 Chronicles 28:12

8) A Jewish exile who returned from Babylon to Judah under Ezra.

Only reference: Ezra 8:12

9) A Levite worship leader in whose room Ezra fasted over Judah's sins.

Only reference: Ezra 10:6

10) Son of Tobiah, an enemy of Israel during the rebuilding of Jerusalem's walls under Nehemiah.

Only reference: Nehemiah 6:18

11) A high priest and descendant of the high priest Jeshua (3), who went to Jerusalem with Zerubbabel. Same as Jonathan (10).

First reference: Nehemiah 12:22 / Last reference: Nehemiah 12:23

👥 JOHN

\# of times mentioned: 133
\# of MEN by this name: 4

1) Called "the Baptist," John was Jesus' cousin. He was born to the elderly couple Zacharias and Elisabeth after an angel told the doubtful Zacharias of the expected birth then temporarily struck him dumb for unbelief.

Before Jesus began His ministry, John preached a message of repentance in the desert and, in the Jordan River, baptized those who confessed their sins. He also confronted the Pharisees and Sadducees with their lack of repentance. John foretold that another more worthy than he would baptize with the Holy Spirit. He unwillingly baptized Jesus and saw the Spirit of God descend on Him.

Because John had objected to Herod the tetrarch's marriage to Herod's brother's wife Herodias, the ruler threw John into prison. Yet Herod was afraid to kill John, because the people believed he was a prophet. From prison, John sent word to ask Jesus if He was the expected Messiah. Jesus replied by telling the messengers to report on the healings they had seen and the preaching they had heard.

When Herod's stepdaughter danced before his birthday guests, Herod offered to give her whatever she wanted. Her mother, Herodias, pressed her to ask for John the Baptist's head. Herod reluctantly gave her what she asked for. John's disciples took his body and buried it.

First reference: Matthew 3:1 / Last reference: Acts 19:4 / Key references: Matthew 3:7–10; 11:2–4; 14:1–12; Mark 1:6–8; Luke 1:5–20

2) A son of Zebedee and brother of James, John became Jesus' disciple when the Master called the brothers to leave their fishing boat and follow Him. Describing himself in his Gospel as the disciple whom Jesus loved, John indicated their intimate relationship. As his closest disciples, he, James, and Peter experienced events such as the healings of Peter's mother-in-law and Jairus's daughter and the transfiguration of Jesus.

Jesus called Zebedee's sons the Sons of Thunder, perhaps for their quick-tempered personalities. When a town refused to house the Master and His men, the brothers wanted to call down fire on them. These two overly confident men asked Jesus if they could sit at his left and right hands in glory.

John and James fell asleep in the Garden of Gethsemane as Jesus prayed before His arrest. John may also have been the "another disciple" who was known to the high priest and brought Peter into the courtyard during Jesus' trial (John 18:15). At the crucifixion, Jesus placed His mother, Mary, in John's care.

After Jesus' death and resurrection, John was often with Peter. Together they investigated the empty tomb and went fishing while they awaited their new ministry. John was with Peter when he healed the beggar at the temple gate.

John wrote the Gospel and letters that bear his name and the book of Revelation.

First reference: Matthew 4:21 / Last reference: Revelation 22:8 / Key references: Matthew 4:21–22; 17:1–3; Mark 10:35–37; John 13:23; 19:26; 20:1–2

3) A member of the family of the high priest Caiaphas, or Annas.

Only reference: Acts 4:6

4) Also called Mark, he joined his cousin Barnabas and the apostle Paul on Paul's first missionary journey but left them at Perga. This caused Paul to lose confidence in John Mark for a time.

First reference: Acts 12:12 / Last reference: Acts 15:37

👥 JOIADA

\# of times mentioned: 4
\# of MEN by this name: 1

Meaning: Jehovah knows

A high priest and descendant of the priest Jeshua.

First reference: Nehemiah 12:10 / Last reference: Nehemiah 13:28

👥 JOIAKIM

\# of times mentioned: 4
\# of MEN by this name: 1

Meaning: Jehovah will raise

A high priest and descendant of the high priest Jeshua (3). Joiakim returned to Jerusalem with Zerubbabel.

First reference: Nehemiah 12:10 / Last reference: Nehemiah 12:26

👥 JOIARIB

of times mentioned: 5
# of MEN by this name: 3

Meaning: Jehovah will contend

1) A Jewish exile charged with finding Levites and temple servants to travel to Jerusalem with Ezra.

Only reference: Ezra 8:16

2) A Jewish exile from the tribe of Judah who re-settled Jerusalem.

Only reference: Nehemiah 11:5

3) An exiled priest who returned to Judah under Zerubbabel.

First reference: Nehemiah 11:10 / Last reference: Nehemiah 12:19

📍 JOKDEAM

of times mentioned: OT 1

Meaning: Burning of the people

A city that became part of the inheritance of the tribe of Judah following the conquest of the Promised Land.

Only reference: Joshua 15:56

👥 JOKIM

of times mentioned: 1
# of MEN by this name: 1

Meaning: Jehovah will establish

A descendant of Abraham through Jacob's son Judah. Jokim was a potter.

Only reference: 1 Chronicles 4:22

📍 JOKMEAM

of times mentioned: OT 1

Meaning: The people will be raised
One of the six cities of refuge established in Israel for those who had committed accidental murder. Jokmeam was given to the Levites by the tribe of Ephraim.

Only reference: 1 Chronicles 6:68

📍 JOKNEAM

of times mentioned: OT 4

Meaning: People will be lamented

1) Jokneam of Carmel was a city on the west side of the Jordan River. After the Israelites conquered it, it became part of the inheritance of the tribe of Zebulun. Jokneam and its suburbs became one of the forty-eight cities given to the Levites as God had commanded.

First reference: Joshua 12:22 / Last reference: Joshua 21:34

2) Under King Solomon's governmental organization, a city responsible for supplying provisions for the king.

Only reference: 1 Kings 4:12

👥 JOKSHAN

of times mentioned: 4
# of MEN by this name: 1

Meaning: Insidious

A son of Abraham by his second wife, Keturah.

First reference: Genesis 25:2 / Last reference: 1 Chronicles 1:32

👥 JOKTAN

of times mentioned: 6
# of MEN by this name: 1

Meaning: He will be made little

A descendant of Noah through his son Shem. Joktan had thirteen sons.

First reference: Genesis 10:25 / Last reference: 1 Chronicles 1:23

📍 JOKTHEEL

of times mentioned: OT 2

Meaning: Veneration of God

1) A city that became part of the inheritance of the tribe of Judah following the conquest of the Promised Land.

Only reference: Joshua 15:38

2) A name that King Amaziah of Judah gave to the city of Selah after he conquered it. Same as Sela and Selah.

Only reference: 2 Kings 14:7

👥 JONA

of times mentioned: 1
# of MEN by this name: 1

Meaning: A dove

Greek form of the name Jonah, used in the New Testament.

Only reference: John 1:42

👥 JONADAB

of times mentioned: 12
# of MEN by this name: 2

Meaning: Jehovah largessed

1) A friend and cousin of David's son Amnon, "a very subtil man" (2 Samuel 13:3) who advised him to pretend to be ill so his half sister Tamar would come to him. He reported Amnon's death to King David, telling him that Absalom had killed his brother.

First reference: 2 Samuel 13:3 / Last reference: 2 Samuel 13:35

2) The Rechabite who commanded his descendants not to drink any wine.

First reference: Jeremiah 35:6 / Last reference: Jeremiah 35:19

👥 JONAH

of times mentioned: 19
# of MEN by this name: 1

Meaning: A dove

An Old Testament minor prophet whom God commanded to preach in Nineveh, home of Israel's Assyrian enemies. Fearing God would give mercy to his enemies, Jonah fled on a ship headed for Tarshish. When a tempest struck the ship, the sailors threw Jonah overboard. Jonah was swallowed by a fish. When he praised God, the fish vomited him onto land.

Jonah went to Nineveh, and the people repented. The angry prophet, wanting to die, fled the city. God pointed out that Jonah had more compassion for a plant that died than for the people of the city. Same as Jona and Jonas (1).

First reference: 2 Kings 14:25 / Last reference: Jonah 4:9 / Key references: Jonah 1:10–15; 4:10–11

👥 JONAN

of times mentioned: 1
# of MEN by this name: 1

Genealogy of Jesus: Yes (Luke 3:30)

A descendant of Abraham through Isaac; forebear of Jesus' earthly father, Joseph.

Only reference: Luke 3:30

👥 JONAS

of times mentioned: 12
# of MEN by this name: 2

1) The Greek form of Jonah, used in the New Testament.

First reference: Matthew 12:39 / Last reference: Luke 11:32

2) Father of Simon Peter.

First reference: John 21:15 / Last reference: John 21:17

👥 JONATHAN

of times mentioned: 121
# of MEN by this name: 14

Meaning: Jehovah given

1) A priest to the idolatrous tribe of Dan in the time of the judges.

Only reference: Judges 18:30

2) Eldest son of King Saul. He and his armor bearer attacked the Philistines at Michmash and brought them into confusion so Saul and his men could attack them. Jonathan and David became great friends, and Jonathan made a covenant with him. When Saul jealously tried to kill David, Jonathan warned his friend. He spoke well of David to his father and earned him a reprieve, but again Saul's anger raged against David, who fled. David later consulted Jonathan, who spoke to his father, then warned David away for good. When Saul again fought the Philistines, Jonathan was killed in battle.

First reference: 1 Samuel 13:2 / Last reference: Jeremiah 38:26 / Key references: 1 Samuel 14:6–15; 18:1–4; 20:1–23; 31:2

3) Son of Abiathar, the high priest during King David's reign. He acted as messenger to David for the counselor Hushai. When David made Solomon king, Jonathan brought the news to David's son Adonijah.

First reference: 2 Samuel 15:27 / Last reference: 1 Kings 1:43

4) David's nephew, who killed a Philistine giant from Gath.

First reference: 2 Samuel 21:21 / Last reference: 1 Chronicles 20:7

5) One of King David's valiant warriors.

First reference: 2 Samuel 23:32 / Last reference: 1 Chronicles 11:34

6) A descendant of Abraham through Jacob's son Judah.

First reference: 1 Chronicles 2:32 / Last reference: 1 Chronicles 2:33

7) David's uncle and counselor, who took care of the king's sons.

Only reference: 1 Chronicles 27:32

8) Forefather of a Jewish exile who returned from Babylon to Judah under Ezra.

Only reference: Ezra 8:6

9) A man who joined Ezra in urging the Israelites to give up their "strange" (foreign) wives.

Only reference: Ezra 10:15

10) A high priest and descendant of the priest Jeshua who went to Jerusalem with Zerubbabel. Same as Johanan (11).

Only reference: Nehemiah 12:11

11) Forefather of a priest who returned to Jerusalem under Zerubbabel.

Only reference: Nehemiah 12:14

12) Father of a priest who helped to dedicate the rebuilt walls of Jerusalem by playing a musical instrument.

Only reference: Nehemiah 12:35

13) The scribe in whose home Jeremiah was imprisoned.

First reference: Jeremiah 37:15 / Last reference: Jeremiah 37:20

14) A captain of Israel's forces under Nebuchadnezzar's governor Gedaliah.

Only reference: Jeremiah 40:8

⭘ JOPPA

of times mentioned: OT 3 / NT 10

Meaning: Beautiful

A Mediterranean seaport city in the territory of the tribe of Dan. Huram (or Hiram) of Tyre shipped cedar logs to King Solomon through Joppa for his building projects in Jerusalem. When the Israelites rebuilt the temple following the Babylonian Exile, they used the same route. To escape God's command to go to Nineveh, the prophet Jonah went to Joppa, seeking a ship bound for Tarshish.

The disciple Tabitha (Dorcas) lived in Joppa. When she died, her friends called Peter to come and heal her. At Simon the tanner's house in Joppa, Peter saw a vision in which God told him, "What God hath cleansed, that call not thou common" (Acts 10:15). From this the apostle understood that he should accept Gentiles who believed in Jesus. Therefore he received the messengers of the centurion Cornelius, visited his household, and preached there. When the Holy Spirit fell upon his hearers, Peter baptized them.

First reference: 2 Chronicles 2:16 / Last reference: Acts 11:13 / Key references: Jonah 1:3; Acts 9:36–38; 10

👥 JORAH

of times mentioned: 1
# of MEN by this name: 1

Meaning: Rainy

Forefather of an exiled family that returned to Judah under Zerubbabel.

Only reference: Ezra 2:18

👥 JORAI

of times mentioned: 1
# of MEN by this name: 1

Meaning: Rainy

A descendant of Abraham through Jacob's son Gad.

Only reference: 1 Chronicles 5:13

👥 JORAM

of times mentioned: 29
# of MEN by this name: 4

Meaning: Jehovah raised

1) The son of the king of Hamath who brought gifts to David.

Only reference: 2 Samuel 8:10

2) King of Judah and son of King Jehoshaphat. Edom revolted during his reign. When Joram fought them, his troops fled. Same as Jehoram (1).

First reference: 2 Kings 8:21 / Last reference: Matthew 1:8

Genealogy of Jesus: Yes (Matthew 1:8)

3) Son of King Ahab and king of Israel. When he went to war with King Ahaziah of Judah against the Syrians, Joram was wounded. While he was recovering in Jezreel, he was killed by Jehu, who took his throne. Same as Jehoram (2).

First reference: 2 Kings 8:16 / Last reference: 2 Chronicles 22:7 / Key references: 2 Kings 8:28–29; 9:21–24

4) A Levite worship leader who worked in the temple treasury during King David's reign.

Only reference: 1 Chronicles 26:25

📍 JORDAN

of times mentioned: OT 183 / NT 15

Meaning: A descender

A river flowing from Palestine's Lake Huleh south to the Sea of Galilee and on to the Dead Sea; the Jordan River defined the eastern edge of Canaan. Abram's nephew Lot settled in the well-watered plain of the Jordan, north of the Dead Sea, when his uncle commanded him to choose his own land.

On their way toward Canaan, the Israelites conquered lands east of the Jordan River, including the eastern part of the Amorite holdings. Before they crossed into Canaan, the tribes of Reuben and Gad asked Moses for lands east of the Jordan River as their inheritance. After these tribes agreed to help in the conquest of Canaan, Moses allowed them this inheritance (Numbers 32). Following the conquest of the Promised Land, most of Israel's land lay west of the Jordan. Only Reuben, Gad, and some of Manasseh's land lay to the east, encompassing Gilead and Bashan.

Under Joshua, Israel crossed the Jordan River into Canaan. God commanded that the ark of the covenant be carried into the Jordan and remain in the channel while Israel crossed over. The waters stood up in a heap so the people could pass safely. From the riverbed, God told Joshua to take twelve stones that were made into a memorial of the crossing.

Before the prophet Elijah was taken up into heaven in a fiery chariot, he and his disciple, Elisha, crossed the Jordan River. On their way across, Elijah struck the river with his mantle, and the water divided. On his way back, alone, Elisha performed the same miracle.

The prophet Elijah told the Syrian captain Naaman to wash himself seven times in the Jordan River to be healed of leprosy. Though Naaman would have preferred to wash in one of the rivers of his own land, his servants persuaded him to follow the prophet's directions, and the captain was healed.

John the Baptist performed many baptisms in the Jordan River, including the baptism of Jesus.

First reference: Genesis 13:10 / Last reference: John 10:40 / Key references: Joshua 1:2; 3:11–17; 2 Kings 2:6–14; 5:1–14; Matthew 3:6, 13

📍 JORIM

of times mentioned: 1

# of MEN by this name: 1

Genealogy of Jesus: Yes (Luke 3:29)

A descendant of Abraham through Isaac; the forebear of Jesus' earthly father, Joseph.

Only reference: Luke 3:29

👥 JORKOAM

of times mentioned: 1
# of MEN by this name: 1

Meaning: People will be poured forth

A descendant of Abraham through Jacob's son Judah.

Only reference: 1 Chronicles 2:44

👥 JOSABAD

of times mentioned: 1
# of MEN by this name: 1

Meaning: Jehovah endowed

A "mighty man" who supported the future king David during his conflict with Saul.

Only reference: 1 Chronicles 12:4

👥 JOSAPHAT

of times mentioned: 2
# of MEN by this name: 1

Genealogy of Jesus: Yes (Matthew 1:8)

A descendant of Abraham through Isaac; forebear of Jesus' earthly father, Joseph.

Only reference: Matthew 1:8

👥 JOSE

of times mentioned: 1
# of MEN by this name: 1

Genealogy of Jesus: Yes (Luke 3:29)

A descendant of Abraham through Isaac; forebear of Jesus' earthly father, Joseph.

Only reference: Luke 3:29

👥 JOSEDECH

of times mentioned: 6
# of MEN by this name: 1

Meaning: Jehovah righted

Father of the high priest Joshua, who took part in rebuilding the temple.

First reference: Haggai 1:1 / Last reference: Zechariah 6:11

👥 JOSEPH

of times mentioned: 250
# of MEN by this name: 11

Meaning: Let him add

1) Son of Jacob and Rachel. Joseph was Jacob's favorite son, which made his other sons jealous. Joseph angered his brothers when he told them of his dream that he would rule over them. While watching their flocks, the brothers plotted to kill Joseph. They threw him into an empty pit then sold him to some passing traders. Killing a goat, they dipped Joseph's robe in it and told Jacob he had been killed by a wild animal.

Carried to Egypt, Joseph became a slave to the captain of Pharaoh's guard. After the captain's wife accused him of trying to seduce her, Joseph landed in prison, where he interpreted the dreams of two of Pharaoh's servants. Given an opportunity to interpret Pharaoh's dream, he became second in command in Egypt. During the famine he had predicted, Joseph's ten half brothers came to buy food from him and did not recognize him. Joseph tested them, to be certain they would not treat his full brother, Benjamin, as they had treated him. The brothers passed the test, and Joseph revealed himself. The family was reunited in Egypt, where they settled in Goshen.

First reference: Genesis 30:24 / Last reference: Hebrews 11:22 / Key references: Genesis 37:3–8, 24–28; 41:14–40; 42:6–28; 44:16–34; 45:3–10

2) Father of one of the twelve spies sent by Moses to spy out the land of Canaan.

Only reference: Numbers 13:7

3) A son of King David's musician Asaph, "which prophesied according to the order of the king" (1 Chronicles 25:2).

First reference: 1 Chronicles 25:2 / Last reference: 1 Chronicles 25:9

4) An exiled Israelite who married a "strange" (foreign) woman.

Only reference: Ezra 10:42

5) Forefather of a priest who returned to Jerusalem under Zerubbabel.

Only reference: Nehemiah 12:14

6) Husband of Mary and the earthly father of Jesus. The carpenter Joseph was betrothed to Mary when she conceived Jesus. He planned to divorce her quietly, but an angel told him not to fear marrying her, for she would bear the Messiah. With Mary, he traveled to Bethlehem, where the child was born. He was with Mary when Jesus was dedicated at the temple and when they visited the temple when Jesus was twelve years old.

First reference: Matthew 1:16 / Last reference: John 6:42 / Key references: Matthew 1:18–25; Luke 2:4–7

Genealogy of Jesus: Yes (Matthew 1:16)

7) A wealthy man of Arimathea and member of the Sanhedrin who became Jesus' disciple. After Jesus' death, Joseph went to Pilate and asked for His body, which Joseph laid in his own tomb.

First reference: Matthew 27:57 / Last reference: John 19:38

8) A descendant of Abraham through Isaac; forebear of Jesus' earthly father, Joseph.

Only reference: Luke 3:24

Genealogy of Jesus: Yes (Luke 3:24)

9) Another descendant of Abraham through Isaac; another forebear of Jesus' earthly father, Joseph.

Only reference: Luke 3:26

Genealogy of Jesus: Yes (Luke 3:26)

10) Another descendant of Abraham through Isaac; another forebear of Jesus' earthly father, Joseph.

Only reference: Luke 3:30

Genealogy of Jesus: Yes (Luke 3:30)

11) A potential apostolic replacement for Judas Iscariot who lost by lot to the other candidate, Matthias. Same as Barsabas and Justus (1).

Only reference: Acts 1:23

👥 JOSES

of times mentioned: 6
# of MEN by this name: 3

1) One of four brothers of Jesus, as recorded in the Gospels of Matthew and Mark.

First reference: Matthew 13:55 / Last reference: Mark 6:3

2) Son of one of the Marys who witnessed Jesus' crucifixion.

First reference: Matthew 27:56 / Last reference: Mark 15:47

3) Another name for Barnabas.

Only reference: Acts 4:36

👥 JOSHAH

of times mentioned: 1
# of MEN by this name: 1

Meaning: Jehovah set

A descendant of Abraham through Jacob's son Simeon.

Only reference: 1 Chronicles 4:34

👥 JOSHAPHAT

of times mentioned: 1
# of MEN by this name: 1

Meaning: Jehovah judged

One of King David's valiant warriors.

Only reference: 1 Chronicles 11:43

👥 JOSHAVIAH

of times mentioned: 1
# of MEN by this name: 1

Meaning: Jehovah set

One of King David's valiant warriors.

Only reference: 1 Chronicles 11:46

👥 JOSHBEKASHAH

of times mentioned: 2
# of MEN by this name: 1

Meaning: Hard seat

A son of King David's musician Heman, who was "under the hands of [his] father for song in the house of the LORD" (1 Chronicles 25:6).

First reference: 1 Chronicles 25:4 / Last reference: 1 Chronicles 25:24

👥 JOSHUA

of times mentioned: 216
# of MEN by this name: 4

Meaning: Jehovah saved

1) Moses' right-hand man, Joshua son of Nun led Israel to victory against the Amalekites. He spied out Canaan before the Israelites entered it and came back with a positive report. For his faith, he was one of only two men of his generation who entered the Promised Land.

God chose Joshua to succeed Moses as Israel's leader. After Moses' death, Joshua led the Israelites into the Promised Land. After they crossed the Jordan River, Joshua led his warriors to attack Jericho using trumpets, the ark of the covenant, and their own voices. The walls fell flat from God's power. Through their own disobedience, the Israelites lost at Ai; then they won, when they obeyed God. Joshua renewed their covenant with God and wrote a copy of Moses' law then continued to conquer the new land. As they fought the king of Jerusalem and his allies, Joshua needed a longer day and asked God to make the sun stand still. It remained in place until Israel won.

When Joshua was old and the land had not all been conquered, God promised to win the land for His people, so Joshua allotted all the lands to the tribes of Israel and charged the people to obey God. Same as Hoshea (1) and Jesus (2).

First reference: Exodus 17:9 / Last reference: 1 Kings 16:34 / Key references: Numbers 14:6–7, 30; 27:18–23; Joshua 6:2–21; 10:12–13; 13:1, 6; 24:15

2) Owner of the land where an ox cart bearing the ark of the covenant stopped when the Philistines sent it to Israel.

First reference: 1 Samuel 6:14 / Last reference: 1 Samuel 6:18

3) Governor of the city of Jerusalem under King Josiah.

Only reference: 2 Kings 23:8

4) The high priest who served under Governor Zerubbabel. Through their leadership, Israel rebuilt the temple. The prophet Zechariah saw a vision of Joshua. Satan accused him as he stood in filthy garments, but an angel reclothed him in clean clothes that symbolized righteousness.

First reference: Haggai 1:1 / Last reference: Zechariah 6:11 / Key references: Haggai 1:14; Zechariah 3:1–10

👥 JOSIAH

of times mentioned: 53
# of MEN by this name: 2

Meaning: Founded of God

1) Son of King Amon of Judah, Josiah became king when he was eight years old and followed the Lord closely through his life. Josiah collected money and repaired the temple. When the book of the law was discovered by Hilkiah the priest, Josiah had it read to him and consulted the prophetess Huldah. Then Josiah read the book to the elders of his nation, made a covenant to follow the Lord, and caused his people to follow his example. He put down idolatry in the land and celebrated the Passover.

Josiah died in battle against Necho, king of Egypt, who fought at Carchemish.

First reference: 1 Kings 13:2 / Last reference: Zephaniah 1:1 / Key references: 2 Kings 22:1–2, 10–13; 23:1–3, 5, 21, 29; 2 Chronicles 34:1–3, 31–33; 35:20–24

2) The man in whose house the high priest Joshua received a prophecy from Zechariah.

Only reference: Zechariah 6:10

👥 JOSIAS

of times mentioned: 2
# of MEN by this name: 1

Genealogy of Jesus: Yes (Matthew 1:10–11)

Meaning: Founded of God

A descendant of Abraham through Isaac; forebear of Jesus' earthly father, Joseph.

First reference: Matthew 1:10 / Last reference: Matthew 1:11

👥 JOSIBIAH

of times mentioned: 1
# of MEN by this name: 1

Meaning: Jehovah will cause to dwell

A descendant of Abraham through Jacob's son Simeon.

Only reference: 1 Chronicles 4:35

👥 JOSIPHIAH

of times mentioned: 1
# of MEN by this name: 1

Meaning: God is adding

Forefather of a Jewish exile who returned from Babylon to Judah under Ezra.

Only reference: Ezra 8:10

📍 JOTBAH

of times mentioned: OT 1

Meaning: Pleasantness

Hometown of Meshullemeth, the mother of King Amon of Judah.

Only reference: 2 Kings 21:19

📍 JOTBATH

of times mentioned: OT 1

Meaning: Pleasantness

A campsite of the Israelites during the Exodus, Jotbath was "a land of rivers of waters." Same as Jotbathah.

Only reference: Deuteronomy 10:7

📍 JOTBATHAH

of times mentioned: OT 2

Meaning: Pleasantness

A campsite of the Israelites on their way to the Promised Land. Same as Jotbath.

First reference: Numbers 33:33 / Last reference: Numbers 33:34

👥 JOTHAM

of times mentioned: 24
# of MEN by this name: 3

Meaning: Jehovah is perfect

1) The youngest son of Jerubbaal (also known as Gideon). Jotham hid from his brother Abimelech, who tried to kill all his brothers.

First reference: Judges 9:5 / Last reference: Judges 9:57

2) Son of Azariah, the king of Judah, Jotham governed for his father, who had become a leper. After he inherited the throne, he built the upper gate of the temple and obeyed God, but he did not destroy idolatry in the land. He defeated the Ammonites and received tribute from them.

First reference: 2 Kings 15:5 / Last reference: Micah 1:1 / Key references: 2 Kings 15:32–35; 2 Chronicles 27:1–5

3) A descendant of Abraham through Jacob's son Judah.

Only reference: 1 Chronicles 2:47

👥 JOZABAD

of times mentioned: 9
# of MEN by this name: 8

Meaning: Jehovah has conferred

1) A mighty man of valor who joined David at Ziklag.

Only reference: 1 Chronicles 12:20

2) An overseer of the temple treasury during King Hezekiah's reign.

Only reference: 2 Chronicles 31:13

3) A descendant of Abraham through Jacob's son Levi. Jozabad was among those who distributed sacrificial animals to fellow Levites preparing to celebrate the Passover under King Josiah.

Only reference: 2 Chronicles 35:9

4) A Levite who weighed the temple vessels after the Babylonian Exile.

Only reference: Ezra 8:33

5) An exiled Israelite priest who married a "strange" (foreign) woman.

Only reference: Ezra 10:22

6) An exiled Levite who married a "strange" (foreign) woman.

Only reference: Ezra 10:23

7) A Levite who helped Ezra to explain the law to exiles after they returned to Jerusalem.

Only reference: Nehemiah 8:7

8) A Levite who oversaw the outside of the Jerusalem temple in the time of Nehemiah.

Only reference: Nehemiah 11:16

👥 JOZACHAR

of times mentioned: 1
# of MEN by this name: 1

Meaning: Jehovah remembered

A servant of King Joash of Judah who conspired against him and murdered him.

Only reference: 2 Kings 12:21

👥 JOZADAK

of times mentioned: 5
# of MEN by this name: 1

Meaning: Jehovah righted

Father of Jeshua, the high priest who returned to Israel with Zerubbabel.

First reference: Ezra 3:2 / Last reference: Nehemiah 12:26

👥 JUBAL

of times mentioned: 1
# of MEN by this name: 1

Meaning: Stream

A descendant of Cain through Lamech and his wife Adah. Jubal was "the father of all such as handle the harp and organ."

Only reference: Genesis 4:21

👥 JUCAL

of times mentioned: 1
# of MEN by this name: 1

Meaning: Potent

A prince of Judah who urged King Zedekiah to kill Jeremiah because of his negative prophecy.

Only reference: Jeremiah 38:1

👥 JUDA

of times mentioned: 4
# of MEN by this name: 4

Meaning: Judah

1) One of four brothers of Jesus, as recorded in Mark's Gospel. Same as Judas (2).

Only reference: Mark 6:3

2) Son of Jacob and ancestor of Jesus.

Only reference: Luke 3:26

Genealogy of Jesus: Yes (Luke 3:26)

3) A descendant of David and another ancestor of Jesus.

Only reference: Luke 3:30

Genealogy of Jesus: Yes (Luke 3:30)

4) A descendant of Abraham through Isaac; forebear of Jesus' earthly father, Joseph.

Only reference: Luke 3:33

Genealogy of Jesus: Yes (Luke 3:33)

♀ JUDAEA

of times mentioned: NT 43

A Roman district, part of the province of Syria, that included Jerusalem and Bethlehem, which was ruled by King Herod the Great. Following Herod's death, his son Archelaus ruled in his place. Fearing the ruler's revenge, Joseph took Mary and Jesus to Galilee when they discovered that Archelaus was ruling Judaea. Later, Pontius Pilate became governor there.

John the Baptist preached and baptized in Judaea's wilderness, and many from this area followed Jesus. There He baptized them and preached the Sermon on the Mount. Jesus warned the Judaeans that when they saw the abomination of desolation prophesied by Daniel, they should flee to the mountains. Though Judaea had become a dangerous place for Jesus, He chose to return there to raise Lazarus, despite the warnings of His disiciples.

Following the death of Stephen, the Christians of Jerusalem were scattered through Judaea and elsewhere because of persecution.

The Judaizers, who wanted Gentiles to receive circumcision, came from Judaea. They attempted to "correct" Paul's missionary efforts with non-Jewish people. Sometimes translated "Judah." Same as Judea.

First reference: Matthew 2:1 / Last reference: 1 Thessalonians 2:14 / Key references: Matthew 3:1; Mark 3:7; Luke 6:17; John 11:7

👥 JUDAH

of times mentioned: 49
# of MEN by this name: 7

Meaning: Celebrated

1) The fourth son of Jacob and Leah. Judah convinced his brothers not to kill Joseph but to sell him to some Midianite traders instead. Because Judah would not give his widowed daughter-in-law his third son as a husband, she sat by the roadside and pretended she was a harlot. Judah went to her and she had twins. In Egypt, Judah spoke up for Benjamin when he was accused of stealing Joseph's cup and offered himself in Benjamin's place. His father's final blessing described Judah as one whom his brothers would praise.

First reference: Genesis 29:35 / Last reference: Jeremiah 38:22 / Key references: Genesis 37:26–27; 44:18–34; 49:8–9

2) Father of several men who oversaw the workmen rebuilding the temple after the Babylonian Exile.

Only reference: Ezra 3:9

3) An exiled Levite who married a "strange" (foreign) woman.

Only reference: Ezra 10:23

4) A descendant of Benjamin who was chosen by lot to resettle Jerusalem after returning from the Babylonian Exile.

Only reference: Nehemiah 11:9

5) A Levite who returned to Judah with Zerubbabel.

Only reference: Nehemiah 12:8

6) A leader of Judah who took part in the dedication of Jerusalem's rebuilt wall.

Only reference: Nehemiah 12:34

7) A priest who helped to dedicate the rebuilt walls of Jerusalem by playing a musical instrument.

Only reference: Nehemiah 12:36

♀ JUDAH

of times mentioned: OT 581

Meaning: Celebrated

When Solomon's son Rehoboam inherited the kingdom of Israel and began to rule it unwisely, all the tribes except Judah, Simeon, and part of Benjamin broke off. The northern tribes followed Jeroboam, who was crowned king of Israel. Rehoboam subsequently ruled over the nation of Judah.

Rehoboam wisely built fortified cities to defend his nation. During his reign, Shishak, king of Egypt, attacked Jerusalem and took away the treasures of the temple and the king's house. In addition, Rehoboam and Jeroboam were constantly at war.

The priests and Levites of Israel were thrown out after Jeroboam's institution of idolatry as the national religion. They reacted by moving to Judah and Jerusalem.

Judah had a succession of good and bad kings and one bad queen. Idolatry was a constant threat to the kingdom, and some rulers gave in to it easily. Judah faced numerous enemies: Israel, Syria, Assyria, and Babylon. Though the Assyrian king

Sennacherib tried to take Jerusalem, he was unsuccessful. But the Chaldean king Nebuchadnezzar put down the rebellious King Zedekiah of Judah. Judah's king was captured, his sons were killed as he watched, his eyes were put out, and he was taken prisoner to Babylon. Jerusalem's temple was destroyed, along with the king's house and the great homes of the city. Many of Judah's people were taken captive to Babylon, along with their king. The top spiritual leaders of Jerusalem were killed.

After Israel's return from the Babylonian Exile, Judah was a district in the Persian Empire.

First reference: 1 Kings 12:17 / Last reference: Malachi 3:4 / Key references: 1 Kings 12; 2 Kings 25; 2 Chronicles 11:1–15

👥 JUDAS

of times mentioned: 33
# of MEN by this name: 7

Meaning: Celebrated

1) The disciple who betrayed Jesus, usually identified as Judas Iscariot. He was given his position by Jesus and was put in charge of the money, but he was not honest with it (John 12:6).

Judas went to the chief priests and promised to betray Jesus for forty pieces of silver. At the Last Supper, Jesus predicted Judas's betrayal and even handed him a morsel of food to indicate his identity as the betrayer. Sorrowful at his own betrayal, following Jesus' death, Judas returned the money to the priests and hanged himself. Same as Iscariot.

First reference: Matthew 10:4 / Last reference: Acts 1:25 / Key references: Matthew 27:3–5; Mark 14:10; John 13:2, 26

2) One of four brothers of Jesus, as recorded by Matthew's Gospel. Same as Juda (1).

Only reference: Matthew 13:55

3) Identified as "the brother of James," another of Jesus' disciples, not to be confused with Judas Iscariot. He was with the disciples in the upper room after Jesus' resurrection. Same as Lebbaeus and Thaddaeus.

First reference: Luke 6:16 / Last reference: Acts 1:13

4) A man of Galilee whom Gamaliel used as an example of fleetingly popular religious figures.

Only reference: Acts 5:37

5) A man of Damascus with whom Saul stayed while he was blinded.

Only reference: Acts 9:11

6) Judas surnamed Barsabbas. The Jerusalem Council sent Judas to Antioch with Paul and Barnabas to address the issue of Gentile circumcision.

First reference: Acts 15:22 / Last reference: Acts 15:32

7) A Greek form of the name Judah. Same as Judah (1).

First reference: Matthew 1:2 / Last reference: Matthew 1:3

👥 JUDE

of times mentioned: 1
# of MEN by this name: 1

A disciple of Jesus, author of the epistle of Jude, and the brother of James. Same as Judas (3), Lebbaeus, and Thaddeus.

Only reference: Jude 1:1

📍 JUDEA

of times mentioned: OT 1

Meaning: Celebrated

Following the Babylonian Exile, the land of Judah became a Persian province called Judea. In some Bible versions it is translated "Judah." Same as Judaea.

Only reference: Ezra 5:8

👥 JUDITH

of times mentioned: 1
# of WOMEN by this name: 1

Meaning: Jew, descendant of Judah

One of Esau's Hittite wives, the daughter of Beeri.

Only reference: Genesis 26:34

JULIA

of times mentioned: 1
# of WOMEN by this name: 1

A Christian acquaintance of the apostle Paul, greeted in his letter to the Romans.

Only reference: Romans 16:15

JULIUS

of times mentioned: 2
# of MEN by this name: 1

A Roman centurion who guarded Paul when he sailed to Rome.

First reference: Acts 27:1 / Last reference: Acts 27:3

JUNIA

of times mentioned: 1
# of WOMEN by this name: 1

A Roman Christian who spent time in jail with the apostle Paul and who also may have been related to Paul.

Only reference: Romans 16:7

JUSHABHESED

of times mentioned: 1
# of MEN by this name: 1

Meaning: Jehovah is perfect

A descendant of Abraham through Jacob's son Judah, in the line of the nation of Judah's third-to-last king, Jeconiah (also known as Jehoiachin).

Only reference: 1 Chronicles 3:20

JUSTUS

of times mentioned: 3
# of MEN by this name: 3

Meaning: Just

1) Surname for Joseph (11), a potential apostolic replacement for Judas Iscariot who lost by lot to the other candidate, Matthias. Same as Barsabas (1).

Only reference: Acts 1:23

2) A Corinthian Christian in whose home Paul stayed.

Only reference: Acts 18:7

3) A Christian Jew and fellow worker with the apostle Paul in Rome. Paul called Justus, also known as Jesus, "a comfort unto me."

Only reference: Colossians 4:11

JUTTAH

of times mentioned: OT 2

Meaning: Extended

A city that became part of the inheritance of the tribe of Judah following the conquest of the Promised Land. It later became one of the forty-eight cities given to the Levites as God had commanded.

First reference: Joshua 15:55 / Last reference: Joshua 21:16

KABZEEL

of times mentioned: OT 3

Meaning: God has gathered

A city that became part of the inheritance of the tribe of Judah following the conquest of the Promised Land. It was the home of Benaiah, one of David's three most valiant warriors.

First reference: Joshua 15:21 / Last reference: 1 Chronicles 11:22

KADESH

of times mentioned: OT 17

Meaning: Sanctuary

A place in the Desert of Zin from which Chedorlaomer, king of Elam, and his allies attacked the Amalekites and Amorites. From Kadesh, Moses sent the twelve spies into the Promised Land. After Israel refused to enter the Promised Land, the Israelites lived in a camp in Kadesh "many days" (Deuteronomy 1:46). Miriam died in Kadesh, and the rock of Meribah, which Moses disobediently struck two times, was near here.

When Israel wanted to pass through Edom on the way to the Promised Land, Moses sent the king of Edom a message from Kadesh, asking permission. He described Kadesh as "a city in the uttermost of thy border."

When Ezekiel described the extent of the restored Jerusalem, he used Kadesh as a border marker. Same as En-mishpat, Kadesh-barnea, and Kedesh (4).

First reference: Genesis 14:7 / Last reference: Ezekiel 48:28 / Key reference: Numbers 20:14–17

KADESH-BARNEA

of times mentioned: OT 10

Meaning: Desert of a fugitive

The site of the Israelite camp from which Moses sent the twelve spies into the Promised Land. In Kadesh-barnea, Moses promised Caleb the mountain of Hebron as an inheritance. Because they had refused to enter the land when God originally commanded them to, it took the Israelites thirty-eight years to travel from Kadesh-barnea to the brook Zered. Same as En-mishpat, Kadesh, and Kedesh (4).

First reference: Numbers 32:8 / Last reference: Joshua 15:3

KADMIEL

of times mentioned: 8
# of MEN by this name: 3

Meaning: Presence of God

1) Head of a Levite family whose descendants returned from captivity with Zerubbabel.

First reference: Ezra 2:40 / Last reference: Nehemiah 7:43

2) A man who supervised the workmen in the temple when it was rebuilt under Zerubbabel.

Only reference: Ezra 3:9

3) One of a group of Levites who led a revival among the Israelites in the time of Nehemiah.

First reference: Nehemiah 9:4 / Last reference: Nehemiah 12:24

KALLAI

of times mentioned: 1
# of MEN by this name: 1

Meaning: Frivolous

Forefather of a priest who returned to Jerusalem under Zerubbabel.

Only reference: Nehemiah 12:20

KANAH

of times mentioned: OT 3

Meaning: Reediness

1) A river that formed a portion of the border of the inheritance of the tribes of Ephraim and Manasseh.

First reference: Joshua 16:8 / Last reference: Joshua 17:9

2) A city that became part of the inheritance of the tribe of Asher following the conquest of the Promised Land.

Only reference: Joshua 19:28

KAREAH

of times mentioned: 13
# of MEN by this name: 1

Meaning: Bald

Father of Johanan and Jonathan, captains of the Israelite forces under Governor Gedaliah, who was placed in authority by King Nebuchadnezzar of Babylon.

First reference: Jeremiah 40:8 / Last reference: Jeremiah 43:5

KARKAA

of times mentioned: OT 1

Meaning: Ground floor

A city that formed part of the border of the tribe of Judah's territory.

Only reference: Joshua 15:3

♀ KARKOR

of times mentioned: OT 1

Meaning: Foundation

A place where the Midianite kings Zebah and Zalmunna gathered their troops against Gideon, after the Midianite–Amalekite army had lost 120,000 men. The Israelites attacked them and both kings fled, then were captured.

Only reference: Judges 8:10

♀ KARNAIM

of times mentioned: OT 1

A city where Chedorlaomer, king of Elam, and his Mesopotamian allies conquered the Rephaims.

Only reference: Genesis 14:5

♀ KARTAH

of times mentioned: OT 1

Meaning: City

One of the forty-eight cities given to the Levites as God had commanded. Kartah was given to them by the tribe of Zebulun.

Only reference: Joshua 21:34

♀ KARTAN

of times mentioned: OT 1

Meaning: City plot

One of the forty-eight cities given to the Levites as God had commanded. Kartan was given to them by the tribe of Naphtali.

Only reference: Joshua 21:32

♀ KATTATH

of times mentioned: OT 1

Meaning: Littleness

A city that became part of the inheritance of Zebulun when Joshua cast lots in Shiloh to provide

territory for the seven tribes that had yet to receive their land.

Only reference: Joshua 19:15

👥 KEDAR

of times mentioned: 2
# of MEN by this name: 1

Meaning: Dusky

A descendant of Abraham through Ishmael, Abraham's son with his surrogate wife, Hagar.

First reference: Genesis 25:13 / Last reference: 1 Chronicles 1:29

👥 KEDEMAH

of times mentioned: 2
# of MEN by this name: 1

Meaning: Precedence

A descendant of Abraham through Ishmael, Abraham's son with his surrogate wife, Hagar.

First reference: Genesis 25:15 / Last reference: 1 Chronicles 1:31

♀ KEDEMOTH

of times mentioned: OT 4

Meaning: Beginnings

1) A wilderness area from which Moses sent messengers to the Amorite king Sihon, asking him to allow Israel to pass through his territory.

Only reference: Deuteronomy 2:26

2) A border city of the tribe of Reuben that became one of the forty-eight cities given to the Levites as God had commanded.

First reference: Joshua 13:18 / Last reference: 1 Chronicles 6:79

♀ KEDESH

of times mentioned: OT 11

Meaning: A sanctum

1) A kingdom on the west side of the Jordan River that was conquered by Joshua and his troops. It became a fortified ("fenced" in the KJV) city in the inheritance of the tribe of Naphtali.

First reference: Joshua 12:22 / Last reference: Joshua 19:37

2) One of the six cities of refuge established in Israel for those who had committed accidental murder. Kedesh was in the land of the tribe of Naphtali. Before the battle with Sisera and his troops, Barak called the men of Zebulun and Naphtali to come to this Galilean city. Heber the Kenite had pitched his tent nearby.

Tiglath-pileser, king of Assyria, conquered Kedesh, and its people were taken captive to Assyria. Same as Kedesh-Naphtali.

First reference: Joshua 20:7 / Last reference: 1 Chronicles 6:76

3) One of the forty-eight cities given to the Levites as God had commanded. Kedesh was given to them by the tribe of Issachar.

Only reference: 1 Chronicles 6:72

4) A city that became part of the inheritance of the tribe of Judah following the conquest of the Promised Land. Same as En-mishpat, Kadesh, and Kadesh-barnea.

Only reference: Joshua 15:23

📍 KEDESH-NAPHTALI

of times mentioned: OT 1

Meaning: A sanctum my wrestling

A city from which the prophet Deborah called Barak when he and the tribes of Naphtali and Zebulun were to fight Sisera and his troops. Same as Kedesh (2).

Only reference: Judges 4:6

📍 KEHELATHAH

of times mentioned: OT 2

Meaning: Convocation

A campsite of the Israelites on their way to the Promised Land.

First reference: Numbers 33:22 / Last reference: Numbers 33:23

👥 KEILAH

of times mentioned: 1
# of MEN by this name: 1

Meaning: Enclosing, citadel

Called a Garmite, Keilah was a descendant of Abraham through Jacob's son Judah.

Only reference: 1 Chronicles 4:19

📍 KEILAH

of times mentioned: OT 17

Meaning: Enclosing or citadel

A city that became part of the inheritance of the tribe of Judah following the conquest of the Promised Land.

After David fled from King Saul, the Philistines attacked Keilah. David inquired twice of the Lord, who told him to attack the Philistines and He would deliver the enemy into David's hands. Israel slaughtered the Philistines and saved the city. Saul planned to capture David in Keilah. But David again inquired of God and learned the people of the city would turn him over to Saul, so he and his men left.

First reference: Joshua 15:44 / Last reference: Nehemiah 3:18 / Key reference: 1 Samuel 23:1–13

👥 KELAIAH

of times mentioned: 1
# of MEN by this name: 1

Meaning: Insignificance

An exiled Levite who married a "strange" (foreign) woman. Same as Kelita (1).

Only reference: Ezra 10:23

👥 KELITA

of times mentioned: 3
# of MEN by this name: 2

Meaning: Maiming

1) An exiled Levite who married a "strange" (foreign) woman. Same as Kelaiah.

Only reference: Ezra 10:23

2) A Levite who helped Ezra to explain the law to exiles returned to Jerusalem.

First reference: Nehemiah 8:7 / Last reference: Nehemiah 10:10

👥 KEMUEL

of times mentioned: 3
# of MEN by this name: 3

Meaning: Raised of God

1) A son of Abraham's brother Nahor.

Only reference: Genesis 22:21

2) Prince of the tribe of Ephraim when the Israelites entered the Promised Land.

Only reference: Numbers 34:24

3) Father of Hashabiah, a ruler over the Levites during King David's reign.

Only reference: 1 Chronicles 27:17

👥 KENAN

of times mentioned: 1
# of MEN by this name: 1

Meaning: A nest

A descendant of Adam through his son Seth. Kenan was the sixth-longest-lived person in the Bible at 910 years.

Only reference: 1 Chronicles 1:2

📍 KENATH

of times mentioned: OT 2

Meaning: Possession

A city that Nobah took, along with its surrounding villages. He renamed the city for himself. Same as Nobah.

First reference: Numbers 32:42 / Last reference: 1 Chronicles 2:23

👥 KENAZ

of times mentioned: 11
# of MEN by this name: 4

Meaning: Hunter

1) A descendant of Abraham's grandson Esau.

First reference: Genesis 36:11 / Last reference: 1 Chronicles 1:36

2) A "duke of Edom," a leader in the family line of Esau.

First reference: Genesis 36:42 / Last reference: 1 Chronicles 1:53

3) Younger brother of Caleb and father of Othniel, the first judge of Israel after Caleb's death.

First reference: Joshua 15:17 / Last reference: 1 Chronicles 4:13

4) A descendant of Abraham through Jacob's son Judah and through Caleb.

Only reference: 1 Chronicles 4:15

📍 KEREN-HAPPUCH

of times mentioned: 1
# of WOMEN by this name: 1

Meaning: Horn of cosmetic

A daughter of Job. Keren-happuch was the youngest of three daughters born to Job when God restored his fortunes. Keren-happuch and her two sisters, Jemima and Kezia, were said to be more beautiful than any women "in all the land" (Job 42:15).

Only reference: Job 42:14

📍 KERIOTH

of times mentioned: OT 3

Meaning: Buildings

1) A city that became part of the inheritance of the tribe of Judah following the conquest of the Promised Land.

Only reference: Joshua 15:25

2) A Moabite city that Jeremiah foretold would be judged. The city would be taken, and its men would be as weak as a woman in labor.

First reference: Jeremiah 48:24 / Last reference: Jeremiah 48:41

👥 KEROS

of times mentioned: 2
# of MEN by this name: 1

Meaning: Ankled

Forefather of an exiled family that returned to Judah under Zerubbabel.

First reference: Ezra 2:44 / Last reference: Nehemiah 7:47

👥 KETURAH

of times mentioned: 4
# of WOMEN by this name: 1

Meaning: Perfumed

Abraham's concubine (1 Chronicles 1:32) and wife (Genesis 25:1). He may have married her following Sarah's death, but her children were not part of God's promised line.

First reference: Genesis 25:1 / Last reference: 1 Chronicles 1:33

👥 KEZIA

of times mentioned: 1
# of WOMEN by this name: 1

Meaning: Cassia

A daughter of Job. Kezia was the second of three daughters born to Job when God restored his fortunes. Kezia and her two sisters, Jemima and Keren-happuch, were said to be more beautiful than any other women "in all the land" (Job 42:15).

Only reference: Job 42:14

📍 KEZIZ

of times mentioned: OT 1

Meaning: Abrupt

A valley that became part of the inheritance of Benjamin when Joshua cast lots in Shiloh to provide territory for the seven tribes that had yet to receive their land.

Only reference: Joshua 18:21

📍 KIBROTH-HATTAAVAH

of times mentioned: OT 5

Meaning: Graves of the longing

A campsite of the Israelites on their way to the Promised Land. Here God sent a plague on His people for their greediness in collecting the quail He had sent for them to eat.

First reference: Numbers 11:34 / Last reference: Deuteronomy 9:22

📍 KIBZAIM

of times mentioned: OT 1

Meaning: A double heap

One of the forty-eight cities given to the Levites as God had commanded. Kibzaim was given to them by the tribe of Ephraim.

Only reference: Joshua 21:22

📍 KIDRON

of times mentioned: OT 11

Meaning: Dusky place

A brook and valley just east of Jerusalem, between Jerusalem and the Mount of Olives, that David passed over when he left Jerusalem to keep his rebellious son Absalom from destroying the city. Kings Asa and Josiah burned idols near the Kidron Brook. Josiah also burned former kings' pagan altars there. When the temple was purified under King Hezekiah's rule, the priests used this area for ridding the nation of all the unclean things that had been in the temple. Jeremiah predicted that when Jerusalem was rebuilt, this area would be holy to the Lord. Same as Cedron.

First reference: 2 Samuel 15:23 / Last reference: Jeremiah 31:40

♀ KINAH

of times mentioned: OT 1

Meaning: Short

A city that became part of the inheritance of the tribe of Judah following the conquest of the Promised Land.

Only reference: Joshua 15:22

♀ KIR

of times mentioned: OT 4

Meaning: Fortress

1) Tiglath-pileser, king of Assyria, took the people of Damascus captive and brought them to this district of his own land. According to the prophet Amos, God brought them out of Kir.

First reference: 2 Kings 16:9 / Last reference: Amos 9:7

2) A city of Moab that the prophet Isaiah foretold would be destroyed and "brought to silence."

Only reference: Isaiah 15:1

♀ KIR-HARASETH

of times mentioned: OT 1

Meaning: Fortress of earthenware

A Moabite city that was conquered by King Jehoram of Israel and his allies, King Jehoshaphat of Judah and the king of Edom. After Mesha, king of Moab, sacrificed his son on the city wall and the fighting became very intense, the Israelites withdrew. Same as Kir-haraseth, Kir-haresh, and Kir-heres.

Only reference: 2 Kings 3:25

♀ KIR-HARESETH

of times mentioned: OT 1

Meaning: Fortress of earthenware

A Moabite city that the prophet Isaiah foretold would be stricken because of that nation's pride. Same as Kir-haraseth, Kir-haresh, and Kir-heres.

Only reference: Isaiah 16:7

♀ KIR-HARESH

of times mentioned: OT 1

Meaning: Fortress of earthenware

A Moabite city over which the prophet Isaiah lamented. Same as Kir-haraseth, Kir-hareseth, and Kir-heres.

Only reference: Isaiah 16:11

♀ KIR-HERES

of times mentioned: OT 2

Meaning: Fortress of earthenware

The prophet Jeremiah mourned for this Moabite city, whose riches had perished. Same as Kir-haraseth, Kir-hareseth, and Kir-haresh.

First reference: Jeremiah 48:31 / Last reference: Jeremiah 48:36

♀ KIRIATHAIM

of times mentioned: OT 4

Meaning: Double city

1) King Chedorlaomer of Elam and his Mesopotamian allies attacked the Emims, a race of giants who inhabited this plain.

Only reference: Genesis 14:5

2) A city of Moab that the prophet Jeremiah foretold would be conquered. God's judgment would come upon it in part because Moab declared that Judah was like all the heathen nations.

First reference: Jeremiah 48:1 / Last reference: Ezekiel 25:9

♀ KIRIOTH

of times mentioned: OT 1

Meaning: Buildings

A Moabite city with palaces that Amos foretold would be burned with tumult, shouting, and "the sound of the trumpet."

Only reference: Amos 2:2

📍 KIRJATH

of times mentioned: OT 1

Meaning: City

A city that became part of the inheritance of Benjamin when Joshua cast lots in Shiloh to provide territory for the seven tribes that had yet to receive their land.

Only reference: Joshua 18:28

📍 KIRJATHAIM

of times mentioned: OT 3

Meaning: Double city

1) A city built by the tribe of Reuben, Kirjathaim was on the tribe's border, between Mephaath and Sibmah.

First reference: Numbers 32:37 / Last reference: Joshua 13:19

2) One of the forty-eight cities given to the Levites as God had commanded. Kirjathaim was given to them by the tribe of Naphtali.

Only reference: 1 Chronicles 6:76

📍 KIRJATH-ARBA

of times mentioned: OT 6

Meaning: City of Arba or city of the four giants

A city of the Anakims, among whom Arba was a great man. Here Sarah died. Kirjath-arba became part of the inheritance of the tribe of Judah following the conquest of the Promised Land. It became one of the six cities of refuge established in Israel for those who had committed accidental murder. After the death of Joshua, Judah fought the Canaanites of this city. It was resettled following the Babylonian exile. Same as Arbah and Hebron.

First reference: Genesis 23:2 / Last reference: Nehemiah 11:25

📍 KIRJATH-ARIM

of times mentioned: OT 1

Meaning: City of forests or city of towns

A city in Judah to which captives returned after the Babylonian Exile.

Only reference: Ezra 2:25

📍 KIRJATH-BAAL

of times mentioned: OT 2

Meaning: City of Baal

A city that became part of the inheritance of the tribe of Judah following the conquest of the Promised Land. Kirjath-baal became part of the inheritance of Benjamin when Joshua cast lots in Shiloh to provide territory for the seven tribes that had yet to receive their land. Same as Baalah (1), Baale of Judah, and Kirjath-jearim.

First reference: Joshua 15:60 / Last reference: Joshua 18:14

📍 KIRJATH-HUZOTH

of times mentioned: OT 1

Meaning: City of streets

A Moabite city where King Balak brought the prophet Balaam after he asked Balaam to curse Israel. Balak made offerings of oxen and sheep and took Balaam to the high places of Baal. But Balaam would not curse Israel.

Only reference: Numbers 22:39

👥 KIRJATH-JEARIM

of times mentioned: 3
# of MEN by this name: 1

Meaning: City of forests

A descendant of Abraham through Jacob's son Judah.

First reference: 1 Chronicles 2:50 / Last reference: 1 Chronicles 2:53

📍 KIRJATH-JEARIM

of times mentioned: OT 15

Meaning: City of forests or city of towns

A city of the Gibeonites that the Israelites did not conquer because they had made a covenant with these people. The Gibeonites persuaded Joshua they had come from far away when really they were close neighbors. Later the city became part of the inheritance of the tribe of Judah. Here the tribe of Dan camped when they went to the house of Micah and stole his priest and idols.

When the Philistines returned the ark of the covenant to Israel, the ox cart came to Beth-shemesh. God killed some of the men of that town because they had looked into the ark. So the people of Beth-shemesh sent a message to Kirjath-jearim to bring the ark of the covenant into their city. The ark stayed there twenty years until David took it to Jerusalem. Same as Baalah (1), Baale of Judah, and Kirjath-baal.

First reference: Joshua 9:17 / Last reference: Jeremiah 26:20 / Key references: Judges 18:12; 1 Samuel 6:21–7:2; 1 Chronicles 13:5–6

📍 KIRJATH-SANNAH

of times mentioned: OT 1

Meaning: City of branches or city of a book

A city that became part of the inheritance of the tribe of Judah following the conquest of the Promised Land. Same as Debir and Kirjath-sepher.

Only reference: Joshua 15:49

📍 KIRJATH-SEPHER

of times mentioned: OT 4

Meaning: City of branches or city of a book

A city of Judah that was not fully conquered at the time Joshua died. When he went up against Kirjath-sepher, Caleb promised that whatever man conquered this city would gain his daughter Achsah as his wife. Caleb's brother Othniel captured the city and gained his bride. Same as Debir and Kirjath-sannah.

First reference: Joshua 15:15 / Last reference: Judges 1:12

👥 KISH

of times mentioned: 21
# of MEN by this name: 5

Meaning: A bow

1) A Benjaminite, the father of King Saul. Seeking his father's donkeys, Saul came to Samuel, who anointed him king. Kish's brother was Abner, Saul's battle commander. Saul and his son Jonathan were buried in Kish's tomb. Same as Cis.

First reference: 1 Samuel 9:1 / Last reference: 1 Chronicles 26:28 / Key references: 1 Samuel 14:50–51; 2 Samuel 21:14

2) A descendant of Abraham through Jacob's son Benjamin.

First reference: 1 Chronicles 8:30 / Last reference: 1 Chronicles 9:36

3) A descendant of Abraham through Jacob's son Levi.

First reference: 1 Chronicles 23:21 / Last reference: 1 Chronicles 24:29

4) Another descendant of Abraham through Jacob's son Levi. Kish was among the Levites who cleansed the temple during the revival of King Hezekiah's day.

Only reference: 2 Chronicles 29:12

5) A forefather of Mordecai, Esther's cousin.

Only reference: Esther 2:5

👥 KISHI

of times mentioned: 1
# of MEN by this name: 1

Meaning: War, battle

A descendant of Abraham through Jacob's son Levi.

Only reference: 1 Chronicles 6:44

📍 KISHION

of times mentioned: OT 1

Meaning: Hard place

A city that became part of the inheritance of Issachar when Joshua cast lots in Shiloh to provide territory for the seven tribes that had yet to receive their land. Same as Kishon (1).

Only reference: Joshua 19:20

📍 KISHON

of times mentioned: OT 6

Meaning: Hard place (1) or winding (2)

1) One of the forty-eight cities given to the Levites as God had commanded. Kishon was given to them by the tribe of Issachar. Same as Kishion.

Only reference: Joshua 21:28

2) A river in the middle of Palestine, running from Mount Gilboa north to the Mediterranean Sea. Sisera gathered his army from Harosheth to this river, where he engaged in battle with Barak and his troops. Barak and Deborah's song tells us that the river swept some of the warriors away.

At this river, after his confrontation with the prophets of Baal on Mount Carmel, the prophet Elijah killed the pagan prophets. Same as Kison.

First reference: Judges 4:7 / Last reference: 1 Kings 18:40

📍 KISON

of times mentioned: OT 1

Meaning: Winding

A river near which Barak, the leader of Israel's army, defeated King Jabin of Hazor and his commander Sisera. Same as Kishon (2).

Only reference: Psalm 83:9

📍 KITHLISH

of times mentioned: OT 1

Meaning: Wall of a man

A city that became part of the inheritance of the tribe of Judah following the conquest of the Promised Land.

Only reference: Joshua 15:40

📍 KITRON

of times mentioned: OT 1

Meaning: Fumigative

A city from which the tribe of Zebulun never drove out the native Canaanites.

Only reference: Judges 1:30

👥 KITTIM

of times mentioned: 2
# of MEN by this name: 1

Meaning: Islander

A descendant of Noah through his son Japheth.

First reference: Genesis 10:4 / Last reference: 1 Chronicles 1:7

👥 KOHATH

of times mentioned: 32
# of MEN by this name: 1

Meaning: Allied

A son of Levi. Kohath's family was designated by God to care for the most holy things of the tabernacle.

First reference: Genesis 46:11 / Last reference: 1 Chronicles 23:12 / Key references: Numbers 4:15; 7:9

👥 KOLAIAH

of times mentioned: 2
# of MEN by this name: 2

Meaning: Voice of God

1) Ancestor of a Benjaminite who was chosen by lot to resettle Jerusalem after returning from the Babylonian Exile.

Only reference: Nehemiah 11:7

2) Father of Ahab, a false prophet at the time of the Babylonian Exile.

Only reference: Jeremiah 29:21

👥 KORAH

of times mentioned: 37
# of MEN by this name: 5

Meaning: To make bald

1) A son of Esau.

First reference: Genesis 36:5 / Last reference:
1 Chronicles 1:35

2) A descendant of Esau and a "duke" of Edom.

Only reference: Genesis 36:16

3) A descendant of Levi and Kohath who opposed
Moses when the prophet said all the Israelites were
not holy. Moses commanded Korah and his company to come before the Lord, with their censers
filled with incense, and stand in the door of the
tabernacle. God warned Moses and Aaron to stand
back while He consumed these rebels. Though the
prophet and priest prayed for them, God made the
earth swallow all 250 men, along with their tents.

First reference: Exodus 6:21 / Last reference:
1 Chronicles 9:19 / Key references: Numbers
16:1–11, 16–19, 32–35; 26:9–11

4) A descendant of Judah through his son Perez.

Only reference: 1 Chronicles 2:43

5) A descendant of Abraham through Jacob's son
Levi. Korah's sons are named in the titles of eleven
Psalms: 42, 44–49, 84–85, and 87–88.

First reference: 1 Chronicles 6:22 / Last reference:
Psalm 88 (title)

👥 KORE

of times mentioned: 4
# of MEN by this name: 2

1) Father of Shallum, a tabernacle gatekeeper.

First reference: 1 Chronicles 9:19 / Last reference:
1 Chronicles 26:19

2) A Levite worship leader who kept the temple's
east gate under King Hezekiah and had charge of
the freewill and most holy offerings.

Only reference: 2 Chronicles 31:14

👥 KOZ

of times mentioned: 4
# of MEN by this name: 2

1) Forefather of an exile who returned to Jerusalem
with Zerubbabel. Koz lost his role as a priest when
his genealogical record could not be found.

First reference: Ezra 2:61 / Last reference:
Nehemiah 7:63

2) Forefather of a man who repaired Jerusalem's
walls under Nehemiah.

First reference: Nehemiah 3:4 / Last reference:
Nehemiah 3:21

👥 KUSHAIAH

of times mentioned: 1
# of MEN by this name: 1

Meaning: Entrapped of God

Father of a Levite musician appointed during King
David's reign.

Only reference: 1 Chronicles 15:17

👥 LAADAH

of times mentioned: 1
# of MEN by this name: 1

A descendant of Abraham through Jacob's son
Judah.

Only reference: 1 Chronicles 4:21

👥 LAADAN

of times mentioned: 7
# of MEN by this name: 2

1) A descendant of Abraham through Joseph's son
Ephraim.

Only reference: 1 Chronicles 7:26

2) A Levite worship leader who was part of David's
reorganization of the Levites.

First reference: 1 Chronicles 23:7 / Last reference:
1 Chronicles 26:21

LABAN

of times mentioned: 55
# of MEN by this name: 1

Meaning: To be white or to make bricks

Called Laban the Syrian (Genesis 25:20), this brother of Rebekah approved of her marriage to Isaac. When Rebekah's son Esau became angry at his brother, Jacob, for stealing their father's blessing from him, Isaac sent Jacob to Laban.

Jacob loved Rachel, Laban's second daughter, and offered to work for him for seven years in order to win her. At the end of that time, Laban tricked Jacob into marrying his first daughter, Leah. Then he offered Rachel to Jacob for another seven years of service.

When Jacob wanted to go home, Laban asked him to stay, recognizing that God had blessed him because Jacob was in his camp. Jacob, in turn, tricked Laban into giving him the best of his flocks. Jacob saw the anger of Laban and his sons, and God called him to return home, so he left. Laban pursued Jacob and confronted him for slipping away without warning and taking his household gods. Laban did not find the gods because Rachel, who had taken them, was sitting on them. He made a covenant with Jacob. Then, blessing them, Laban departed.

First reference: Genesis 24:29 / Last reference: Genesis 46:25 / Key references: Genesis 28:2; 29:18–28; 30:31–43

📍 LABAN

of times mentioned: OT 1

Meaning: White

A place in the wilderness "over against the Red Sea." Near here Moses reviewed the Law with the Israelites before they entered the Promised Land.

Only reference: Deuteronomy 1:1

📍 LACHISH

of times mentioned: OT 24

An Amorite city ruled by Japhia when Joshua and his troops conquered the Promised Land. Japhia joined with Adoni-zedek and his other allies in attacking Gibeon. Joshua and his forces came to Gibeon's aid because they had an agreement with that city. Japhia was one of the five kings who fled to the cave at Makkedah and became trapped there. After the battle, all five kings were killed by Joshua. The Israelites besieged Lachish, took it in two days, and killed all its inhabitants. The city became part of the inheritance of the tribe of Judah following the conquest of the Promised Land.

King Rehoboam fortified Lachish to defend his nation. King Amaziah of Judah fled from a conspiracy in Jerusalem, escaped to Lachish, and was killed there by his enemies. Sennacherib, king of Assyria, laid siege to Lachish as his messengers visited Jerusalem, to threaten that city with attack.

First reference: Joshua 10:3 / Last reference: Micah 1:13 / Key reference: Joshua 10:3–35

👥 LAEL

of times mentioned: 1
# of MEN by this name: 1

Meaning: Belonging to God

Chief of the Gershonites when Moses led Israel.

Only reference: Numbers 3:24

👥 LAHAD

of times mentioned: 1
# of MEN by this name: 1

Meaning: To glow, to be earnest

A descendant of Abraham through Jacob's son Judah.

Only reference: 1 Chronicles 4:2

📍 LAHAI-ROI

of times mentioned: OT 2

Meaning: Of the Living One, my seer

Isaac lived near this well in the south country, near Beersheba. Same as Beer-lahai-roi.

First reference: Genesis 24:62 / Last reference: Genesis 25:11

♀ LAHMAM

of times mentioned: OT 1

Meaning: Foodlike

A city that became part of the inheritance of the tribe of Judah following the conquest of the Promised Land.

Only reference: Joshua 15:40

☷ LAHMI

of times mentioned: 1
# of MEN by this name: 1

Meaning: Foodful

Brother of the Philistine giant Goliath. Lahmi was killed in battle by King David's warrior Elhanan. Lahmi's spear handle "was like a weaver's beam."

Only reference: 1 Chronicles 20:5

☷ LAISH

of times mentioned: 2
# of MEN by this name: 1

Meaning: Crushing

Father of Phalti, Michal's second husband, whom she was forced to leave to return to her first husband, King David.

First reference: 1 Samuel 25:44 / Last reference: 2 Samuel 3:15

♀ LAISH

of times mentioned: OT 5

Meaning: Crushing

A Sidonian (or Zidonian) city captured and burned by the tribe of Dan. The tribe renamed it the city of Dan, rebuilt it, and lived there. Same as Leshem.

First reference: Judges 18:7 / Last reference: Isaiah 10:30

♀ LAKUM

of times mentioned: OT 1

Meaning: Stop up by a barricade (perhaps a fortification)

A city that became part of the inheritance of Naphtali when Joshua cast lots in Shiloh to provide territory for the seven tribes that had yet to receive their land.

Only reference: Joshua 19:33

☷ LAMECH

of times mentioned: 12
# of MEN by this name: 1

Genealogy of Jesus: Yes (Luke 3:36)

Meaning: Uncertain

A descendant of Cain through his son Enoch. Lamech's father was Methuselah, and Lamech was the father of Noah. Lamech is the first man whom the Bible records as having more than one wife.

First reference: Genesis 4:18 / Last reference: Luke 3:36 / Key references: Genesis 4:19; 5:28–29

♀ LAODICEA

of times mentioned: NT 6

Meaning: Just people

A city of the Roman province of Phrygia. Paul had not yet visited the church in Laodicea when he wrote the Colossians. Paul told the nearby church at Colossae that Epaphras, "a servant of Christ" (Colossians 4:12), had a great zeal for their congregation and the church at Laodicea. The epistle to the Colossians was written to be read in both churches. In the book of Revelation, John relays Jesus' message to the church in Laodicea.

First reference: Colossians 2:1 / Last reference: Revelation 1:11

☷ LAPIDOTH

of times mentioned: 1
# of MEN by this name: 1

Meaning: To shine, or a lamp or flame

Husband of Israel's only female judge, Deborah.

Only reference: Judges 4:4

📍 LASEA

of times mentioned: NT 1

A Cretan city near the port called the Fair Havens, where Paul and his companions took shelter before a storm.

Only reference: Acts 27:8

📍 LASHA

of times mentioned: OT 1

Meaning: To break through; a boiling spring

An early border place in the land settled by the descendants of Noah's grandson Canaan.

Only reference: Genesis 10:19

📍 LASHARON

of times mentioned: OT 1

Meaning: Plain

A Canaanite city on the west side of the Jordan River that was conquered by Joshua and his army.

Only reference: Joshua 12:18

👥 LAZARUS

of times mentioned: 11
# of MEN by this name: 1

The brother of Mary and Martha, Lazarus was loved by Jesus, who often came to visit the family. When Lazarus became ill, his sisters sent for Jesus, who waited several days before arriving. By the time He appeared in Bethany, Lazarus had died. Jesus promised to Martha, "Thy brother shall rise again" (John 11:23) and told her He was the resurrection and the life. After weeping at Lazarus's tomb, Jesus had the stone removed from the mouth of this cave then called Lazarus forth. Lazarus walked out, still bound by the grave clothes.

This Lazarus is not to be confused with the beggar named Lazarus in Jesus' parable in Luke 16.

First reference: John 11:1 / Last reference: John 12:17

👥 LEAH

of times mentioned: 34
# of WOMEN by this name: 1

Meaning: Weary

Laban's tender-eyed daughter who was less beautiful than her sister, Rachel. Though Jacob loved Rachel and arranged to marry her, Laban insisted that Jacob marry Leah first. He tricked Jacob into marriage with Leah but then allowed him to marry Rachel, too. Leah had four children, while Rachel was barren. When Rachel gave Jacob her maid, Bilhah, to have children with him and Leah had had no more children, Leah gave her maid, Zilpah, to Jacob, too. But Leah later had two more sons and a daughter.

When Jacob returned to his home after serving Laban for many years, he placed Leah in more danger than her sister as they neared Jacob's wronged brother, Esau. Leah's daughter, Dinah, was raped by the prince of Shechem, and Leah's sons Simeon and Levi killed the men of Shechem. Leah was buried at Machpelah with Abraham, Sarah, Isaac, and Rebekah.

First reference: Genesis 29:16 / Last reference: Ruth 4:11 / Key references: Genesis 29:20–28, 31–35; 30:9, 17–21; 33:1–2; 34:1–2; 49:31

👥 LEBANA

of times mentioned: 1
# of MEN by this name: 1

Meaning: The white, the moon

Forefather of a family that returned to Jerusalem with Zerubbabel. Same as Lebanah.

Only reference: Nehemiah 7:48

👥 LEBANAH

of times mentioned: 1
# of MEN by this name: 1

Meaning: The white, the moon

Forefather of a family that returned to Jerusalem with Zerubbabel. Same as Lebana.

Only reference: Ezra 2:45

📍 LEBANON

of times mentioned: OT 71

Meaning: The white mountain

A Syrian mountain range of northern Palestine that runs along the Mediterranean Sea; it consists of two lines of mountains, the Lebanon Mountains in the west and the Anti-Lebanon Mountains in the east, with a valley between them. This was a richly wooded land in the Old Testament era and is used in scripture as a sign of a land filled with plenty.

God promised Israel that it would own the land to Lebanon. When Israel began to claim the Promised Land, the kings of this area fought Joshua and his troops. When Joshua was old, God promised to drive out the inhabitants of Lebanon, from Baal-gad to the entering into Hamath. But God left the nations of this area "to prove Israel" (Judges 3:1, 3).

Lebanon was famed for its cedar trees. When King Solomon began to build the temple in Jerusalem, he arranged with King Hiram of Tyre to have Lebanon cedar, fir, and algum trees cut and floated down by sea to Israel. When the temple was rebuilt after the Babylonian Exile, Israel again secured timber from Lebanon.

The prophets foretold Lebanon's destruction by the Lord.

First reference: Deuteronomy 1:7 / Last reference: Zechariah 11:1 / Key references: Joshua 1:4; 1 Kings 5:1–10; 2 Chronicles 2:8, 16

👥 LEBBAEUS

of times mentioned: 1
# of MEN by this name: 1

Meaning: Uncertain

Also called Thaddaeus, he was one of Jesus' twelve disciples, as listed by Matthew. Apparently called "Judas, the brother of James" in Luke's Gospel and the book of Acts. Same as Judas (3) and Jude.

Only reference: Matthew 10:3

📍 LEBONAH

of times mentioned: OT 1

Meaning: Frankincense

A place near Shiloh and Bethel. The Israelites fought the tribe of Benjamin and refused to allow their daughters to marry into that tribe because it condoned the abuse and killing of a Levite's concubine at Gibeah. Afterward they debated how the few men left in Benjamin should find wives. South of Lebonah there was an annual feast, and the Israelites decided that here the men of Benjamin should capture wives from the daughters of Shiloh.

Only reference: Judges 21:19

👥 LECAH

of times mentioned: 1
# of MEN by this name: 1

Meaning: A journey

A descendant of Abraham through Jacob's son Judah.

Only reference: 1 Chronicles 4:21

👥 LEHABIM

of times mentioned: 2
# of MEN by this name: 1

Meaning: Flames

A descendant of Noah through his son Ham.

First reference: Genesis 10:13 / Last reference: 1 Chronicles 1:11

📍 LEHI

of times mentioned: OT 3

Meaning: To be soft; the cheek; jawbone

A place in Judah where Samson battled the Philistines and killed a thousand men with the jawbone of a donkey.

First reference: Judges 15:9 / Last reference: Judges 15:19

👥 LEMUEL

of times mentioned: 2
# of MEN by this name: 1

Meaning: Belonging to God

An otherwise unknown king credited with writing Proverbs 31. Lemuel credited the words to "the prophecy that his mother taught him" (Proverbs 31:1).

First reference: Proverbs 31:1 / Last reference: Proverbs 31:4

📍 LESHEM

of times mentioned: OT 1

Meaning: A gem, perhaps a jacinth

A city captured by the tribe of Dan. They renamed the city Dan, after their forefather. Same as Laish.

Only reference: Joshua 19:47

👥 LETUSHIM

of times mentioned: 1
# of MEN by this name: 1

Meaning: Oppressed

A descendant of Abraham and his wife Keturah.

Only reference: Genesis 25:3

👥 LEUMMIM

of times mentioned: 1
# of MEN by this name: 1

Meaning: Night specter

A descendant of Abraham and his wife Keturah.

Only reference: Genesis 25:3

👥 LEVI

of times mentioned: 21
# of MEN by this name: 4

Meaning: Attached

1) Leah and Jacob's third child. After Dinah was raped by the prince of Shechem, Levi and his brother Simeon attacked the men of the city and killed them. Through his line, God established the priests and Levites, beginning with Aaron and his sons.

First reference: Genesis 29:34 / Last reference: Ezra 8:18 / Key reference: Genesis 34:25

2) The son of Alphaeus, a tax collector who became Jesus' disciple. He left his work when Jesus called him to follow Him. Same as Matthew.

First reference: Mark 2:14 / Last reference: Luke 5:29

3) A descendant of Abraham through Isaac; forebear of Jesus' earthly father, Joseph.

Only reference: Luke 3:24

Genealogy of Jesus: Yes (Luke 3:24)

4) Another descendant of Abraham through Isaac; another forebear of Jesus' earthly father, Joseph.

Only reference: Luke 3:29

Genealogy of Jesus: Yes (Luke 3:29)

📍 LIBNAH

of times mentioned: OT 18

Meaning: A whitish tree, perhaps the storax

1) A campsite of the Israelites on their way to the Promised Land.

First reference: Numbers 33:20 / Last reference: Numbers 33:21

2) A Canaanite city conquered by Joshua and his troops. Libnah became part of the inheritance of the tribe of Judah following the conquest of the Promised Land. It became one of the forty-eight cities given to the Levites as God had commanded.

Libnah revolted against the rule of wicked King Jehoram (Joram) of Judah, who did not follow the Lord. Later, King Sennacherib of Assyria besieged the city after he fought Lachish and before he attacked Jerusalem.

First reference: Joshua 10:29 / Last reference: Jeremiah 52:1 / Key reference: Joshua 10:29–31

👥 LIBNI

of times mentioned: 5
# of MEN by this name: 2

Meaning: White

1) A descendant of Abraham through Jacob's son Levi.

First reference: Exodus 6:17 / Last reference: 1 Chronicles 6:20

2) Another descendant of Abraham through Jacob's son Levi.

Only reference: 1 Chronicles 6:29

📍 LIBYA

of times mentioned: OT 2 / NT 1

Meaning: Put, a son of Ham

A country west of Egypt that Ezekiel foretold would fall by the sword, along with Egypt, Persia, and Ethiopia. People from Libya were part of the crowd that observed the coming of the Holy Spirit at Pentecost.

First reference: Ezekiel 30:5 / Last reference: Acts 2:10

👥 LIKHI

of times mentioned: 1
# of MEN by this name: 1

Meaning: Learned

A descendant of Abraham through Joseph's son Manasseh.

Only reference: 1 Chronicles 7:19

👥 LINUS

of times mentioned: 1
# of MEN by this name: 1

A Christian whose greetings Paul passed on to Timothy when Paul wrote his second letter to the young pastor.

Only reference: 2 Timothy 4:21

👥 LO-AMMI

of times mentioned: 1
# of MEN by this name: 1

Meaning: Not my people

The third child of the prophet Hosea's adulterous wife, Gomer. God gave the boy the prophetic name Lo-ammi to indicate that the Jewish people "are not

my people, and I will not be your God."

Only reference: Hosea 1:9

📍 LOD

of times mentioned: OT 4

A city built by the sons of Elpaal, who were of the tribe of Benjamin. Lod was resettled by the tribe of Benjamin following the Babylonian Exile.

First reference: 1 Chronicles 8:12 / Last reference: Nehemiah 11:35

📍 LO-DEBAR

of times mentioned: OT 3

Meaning: Pastureless

A city where Mephibosheth, Jonathan's son, lived in the home of Machir, son of Ammiel, until King David brought Mephibosheth to Jerusalem.

First reference: 2 Samuel 9:4 / Last reference: 2 Samuel 17:27

👥 LOIS

of times mentioned: 1
# of WOMEN by this name: 1

Meaning: Uncertain

Grandmother of the apostle Paul's protégé Timothy. Paul described Lois as a person of "unfeigned faith."

Only reference: 2 Timothy 1:5

👥 LO-RUHAMAH

of times mentioned: 2
# of WOMEN by this name: 1

Meaning: Not pitied

The second child of the prophet Hosea's adulterous wife, Gomer. God gave the girl the prophetic name Lo-ruhamah to indicate that "I will no more have mercy upon the house of Israel" (Hosea 1:6).

First reference: Hosea 1:6 / Last reference: Hosea 1:8

LOT

of times mentioned: 37
# of MEN by this name: 1

Abram's nephew, who traveled with him to the Promised Land. Once their grazing area was unable to support all their flocks, Lot chose to move to the plain of the Jordan River and live near Sodom.

An alliance of Canaanite kings attacked Sodom and Gomorrah and captured Lot, his people, and his goods. When Abram heard about this, he went to Lot's rescue and regained everything. Lot returned to Sodom, where two angels visited him. Lot offered them his hospitality, but the men of Sodom demanded that he bring the two angels out so they could know them. Instead, Lot offered the men his two virgin daughters, whom they refused. The angels blinded the men and told Lot they were about to destroy the city. Lot tried to gather his extended family, but his sons-in-law would not listen. So Lot took his wife and daughters and left the city. They were warned not to look back, but his wife did and was turned into a pillar of salt.

After the destruction of the cities of the plain, Lot's daughters lay with their father. The children of these unions became the founders of the Moabites and Ammonites.

First reference: Genesis 11:27 / Last reference: 2 Peter 2:7 / Key references: Genesis 13:5–11; 14:14–16; 19:1–38

LOTAN

of times mentioned: 7
# of MEN by this name: 1

Meaning: Covering

A descendant of Seir, who lived in Esau's "land of Edom."

First reference: Genesis 36:20 / Last reference: Chronicles 1:39

LUCAS

of times mentioned: 1
# of MEN by this name: 1

A variation on the name Luke; a biblical writer and traveling companion of the apostle Paul.

Only reference: Philemon 1:24

LUCIUS

of times mentioned: 2
# of MEN by this name: 2

Meaning: Illuminative

1) Called Lucius of Cyrene, he was a prophet or teacher who ministered in Antioch when Paul and Barnabas were chosen for missionary work.

Only reference: Acts 13:1

2) A relative of Paul who lived in Rome and was greeted in the apostle's letter to the Romans.

Only reference: Romans 16:21

LUD

of times mentioned: 2
# of MEN by this name: 1

A descendant of Noah through his son Shem.

First reference: Genesis 10:22 / Last reference: 1 Chronicles 1:17

LUDIM

of times mentioned: 2
# of MEN by this name: 1

Meaning: A Ludite

A descendant of Noah through his son Ham.

First reference: Genesis 10:13 / Last reference: 1 Chronicles 1:11

♀ LUHITH

of times mentioned: OT 2

Meaning: Floored

A Moabite hill or city that probably was near Zoar and Horonaim.

First reference: Isaiah 15:5 / Last reference: Jeremiah 48:5

♀ LUKE

of times mentioned: 2

# of MEN by this name: 1

Known as the "beloved physician," Luke was probably a Gentile believer who became a companion of Paul. Writer of a Gospel and the book of Acts, he was also an excellent historian, as is shown by the exactness with which he describes the details of the Gospel events and the places where they happened. The use of "we" in Acts 16:10 indicates that Luke joined Paul and Silas on their missionary journey. He was with Paul during his imprisonment in Rome. Same as Lucas.

First reference: Colossians 4:14 / Last reference: 2 Timothy 4:11

◉ LUZ

of times mentioned: OT 8

Meaning: Probably derived from a nut tree, perhaps the almond

1) Luz is the Canaanite name for the city that Jacob called Bethel. After his sons revenged the rape of Dinah, God told Jacob to take his household to this city and build an altar there. Later Jacob testified to Joseph that God appeared to him there and blessed him (Genesis 48:3). Luz became part of the inheritance of the tribe of Benjamin following the conquest of the Promised Land. Same as Bethel.

First reference: Genesis 28:19 / Last reference: Judges 1:23

2) A city built in the land of the Hittites by the man who showed the spies of the house of Joseph how to enter the city of Bethel (which was also called Luz).

Only reference: Judges 1:26

◉ LYCAONIA

of times mentioned: NT 2

Meaning: Perhaps derived remotely from wolf

An area of Asia Minor that included the cities of Lystra and Derbe. The people there must have spoken a distinctive dialect, since Luke specifically mentions their unusual speech.

First reference: Acts 14:6 / Last reference: Acts 14:11

◉ LYCIA

of times mentioned: NT 1

Meaning: Perhaps derived remotely from wolf

A Roman province in Asia Minor that included the city of Myra. The centurion in charge of getting Paul to Rome found a ship in Myra to take them to their destination.

Only reference: Acts 27:5

◉ LYDDA

of times mentioned: NT 3

A Judean city where Peter healed a man named Aeneas. Many people came to the Lord through this miracle. Then believers asked Peter to come to Joppa to heal Tabitha.

First reference: Acts 9:32 / Last reference: Acts 9:38

👥 LYDIA

of times mentioned: 2
# of WOMEN by this name: 1

A woman of Thyatira who sold goods dyed with an expensive purple color. After hearing Paul's preaching, she became a Christian believer.

First reference: Acts 16:14 / Last reference: Acts 16:40

👥 LYSANIAS

of times mentioned: 1
# of MEN by this name: 1

Meaning: Grief dispelling

Tetrarch of Abilene when John the Baptist began preaching.

Only reference: Luke 3:1

👥 LYSIAS

of times mentioned: 3
# of MEN by this name: 1

Meaning: Uncertain

The Roman soldier who heard information from Paul's nephew about a plot to kill Paul. Lysias sent Paul to the governor, Felix, in Caesarea. Also called Claudius Lysias. See Claudius (2).

First reference: Acts 23:26 / Last reference: Acts 24:22

📍 LYSTRA

of times mentioned: NT 6

A Lycaonian city to which Paul and Barnabas fled after the Jews of Iconium tried to stone them. In Lystra Paul healed a lame man. The people of the city responded by declaring Paul and Barnabas gods. But the Jews of Antioch and Iconium followed the apostles to Lystra and stoned Paul. Though they left Lystra, Paul and Barnabas later returned to encourage the believers there.

The Christians of Lystra and Iconium gave a good report about Timothy, so Paul took him on his missionary travels.

First reference: Acts 14:6 / Last reference: 2 Timothy 3:11

👥 MAACAH

of times mentioned: 2
# of MEN by this name: 1
# of WOMEN by this name: 1

Meaning: Depression

1) One of David's wives who was daughter of Talmai, the king of Geshur, and mother of Absalom. Same as Maachah (6).

Only reference: 2 Samuel 3:3

2) A king who provided hired soldiers to the Ammonites when they attacked King David.

Only reference: 2 Samuel 10:6

📍 MAACAH

of times mentioned: OT 1

Meaning: Depression

A small Syrian kingdom north of Lake Huleh that supported the Ammonites after their king insulted King David's messengers. The Syrians fled before Israel's battle commander Joab and his troops. Same as Maachah.

Only reference: 2 Samuel 10:8

👥 MAACHAH

of times mentioned: 18
# of MEN by this name: 4
# of WOMEN by this name: 6

Meaning: Depression

1) A son of Nahor (2), Abraham's brother, by his concubine Reumah.

Only reference: Genesis 22:24

2) Father of Achish, a king of Gath with whom David once sought refuge.

Only reference: 1 Kings 2:39

3) A daughter of David's son Absalom and the favorite among King Rehoboam's eighteen wives and sixty concubines.

First reference: 1 Kings 15:2 / Last reference: 2 Chronicles 11:22

4) Mother of King Asa of Judah.

First reference: 1 Kings 15:13 / Last reference: 2 Chronicles 15:16

5) A concubine of Caleb, the brother of Jerahmeel.

Only reference: 1 Chronicles 2:48

6) One of David's wives who was daughter of Talmai, the king of Geshur, and mother of Absalom. Same as Maacah (1).

Only reference: 1 Chronicles 3:2

7) Wife of a descendant of Manasseh named Machir.

First reference: 1 Chronicles 7:15 / Last reference: 1 Chronicles 7:16

8) Wife of Jehiel, the leader of Gibeon.

First reference: 1 Chronicles 8:29 / Last reference: 1 Chronicles 9:35

9) Father of one of King David's valiant warriors.

Only reference: 1 Chronicles 11:43

10) Father of a leader of the Simeonites who served under David.

Only reference: 1 Chronicles 27:16

📍 MAACHAH

of times mentioned: OT 1

Meaning: Depression

A small Syrian kingdom north of Lake Huleh that supported the Ammonites after their king insulted King David's messengers. The Syrians fled before Israel's battle commander Joab and his troops. Same as Maacah.

Only reference: 1 Chronicles 19:7

👥 MAADAI

of times mentioned: 1
# of MEN by this name: 1

Meaning: Ornamental

An exiled Israelite who married a "strange" (foreign) woman.

Only reference: Ezra 10:34

👥 MAADIAH

of times mentioned: 1
# of MEN by this name: 1

Meaning: Ornament of God

A chief priest who went up to Jerusalem with Zerubbabel.

Only reference: Nehemiah 12:5

👥 MAAI

of times mentioned: 1
# of MEN by this name: 1

Meaning: Sympathetic

A priest who helped to dedicate the rebuilt walls of Jerusalem by playing a musical instrument.

Only reference: Nehemiah 12:36

📍 MAALEH-ACRABBIM

of times mentioned: OT 1

Meaning: Steep of scorpions

A pass that formed part of the southern border of the tribe of Judah's territory.

Only reference: Joshua 15:3

📍 MAARATH

of times mentioned: OT 1

Meaning: Waste

A city that became part of the inheritance of the tribe of Judah following the conquest of the Promised Land.

Only reference: Joshua 15:59

👥 MAASEIAH

of times mentioned: 25
# of MEN by this name: 21

Meaning: Work of God

1) A Levite musician who performed in celebration when King David brought the ark of the covenant to Jerusalem.

First reference: 1 Chronicles 15:18 / Last reference: 1 Chronicles 15:20

2) A captain of hundreds under Jehoiada the priest, who crowned King Joash.

Only reference: 1 Chronicles 23:1

3) An official under King Uzziah, who prepared his army.

Only reference: 2 Chronicles 26:11

4) A son of King Ahaz, who was killed in a battle with Syria.

Only reference: 2 Chronicles 28:7

5) Jerusalem's governor who repaired the temple at King Josiah's command.

Only reference: 2 Chronicles 34:8

6) An exiled Israelite priest who married a "strange" (foreign) woman.

Only reference: Ezra 10:18

7) Another exiled Israelite priest who married a "strange"(foreign) woman.

Only reference: Ezra 10:21

8) Another exiled Israelite priest who married a "strange"(foreign) woman.

Only reference: Ezra 10:22

9) An exiled Israelite who married a "strange" (foreign) woman.

Only reference: Ezra 10:30

10) A rebuilder of the walls of Jerusalem under Nehemiah.

Only reference: Nehemiah 3:23

11) A priest who assisted Ezra in reading the book of the law to the people of Jerusalem.

Only reference: Nehemiah 8:4

12) A Levite who helped Ezra to explain the law to exiles returned to Jerusalem.

Only reference: Nehemiah 8:7

13) A Jewish leader who renewed the covenant under Nehemiah.

Only reference: Nehemiah 10:25

14) A Jewish exile from the tribe of Judah who re-settled Jerusalem in the time of Nehemiah.

Only reference: Nehemiah 11:5

15) Ancestor of a Benjaminite who was chosen by lot to resettle Jerusalem after returning from the Babylonian Exile.

Only reference: Nehemiah 11:7

16) A priest who helped to dedicate the rebuilt wall of Jerusalem by giving thanks.

Only reference: Nehemiah 12:41

17) A priest who gave thanks with a trumpet at the dedication of Jerusalem's rebuilt wall.

Only reference: Nehemiah 12:42

18) Father of the priest Zephaniah, who served during the reign of King Zedekiah of Judah.

First reference: Jeremiah 21:1 / Last reference: Jeremiah 37:3

19) A false prophet whom Jeremiah prophesied against.

Only reference: Jeremiah 29:21

20) Father of a temple "porter" (doorkeeper) during the reign of King Jehoiakim of Judah.

Only reference: Jeremiah 35:4

21) Forefather of Baruch, scribe of the prophet Jeremiah.

First reference: Jeremiah 32:12 / Last reference: Jeremiah 51:59

👥 MAASIAI

\# of times mentioned: 1
\# of MEN by this name: 1

Meaning: Operative

Forefather of a Levite who returned to Jerusalem following the Babylonian captivity.

Only reference: 1 Chronicles 9:12

👥 MAATH

\# of times mentioned: 1
\# of MEN by this name: 1

Genealogy of Jesus: Yes (Luke 3:26)

A descendant of Abraham through Isaac; forebear of Jesus' earthly father, Joseph.

Only reference: Luke 3:26

👥 MAAZ

\# of times mentioned: 1
\# of MEN by this name: 1

Meaning: Closure

A descendant of Abraham through Jacob's son Judah and Judah's son Pharez.

Only reference: 1 Chronicles 2:27

👥 MAAZIAH

of times mentioned: 2
# of MEN by this name: 2

Meaning: Rescue of God

1) One of twenty-four priests in David's time who was chosen by lot to serve in the tabernacle.

Only reference: 1 Chronicles 24:18

2) A priest who renewed the covenant under Nehemiah.

Only reference: Nehemiah 10:8

📍 MACEDONIA

of times mentioned: NT 28

Famed homeland of Alexander the Great, in the New Testament era Macedonia was a Roman province north of Greece; it included the cities of Philippi, Berea, and Thessalonica. The apostle Paul began his ministry there after he had a vision of a Macedonian who requested him to come to his land. In response, Paul and his ministry companions traveled to Philippi, the chief city of the eastern part of the province. There Lydia became the first European convert (Acts 16:14–15).

But ministry in Macedonia was not always easy. The apostle declared that in Macedonia "our flesh had no rest, but we were troubled on every side" (2 Corinthians 7:5). During his first visit to Philippi, Paul and Silas were beaten and imprisoned. But their suffering bore fruit, as their jailor came to faith. Paul and Silas moved on to Thessalonica, where a multitude of devout Greeks believed, not a few of whom were the chief women of the city. Trouble again arose, and Paul and Silas moved on to Berea, where the Jews to whom he preached studied the scriptures to see if he spoke the truth.

But again, after some people believed, Paul's opponents from Thessalonica stirred up trouble, so Paul traveled on, leaving Timothy and Silas to continue the ministry. Paul took Macedonians Gaius and Aristarchus as companions in his ministry. They visited Ephesus with Paul and became part of the riot inspired by the silversmith Demetrius (Acts 19:29). After the uproar died down, Paul returned to the Macedonian ministry.

The Thessalonians became examples to the fledgling church of Macedonia as they turned away from idolatry. And the apostle commends them as successful Gospel preachers (1 Thessalonians 1:8). The churches of this province also gave to the collection of funds for the beleaguered church of Jerusalem.

Paul closely connected his visits to Macedonia with those to Corinth, and he spoke to the churches about each other. The apostle confronted Corinthian pride, telling the church at Corinth that where it did not provide for him, Macedonia supplied his needs. But Philippi had also provided for him when Macedonia failed.

First reference: Acts 16:9 / Last reference: 1 Timothy 1:3 / Key references: Acts 16:9–12; 2 Corinthians 7:5

👥 MACHBANAI

of times mentioned: 1
# of MEN by this name: 1

Meaning: Native of Macbena

One of several warriors from the tribe of Gad who left Saul to join David during his conflict with the king. Machbanai and his companions were "men of might. . .whose faces were like the faces of lions" (1 Chronicles 12:8).

Only reference: 1 Chronicles 12:13

👥 MACHBENAH

of times mentioned: 1
# of MEN by this name: 1

Meaning: Knoll

A descendant of Abraham through Jacob's son Judah.

Only reference: 1 Chronicles 2:49

👥 MACHI

of times mentioned: 1
# of MEN by this name: 1

Meaning: Pining

Father of one of the twelve spies sent by Moses to spy out the land of Canaan.

Only reference: Numbers 13:15

👥 MACHIR

of times mentioned: 22
# of MEN by this name: 2

Meaning: Salesman

1) A grandson of Joseph through his son Manasseh and his Syrian concubine. Machir's family took Gilead from the Amorites. Moses gave him the land, and he lived there.

First reference: Genesis 50:23 / Last reference: 1 Chronicles 7:17 / Key references: Numbers 32:39–40; 1 Chronicles 7:14

2) A man who brought food and supplies to King David and his soldiers as they fled from the army of David's son Absalom.

First reference: 2 Samuel 9:4 / Last reference: 2 Samuel 17:27

👥 MACHNADEBAI

of times mentioned: 1
# of MEN by this name: 1

Meaning: What is like a liberal man?

An exiled Israelite who married a "strange" (foreign) woman.

Only reference: Ezra 10:40

📍 MACHPELAH

of times mentioned: OT 6

Meaning: A fold

A cave of Shechem that, along with the surrounding field, Abraham bought from Ephron the Hittite as a burial place for Sarah. Also buried there were Abraham, Isaac, Rebekah, and Leah. Joseph brought the body of his father, Jacob, out of Egypt to be buried at Machpelah as well.

First reference: Genesis 23:9 / Last reference: Genesis 50:13

👥 MADAI

of times mentioned: 2
# of MEN by this name: 1

Meaning: Mede
A grandson of Noah through his son Japheth.

First reference: Genesis 10:2 / Last reference: 1 Chronicles 1:5

📍 MADIAN

of times mentioned: NT 1

A variation of the name Midian. Moses fled here after he killed an Egyptian. Same as Midian.

Only reference: Acts 7:29

👥 MADMANNAH

of times mentioned: 1
# of MEN by this name: 1

A descendant of Abraham through Jacob's son Judah.

Only reference: 1 Chronicles 2:49

📍 MADMANNAH

of times mentioned: OT 1

Meaning: Dunghill

A city that became part of the inheritance of the tribe of Judah following the conquest of the Promised Land.

Only reference: Joshua 15:31

📍 MADMEN

of times mentioned: OT 1

Meaning: Dunghill

A Moabite town whose people the prophet Jeremiah foresaw being cut down and pursued with a sword.

Only reference: Jeremiah 48:2

📍 MADMENAH

of times mentioned: OT 1

Meaning: Dunghill

The people of this place would flee before the Assyrians, according to the prophet Isaiah's prophecy.

Only reference: Isaiah 10:31

MADON

of times mentioned: OT 2

Meaning: Extensiveness (that is, height)

A Canaanite city whose king supported Jabin, king of Hazor, when Israel arrived in the Promised Land. Joshua and his troops conquered Madon.

First reference: Joshua 11:1 / Last reference: Joshua 12:19

MAGBISH

of times mentioned: 1
# of MEN by this name: 1

Meaning: Stiffening

Forefather of an exiled family that returned to Judah under Zerubbabel.

Only reference: Ezra 2:30

MAGDALA

of times mentioned: NT 1

Meaning: The tower

A city on the Sea of Galilee that was the home of Mary Magdalene.

Only reference: Matthew 15:39

MAGDALENE

of times mentioned: 12
# of WOMEN by this name: 1

Meaning: Woman of Magdala

Surname of Mary (2).

First reference: Matthew 27:56 / Last reference: John 20:18

MAGDIEL

of times mentioned: 2
# of MEN by this name: 1

Meaning: Preciousness of God

A "duke of Edom," a leader in the family line of Esau.

First reference: Genesis 36:43 / Last reference: 1 Chronicles 1:54

MAGOG

of times mentioned: 2
# of MEN by this name: 1

A son of Japheth and a grandson of Noah.

First reference: Genesis 10:2 / Last reference: 1 Chronicles 1:5

MAGOR-MISSABIB

of times mentioned: 1
# of MEN by this name: 1

Meaning: Afright from around

A name God gave Pashur (3), the "chief governor" of the temple, when he put the prophet Jeremiah in the stocks.

Only reference: Jeremiah 20:3

MAGPIASH

of times mentioned: 1
# of MEN by this name: 1

Meaning: Exterminator of the moth

A Jewish leader who renewed the covenant under Nehemiah.

Only reference: Nehemiah 2:10

MAHALAH

of times mentioned: 1
# of MEN by this name: 1

Meaning: Sickness

A descendant of Abraham through Joseph's son Manasseh.

Only reference: 1 Chronicles 7:18

👥 MAHALALEEL

\# of times mentioned: 7
\# of MEN by this name: 2

Meaning: Praise of God

1) A descendant of Adam through his son Seth.

First reference: Genesis 5:12 / Last reference: 1 Chronicles 1:2

2) A Jewish exile from the tribe of Judah who resettled Jerusalem.

Only reference: Nehemiah 11:4

👥 MAHALATH

\# of times mentioned: 2
\# of WOMEN by this name: 2

Meaning: Sickness

1) A daughter of Ishmael who married Esau.

Only reference: Genesis 28:9

2) Granddaughter of David and wife of Rehoboam, king of Judah.

Only reference: 2 Chronicles 11:18

👥 MAHALI

\# of times mentioned: 1
\# of MEN by this name: 1

Meaning: Sick

A grandson of Levi and a great-grandson of Jacob.

Only reference: Exodus 6:19

📍 MAHANAIM

\# of times mentioned: OT 13

Meaning: Double camp

A place east of the Jordan River where Jacob met angels of God after making a covenant with his father-in-law, Laban. Mahanaim became a border indicator for the tribes of Gad and Manasseh and later became one of the six cities of refuge established in Israel for those who had committed accidental murder. Mahanaim was given to the Levites by the tribe of Gad.

Here Abner made Ish-bosheth king of Gilead. When King David fled from his son Absalom, supporters brought David's men supplies in Mahanaim.

First reference: Genesis 32:2 / Last reference: 1 Chronicles 6:80 / Key references: 2 Samuel 2:8–11; 17:26–27

📍 MAHANEH-DAN

\# of times mentioned: OT 1

Meaning: Camp of Dan

A place behind Kirjath-jearim where the Danites camped before they stole the idols from Micah in Mount Ephraim.

Only reference: Judges 18:12

👥 MAHARAI

\# of times mentioned: 3
\# of MEN by this name: 1

Meaning: Hasty

A commander in King David's army, overseeing twenty-four thousand men in the tenth month of each year.

First reference: 2 Samuel 23:28 / Last reference: 1 Chronicles 27:13

👥 MAHATH

\# of times mentioned: 3
\# of MEN by this name: 2

Meaning: Erasure

1) A descendant of Abraham through Jacob's son Levi.

First reference: 1 Chronicles 6:35 / Last reference: 2 Chronicles 29:12

2) An overseer of temple offerings under King Hezekiah.

Only reference: 2 Chronicles 31:13

 MAHAZIOTH

of times mentioned: 2
# of MEN by this name: 1

Meaning: Visions

A son of King David's musician Heman, "under the hands of [his] father for song in the house of the LORD" (1 Chronicles 25:6).

First reference: 1 Chronicles 25:4 / Last reference: 1 Chronicles 25:30

MAHER-SHALAL-HASH-BAZ

of times mentioned: 2
# of MEN by this name: 1

Meaning: Hasting is he to the booty

A son of the prophet Isaiah, named at God's command to describe the Assyrian attack on Damascus and Samaria.

First reference: Isaiah 8:1 / Last reference: Isaiah 8:3

MAHLAH

of times mentioned: 4
# of WOMEN by this name: 1

Meaning: Sickness

One of Zelophehad's five daughters who received his inheritance because he had no sons. Each had to marry within their tribe, Manasseh.

First reference: Numbers 26:33 / Last reference: Joshua 17:3

MAHLI

of times mentioned: 11
# of MEN by this name: 2

Meaning: Sick

1) A descendant of Abraham through Jacob's son Levi. His father was Merari.

First reference: Numbers 3:20 / Last reference: Ezra 8:18

2) Forefather of the sons of Merari, who ministered in the tabernacle, and a descendant of Levi.

First reference: 1 Chronicles 6:47 / Last reference: 1 Chronicles 24:30

MAHLON

of times mentioned: 4
# of MEN by this name: 1

Meaning: Sick

A son of Naomi and her husband, Elimelech. Mahlon, his father, and his brother died in Moab, forcing Naomi and Mahlon's wife, Ruth, to return to Bethlehem.

First reference: Ruth 1:2 / Last reference: Ruth 4:10

MAHOL

of times mentioned: 1
# of MEN by this name: 1

Meaning: Dancing

The father of two wise men who were not as wise as Solomon.

Only reference: 1 Kings 4:31

MAKAZ

of times mentioned: OT 1

Meaning: End

Under King Solomon's governmental organization, a town responsible for supplying provisions for the king.

Only reference: 1 Kings 4:9

MAKHELOTH

of times mentioned: OT 2

Meaning: Assemblies

A campsite of the Israelites on their way to the Promised Land.

First reference: Numbers 33:25 / Last reference: Numbers 33:26

📍 MAKKEDAH

of times mentioned: OT 9

Meaning: Herding fold

Site of a cave where Joshua trapped five Amorite kings who fled during battle. Later, Joshua killed them here.

First reference: Joshua 10:10 / Last reference: Joshua 15:41

📍 MAKTESH

of times mentioned: OT 1

Meaning: Dell

A district in or near Jerusalem that the prophet Zephaniah foresaw would howl at the destruction of its merchants.

Only reference: Zephaniah 1:11

👥 MALACHI

of times mentioned: 1
# of MEN by this name: 1

Meaning: Ministrative

Writer of the last book of the Old Testament. Malachi lived in the time of Nehemiah and Ezra.

Only reference: Malachi 1:1

👥 MALCHAM

of times mentioned: 1
# of MEN by this name: 1

A descendant of Abraham through Jacob's son Benjamin.

Only reference: 1 Chronicles 8:9

👥 MALCHIAH

of times mentioned: 9
# of MEN by this name: 7

Meaning: King of [appointed by] God
1) Forefather of the temple musician Asaph.

Only reference: 1 Chronicles 6:40

2) An exiled Israelite who married a "strange" (foreign) woman.

First reference: Ezra 10:25 / Last reference: Nehemiah 11:12

3) Another exiled Israelite who married a "strange" (foreign) woman.

Only reference: Ezra 10:31

4) A man who repaired Jerusalem's walls under Nehemiah.

Only reference: Nehemiah 3:14

5) A goldsmith's son who repaired Jerusalem's walls under Nehemiah.

Only reference: Nehemiah 3:31

6) A priest who assisted Ezra in reading the book of the law to the people of Jerusalem.

Only reference: Nehemiah 8:4

7) Owner of the dungeon in which the prophet Jeremiah was imprisoned.

First reference: Jeremiah 38:1 / Last reference: Jeremiah 38:6

👥 MALCHIEL

of times mentioned: 3
# of MEN by this name: 1

Meaning: King of [appointed by] God

A descendant of Abraham through Jacob's son Asher. His father was Beriah.

First reference: Genesis 46:17 / Last reference: 1 Chronicles 7:31

👥 MALCHIJAH

of times mentioned: 6
# of MEN by this name: 5

Meaning: King of [appointed by] God

1) Forefather of a priest who returned to Jerusalem after the Babylonian captivity.

Only reference: 1 Chronicles 9:12

2) One of twenty-four priests in David's time who was chosen by lot to serve in the tabernacle.

Only reference: 1 Chronicles 24:9

3) An exiled Israelite who married a "strange" (foreign) woman.

Only reference: Ezra 10:25

4) A rebuilder of the walls of Jerusalem under Nehemiah.

Only reference: Nehemiah 3:11

5) A priest who helped to dedicate the rebuilt wall of Jerusalem by giving thanks.

First reference: Nehemiah 10:3 / Last reference: Nehemiah 12:42

 MALCHIRAM

of times mentioned: 1
# of MEN by this name: 1

Meaning: King of a high one (or exaltation)

A descendant of Abraham through Jacob's son Judah, in the line of the nation of Judah's third-to-last king, Jeconiah (also known as Jehoiachin).

Only reference: 1 Chronicles 3:18

MALCHI-SHUA

of times mentioned: 3
# of MEN by this name: 1

A son of King Saul. Same as Melchi-shua.

First reference: 1 Chronicles 8:33 / Last reference: 1 Chronicles 10:2

MALCHUS

of times mentioned: 1
# of MEN by this name: 1

The high priest's servant whose ear Simon Peter cut off when Jesus was arrested.

Only reference: John 18:10

MALELEEL

of times mentioned: 1
# of MEN by this name: 1

Genealogy of Jesus: Yes (Luke 3:37)

A descendant of Abraham through Isaac; forebear of Jesus' earthly father, Joseph.

Only reference: Luke 3:37

MALLOTHI

of times mentioned: 2
# of MEN by this name: 1

Meaning: I have talked; loquacious

A son of King David's musician Heman, who was "under the hands of [his] father for song in the house of the LORD" (1 Chronicles 25:6).

First reference: 1 Chronicles 25:4 / Last reference: 1 Chronicles 25:26

MALLUCH

of times mentioned: 6
# of MEN by this name: 5

Meaning: Regnant

1) A descendant of Levi and a forefather of the sons of Merari who ministered in the tabernacle.

Only reference: 1 Chronicles 6:44

2) An exiled Israelite who married a "strange" (foreign) woman.

Only reference: Ezra 10:29

3) Another exiled Israelite who married a "strange" (foreign) woman.

Only reference: Ezra 10:32

4) A priest who renewed the covenant under Nehemiah.

First reference: Nehemiah 10:4 / Last reference: Nehemiah 12:2

5) A Jewish leader who renewed the covenant under Nehemiah.

Only reference: Nehemiah 10:27

👥 MAMRE

of times mentioned: 2
# of MEN by this name: 1

Meaning: Lusty (meaning vigorous)

An Amorite ally of Abram who went with him to recover Abram's nephew Lot from the king of Sodom.

First reference: Genesis 14:13 / Last reference: Genesis 14:24

📍 MAMRE

of times mentioned: OT 8

Meaning: Lusty (meaning vigorous)

A plain in Hebron where Abram (later called Abraham) lived and built an altar. Here he received the news that Sarah would have a child. Near Mamre, Sarah, Abraham, Isaac, Rebekah, Leah, and Jacob would be buried.

First reference: Genesis 13:18 / Last reference: Genesis 50:13

👥 MANAEN

of times mentioned: 1
# of MEN by this name: 1

A prophet or teacher at Antioch when Barnabas and Saul were commissioned as missionaries.

Only reference: Acts 13:1

👥 MANAHATH

of times mentioned: 2
# of MEN by this name: 1

Meaning: Rest

A descendant of Seir, who lived in Esau's "land of Edom."

First reference: Genesis 36:23 / Last reference: 1 Chronicles 1:40

📍 MANAHATH

of times mentioned: OT 1

Meaning: To rest

A Benjaminite city to which the people of Geba were taken as captives.

Only reference: 1 Chronicles 8:6

👥 MANASSEH

of times mentioned: 55
# of MEN by this name: 5

Meaning: Causing to forget

1) The elder child of Joseph and Asenath who was adopted, with his brother Ephraim, by Joseph's father, Jacob. When Jacob blessed the two boys, he gave Ephraim the greater blessing. But he prophesied that both nations that came from the boys would be great.

First reference: Genesis 41:51 / Last reference: 1 Chronicles 7:17 / Key reference: Genesis 48:17–19

2) A priest of the tribe of Dan, which worshipped idols, in the period of the judges.

Only reference: Judges 18:30

3) King of Judah and son of King Hezekiah, Manasseh was an evil ruler who erected pagan altars in the temple and led his nation into idolatry. He burned his own sons as offerings to the idols and became involved in witchcraft. The Lord caused the Assyrian army to capture Manasseh and bring him to Babylon. Manasseh repented, and God brought him back to Jerusalem. Manasseh removed the idols from Jerusalem, repaired God's altar, and commanded his nation to follow God.

First reference: 2 Kings 20:21 / Last reference: Jeremiah 15:4 / Key reference: 2 Chronicles 33:1–20

4) An exiled Israelite who married a "strange" (foreign) woman.

Only reference: Ezra 10:30

5) Another exiled Israelite who married a "strange" (foreign) woman.

Only reference: Ezra 10:33

⚲ MANASSEH

of times mentioned: OT 91

Meaning: Causing to forget

The land of the tribe of Manasseh, which included the conquered kingdom of Og of Bashan. This tribe's split inheritance lay on both the east and west sides of the Jordan River. Before the conquest of the land west of the Jordan River, Manasseh evidently joined with Reuben and Gad in desiring land east of the Jordan River. The sons of Machir, the firstborn son of Manasseh, conquered Gilead, displacing the Amorites. So Moses gave this northeastern corner of Israel's conquest to Machir and his descendants. Jair and Nobah added to their land, winning a further city and villages (Numbers 32:39–42). Moses confirmed Manasseh's inheritance (Numbers 34:13–15).

This was the largest portion of the tribe's holdings, but the rest of the tribe received land west of the Jordan, in a territory north of Ephraim and Dan, stretching from the Jordan River to the Mediterranean Sea. Manasseh thrived in the Promised Land.

But the tribe of Manasseh never drove out some of the original inhabitants of their cities and therefore fell into idolatry. So God sent the Assyrian king Pul (Tiglath-pileser III), who took captive the people of Manasseh east of the Jordan River and exported them to his own land (1 Chronicles 5:25–26). When Josiah became king of Judah, he destroyed idolatrous images in the towns of Manasseh and burned the pagan priests on their altars.

First reference: Numbers 1:10 / Last reference: Ezekiel 48:5 / Key references: Joshua 17:1–17; 2 Chronicles 34:4–6

👥 MANASSES

of times mentioned: 2
# of MEN by this name: 1

Genealogy of Jesus: Yes (Matthew 1:10)

Meaning: Causing to forget

A descendant of Abraham through Isaac; forebear of Jesus' earthly father, Joseph. Greek form of Manasseh.

Only reference: Matthew 1:10

👥 MANOAH

of times mentioned: 18
# of MEN by this name: 1

Meaning: Rest

The father of Samson, whose wife was barren. The woman received a visit from the angel of the Lord, telling her not to have strong drink or anything unclean, because the child she would bear would be a Nazarite. When Manoah heard this, he prayed that God would send the angel again, so he could know what to do when the child was born. Again the angel appeared to the woman, and she brought her husband to Him. When Manoah received the instructions, he recognized that he had seen God and made an offering to Him.

First reference: Judges 13:2 / Last reference: Judges 16:31 / Key reference: Judges 13

👥 MAOCH

of times mentioned: 1
# of MEN by this name: 1

Meaning: Oppressed

Father of Achish, the Philistine king of Gath with whom David sought refuge.

Only reference: 1 Samuel 27:2

👥 MAON

of times mentioned: 2
# of MEN by this name: 1

Meaning: A residence

A descendant of Abraham through Jacob's son Judah.

Only reference: 1 Chronicles 2:45

⚲ MAON

of times mentioned: OT 6

Meaning: A residence

1) A village that became part of the inheritance of the tribe of Judah following the conquest of the Promised Land. Maon was the home of Nabal, the wealthy man who refused to help David and

his men, though they had protected Nabal's lands during David's warfare with Saul.

First reference: Joshua 15:55 / Last reference: 1 Samuel 25:2

2) A wilderness in the plain south of Jeshimon. Here King Saul pursued David, who fled until the king was distracted by a Philistine attack.

First reference: 1 Samuel 23:24 / Last reference: 1 Samuel 23:25

🏿 MARA

of times mentioned: 1
# of WOMEN by this name: 1

Meaning: Bitter

A name Ruth gave herself after the men of her family died and she felt that God had dealt bitterly with her.

Only reference: Ruth 1:20

📍 MARAH

of times mentioned: OT 5

Meaning: Bitter

A campsite of the Israelites on their way to the Promised Land. The waters here were bitter.

First reference: Exodus 15:23 / Last reference: Numbers 33:9

📍 MARALAH

of times mentioned: OT 1

Meaning: Earthquake

A city that became part of the inheritance of Zebulun when Joshua cast lots in Shiloh to provide territory for the seven tribes that had yet to receive their land.

Only reference: Joshua 19:11

🏿 MARCUS

of times mentioned: 3
# of MEN by this name: 1

Latin form of Mark. Same as Mark.

First reference: 1 Colossians 4:10 / Last reference: 1 Peter 5:13

🏿 MARESHAH

of times mentioned: 2
# of MEN by this name: 2

Meaning: Summit

1) A descendant of Abraham through Jacob's son Judah.

Only reference: 1 Chronicles 2:42

2) Another descendant of Abraham through Jacob's son Judah.

Only reference: 1 Chronicles 4:21

📍 MARESHAH

of times mentioned: OT 6

Meaning: Summit

A city that became part of the inheritance of the tribe of Judah following the conquest of the Promised Land. King Rehoboam of Judah fortified Mareshah to defend his nation. Here King Asa of Judah met in battle with Zerah the Ethiopian. The prophet Micah foretold this city's conquest by Assyria.

First reference: Joshua 15:44 / Last reference: Micah 1:15

🏿 MARK

of times mentioned: 5
# of MEN by this name: 1

Nephew of Barnabas and fellow missionary with Barnabas and Saul. At Pamphylia, Mark left the mission. When his uncle wanted to bring him on a second journey, Paul objected. So Barnabas took Mark back with him to Cyprus. Mark was the writer of the Gospel that bears his name. Same as Marcus.

First reference: Acts 12:12 / Last reference: 2 Timothy 4:11

📍 MAROTH

of times mentioned: OT 1

Meaning: Bitter springs

A Judean city that awaited good but saw evil come upon it when the Assyrians attacked.

Only reference: Micah 1:12

👥 MARSENA

of times mentioned: 1
# of MEN by this name: 1

One of seven Persian princes serving under King Ahasuerus.

Only reference: Esther 1:14

📍 MARS' HILL

of times mentioned: NT 1

Also called "the Areopagus," this hill near Athens's Acropolis was where the ancient Athenian court and council met. In Paul's day, the council was in charge of religious matters in the city. Paul had taught Christ in the synagogues; the philosophers of Athens heard his message and began to debate with him about the "foreign gods" he was preaching (Acts 17:18 NIV). They brought him to a meeting of the council of the Areopagus at Mars' Hill and asked him about his teaching. The apostle took the opportunity to speak to them about Christ, and a few people came to the Lord as a result of his message. Same as Areopagus.

Only reference: Acts 17:22

👥 MARTHA

of times mentioned: 13
# of WOMEN by this name: 1

Meaning: Mistress

Sister of Lazarus and Mary (5). Jesus became friendly with the family when Martha invited Him to her home in Bethany. Martha, encumbered with serving, asked Jesus to tell Mary to help her, but Jesus pointed out that Mary had chosen the better part—listening to His teaching.

When their brother became ill, Martha and Mary called for Jesus. While He delayed, Lazarus died. When Jesus reached Bethany, Martha commented, "If thou hadst been here, my brother had not died" (John 11:21). Jesus pointed out that He was the resurrection and brought her brother back to life.

First reference: Luke 10:38 / Last reference: John 12:2 / Key references: Luke 10:38–42; John 11:1–44

👥 MARY

of times mentioned: 54
# of WOMEN by this name: 7

1) Jesus' mother, who as a virgin received the news from an angel that she would bear the Messiah. Mary traveled to Bethlehem with her betrothed, Joseph. Jesus was born there, and there Mary saw the shepherds and kings worship Him.

When she and Joseph brought Jesus to the temple, Mary heard Simeon's and Anna's prophecies about her son. When Jesus was twelve years old, the couple brought Him to the temple, did not realize He had not left with their group, and had to return for Him.

Mary stood by the cross and saw her son crucified. She was also in the upper room, praying with the disciples after His ascension.

Genealogy of Jesus: Yes (Matthew 1:16)

First reference: Matthew 1:16 / Last reference: Acts 1:14 / Key references: Matthew 1:18–25; Luke 1:26–35; 2; John 19:25

2) Called Mary Magdelene, Jesus cast seven devils out of her. Mary was present throughout the crucifixion of Jesus. Following His resurrection, she came to the tomb with the other women to anoint His body and saw the angels who reported that Jesus had risen from the dead. She and the other women told the disciples. As Mary wept at the tomb, Jesus appeared to her. She did not recognize Him until He spoke her name.

First reference: Matthew 27:56 / Last reference: John 20:18 / Key references: Mark 15:40–41; 16:9; Luke 24:10–11; John 20:1–18

3) Mary, the mother of James and Joses, was with Mary Magdelene and other women at the crucifixion of Jesus and at the tomb following His resurrection.

First reference: Matthew 27:56 / Last reference: Luke 24:10

4) Wife of Cleophas. Possibly the same as Mary (3).

Only reference: John 19:25

5) The sister of Lazarus and Martha, Mary of Bethany listened at Jesus' feet while her sister became encumbered in household matters. When their brother became ill, Martha and Mary called for Jesus. While He delayed, Lazarus died. Mary saw her brother, Lazarus, resurrected by Jesus and anointed Him with spikenard before His death.

First reference: Luke 10:39 / Last reference: John 12:3 / Key references: Luke 10:39–42; John 11:28–32; 12:3

6) Mother of John (4).

Only reference: Acts 12:12

7) A Christian whom Paul greeted in his letter to the church at Rome.

Only reference: Romans 16:6

👥 MASH

of times mentioned: 1
# of MEN by this name: 1

A descendant of Noah through his son Shem.

Only reference: Genesis 10:23

📍 MASHAL

of times mentioned: OT 1

Meaning: Request

One of the forty-eight cities given to the Levites as God had commanded. Mashal was given to them by the tribe of Asher.

Only reference: 1 Chronicles 6:74

📍 MASREKAH

of times mentioned: OT 2

Meaning: Vineyard

Home of an Edomite king, Samlah, who inherited his throne from Hadad, son of Bedad.

First reference: Genesis 36:36 / Last reference: 1 Chronicles 1:47

👥 MASSA

of times mentioned: 2
# of MEN by this name: 1

Meaning: Burden

A son of Ishmael.

First reference: Genesis 25:14 / Last reference: 1 Chronicles 1:30

📍 MASSAH

of times mentioned: OT 4

Meaning: A testing

Another name for Meribah, where God's people murmured against Him. Their grumbling provoked Him to wrath, though He provided water for them there.

First reference: Exodus 17:7 / Last reference: Deuteronomy 33:8

👥 MATHUSALA

of times mentioned: 1
# of MEN by this name: 1

Genealogy of Jesus: Yes (Luke 3:37)

A descendant of Abraham through Isaac; forebear of Jesus' earthly father, Joseph.

Only reference: Luke 3:37

👥 MATRED

of times mentioned: 2
# of WOMEN by this name: 1

Meaning: Propulsive

Mother-in-law of a king of Edom, "before there reigned any king over the children of Israel" (Genesis 36:31).

First reference: Genesis 36:39 / Last reference: 1 Chronicles 1:50

MATRI

of times mentioned: 1
# of MEN by this name: 1

A forefather of King Saul.

Only reference: 1 Samuel 10:21

MATTAN

of times mentioned: 3
# of MEN by this name: 2

1) A priest of Baal killed by the people of Judah after Jehoiada made a covenant between them, King Joash, and God.

First reference: 2 Kings 11:18 / Last reference: 2 Chronicles 23:17

2) Father of Shephatiah, who threw Jeremiah into a dungeon.

Only reference: Jeremiah 38:1

MATTANAH

of times mentioned: OT 2

Meaning: A present; an offering; a bribe

A camp of the Israelites during their forty years in the wilderness.

First reference: Numbers 21:18 / Last reference: Numbers 21:19

MATTANIAH

of times mentioned: 16
# of MEN by this name: 9

Meaning: Gift of God

1) When Nebuchadnezzar, king of Babylon, conquered Judah, Mattaniah was made king in his uncle Jehoiachin's place and renamed Zedekiah.

Only reference: 2 Kings 24:17

2) A Jewish exile from the tribe of Levi who resettled Jerusalem.

First reference: 1 Chronicles 9:15 / Last reference: Nehemiah 12:35

3) A son of King David's musician Heman, who was "under the hands of [his] father for song in the house of the LORD" (1 Chronicles 25:6).

First reference: 1 Chronicles 25:4 / Last reference: 1 Chronicles 25:16

4) A descendant of Abraham through Jacob's son Levi. Mattaniah was among the Levites who cleansed the Jerusalem temple during the revival of King Hezekiah's day.

Only reference: 2 Chronicles 29:13

5) An exiled Israelite who married a "strange" (foreign) woman.

Only reference: Ezra 10:26

6) Another exiled Israelite who married a "strange" (foreign) woman.

Only reference: Ezra 10:27

7) Another exiled Israelite who married a "strange" (foreign) woman.

Only reference: Ezra 10:30

8) Another exiled Israelite who married a "strange" (foreign) woman.

Only reference: Ezra 10:37

9) Forefather of one of the temple treasurers appointed by Nehemiah.

Only reference: Nehemiah 13:13

MATTATHA

of times mentioned: 1
# of MEN by this name: 1

Genealogy of Jesus: Yes (Luke 3:31)

Meaning: Gift of God

A descendant of Abraham through Isaac; forebear of Jesus' earthly father, Joseph.

Only reference: Luke 3:31

MATTATHAH

of times mentioned: 1
# of MEN by this name: 1

Meaning: Gift of God

An exiled Israelite who married a "strange" (foreign) woman.

Only reference: Ezra 10:33

👥 MATTATHIAS

of times mentioned: 2
# of MEN by this name: 2

Meaning: Gift of God

1) A descendant of Abraham through Isaac; forebear of Jesus' earthly father, Joseph.

Only reference: Luke 3:25

Genealogy of Jesus: Yes (Luke 3:25)

2) Another descendant of Abraham through Isaac; another forebear of Jesus' earthly father, Joseph.

Only reference: Luke 3:26

Genealogy of Jesus: Yes (Luke 3:26)

👥 MATTENAI

of times mentioned: 3
# of MEN by this name: 3

Meaning: Liberal

1) An exiled Israelite who married a "strange" (foreign) woman.

Only reference: Ezra 10:33

2) Another exiled Israelite who married a "strange" (foreign) woman.

Only reference: Ezra 10:37

3) Forefather of a priest who returned to Jerusalem under Zerubbabel.

Only reference: Nehemiah 12:19

👥 MATTHAN

of times mentioned: 2
# of MEN by this name: 1

Genealogy of Jesus: Yes (Matthew 1:15)

A descendant of Abraham through Isaac; forebear of Jesus' earthly father, Joseph.

Only reference: Matthew 1:15

👥 MATTHAT

of times mentioned: 2
# of MEN by this name: 2

Meaning: Gift of God

1) A descendant of Abraham through Isaac; forebear of Jesus' earthly father, Joseph.

Only reference: Luke 3:24

Genealogy of Jesus: Yes (Luke 3:24)

2) Another descendant of Abraham through Isaac; forebear of Jesus' earthly father, Joseph.

Only reference: Luke 3:29

Genealogy of Jesus: Yes (Luke 3:29)

👥 MATTHEW

of times mentioned: 5
# of MEN by this name: 1

A tax collector (or publican), also called Levi, who left his tax booth to follow Jesus. Disciple Matthew was in the upper room, following Jesus' resurrection, praying. Although Matthew does not list himself as the writer of the Gospel named after him, the early church ascribed it to him. Same as Levi (2).

First reference: Matthew 9:9 / Last reference: Acts 1:13

👥 MATTHIAS

of times mentioned: 2
# of MEN by this name: 1

One of two potential apostolic replacements for Judas Iscariot. Matthias won the position but is not mentioned afterward in scripture.

First reference: Acts 1:23 / Last reference: Acts 1:26

👥 MATTITHIAH

of times mentioned: 8
# of MEN by this name: 5

Meaning: Gift of God

1) A Levite official in charge of the things baked in the temple sanctuary.

Only reference: 1 Chronicles 9:31

2) A Levite musician who performed in celebration when King David brought the ark of the covenant to Jerusalem.

First reference: 1 Chronicles 15:18 / Last reference: 1 Chronicles 16:5

3) A son of King David's musician Jeduthun, "who prophesied with a harp, to give thanks and to praise the LORD" (1 Chronicles 25:3).

First reference: 1 Chronicles 25:3 / Last reference: 1 Chronicles 25:21

4) An exiled Israelite who married a "strange" (foreign) woman.

Only reference: Ezra 10:43

5) A priest who assisted Ezra in reading the book of the law to the people of Jerusalem.

Only reference: Nehemiah 8:4

● MEAH

of times mentioned: OT 2

Meaning: A hundred or a hundredth

A tower in Jerusalem that was sanctified by the high priest Eliashib and dedicated by Nehemiah.

First reference: Nehemiah 3:1 / Last reference: Nehemiah 12:39

● MEARAH

of times mentioned: OT 1

Meaning: Cave

A place near Sidon that Israel had not yet possessed when Joshua was old.

Only reference: Joshua 13:4

 MEBUNNAI

of times mentioned: 1
# of MEN by this name: 1

Meaning: Built up

One of King David's warriors known as the "mighty men."

Only reference: 2 Samuel 23:27

👥 MEDAD

of times mentioned: 2
# of MEN by this name: 1

Meaning: Loving, affectionate

A man who prophesied after God sent the Israelites quail to eat in the wilderness.

First reference: Numbers 11:26 / Last reference: Numbers 11:27

👥 MEDAN

of times mentioned: 2
# of MEN by this name: 1

Meaning: Discord, strife

A son of Abraham by his second wife, Keturah.

First reference: Genesis 25:2 / Last reference: 1 Chronicles 1:32

● MEDEBA

of times mentioned: OT 5

Meaning: Water of quiet

An Amorite city that became part of the inheritance of the tribe of Reuben. After the new king of Ammon offended David's messengers, he hired the king of Maacha and his troops as mercenaries. Maacha's men assembled against Israel at Medeba.

First reference: Numbers 21:30 / Last reference: Isaiah 15:2

📍 MEDIA

of times mentioned: OT 6

Meaning: Madai (in Hebrew)

A Mesopotamian nation that lay northeast of Babylon and north of Elam. Media was conquered by the Assyrians, whose king, Shalmaneser, transported the conquered Israelites to Media. For a time the Media established themselves as an independent nation but were again conquered by Persia. The army and leaders of Media were part of the Persian king Ahasuerus's feast.

First reference: Esther 1:3 / Last reference: Daniel 8:20

📍 MEGIDDO

of times mentioned: OT 11

Meaning: Rendezvous

A fortress city northwest of Taanach that guarded a strategic mountain pass west of the Jordan River, Megiddo was conquered by Joshua and his troops. Though it was within the tribe of Issachar's territory, Megiddo became part of the inheritance of the tribe of Manasseh. The tribe did not drive out its original inhabitants.

Deborah and Barak's victory song says, "The kings of Canaan fought at Taanach by the waters of Megiddo" (Judges 5:19 NIV), but the kings did not leave the field with plunder. Instead Israel was victorious. During King Solomon's rule, Baana was the provisions officer in charge of Megiddo.

Fleeing from Jehu, King Azahiah of Judah was set upon by Jehu's men and died in Megiddo. King Josiah of Judah also died here in a battle with Pharaoh Necho, having been shot by the pharaoh's archers.

First reference: Joshua 12:21 / Last reference: 2 Chronicles 35:22

📍 MEGIDDON

of times mentioned: OT 1

Meaning: Rendezvous

The prophet Zechariah compares the day when Israel will recognize the crucified Messiah to the great mourning in this valley. Same as Megiddo.

Only reference: Zechariah 12:11

👥 MEHETABEEL

of times mentioned: 1
# of MEN by this name: 1

Meaning: Bettered of God

Forefather of Shemaiah, who falsely told Nehemiah that he would be killed.

Only reference: Nehemiah 6:10

👥 MEHETABEL

of times mentioned: 2
# of WOMEN by this name: 1

Meaning: Bettered of God

Wife of a king of Edom, "before there reigned any king over the children of Israel" (Genesis 36:31).

First reference: Genesis 36:39 / Last reference: 1 Chronicles 1:50

👥 MEHIDA

of times mentioned: 2
# of MEN by this name: 1

Meaning: Junction

Forefather of an exiled family that returned to Judah under Zerubbabel.

First reference: Ezra 2:52 / Last reference: Nehemiah 7:54

👥 MEHIR

of times mentioned: 1
# of MEN by this name: 1

Meaning: Price

A descendant of Abraham through Jacob's son Judah.

Only reference: 1 Chronicles 4:11

📍 MEHUJAEL

of times mentioned: 2
# of MEN by this name: 1

Meaning: Smitten of God

A descendant of Cain through his son Enoch.

Only reference: Genesis 4:18

 MEHUMAN

of times mentioned: 1
# of MEN by this name: 1

A eunuch serving the Persian king Ahasuerus in Esther's time.

Only reference: Esther 1:10

MEHUNIM

of times mentioned: 1
# of MEN by this name: 1

Meaning: A Muenite or inhabitant of Maon

Forefather of an exiled family that returned to Judah under Zerubbabel.

Only reference: Ezra 2:50

ME-JARKON

of times mentioned: OT 1

Meaning: Water of the yellowness

A town that became part of the inheritance of Dan when Joshua cast lots in Shiloh to provide territory for the seven tribes that had yet to receive their land.

Only reference: Joshua 19:46

MEKONAH

of times mentioned: OT 1

Meaning: A base

A town of Judah resettled by the Jews after the Babylonian Exile.

Only reference: Nehemiah 11:28

MELATIAH

of times mentioned: 1
# of MEN by this name: 1

Meaning: God has delivered

A man who repaired Jerusalem's walls under Nehemiah.

Only reference: Nehemiah 3:7

MELCHI

of times mentioned: 2
# of MEN by this name: 2

Meaning: My king

1) A descendant of Abraham through Isaac; forebear of Jesus' earthly father, Joseph.

Only reference: Luke 3:24

Genealogy of Jesus: Yes (Luke 3:24)

2) Another descendant of Abraham through Isaac; forebear of Jesus' earthly father, Joseph.

Only reference: Luke 3:28

Genealogy of Jesus: Yes (Luke 3:28)

MELCHIAH

of times mentioned: 1
# of MEN by this name: 1

Meaning: King of (appointed by) God

Forefather of Pashur, who served King Zedekiah of Judah.

Only reference: Jeremiah 21:1

MELCHISEDEC

of times mentioned: 9
# of MEN by this name: 1

Meaning: King of right

King and high priest of Salem who blessed Abram after he recovered his nephew Lot (Genesis 14:18; Hebrews 7:1). The writer of Hebrews refers to Jesus as high priest "after the order of Melchisedec," since He was not a priest from the line of Levi. Same as Melchizedek.

First reference: Hebrews 5:6 / Last reference: Hebrews 7:21

 MELCHI-SHUA

of times mentioned: 2
# of MEN by this name: 1

Meaning: King of wealth

A son of King Saul. He was killed by the Philistines along with his father and two brothers. Same as Malchi-shua.

First reference: 1 Samuel 14:49 / Last reference: 1 Samuel 31:2

 MELCHIZEDEK

of times mentioned: 2
# of MEN by this name: 1

Meaning: King of right

Hebrew form of the name Melchisedec.

First reference: Genesis 14:18 / Last reference: Psalm 110:4

 MELEA

of times mentioned: 1
# of MEN by this name: 1

Genealogy of Jesus: Yes (Luke 3:31)

A descendant of Abraham through Isaac; forebear of Jesus' earthly father, Joseph.

Only reference: Luke 3:31

 MELECH

of times mentioned: 2
# of MEN by this name: 1

Meaning: King

A descendant of Abraham through Jacob's son Benjamin, in the line of King Saul and his son Jonathan.

First reference: 1 Chronicles 8:35 / Last reference: 1 Chronicles 9:41

MELICU

of times mentioned: 1
# of MEN by this name: 1

Meaning: Regnant

Forefather of a household of priests who returned to Jerusalem under Zerubbabel.

Only reference: Nehemiah 12:14

⚲ MELITA

of times mentioned: NT 1

The island on which Paul and his fellow travelers to Rome landed after they were shipwrecked. The people of Melita were kind to them.

Only reference: Acts 28:1

MELZAR

of times mentioned: 2
# of MEN by this name: 1

A Babylonian official in charge of Daniel and his three friends.

First reference: Daniel 1:11 / Last reference: Daniel 1:16

⚲ MEMPHIS

of times mentioned: OT 1

An ancient Egyptian city, capital of the northern part of that country, that was famed for its burial places. The prophet Hosea foretold that Memphis would bury the people of Israel who had turned away from God.

Only reference: Hosea 9:6

MEMUCAN

of times mentioned: 3
# of MEN by this name: 1

One of seven Persian princes serving under King Ahasuerus.

First reference: Esther 1:14 / Last reference: Esther 1:21

 MENAHEM

of times mentioned: 8
# of MEN by this name: 1

Meaning: Comforter

A king of Israel who usurped the throne from King Shallum. During his ten-year reign, the idolatrous Menahem did evil. To keep his throne, he raised money from the wealthy men of Israel and gave it to Pul, the king of Assyria, as tribute.

First reference: 2 Kings 15:14 / Last reference: 2 Kings 15:23

MENAN

of times mentioned: 1
# of MEN by this name: 1

Genealogy of Jesus: Yes (Luke 3:31)

A descendant of Abraham through Isaac; forebear of Jesus' earthly father, Joseph.

Only reference: Luke 3:31

MEONENIM

of times mentioned: OT 1

Meaning: To cover; to cloud over; to act covertly (that is, to practice magic)

A plain near Shechem.

Only reference: Judges 9:37

MEONOTHAI

of times mentioned: 1
# of MEN by this name: 1

Meaning: Habitative

A descendant of Abraham through Jacob's son Judah.

Only reference: 1 Chronicles 4:14

MEPHAATH

of times mentioned: OT 4

Meaning: Illuminative

One of the forty-eight cities given to the Levites as God had commanded. Mephaath was given to them by the tribe of Reuben. In his oracle against Moab, the prophet Jeremiah foresaw judgment falling on Mephaath.

First reference: Joshua 13:18 / Last reference: Jeremiah 48:21

MEPHIBOSHETH

of times mentioned: 15
# of MEN by this name: 2

Meaning: Dispeller of shame

1) Grandson of King Saul and son of Jonathan. As a child, Mephibosheth was dropped by his nurse and became lame. When David took the throne of Israel, he treated Mephibosheth kindly because of his friendship with Jonathan.

When Absalom ousted David from Jerusalem, Mephibosheth's servant Ziba reported that Mephibosheth remained in Jerusalem, confident he would be made king. David gave Mephibosheth's land to Ziba. When David returned to Jerusalem, Mephibosheth claimed that Ziba had deceived him and lied to David. The king ordered the two men to split the land, but Mephibosheth agreed that Ziba should have all, as long as David had returned in peace. Same as Merib-baal.

First reference: 2 Samuel 4:4 / Last reference: 2 Samuel 21:7 / Key references: 2 Samuel 9:6–10; 16:3–4; 19:24–30

2) One of King Saul's sons whom David handed over to the Gibeonites, who sought vengeance on Saul's house.

Only reference: 2 Samuel 21:8

MERAB

of times mentioned: 3
# of WOMEN by this name: 1

Meaning: Increase

King Saul's firstborn daughter who was promised to David but married another man.

First reference: 1 Samuel 14:49 / Last reference: 1 Samuel 18:19

 MERAIAH

of times mentioned: 1
# of MEN by this name: 1

Meaning: Rebellion

A priest in the days of the high priest Joiakim.

Only reference: Nehemiah 12:12

MERAIOTH

of times mentioned: 7
# of MEN by this name: 3

Meaning: Rebellious

1) Forefather of Ezra (2) and a descendant of Abraham through Jacob's son Levi.

First reference: 1 Chronicles 6:6 / Last reference: Ezra 7:3

2) Forefather of a priest who returned to Jerusalem following the Babylonian captivity.

First reference: 1 Chronicles 9:11 / Last reference: Nehemiah 11:11

3) A descendant of Abraham through Jacob's son Levi, and a priest through the line of Aaron.

Only reference: Nehemiah 12:15

MERARI

of times mentioned: 39
# of MEN by this name: 1

Meaning: Bitter

Levi's third son. His family was in charge of the boards, bars, pillars, sockets, and vessels of the tabernacle, along with the pillars of the court and their sockets, pins, and cords.

First reference: Genesis 46:11 / Last reference: Ezra 8:19 / Key references: Exodus 6:19; Numbers 3:33–37

MERATHAIM

of times mentioned: OT 1

Meaning: Double bitterness

A name for Babylon that the prophet Jeremiah used when he foretold Israel's return to its land and the righteousness of Israel and Judah. God commanded the two nations to destroy Merathaim.

Only reference: Jeremiah 50:21

MERED

of times mentioned: 2
# of MEN by this name: 1

Meaning: Rebellion

A descendant of Abraham through Jacob's son Judah.

First reference: 1 Chronicles 4:17 / Last reference: 1 Chronicles 4:18

MEREMOTH

of times mentioned: 6
# of MEN by this name: 3

Meaning: Heights

1) A priest's son who weighed the valuable utensils that King Artaxerxes of Persia and his officials had given Ezra to take back to Jerusalem's temple.

First reference: Ezra 8:33 / Last reference: Nehemiah 3:21

2) An exiled Israelite who married a "strange" (foreign) woman.

Only reference: Ezra 10:36

3) A priest who renewed the covenant under Nehemiah.

First reference: Nehemiah 10:5 / Last reference: Nehemiah 12:3

MERES

of times mentioned: 1
# of MEN by this name: 1

One of seven Persian princes serving under King Ahasuerus.

Only reference: Esther 1:14

📍 MERIBAH

of times mentioned: OT 6

Meaning: Quarrel

1) The rock of Horeb that God commanded Moses to strike to provide water for His people in the wilderness. Because the Israelites quarreled and tested God there, Moses called the place Massah (meaning "a testing") and Meribah (meaning "quarrel").

Only reference: Exodus 17:7

2) During the Israelites' forty years in the desert, in a second incident in the desert of Zin, God commanded Moses to speak to a rock that would produce water. Instead Moses struck the rock twice. Here God provided the water but told Moses and Aaron they would not enter the Promised Land. Same as Meribah-kadesh.

First reference: Numbers 20:13 / Last reference: Psalm 81:7

📍 MERIBAH-KADESH

of times mentioned: OT 1

A place in the wilderness (or desert) of Zin where the Israelites disobeyed God. Same as Meribah (2).

Only reference: Deuteronomy 32:51

👥 MERIBBAAL

of times mentioned: 4
# of MEN by this name: 1

Meaning: Quarreler of Baal

A descendant of Abraham through Jacob's son Benjamin, in the line of King Saul and his son Jonathan. Same as Mephibosheth (1).

First reference: 1 Chronicles 8:34 / Last reference: 1 Chronicles 9:40

👥 MERODACH-BALADAN

of times mentioned: 1
# of MEN by this name: 1

King of Babylon during the reign of King Hezekiah of Judah.

Only reference: Isaiah 39:1

📍 MEROM

of times mentioned: OT 2

Meaning: Altitude, elevated place, or elation

The "waters of Merom" were the site of a battle between Jabin, king of Hazor, and his allies and Joshua and his troops. The Israelites defeated their enemies and chased them to Zidon and beyond. Some have identified Merom with Lake Huleh, but the Jewish historian Josephus places the Israelites' camp elsewhere.

First reference: Joshua 11:5 / Last reference: Joshua 11:7

📍 MEROZ

of times mentioned: OT 1

A city on which Deborah and Barak called down a curse because its inhabitants did not assist in Israel's battle with Sisera.

Only reference: Judges 5:23

👥 MESHA

of times mentioned: 3
# of MEN by this name: 3

Meaning: Safety

1) A king of Moab at the time of King Jehoram of Israel.

Only reference: 2 Kings 3:4

2) A descendant of Abraham through Jacob's son Judah.

Only reference: 1 Chronicles 2:42

3) A descendant of Benjamin and son of Shaharaim.

Only reference: 1 Chronicles 8:9

📍 MESHA

of times mentioned: OT 1

Meaning: A sowing or a possession

A place where Shem's descendants lived.

Only reference: Genesis 10:30

👥 MESHACH

of times mentioned: 15
# of MEN by this name: 1

The Babylonian name for Mishael, one of Daniel's companions in exile. Daniel had King Nebuchadnezzar make Meshach a ruler in Babylon. When some Chaldeans accused Meshach and his friends, fellow Jews and corulers Shadrach and Abed-nego, of not worshipping the king's golden idol, the three faithful Jews were thrown into a furnace. God protected His men, who were not even singed. The king recognized the power of their God and promoted them in his service. Same as Mishael.

First reference: Daniel 1:7 / Last reference: Daniel 3:30 / Key reference: Daniel 3:16–18

👥 MESHECH

of times mentioned: 3
# of MEN by this name: 2

1) One of Noah's grandsons through his son Japheth.

First reference: Genesis 10:2 / Last reference: 1 Chronicles 1:5

2) A descendant of Noah through his son Shem.

Only reference: 1 Chronicles 1:17

👥 MESHELEMIAH

of times mentioned: 4
# of MEN by this name: 1

Meaning: Ally of God

A Levite "porter" (doorkeeper) in the house of the Lord.

First reference: 1 Chronicles 9:21 / Last reference: 1 Chronicles 26:9

👥 MESHEZABEEL

of times mentioned: 3
# of MEN by this name: 2

Meaning: Delivered of God

1) Forefather of a man who repaired Jerusalem's walls under Nehemiah.

Only reference: Nehemiah 3:4

2) A Levite who renewed the covenant under Nehemiah.

First reference: Nehemiah 10:21 / Last reference: Nehemiah 11:24

📍 MESHILLEMITH

of times mentioned: 1
# of MEN by this name: 1

Meaning: Reconciliation

Forefather of a priest who returned to Jerusalem after the Babylonian captivity.

Only reference: 1 Chronicles 9:12

👥 MESHILLEMOTH

of times mentioned: 2
# of MEN by this name: 2

Meaning: Reconciliations

1) A man of the tribe of Ephraim whose son Berechiah counseled his nation of Israel against enslaving fellow Jews from Judah who were captured in a civil war.

Only reference: 2 Chronicles 28:12

2) A forefather of Amashai, who worked in the temple following Judah's return from exile.

Only reference: Nehemiah 11:13

👥 MESHOBAB

of times mentioned: 1
# of MEN by this name: 1

Meaning: Returned

A descendant of Abraham through Jacob's son Simeon.

Only reference: 1 Chronicles 4:34

👥 MESHULLAM

of times mentioned: 25
# of MEN by this name: 21

Meaning: Allied

1) Forefather of a scribe who worked for King Josiah.

Only reference: 2 Kings 22:3

2) A descendant of Abraham through Jacob's son Judah, in the line of the nation of Judah's third-to-last king, Jeconiah (also known as Jehoiachin).

Only reference: 1 Chronicles 3:19

3) A descendant of Abraham through Jacob's son Gad.

Only reference: 1 Chronicles 5:13

4) A descendant of Benjamin and a chief of that tribe who lived in Jerusalem.

Only reference: 1 Chronicles 8:17

5) Father of a Benjaminite who was chosen by lot to resettle Jerusalem after returning from the Babylonian Exile.

Only reference: 1 Chronicles 9:7

6) A descendant of Abraham through Jacob's son Benjamin.

Only reference: 1 Chronicles 9:8

7) Forefather of a priest who returned to Jerusalem under Zerubbabel.

First reference: 1 Chronicles 9:11 / Last reference: Nehemiah 11:11

8) Another forefather of a priest who returned to Jerusalem under Zerubbabel.

Only reference: 1 Chronicles 9:12

9) Forefather of several Kohathites who rebuilt the temple under King Josiah.

Only reference: 2 Chronicles 34:12

10) A Jewish leader whom Ezra requested to send Levites to join the exiles returning to Jerusalem.

Only reference: Ezra 8:16

11) A Levite who urged the Israelites to give up their "strange" (foreign) wives.

Only reference: Ezra 10:15

12) An exiled Israelite who married a "strange" (foreign) woman.

Only reference: Ezra 10:29

13) A man who repaired Jerusalem's walls under Nehemiah. His daughter married Tobiah, one of Judah's enemies who tried to stop the walls from being rebuilt.

First reference: Nehemiah 3:4 / Last reference: Nehemiah 6:18

14) Another man who repaired Jerusalem's walls under Nehemiah.

Only reference: Nehemiah 3:6

15) A priest who assisted Ezra in reading the book of the law to the people of Jerusalem.

Only reference: Nehemiah 8:4

16) A Jewish leader who renewed the covenant under Nehemiah.

Only reference: Nehemiah 10:7

17) A Levite who renewed the covenant under Nehemiah.

Only reference: Nehemiah 10:20

18) Forefather of a Jewish exile from the tribe of Benjamin who resettled Jerusalem.

Only reference: Nehemiah 11:7

19) A priest who helped to dedicate Jerusalem's rebuilt wall.

First reference: Nehemiah 12:13 / Last reference: Nehemiah 12:33

20) A priest who returned to Jerusalem with Zerubbabel after the exile.

Only reference: Nehemiah 12:16

21) A Levite "porter" (doorkeeper) at the temple gates in Nehemiah's day.

Only reference: Nehemiah 12:25

👥 MESHULLEMETH

of times mentioned: 1
# of WOMEN by this name: 1

Meaning: A mission or a favorable release

Mother of King Amon of Judah.

Only reference: 2 Kings 21:19

MESOPOTAMIA

of times mentioned: OT 5 / NT 2

Meaning: In the middle of two rivers

The territory between the Tigris and Euphrates Rivers. From this area came a number of great ancient empires, including the Old Babylonian, Assyrian, and Neo-Babylonian empires. Abraham, who was originally from Ur, a city of Mesopotamia, sent a servant to the city of Nahor, also in Mesopotamia, to find a bride from his own family for his son Isaac.

In the time of the judges, when Israel sinned, God put the nation under the hand of Mesopotamia's king for eight years. Othniel delivered Israel from his rule. The Mesopotamians joined the Ammonites in war against King David.

People from Mesopotamia saw the Christians filled with the Holy Spirit at Pentecost. See Assyria and Babylon.

First reference: Genesis 24:10 / Last reference: Acts 7:2

METHEG-AMMAH

of times mentioned: OT 1

Meaning: Bit of the metropolis

A figurative name for a major city that King David won in a battle with the Philistines.

Only reference: 2 Samuel 8:1

METHUSAEL

of times mentioned: 2
# of MEN by this name: 1

Meaning: Man who is of God

A descendant of Adam through his son Cain.

Only reference: Genesis 4:18

METHUSELAH

of times mentioned: 6
# of MEN by this name: 1

Meaning: Man of a dart

A descendant of Seth who lived for 969 years, the longest recorded life span in the Bible.

First reference: Genesis 5:21 / Last reference: 1 Chronicles 1:3

MEUNIM

of times mentioned: 1
# of MEN by this name: 1

Meaning: A Meunite

Forefather of an exiled family that returned to Judah under Zerubbabel.

Only reference: Nehemiah 7:52

MEZAHAB

of times mentioned: 2
# of WOMEN by this name: 1

Meaning: Water of gold

Grandmother of a wife of a king of Edom, "before there reigned any king over the children of Israel" (Genesis 36:31).

First reference: Genesis 36:39 / Last reference: 1 Chronicles 1:50

MIAMIN

of times mentioned: 2
# of MEN by this name: 2

Meaning: From the right hand

1) An exiled Israelite who married a "strange" (foreign) woman.

Only reference: Ezra 10:25

2) A chief priest who went up to Jerusalem with Zerubbabel.

Only reference: Nehemiah 12:5

MIBHAR

of times mentioned: 1
# of MEN by this name: 1

Meaning: Select, the best

One of King David's warriors known as the "mighty men."

Only reference: 1 Chronicles 11:38

MIBSAM

of times mentioned: 3
# of MEN by this name: 2

Meaning: Fragrant

1) The fourth son of Ishmael.

First reference: Genesis 25:13 / Last reference:
1 Chronicles 1:29

2) A descendant of Abraham through Jacob's son
Simeon.

Only reference: 1 Chronicles 4:25

MIBZAR

of times mentioned: 2
# of MEN by this name: 1

Meaning: Fortification, castle, or fortified city

A "duke of Edom," a leader in the family line of
Esau.

First reference: Genesis 36:42 / Last reference:
1 Chronicles 1:53

MICAH

of times mentioned: 31
# of MEN by this name: 7

Meaning: Who is like God?

1) A man of Mount Ephraim who took eleven hundred shekels from his mother. When he returned them, she had two idols made for him. Micah consecrated one of his sons to be his priest. When a Levite came to his area, Micah hired him as a priest and consecrated him. Some men from Dan stole his idols and took the priest, who went with them willingly. Though Micah and his neighbors tried to recover the items, the Danites were too strong. The thieves set up the idol in Laish, a city they had conquered.

First reference: Judges 17:1 / Last reference: Judges
18:27 / Key references: Judges 17:1–6, 10–12;
18:17–27

2) A descendant of Abraham through Jacob's son
Reuben.

Only reference: 1 Chronicles 5:5

3) A descendant of Abraham through Jacob's son
Benjamin, in the line of King Saul and his son
Jonathan.

First reference: 1 Chronicles 8:34 / Last reference:
1 Chronicles 9:41

4) A Jewish exile from the tribe of Levi who resettled Jerusalem.

Only reference: 1 Chronicles 9:15

5) A descendant of Levi's son Kohath. Micah was
the head of his father's household.

Only reference: 1 Chronicles 23:20

6) Father of Abdon, whom King Josiah sent to
Huldah the prophetess to ask about the book of the
law he had discovered.

Only reference: 2 Chronicles 34:20

7) Called Micah the Morasthite, this Old
Testament minor prophet ministered during the
reign of Hezekiah, king of Judah.

First reference: Jeremiah 26:18 / Last reference:
Micah 1:1

MICAIAH

of times mentioned: 18
# of MEN by this name: 1

A prophet whom King Ahab of Israel hated because he never prophesied anything good to him.
When King Jehoshaphat of Israel asked Ahab
for a prophet who would tell the truth, Ahab had
Micaiah called. Though Ahab's messenger warned
him to give a good message, the prophet would
only say what God told him. Micaiah mocked the
false prophets' message then told Ahab that if he
attacked Ramoth-gilead, his soldiers would be scattered. Micaiah condemned the lying prophets and
was struck by one of their number. Micaiah prophesied against him.

First reference: 1 Kings 22:8 / Last reference:
2 Chronicles 18:27 / Key references: 1 Kings
22:13–17; 2 Chronicles 18:1–16

MICHA

of times mentioned: 4
# of MEN by this name: 3

1) Son of Mephibosheth and grandson of King Saul's son Jonathan.

Only reference: 2 Samuel 9:12

2) A Jewish leader who renewed the covenant under Nehemiah.

Only reference: Nehemiah 10:11

3) A Jewish exile of the tribe of Levi who resettled Jerusalem.

First reference: Nehemiah 11:17 / Last reference: Nehemiah 11:22

👥 MICHAEL

of times mentioned: 10
# of MEN by this name: 10

Meaning: Who is like God?

1) Father of one of the twelve spies sent by Moses to spy out the land of Canaan.

Only reference: Numbers 13:13

2) A descendant of Abraham through Jacob's son Gad.

Only reference: 1 Chronicles 5:13

3) Another descendant of Abraham through Jacob's son Gad.

Only reference: 1 Chronicles 5:14

4) Father of a temple musician appointed by King David.

Only reference: 1 Chronicles 6:40

5) A descendant of Abraham through Jacob's son Issachar.

Only reference: 1 Chronicles 7:3

6) A descendant of Abraham through Jacob's son Benjamin.

Only reference: 1 Chronicles 8:16

7) A mighty man of valor who defected to David at Ziklag.

Only reference: 1 Chronicles 12:20

8) Father or a ruler of the tribe of Issachar in David's time.

Only reference: 1 Chronicles 27:18

9) A son of Judah's king Jehoshaphat, Michael was given "great gifts of silver, and of gold, and of precious things" by his father (2 1 Chronicles 21:3).

Only reference: 2 Chronicles 21:2

10) Forefather of a Jewish exile who returned from Babylon to Judah under Ezra.

Only reference: Ezra 8:8

👥 MICHAH

of times mentioned: 3
# of MEN by this name: 1

Meaning: Who is like God?

A Levite worship leader during David's reign. Lots were cast to determine Michah's duties.

First reference: 1 Chronicles 24:24 / Last reference: 1 Chronicles 24:25

👥 MICHAIAH

of times mentioned: 7
# of MEN by this name: 4
# of WOMEN by this name: 1

Meaning: Who is like God?

1) Father of Achbor. Same as Micah (6).

Only reference: 2 Kings 22:12

2) Mother of King Abijah of Judah.

Only reference: 2 Chronicles 13:12

3) A prince of Judah sent by King Jehoshaphat to teach the law of the Lord throughout the nation.

Only reference: 2 Chronicles 17:7

4) A priest who helped to dedicate the rebuilt wall of Jerusalem by giving thanks.

First reference: Nehemiah 12:35 / Last reference: Nehemiah 12:41

5) A man who heard the prophet Jeremiah's words, read by his scribe, and related them to Judah's princes.

First reference: Jeremiah 36:11 / Last reference: Jeremiah 36:13

 MICHAL

of times mentioned: 18
# of WOMEN by this name: 1

Meaning: Rivulet

Daughter of King Saul and wife of David. To win her, David had to give Saul a hundred Philistine foreskins; he killed two hundred of the enemy, fulfilling the king's request twice over.

When Saul sought to kill David, Michal warned her husband and let him out a window. She told Saul's men that David was sick. Discovered, she claimed David threatened to kill her.

Saul married Michal to Phalti. When David sent for her, after he became king, she was returned to him. But David danced before the ark, and Michal despised and berated him. She had no children.

First reference: 1 Samuel 14:49 / Last reference: 1 Chronicles 15:29 / Key references: 1 Samuel 18:20–27; 19:11–12; 25:44

MICHMAS

of times mentioned: OT 2

Meaning: Hidden

A city whose people returned to Israel after the Babylonian Exile. Same as Michmash.

First reference: Ezra 2:27 / Last reference: Nehemiah 7:31

MICHMASH

of times mentioned: OT 9

Meaning: Hidden

A village of Israel where Saul's troops gathered to fight the Philistines. Afterward the Philisitnes set up a garrison at the pass of Michmash. Jonathan and his armor bearer attacked the Philistines here, and in the ensuing battle their enemies fled. Michmash was resettled by the tribe of Benjamin following the Babylonian Exile. Same as Michmas.

First reference: 1 Samuel 13:2 / Last reference: Isaiah 10:28

MICHMETHAH

of times mentioned: OT 2

Meaning: Concealment

A city on the border of the territory of the tribes of Ephraim and Manasseh.

First reference: Joshua 16:6 / Last reference: Joshua 17:7

MICHRI

of times mentioned: 1
# of MEN by this name: 1

Meaning: Salesman

Forefather of one of Benjamin's descendants who returned to Jerusalem after the Babylonian Exile.

Only reference: 1 Chronicles 9:8

MIDDIN

of times mentioned: OT 1

Meaning: A contest or a quarrel

A city that became part of the inheritance of the tribe of Judah following the conquest of the Promised Land.

Only reference: Joshua 15:61

MIDIAN

of times mentioned: 4
# of MEN by this name: 1

Meaning: Brawling, contentious

A son of Abraham by his second wife, Keturah.

First reference: Genesis 25:2 / Last reference: 1 Chronicles 1:33

MIDIAN

of times mentioned: OT 35

Meaning: A contest or a quarrel

A land east of the Sinai Peninsula, in the northwest portion of Arabia. Midian lay east of the Gulf of

Aqaba and south of Edom. Moses fled here after he killed an Egyptian. He married Zipporah, daughter of the Midian priest Jethro. When Israel conquered the Promised Land, Midianites sought to lure Israel into idolatry and intermarriage. Cozbi, daughter of a Midianite prince, was killed when an Israelite brought her to his tent as Moses called Israel to turn away from foreign women.

God called Moses to fight Midian, bringing His vengeance down on it. Israel killed Midian's five kings and their prophet Balaam, who had plotted with Midian and Moab to draw Israel into pagan practices. Israel killed the Midianite men but brought the women and children as captives to their camp. Moses reminded them that these women had caused Israel's downfall. He commanded them to kill all but the women who were virgins.

After the prophetess Deborah and the battle commander Barak freed Israel from the rule of Canaan, God gave the nation over to Midian for seven years. Then God called Gideon to fight the Midianites and liberate Israel from their rule. With three hundred men he attacked the Midian campsite at night, and the enemy ran. Following the attack, Israel captured and killed two of Midian's kings and made peace with two more. During Solomon's reign, Midian supported Hadad the Edomite against Israel. Same as Madian.

First reference: Genesis 36:35 / Last reference: Habakkuk 3:7 / Key references: Numbers 25; 31:1–18; Judges 7:8–8:28

♀ MIGDAL-EL

of times mentioned: OT 1

Meaning: Tower of God

A fortified or walled city that became part of the inheritance of Naphtali when Joshua cast lots in Shiloh to provide territory for the seven tribes that had yet to receive their land.

Only reference: Joshua 19:38

♀ MIGDAL-GAD

of times mentioned: OT 1

Meaning: Tower of fortune

A city that became part of the inheritance of the tribe of Judah following the conquest of the Promised Land.

Only reference: Joshua 15:37

♀ MIGDOL

of times mentioned: OT 4

1) A campsite of the Israelites on their way to the Promised Land. Migdol lay on the northeastern border of Egypt.

First reference: Exodus 14:2 / Last reference: Numbers 33:7

2) A city in Egypt where the people of Judah settled after their nation was devastated by the Babylonians. Jeremiah prophesied that because they did not follow the Lord, they would die in Egypt.

First reference: Jeremiah 44:1 / Last reference: Jeremiah 46:14

♀ MIGRON

of times mentioned: OT 2

Meaning: Precipice

A town on the outskirts of Gibeah. Here, under a pomegranate tree, Saul tarried while Jonathan attacked a Philistine outpost.

First reference: 1 Samuel 14:2 / Last reference: Isaiah 10:28

👥 MIJAMIN

of times mentioned: 2
# of MEN by this name: 2

1) One of twenty-four priests in David's time who was chosen by lot to serve in the tabernacle.

Only reference: 1 Chronicles 24:9

2) A priest who renewed the covenant under Nehemiah.

Only reference: Nehemiah 10:7

👥 MIKLOTH

of times mentioned: 4
# of MEN by this name: 2

Meaning: Rods

1) A descendant of Abraham through Jacob's son Benjamin.

First reference: 1 Chronicles 8:32 / Last reference: 1 Chronicles 9:38

2) One of David's officers who served him during the second month.

Only reference: 1 Chronicles 27:4

👥 MIKNEIAH

of times mentioned: 2
# of MEN by this name: 1

Meaning: Possession of God

A Levite musician who performed in celebration when King David brought the ark of the covenant to Jerusalem.

First reference: 1 Chronicles 15:18 / Last reference: 1 Chronicles 15:21

👥 MILALAI

of times mentioned: 1
# of MEN by this name: 1

Meaning: Talkative

A priest who helped to dedicate the rebuilt walls of Jerusalem by playing a musical instrument.

Only reference: Nehemiah 12:36

👥 MILCAH

of times mentioned: 11
# of WOMEN by this name: 2

Meaning: Queen

1) Wife of Nahor (2), Abraham's brother. The couple had eight children together. Milcah was Rebekah's grandmother.

First reference: Genesis 11:29 / Last reference: Genesis 24:47

2) One of Zelophehad's five daughters who received his inheritance because he had no sons. Each had to marry within their tribe, Manasseh.

First reference: Numbers 26:33 / Last reference: Joshua 17:3

📍 MILETUM

of times mentioned: NT 1

A city south of Ephesus where Paul told Timothy he had left his companion Trophimus, who was sick. Same as Miletus.

Only reference: 2 Timothy 4:20

📍 MILETUS

of times mentioned: NT 2

A city south of Ephesus where Paul met with the Ephesian elders before he left for Jerusalem. Same as Melitum.

First reference: Acts 20:15 / Last reference: Acts 20:17

📍 MILLO

of times mentioned: OT 10

Meaning: A rampart (that is, a citadel)

1) A fortification somewhere in the area of Shechem, where the men of Millo supported Abimelech as king after Gideon died. It is called Beth Millo in some translations.

First reference: Judges 9:6 / Last reference: Judges 9:20

2) A fortification of ancient Jerusalem. David lived here after the Israelites first made him their king. He rebuilt Jerusalem around Millo. King Solomon repaired the breaches in the fort's wall and refortified it.

Joash, king of Judah, was killed at Millo. King Hezekiah of Judah repaired Millo as the Assyrians threatened his nation.

First reference: 2 Samuel 5:9 / Last reference: 2 Chronicles 32:5

👥 MINIAMIN

of times mentioned: 3
# of MEN by this name: 2

Meaning: From the right hand

1) A priest in the time of King Hezekiah who helped to distribute the people's freewill offerings

to his fellow priests.

Only reference: 2 Chronicles 31:15

2) A priest who helped to dedicate the rebuilt wall of Jerusalem by giving thanks.

First reference: Nehemiah 12:17 / Last reference: Nehemiah 12:41

◉ MINNI

of times mentioned: OT 1

An Armenian province that the prophet Jeremiah called to attack Babylon as part of God's judgment of that nation.

Only reference: Jeremiah 51:27

◉ MINNITH

of times mentioned: OT 2

Meaning: Enumeration

An Ammonite town where Jephthah the Gileadite ended his battle that subdued the Ammonites. Minnith grew wheat that was exported to Tyre.

First reference: Judges 11:33 / Last reference: Ezekiel 27:17

◉ MIPHKAD

of times mentioned: OT 1

Meaning: Assignment

A gate in Jerusalem during Nehemiah's rebuilding of the city that designated the area to be repaired by Malchiah.

Only reference: Nehemiah 3:31

👥 MIRIAM

of times mentioned: 15
# of WOMEN by this name: 2

Meaning: Rebelliously

1) The sister of Moses and Aaron and a prophetess of Israel. Miriam led the praises after Israel crossed the Red Sea. She and Aaron objected to Moses' marrying an Ethiopian woman. "Hath the

LORD indeed spoken only by Moses?" they asked, seeking acknowledgment of their own prophetic gifts (Numbers 12:2). The Lord became angry, confronted them publicly, and made Miriam leprous. Moses prayed for her. God had her stay outside the camp for a week until she was healed. She died in the Desert of Zin.

First reference: Exodus 15:20 / Last reference: Micah 6:4 / Key references: Exodus 15:20–21; Numbers 12:1–15; 20:1

2) A descendant of Jacob through his son Judah.

Only reference: 1 Chronicles 4:17

👥 MIRMA

of times mentioned: 1
# of MEN by this name: 1

Meaning: Deceiving, fraud

A descendant of Abraham through Jacob's son Benjamin.

Only reference: 1 Chronicles 8:10

◉ MISGAB

of times mentioned: OT 1

Meaning: A cliff; altitude; refuge

A place in Moab that the prophet Jeremiah described as "confounded and dismayed" in his prophecy against that nation.

Only reference: Jeremiah 48:1

◉ MISHAL

of times mentioned: OT 1

One of the forty-eight cities given to the Levites as God had commanded. Mishal was given to them by the tribe of Asher.

Only reference: Joshua 21:30

👥 MISHAEL

of times mentioned: 8
# of MEN by this name: 3

Meaning: Who is what God is?

1) A cousin of Moses. When God killed Aaron's two oldest sons, Mishael and his brother carried them from the sanctuary.

First reference: Exodus 6:22 / Last reference: Leviticus 10:4

2) A friend of the prophet Daniel who would not defile himself by eating the king's meat. Along with two others, he would not worship an idol and was cast into the fiery furnace by King Nebuchadnezzar. Also called Meshach.

First reference: Daniel 1:6 / Last reference: Daniel 2:17

3) A priest who assisted Ezra in reading the book of the law to the people of Jerusalem.

Only reference: Nehemiah 8:4

👥 MISHAM

of times mentioned: 1
# of MEN by this name: 1

Meaning: Inspection

A descendant of Abraham through Jacob's son Benjamin.

Only reference: 1 Chronicles 8:12

👥 MISHMA

of times mentioned: 4
# of MEN by this name: 1

Meaning: A report, hearing

A descendant of Abraham through Jacob's son Simeon.

First reference: Genesis 25:14 / Last reference: 1 Chronicles 4:26

👥 MISHMANNAH

of times mentioned: 1
# of MEN by this name: 1

Meaning: Fatness

One of several warriors from the tribe of Gad who left Saul to join David during his conflict with the king. Mishmannah and his companions were "men of might. . .whose faces were like the faces of lions" (1 Chronicles 12:8).

Only reference: 1 Chronicles 12:10

👥 MISPERETH

of times mentioned: 1
# of MEN by this name: 1

Meaning: Enumeration

Forefather of an exiled family that returned to Judah under Zerubbabel.

Only reference: Nehemiah 7:7

📍 MISREPHOTH-MAIM

of times mentioned: OT 2

Meaning: Burnings of water

Joshua and his troops chased their Canaanite enemies to this place after the battle at the waters of Merom. When Joshua was old, Misrephoth-maim had not yet been possessed by Israel.

First reference: Joshua 11:8 / Last reference: Joshua 13:6

📍 MITHCAH

of times mentioned: OT 2

Meaning: Sweetness

A campsite of the Israelites on their way to the Promised Land.

First reference: Numbers 33:28 / Last reference: Numbers 33:29

👥 MITHREDATH

of times mentioned: 2
# of MEN by this name: 1

Treasurer for Cyrus, king of Persia. He joined in writing a letter of complaint to King Artaxerxes about the rebuilding of Jerusalem.

First reference: Ezra 1:8 / Last reference: Ezra 4:7

📍 MITYLENE

of times mentioned: NT 1

A city on the Greek island of Lesbos. Paul stopped here on his way to Jerusalem at the end of his third missionary journey.

Only reference: Acts 20:14

📍 MIZAR

of times mentioned: OT 1

Meaning: Petty; short (time)

A hill or mountain that the psalmist remembered as he longed for God.

Only reference: Psalm 42:6

📍 MIZPAH

of times mentioned: OT 23

1) A heap of stones set up by Laban and Jacob as a sign of the covenant between them. Same as Galeed and Jegar-sahadutha.

Only reference: Genesis 31:49

2) A city of Benjamin built by King Asa of Judah with stones and timber that King Baasha of Israel had been using to build Ramah.

First reference: 1 Kings 15:22 / Last reference: Nehemiah 3:7

3) At his home base in Mizpah, Gedaliah, the ruler placed over Judah by Babylon's king Nebuchadnezzar, was visited by the captains of Judah's armies. He encouraged them not to fear serving Nebuchadnezzar. But because the Israelites dreaded their Chaldean overlords, Ishmael, son of Nethaniah, and his men in Mizpah killed Gedaliah and his followers.

Ishmael also met eighty men who were headed to Jerusalem with offerings for the Lord. Ishmael left Mizpah, met the men, and invited them into the city, where he killed all but ten of the group. Then he made the rest of the inhabitants of the city captives. Army officer Johanan discovered Ishmael's crimes and fought him and his men. The people of Mizpah supported Johanan, but Ishmael and a few of his men escaped.

First reference: 2 Kings 25:23 / Last reference: Hosea 5:1 / Key references: Jeremiah 40:8–10; 41:1–15

4) The territory co-ruled by Shallum, who made repairs to the gate of the fountain in Jerusalem under Nehemiah's rule.

Only reference: Nehemiah 3:15

5) An area ruled by Ezer, who made repairs in Jerusalem under Nehemiah's rule.

Only reference: Nehemiah 3:19

👥 MIZPAR

of times mentioned: 1
# of MEN by this name: 1

Meaning: Number

Forefather of an exiled family that returned to Judah under Zerubbabel.

Only reference: Ezra 2:2

📍 MIZPEH

of times mentioned: OT 23

1) A Hivite valley near Mount Hermon where Joshua and the Israelites fought Jabin, king of Hazor, and his allies.

First reference: Joshua 11:3 / Last reference: Joshua 11:8

2) A city that became part of the inheritance of the tribe of Judah following the conquest of the Promised Land. Here the Israelites gathered before they went to war against the Benjaminites, who had abused and killed a Levite's concubine. In Mizpeh the Israelites swore that they would never give their daughters as wives to the Benjaminites.

The prophet Samuel called the Israelites to Mizpeh after he told them to give up idolatry. As they were confessing their sin, the Philistines took advantage of the opportunity to attack. The Lord thundered over the Philistines, terrifying them. Israel's army engaged and subdued its enemies. Mizpeh became part of Samuel's regular circuit court as he judged Israel. When Israel demanded a king, Samuel called the people to Mizpeh, where Saul was chosen to rule the nation.

First reference: Joshua 15:38 / Last reference: 1 Samuel 10:17 / Key reference: Judges 20:1–3

3) A city that became part of the inheritance of Benjamin when Joshua cast lots in Shiloh to provide territory for the seven tribes that had yet to receive their land.

Only reference: Joshua 18:26

4) A city where Israel camped before Jephthah the Gileadite led them into battle against the Ammonites. Mizpeh was Jephthah's hometown.

First reference: Judges 10:17 / Last reference: Judges 11:34

5) A city in Moab where David went to ask the king of Moab to protect his parents while he battled King Saul.

Only reference: 1 Samuel 22:3

👥 MIZRAIM

of times mentioned: 4
# of MEN by this name: 1

Meaning: Upper and Lower Egypt

A descendant of Noah through his son Ham.

First reference: Genesis 10:6 / Last reference: 1 Chronicles 1:11

👥 MIZZAH

of times mentioned: 3
# of MEN by this name: 1

Meaning: To faint with fear

A descendant of Abraham's grandson Esau, whose blessing as older brother was taken by the scheming Jacob.

First reference: Genesis 36:13 / Last reference: 1 Chronicles 1:37

👥 MNASON

of times mentioned: 1
# of MEN by this name: 1

An elderly Christian from Cyprus who accompanied Paul to Jerusalem.

Only reference: Acts 21:16

👥 MOAB

of times mentioned: 1
# of MEN by this name: 1

Meaning: From her (the mother's) father

Son of one of Lot's daughters who lay with her father and became pregnant. Moab became the forefather of the Moabites.

Only reference: Genesis 19:37

📍 MOAB

of times mentioned: OT 169

Meaning: From her (the mother's) father

At the time of the Israelites' return to the Promised Land, this nation, which was composed of the descendants of Lot and his older daughter (Genesis 19:37), lay east of the Dead Sea and below the Arnon River. Though it had once covered land north of the river, the Amorite king Sihon had taken Heshbon and the land to the north from Moab's grasp.

At God's command, when they headed for the Promised Land, the Israelites skirted Moab and went through the Amorites' territory. But Moab's king Balak feared the Israelites and asked the pagan prophet Balaam to curse them. When Balaam could not, he counseled Balak to lead Israel into idolatry (Numbers 31:16). His tactic was successful and its effects were long lasting.

Following the death of the judge Othniel, Moab's king Eglon put together an alliance of nations that attacked Israel. As the loser, Israel served Moab for eighteen years until Gera delivered the nation. Ehud killed Eglon, raised up the men of Mount Ephraim, and subdued their former overlords.

Moab periodically took up arms against God's people. It joined Sisera in his attack on Israel. Saul defended his nation from Moab. But when David escaped to the cave Adullam, he asked the king to allow his parents to live in Moab until he could settle his own future. David's parents remained in Moab as long as David was in that land. But as Israel's king, David fought Moab, which became a tributary to Israel.

After Ahab's death Moab rebelled, and Israel and Judah joined forces against King Mesha of Moab. When the battle went against him, Mesha made a sacrifice of his eldest son, and Israel and Judah withdrew. Moab and the Ammonites fought

King Jehoshaphat of Judah. After the nation sought God, Jehoshaphat's army destroyed its enemies.

The prophets speak often of Moab. Isaiah prophesied its destruction and the grief of its people. Jeremiah foretold that Moab's cities would be destroyed and its people would flee. Amos foresaw that Moab would "die with tumult" (Amos 2:2).

First reference: Genesis 36:35 / Last reference: Zephaniah 2:9 / Key references: Numbers 21:26; 22:1–20; Isaiah 15–16; Jeremiah 48:42

👥 MOADIAH

of times mentioned: 1
# of MEN by this name: 1

Meaning: Assembly of God

A priest under the leadership of Joiakim, following the return from exile.

Only reference: Nehemiah 12:17

📍 MOLADAH

of times mentioned: OT 4

Meaning: Birth

A city that became part of the inheritance of the tribe of Judah following the conquest of the Promised Land. It was given to the tribe of Simeon when Joshua cast lots in Shiloh to provide territory for the seven tribes that had yet to receive their land. Moladah was resettled by the Jews after the Babylonian Exile.

First reference: Joshua 15:26 / Last reference: Nehemiah 11:26

👥 MOLID

of times mentioned: 1
# of MEN by this name: 1

Meaning: Genitor

A descendant of Abraham through Jacob's son Judah.

Only reference: 1 Chronicles 2:29

👥 MORDECAI

of times mentioned: 60
# of MEN by this name: 2

1) An exiled Israelite who returned to Judah under Zerubbabel.

First reference: Ezra 2:2 / Last reference: Nehemiah 7:7

2) Cousin of Queen Esther, who was wife of the Persian king Ahasuerus. Though he was an exiled Jew, Mordecai was faithful to his king and warned him of a plot against him by some officers of the king's household. Then Mordecai discovered a plot against the Jews, set up by the king's scheming counselor, Haman. Mordecai warned Esther and encouraged her to confront the king for the good of her people. Before the king and Haman came to the banquet at which she intended to reveal Haman's plans, the king discovered that Mordecai had never been honored for his role in foiling the plot against him. The king commanded Haman to honor Mordecai by publicly proclaiming his deeds.

When Esther revealed Haman's plan against the Jews to her husband, he became angry and commanded that Haman be hanged on the gallows his counselor had prepared for Mordecai. Then he commanded Mordecai to write a law that would defend the Jews against attack and made him first counselor in Haman's place. Mordecai received all Haman's household as a reward.

First reference: Esther 2:5 / Last reference: Esther 10:3 / Key reference: Esther 4:13–14

📍 MOREH

of times mentioned: OT 3

Meaning: An archer; also a teacher or teaching

1) A Canaanite plain where God promised Abraham He would give the land to his descendants.

First reference: Genesis 12:6 / Last reference: Deuteronomy 11:30

2) A hill near the Midianite encampment attacked by Gideon and his three hundred men whom God had chosen by the way they drank water.

Only reference: Judges 7:1

♀ MORESHETH-GATH

of times mentioned: OT 1

Meaning: Possession of Gath

The prophet Micah poetically declared that this place would receive presents (that is, a dowry) because it was going into exile.

Only reference: Micah 1:14

♀ MORIAH

of times mentioned: OT 2

Meaning: Seen of God

The land where God sent Abraham to sacrifice his son Isaac, then provided a ram for the sacrifice instead. On Mount Moriah, in the place where the threshing floor of Ornan the Jebusite had been, Solomon built Jerusalem's temple. Same as Jehovah-jireh.

First reference: Genesis 22:2 / Last reference: 2 Chronicles 3:1

♀ MOSERA

of times mentioned: OT 1

Meaning: Correction or corrections

A place in the wilderness where Aaron died and was buried.

Only reference: Deuteronomy 10:6

♀ MOSEROTH

of times mentioned: OT 2

Meaning: Correction or corrections

A campsite of the Israelites on their way to the Promised Land.

First reference: Numbers 33:30 / Last reference: Numbers 33:31

👥 MOSES

of times mentioned: 848
# of MEN by this name: 1

Meaning: Drawing out (of the water), rescued

The Old Testament prophet through whom God gave Israel the law. Because Pharaoh commanded that all male newborn Israelites should be killed, Moses' mother placed him in a basket in the Nile River. There he was found by an Egyptian princess, who raised him. Once grown, Moses killed a man for abusing an Israelite slave and fled to Midian, where he met God in a burning bush. The Lord sent Moses back to Egypt, where his brother Aaron became his spokesman.

As God's prophet in Egypt, Moses confronted Pharaoh. God visited ten plagues on Egypt because Egypt's ruler would not let Israel go. After all Egypt's firstborn died, Pharaoh finally sent Israel away. But Egyptian troops followed, planning to recapture them. God parted the Red Sea's waters for His people, but the Egyptians were caught in the returning waves. On the way to the Promised Land, God gave His people the Ten Commandments and other laws. At their goal, ten spies sent into Canaan discouraged Israel from entering their Promised Land. So Moses and his people wandered in the desert for forty years. Moses died on Mount Nebo, just before Israel finally entered the Promised Land.

First reference: Exodus 2:10 / Last reference: Revelation 15:3 / Key references: Exodus 3:2–18; 11:4–10; 12:29–30; 14:21–27; 20:1–17; Deuteronomy 34:5

👥 MOZA

of times mentioned: 5
# of MEN by this name: 2

1) A descendant of Abraham through Jacob's son Judah.

Only reference: 1 Chronicles 2:46

2) A descendant of Abraham through Jacob's son Benjamin, in the line of King Saul and his son Jonathan.

First reference: 1 Chronicles 8:36 / Last reference: 1 Chronicles 9:43

♀ MOZAH

of times mentioned: OT 1

Meaning: Drained

A city that became part of the inheritance of Benjamin when Joshua cast lots in Shiloh to provide territory for the seven tribes that had yet to receive their land.

Only reference: Joshua 18:26

👥 MUPPIM

of times mentioned: 1
# of MEN by this name: 1

Meaning: Wavings

A son of Benjamin and descendant of Abraham.

Only reference: Genesis 46:21

👥 MUSHI

of times mentioned: 8
# of MEN by this name: 1

Meaning: Sensitive

A descendant of Abraham through Jacob's son Levi.

First reference: Exodus 6:19 / Last reference: 1 Chronicles 24:30

📍 MYRA

of times mentioned: NT 1

A city of Lycia where Paul and his companions stopped on their voyage to Rome. Here the centurion who was in charge of their journey found an Alexandrian ship headed for Italy.

Only reference: Acts 27:5

📍 MYSIA

of times mentioned: NT 2

A northwestern region of the Roman province of Asia. Paul and Silas visited Mysia before they were called to Macedonia.

First reference: Acts 16:7 / Last reference: Acts 16:8

👥 NAAM

of times mentioned: 1
# of MEN by this name: 1

Meaning: Pleasure

A descendant of Abraham through Jacob's son Judah. Naam was Caleb's son.

Only reference: 1 Chronicles 4:15

👥 NAAMAH

of times mentioned: 4
# of WOMEN by this name: 2

Meaning: Pleasantness

1) A descendant of Cain and sister of Tubal-cain.

Only reference: Genesis 4:22

2) Mother of King Rehoboam, she was an Ammonite.

First reference: 1 Kings 14:21 / Last reference: 2 Chronicles 12:13

📍 NAAMAH

of times mentioned: OT 1

Meaning: Pleasantness

A city that became part of the inheritance of the tribe of Judah following the conquest of the Promised Land.

Only reference: Joshua 15:41

👥 NAAMAN

of times mentioned: 17
# of MEN by this name: 4

Meaning: Pleasantness

1) A son of Benjamin and a descendant of Abraham.

Only reference: Genesis 46:21

2) A descendant of Abraham through Jacob's son Benjamin.

First reference: Numbers 26:40 / Last reference: 1 Chronicles 8:4

3) Another descendant of Abraham through Jacob's son Benjamin.

Only reference: 1 Chronicles 8:7

4) Leprous captain of the Syrian army who came to the prophet Elisha for healing. Angered that Elisha told him to wash seven times in the Jordan River, he had to be persuaded to obey. When he did, he was healed.

First reference: 2 Kings 5:1 / Last reference: Luke 4:27

NAARAH

of times mentioned: 3
# of WOMEN by this name: 1

Meaning: Girl

Wife of Ashur, who was a descendant of Abraham through Jacob's son Judah.

First reference: 1 Chronicles 4:5 / Last reference: 1 Chronicles 4:6

NAARAI

of times mentioned: 1
# of MEN by this name: 1

Meaning: Youthful

One of King David's valiant warriors.

Only reference: 1 Chronicles 11:37

NAARAN

of times mentioned: OT 1

Meaning: Youthful

A city on the border of the tribe of Ephraim's territory. Naaran lay east of Bethel. Same as Naarath.

Only reference: 1 Chronicles 7:28

NAARATH

of times mentioned: OT 1

Meaning: A girl (from infancy to adolescence)

A city on the border of the tribe of Ephraim's territory. Same as Naaran.

Only reference: Joshua 16:7

NAASHON

of times mentioned: 1
# of MEN by this name: 1

Meaning: Enchanter

Brother of Elisheba, Aaron's wife.

Only reference: Exodus 6:23

NAASSON

of times mentioned: 3
# of MEN by this name: 1

Genealogy of Jesus: Yes (Luke 3:32)

A descendant of Abraham through Isaac; forebear of Jesus' earthly father, Joseph.

First reference: Matthew 1:4 / Last reference: Luke 3:32

NABAL

of times mentioned: 22
# of MEN by this name: 1

Meaning: Dolt

The churlish first husband of Abigail. Nabal refused to give David and his men anything in return for their protection of his lands during David's battles with Saul. Nabal's wife stepped in and generously provided them with food. When her husband heard what she had done, "his heart died within him" (1 Samuel 25:37). Ten days later, he died.

First reference: 1 Samuel 25:3 / Last reference: 2 Samuel 3:3 / Key references: 1 Samuel 25:5–11, 37–38

NABOTH

of times mentioned: 22
# of MEN by this name: 1

Meaning: Fruits

Owner of a vineyard that was coveted by King Ahab of Israel. When Naboth refused to trade his inheritance for another vineyard, Ahab became sulky. Discovering her husband in this mood, Queen Jezebel conspired to get Naboth's property.

She ordered the leaders of Naboth's town to get two men to accuse Naboth of blasphemy. After the innocent man had been stoned, Ahab took possession of his land.

First reference: 1 Kings 21:1 / Last reference: 2 Kings 9:26 / Key references: 1 Kings 21:2–4, 7–16

👥 NACHON

of times mentioned: 1
# of MEN by this name: 1

Meaning: Prepared

Owner of the threshing floor at which Uzzah died for touching the ark of the covenant.

Only reference: 2 Samuel 6:6

👥 NACHOR

of times mentioned: 2
# of MEN by this name: 2

Meaning: Snorer

1) Brother of Abraham. Same as Nahor (2).

Only reference: Joshua 24:2

2) A descendant of Abraham through Isaac; forebear of Jesus' earthly father, Joseph.

Only reference: Luke 3:34

Genealogy of Jesus: Yes (Luke 3:34)

👥 NADAB

of times mentioned: 20
# of MEN by this name: 4

Meaning: Liberal

1) A son of Aaron who, along with his brother Abihu, offered strange fire before the Lord. God sent fire from His presence to consume them, and they died.

First reference: Exodus 6:23 / Last reference: 1 Chronicles 24:2 / Key reference: Numbers 3:4

2) Son of Jeroboam, king of Israel, who inherited Jeroboam's throne. Nadab did evil and made his country sin. Baasha conspired against Nadab and killed him at Gibbethon before usurping his throne.

First reference: 1 Kings 14:20 / Last reference: 1 Kings 15:31

3) A descendant of Abraham through Jacob's son Judah.

First reference: 1 Chronicles 2:28 / Last reference: 1 Chronicles 2:30

4) A descendant of Abraham through Jacob's son Benjamin.

First reference: 1 Chronicles 8:30 / Last reference: 1 Chronicles 9:36

👥 NAGGE

of times mentioned: 1
# of MEN by this name: 1

Genealogy of Jesus: Yes (Luke 3:25)

A descendant of Abraham through Isaac; forebear of Jesus' earthly father, Joseph.

Only reference: Luke 3:25

📍 NAHALAL

of times mentioned: OT 1

Meaning: Pasture

One of the forty-eight cities given to the Levites as God had commanded. Nahalal was given to them by the tribe of Zebulun. Same as Nahallal and Nahalol.

Only reference: Joshua 21:35

📍 NAHALIEL

of times mentioned: OT 1

Meaning: Valley of God

A campsite of the Israelites during their years in the wilderness.

Only reference: Numbers 21:19

📍 NAHALLAL

of times mentioned: OT 1

Meaning: Pasture

A city that became part of the inheritance of Zebulun when Joshua cast lots in Shiloh to provide territory for the seven tribes that had yet to receive their land. Same as Nahalal and Nahalol.

Only reference: Joshua 19:15

NAHALOL

of times mentioned: OT 1

Meaning: Pasture

A city that became part of the inheritance of the tribe of Zebulun. The people of Zebulun never drove the Canaanites out of Nahalol. Same as Nahalal and Nahallal.

Only reference: Judges 1:30

NAHAM

of times mentioned: 1
# of MEN by this name: 1

A descendant of Jacob through his son Judah.

Only reference: 1 Chronicles 4:19

NAHAMANI

of times mentioned: 1
# of MEN by this name: 1

Meaning: Consolatory

Forefather of an exiled family that returned to Judah under Zerubbabel.

Only reference: Nehemiah 7:7

NAHARAI

of times mentioned: 1
# of MEN by this name: 1

Meaning: Snorer

One of King David's valiant warriors. Same as Nahari.

Only reference: 1 Chronicles 11:39

NAHARI

of times mentioned: 1
# of MEN by this name: 1

Meaning: Snorer

One of King David's valiant warriors. Same as Naharai.

Only reference: 2 Samuel 23:37

NAHASH

of times mentioned: 9
# of MEN by this name: 3

1) King of the Ammonites. Saul raised an army against him, won, and was made king over Gilgal.

First reference: 1 Samuel 11:1 / Last reference: 1 Samuel 12:12

2) Father of a man who brought food and supplies to King David and his soldiers as they fled from the army of David's son Absalom.

First reference: 2 Samuel 10:2 / Last reference: 1 Chronicles 19:2

3) Grandfather of Absalom's commander Amasa.

Only reference: 2 Samuel 17:25

NAHATH

of times mentioned: 5
# of MEN by this name: 3

Meaning: Quiet

1) A descendant of Abraham's grandson Esau, whose blessing as older brother was taken by the scheming Jacob.

First reference: Genesis 36:13 / Last reference: 1 Chronicles 1:37

2) A descendant of Abraham through Jacob's son Levi.

Only reference: 1 Chronicles 6:26

3) A temple overseer during the reign of King Hezekiah of Judah.

Only reference: 2 Chronicles 31:13

NAHBI

of times mentioned: 1
# of MEN by this name: 1

Meaning: Occult

One of the twelve spies sent by Moses to spy out the land of Canaan.

Only reference: Numbers 13:14

NAHOR

of times mentioned: 17
# of MEN by this name: 2

Meaning: Snorer

1) Grandfather of Abram (Abraham).

First reference: Genesis 11:22 / Last reference: 1 Chronicles 1:26

2) Brother of Abram (Abraham) and son of Terah. He married Milcah. When Abram left Haran, Nahor stayed behind. He had eight sons with Milcah and four with his concubine. His son Laban became Jacob's father-in-law. Same as Nachor (1).

First reference: Genesis 11:26 / Last reference: Genesis 31:53 / Key references: Genesis 22:20; 24:15

NAHSHON

of times mentioned: 9
# of MEN by this name: 1

Meaning: Enchanter

Captain and prince of the tribe of Judah, he was appointed by God through Moses. Nahshon was a forefather of Boaz.

First reference: Numbers 1:7 / Last reference: 1 Chronicles 2:11

NAHUM

of times mentioned: 1
# of MEN by this name: 1

Meaning: Comfortable

An Old Testament minor prophet who came from Elkosh. He preached to Judah after Assyria had captured Israel.

Only reference: Nahum 1:1

NAIN

of times mentioned: NT 1

A Galilean city. As Jesus and a crowd of followers approached the city gate, a funeral procession for a young man came out. Jesus had compassion on his mother, a widow, and brought her son back to life.

Only reference: Luke 7:11

NAIOTH

of times mentioned: OT 6

Meaning: Residence

After David's wife Michal saved him from King Saul's attempts to kill him, David escaped to the prophet Samuel in Ramah. Together the two men went to Naioth, a place where prophets lived, in or near Ramah. When Saul heard that David was there, he sent men to capture him. Though he sent three groups of men, before they could capture David they all began to prophesy. When Saul went himself, he also prophesied. Meanwhile, David left Naioth to seek Jonathan's help.

First reference: 1 Samuel 19:18 / Last reference: 1 Samuel 20:1

NAOMI

of times mentioned: 21
# of WOMEN by this name: 1

Meaning: Pleasant

Elimelech's wife, Naomi, and her family moved to Moab during a famine. Following the deaths of her husband and two sons, Naomi and her daughter-in-law Ruth returned to Bethlehem. Ruth supported them by gleaning fields until Boaz, Elimelech's relative, became their kinsman-redeemer, buying Elimelech's inherited land and marrying Ruth. Naomi became nurse to their son, Obed, who was considered her grandson.

First reference: Ruth 1:2 / Last reference: Ruth 4:17 / Key references: Ruth 1:6, 20–22; 2:1–2; 4:3–6, 14–17

👥 NAPHISH

of times mentioned: 2
# of MEN by this name: 1

Meaning: Refreshed

A son of Ishmael.

First reference: Genesis 25:15 / Last reference:
1 Chronicles 1:31

👥 NAPHTALI

of times mentioned: 8
# of MEN by this name: 1

Meaning: My wrestling

A son of Jacob and founder of one of Israel's twelve
tribes. Naphtali was the second son of Bilhah,
Rachel's maid. When his father blessed him, he
called Napthali "a hind let loose; he giveth godly
words" (Genesis 49:21).

First reference: Genesis 30:8 / Last reference:
Ezekiel 48:34

📍 NAPHTALI

of times mentioned: OT 41

Meaning: My wrestling

The land belonging to the tribe of Naphtali was one
of the northernmost inheritances, lying between
Asher and the northeastern lands of Manasseh,
with Zebulun and Issachar on its southern flank.
The western shore of the Sea of Galilee and the
northernmost section of the west bank of the Jordan
River were part of its territory. Kedesh, Hazor, Dan,
and Merom lay within Naphtali's borders. The tribe
did not drive out the original inhabitants of Beth-
shemesh and Beth-anath, but lived among them
and made them pay tribute.

Under King Solomon's governmental organization, the territory of Naphtali was responsible for
supplying provisions for the king.

Ben-hadad, king of Syria, allied himself with
King Asa of Judah and fought against Naphtali.
During the reign of Pekah, king of Israel, the
Assyrian king Tiglath-pileser conquered Naphtali
and carried its inhabitants to his own land.

Josiah, king of Judah, broke down the idols of
Manasseh, Ephraim, and Simeon as far as Naphtali

and burned the bones of the pagan priests on their
own altars.

First reference: Numbers 1:15 / Last reference:
Ezekiel 48:4 / Key references: 1 Kings 15:20;
2 Kings 15:29; 2 Chronicles 34:1–6

👥 NARCISSUS

of times mentioned: 1
# of MEN by this name: 1

Meaning: Narcissus (flower)

Head of a household of believers, Narcissus was
greeted by Paul in his letter to the Romans.

Only reference: Romans 16:11

👥 NATHAN

of times mentioned: 43
# of MEN by this name: 10

Meaning: Given

1) A son of King David, born in Jerusalem.

First reference: 2 Samuel 5:14 / Last reference:
Luke 3:31

Genealogy of Jesus: Yes (Luke 3:31)

2) The prophet who confronted King David about
his sin with Bath-sheba. Though Nathan had encouraged David to build the temple, he had to
tell the king that his son would build it at God's
command. When David sinned with Bath-sheba,
the prophet told him a parable that described his
sin against her husband, Uriah. As the king became angry about the wrong, Nathan revealed it as
David's own, and the king repented. Nathan warned
Bath-sheba when her son Solomon's claim to the
throne was endangered by his brother Adonijah.
Together the prophet and Bath-sheba told David
of the threat.

First reference: 2 Samuel 7:2 / Last reference:
Psalm 51 (title) / Key references: 2 Samuel 7:3–12;
12:1–15; 1 Kings 1:11–14, 23–27

3) Father of Igal, one of David's mighty men.

Only reference: 2 Samuel 23:36

4) Father of a prince who commanded King
Solomon's officers.

Only reference: 1 Kings 4:5

5) Father of an officer under King Solomon who was also the king's friend.

Only reference: 1 Kings 4:5

6) A descendant of Abraham through Jacob's son Judah. Nathan descended from the line of an unnamed Israelite woman and her Egyptian husband, Jarha.

Only reference: 1 Chronicles 2:36

7) Brother of a valiant man in King David's army.

Only reference: 1 Chronicles 11:38

8) A Jewish exile charged with finding Levites and temple servants to travel to Jerusalem with Ezra.

Only reference: Ezra 8:16

9) An exiled Israelite who married a "strange" (foreign) woman.

Only reference: Ezra 10:39

10) One who will mourn at the piercing of the Messiah when God defends Jerusalem.

Only reference: Zechariah 12:12

NATHANAEL

of times mentioned: 6
# of MEN by this name: 1

A disciple from Cana who first heard of Jesus from His disciple Philip and wondered, "Can there be any good thing come out of Nazareth?" (John 1:46). Jesus described him as an Israelite in whom there was no guile. Quickly Nathanael recognized Jesus as Son of God and King of Israel and followed Him. Probably the same as Bartholomew.

First reference: John 1:45 / Last reference: John 21:2

NATHAN-MELECH

of times mentioned: 1
# of MEN by this name: 1

Meaning: Given of the king

A court official under 2 King Josiah of Judah.

Only reference: 2 Kings 23:11

NAUM

of times mentioned: 1
# of MEN by this name: 1

Genealogy of Jesus: Yes (Luke 3:25)

A descendant of Abraham through Isaac; forebear of Jesus' earthly father, Joseph.

Only reference: Luke 3:25

NAZARETH

of times mentioned: NT 29

In this village of Galilee, the virgin Mary heard the news that she would bear the Messiah. After the death of Herod the Great, Joseph brought Mary and Jesus out of Egypt and back to live in Nazareth, which was beyond the reach of Archelaus, son of Herod the Great.

Here Jesus announced the beginning of His ministry and the fulfillment of the promise of the Good News and liberty for God's people. Furious, the people of His hometown tried to kill Him (Luke 4:28–29). Matthew's account tells us that their unbelief caused Him not to do many miracles there (Matthew 13:58). Though Jesus moved to Capernaum and stayed there during His early ministry, He is frequently referred to in scripture as Jesus of Nazareth.

Nathanael had no good opinion of the village and wondered if anything good could come from it (John 1:46).

First reference: Matthew 2:23 / Last reference: Acts 26:9 / Key references: Matthew 2:19–23; Luke 1:26–29; 4:16–19

NEAH

of times mentioned: OT 1

Meaning: Motion

A city that became part of the inheritance of Zebulun when Joshua cast lots in Shiloh to provide territory for the seven tribes that had yet to receive their land.

Only reference: Joshua 19:13

♀ NEAPOLIS

of times mentioned: NT 1

Meaning: A youth (up to about forty years)

The port of Philippi. Paul and his companions stopped in Neapolis on their way to the important city of Macedonia.

Only reference: Acts 16:11

👥 NEARIAH

of times mentioned: 3
# of MEN by this name: 2

Meaning: Servant of God

1) A descendant of Abraham through Jacob's son Judah, in the line of the nation of Judah's third-to-last king, Jeconiah (also known as Jehoiachin).

First reference: 1 Chronicles 3:22 / Last reference: 1 Chronicles 3:23

2) A captain over the sons of Simeon during the reign of King Hezekiah of Judah.

Only reference: 1 Chronicles 4:42

👥 NEBAI

of times mentioned: 1
# of MEN by this name: 1

Meaning: Fruitful

An Israelite who signed an agreement declaring that the exiles from Babylon would repent and obey God.

Only reference: Nehemiah 10:19

👥 NEBAIOTH

of times mentioned: 1
# of MEN by this name: 1

Meaning: Fruitfulness

A variant spelling of Nebajoth.

Only reference: 1 Chronicles 1:29

👥 NEBAJOTH

of times mentioned: 3
# of MEN by this name: 1

Meaning: Fruitfulness

Ishmael's firstborn son. Nebajoth's sister married Esau. Same as Nebaioth.

First reference: Genesis 25:13 / Last reference: Genesis 36:3

♀ NEBALLAT

of times mentioned: OT 1

Meaning: Foolish secrecy

A town of Benjamin resettled by the Jews after the Babylonian Exile.

Only reference: Nehemiah 11:34

👥 NEBAT

of times mentioned: 25
# of MEN by this name: 1

Meaning: Regard

Father of King Jeroboam (1). Jeroboam was King Solomon's servant, a mighty man of valor, and king over Israel after Solomon's death and the division of his kingdom.

First reference: 1 Kings 11:26 / Last reference: 2 Chronicles 13:6

👥 NEBO

of times mentioned: 1
# of MEN by this name: 1

Father of several exiled Israelites who married "strange" (foreign) women.

Only reference: Ezra 10:43

♀ NEBO

of times mentioned: OT 11

Meaning: Name of a Babylonian god

1) A city east of the Jordan River that the Reubenites requested as part of their inheritance because it had good grazing land for cattle. After inheriting Nebo, the Reubenites built it up. Isaiah foretold that Moab would howl over the city, and Ezekiel foresaw that it would be spoiled in war.

First reference: Numbers 32:3 / Last reference: Jeremiah 48:22

2) Mount Nebo was a Moabite mountain near Jericho. Before he died in Moab, Moses went from the plains of Moab to Mount Nebo and on to Mount Pisgah, where he got a clear view of the new land his people would inherit.

First reference: Deuteronomy 32:49 / Last reference: Deuteronomy 34:1

3) A city in Judah to which captives returned after the Babylonian Exile.

First reference: Ezra 2:29 / Last reference: Nehemiah 7:33

👥 NEBUCHADNEZZAR

\# of times mentioned: 60
\# of MEN by this name: 1

Twice this king of Babylon besieged Jerusalem, took its king, and brought Judah's people into exile. King Jehoiakim of Judah had been Nebuchadnezzar's vassal for three years when he rebelled. Nebuchadnezzar attacked Jerusalem and took him and his family, with his servants, princes, and officers. He left only the poorest people in the nation's capital. Babylon's king also took the treasures of the palace and temple.

Zedekiah, made king by Nebuchadnezzar, also rebelled. When his city was starving, the king and his soldiers fled. Nebuchadnezzar pursued, captured Zedekiah, killed his sons before him, put out his eyes, and carried him to Babylon.

The prophet Daniel was one of Nebuchadnezzar's captives. He received a vision of the king's dream and interpreted it. Nebuchadnezzar made him a great man in Babylon. When Daniel's three friends, Shadrach, Meshach, and Abed-nego, refused to worship an idol, Nebuchadnezzar had them thrown into a fiery furnace, but they were not consumed. Amazed, the king declared that no one should speak anything amiss about their God and then promoted the three men to higher positions. Daniel prophesied that Nebuchadnezzar would be driven out from among people and eat grass until he recognized the Lord as the supreme God. Same as Nebuchadrezzar.

First reference: 2 Kings 24:1 / Last reference: Daniel 5:18 / Key references: 2 Kings 24:1, 10, 12–14; 2 Kings 25:1, 6–7, 9–10; Daniel 2:28–48; 3:13–30; 4:25–36

👥 NEBUCHADREZZAR

\# of times mentioned: 31
\# of MEN by this name: 1

King of Babylon. Variant spelling for Nebuchadnezzar.

First reference: Jeremiah 21:2 / Last reference: Ezekiel 30:10 / Key references: Jeremiah 21:7; 39:1; 52:12; Ezekiel 26:7

👥 NEBUSHASBAN

\# of times mentioned: 1
\# of MEN by this name: 1

A Babylonian official who, at King Nebuchadnezzar's command, showed kindness to the prophet Jeremiah.

Only reference: Jeremiah 39:13

👥 NEBUZAR-ADAN

\# of times mentioned: 15
\# of MEN by this name: 1

Captain of the guard for King Nebuchadnezzar of Babylon. He burned Jerusalem when Nebuchadnezzar attacked King Zedekiah of Judah. Nebuzar-adan carried the Israelite captives to Babylon. He brought some important prisoners to his king, who killed them. Before he left Israel, Nebuzar-adan commanded the captain of the guard there not to harm the prophet Jeremiah, and Jeremiah was freed into Gedaliah's care.

First reference: 2 Kings 25:8 / Last reference: Jeremiah 52:30 / Key references: 2 Kings 25:8–12, 18–21; Jeremiah 39:11–12

👥 NECHO

\# of times mentioned: 3
\# of MEN by this name: 1

A king of Egypt who attacked Carchemish. King Josiah of Judah fought him and was killed in the battle. Necho made Jehoiakim king in Josiah's place.

First reference: 2 Chronicles 35:20 / Last reference: 2 Chronicles 36:4

👥 NEDABIAH

of times mentioned: 1
# of MEN by this name: 1

Meaning: Largesse of God

A descendant of Abraham through Jacob's son Judah, in the line of the nation of Judah's third-to-last king, Jeconiah (also known as Jehoiachin).

Only reference: 1 Chronicles 3:18

👥 NEHEMIAH

of times mentioned: 8
# of MEN by this name: 3

Meaning: Consolation of God

1) Forefather of an exiled family that returned to Judah under Zerubbabel.

First reference: Ezra 2:2 / Last reference: Nehemiah 7:7

2) Sent at his own request, by the Persian king Artaxerxes, to rebuild Jerusalem, Nehemiah became the governor of Jerusalem. Under his rule, Jerusalem's walls were rebuilt.

First reference: Nehemiah 1:1 / Last reference: Nehemiah 12:47

3) A man who repaired Jerusalem's walls under Nehemiah.

Only reference: Nehemiah 3:16

👥 NEHUM

of times mentioned: 1
# of MEN by this name: 1

Meaning: Comforted

Forefather of an exiled family that returned to Judah under Zerubbabel.

Only reference: Nehemiah 7:7

👥 NEHUSHTA

of times mentioned: 1
# of WOMEN by this name: 1

Meaning: Copper

Mother of King Jehoiachin of Judah.

Only reference: 2 Kings 24:8

📍 NEIEL

of times mentioned: OT 1

Meaning: Moved of God

A city that became part of the inheritance of Asher when Joshua cast lots in Shiloh to provide territory for the seven tribes that had yet to receive their land.

Only reference: Joshua 19:27

📍 NEKEB

of times mentioned: OT 1

Meaning: Dell

A city that became part of the inheritance of Naphtali when Joshua cast lots in Shiloh to provide territory for the seven tribes that had yet to receive their land.

Only reference: Joshua 19:33

👥 NEKODA

of times mentioned: 4
# of MEN by this name: 2

Meaning: Distinction, marked

1) Forefather of an exiled family that returned to Judah under Zerubbabel.

First reference: Ezra 2:48 / Last reference: Nehemiah 7:50

2) Another forefather of an exiled family that returned to Judah under Zerubbabel.

First reference: Ezra 2:60 / Last reference: Nehemiah 7:62

 NEMUEL

of times mentioned: 3
# of MEN by this name: 2

Meaning: Day of God

1) A Reubenite counted in the census taken by Moses and Aaron.

Only reference: Numbers 26:9

2) A descendant of Abraham through Jacob's son Simeon. Same as Jemuel.

First reference: Numbers 26:12 / Last reference: 1 Chronicles 4:24

NEPHEG

of times mentioned: 4
# of MEN by this name: 2

Meaning: To spring forth; a sprout

1) A descendant of Abraham through Jacob's son Levi.

Only reference: Exodus 6:21

2) A son of King David, born in Jerusalem.

First reference: 2 Samuel 5:15 / Last reference: 1 Chronicles 14:6

NEPHISHESIM

of times mentioned: 1
# of MEN by this name: 1

Meaning: To scatter; expansions

Forefather of an exiled family that returned to Judah under Zerubbabel.

Only reference: Nehemiah 7:52

NEPHTHALIM

of times mentioned: NT 2

Meaning: To fall down

On the borders of Nephthalim, the land of the tribe of Naphtali, Jesus lived at the beginning of His ministry. By doing so He fulfilled a prophecy that the people of this area would see a great light.

First reference: Matthew 4:13 / Last reference: Matthew 4:15

NEPHTOAH

of times mentioned: OT 2

Meaning: Opened

A spring of water near Jerusalem that was on the border of the tribe of Judah's territory.

First reference: Joshua 15:9 / Last reference: Joshua 18:15

NEPHUSIM

of times mentioned: 1
# of MEN by this name: 1

Meaning: To scatter; expansions

Forefather of an exiled family that returned to Judah under Zerubbabel.

Only reference: Ezra 2:50

NER

of times mentioned: 16
# of MEN by this name: 1

Meaning: Lamp

Grandfather of King Saul and father of Abner, Saul's army commander, who was called Abner son of Ner.

First reference: 1 Samuel 14:50 / Last reference: 1 Chronicles 26:28

NEREUS

of times mentioned: 1
# of MEN by this name: 1

Meaning: Wet

A Christian whom Paul greeted in his letter to the church at Rome.

Only reference: Romans 16:15

👥 NERGAL-SHAREZER

of times mentioned: 3
# of MEN by this name: 2

1) A prince of Babylon who besieged Jerusalem during the reign of King Zedekiah of Judah.

Only reference: Jeremiah 39:3

2) Another Babylonian prince who took part in the destruction of Jerusalem under King Nebuchadnezzar. Nergal-sharezer was an official who, at Nebuchadnezzar's command, showed kindness to the prophet Jeremiah.

First reference: Jeremiah 39:3 / Last reference: Jeremiah 39:13

👥 NERI

of times mentioned: 1
# of MEN by this name: 1

Genealogy of Jesus: Yes (Luke 3:27)

A descendant of Abraham through Isaac; forebear of Jesus' earthly father, Joseph.

Only reference: Luke 3:27

👥 NERIAH

of times mentioned: 10
# of MEN by this name: 1

Meaning: Light of God

Father of Baruch, the scribe of the prophet Jeremiah.

First reference: Jeremiah 32:12 / Last reference: Jeremiah 51:59

👥 NETHANEEL

of times mentioned: 14
# of MEN by this name: 10

Meaning: Given of God

1) Head of the tribe of Issachar during Israel's wandering after they failed to enter the Promised Land.

First reference: Numbers 1:8 / Last reference: Numbers 10:15

2) A descendant of Abraham through Jacob's son Judah.

Only reference: 1 Chronicles 2:14

3) A priest who blew a trumpet before the ark of the covenant when David brought it to Jerusalem.

Only reference: 1 Chronicles 15:24

4) A descendant of Abraham through Jacob's son Levi.

Only reference: 1 Chronicles 24:6

5) A Levite "porter" (doorkeeper) in the house of the Lord.

Only reference: 1 Chronicles 26:4

6) A prince of Judah sent by King Jehoshaphat to teach the law of the Lord throughout the nation.

Only reference: 2 Chronicles 17:7

7) A chief Levite who provided for the first Passover celebration under King Josiah of Judah.

Only reference: 2 Chronicles 35:9

8) An exiled Israelite priest who married a "strange" (foreign) woman.

Only reference: Ezra 10:22

9) Forefather of a priest who returned to Jerusalem under Zerubbabel.

Only reference: Nehemiah 12:21

10) A priest who helped to dedicate the rebuilt walls of Jerusalem by playing a musical instrument.

Only reference: Nehemiah 12:36

👥 NETHANIAH

of times mentioned: 20
# of MEN by this name: 4

Meaning: Given of God

1) The father of a man named Ishmael, who killed the Judean governor placed over the land by the Babylonian king Nebuchadnezzar.

First reference: 2 Kings 25:23 / Last reference: Jeremiah 41:18 / Key reference: Jeremiah 41:1–2

2) A son of King David's musician Asaph, "which prophesied according to the order of the king" (1 Chronicles 25:2).

First reference: 1 Chronicles 25:2 / Last reference: 1 Chronicles 25:12

3) A Levite sent by King Jehoshaphat to teach the law of the Lord throughout the nation of Judah.

Only reference: 2 Chronicles 17:8

4) Father of Jehudi. His son carried a message from King Josiah's court to Jeremiah's scribe, commanding him to read to Judah's princes the word that God sent through the prophet.

Only reference: Jeremiah 36:14

📍 NETOPHAH

of times mentioned: OT 2

Meaning: Distillation

A city in Judah to which captives returned after the Babylonian Exile.

First reference: Ezra 2:22 / Last reference: Nehemiah 7:26

👥 NEZIAH

of times mentioned: 2
# of MEN by this name: 1

Meaning: Conspicuous

Forefather of an exiled family that returned to Judah under Zerubbabel.

First reference: Ezra 2:54 / Last reference: Nehemiah 7:56

📍 NEZIB

of times mentioned: OT 1

Meaning: Station

A city that became part of the inheritance of the tribe of Judah following the conquest of the Promised Land.

Only reference: Joshua 15:43

📍 NIBSHAN

of times mentioned: OT 1

A city that became part of the inheritance of the tribe of Judah following the conquest of the Promised Land.

Only reference: Joshua 15:62

👥 NICANOR

of times mentioned: 1
# of MEN by this name: 1

Meaning: Victorious

One of seven men, "full of the Holy Ghost and wisdom," selected to serve needy Christians in Jerusalem while the twelve disciples devoted themselves to prayer, and to the ministry of the word." (Acts 6:3–4).

Only reference: Acts 6:5

📍 NICOPOLIS

of times mentioned: NT 1

Meaning: Victorious city

A Greek city where Paul planned to spend the winter when he wrote his epistle to Titus. Though the greeting of Paul's letter describes it as a Macedonian city, scholars believe Nicopolis was probably the Roman-built city at Epirus.

Only reference: Titus 3:12

👥 NIGER

of times mentioned: 1
# of MEN by this name: 1

Meaning: Black

A prophet and teacher in the church at Antioch in the time of the apostle Paul. Also called Simeon (4).

Only reference: Acts 13:1

📍 NIMRAH

of times mentioned: OT 1

Meaning: Clear water

A city east of the Jordan River that the Reubenites and Gadites requested as part of their inheritance because it had good grazing land for cattle.

Only reference: Numbers 32:3

♀ NIMRIM

of times mentioned: OT 2

Meaning: Clear waters

A Moabite stream that the prophets Isaiah and Jeremiah foretold would become desolate because of God's judgment.

First reference: Isaiah 15:6 / Last reference: Jeremiah 48:34

👥 NIMROD

of times mentioned: 4
# of MEN by this name: 1

A descendant of Noah through his son Ham. Nimrod was "mighty upon the earth" (1 Chronicles 1:10), and he built the city of Nineveh.

First reference: Genesis 10:8 / Last reference: Micah 5:6

👥 NIMSHI

of times mentioned: 5
# of MEN by this name: 1

Meaning: Extricated

Father of King Jehu of Israel, whom God anointed to kill off the line of King Ahab of Israel.

First reference: 1 Kings 19:16 / Last reference: 2 Chronicles 22:7

♀ NINEVE

of times mentioned: NT 1

Meaning: Greek form of Nineveh

Jesus warned the Jews that the people of Nineve, who had repented under Jonah's message, would rise up in judgment of them because they did not repent when they heard His preaching. Same as Nineveh.

Only reference: Luke 11:32

♀ NINEVEH

of times mentioned: OT 17 / NT 1

An ancient city built by Asshur that became the capital of the Assyrian Empire. Nineveh was located on the Tigris River's eastern bank. When the Assyrian king Sennacherib attacked Jerusalem, God killed his troops, so the frightened king returned to Nineveh.

God sent Jonah to preach repentance to this large city, which took a journey of three days to cross. Amazingly, Nineveh's king declared that everyone in the city should repent, and the people repented, fasting and putting on sackcloth. Therefore God did not destroy the city as He had warned He would do.

But about a century later, the prophet Nahum spoke of God's anger at the city, which had become the Lord's enemy, and foretold its destruction.

Matthew records Jesus' warning to the Jews that the people of Nineveh would judge them for their lack of repentance. Same as Nineve.

First reference: Genesis 10:11 / Last reference: Matthew 12:41 / Key references: 2 Kings 19:36; Jonah 3; Nahum 1:1–2:1; 3:7

♀ NO

of times mentioned: OT 5

Another name for Upper (southern) Egypt's capital, Thebes. The prophet Jeremiah warned that Egypt, including No, would be destroyed from the north. The prophet Ezekiel foresaw the city being judged and its inhabitants being "cut off" and "rent asunder." The prophet Nahum asked Nineveh if it was better than No, which was carried into captivity.

First reference: Jeremiah 46:25 / Last reference: Nahum 3:8

👥 NOADIAH

of times mentioned: 2
# of MEN by this name: 1
# of WOMEN by this name: 1

Meaning: Convened of God

1) A Levite who weighed the temple vessels after the Babylonian Exile.

Only reference: Ezra 8:33

2) A prophetess who opposed Nehemiah as he rebuilt Jerusalem's wall.

Only reference: Nehemiah 6:14

NOAH

\# of times mentioned: 53
\# of MEN by this name: 1
\# of WOMEN by this name: 1

Meaning: Rest

1) The man God chose to build an ark that would save both animals and people. God gave Noah specific building directions. When his boat-building project was finished, he and his family entered the ark and brought in seven of every clean animal and two of the unclean. God caused it to rain for forty days and nights until the world was flooded and everything else on earth was destroyed. For 150 days the ark floated, until the waters abated and the vessel rested on the mountains of Ararat. Noah tested the land by sending out a raven and then a dove. When the dove did not return, he knew that dry land had appeared. God commanded Noah and his family to leave the ark, and they went out. Noah made a sacrifice. Then God promised Noah and his sons that He would never curse the earth by flood again. Same as Noe.

First reference: Genesis 5:29 / Last reference: 2 Peter 2:5 / Key references: Genesis 6:8–9, 14–16; 7:2–5, 24; 8:6–12, 20; 9:11–17

2) One of Zelophehad's five daughters who received his inheritance because he had no sons. Each had to marry within their tribe, which was Manasseh.

First reference: Numbers 26:33 / Last reference: Joshua 17:3

NOB

\# of times mentioned: OT 6

Meaning: Fruit

At this "city of the priests" (1 Samuel 22:19), David came to the high priest, Ahimelech, when he was fleeing from King Saul's wrath. At David's request, the priest gave him the showbread from the altar as well as Goliath's sword. After David fled to Gath, Saul heard from Doeg the Edomite that the priest had supported his enemy. The king commanded Doeg to kill the priests of Nob. The Edomite killed eighty-five priests, as well as men, women, and children and the city's animals.

The tribe of Benjamin resettled Nob after the Babylonian Exile.

First reference: 1 Samuel 21:1 / Last reference: Isaiah 10:32

NOBAH

\# of times mentioned: 2
\# of MEN by this name: 1

Meaning: A bark

A man who took Kenath and its villages for his inheritance when Moses divided the Promised Land between the tribes.

Only reference: Numbers 32:42

NOBAH

\# of times mentioned: OT 1

Meaning: A bark

After he conquered Kenath and its villages, the warrior Nobah renamed the town after himself (Numbers 32:42). Same as Kenath.

Only reference: Judges 8:11

NOD

\# of times mentioned: OT 1

Meaning: Vagrancy

A land east of Eden where Cain lived after he murdered his brother Abel.

Only reference: Genesis 4:16

NOE

\# of times mentioned: 5
\# of MEN by this name: 1

Meaning: Noah

Greek spelling of Noah, used in the New Testament.

First reference: Matthew 24:37 / Last reference: Luke 17:27

NOGAH

of times mentioned: 2
# of MEN by this name: 1

Meaning: Brilliancy

A son of King David, born in Jerusalem.

First reference: 1 Chronicles 3:7 / Last reference:
1 Chronicles 14:6

NOHAH

of times mentioned: 1
# of MEN by this name: 1

Meaning: Quietude

A descendant of Abraham through Jacob's son
Benjamin. Nohah was Benjamin's fourth son.

Only reference: 1 Chronicles 8:2

NON

of times mentioned: 1
# of MEN by this name: 1

Meaning: Perpetuity

Variant spelling of Nun, father of the Israelite leader
Joshua.

Only reference: 1 Chronicles 7:27

NOPH

of times mentioned: OT 7

Another name for Memphis, the ancient capital of
Lower (northern) Egypt. In an oracle about Egypt,
Isaiah declared that Noph's princes had been deceived and they had seduced their nation.
 Following the Babylonian conquest of Judah,
some of the Jews fled into Egypt and lived at Noph.
But Jeremiah prophesied that Nebuchadnezzar
would conquer Egypt as well, and Nopf would be
desolate. Ezekiel also predicted the city's destruction.

First reference: Isaiah 19:13 / Last reference:
Ezekiel 30:16

NOPHAH

of times mentioned: OT 1

Meaning: A gust

A Moabite city that the Amorites had taken from
them. The Israelites destroyed Nophah when they
conquered the Amorite lands on their way to the
Promised Land.

Only reference: Numbers 21:30

NUN

of times mentioned: 29
# of MEN by this name: 1

Meaning: Perpetuity

A descendant of Abraham through Joseph's son
Ephraim and the father of the Israelite leader
Joshua. Same as Non.

First reference: Exodus 33:11 / Last reference:
Nehemiah 8:17

NYMPHAS

of times mentioned: 1
# of WOMEN by this name: 1

Meaning: Nymph given

A Colossian Christian who had a house church in
her home.

Only reference: Colossians 4:15

OBADIAH

of times mentioned: 20
# of MEN by this name: 13

Meaning: Serving God

1) "Governor" of King Ahab of Israel's household
and a man who feared God. Obadiah hid one hundred prophets in a cave when Queen Jezebel sought
to kill them. Looking for water for Ahab's cattle, he
met Elijah, who sent him to the king with the news
that he had returned to Israel.

First reference: 1 Kings 18:3 / Last reference:
1 Kings 18:16

2) A descendant of Abraham through Jacob's son Judah, in the line of the nation's third-to-last king, Jeconiah (also known as Jehoiachin).

Only reference: 1 Chronicles 3:21

3) A descendant of Abraham through Jacob's son Issachar.

Only reference: 1 Chronicles 7:3

4) A descendant of Abraham through Jacob's son Benjamin, in the line of King Saul and his son Jonathan.

First reference: 1 Chronicles 8:38 / Last reference: 1 Chronicles 9:44

5) A Jewish exile from the tribe of Levi who resettled Jerusalem.

Only reference: 1 Chronicles 9:16

6) One of several warriors from the tribe of Gad who left Saul to join David during his conflict with the king. Obadiah and his companions were "men of might. . .whose faces were like the faces of lions" (1 1 Chronicles 12:8).

Only reference: 1 Chronicles 12:9

7) Ruler of the tribe of Zebulun in the days of King David.

Only reference: 1 Chronicles 27:19

8) A prince of Judah sent by King Jehoshaphat to teach the law of the Lord throughout the nation.

Only reference: 2 Chronicles 17:7

9) An overseer of the men who repaired the temple under King Josiah of Judah.

Only reference: 2 Chronicles 34:12

10) A Jewish exile who returned from Babylon to Judah under Ezra.

Only reference: Ezra 8:9

11) A priest who renewed the covenant under Nehemiah.

Only reference: Nehemiah 10:5

12) A Levite "porter" (doorkeeper) in the house of the Lord.

Only reference: Nehemiah 12:25

13) An Old Testament minor prophet who spoke God's words against Edom.

Only reference: Obadiah 1:1

👥 OBAL

of times mentioned: 1
# of MEN by this name: 1

A descendant of Noah through his son Shem.

Only reference: Genesis 10:28

👥 OBED

of times mentioned: 13
# of MEN by this name: 5

Meaning: Serving

1) A descendant of Abraham through Isaac; forebear of Jesus' earthly father, Joseph.

First reference: Ruth 4:17 / Last reference: Luke 3:32

Genealogy of Jesus: Yes (Luke 3:32)

2) A descendant of Abraham through Jacob's son Judah. Obed descended from the line of an unnamed Israelite woman and her Egyptian husband, Jarha.

First reference: 1 Chronicles 2:37 / Last reference: 1 Chronicles 2:38

3) One of King David's warriors known as the "mighty men."

Only reference: 1 Chronicles 11:47

4) A Levite "porter" (doorkeeper) in the house of the Lord.

Only reference: 1 Chronicles 26:7

5) Father of a captain of hundreds under the priest Jehoiada.

Only reference: 2 Chronicles 23:1

👥 OBED-EDOM

of times mentioned: 20
# of MEN by this name: 3

Meaning: Worker of Edom

1) Owner of a house where the ark of the covenant was kept for three months before David brought it to Jerusalem. God blessed Obed-edom's household while it held the ark.

First reference: 2 Samuel 6:10 / Last reference: 1 Chronicles 15:25

2) A Levite musician who performed in celebration when King David brought the ark of the covenant to Jerusalem. He was also gatekeeper at Jerusalem's South Gate.

First reference: 1 Chronicles 15:18 / Last reference: 1 Chronicles 26:15

3) A man who worked in the temple treasury when Joash, king of Israel, invaded and looted the temple.

Only reference: 2 Chronicles 25:24

OBIL

of times mentioned: 1
# of MEN by this name: 1

Meaning: Mournful

A servant of King David, Obil was in charge of the royal camels.

Only reference: 1 Chronicles 27:30

📍 OBOTH

of times mentioned: OT 4

Meaning: Water skins

A campsite of the Israelites on their way to the Promised Land.

First reference: Numbers 21:10 / Last reference: Numbers 33:44

👥 OCRAN

of times mentioned: 5
# of MEN by this name: 1

Meaning: Muddler

Father of Pagiel, a chief of the tribe of Asher who helped Moses take a census of Israel.

First reference: Numbers 1:13 / Last reference: Numbers 10:26

ODED

of times mentioned: 3
# of MEN by this name: 2

Meaning: Reiteration

1) Father of Azariah (10) the prophet.

First reference: 2 Chronicles 15:1 / Last reference: 2 Chronicles 15:8

2) A prophet who warned the Israelites not to enslave their fellow Jewish citizens whom they had captured when King Pekah led them into battle.

Only reference: 2 Chronicles 28:9

👥 OG

of times mentioned: 22
# of MEN by this name: 1

Meaning: Round

The Amorite king of Bashan, whom Moses defeated after Israel failed to enter the Promised Land. Israel took sixty cities from him. News of Og's destruction spread to Rahab and the Gibeonites, who feared Israel's power.

First reference: Numbers 21:33 / Last reference: Psalm 136:20 / Key references: Deuteronomy 3:1–4; Joshua 2:10; 9:10

👥 OHAD

of times mentioned: 2
# of MEN by this name: 1

Meaning: Unity

A son of Simeon and descendant of Abraham.

First reference: Genesis 46:10 / Last reference: Exodus 6:15

👥 OHEL

of times mentioned: 1
# of MEN by this name: 1

Meaning: A tent

A descendant of Abraham through Jacob's son Judah, in the line of the nation of Judah's third-to-last king, Jeconiah (also known as Jehoiachin). Only reference: 1 Chronicles 3:20

OLIVET

of times mentioned: OT 1 / NT 1

Meaning: An olive (as yielding illuminating oil)

A mountain ridge east of Jerusalem. King David fled from his son Absalom, grieving as he ascended the Olivet ridge. Luke describes it as "a Sabbath day's journey" outside the city. From here Jesus ascended into heaven. Also called the Mount of Olives.

First reference: 2 Samuel 15:30 / Last reference: Acts 1:12

 OLYMPAS

# of times mentioned: 1
# of MEN by this name: 1

Meaning: Olympian bestowed or heaven descended

A Christian whom Paul greeted in his letter to the church at Rome.

Only reference: Romans 16:15

 OMAR

# of times mentioned: 3
# of MEN by this name: 1

Meaning: Talkative

A descendant of Abraham's grandson Esau, whose blessing as older brother was taken by the scheming Jacob.

First reference: Genesis 36:11 / Last reference: 1 Chronicles 1:36

OMRI

of times mentioned: 18
# of MEN by this name: 4

Meaning: Heaping

1) Commander of Israel's army under King Elah. After Zimri killed Elah, the people made Omri king. Omri and his army besieged Zimri at Tirzah and took the city. Omri overcame those who supported Tibni for king. He did evil and made Israel sin.

First reference: 1 Kings 16:16 / Last reference: Micah 6:16 / Key reference: 1 Kings 16:16–22

2) A descendant of Abraham through Jacob's son Benjamin. A son of Beker.

Only reference: 1 Chronicles 7:8

3) Father of a returned exile, Uthai, who was head of his father's household.

Only reference: 1 Chronicles 9:4

4) A ruler of the tribe of Issachar under David.

Only reference: 1 Chronicles 27:18

ON

of times mentioned: 1
# of MEN by this name: 1

Meaning: Ability, power, wealth

Forefather of Korah (3).

Only reference: Numbers 16:1

 ON

# of times mentioned: OT 3

An Egyptian city northeast of Memphis. On was the home of Joseph's wife, Asenath. Her father was a priest there. Same as Aven (1).

First reference: Genesis 41:45 / Last reference: Genesis 46:20

ONAM

of times mentioned: 4
# of MEN by this name: 2

Meaning: Strong

1) A descendant of Seir, who lived in Esau's "land of Edom."

First reference: Genesis 36:23 / Last reference: 1 Chronicles 1:40

2) A descendant of Abraham through Jacob's son Judah.
First reference: 1 Chronicles 2:26 / Last reference: 1 Chronicles 2:28

👥 ONAN

of times mentioned: 8
# of MEN by this name: 1

Meaning: Strong

Second son of Jacob's son Judah and his Canaanite wife. Onan refused to sire a son with his brother's widow, whom he had married, because the boy would be considered his brother's child. God put Onan to death for this.

First reference: Genesis 38:4 / Last reference: 1 Chronicles 2:3

👥 ONESIMUS

of times mentioned: 2
# of MEN by this name: 1

Meaning: Profitable

A slave of Philemon, Onesimus fled his master and met Paul, who led him to Christ. In his epistle to Philemon, Paul interceded for Onesimus.

First reference: Colossians 4:9 / Last reference: Philemon 1:10

👥 ONESIPHORUS

of times mentioned: 2
# of MEN by this name: 1

Meaning: Profit bearer

An Ephesian Christian whose household refreshed Paul. Onesiphorus visited Paul while he was imprisoned in Rome.

First reference: 2 Timothy 1:16 / Last reference: 2 Timothy 4:19

📍 ONO

of times mentioned: OT 5

Meaning: Strong

1) A village built by the Benjaminites. It was resettled by them after the Babylonian Exile.

First reference: 1 Chronicles 8:12 / Last reference: Nehemiah 11:35

2) A plain that may be the valley of the craftsmen mentioned in Nehemiah 11:35. In one of the villages here, Sanballat and Geshem wanted to meet Nehemiah to do him harm, but he did not fall for their ploy.

Only reference: Nehemiah 6:2

📍 OPHEL

of times mentioned: OT 5

Meaning: A mound

A walled part of Jerusalem near the Temple Mount. It was the home of the Nethinims, who were temple servants.

First reference: 2 Chronicles 27:3 / Last reference: Nehemiah 11:21

👥 OPHIR

of times mentioned: 2
# of MEN by this name: 1

A descendant of Noah through his son Shem.

First reference: Genesis 10:29 / Last reference: 1 Chronicles 1:23

📍 OPHIR

of times mentioned: OT 11

A place, possibly in Arabia, Africa, or India, that became a byword for its trade in fine gold. Hiram (or Huram), king of Tyre, sent his navy to bring the precious metal and stones and almug trees from Ophir. King David collected stores of Ophir's gold to line the temple that his son Solomon would build. Solomon joined with Huram to acquire 450 additional talents of gold. King Jehoshaphat of Judah attempted to raise a navy to become part of this trade, but it was destroyed at the port of Eziongeber.

First reference: 1 Kings 9:28 / Last reference: Isaiah 13:12

📍 OPHNI

of times mentioned: OT 1

Meaning: An inhabitant of Ophen

A city that became part of the inheritance of Benjamin when Joshua cast lots in Shiloh to provide territory for the seven tribes that had yet to receive their land.

Only reference: Joshua 18:24

👥 OPHRAH

of times mentioned: 1
# of MEN by this name: 1

Meaning: A female fawn

A descendant of Abraham through Jacob's son Judah.

Only reference: 1 Chronicles 4:14

📍 OPHRAH

of times mentioned: OT 7

Meaning: A female fawn

1) A city that became part of the inheritance of Benjamin when Joshua cast lots in Shiloh to provide territory for the seven tribes that had yet to receive their land.

First reference: Joshua 18:23 / Last reference: 1 Samuel 13:17

2) A city called Ophrah of the Abiezrites where an angel visited Gideon and called him a "mighty man of valour" (Judges 6:12). Gideon built an altar there and named it Jehovah-shalom. After Gideon was buried in Ophrah, his son Abimelech killed sixty-nine of his seventy brothers in their father's home.

First reference: Judges 6:11 / Last reference: Judges 9:5

👥 OREB

of times mentioned: 5
# of MEN by this name: 1

Meaning: Mosquito

A prince of Midian who was killed by the tribe of Ephraim when Gideon called the tribe to fight that nation.

First reference: Judges 7:25 / Last reference: Psalm 83:11

📍 OREB

of times mentioned: OT 1

Meaning: A raven

A rock where the Midianites were slaughtered. Isaiah compares this event to the scourge God will stir up against Assyria.

Only reference: Isaiah 10:26

👥 OREN

of times mentioned: 1
# of MEN by this name: 1

A descendant of Abraham through Jacob's son Judah.

Only reference: 1 Chronicles 2:25

👥 ORNAN

of times mentioned: 12
# of MEN by this name: 1

Meaning: Strong

The owner of a threshing floor where King David saw the angel of the Lord, after he had sinned by taking a census. The angel commanded David to build an altar there, so David tried to buy the land from Ornan. Ornan refused his money, but David insisted and paid him 600 shekels for the land. Same as Araunah.

First reference: 1 Chronicles 21:15 / Last reference: 2 Chronicles 3:1

👥 ORPAH

of times mentioned: 2
# of WOMEN by this name: 1

Meaning: Mane

Naomi's daughter-in-law who did not follow her to Bethlehem.

First reference: Ruth 1:4 / Last reference: Ruth 1:14

👥 OSEE

of times mentioned: 1
# of MEN by this name: 1

Greek form of the name Hoshea.

Only reference: Romans 9:25

👥 OSHEA

of times mentioned: 2
# of MEN by this name: 1

Meaning: Deliverer

Variant spelling of the name Joshua. Same as Joshua (1).

First reference: Numbers 13:8 / Last reference: Numbers 13:16

👥 OTHNI

of times mentioned: 1
# of MEN by this name: 1

Meaning: To force, forcible

A Levite "porter" (doorkeeper) in the house of the Lord whose father was Shemiah.

Only reference: 1 Chronicles 26:7

👥 OTHNIEL

of times mentioned: 6
# of MEN by this name: 1

Meaning: Force of God

Caleb's brother, who by capturing Kirjath-sepher won the hand of Caleb's daughter, Achsah, in marriage. Othniel delivered Israel from the king of Mesopotamia and judged Israel for forty years.

First reference: Joshua 15:17 / Last reference: 1 Chronicles 4:13

👥 OZEM

of times mentioned: 2
# of MEN by this name: 2

Meaning: To be strong, strength

1) King David's brother, Jesse's sixth son.

Only reference: 1 Chronicles 2:15

2) A descendant of Abraham through Jacob's son Judah.

Only reference: 1 Chronicles 2:25

👥 OZIAS

of times mentioned: 2
# of MEN by this name: 1

Genealogy of Jesus: Yes (Matthew 1:8–9)

A descendant of Abraham through Isaac; forebear of Jesus' earthly father, Joseph.

First reference: Matthew 1:8 / Last reference: Matthew 1:9

👥 OZNI

of times mentioned: 1
# of MEN by this name: 1

Meaning: Having quick ears

A descendant of Abraham through Jacob's son Gad.

Only reference: Numbers 26:16

👥 PAARAI

of times mentioned: 1
# of MEN by this name: 1

Meaning: Yawning

One of King David's warriors known as the "mighty men."

Only reference: 2 Samuel 23:35

📍 PADAN

of times mentioned: OT 1

Meaning: A plateau

A name for Padan-aram that Jacob uses when he tells of his leaving there for his homeland. Same as Padan-aram.

Only reference: Genesis 48:7

📍 PADAN-ARAM

of times mentioned: OT 10

Meaning: The tableland of Aram

An area of northern Mesopotamia around the city of Haran, Padan-aram was Rebekah's homeland before she married Isaac. When Jacob needed a bride, his father sent him to Padan-aram to marry one of Laban's daughters. Jacob remained there fourteen years, serving his father-in-law for his two daughters, Leah and Rachel. During these years, Jacob's twelve sons were born. When Jacob left Padanaram, God blessed him and gave him the covenant name Israel. Same as Padan.

First reference: Genesis 25:20 / Last reference: Genesis 46:15

👥 PADON

of times mentioned: 2
# of MEN by this name: 1

Meaning: Ransom

Forefather of an exiled family that returned to Judah under Zerubbabel.

First reference: Ezra 2:44 / Last reference: Nehemiah 7:47

👥 PAGIEL

of times mentioned: 5
# of MEN by this name: 1

Meaning: Accident of God

A chief of the tribe of Asher who helped Moses take a census of Israel.

First reference: Numbers 1:13 / Last reference: Numbers 10:26

👥 PAHATH-MOAB

of times mentioned: 6
# of MEN by this name: 3

Meaning: Pit of Moab

1) Father of a man who repaired Jerusalem's walls under Nehemiah. Some of his descendants married "strange" (foreign) women.

First reference: Ezra 2:6 / Last reference: Nehemiah 7:11

2) Forefather of a Jewish exile who returned from Babylon to Judah under Ezra.

Only reference: Ezra 8:4

3) A Jewish leader who renewed the covenant under Nehemiah.

Only reference: Nehemiah 10:14

📍 PAI

of times mentioned: OT 1

Meaning: Screaming

The capital city of Hadad, king of Edom.

Only reference: 1 Chronicles 1:50

👥 PALAL

of times mentioned: 1
# of MEN by this name: 1

Meaning: Judge

A man who repaired Jerusalem's walls under Nehemiah.

Only reference: Nehemiah 3:25

📍 PALESTINA

of times mentioned: OT 3

Meaning: Rolling (that is, migratory)

A name for the land of the Philistines, the strip of land next to the Mediterranean Sea. The song of Moses and the Israelites, following the crossing of the Red Sea, spoke of the sorrow that would engulf the people of this land as Israel came to the Promised Land. The prophet Isaiah prophesied against Palestina. By the time of the New Testament, the name had come to describe the entire land of the Jews. Same as Palestine.

First reference: Exodus 15:14 / Last reference: Isaiah 14:31

⚲ PALESTINE

of times mentioned: OT 1

Meaning: Rolling (that is, migratory)

An ancient name for the land of the Philistines, the strip of land next to the Mediterranean Sea. By the time of the New Testament, the name had come to describe the entire land of the Jews. The name Palestine is used only once in scripture, when the prophet Joel speaks of God's judgment of Palestine for its sins. Same as Palestina.

Only reference: Joel 3:4

⚎ PALLU

of times mentioned: 4
# of MEN by this name: 1

Meaning: Distinguished

A descendant of Abraham through Jacob's son Reuben.

First reference: Exodus 6:14 / Last reference: 1 Chronicles 5:3

⚎ PALTI

of times mentioned: 1
# of MEN by this name: 1

Meaning: Delivered

A spy from the tribe of Benjamin who reported that Israel could not take the Promised Land.

Only reference: Numbers 13:9

⚎ PALTIEL

of times mentioned: 1
# of MEN by this name: 1

Meaning: Deliverance of God

Prince of the tribe of Issachar when the Israelites entered the Promised Land.

Only reference: Numbers 34:26

⚲ PAMPHYLIA

of times mentioned: NT 5

Meaning: Every tribal (meaning heterogeneous)

A province on the southern coast of Asia Minor, between Lycia and Cilicia. At Pentecost, people from this province heard the Christians speak in their own tongue. Paul and Barnabas first brought the Gospel to Pamphylia when they preached in the city of Perga. Mark had joined them on this mission but left them here, so Paul refused to take him on his next journey. On his way to Rome, Paul sailed past Pamphylia.

First reference: Acts 2:10 / Last reference: Acts 27:5

⚲ PANNAG

of times mentioned: OT 1

Meaning: Pastry

Some scholars believe this is the name of a pastry, while others connect it with a place between Damascus and Baalbec.

Only reference: Ezekiel 27:17

⚲ PAPHOS

of times mentioned: NT 2

Cyprus's capital city, where Paul and Barnabas confronted the Jewish sorcerer Elymas, who was perverting the Gospel message. When the two apostles declared the Gospel to the proconsul, Sergius Paulus, Elymas tried to turn him away from the truths of the Gospel. Paul saw Elymas as God's enemy, confronted him, and told him he would be blind for a time. The sorcerer lost his sight, and the proconsul believed.

First reference: Acts 13:6 / Last reference: Acts 13:13

⚲ PARAH

of times mentioned: OT 1

Meaning: Heifer

A city that became part of the inheritance of Benjamin when Joshua cast lots in Shiloh to provide territory for the seven tribes that had yet to receive their land.

Only reference: Joshua 18:23

📍 PARAN

of times mentioned: OT 11

Meaning: Ornamental

The wilderness in Sinai where Ishmael and his mother lived after Abraham sent Hagar away with the boy. During the Exodus, Israel camped here while the twelve spies investigated the Promised Land. After Samuel died, David went to Paran, where he asked Nabal for food and was refused. Nabal's wife, Abigail, came to David's rescue and prevented him from fighting her foolish husband. King Solomon's opponent, Hadad the Edomite, was supported by men of Paran when he fled to Egypt as a boy.

First reference: Genesis 21:21 / Last reference: Habakkuk 3:3

📍 PARBAR

of times mentioned: OT 1

Translated "at Parbar westward" in the KJV and "as far as the court to the west" in the NIV, this somewhat obscure phrase refers to an area near the temple, perhaps a suburb by the west wall.

Only reference: 1 Chronicles 26:18

👥 PARMASHTA

of times mentioned: 1
# of MEN by this name: 1

One of ten sons of Haman, the villain of the story of Esther.

Only reference: Esther 9:9

👥 PARMENAS

of times mentioned: 1
# of MEN by this name: 1

Meaning: Constant

One of seven men, "full of the Holy Ghost and wisdom," selected to serve needy Christians in Jerusalem while the twelve disciples devoted themselves "to prayer, and to the ministry of the word" (Acts 6:3–4).

Only reference: Acts 6:5

👥 PARNACH

of times mentioned: 1
# of MEN by this name: 1

Forefather of Elizaphan, prince of the tribe of Zebulun when the Israelites entered the Promised Land.

Only reference: Numbers 34:25

👥 PAROSH

of times mentioned: 5
# of MEN by this name: 4

Meaning: A flea

1) Forefather of an exiled family that returned to Judah under Zerubbabel.

First reference: Ezra 2:3 / Last reference: Nehemiah 7:8

2) An exiled Israelite who married a "strange" (foreign) woman.

Only reference: Ezra 10:25

3) Father of a man who repaired Jerusalem's walls under Nehemiah.

Only reference: Nehemiah 3:25

4) A Jewish leader who renewed the covenant under Nehemiah.

Only reference: Nehemiah 10:14

👥 PARSHANDATHA

of times mentioned: 1
# of MEN by this name: 1

One of ten sons of Haman, the villain of the story of Esther.

Only reference: Esther 9:7

👥 PARUAH

of times mentioned: 1
# of MEN by this name: 1

Meaning: Blossomed

Father of one of King Solomon's officers who provided food for the royal household.

Only reference: 1 Kings 4:17

📍 PARVAIM

of times mentioned: OT 1

A place from which King Solomon brought gold to decorate the temple.

Only reference: 2 Chronicles 3:6

👥 PASACH

of times mentioned: 1
# of MEN by this name: 1

Meaning: Divider

A descendant of Abraham through Jacob's son Asher.

Only reference: 1 Chronicles 7:33

📍 PAS-DAMMIM

of times mentioned: OT 1

Meaning: Palm (that is, dell) of bloodshed

A place where David and his men fought the Philistines in a field of barley. After fleeing from their enemy, David's troops turned and made their stand in the middle of the field, and God gave them the victory. David's mighty man Eleazar was with him at this battle.

Only reference: 1 Chronicles 11:13

👥 PASEAH

of times mentioned: 3
# of MEN by this name: 3

Meaning: Limping

1) A descendant of Abraham through Jacob's son Judah.

Only reference: 1 Chronicles 4:12

2) Forefather of an exiled family that returned to Judah under Zerubbabel.

Only reference: Ezra 2:49

3) Father of a man who repaired Jerusalem's walls under Nehemiah.

Only reference: Nehemiah 3:6

👥 PASHUR

of times mentioned: 14
# of MEN by this name: 4

Meaning: Liberation

1) Forefather of a priest who resettled Jerusalem after the Babylonian Exile.

First reference: 1 Chronicles 9:12 / Last reference: Nehemiah 11:12

2) A priest who renewed the covenant under Nehemiah.

Only reference: Nehemiah 10:3

3) A priest and "chief governor" of the temple who responded to Jeremiah's prophecies by hitting him and putting him in the stocks near the temple. When Pashur removed him from the stocks, the prophet gave him a new name, Magor-missabib, meaning "afright from around," because he would become a terror to himself and others as God gave Judah over to Babylon.

First reference: Jeremiah 20:1 / Last reference: Jeremiah 38:1

4) A prince of Judah who sought to have King Zedekiah kill Jeremiah because of his negative prophecy.

First reference: Jeremiah 21:1 / Last reference: Jeremiah 38:1

📍 PATARA

of times mentioned: NT 1

A city on the coast of Asia Minor in the Roman province of Lycia. On his way to Jerusalem, Paul stopped here to board a ship headed for Phoenicia.

Only reference: Acts 21:1

📍 PATHROS

of times mentioned: OT 5

A name for Upper (southern) Egypt. From here God promised to recover a remnant of His people when Christ's kingdom is established. But the prophet Jeremiah prophesied to the Jews of his day, who had fled from the Babylonians to Egypt, that they would be destroyed. When Ezekiel prophesied against Egypt, he foretold that after its destruction, God would gather a remnant of that nation in Pathros.

First reference: Isaiah 11:11 / Last reference: Ezekiel 30:14

📍 PATMOS

of times mentioned: NT 1

An island in the Aegean Sea, west of Asia Minor and southwest of the island of Samos. Here John was imprisoned for the sake of the Gospel and received the revelation that became the last book of the New Testament.

Only reference: Revelation 1:9

👥 PATROBAS

of times mentioned: 1
# of MEN by this name: 1

Meaning: Father's life

A Christian whom Paul greeted in his letter to the church at Rome.

Only reference: Romans 16:14

📍 PAU

of times mentioned: OT 1

Meaning: Screaming

An Edomite city ruled by King Hadar.

Only reference: Genesis 36:39

👥 PAUL

of times mentioned: 157
# of MEN by this name: 1

Meaning: Little

Latin name for Saul; God's chosen apostle to the Gentiles. Paul zealously persecuted Christians until he became one himself as he traveled to Damascus and was confronted by Jesus. Scripture begins calling him Paul when he and Barnabas set out on Paul's first missionary journey, to Galatia. Paul and Barnabas disagreed over bringing John Mark on a second missionary venture and split up. Paul brought Silas and Timothy on his next journey and later added Luke to the group. After Paul received a vision, they traveled to Macedonia. The apostle and his disciples made two more missionary journeys to the churches of Asia and Greece. He communicated with the churches through his epistles to the Romans, Corinthians, Galatians, Colossians, Thessalonians, and a letter to Titus. These form part of his contribution to the New Testament.

Constrained by the Spirit, Paul went to Jerusalem. In the temple he was rescued from a riot by the Roman tribune, who arrested him. Following a plot to kill him, Paul was sent to Caesarea, where he stayed two years while Felix delayed making a decision on his case. Paul appealed to Caesar, but on his way to Rome was shipwrecked. He finally arrived in Rome, where he lived for two years. He may have been released but then rearrested. During his time in prison, he wrote additional epistles that became scripture: Ephesians, probably Philippians, the letters to Timothy, and Philemon. Church tradition records that the emperor Nero martyred Paul. Same as Saul (3).

First reference: Acts 13:9 / Last reference: 2 Peter 3:15 / Key references: Acts 15:1–21; 17:22–33; 21:27–35; 25:8; 28:30–31

👥 PAULUS

of times mentioned: 1
# of MEN by this name: 1

Meaning: Little

Sergius Paulus was a proconsul of Cyprus who called on Barnabas and Saul to share their faith with him.

Only reference: Acts 13:7

PEDAHEL

of times mentioned: 1
# of MEN by this name: 1

Meaning: God has ransomed

Prince of the tribe of Naphtali when the Israelites entered the Promised Land.

Only reference: Numbers 34:28

PEDAHZUR

of times mentioned: 5
# of MEN by this name: 1

Meaning: A rock (God) has ransomed

Father of a chief of the tribe of Benjamin who helped Moses take a census.

First reference: Numbers 1:10 / Last reference: Numbers 10:23

PEDAIAH

of times mentioned: 8
# of MEN by this name: 6

Meaning: God has ransomed

1) Grandfather of King Jehoiakim of Judah.

Only reference: 2 Kings 23:36

2) A descendant of Abraham through Jacob's son Judah, in the line of the nation of Judah's third-to-last king, Jeconiah (also known as Jehoiachin).

First reference: 1 Chronicles 3:18 / Last reference: 1 Chronicles 3:19

3) Father of a leader of the half tribe of Manasseh under King David.

Only reference: 1 Chronicles 27:20

4) A man who repaired Jerusalem's walls under Nehemiah.

Only reference: Nehemiah 3:25

5) A priest who assisted Ezra in reading the book of the law to the people of Jerusalem. Nehemiah also appointed him one of the temple treasurers.

First reference: Nehemiah 8:4 / Last reference: Nehemiah 13:13

6) An exile of Benjamin's line who returned to Jerusalem and lived there.

Only reference: Nehemiah 11:7

PEKAH

of times mentioned: 11
# of MEN by this name: 1

Meaning: Watch

Captain of King Pekahiah of Israel, Pekah conspired against his king, killed him, and usurped his throne. Pekah was an evil king. The Assyrian king Tigleth-pileser conquered portions of Israel during Pekah's reign.

First reference: 2 Kings 15:25 / Last reference: Isaiah 7:1

PEKAHIAH

of times mentioned: 3
# of MEN by this name: 1

Meaning: God has answered

Evil ruler of Israel who succeeded his father, Menahem, as king. Pekah consipired against Pekahiah and usurped his throne.

First reference: 2 Kings 15:22 / Last reference: 2 Kings 15:26

PEKOD

of times mentioned: OT 2

Meaning: Punishment

A symbolic name for the Babylonians (or Chaldeans), used by the prophets as they foretold God's judgment of Babylon.

First reference: Jeremiah 50:21 / Last reference: Ezekiel 23:23

PELAIAH

of times mentioned: 3
# of MEN by this name: 3

Meaning: God has distinguished

1) A descendant of Abraham through Jacob's son Judah, in the line of the nation of Judah's third-to-last king, Jeconiah (also known as Jehoiachin).

Only reference: 1 Chronicles 3:24

2) A Levite who helped Israel to understand the law after Ezra read it to them.

Only reference: Nehemiah 8:7

3) A Levite who helped Ezra to explain the law to exiles returned to Jerusalem.

Only reference: Nehemiah 10:10

👥 PELALIAH

of times mentioned: 1
# of MEN by this name: 1

Meaning: God has judged

Forefather of a priest who returned to Jerusalem after the Babylonian Exile.

Only reference: Nehemiah 11:12

👥 PELATIAH

of times mentioned: 5
# of MEN by this name: 4

Meaning: God has delivered

1) A descendant of Abraham through Jacob's son Judah, in the line of the nation of Judah's third-to-last king, Jeconiah (also known as Jehoiachin).

Only reference: 1 Chronicles 3:21

2) A descendant of King David through David's son Solomon.

Only reference: 1 Chronicles 4:42

3) A Jewish leader who renewed the covenant under Nehemiah.

Only reference: Nehemiah 10:22

4) A prince of Judah and a wicked counselor who died as Ezekiel prophesied against Jerusalem.

First reference: Ezekiel 11:1 / Last reference: Ezekiel 11:13

👥 PELEG

of times mentioned: 7
# of MEN by this name: 1

Meaning: Earthquake

A descendant of Noah through his son Ham. Same as Phalec.

First reference: Genesis 10:25 / Last reference: 1 Chronicles 1:25

👥 PELET

of times mentioned: 2
# of MEN by this name: 2

Meaning: Escape

1) A descendant of Abraham through Jacob's son Judah.

Only reference: 1 Chronicles 2:47

2) A "mighty man" who supported the future king David during his conflict with Saul.

Only reference: 1 Chronicles 12:3

👥 PELETH

of times mentioned: 2
# of MEN by this name: 1

Meaning: To flee, swiftness

Forefather of a Reubenite who joined Korah in rebellion against Moses.

First reference: Numbers 16:1 / Last reference: 1 Chronicles 2:33

📍 PENIEL

of times mentioned: OT 1

Meaning: Face of God

The place near the ford of the Jabbok River where Jacob wrestled with a man and was given the name Israel. The man wrenched Jacob's hip near the tendon, ending the match, and he told Jacob he had struggled with God and man and had overcome. Jacob declared he had met God face-to-face, and his life was preserved. Same as Penuel.

Only reference: Genesis 32:30

 PENINNAH

of times mentioned: 3
# of WOMEN by this name: 1

Meaning: A pearl; round

Elkanah's wife who had children and provoked his wife Hannah, who was barren.

First reference: 1 Samuel 1:2 / Last reference: 1 Samuel 1:4

PENUEL

of times mentioned: 2
# of MEN by this name: 2

Meaning: Face of God

1) A descendant of Abraham through Jacob's son Judah.

Only reference: 1 Chronicles 4:4

2) A descendant of Abraham through Jacob's son Benjamin.

Only reference: 1 Chronicles 8:25

PENUEL

of times mentioned: OT 5

Meaning: Face of God

The place near the ford of the Jabbok River where Jacob wrestled with a man and was given the name Israel. The man wrenched Jacob's hip near the tendon, ending the match, and Jacob left the place limping.

When Gideon asked the men of the city of Penuel to help his army, they refused. Gideon promised that when he finished chasing the kings of Midian, he would break down their tower. He kept his promise, destroying the tower and killing the men of the city. Same as Peniel.

First reference: Genesis 32:31 / Last reference: Judges 8:17

PEOR

of times mentioned: OT 1

Meaning: A gap

A Moabite mountain to which King Balak brought Balaam. The king wanted the pagan prophet to curse the Israelites before they entered the Promised Land.

Only reference: Numbers 23:28

PERAZIM

of times mentioned: OT 1

The prophet Isaiah reminded the people of Judah that God had risen up in anger on this mountain. The Lord would rise up again to do His work, the prophet told them. Perhaps the same as Baal-perazim.

Only reference: Isaiah 28:21

PERESH

of times mentioned: 1
# of MEN by this name: 1

A descendant of Abraham through Joseph's son Manasseh.

Only reference: 1 Chronicles 7:16

PEREZ

of times mentioned: 3
# of MEN by this name: 2

Meaning: A break

1) Forefather of a commander in David's army. Same as Phares and Pharez.

Only reference: 1 Chronicles 27:3

2) A Jewish exile from the tribe of Judah who re-settled Jerusalem.

First reference: Nehemiah 11:4 / Last reference: Nehemiah 11:6

PEREZ-UZZA

of times mentioned: OT 1

Meaning: Break of Uzza

The threshing floor of Chidon (also called Nachon), where Uzza put out his hand to steady the ark of the covenant as the oxen stumbled. God killed Uzza.

Angered at God's wrath against the man, King David gave the place this name. Same as Perez-uzzah.

Only reference: 1 Chronicles 13:11

📍 PEREZ-UZZAH

of times mentioned: OT 1

Meaning: Break of Uzza

The threshing floor of Nachon (also called Chidon), where Uzza put out his hand to steady the ark of the covenant as the oxen stumbled. God killed Uzza. Angered at God's wrath against the man, King David gave the place this name. Same as Perez-uzza.

Only reference: 2 Samuel 6:8

📍 PERGA

of times mentioned: NT 3

Meaning: A tower

A city of Pamphylia and a stop on the first missionary journey of Paul and Barnabas. At this city, John Mark left Barnabas and Paul and returned to Jerusalem. The two apostles later returned to the city on a preaching mission.

First reference: Acts 13:13 / Last reference: Acts 14:25

📍 PERGAMOS

of times mentioned: NT 2

Meaning: Fortified

A city in the Roman province of Mysia in Asia Minor. It is only mentioned in Revelation, in the letter to the seven churches of Asia Minor. Though the Christians of Pergamos held fast to God's name, their doctrine was not pure.

First reference: Revelation 1:11 / Last reference: Revelation 2:12

👥 PERIDA

of times mentioned: 1
# of MEN by this name: 1

Meaning: Dispersion

Forefather of an exiled family—former servants of Solomon—that returned to Judah under Zerubbabel. Same as Peruda.

Only reference: Nehemiah 7:57

📍 PERSIA

of times mentioned: OT 29

An empire whose original nation lay on the Persian Gulf. It began after Cyrus, later called the Great, became ruler of a small Elamite province; the Persians rebelled against the Medes and began to establish a territory that eventually reached Asia Minor. In the first year of his rule, Cyrus declared that God had charged him with building a temple in Judah. He encouraged the leaders of Judah and Benjamin, along with the priests and Levites, to rebuild the temple. He also returned the temple vessels that Nebuchadnezzar had taken from Jerusalem.

The elderly prophet Daniel was still in Babylonia when Cyrus sent Jews back to their homeland to rebuild the temple. In the third year of this king's rule, the prophet received a vision that described a powerful evil being as the prince of Persia. Daniel foresaw the subsequent rulers of the Persian Empire and the conquest of the Macedonian Alexander the Great.

The Persian king Xerxes I was the Ahasuerus who became Esther's husband. He made her queen after his wife Vashti failed to obey him. When Esther's cousin Mordecai proved his faithfulness by revealing plots against the king, he was rewarded by being made a powerful leader in the Persian Empire.

Opponents of the temple's rebuilding complained to Xerxes' son, King Artaxerxes. Construction of the temple stopped until King Darius took over the rule of Persia. But Artaxerxes made Ezra spiritual leader and Nehemiah governor of Judah.

First reference: 2 Chronicles 36:20 / Last reference: Daniel 11:2 / Key references: 2 Chronicles 36:20–23; Ezra 1:1–11

👥 PERSIS

of times mentioned: 1
# of WOMEN by this name: 1

A Christian whom Paul greeted and commended in his letter to the church at Rome.

Only reference: Romans 16:12

👥 PERUDA

of times mentioned: 1
# of MEN by this name: 1

Meaning: Dispersions

Forefather of an exiled family that returned to Judah under Zerubbabel. Same as Perida.

Only reference: Ezra 2:55

👥 PETER

of times mentioned: 162
# of MEN by this name: 1

Meaning: A piece of rock

Jesus' disciple, also called Simon Peter and Simon Bar-Jonah, who was called from his fishing, along with his brother Andrew, to become a fisher of men. The brothers were among Jesus' most intimate disciples. Peter walked on water to meet Jesus after the feeding of the five thousand. He was the first to call Jesus "the Christ." With James and John, he witnessed the transfiguration of Jesus. In the Garden of Gethsemane, Peter fell asleep while Jesus prayed. As Jesus was arrested, Peter cut off the ear of the high priest's servant. While Jesus stood before Caiaphas in an illegal trial, three times Peter denied being His disciple. After the resurrection of Jesus, Peter and John checked the empty tomb. Later Jesus confronted Peter about his love for Him and reconfirmed his ministry.

Following the giving of the Great Commission, Peter spoke out boldly in his Pentecost sermon. He healed the lame beggar at the temple gate and refused to stop preaching when the Jewish Council arrested him. He had a vision about the acceptance of Gentile believers in the church but later failed to support them.

He wrote the books of 1 and 2 Peter. Same as Cephas.

First reference: Matthew 4:18 / Last reference: 2 Peter 1:1 / Key references: Matthew 14:28–33; 16:16; 17:1–8; John 18:10; 20:1–7; 21:15–19; Acts 2:14–41; 3:1–8; 4:13–20; 10:1–11:18

👥 PETHAHIAH

of times mentioned: 4
# of MEN by this name: 4

Meaning: God has opened

1) One of twenty-four priests in David's time who was chosen by lot to serve in the tabernacle.

Only reference: 1 Chronicles 24:16

2) An exiled Levite who married a "strange" (foreign) woman.

Only reference: Ezra 10:23

3) One of a group of Levites who led a revival among the Israelites in the time of Nehemiah.

Only reference: Nehemiah 9:5

4) A man of the tribe of Judah who was Israel's representative with King Artaxerxes of Persia.

Only reference: Nehemiah 11:24

📍 PETHOR

of times mentioned: OT 2

The Mesopotamian hometown of the pagan prophet Balaam. King Balak of Moab sent messengers here to bring Balaam to Moab to curse the Israelites before they entered the Promised Land.

First reference: Numbers 22:5 / Last reference: Deuteronomy 23:4

👥 PETHUEL

of times mentioned: 1
# of MEN by this name: 1

Meaning: Enlarged of God

Father of the Old Testament minor prophet Joel.

Only reference: Joel 1:1

👥 PEULTHAI

of times mentioned: 1
# of MEN by this name: 1

Meaning: Laborious

A Levite "porter" (doorkeeper) in the house of the Lord.

Only reference: 1 Chronicles 26:5

👥 PHALEC

of times mentioned: 1
# of MEN by this name: 1

Genealogy of Jesus: Yes (Luke 3:35)

A descendant of Abraham through Isaac; forebear of Jesus' earthly father, Joseph. Same as Peleg.

Only reference: Luke 3:35

👥 PHALLU

of times mentioned: 1
# of MEN by this name: 1

Meaning: Distinguished

A descendant of Abraham and grandson of Jacob through his son Reuben.

Only reference: Genesis 46:9

👥 PHALTI

of times mentioned: 1
# of MEN by this name: 1

Meaning: Delivered

Michal's second husband, whom Saul married her to after David fled. Same as Phaltiel.

Only reference: 1 Samuel 25:44

👥 PHALTIEL

of times mentioned: 1
# of MEN by this name: 1

Meaning: Deliverance of God

Michal's second husband, from whom King David claimed her. Same as Phalti.

Only reference: 2 Samuel 3:15

👥 PHANUEL

of times mentioned: 1
# of MEN by this name: 1

Father of the prophetess Anna, who saw the baby Jesus in the temple.

Only reference: Luke 2:36

👥 PHARAOH-HOPHRA

of times mentioned: 1
# of MEN by this name: 1

The king of Egypt who Jeremiah prophesied would be given into the hands of his enemies.

Only reference: Jeremiah 44:30

👥 PHARAOH-NECHO

of times mentioned: 1
# of MEN by this name: 1

The king of Egypt whom Jeremiah prophesied God would take vengeance against. Same as Pharaoh-nechoh.

Only reference: Jeremiah 46:2

👥 PHARAOH-NECHOH

of times mentioned: 4
# of MEN by this name: 1

The king of Egypt who fought Assyria and King Josiah of Judah. Josiah was killed, and Pharaoh-nechoh made Jehoiakim king in his place. Same as Pharaoh-necho.

First reference: 2 Kings 23:29 / Last reference: 2 Kings 23:35

👥 PHARES

of times mentioned: 3
# of MEN by this name: 1

Genealogy of Jesus: Yes (Matthew 1:3)

A descendant of Abraham through Isaac; forebear of Jesus' earthly father, Joseph. Same as Perez and Pharez.

First reference: Matthew 1:3 / Last reference: Luke 3:33

👥 PHAREZ

of times mentioned: 12
# of MEN by this name: 1

A grandson of Jacob, born to Jacob's son Judah and Judah's daughter-in-law Tamar. Same as Perez and Phares.

First reference: Genesis 38:29 / Last reference: 1 Chronicles 9:4

 PHAROSH

of times mentioned: 1
# of MEN by this name: 1

Meaning: A flea

Forefather of a family of exiles who returned to Jerusalem under Ezra.

Only reference: Ezra 8:3

PHARPAR

of times mentioned: OT 1

Meaning: Rushing or rapid

A river of Damascus that Naaman of Syria would have preferred to wash in, rather than the Jordan River. His servants convinced him that the prophet Elisha was not being unreasonable. When he washed in the Jordan River, Naaman was cured of his leprosy.

Only reference: 2 Kings 5:12

PHASEAH

of times mentioned: 1
# of MEN by this name: 1

Meaning: Limping

Forefather of an exiled family that returned to Judah under Zerubbabel.

Only reference: Nehemiah 7:51

PHEBE

of times mentioned: 1
# of WOMEN by this name: 1

Meaning: Bright

A believer whom Paul recommended that the Roman church assist.

Only reference: Romans 16:1

PHENICE

of times mentioned: NT 3

Meaning: Palm country

1) Another name for Phenicia. Some Christians went to Phenice following the death of Stephen. Paul and Barnabas passed through here on their way to Jerusalem. Same as Phenicia.

First reference: Acts 11:19 / Last reference: Acts 15:3

2) When Paul was traveling to Rome, the master of the ship left Fair Havens and tried to make this port on Crete, where he was planning to spend the winter.

Only reference: Acts 27:12

PHENICIA

of times mentioned: NT 1

Meaning: Palm country

Paul and his companions sailed to this land north of Israel, on the coast of the Mediterranean Sea, as they traveled to Jerusalem. Same as Phenice (1).

Only reference: Acts 21:2

PHICHOL

of times mentioned: 3
# of MEN by this name: 1

Meaning: Mouth of all

Commander of the Philistine king Abimelech's army in the time of Abraham and Isaac.

First reference: Genesis 21:22 / Last reference: Genesis 26:26

PHILADELPHIA

of times mentioned: NT 2

Meaning: Fraternal affection

A city where one of the seven churches of Asia Minor met. In the book of Revelation, Jesus commended and encouraged this church, which had kept His word and avoided denying His name. As a result, God would protect them from the trials that lay ahead. But the Lord also warned the church to hold on to what they already had so they would not lose their crown.

First reference: Revelation 1:11 / Last reference: Revelation 3:7

👥 PHILEMON

of times mentioned: 1
# of MEN by this name: 1

Meaning: Friendly

Christian owner of the escaped slave Onesimus. Paul wrote Philemon an epistle appealing for the slave.

Only reference: Philemon 1:1

👥 PHILETUS

of times mentioned: 1
# of MEN by this name: 1

Meaning: Amiable

A false teacher who opposed Paul, teaching that Christians would not be physically resurrected.

Only reference: 2 Timothy 2:17

👥 PHILIP

of times mentioned: 36
# of MEN by this name: 3

Meaning: Fond of horses

1) A disciple of Jesus who introduced the soon-to-be-disciple Nathanael to Him. Jesus asked Philip where they could buy bread to feed the five thousand, and Philip was at a loss. In Jerusalem, some Greeks who wanted to see Jesus came to Philip for an introduction. When Jesus told the disciples, "If ye had known me, ye should have known my Father also" (John 14:7), Philip wanted Him to show them the Father.

First reference: Matthew 10:3 / Last reference: Acts 1:13 / Key references: John 1:43–48; 6:5–7; 12:21–22; 14:8–9

2) Also called Herod Philip I, this tetrarch of Iturea and Trachonitis was a son of Herod the Great. His wife, Herodias, left him and married his half brother, Herod.

First reference: Matthew 14:3 / Last reference: Luke 3:1

3) One of seven men, "full of the Holy Ghost and wisdom," selected to serve needy Christians in Jerusalem while the twelve disciples devoted themselves "to prayer, and to the ministry of the word" (Acts 6:3–4). He preached to the Ethiopian eunuch and baptized him. Also called Philip the evangelist.

First reference: Acts 6:5 / Last reference: Acts 21:8 / Key references: Acts 8:5–8, 26–39

📍 PHILIPPI

of times mentioned: NT 6

Meaning: Fond of horses

1) Also known as Caesarea Philippi, this city northeast of Lake Huleh was built by Herod the Great. Near here Jesus asked His disciples who people were saying the Son of man was. Same as Caesarea (1).

First reference: Matthew 16:13 / Last reference: Mark 8:27

2) A chief city of northeastern Macedonia that Paul and his fellow laborers visited to preach the Gospel. Here Lydia became a convert, and a slave girl with a spirit of divination was healed. But the slave's owners dragged Paul and Silas before the magistrates, and the two men were imprisoned. Their jailor was converted before these prisoners were released by the magistrates. From this city Paul wrote the books of 1 and 2 Corinthians. Paul wrote an epistle to the believers of Philippi while he was in Rome.

First reference: Acts 16:12 / Last reference: 1 Thessalonians 2:2

📍 PHILISTIA

of times mentioned: OT 3

Meaning: Rolling (that is, migratory)

The country of the Philistines that hugged the coast of the Mediterranean Sea, south of Mount Carmel and west of Judah. Though there are frequent references to the Philistines in scripture, the name Philistia only appears in the Psalms, where the psalmist describes God's triumph over that nation and speaks of people of Philistia coming to know God.

First reference: Psalm 60:8 / Last reference: Psalm 108:9

👥 PHILOLOGUS

\# of times mentioned: 1
\# of MEN by this name: 1

Meaning: Fond of words

A Christian whom Paul greeted in his letter to the church at Rome.

Only reference: Romans 16:15

👥 PHINEHAS

\# of times mentioned: 25
\# of MEN by this name: 3

Meaning: Mouth of a serpent

1) Son of the high priest Eleazar and grandson of Aaron. He killed Zimri (1), who brought a Midianite woman before Moses while God was judging those who had fallen into idolatry. Because of Phinehas's act, God turned His wrath from Israel.

First reference: Exodus 6:25 / Last reference: Psalm 106:30 / Key reference: Numbers 25:6–9

2) Son of the high priest Eli, who honored Phinehas and his brother Hophni more than the Lord. The brothers did not know the Lord, misused their priestly office, and disobeyed the law. A man of God prophesied that they would die in the same day. When the Philistines attacked and took the ark of the covenant, both were killed.

First reference: 1 Samuel 1:3 / Last reference: 1 Samuel 14:3

3) Father of a Levite who weighed the temple vessels after the Babylonian Exile.

Only reference: Ezra 8:33

👥 PHLEGON

\# of times mentioned: 1
\# of MEN by this name: 1

Meaning: Blazing

A Christian whom Paul greeted in his letter to the church at Rome.

Only reference: Romans 16:14

📍 PHRYGIA

\# of times mentioned: NT 3

People from this area of western central Asia Minor witnessed the coming of the Holy Spirit at Pentecost. Paul and Silas preached in Phrygia, and the apostle returned to this area after he preached in Antioch. From Laodicea, a city in Phrygia, Paul wrote the book of 1 Timothy.

First reference: Acts 2:10 / Last reference: Acts 18:23

👥 PHURAH

\# of times mentioned: 2
\# of MEN by this name: 1

Meaning: Foliage

Gideon's servant who, before Israel attacked the enemy, went with Gideon to the Midianite camp to hear what the soldiers said about him.

First reference: Judges 7:10 / Last reference: Judges 7:11

👥 PHUT

\# of times mentioned: 2
\# of MEN by this name: 1

Meaning: Meaning

Grandson of Noah through his son Ham.

First reference: Genesis 10:6 / Last reference: Ezra 27:10

📍 PHUT

\# of times mentioned: OT 1

The land belonging to a descendant of Ham of the same name. The men of Phut were in Tyre's army.

Only reference: Ezekiel 27:10

👥 PHUVAH

\# of times mentioned: 1
\# of MEN by this name: 1

Meaning: A blast

A descendant of Abraham through Jacob's son Issachar.

Only reference: Genesis 46:13

👥 PHYGELLUS

\# of times mentioned: 1
\# of MEN by this name: 1

Meaning: Fugitive

An Asian Christian who turned away from Paul.

Only reference: 2 Timothy 1:15

📍 PI-BESETH

\# of times mentioned: OT 1

An Egyptian city whose young men would be killed and whose remaining population would be taken captive, according to Ezekiel's prophecy.

Only reference: Ezekiel 30:17

📍 PI-HAHIROTH

\# of times mentioned: OT 4

Meaning: Mouth of the gorges

A place where the Israelites camped before they crossed the Red Sea.

First reference: Exodus 14:2 / Last reference: Numbers 33:8

👥 PILATE

\# of times mentioned: 56
\# of MEN by this name: 1

Meaning: Close pressed

Procurator (governor) of Judea before whom Jesus appeared after His trial before the Jewish religious authorities. When Pilate heard Jesus was a Galilean, he sent Jesus to Herod, who had his soldiers mock Him and return Him to Pilate. Pilate questioned Jesus briefly and understood He was innocent. Though Pilate knew envy had spurred the Jewish leaders to condemn Jesus, fearing these leaders, he gave the crowd a choice of prisoners to be released: Jesus or Barabbas. His wife warned him against condemning Jesus, but Pilate still gave Him over to be crucified. Same as Pontius Pilate.

First reference: Matthew 27:2 / Last reference: 1 Timothy 6:13 / Key references: Matthew 27:11–26; Luke 23:6–11; John 18:29–19:15

👥 PILDASH

\# of times mentioned: 1
\# of MEN by this name: 1

Son of Nahor and nephew of Abraham.

Only reference: Genesis 22:22

👥 PILEHA

\# of times mentioned: 1
\# of MEN by this name: 1

Meaning: Slicing

A Jewish leader who renewed the covenant under Nehemiah.

Only reference: Nehemiah 10:24

👥 PILTAI

\# of times mentioned: 1
\# of MEN by this name: 1

Meaning: A Paltite or descendant of Palti

A chief priest under Joiakim in the days of Zerubbabel.

Only reference: Nehemiah 12:17

👥 PINON

\# of times mentioned: 2
\# of MEN by this name: 1

Meaning: Perplexity

Forefather of a priest who returned to Jerusalem under Zerubbabel.

First reference: Genesis 36:41 / Last reference:
1 Chronicles 1:52

👥 PIRAM

of times mentioned: 1
# of MEN by this name: 1

Meaning: Wildly

A "duke of Edom," a leader in the family line of
Esau.

Only reference: Joshua 10:3

📍 PIRATHON

of times mentioned: OT 1

Meaning: Chieftancy

Home and burial place of the judge Abdon.

Only reference: Judges 12:15

📍 PISGAH

of times mentioned: OT 5

Meaning: A cleft

A Moabite mountain northeast of the Dead Sea
where the Israelites stopped while Moses asked the
Amorite king Sihon if they could travel through his
land. King Balak of Moab brought Balaam here to
make sacrifices when he wanted Balaam to curse
the Israelites as Joshua led them to the Promised
Land. Before entering Canaan, Israel conquered the
Amorite land "even unto the sea of the plain, under
the springs of Pisgah" (Deuteronomy 4:49).

On Pisgah, Moses climbed to a vantage point
from which he could view the Promised Land just
before he died.

First reference: Numbers 21:20 / Last reference:
Deuteronomy 34:1

📍 PISIDIA

of times mentioned: NT 2

An area of Asia Minor that lay directly north of
Pamphylia. Paul and Barnabas visited Pisidia's syn-
agogue, where Paul preached to the congregation.
They later returned to Antioch of Pisidia, where

they ordained church leaders and encouraged believers.

First reference: Acts 13:14 / Last reference: Acts
14:24

📍 PISON

of times mentioned: OT 1

Meaning: Dispersive

One of the four rivers fed by Eden's river. The Pison
flowed in the land of Havilah, which was known
for its gold.

Only reference: Genesis 2:11

👥 PISPAH

of times mentioned: 1
# of MEN by this name: 1

Meaning: Dispersion

A descendant of Abraham through Jacob's son
Asher.

Only reference: 1 Chronicles 7:38

📍 PITHOM

of times mentioned: OT 1

During their enslavement, the Israelites built this
store city in northeastern Egypt.

Only reference: Exodus 1:11

👥 PITHON

of times mentioned: 2
# of MEN by this name: 1

Meaning: Expansive

A descendant of Abraham through Jacob's son
Benjamin, in the line of King Saul and his son
Jonathan.

First reference: 1 Chronicles 8:35 / Last reference:
1 Chronicles 9:41

👥 POCHERETH

of times mentioned: 2
# of MEN by this name: 1

Meaning: To entrap

An Israelite who returned to Jerusalem under Zerubbabel.

First reference: Ezra 2:57 / Last reference: Nehemiah 7:59

👥 PONTIUS PILATE

of times mentioned: 4
# of MEN by this name: 1

Meaning: Pontius, "bridged"; Pilate, "close pressed"

Pilate's family name and first name. Same as Pilate.

First reference: Matthew 27:2 / Last reference: 1 Timothy 6:13

📍 PONTUS

of times mentioned: NT 3

Meaning: A sea

People from this Roman province of Asia Minor witnessed the coming of the Holy Spirit at Pentecost. Pontus was the birthplace of Paul's fellow laborer Aquila. The apostle Peter wrote his first epistle to the Christians in Pontus and other provinces of Asia Minor.

First reference: Acts 2:9 / Last reference: 1 Peter 1:1

👥 PORATHA

of times mentioned: 1
# of MEN by this name: 1

One of ten sons of Haman, the villain of the story of Esther.

Only reference: Esther 9:8

👥 PORCIUS FESTUS

of times mentioned: 1
# of MEN by this name: 1

Meaning: Porcius, "swinish"; Festus, "festal"

Governor of Judea who heard Paul's case and sent him to Caesar. Also called Festus.

Only reference: Acts 24:27

👥 POTIPHAR

of times mentioned: 2
# of MEN by this name: 1

The officer of Pharaoh and captain of Pharaoh's guard, Potiphar became master to the enslaved Joseph (1).

First reference: Genesis 37:36 / Last reference: Genesis 39:1

👥 POTIPHERAH

of times mentioned: 3
# of MEN by this name: 1

Egyptian priest of On and father-in-law of Joseph (1).

First reference: Genesis 41:45 / Last reference: Genesis 46:20

📍 PRAETORIUM

of times mentioned: NT 1

Meaning: Governor's courtroom

The hall where Pilate's soldiers humiliated Jesus with a purple robe, crown of thorns, mockery, and beatings before His crucifixion. It is also translated "judgment hall" (John 18:28) and "the common hall" (Matthew 27:27).

Only reference: Mark 15:16

👥 PRISCA

of times mentioned: 1
# of WOMEN by this name: 1

With her husband, Aquila, she was a coworker of Paul. Same as Priscilla.

Only reference: 2 Timothy 4:19

👥 PRISCILLA

of times mentioned: 5
# of WOMEN by this name: 1

Wife of Aquila. This tent-making couple worked with the apostle Paul in their craft and in spreading the Gospel. They founded a house church in their home. Same as Prisca.

First reference: Acts 18:2 / Last reference:
1 Corinthians 16:19

👥 PROCHORUS

of times mentioned: 1
# of MEN by this name: 1

Meaning: Before the dance

One of seven men, "full of the Holy Ghost and wisdom," selected to serve needy Christians in Jerusalem while the twelve disciples devoted themselves "to prayer, and to the ministry of the word" (Acts 6:3–4).

Only reference: Acts 6:5

📍 PTOLEMAIS

of times mentioned: NT 1

Meaning: Ptolemy

A Phoenician seacoast town south of Tyre. On his way to Jerusalem, Paul stopped here for a day. Same as Accho.

Only reference: Acts 21:7

👥 PUA

of times mentioned: 1
# of MEN by this name: 1

Meaning: A blast

A descendant of Abraham through Jacob's son Issachar. Same as Puah (1).

Only reference: Numbers 26:23

👥 PUAH

of times mentioned: 3
# of MEN by this name: 2
# of WOMEN by this name: 1

Meaning: A blast

1) A descendant of Abraham through Jacob's son Issachar. Same as Pua.

Only reference: 1 Chronicles 7:1

2) Father of Israel's sixth judge, Tola.

Only reference: Judges 10:1

3) A Hebrew midwife who did not obey the king of Egypt's command to kill all male Israelite babies.

Only reference: Exodus 1:15

👥 PUBLIUS

of times mentioned: 2
# of MEN by this name: 1

Meaning: Popular

The chief official of Melita who housed Paul and his companions after they were shipwrecked on their way to Rome.

First reference: Acts 28:7 / Last reference: Acts 28:8

👥 PUDENS

of times mentioned: 1
# of MEN by this name: 1

Meaning: Modest

A Christian to whom Paul sent greetings when he wrote Timothy.

Only reference: 2 Timothy 4:21

👥 PUL

of times mentioned: 3
# of MEN by this name: 1

The king of Assyria who extracted tribute from Israel then brought the nation into exile. Possibly the same as Tiglath-pileser.

First reference: 2 Kings 15:19 / Last reference:
1 Chronicles 5:26

PUL

of times mentioned: OT 1

A north African nation to which God promises to send survivors of persecution. They will declare God's glory when He executes His final judgment of the world.

Only reference: Isaiah 66:19

PUNON

of times mentioned: OT 2

Meaning: Perplexity

A campsite of the Israelites on their way to the Promised Land.

First reference: Numbers 33:42 / Last reference: Numbers 33:43

PUT

of times mentioned: 1
# of MEN by this name: 1

A grandson of Noah through his son Ham.

Only reference: 1 Chronicles 1:8

PUTEOLI

of times mentioned: NT 1

Meaning: Little wells (that is, mineral springs)

An Italian port where the apostle Paul ended his sea voyage and began his journey by land to Rome.

Only reference: Acts 28:13

PUTIEL

of times mentioned: 1
# of MEN by this name: 1

Meaning: Contempt of God

Father-in-law of Aaron's son Eleazar.

Only reference: Exodus 6:25

QUARTUS

of times mentioned: 1
# of MEN by this name: 1

Meaning: Fourth

A Christian in Corinth who sent his greetings to fellow believers in Paul's letter to Rome.

Only reference: Romans 16:23

RAAMAH

of times mentioned: 4
# of MEN by this name: 1

Meaning: Mane

A descendant of Noah through his son Ham.

First reference: Genesis 10:7 / Last reference: 1 Chronicles 1:9

RAAMAH

of times mentioned: OT 1

Meaning: Name of a grandson of Ham

A nation of traders on the Persian Gulf who brought precious goods to Tyre.

Only reference: Ezekiel 27:22

RAAMIAH

of times mentioned: 1
# of MEN by this name: 1

Meaning: God has shaken

A Jewish exile who returned to Judah under Zerubbabel.

Only reference: Nehemiah 7:7

RAAMSES

of times mentioned: OT 1

During their enslavement, the Israelites built this store city in northeastern Egypt.

Only reference: Exodus 1:11

📍 RABBAH

of times mentioned: OT 13

Meaning: Great

1) A royal Ammonite city on the border of the tribe of Reuben's territory. Joab besieged Rabbah while King David stayed behind in Jerusalem and fell into sin with Bathsheba. Joab won the city and called on David to encamp against it, so that the king, not the battle commander, would receive praise. David received the crown of Rabbah's king and took great spoils from the city.

The prophet Jeremiah foretold that war would come to Rabbah, and it would become a desolate heap. He called on the city's women to mourn for the loss of their leaders (Jeremiah 49:2–3). Ezekiel prophesied that Ammon would be attacked and delivered over to men from the east. He foresaw Rabbah turned into a stable for camels under God's judging hand (Ezekiel 25:5). Amos saw God kindling a fire in the walls of the city and its leaders going into captivity. Same as Rabbath.

First reference: Joshua 13:25 / Last reference: Amos 1:14 / Key reference: 2 Samuel 12:26–29

2) A city that became part of the inheritance of the tribe of Judah following the conquest of the Promised Land.

Only reference: Joshua 15:60

📍 RABBATH

of times mentioned: OT 2

Meaning: Great

An Ammonite city where Og, king of Bashan, had his nine-cubit-long bedstead. The prophet Ezekiel foretold Babylon's attack on Rabbath and Judah. Same as Rabbah (1).

First reference: Deuteronomy 3:11 / Last reference: Ezekiel 21:20

📍 RABBITH

of times mentioned: OT 1

Meaning: Multitude

A city that became part of the inheritance of Issachar when Joshua cast lots in Shiloh to provide territory for the seven tribes that had yet to receive their land.

Only reference: Joshua 19:20

👥 RABMAG

of times mentioned: 2
# of MEN by this name: 1

Meaning: Chief magician

A Babylonian prince who took part in the destruction of Jerusalem under King Nebuchadnezzar. Rabmag was an official who also, at Nebuchadnezzar's command, showed kindness to the prophet Jeremiah.

First reference: Jeremiah 39:3 / Last reference: Jeremiah 39:13

👥 RABSARIS

of times mentioned: 3
# of MEN by this name: 2

Meaning: Chief eunuch

1) A Babylonian prince who took part in the destruction of Jerusalem under King Nebuchadnezzar. Rabsaris was an official who also, at Nebuchadnezzar's command, showed kindness to the prophet Jeremiah.

First reference: Jeremiah 39:3 / Last reference: Jeremiah 39:13

2) An Assyrian military commander who participated in King Sennacherib's failed attempt to take Jerusalem in the days of King Hezekiah and the prophet Isaiah.

Only reference: 2 Kings 18:17

👥 RAB-SHAKEH

of times mentioned: 16
# of MEN by this name: 1

Meaning: Chief butler

An Assyrian field commander sent by King Sennacherib to attack King Hezekiah at Jerusalem. He attempted to get Hezekiah and his people to surrender to Assyria and fight with that nation. Same as Rabsakeh.

First reference: 2 Kings 18:17 / Last reference: 2 Kings 19:8

👥 RABSHAKEH

of times mentioned: 16
# of MEN by this name: 1

Meaning: Chief butler

A variant spelling of the name of the Assyrian military commander Rab-shakeh.

First reference: Isaiah 36:2 / Last reference: Isaiah 37:8

👥 RACHAB

of times mentioned: 1
# of WOMEN by this name: 1

Genealogy of Jesus: Yes (Matthew 1:5)

Meaning: Proud

Greek form of the name Rahab, used in the New Testament.

Only reference: Matthew 1:5

📍 RACHAL

of times mentioned: OT 1

Meaning: Merchant

A city of Judah to which David sent some of the spoils from his warfare with the Amalekites.

Only reference: 1 Samuel 30:29

👥 RACHEL

of times mentioned: 47
# of WOMEN by this name: 1

Meaning: Ewe

Daughter of Laban and wife of Jacob. When Jacob came to Haran, he fell in love with the beautiful Rachel. He agreed to work for Laban for seven years to win her. But when it was time for the marriage, Laban fooled him by putting his sister, Leah, in Rachel's place. Jacob agreed to work seven more years to gain Rachel and finally received her as his bride.

While Leah had children, Rachel remained barren, so Rachel gave her maid, Bilhah, to Jacob, to bear children for her. Finally God enabled Rachel to conceive, and she bore Joseph. Jacob decided to move his family back to his own homeland. When Laban discovered they had left secretly, he followed, partly in search of the idols Rachel had stolen and partly to make sure all would be well with his daughters. When they planned to meet Jacob's brother, Esau, whom he had wronged, Jacob put Rachel in the safest part of the caravan. As they traveled to Ephrath (Bethlehem), Rachel gave birth to her second son, whom she called Ben-oni, but Jacob renamed him Benjamin. Rachel died following this difficult childbirth and was buried there. Same as Rahel.

First reference: Genesis 29:6 / Last reference: Matthew 2:18 / Key references: Genesis 29:16–30; 30:1–8; 31:34; 33:2; 35:16–19

👥 RADDAI

of times mentioned: 1
# of MEN by this name: 1

Meaning: Domineering

Fifth son of Jesse and older brother of King David.

Only reference: 1 Chronicles 2:14

👥 RAGAU

of times mentioned: 1
# of MEN by this name: 1

Genealogy of Jesus: Yes (Luke 3:35)

Meaning: Friend

Greek form of the name Reu, used in the New Testament.

Only reference: Luke 3:35

👥 RAGUEL

of times mentioned: 1
# of MEN by this name: 1

Meaning: Friend of God

Father-in-law of Moses. Same as Reuel and Jethro.

Only reference: Numbers 10:29

👥 RAHAB

of times mentioned: 7
# of WOMEN by this name: 1

Genealogy of Jesus: Yes (Matthew 1:5)

Meaning: Proud

A prostitute of Jericho who hid the two spies whom Joshua sent to look over the city before Israel attacked it. When the king of Jericho was warned of their presence, Rahab hid the men on her roof and informed the king they had left. Rahab told the spies that she feared Israel and asked them to be kind to her family. The men promised she and her family would be spared if she hung a scarlet cord from her window when Israel attacked. When Jericho fell to Joshua's troops, he kept the spies' promise. Same as Rachab.

First reference: Joshua 2:1 / Last reference: James 2:25

📍 RAHAB

of times mentioned: OT 3

Meaning: Boaster

A name for Egypt that reflects that nation's pride. Psalm 87 looks forward to a day when Rahab will worship the Lord. Psalm 89:10 and Isaiah 51:9 speak of Rahab being broken and cut.

First reference: Psalm 87:4 / Last reference: Isaiah 51:9

👥 RAHAM

of times mentioned: 1
# of MEN by this name: 1

Meaning: Pity

A descendant of Abraham through Jacob's son Judah.

Only reference: 1 Chronicles 2:44

👥 RAHEL

of times mentioned: 1
# of WOMEN by this name: 1

Meaning: Ewe

A variant spelling of the name of Jacob's wife Rachel.

Only reference: Jeremiah 31:15

👥 RAKEM

of times mentioned: 1
# of MEN by this name: 1

Meaning: Parti-colored

A descendant of Abraham through Joseph's son Manasseh.

Only reference: 1 Chronicles 7:16

📍 RAKKATH

of times mentioned: OT 1

Meaning: A beach (as with an expanded stony area)

A fortified or walled city that became part of the inheritance of Naphtali when Joshua cast lots in Shiloh to provide territory for the seven tribes that had yet to receive their land.

Only reference: Joshua 19:35

📍 RAKKON

of times mentioned: OT 1

Meaning: Thinness

A city that became part of the inheritance of Dan when Joshua cast lots in Shiloh to provide territory for the seven tribes that had yet to receive their land.

Only reference: Joshua 19:46

👥 RAM

of times mentioned: 7
# of MEN by this name: 3

Meaning: High

1) Forefather of Boaz, Jesse, and David.

First reference: Ruth 4:19 / Last reference: 1 Chronicles 2:10

2) A descendant of Abraham through Jacob's son Judah.

First reference: 1 Chronicles 2:25 / Last reference: 1 Chronicles 2:27

3) Family head of Job's accusing "friend," Elihu.

Only reference: Job 32:2

⚲ RAMA

of times mentioned: NT 1

A city of the tribe of Ephraim spoken of in a prophecy in Jeremiah 31:15 that describes Rachel weeping for her children. Matthew compares it to the mourning after Herod killed the children of Bethlehem and the surrounding area. Same as Ramah (3).

Only reference: Matthew 2:18

⚲ RAMAH

of times mentioned: OT 36

Meaning: Height (as a seat of idolatry)

1) A city that became part of the inheritance of Benjamin when Joshua cast lots in Shiloh to provide territory for the seven tribes that had yet to receive their land. The prophet Deborah lived near Ramah. When King Baasha of Israel began to fortify the city to control who went in and out of Israel, King Asa of Judah arranged with Ben-hadad, king of Syria, to attack cities of Israel. As Baasha left to fight Ben-hadad, Asa brought his people to Ramah. They carried away the building materials and fortified their own cities with them. After the Babylonian Exile, the people of Ramah returned and resettled their city. The Babylonians imprisoned the prophet Jeremiah in Ramah.

First reference: Joshua 18:25 / Last reference: Hosea 5:8 / Key references: 2 Chronicles 16:1–6; Jeremiah 40:1

2) A fortified or walled city that became part of the inheritance of Naphtali when Joshua cast lots in Shiloh to provide territory for the seven tribes that had yet to receive their land.

First reference: Joshua 19:29 / Last reference: Joshua 19:36

3) Hometown of Elkanah and Hannah, the prophet Samuel's parents. As a child, Samuel lived in Shiloh with Eli the priest, but when the prophet was an adult, Ramah became his home. When Saul sought to kill him, David came to Samuel at his home. Saul tried to send men to take David, but the messengers could not do the deed, but began to prophesy instead. When Saul went himself, he also prophesied. Samuel was buried in his home at Ramah.

A prophecy in Jeremiah 31:15 poetically speaks of Rachel weeping for her children in Ramah. Matthew 2:18 compares it to the mourning after Herod killed the children of Bethlehem and the surrounding area. Same as Rama and Ramathaim-Zophim.

First reference: 1 Samuel 1:19 / Last reference: Jeremiah 31:15 / Key references: 1 Samuel 19:18–24; 25:1

4) A shortened form of Ramoth-gilead, where King Joram of Israel went to be healed of battle wounds. Same as Ramoth-gilead.

First reference: 2 Kings 8:29 / Last reference: 2 Chronicles 22:6

⚲ RAMATH

of times mentioned: OT 1

Meaning: Height (as a seat of idolatry)

A city that became part of the inheritance of Simeon when Joshua cast lots in Shiloh to provide territory for the seven tribes that had yet to receive their land.

Only reference: Joshua 19:8

⚲ RAMATHAIM-ZOPHIM

of times mentioned: OT 1

Meaning: Double height of watchers

Hometown of Elkanah, the prophet Samuel's father. Same as Ramah (3).

Only reference: 1 Samuel 1:1

⚲ RAMATH-LEHI

of times mentioned: OT 1

Meaning: Height of a jawbone

After Samson was captured by the Philistines and brought to Lehi, he killed a thousand of them with the jawbone of a donkey. Then he named the place where he threw the bone Ramath-lehi.

Only reference: Judges 15:17

📍 RAMATH-MIZPEH

of times mentioned: OT 1

Meaning: Height of the watchtower

A city east of the Jordan River that Moses made part of the inheritance of Gad.

Only reference: Joshua 13:26

📍 RAMESES

of times mentioned: OT 4

Joseph established his father, his brothers, and their families in this area of Lower Egypt. Four hundred years later, the Israelites left Rameses to begin their exodus to the Promised Land.

First reference: Genesis 47:11 / Last reference: Numbers 33:5

👥 RAMIAH

of times mentioned: 1
# of MEN by this name: 1

Meaning: God has raised

An exiled Israelite who married a "strange" (foreign) woman.

Only reference: Ezra 10:25

👥 RAMOTH

of times mentioned: 1
# of MEN by this name: 1

Meaning: Elevations

An exiled Israelite who married a "strange" (foreign) woman.

Only reference: Ezra 10:29

📍 RAMOTH

of times mentioned: OT 7

Meaning: Heights

1) One of the six cities of refuge established in Israel for those who had committed accidental murder. Ramoth was given to the Levites by the tribe of Gad.

First reference: Deuteronomy 4:43 / Last reference: 1 Chronicles 6:80

2) One of the forty-eight cities given to the Levites as God had commanded. Ramoth was given to them by the tribe of Issachar.

Only reference: 1 Chronicles 6:73

3) A city of Judah to which David sent some of the spoils from his warfare with the Amalekites.

Only reference: 1 Samuel 30:27

4) A city that King Jehoshaphat of Judah wanted to win back from the Syrians. Same as Ramoth-gilead.

Only reference: 1 Kings 22:3

📍 RAMOTH-GILEAD

of times mentioned: OT 19

Meaning: Heights of Gilead

One of the six cities of refuge established in Israel for those who had committed accidental murder. Ramoth-gilead was given to the Levites by the tribe of Gad.

Under King Solomon's governmental organization, the son of Geber was the officer in charge of providing the king with provisions from this city. King Ahab of Israel joined with Judah's king Jehoshaphat to free Ramoth-gilead from Syria's power. Despite his going into battle in disguise, Ahab was killed by an archer. At Ramoth-gilead, Ahab's son, King Joram, and King Ahaziah of Judah battled the Syrian king Hazael. Joram was wounded in the battle.

Elisha secretly anointed Jehu king of Israel at Ramoth-gilead and told him to fight the house of Ahab. Same as Ramah 4 and Ramoth (4).

First reference: 1 Kings 4:13 / Last reference: 1 Chronicles 22:5 / Key references: 1 Kings 22:4–29; 2 Kings 9:1–14; 2 Chronicles 18

RAPHA

\# of times mentioned: 2
\# of MEN by this name: 2

Meaning: Giant

1) A descendant of Abraham through Jacob's son Benjamin. Rapha was Benjamin's fifth son.

Only reference: 1 Chronicles 8:2

2) A descendant of Abraham through Jacob's son Benjamin, through the line of King Saul and his son Jonathan.

Only reference: 1 Chronicles 8:37

RAPHU

\# of times mentioned: 1
\# of MEN by this name: 1

Meaning: Cured

Father of one of the twelve spies sent by Moses to spy out the land of Canaan.

Only reference: Numbers 13:9

REAIA

\# of times mentioned: 1
\# of MEN by this name: 1

Meaning: God has seen

A descendant of Abraham through Jacob's son Reuben.

Only reference: 1 Chronicles 5:5

REAIAH

\# of times mentioned: 3
\# of MEN by this name: 2

Meaning: God has seen

1) A descendant of Abraham through Jacob's son Judah.

Only reference: 1 Chronicles 4:2

2) Forefather of an exiled family that returned to Judah under Zerubbabel.

First reference: Ezra 2:47 / Last reference: Nehemiah 7:50

REBA

\# of times mentioned: 2
\# of MEN by this name: 1

Meaning: A fourth

A Midianite king killed by the Israelites at God's command.

First reference: Numbers 31:8 / Last reference: Joshua 13:21

REBECCA

\# of times mentioned: 1
\# of WOMEN by this name: 1

Meaning: Fettering by beauty

Greek form of the name Rebekah, used in the New Testament.

Only reference: Romans 9:10

REBEKAH

\# of times mentioned: 30
\# of WOMEN by this name: 1

Meaning: Fettering by beauty

When Abraham's servant came to Nahor, seeking a wife for Abraham's son Isaac, Rebekah watered his camels, proving she was God's choice as the bride. She agreed to marry Isaac and traveled to her new home, where Isaac loved and married her. At first barren, when Rebekah conceived, she had the twins Esau and Jacob. Because she loved her second son best, she conspired with Jacob to get him the eldest son's blessing from his father. When Esau discovered what Jacob had done, he became so angry that Rebekah arranged for Jacob to leave before his brother killed him. Same as Rebecca.

First reference: Genesis 22:23 / Last reference: Genesis 49:31 / Key references: Genesis 24:15–25, 62–67; 25:21–26; 27:5–10, 41–46

👥 RECHAB

of times mentioned: 13
# of MEN by this name: 3

Meaning: Rider

1) A leader of one of the raiding bands of Saul's son Ish-bosheth. Rechab and his brother Baanah killed Ish-bosheth. In turn, David had the brothers killed.

First reference: 2 Samuel 4:2 / Last reference: 2 Samuel 4:9

2) Father of Jonadab, who commanded his descendants not to drink wine.

First reference: 2 Kings 10:15 / Last reference: Jeremiah 35:19

3) Father of a man who repaired Jerusalem's walls under Nehemiah.

Only reference: Nehemiah 3:14

📍 RED SEA

of times mentioned: OT 26 / NT 2

Meaning: A reed

This sea east of Egypt and west of Arabia is first mentioned in scripture when God relented and drove the locusts of the eighth plague against Egypt into the Red Sea. Though scholars have debated what body of water Red (or Reed) Sea refers to and have argued about the route of the Exodus, the miracles the scriptures describe concerning it are no less amazing.

God led Moses and the Israelites to the Red Sea after Pharaoh allowed them to leave Egypt following the tenth plague God sent against the Egyptians. Pharaoh then changed his mind, and he and his troops pursued the Israelites. Moses called on his people to stand still and see God's salvation. As Moses lifted up his rod, the sea parted before them and the Israelites crossed it on dry ground. But when the Egyptians followed, God commanded Moses to stretch his hand over the sea, and Israel's enemies were swallowed up in the water. Then God led His people to "journey into the wilderness by the way of the Red sea" (Deuteronomy 1:40).

God promised His people that He would "set thy bounds from the Red sea even unto the sea of the Philistines" (Exodus 23:31).

Throughout scripture, the crossing of the Red Sea is a picture of God's salvation of Israel. Joshua reminds his nation of God's faithfulness and might as shown in this action. In the book of Nehemiah, the Levites led the people in worship and reminded them that God had heard their cry when their backs were to the Red Sea and they saw Egypt's warriors before them. The psalms use the Red Sea crossing as an example of God's mercy toward Israel. Hebrews reminds the Jewish Christians that Israel passed through the sea by faith.

First reference: Exodus 10:19 / Last reference: Hebrews 11:29 / Key reference: Exodus 13:17–14:31

👥 REELAIAH

of times mentioned: 1
# of MEN by this name: 1

Meaning: Fearful of God

A Jewish exile who returned to Judah under Zerubbabel.

Only reference: Ezra 2:2

👥 REGEM

of times mentioned: 1
# of MEN by this name: 1

Meaning: Stone heap

A descendant of Abraham through Jacob's son Judah.

Only reference: 1 Chronicles 2:47

👥 REGEM-MELECH

of times mentioned: 1
# of MEN by this name: 1

Meaning: King's heap

A messenger sent to the prophet Zechariah to ask if the Jews should fast over their exile in Babylon.

Only reference: Zechariah 7:2

👥 REHABIAH

of times mentioned: 5
# of MEN by this name: 1

Meaning: God has enlarged

A descendant of Abraham through Jacob's son Levi, through the line of Moses.

First reference: 1 Chronicles 23:17 / Last reference: 1 Chronicles 26:25

👥 REHOB

of times mentioned: 3
# of MEN by this name: 2

Meaning: Width

1) Father of Hadadezer, king of Zobah, whom King David conquered.

First reference: 2 Samuel 8:3 / Last reference: 2 Samuel 8:12

2) A Jewish leader who renewed the covenant under Nehemiah.

Only reference: Nehemiah 10:11

📍 REHOB

of times mentioned: OT 7

Meaning: Width (that is, avenue or area)

When Moses sent spies into Canaan, he told them to explore the area from the Desert of Zin to Rehob. The city of Rehob became part of the inheritance of Asher when Joshua cast lots in Shiloh to provide territory for the seven tribes that had yet to receive their land. Later this city became one of the forty-eight cities given to the Levites as God had commanded. The tribe of Asher did not drive out the Canaanites who lived here when they conquered the Promised Land; instead they lived under the Rehobites' pagan influence.

First reference: Numbers 13:21 / Last reference: 1 Chronicles 6:75

👥 REHOBOAM

of times mentioned: 50
# of MEN by this name: 1

Meaning: A people has enlarged

A son of King Solomon, Rehoboam inherited the kingdom of Israel. But his proud attitude toward his subjects' request for lower taxes made Israel rebel against him and set up Jeroboam as their king. When Rehoboam wanted to fight Jeroboam, God spoke through the prophet Shemiah and ordered Rehoboam not to. Only the southern kingdom of Judah remained under Rehoboam's rule, and he built up its defenses. The priests and Levites sided with Rehoboam, even moving into Judah, because Jeroboam had set up idols in his nation and rejected God's spiritual leaders. But once Rehoboam had established his power, "he forsook the law of the LORD, and all Israel with him" (2 Chronicles 12:1).

In the fifth year of Rehoboam's reign, Shishak, king of Egypt, attacked Jerusalem. When Shemiah told Judah that God had abandoned their nation because it had abandoned Him, its leaders repented. But God did not free them from Shishak's rule, and he looted all the temple treasures. Yet Rehoboam was not destroyed and Judah became somewhat prosperous. Same as Roboam.

First reference: 1 Kings 11:43 / Last reference: 2 Chronicles 13:7 / Key references: 1 Kings 12:1–24; 14:25–28; 2 Chronicles 11:5–14; 12:1–12

📍 REHOBOTH

of times mentioned: OT 4

Meaning: Streets

1) An ancient Assyrian city built by Asshur. Saul (or Shaul) of Rehoboth ruled over Edom before Israel had kings.

First reference: Genesis 10:11 / Last reference: 1 Chronicles 1:48

2) A well dug by Isaac. It was the first one the local people did not take from him.

Only reference: Genesis 26:22

👥 REHUM

of times mentioned: 8
# of MEN by this name: 4

Meaning: Compassionate

1) An exiled priest who returned to Judah under Zerubbabel.

First reference: Ezra 2:2 / Last reference: Nehemiah 12:3

2) An officer of the Persian king Artaxerxes who joined in opposition to Zerubbabel's rebuilding of the temple in Jerusalem. Rehum wrote a letter to the king calling Jerusalem "a rebellious city" (Ezra 4:15) and causing Artaxerxes to suspend the work.

First reference: Ezra 4:8 / Last reference: Ezra 4:23

3) A Levite who repaired the walls of Jerusalem under Nehemiah.

Only reference: Nehemiah 3:17

4) A Jewish leader who renewed the covenant under Nehemiah.

Only reference: Nehemiah 10:25

👥 REI

of times mentioned: 1
# of MEN by this name: 1

Meaning: Social

A friend of King David who did not join in the attempted coup of David's son Adonijah.

Only reference: 1 Kings 1:8

👥 REKEM

of times mentioned: 4
# of MEN by this name: 2

Meaning: Parti-colored

1) A Midianite king killed by the Israelites at God's command to Moses.

First reference: Numbers 31:8 / Last reference: Joshua 13:21

2) A descendant of Abraham through Jacob's son Judah.

First reference: 1 Chronicles 2:43 / Last reference: 1 Chronicles 2:44

📍 REKEM

of times mentioned: OT 1

Meaning: Variegated color

A city that became part of the inheritance of Benjamin when Joshua cast lots in Shiloh to provide

territory for the seven tribes that had yet to receive their land.

Only reference: Joshua 18:27

👥 REMALIAH

of times mentioned: 13
# of MEN by this name: 1

Meaning: God has bedecked

Father of King Pekah of Israel.

First reference: 2 Kings 15:25 / Last reference: Isaiah 8:6

📍 REMETH

of times mentioned: OT 1

Meaning: Height

A city that became part of the inheritance of Issachar when Joshua cast lots in Shiloh to provide territory for the seven tribes that had yet to receive their land.

Only reference: Joshua 19:21

📍 REMMON

of times mentioned: OT 1

Meaning: Name of a Syrian deity

A city that became part of the inheritance of Simeon when Joshua cast lots in Shiloh to provide territory for the seven tribes that had yet to receive their land.

Only reference: Joshua 19:7

📍 REMMON-METHOAR

of times mentioned: OT 1

Meaning: Remmon (a Syrian deity), the one marked off (that is, which pertains to)

A city that became part of the inheritance of Zebulun when Joshua cast lots in Shiloh to provide territory for the seven tribes that had yet to receive their land.

Only reference: Joshua 19:13

 REPHAEL

of times mentioned: 1
# of MEN by this name: 1

Meaning: God has cured

A Levite "porter" (doorkeeper) in the house of the Lord.

Only reference: 1 Chronicles 26:7

📍 REPHAIM

of times mentioned: OT 6

Meaning: A giant

A valley southwest of Jerusalem that the Philistines raided shortly after David was anointed king of Israel. Twice David fought and defeated them. First, he went to Baal-perazin, and God handed the Philistines over to Israel. The second time, David and his men fought the Philistines from Gibeon to Gezer. During harvesttime, the Philistines again camped in the valley, making Bethlehem their garrison. David assembled his forces at the cave of Adullam.

When David longed for some water from Bethlehem, three of his brave warriors broke through the lines and got it for him. When they brought it to him, he refused to drink and poured it out before God. "Is it not the blood of men who went at the risk of their lives?" he asked (2 Samuel 23:17 NIV).

First reference: 2 Samuel 5:18 / Last reference: Isaiah 17:5

👥 REPHAH

of times mentioned: 1
# of MEN by this name: 1

Meaning: To sustain

A descendant of Abraham through Joseph's son Ephraim.

Only reference: 1 Chronicles 7:25

👥 REPHAIAH

of times mentioned: 5
# of MEN by this name: 5

Meaning: God has cured

1) A descendant of Abraham through Jacob's son Judah, in the line of the nation of Judah's third-to-last king, Jeconiah (also known as Jehoiachin).

Only reference: 1 Chronicles 3:21

2) One of Simeon's descendants who fought the Amalekites and won their lands.

Only reference: 1 Chronicles 4:42

3) A descendant of Abraham through Jacob's son Issachar.

Only reference: 1 Chronicles 7:2

4) A descendant of Jehiel, father of the Gibeonites.

Only reference: 1 Chronicles 9:43

5) A city official of Jerusalem and rebuilder of the walls under Nehemiah.

Only reference: Nehemiah 3:9

📍 REPHIDIM

of times mentioned: OT 5

Meaning: Balusters

A campsite of the Israelites on their way to the Promised Land. There was no water to drink at Rephidim, so God moved Israel to the rock of Horeb. While the Israelites were at Rephidim, they were attacked by the Amalekites. Moses stood on top of the hill, and as long as his arms were raised, Israel prevailed. When he grew tired, Aaron and Hur stood beside him and held up his hands until Joshua won the battle. Moses built an altar here and called it Jehovah-nissi, "God is my banner."

First reference: Exodus 17:1 / Last reference: Numbers 33:15

📍 RESEN

of times mentioned: OT 1

Meaning: To curb; a halter (as restraining)

An ancient Assyrian city built by Asshur.

Only reference: Genesis 10:12

👥 RESHEPH

of times mentioned: 1
# of MEN by this name: 1

Meaning: Lightning

A descendant of Abraham through Joseph's son Ephraim.

Only reference: 1 Chronicles 7:25

👥 REU

of times mentioned: 5
# of MEN by this name: 1

Genealogy of Jesus: Yes (as Ragau)

Meaning: Friend

A descendant of Noah through his son Shem. Same as Ragau.

First reference: Genesis 11:18 / Last reference: 1 Chronicles 1:25

👥 REUBEN

of times mentioned: 26
# of MEN by this name: 1

Meaning: See ye a son

Jacob and Leah's first son. Reuben slept with his father's concubine Bilhah, and Jacob heard of it. When his brothers wanted to kill Joseph, Reuben balked at it. He was sorrowful when he learned his brothers had sold Joseph as a slave, since he had hoped to return him to their father. When Joseph commanded them to bring Benjamin to Egypt in order to buy food, Reuben offered his sons as hostages to his father.

When Jacob blessed his sons, he did not forget Reuben's sin with Bilhah and prophesied that because he was unstable, Reuben would not excel.

First reference: Genesis 29:32 / Last reference: 1 Chronicles 5:3 / Key references: Genesis 37:21–22, 29; 49:3–4

👥 REUEL

of times mentioned: 10
# of MEN by this name: 4

Meaning: Friend of God

1) A son of Esau.

First reference: Genesis 36:4 / Last reference: 1 Chronicles 1:37

2) Father-in-law of Moses. Same as Raguel and Jethro.

Only reference: Exodus 2:18

3) Father of Eliasaph, captain of the tribe of Gad under Moses.

Only reference: Numbers 2:14

4) A descendant of Abraham through Jacob's son Benjamin.

Only reference: 1 Chronicles 9:8

👥 REUMAH

of times mentioned: 1
# of WOMEN by this name: 1

Meaning: Raised

Concubine of Abraham's brother Nahor.

Only reference: Genesis 22:24

📍 REZEPH

of times mentioned: OT 2

Meaning: A red-hot stone for baking

When Rabshekeh brought King Hezekiah of Judah an intimidating message from King Sennacherib of Assyria, he used Rezeph as an example of a fortress that had not withstood Assyria's might.

First reference: 2 Kings 19:12 / Last reference: Isaiah 37:12

👥 REZIA

of times mentioned: 1
# of MEN by this name: 1

Meaning: Delight

A descendant of Abraham through Jacob's son Asher.

Only reference: 1 Chronicles 7:39

REZIN

of times mentioned: 10
# of MEN by this name: 2

Meaning: Delight

1) A king of Syria who attacked Judah during the reigns of Kings Jotham and Ahaz. Rezin was killed in battle with King Tigleth-pileser's troops after Ahaz asked the Assyrian king to come to his aid.

First reference: 2 Kings 15:37 / Last reference: Isaiah 9:11

2) Forefather of an exiled family that returned to Judah under Zerubbabel.

First reference: Ezra 2:48 / Last reference: Nehemiah 7:50

REZON

of times mentioned: 1
# of MEN by this name: 1

Meaning: Prince

A rebel leader in Damascus who became King Solomon's adversary.

Only reference: 1 Kings 11:23

RHEGIUM

of times mentioned: NT 1

A port in southern Italy that Paul passed through on his way to Rome.

Only reference: Acts 28:13

RHESA

of times mentioned: 1
# of MEN by this name: 1

Genealogy of Jesus: Yes (Luke 3:27)

Meaning: God has cured

A descendant of Abraham through Isaac; forebear of Jesus' earthly father, Joseph.

Only reference: Luke 3:27

RHODA

of times mentioned: 1
# of WOMEN by this name: 1

Meaning: Rose

A young woman serving in the Jerusalem home of Mary, mother of John Mark. Responding to a knock at the gate, Rhoda heard the voice of Peter, who had just been miraculously freed from prison while Christians in Mary's home prayed for him. In her excitement, she forgot to let Peter in—and had a hard time convincing those praying that their request had been answered.

Only reference: Acts 12:13

RHODES

of times mentioned: NT 1

Luke mentions this Aegean island, which also had a city by the same name, as a point on Paul's voyage to Jerusalem.

Only reference: Acts 21:1

RIBAI

of times mentioned: 2
# of MEN by this name: 1

Meaning: Contentious

Father of one of King David's valiant warriors.

First reference: 2 Samuel 23:29 / Last reference: 1 Chronicles 11:31

RIBLAH

of times mentioned: OT 11

Meaning: Fruitful; fertile

A city on the border of the Promised Land, in the land of Hamath, where Pharaoh Necho imprisoned King Jehoahaz of Judah. When King Nebuchadnezzar of Babylon captured Jerusalem, King Zedekiah of Judah was brought to Riblah for judgment by his captor. Nebuchadnezzar's men slew Zedekiah's sons as he watched; then they put out Zedekiah's eyes and carried him to Babylon. At Riblah the Babylonians also killed Judah's chief spiritual and temple leaders. Same as Diblath.

First reference: Numbers 34:11 / Last reference: Jeremiah 52:27

👥 RIMMON

of times mentioned: 3
# of MEN by this name: 1

Meaning: Pomegranate

Father of two men who led raiding bands for Ish-bosheth, king of Israel.

First reference: 2 Samuel 4:2 / Last reference: 2 Samuel 4:9

📍 RIMMON

of times mentioned: OT 8

Meaning: Name of a Syrian deity

1) One of the forty-eight cities given to the Levites as God had commanded. Rimmon was given to them by the tribe of Zebulun. Zechariah foresaw that in the day of the Lord, Rimmon would be part of a lifted-up plain where people would live.

First reference: 1 Chronicles 6:77 / Last reference: Zechariah 14:10

2) A rock near Gibeah to which six hundred Benjaminites fled when the Israelites burned their city because they had abused and killed the concubine of a visiting Levite. Later Israel made peace with this errant tribe at the rock.

First reference: Judges 20:45 / Last reference: Judges 21:13

3) A city that became part of the inheritance of the tribe of Judah following the conquest of the Promised Land. Later it became part of Simeon's territory.

First reference: Joshua 15:32 / Last reference: 1 Chronicles 4:32

📍 RIMMON-PAREZ

of times mentioned: OT 2

Meaning: Pomegranate of the breach

A campsite of the Israelites on their way to the Promised Land.

First reference: Numbers 33:19 / Last reference: Numbers 33:20

👥 RINNAH

of times mentioned: 1
# of MEN by this name: 1

Meaning: Creaking

A descendant of Abraham through Jacob's son Judah.

Only reference: 1 Chronicles 4:20

👥 RIPHATH

of times mentioned: 2
# of MEN by this name: 1

A descendant of Noah through his son Japheth.

First reference: Genesis 10:3 / Last reference: 1 Chronicles 1:6

📍 RISSAH

of times mentioned: OT 2

Meaning: A ruin (as dripping to pieces)

A campsite of the Israelites on their way to the Promised Land.

First reference: Numbers 33:21 / Last reference: Numbers 33:22

📍 RITHMAH

of times mentioned: OT 2

Meaning: The Spanish broom

A campsite of the Israelites on their way to the Promised Land.

First reference: Numbers 33:18 / Last reference: Numbers 33:19

👥 RIZPAH

\# of times mentioned: 4
\# of WOMEN by this name: 1

Meaning: Hot stone

A concubine of Saul who, after the king's death, was romanced by Saul's military commander, Abner. When Saul's son Ish-bosheth, king of ten of Israel's tribes, confronted Abner about the liaison with Rizpah, the commander switched his allegiance to David, king of the tribe of Judah. Later, when David ruled all Israel, he allowed men of Gibeon to kill two of Rizpah's sons by Saul in retaliation for an atrocity Saul had committed. The grieving Rizpah spent days outdoors protecting the bodies of her sons from birds and wild animals.

First reference: 2 Samuel 3:7 / Last reference: 2 Samuel 21:11

👥 ROBOAM

\# of times mentioned: 2
\# of MEN by this name: 1

Genealogy of Jesus: Yes (Matthew 1:7)

Meaning: A people has enlarged

Greek form of the name Rehoboam, used in the New Testament. Rehoboam was a son of Solomon and the first king of Judah, the southern portion of divided Israel.

Only reference: Matthew 1:7

📍 ROGELIM

\# of times mentioned: OT 2

Meaning: Fullers (as tramping the cloth in washing)

Hometown of Barzillai, who brought food and other goods to King David as he fled from Absalom's rebellion.

First reference: 2 Samuel 17:27 / Last reference: 2 Samuel 19:31

👥 ROHGAH

\# of times mentioned: 1
\# of MEN by this name: 1

Meaning: Outcry

A descendant of Abraham through Jacob's son Asher.

Only reference: 1 Chronicles 7:34

👥 ROMAMTI-EZER

\# of times mentioned: 2
\# of MEN by this name: 1

Meaning: I have raised up a help

A son of King David's musician Heman, who was "under the hands of [his] father for song in the house of the LORD" (1 Chronicles 25:6).

First reference: 1 Chronicles 25:4 / Last reference: 1 Chronicles 25:31

📍 ROME

\# of times mentioned: NT 13

Meaning: Strength

This city was the center of the New Testament world and the capital of the Roman Empire. Though Rome's political influence dominated New Testament believers, the city of Rome is not frequently mentioned in scripture. "Strangers of Rome" witnessed the coming of the Holy Spirit to believers at Pentecost and heard them speak their own tongue. The Roman emperor Claudius commanded Jews to depart from Rome, so Aquila and his wife, Priscilla, moved to Corinth, where they met the apostle Paul. The apostle longed to visit Rome and wrote to the Christians there, probably while he was in Corinth. He remarked to the fledgling church that the whole world spoke of their faith (Romans 1:8) and that he was ready to preach the Gospel in their city (Romans 1:15).

After Paul's appearance in the temple in Jerusalem enflamed some Jews, a peacekeeping Roman guard stepped in. When the soldiers planned to scourge him, Paul demanded the treatment due a Roman citizen (Acts 22:25). Though he was not freed, God told Paul he would testify about Him in Rome. Before Festus, the Roman procurator of Judea, Paul appealed to Caesar Augustus for judgment. But not until his case was heard by King Herod Agrippa II was Paul sent to Rome under a Roman guard.

From Rome Paul wrote the epistles of Galatians, Ephesians, Philippians, Colossians, 2 Timothy, and Philemon.

First reference: Acts 2:10 / Last reference: 2 Timothy 1:17 / Key references: Acts 18:2; 23:11

👥 ROSH

of times mentioned: 1
# of MEN by this name: 1

Meaning: To shake the head

A descendant of Abraham through Jacob's son Benjamin.

Only reference: Genesis 46:21

👥 RUFUS

of times mentioned: 2
# of MEN by this name: 2

Meaning: Red

1) One of two sons of Simon, a man from Cyrene forced by Roman soldiers to carry Jesus' cross to Golgotha, the crucifixion site.

Only reference: Mark 15:21

2) An acquaintance, "chosen in the Lord," whom the apostle Paul greeted in his letter to the Romans.

Only reference: Romans 16:13

📍 RUMAH

of times mentioned: OT 1

Meaning: Height

Hometown of Zebudah, mother of King Jehoiakim of Judah.

Only reference: 2 Kings 23:36

👥 RUTH

of times mentioned: 13
# of WOMEN by this name: 1

Genealogy of Jesus: Yes (Matthew 1:5)

Meaning: Friend

The Moabite daughter-in-law of Naomi, Ruth married Naomi's son Mahlon while the family lived in Moab during a famine. When Ruth's husband, brother-in-law, and father-in-law died, Naomi decided to move back to Bethlehem. Though her daughter-in-law Orpah went back to her family, Ruth refused to leave Naomi. Together they went to Bethlehem, and there Ruth gleaned the barley harvest to provide food for them. Boaz became aware of Ruth and became kinsman-redeemer for her and Naomi. Ruth married Boaz and had a son, Obed, who was considered Naomi's grandson.

First reference: Ruth 1:4 / Last reference: Matthew 1:5 / Key references: Ruth 1:14–19; 4:1–10, 13–14

👥 SABTA

of times mentioned: 1
# of MEN by this name: 1

A descendant of Noah through his son Ham. Same as Sabtah.

Only reference: 1 Chronicles 1:9

👥 SABTAH

of times mentioned: 1
# of MEN by this name: 1

A descendant of Noah through his son Ham. Same as Sabta.

Only reference: Genesis 10:7

👥 SABTECHA

of times mentioned: 1
# of MEN by this name: 1

A descendant of Noah through his son Ham. Same as Sabtechah.

Only reference: 1 Chronicles 1:9

👥 SABTECHAH

of times mentioned: 1
# of MEN by this name: 1

A descendant of Noah through his son Ham. Same as Sabtecha.

Only reference: Genesis 10:7

👥 SACAR

of times mentioned: 2
# of MEN by this name: 2

Meaning: Recompense

1) Father of one of King David's valiant warriors.

Only reference: 1 Chronicles 11:35

2) A Levite "porter" (doorkeeper) in the house of the Lord.

Only reference: 1 Chronicles 26:4

👥 SADOC

of times mentioned: 2
# of MEN by this name: 1

Genealogy of Jesus: Yes (Matthew 1:4)

Meaning: Just

A descendant of Abraham through Isaac; forebear of Jesus' earthly father, Joseph.

Only reference: Matthew 1:14

👥 SALA

of times mentioned: 1
# of MEN by this name: 1

Genealogy of Jesus: Yes (Luke 3:35)

Meaning: Spear

Greek form of the name Salah, used in the New Testament.

Only reference: Luke 3:35

👥 SALAH

of times mentioned: 6
# of MEN by this name: 1

Genealogy of Jesus: Yes (Luke 3:35)

Meaning: Spear
A descendant of Noah through his son Shem. Same as Sala.

First reference: Genesis 10:24 / Last reference: Genesis 11:15

📍 SALAMIS

of times mentioned: NT 1

Meaning: Vibration (that is, billow)

A city on the east coast of the island of Cyrus where Barnabas and Saul preached the Word of God in the Jewish synagogues.

Only reference: Acts 13:5

👥 SALATHIEL

of times mentioned: 4
# of MEN by this name: 1

Genealogy of Jesus: Yes (Matthew 1:2; Luke 3:27)

Meaning: I have asked God

A descendant of Abraham through Jacob's son Judah, in the line of the nation of Judah's third-to-last king, Jeconiah (also known as Jehoiachin).

First reference: 1 Chronicles 3:17 / Last reference: Luke 3:27

📍 SALCAH

of times mentioned: OT 2

Meaning: Walking

A city ruled by Og, king of Bashan. After the conquest of the Promised Land, it became part of the inheritance of the tribe of Gad. Same as Salchah.

First reference: Joshua 12:5 / Last reference: Joshua 13:11

📍 SALCHAH

of times mentioned: OT 2

Meaning: Walking

A city of King Og of Bashan that became part of the inheritance of the tribe of Gad. Same as Salcah. First reference: Deuteronomy 3:10 / Last reference: 1 Chronicles 5:11

📍 SALEM

of times mentioned: OT 2 / NT 2

Meaning: Peaceful

The city ruled by King Mechizedek, a priest of God who blessed Abraham. Melchizedek also received a tithe of Abraham's spoils of war from the city of Sodom. Same as Jebus, Jebusi, Jerusalem, and Zion.

First reference: Genesis 14:18 / Last reference: Hebrews 7:2

📍 SALIM

of times mentioned: NT 1

Meaning: To agitate; to rock; to topple; or by implication, to destroy

A place near Aenon, the site where John the Baptist baptized believers. Both Salim and Aenon were probably on the west bank of the Jordan River.

Only reference: John 3:23

👥 SALLAI

of times mentioned: 2
# of MEN by this name: 2

Meaning: Weighed

1) A descendant of Benjamin who was chosen by lot to resettle Jerusalem after the Babylonian Exile.

Only reference: Nehemiah 11:8

2) A priest who returned to Jerusalem with Zerubbabel.

Only reference: Nehemiah 12:20

👥 SALLU

of times mentioned: 3
# of MEN by this name: 2

Meaning: Weighed

1) A descendant of Benjamin who was chosen by lot to resettle Jerusalem after the Babylonian Exile.

First reference: 1 Chronicles 9:7 / Last reference: Nehemiah 11:7

2) An exiled priest who returned to Judah under Zerubbabel.

Only reference: Nehemiah 12:7

👥 SALMA

of times mentioned: 4
# of MEN by this name: 1

Meaning: Clothing

Father of Boaz and a descendant of Abraham through Jacob's son Judah. He is called "the father of Bethlehem" (1 Chronicles 2:51). Same as Salmon.

First reference: 1 Chronicles 2:11 / Last reference: 1 Chronicles 2:54

👥 SALMON

of times mentioned: 5
# of MEN by this name: 1

Genealogy of Jesus: Yes (Luke 3:32)

Meaning: Clothing

Father of Boaz, who was Ruth's second husband, and a forefather of Jesus. Same as Salma.

First reference: Ruth 4:20 / Last reference: Luke 3:32

📍 SALMON

of times mentioned: OT 1

Meaning: A phantom (that is, an illusion or resemblance)

A mountain, perhaps near Shechem. The psalmist David compares the snow on this mountain with the way God scattered the kings who opposed him. Same as Zalmon.

Only reference: Psalm 68:14

 SALOME

of times mentioned: 2
# of WOMEN by this name: 1

Meaning: Welfare

A follower of Jesus who witnessed His death on the cross and later brought spices to anoint His body—only to find it gone due to His resurrection.

First reference: Mark 15:40 / Last reference: Mark 16:1

SALMONE

of times mentioned: NT 1

A high place that forms the northeastern point of the island of Crete. Paul passed by here on his voyage to Rome.

Only reference: Acts 27:7

SALU

of times mentioned: 1
# of MEN by this name: 1

Meaning: Weighed

Father of Zimri (1).

Only reference: Numbers 25:14

SAMARIA

of times mentioned: OT 111 / NT 13

Meaning: Watch station

1) The third capital of the northern kingdom of Israel. Sometimes the name is also used to describe the nation (see Samaria [2]). King Omri of Israel bought the hill of Samaria for two talents and built his capital city there, moving the capital from Tirzah.

In Samaria, Omri's son, King Ahab, built an altar to the pagan god Baal, leading his people into pagan worship. When Ben-hadad, king of Syria, put together an alliance of nations and attacked Samaria, an unnamed prophet came to Ahab, calling him to battle. Though Israel won the battle with the Syrians, the prophet warned that Syria would return. Again God promised Israel victory. The second time, Syria was routed, but Ahab made a covenant

with Ben-hadad. God told Ahab that because he did not kill Ben-hadad, Ahab's life would be taken in his place. In a battle at Ramoth-gilead, Ahab was killed by a Syrian archer.

Syria again attacked Israel in an attempt to take the prophet Elisha captive. The prophet asked God to blind the enemy. Elisha then led them into the city of Samaria. When their eyes were opened by the Lord, Elisha made peace between the king and Syria. But Syria again attacked, besieging the city of Samaria and starving the people. Four fearful lepers discovered that in the night the Lord made the Syrians hear the sound of chariots and they fled.

In Samaria, Jehu killed all of Ahab's line, as God had commanded him to do. Jehu called the people of Israel to worship Baal and then had his guard kill all the idolaters. Jehu had all the idols destroyed. But idolatry was not dead in Samaria, for its kings, including Jehu, still did not follow the Lord.

During the reign of King Hosea of Israel, Shalmaneser, king of Assyria, attacked Samaria, besieging it for three years. Finally, as Isaiah had predicted, Assyria took the city and carried away its people as captives.

The prophet Ezekiel compared Samaria's sin to that of Sodom, and the prophet Hosea clearly states that its rebellion against God caused it to become desolate (Hosea 13:16).

The apostle Philip preached Christ to the city of Samaria, and the people began to listen. But a sorcerer, Simon, bewitched them, so many turned to him instead. Peter and John were sent to the city to pray that the Christians there would receive the Holy Spirit. When Simon tried to buy the Holy Spirit, Peter called on him to repent.

First reference: 1 Kings 16:24 / Last reference: Acts 8:14 / Key references: 1 Kings 20; 2 Kings 6:11–23; 7:1–16; 10:11–29; Ezekiel 16:46–55

2) Another name for the northern kingdom of Israel, taken from the name of its capital. Following Assyria's conquest of the kingdom and deportation of the Jews, people from other lands were settled in Samaria. Though they eventually learned something about the Lord, the Samaritans developed a syncretistic religion, combining their pagan religious practices with Judaism. This impure worship was despised by the people of Judah.

King Josiah of Judah broke down the pagan altars that King Jeroboam of Israel had established in Samaria, and he burned human bones on the altars to pollute them.

When Rabshakeh wanted to convince the people of Jerusalem to support the Assyrians, he used

Samaria as an example of the mighty conquests of King Sennacherib.

God spoke against the false prophets of Samaria through the prophet Jeremiah, but He held out hope for that nation. The prophet Hosea spoke of the destruction of Samaria's idols and its king.

First reference: 1 Kings 13:32 / Last reference: Obadiah 1:19 / Key references: 2 Kings 23:15–19; Jeremiah 23:13; 31:5

3) During the New Testament era, Samaria was the central Roman province of western Palestine. Knowing the Jews' hatred for the Samaritans' theological error, Jesus used the example of the Good Samaritan to teach spiritual truth to the Jews (Luke 10:30–37). On the border between Samaria and Galilee, He healed ten leprous men, of whom only one gave thanks. At Sychar He spoke to a Samaritan woman about living water and declared Himself as the Messiah (John 4:4–26).

At His ascension into heaven, Jesus foretold that His disciples would be His witnesses in Samaria. After the death of Stephen, when the church was scattered, some believers fled to Samaria. Later, Paul and Barnabas traveled through the province and reported on the conversion of Gentiles there.

First reference: Luke 17:11 / Last reference: Acts 15:3

👥 SAMGAR-NEBO

of times mentioned: 1
# of MEN by this name: 1

A Babylonian prince who took part in the destruction of Jerusalem under King Nebuchadnezzar.

Only reference: Jeremiah 39:3

👥 SAMLAH

of times mentioned: 4
# of MEN by this name: 1

Meaning: Dress

A king of Edom, "before there reigned any king over the children of Israel" (Genesis 36:31).

First reference: Genesis 36:36 / Last reference: 1 Chronicles 1:48

📍 SAMOS

of times mentioned: NT 1

An island in the Aegean Sea, southwest of Ephesus. Paul stopped in Samos on his way to Jerusalem.

Only reference: Acts 20:15

📍 SAMOTHRACIA

of times mentioned: NT 1

Meaning: Samos of Thrace

An island of the northeastern Aegean Sea. Paul stopped in Samothracia briefly on his way to Philippi.

Only reference: Acts 16:11

👥 SAMSON

of times mentioned: 39
# of MEN by this name: 1

Meaning: Sunlight

The twelfth judge of Israel, from the time of his conception he was supposed to follow a Nazarite vow, which meant he could not eat or drink anything from a grapevine, drink alcohol, cut his hair, or eat anything unclean. Samson performed amazing feats of strength. When he married, Samson chose a Philistine woman. God used the union to confront the Philistines, who ruled over Israel. Betrayed by his wife, Samson took out his anger on her people, burning their grain and performing more feats of strength.

When he fell in love with Delilah, her fellow Philistines offered her money to find out the source of Samson's strength. Though Samson lied to her several times, he finally admitted that if she shaved his head, he would become weak. She did this, and he lost his strength because God had left him. The Philistines captured Samson, blinded him, and made him a slave. But as his hair grew, his strength returned. Brought to the Philistine temple to perform during their celebration, Samson leaned on the pillars of the temple and brought it down, killing the worshippers and himself.

First reference: Judges 13:24 / Last reference: Hebrews 11:32 / Key references: Judges 13:13; 14:4; 16:4–30

👥 SAMUEL

of times mentioned: 142
# of MEN by this name: 1

Meaning: Heard of God

Prophet and judge of Israel. Samuel was born after his mother, Hannah, petitioned God to give her a child and promised to give him up to God's service in return. After Samuel was weaned, Hannah brought him to the priest Eli to live at the temple and serve the Lord. Eli realized that God had spoken to Samuel and encouraged the boy to listen and respond. In his first prophecy, Samuel spoke out against the wickedness of Eli's sons.

Samuel led the Israelites to repent of their idolatry, and he judged Israel during his entire life. But when he became old, his sons were not faithful, and the people of Israel asked for a king. Though Samuel warned them against it, Israel insisted on a king, so God had the prophet anoint Saul. Samuel turned his authority over to Saul and encouraged the people to obey him, though their choice of Saul as a leader was evil.

When Saul disobeyed God, attacking the Amalekites but not destroying them and their cattle, Samuel informed Saul that God had rejected him as king. Samuel anointed David king in Saul's place. The prophet died and was buried in his home at Ramah. Same as Shemuel.

First reference: 1 Samuel 1:20 / Last reference: Hebrews 11:32 / Key references: 1 Samuel 1:11, 19–20, 24–28; 3:1–18; 7:3–6, 15–17; 10:1, 20–25; 12:1–25; 15:26; 16:13

👥 SANBALLAT

of times mentioned: 10
# of MEN by this name: 1

One of Nehemiah's opponents as he rebuilt Jerusalem, Sanballat plotted to fight against Jerusalem, forcing the Israelites to guard the uncompleted walls. Sanballat then accused Nehemiah of fomenting a revolt. When that came to nothing, he hired a man to report that men were coming to kill Nehemiah.

First reference: Nehemiah 2:10 / Last reference: Nehemiah 13:28

📍 SANSANNAH

of times mentioned: OT 1

Meaning: A bough

A city that became part of the inheritance of the tribe of Judah following the conquest of the Promised Land.

Only reference: Joshua 15:31

👥 SAPH

of times mentioned: 1
# of MEN by this name: 1

Meaning: Containing

A son of a Philistine giant killed in battle by one of King David's warriors, Sibbechai.

Only reference: 2 Samuel 21:18

📍 SAPHIR

of times mentioned: OT 1

Meaning: Beautiful

A city of Judah whose shameful behavior, the prophet Micah declared, would cause them to go into exile.

Only reference: Micah 1:11

👥 SAPPHIRA

of times mentioned: 1
# of WOMEN by this name: 1

Meaning: Sapphire

Wife of Ananias (1). The couple agreed to sell property and give only a portion of their gains to the church, while claiming they gave the whole price. When she lied to the apostle Peter, Sapphira died.

Only reference: Acts 5:1

👥 SARA

of times mentioned: 2
# of WOMEN by this name: 1

Meaning: Female noble

Greek form of the name Sarah, used in the New Testament.

First reference: Hebrews 11:1 / Last reference: 1 Peter 3:6

👥 SARAH

of times mentioned: 41
# of WOMEN by this name: 2

Meaning: Female noble

1) The name God gave Sarai, wife of Abram (Abraham), after He promised she would bear a child. Though she was ninety years old, God repeated the promise to give Abraham a son by her. When Sarah heard this, she laughed. A year later she bore Isaac. When Abraham's son Ishmael—child of Sarah's maid, Hagar—mocked Isaac, Sarah feared for her own son and had Hagar and Ishmael sent out of Abraham's camp.

When Sarah died, Abraham bought land from the Hittites and buried her in the cave of Machpelah.

First reference: Genesis 17:15 / Last reference: Romans 9:9 / Key references: Genesis 18:10–15; 21:1–10; 23:1–20

2) A daughter of Asher and granddaughter of Jacob.

Only reference: Numbers 26:46

👥 SARAI

of times mentioned: 17
# of WOMEN by this name: 1

Meaning: Controlling

The barren wife of Abram, Sarai traveled with her husband to Canaan at God's calling. Following a famine, they moved to Egypt, where Abram called her his sister, because he feared he would be killed so that an Egyptian could have her. She was taken by Pharaoh, but God revealed her marriage to him, and he returned her to Abram, sending them away. When Sarai had no children, she gave her maid, Hagar, to Abram to bear children for her. But Hagar despised Sarai and fled. God kept His promise to Abraham that He would give Sarai a son who would be the father of a multitude. He changed her name to Sarah. Same as Sarah.

First reference: Genesis 11:29 / Last reference:

Genesis 17:15 / Key references: Genesis 12:5, 10–20; 16:1–10; 17:15

👥 SARAPH

of times mentioned: 1
# of MEN by this name: 1

Meaning: Burning

A descendant of Abraham through Jacob's son Judah. Saraph was a potter.

Only reference: 1 Chronicles 4:22

📍 SARDIS

of times mentioned: NT 3

A city northeast of Ephesus, in Asia Minor's district of Lydia. It is only mentioned in Revelation, in the letter to the seven churches of Asia Minor. Though the church at Sardis had a reputation for being alive in Christ, Jesus said they were dead and needed to repent. Only a few believers there were not defiled.

First reference: Revelation 1:11 / Last reference: Revelation 3:4

📍 SAREPTA

of times mentioned: NT 1

A Sidonian city to which God sent the prophet Elijah after he fled from Jezebel and a drought began in Israel. In Sarepta, a widow cared for the prophet until the drought ended. Same as Zarephath.

Only reference: Luke 4:26

📍 SARID

of times mentioned: OT 2

Meaning: A survivor

A city that became part of the inheritance of Zebulun when Joshua cast lots in Shiloh to provide territory for the seven tribes that had yet to receive their land.

First reference: Joshua 19:10 / Last reference: Joshua 19:12

 SARGON

of times mentioned: 1
# of MEN by this name: 1

A king of Assyria in the days of the prophet Isaiah.

Only reference: Isaiah 20:1

SARON

of times mentioned: NT 1

Meaning: Sharon

A plain in western Palestine that parallels the eastern coast of the Mediterranean Sea. When Peter healed Aeneas in Lydda, on this plain's eastern edge, many people from Saron believed in Christ. Same as Sharon (1).

Only reference: Acts 9:35

SARSECHIM

of times mentioned: 1
# of MEN by this name: 1

A Babylonian prince who took part in the destruction of Jerusalem under King Nebuchadnezzar.

Only reference: Jeremiah 39:3

SARUCH

of times mentioned: 1
# of MEN by this name: 1

Genealogy of Jesus: Yes (Luke 3:35)

Meaning: Tendril

A descendant of Abraham through Isaac; forebear of Jesus' earthly father, Joseph.

Only reference: Luke 3:35

SAUL

of times mentioned: 422
# of MEN by this name: 3

Meaning: Asked

1) Anointed king of Israel by the prophet Samuel, Saul fought the Philistines throughout his reign. But after the king wrongly made a burnt offering to God at Michmash, Samuel told Saul that because of his sin, his kingdom would not be established forever, and God would seek a man after his own heart. When God ordered Saul to fight the Amalekites and kill all the people and cattle, Saul did not kill their king or cattle. God rejected him as Israel's king, and Samuel anointed David king.

After David killed the giant Goliath, Saul brought him into his court. Though his son Jonathan loved David, Saul became increasingly jealous of the young man and sought to kill him. Eventually David fled the court and began a series of battles with Saul.

When Saul gathered an army to fend off the Philistines, fearful, he sought out a witch at Endor. The king asked her to call up the dead Samuel, from whom he received a disconcerting answer. When Saul went into battle, three of his sons were killed, and he seemed to be losing. Saul's armor bearer refused to kill him, so he fell on his own sword.

First reference: 1 Samuel 9:2 / Last reference: Acts 13:21 / Key references: 1 Samuel 10:1, 17–24; 13:8–14; 15:1–3, 8–14, 35; 18:1–2, 5–11; 28:7–19; 31:1–4

2) A king of Edom, "before there reigned any king over the children of Israel" (Genesis 36:31).

First reference: Genesis 36:37 / Last reference: Genesis 36:38

3) A zealous Jew who witnessed the martyrdom of Stephen and persecuted Christians. As Saul traveled to Damascus, planning to imprison Christians there, Jesus met him and temporarily blinded him. At Damascus, God sent Ananias (2) to restore his sight. After becoming a Christian and being baptized, Saul began to preach the message of Christ in the synagogues. Learning of a conspiracy to kill him, he left Damascus and returned to Jerusalem. Only Barnabas's testimony about his preaching made the disciples believe that he was not plotting against them. Saul was chosen by the Holy Spirit for a missionary journey. At that time scripture begins to call him Paul.

First reference: Acts 7:58 / Last reference: Acts 26:14 / Key references: Acts 8:1, 3; 9:1–20, 23–27; 13:1–3, 9

SCEVA

of times mentioned: 1
# of MEN by this name: 1

Meaning: Left-handed

A Jewish chief priest in Ephesus whose seven sons were beaten by a demon-possessed man during an attempted exorcism.

Only reference: Acts 19:14

👥 SEBA

of times mentioned: 2
# of MEN by this name: 1

A descendant of Noah through his son Ham.

First reference: Genesis 10:7 / Last reference: 1 Chronicles 1:9

📍 SEBA

of times mentioned: OT 2

A kingdom on the west coast of the Red Sea, possibly near Cush, that the psalmist says will bring gifts to Solomon. The prophet Isaiah says God gave Seba for His people's redemption.

First reference: Psalm 72:10 / Last reference: Isaiah 43:3

📍 SECACAH

of times mentioned: OT 1

Meaning: Enclosure

A city that became part of the inheritance of the tribe of Judah following the conquest of the Promised Land.

Only reference: Joshua 15:61

📍 SECHU

of times mentioned: OT 1

Meaning: An observatory

A place probably near Ramah. Here King Saul, wanting to capture David, questioned people regarding the whereabouts of David and the prophet Samuel.

Only reference: 1 Samuel 19:22

👥 SECUNDUS

of times mentioned: 1
# of MEN by this name: 1

Meaning: Second

A man from Thessalonica who was a traveling companion of the apostle Paul.

Only reference: Acts 20:4

👥 SEGUB

of times mentioned: 3
# of MEN by this name: 2

Meaning: Aloft

1) A son of Hiel of Bethel who died when his father set up Jericho's gates.

Only reference: 1 Kings 16:34

2) A descendant of Abraham through Jacob's son Judah.

First reference: 1 Chronicles 2:21 / Last reference: 1 Chronicles 2:22

👥 SEIR

of times mentioned: 2
# of MEN by this name: 1

Meaning: Rough

Forefather of an Edomite family whose sons were Horite chiefs.

First reference: Genesis 36:20 / Last reference: 1 Chronicles 1:38

📍 SEIR

of times mentioned: OT 37

Meaning: Rough

1) A mountainous area originally inhabited by the Horites, Seir lay east of the Arabah Valley. Jacob sent a message to his brother, Esau, at his home in Mount Seir before they were reunited. Esau's descendants, the Edomites, conquered Seir.

Balaam foresaw that Seir would be a possession of the Israelites. But on their way to the Promised

Land, God told the Israelites to treat the land carefully and not provoke the Edomites because He would not give Israel the land. Not until the rule of King David did Israel conquer Edom (2 Samuel 8:11–14).

When the Moabites, Ammonites, and inhabitants of Mount Seir came against Judah, King Jehoshaphat called on God to protect Judah from these people whom God had not allowed the nation of Israel to conquer when it entered the Promised Land. God protected His people from their enemies by ambushing them Himself, causing the Ammonites and Moabites to rise up against the people of Mount Seir and slaughter them.

The people of Seir claimed that Judah was like all pagan nations and rejoiced at its desolation. The prophet Ezekiel promised that God would make the Edomite nation desolate.

First reference: Genesis 14:6 / Last reference: Ezekiel 35:15 / Key references: Genesis 33:14–16; Numbers 24:18; 2 Chronicles 20:5–23; Ezekiel 35:2–15

2) A mountain that formed part of the border of the tribe of Judah's territory.

Only reference: Joshua 15:10

♦ SEIRATH

of times mentioned: OT 1

Meaning: Roughness

A place in Mount Ephraim to which Ehud escaped after he killed Eglon, king of Moab.

Only reference: Judges 3:26

♦ SELA

of times mentioned: OT 1

Meaning: To be lofty

Edom's capital city, from which the prophet Isaiah declared that some escaped Moabites would send a lamb to Jerusalem, indicating submission to Israel. Same as Joktheel and Selah.

Only reference: Isaiah 16:1

♦ SELAH

of times mentioned: OT 1

Meaning: To be lofty

Edom's capital city, which King Amaziah of Judah captured and renamed Joktheel. Same as Joktheel and Sela.

Only reference: 2 Kings 14:7

♦ SELA-HAMMAHLEKOTH

of times mentioned: OT 1

Meaning: Rock of the divisions

A gorge in the wilderness of Maon where David and Saul met. When Saul heard that the Philistines had attacked Israel, he left David there.

Only reference: 1 Samuel 23:28

👥 SELED

of times mentioned: 2
# of MEN by this name: 1

Meaning: Exultation

A descendant of Abraham through Jacob's son Judah.

Only reference: 1 Chronicles 2:30

♦ SELEUCIA

of times mentioned: NT 1

Meaning: From Seleucus (a Syrian king)

A Syrian city that Barnabas and Saul visited on their first missionary journey before they sailed for Cyprus.

Only reference: Acts 13:4

👥 SEM

of times mentioned: 1
# of MEN by this name: 1

Genealogy of Jesus: Yes (Luke 3:36)

Meaning: Name

Greek form of the name Shem, used in the New Testament.

Only reference: Luke 3:36

👥 SEMACHIAH

\# of times mentioned: 1
\# of MEN by this name: 1

Meaning: Supported of God

A Levite "porter" (doorkeeper) in the house of the Lord.

Only reference: 1 Chronicles 26:7

👥 SEMEI

\# of times mentioned: 1
\# of MEN by this name: 1

Genealogy of Jesus: Yes (Luke 3:26)

Meaning: Famous

A descendant of Abraham through Isaac; forebear of Jesus' earthly father, Joseph.

Only reference: Luke 3:26

📍 SENAAH

\# of times mentioned: OT 2

Meaning: Thorny

A city in Judah to which captives returned after the Babylonian Exile.

First reference: Ezra 2:35 / Last reference: Nehemiah 7:38

📍 SENEH

\# of times mentioned: OT 1

Meaning: Thorn

A cliff on one side of a pass that Jonathan and his armor bearer had to cross to get to the Philistines' garrison before their heated battle at Michmash.

Only reference: 1 Samuel 14:4

📍 SENIR

\# of times mentioned: OT 2

Meaning: Peak

The name the Amorites gave Mount Hermon (Deuteronomy 3:9). Same as Hermon, Shenir, Sion (1), and Sirion.

First reference: 1 Chronicles 5:23 / Last reference: Ezekiel 27:5

👥 SENNACHERIB

\# of times mentioned: 13
\# of MEN by this name: 1

The king of Assyria who attacked and captured Judah's fortified cities during King Hezekiah's reign. Hezekiah paid him tribute to withdraw, but Sennacherib sent his commanders to threaten Jerusalem's people and force them to capitulate. Because the commanders spoke against the Lord, the angel of death killed 185,000 Assyrian soldiers, and Sennacherib withdrew to Nineveh.

First reference: 2 Kings 18:13 / Last reference: Isaiah 37:37 / Key references: 2 Chronicles 32:1, 9–19; Isaiah 37:36–37

👥 SENUAH

\# of times mentioned: 1
\# of MEN by this name: 1

Meaning: Pointed

Father of a Benjamite who was chosen by lot to resettle Jerusalem after returning from the Babylonian Exile.

Only reference: Nehemiah 11:9

👥 SEORIM

\# of times mentioned: 1
\# of MEN by this name: 1

Meaning: Barley

One of twenty-four priests in David's time who was chosen by lot to serve in the tabernacle.

Only reference: 1 Chronicles 24:8

◉ SEPHAR

of times mentioned: OT 1

Meaning: Census

A mountain in Arabia on the eastern border of the area where Shem's descendants settled.

Only reference: Genesis 10:30

◉ SEPHARAD

of times mentioned: OT 1

A place of uncertain location where the prophet Obadiah reported that exiles from Jerusalem lived. Obadiah foretold that one day they would possess the cities of the Negeb.

Only reference: Obadiah 1:20

◉ SEPHARVAIM

of times mentioned: OT 6

A Mesopotamian city whose people Shalmaneser, king of Assyria, brought to the conquered northern kingdom of Israel (Samaria) to repopulate it. The new settlers brought their pagan worship with them. When Rabshakeh tried to intimidate Judah, he used the gods of Sepharvaim as examples of deities who had not saved their people and pointed out that Sepharvaim's king had not stopped Assyria.

First reference: 2 Kings 17:24 / Last reference: Isaiah 37:13

👥 SERAH

of times mentioned: 2
# of WOMEN by this name: 1

Meaning: Superfluity

The daughter of Asher, a descendant of Abraham through Jacob.

First reference: Genesis 46:17 / Last reference: 1 Chronicles 7:30

👥 SERAIAH

of times mentioned: 20
# of MEN by this name: 9

Meaning: God has prevailed

1) The scribe in King David's court.

Only reference: 2 Samuel 8:17

2) The high priest during King Zedekiah's reign. He was killed following Nebuchadnezzar's invasion of Jerusalem.

First reference: 2 Kings 25:18 / Last reference: Jeremiah 52:24

3) A captain of Judah's troops whom Nebuchad= nezzar's governor Gedaliah tried to sway to support him.

First reference: 2 Kings 25:23 / Last reference: Jeremiah 40:8

4) A descendant of Abraham through Jacob's son Judah.

First reference: 1 Chronicles 4:13 / Last reference: 1 Chronicles 4:14

5) A descendant of Abraham through Jacob's son Simeon.

Only reference: 1 Chronicles 4:35

6) A priest who renewed the covenant under Nehemiah.

First reference: Ezra 2:2 / Last reference: Nehemiah 12:12

7) A priest who resettled Jerusalem following the Babylonian Exile.

Only reference: Nehemiah 11:11

8) A man whom King Jehoiakim ordered to imprison the prophet Jeremiah and his scribe.

Only reference: Jeremiah 36:26

9) A "quiet prince" who went into exile with King Zedekiah of Judah. At Jeremiah's command, he spoke a prophecy against Babylon.

First reference: Jeremiah 51:59 / Last reference: Jeremiah 51:61

👥 SERED

of times mentioned: 2
# of MEN by this name: 1

Meaning: Trembling

A son of Zebulun and a descendant of Abraham through his son Jacob.

First reference: Genesis 46:14 / Last reference: Numbers 26:26

SERGIUS

of times mentioned: 1
# of MEN by this name: 1

Roman ruler of Cyprus during the apostle Paul's first missionary journey. Sergius Paulus, "a prudent man" (Acts 13:7), asked Paul and Barnabas to share the word of God with him, but a false prophet named Bar-jesus (also known as Elymas) interfered. After Paul pronounced blindness on Bar-jesus, Sergius came to faith.

Only reference: Acts 13:7

SERUG

of times mentioned: 5
# of MEN by this name: 1

Meaning: Tendril

A descendant of Noah through his son Shem. Serug was the great-grandfather of Abraham. He lived 230 years.

First reference: Genesis 11:20 / Last reference: 1 Chronicles 1:26

SETH

of times mentioned: 8
# of MEN by this name: 1

Genealogy of Jesus: Yes (Luke 3:38)

Meaning: Substituted

Adam and Eve's third son, whom Eve bore after Abel was killed by his brother Cain. He became a forefather of Jesus. Same as Sheth (2).

First reference: Genesis 4:25 / Last reference: Luke 3:38 / Key reference: Genesis 4:25–26

SETHUR

of times mentioned: 1
# of MEN by this name: 1

Meaning: Hidden

One of twelve spies sent by Moses to spy out the land of Canaan.

Only reference: Numbers 13:13

SHAALABBIN

of times mentioned: OT 1

Meaning: Foxholes

A town that became part of the inheritance of Dan when Joshua cast lots in Shiloh to provide territory for the seven tribes that had yet to receive their land. Same as Shaalbim.

Only reference: Joshua 19:42

SHAALBIM

of times mentioned: OT 2

Meaning: Foxholes

A town of Dan that was taken by the Amorites. The Ephraimites took up arms in favor of their fellow Jews and made the Amorites subject to Dan. Under King Solomon's governmental organization, the son of Dekar was the officer in charge of supplying the king with provisions from this place. Same as Shaalabbin.

First reference: Judges 1:35 / Last reference: 1 Kings 4:9

SHAAPH

of times mentioned: 2
# of MEN by this name: 1

Meaning: Fluctuation

A descendant of Abraham through Jacob's son Judah.

First reference: 1 Chronicles 2:47 / Last reference: 1 Chronicles 2:49

SHAARAIM

of times mentioned: OT 2

Meaning: Double gates

David pursued the Philistines to this city that was part of the inheritance of the tribe of Simeon.

First reference: 1 Samuel 17:52 / Last reference: 1 Chronicles 4:31

SHAASHGAZ

of times mentioned: 1
# of MEN by this name: 1

A eunuch serving the Persian king Ahasuerus. Shaashgaz oversaw the king's harem, including the future queen Esther.

Only reference: Esther 2:14

SHABBETHAI

of times mentioned: 3
# of MEN by this name: 3

Meaning: Restful

1) A Levite who urged the Israelites to give up their "strange" (foreign) wives.

Only reference: Ezra 10:15

2) A Levite who helped Ezra to explain the law to exiles returned to Jerusalem.

Only reference: Nehemiah 8:7

3) A Levite who oversaw the outside of the Jerusalem temple in the time of Nehemiah.

Only reference: Nehemiah 11:16

SHACHIA

of times mentioned: 1
# of MEN by this name: 1

Meaning: Captivation

A descendant of Abraham through Jacob's son Benjamin.

Only reference: 1 Chronicles 8:10

SHADRACH

of times mentioned: 15
# of MEN by this name: 1

The Babylonian name for Hananiah, one of Daniel's companions in exile. Daniel had King Nebuchadnezzar make Shadrach a ruler in Babylon. When Chaldeans accused Shadrach and his fellow Jews, Meshach and Abed-nego, of not worshipping the king's golden idol, the three faithful men were thrown into a furnace. God protected them, and they were not even singed. Recognizing the power of their God, the king promoted them in his service.

First reference: Daniel 1:7 / Last reference: Daniel 3:30 / Key reference: Daniel 3:16–18

SHAGE

of times mentioned: 1
# of MEN by this name: 1

Father of one of King David's valiant warriors.

Only reference: 1 Chronicles 11:34

SHAHARAIM

of times mentioned: 1
# of MEN by this name: 1

Meaning: Double dawn

A descendant of Abraham through Jacob's son Benjamin. Shaharaim divorced two wives then had children by other wives in the land of Moab.

Only reference: 1 Chronicles 8:8

SHAHAZIMAH

of times mentioned: OT 1

Meaning: Proudly

A city that became part of the inheritance of Issachar when Joshua cast lots in Shiloh to provide territory for the seven tribes that had yet to receive their land.

Only reference: Joshua 19:22

⚲ SHALEM

of times mentioned: OT 1

Meaning: Complete (figuratively, friendly)

A city of Shechem where Jacob bought land and erected an altar called El-elohe-Israel.

Only reference: Genesis 33:18

⚲ SHALIM

of times mentioned: OT 1

Meaning: Foxes

A district that the future King Saul passed through as he searched for his father's missing donkeys.

Only reference: 1 Samuel 9:4

⚲ SHALISHA

of times mentioned: OT 1

Meaning: Trebled land

A district that the future King Saul passed through as he searched for his father's missing donkeys.

Only reference: 1 Samuel 9:4

⚲ SHALLECHETH

of times mentioned: OT 1

Meaning: A felling of trees

A gate at the temple in Jerusalem, "by the causeway of the going up," or "on the road that goes up" (ESV).

Only reference: 1 Chronicles 26:16

👥 SHALLUM

of times mentioned: 27
# of MEN by this name: 14

Meaning: Retribution

1) The fifth-to-last king of the northern kingdom of Israel. Shallum obtained the throne by assassinating King Zachariah. Shallum was himself assassinated only one month later.

First reference: 2 Kings 15:10 / Last reference: 2 Kings 15:15

2) Husband of the prophetess Huldah during the reign of King Josiah of Judah.

First reference: 2 Kings 22:14 / Last reference: 2 Chronicles 34:22

3) A descendant of Abraham through Jacob's son Judah. Shallum descended from the line of an unnamed Israelite woman and her Egyptian husband, Jarha.

First reference: 1 Chronicles 2:40 / Last reference: 1 Chronicles 2:41

4) Fourth son of Judah's king Josiah who inherited the throne from his father. Same as Jehoahaz (2).

First reference: 1 Chronicles 3:15 / Last reference: Jeremiah 22:11

5) A descendant of Abraham through Jacob's son Simeon.

Only reference: 1 Chronicles 4:25

6) A descendant of Abraham through Jacob's son Levi, and a priest through the line of Aaron. Shallum was a forefather of Ezra (2).

First reference: 1 Chronicles 6:12 / Last reference: Ezra 7:2

7) A descendant of Abraham through Jacob's son Naphtali.

Only reference: 1 Chronicles 7:13

8) A Jewish exile from the tribe of Levi who resettled Jerusalem.

First reference: 1 Chronicles 9:17 / Last reference: Nehemiah 7:45

9) A man of the tribe of Ephraim whose son Jehizkiah counseled his nation of Israel against enslaving fellow Jews from Judah who were captured in a civil war.

Only reference: 2 Chronicles 28:12

10) An exiled Levite who married a "strange" (foreign) woman.

Only reference: Ezra 10:24

11) Another exiled Israelite who married a "strange" (foreign) woman.

Only reference: Ezra 10:42

12) A city official who, with the aid of his daughters, helped to rebuild the walls of Jerusalem under Nehemiah.

Only reference: Nehemiah 3:12

13) The prophet Jeremiah's uncle.

Only reference: Jeremiah 32:7

14) Father of Maaseiah, a temple doorkeeper during Jeremiah's ministry.

Only reference: Jeremiah 35:4

👥 SHALLUN

of times mentioned: 1
# of MEN by this name: 1

Meaning: Retribution

A rebuilder of the walls of Jerusalem under Nehemiah. Shallun repaired the Fountain Gate, with its locks and bars, as well as the wall near the Pool of Siloam.

Only reference: Nehemiah 3:15

👥 SHALMAI

of times mentioned: 2
# of MEN by this name: 1

Meaning: Clothed

Forefather of an exiled family that returned to Judah under Zerubbabel.

First reference: Ezra 2:46 / Last reference: Nehemiah 7:48

👥 SHALMAN

of times mentioned: 1
# of MEN by this name: 1

A variant spelling of Shalmaneser, who was king of Assyria. The prophet Hosea described Shalman's viciousness in battle: "The mother was dashed in pieces upon her children" (Hosea 10:14).

Only reference: Hosea 10:14

👥 SHALMANESER

of times mentioned: 2
# of MEN by this name: 1

The king of Assyria who imprisoned King Hoshea of Israel and besieged, then captured, Samaria. He brought Israel into exile. Same as Shalman.

First reference: 2 Kings 17:3 / Last reference: 2 Kings 18:9

👥 SHAMA

of times mentioned: 1
# of MEN by this name: 1

Meaning: Obedient

One of King David's valiant warriors.

Only reference: 1 Chronicles 11:44

👥 SHAMARIAH

of times mentioned: 1
# of MEN by this name: 1

A son of Judah's king Rehoboam and a grandson of Solomon.

Only reference: 2 Chronicles 11:19

👥 SHAMED

of times mentioned: 1
# of MEN by this name: 1

Meaning: Preserved

A descendant of Abraham through Jacob's son Benjamin.

Only reference: 1 Chronicles 8:12

👥 SHAMER

of times mentioned: 2
# of MEN by this name: 2

Meaning: Preserved

1) A descendant of Abraham through Jacob's son Levi.

Only reference: 1 Chronicles 6:46

2) A descendant of Abraham through Jacob's son Asher.

Only reference: 1 Chronicles 7:34

👥 SHAMGAR

of times mentioned: 2
# of MEN by this name: 1

The third judge of Israel. Shamgar killed six hundred Philistines with an ox goad.

First reference: Judges 3:31 / Last reference: Judges 5:6

👥 SHAMHUTH

of times mentioned: 1
# of MEN by this name: 1

Meaning: Desolation

A commander in King David's army, overseeing twenty-four thousand men in the fifth month of each year.

Only reference: 1 Chronicles 27:8

👥 SHAMIR

of times mentioned: 1
# of MEN by this name: 1

Meaning: Observed

A descendant of Abraham through Jacob's son Levi.

Only reference: 1 Chronicles 24:24

📍 SHAMIR

of times mentioned: OT 3

Meaning: A thorn

1) A city that became part of the inheritance of the tribe of Judah following the conquest of the Promised Land.

Only reference: Joshua 15:48

2) A city on Mount Ephraim where the judge Tola lived and was buried.

First reference: Judges 10:1 / Last reference: Judges 10:2

👥 SHAMMA

of times mentioned: 1
# of MEN by this name: 1

Meaning: Desolation

A descendant of Abraham through Jacob's son Asher.

Only reference: 1 Chronicles 7:37

👥 SHAMMAH

of times mentioned: 8
# of MEN by this name: 4

Meaning: Consternation

1) A descendant of Abraham's grandson Esau, whose blessing as older brother was taken by the scheming Jacob.

First reference: Genesis 36:13 / Last reference: 1 Chronicles 1:37

2) The third son of Jesse and an older brother of King David. Shammah served as a soldier in King Saul's army. Same as Shimea (1) and Shimeah (1).

First reference: 1 Samuel 16:9 / Last reference: 1 Samuel 17:13

3) One of King David's warriors known as the "mighty men." Shammah defeated a troop of Philistines in a lentil field.

First reference: 2 Samuel 23:11 / Last reference: 2 Samuel 23:33

4) One of King David's valiant warriors.

Only reference: 2 Samuel 23:25

👥 SHAMMAI

of times mentioned: 6
# of MEN by this name: 3

Meaning: Destructive

1) A descendant of Abraham through Jacob's son Judah.

First reference: 1 Chronicles 2:28 / Last reference: 1 Chronicles 2:32

2) Another descendant of Abraham through Jacob's son Judah.

First reference: 1 Chronicles 2:44 / Last reference: 1 Chronicles 2:45

3) Yet another descendant of Abraham through Jacob's son Judah.

Only reference: 1 Chronicles 4:17

👥 SHAMMOTH

of times mentioned: 1
# of MEN by this name: 1

Meaning: Ruins

One of King David's valiant warriors.

Only reference: 1 Chronicles 11:27

👥 SHAMMUA

of times mentioned: 4
# of MEN by this name: 4

Meaning: Renowned

1) One of twelve spies sent by Moses to spy out the land of Canaan.

Only reference: Numbers 13:4

2) A son of King David, born in Jerusalem. Same as Shammuah.

Only reference: 1 Chronicles 14:4

3) Forefather of a Jewish exile from the tribe of Levi who resettled Jerusalem.

Only reference: Nehemiah 11:17

4) Forefather of a priest who returned to Jerusalem under Zerubbabel.

Only reference: Nehemiah 12:18

👥 SHAMMUAH

of times mentioned: 1
# of MEN by this name: 1

Meaning: Renowned

A son of King David, born in Jerusalem. Same as Shammua (2).

Only reference: 2 Samuel 5:14

👥 SHAMSHERAI

of times mentioned: 1
# of MEN by this name: 1

Meaning: Sunlike

A descendant of Abraham through Jacob's son Benjamin.

Only reference: 1 Chronicles 8:26

👥 SHAPHAM

of times mentioned: 1
# of MEN by this name: 1

Meaning: Baldly

A descendant of Abraham through Jacob's son Gad.

Only reference: 1 Chronicles 5:12

👥 SHAPHAN

of times mentioned: 30
# of MEN by this name: 4

Meaning: Rock-rabbit

1) Scribe for King Josiah of Judah, Shaphan brought the high priest Hilkiah the money the Levites collected to refurbish the temple. The priest reported that he had found the book of the law in the temple. Following the king's orders, Shaphan consulted with Huldah the prophetess.

First reference: 2 Kings 22:3 / Last reference: Jeremiah 36:12

2) Father of Ahikam, who consulted the prophetess Huldah at King Josiah's command.

First reference: 2 Kings 22:12 / Last reference: Jeremiah 43:6

3) Father of Elasah, a messenger whom Jeremiah sent to Babylon.

Only reference: Jeremiah 29:3

4) Father of Jaazaniah who burned incense, though he was not a priest. Possibly the same as Shaphan (1).

Only reference: Ezekiel 8:11

👥 SHAPHAT

of times mentioned: 8
# of MEN by this name: 5

Meaning: Judge

1) One of twelve spies sent by Moses to spy out the land of Canaan.

Only reference: Numbers 13:5

2) Father of the prophet Elisha.

First reference: 1 Kings 19:16 / Last reference: 2 Kings 6:31

3) A descendant of Abraham through Jacob's son Judah, in the line of the nation of Judah's third-to-last king, Jeconiah (also known as Jehoiachin).

Only reference: 1 Chronicles 3:22

4) A descendant of Abraham through Jacob's son Gad.

Only reference: 1 Chronicles 5:12

5) King David's chief shepherd over herds in the valleys.

Only reference: 1 Chronicles 27:29

📍 SHAPHER

of times mentioned: OT 2

Meaning: Beauty

A mountain where the Israelites camped on their way to the Promised Land.

First reference: Numbers 33:23 / Last reference: Numbers 33:24

👥 SHARAI

of times mentioned: 1
# of MEN by this name: 1

Meaning: Hostile

An exiled Israelite who married a "strange" (foreign) woman.

Only reference: Ezra 10:40

📍 SHARAIM

of times mentioned: OT 1

Meaning: Double gates

A city that became part of the inheritance of the tribe of Judah following the conquest of the Promised Land.

Only reference: Joshua 15:36

👥 SHARAR

of times mentioned: 1
# of MEN by this name: 1

Meaning: Hostile

Father of one of King David's valiant warriors.

Only reference: 2 Samuel 23:33

👥 SHAREZER

of times mentioned: 2
# of MEN by this name: 1

Son of the Assyrian king Sennacherib, who, with his brother Adrammelech, killed his father with a sword. After the assassination, Sharezer fled to Armenia.

First reference: 2 Kings 19:37 / Last reference: Isaiah 37:38

SHARON

of times mentioned: OT 6

1) A plain of western Palestine that parallels the eastern part of the Mediterranean Sea. The "rose of Sharon" (Song of Solomon 2:1) was a flowering bulb that grew on this plain. Isaiah predicted that the plain will be like a wilderness when God fills "Zion with judgment and righteousness" (Isaiah 33:5), and Sharon will see God's glory. Flocks will be kept there for God's people. Same as Saron.

First reference: 1 Chronicles 27:29 / Last reference: Isaiah 65:10

2) An area of "pasturelands" (ESV and NIV) in the land of the tribe of Gad. Scripture gives no clear description of Sharon's location.

Only reference: 1 Chronicles 5:16

📍 SHARUHEN

of times mentioned: OT 1

Meaning: Abode of pleasure

A city that became part of the inheritance of Simeon when Joshua cast lots in Shiloh to provide territory for the seven tribes that had yet to receive their land.

Only reference: Joshua 19:6

👥 SHASHAI

of times mentioned: 1
# of MEN by this name: 1

Meaning: Whitish

An exiled Israelite who married a "strange" (foreign) woman.

Only reference: Ezra 10:40

👥 SHASHAK

of times mentioned: 2
# of MEN by this name: 1

Meaning: Pedestrian

A descendant of Abraham through Jacob's son Benjamin.

First reference: 1 Chronicles 8:14 / Last reference: 1 Chronicles 8:25

👥 SHAUL

of times mentioned: 7
# of MEN by this name: 3

Meaning: Asked

1) A descendant of Abraham through Jacob's son Simeon. Shaul was born to Simeon and a "Canaanitish" woman.

First reference: Genesis 46:10 / Last reference: 1 Chronicles 4:24

2) A king of Edom in the days before Israel had a king.

First reference: 1 Chronicles 1:48 / Last reference: 1 Chronicles 1:49

3) A descendant of Abraham through Jacob's son Levi.

Only reference: 1 Chronicles 6:24

📍 SHAVEH

of times mentioned: OT 2

Meaning: Plain

A valley, also called the King's Dale, where Chedorlaomer, king of Elam, and his Mesopotamian allies overcame the Emims.

First reference: Genesis 14:5 / Last reference: Genesis 14:17

👥 SHAVSHA

of times mentioned: 1
# of MEN by this name: 1

Meaning: Joyful

A scribe serving in the government of King David.

Only reference: 1 Chronicles 18:16

👥 SHEAL

of times mentioned: 1
# of MEN by this name: 1

Meaning: Request

An exiled Israelite who married a "strange" (foreign) woman.

Only reference: Ezra 10:29

👥 SHEALTIEL

of times mentioned: 9
# of MEN by this name: 1

Meaning: I have asked God

Father of Zerubbabel, governor of Judah after the Babylonian Exile.

First reference: Ezra 3:2 / Last reference: Haggai 2:23

👥 SHEARIAH

of times mentioned: 2
# of MEN by this name: 1

Meaning: God has stormed

A descendant of Abraham through Jacob's son Benjamin, through the line of King Saul and his son Jonathan.

First reference: 1 Chronicles 8:38 / Last reference: 1 Chronicles 9:44

👥 SHEAR-JASHUB

of times mentioned: 1
# of MEN by this name: 1

Meaning: A remnant will return

Son of Isaiah who joined the prophet in delivering a message to Judah's king Ahaz.

Only reference: Isaiah 7:3

👥 SHEBA

of times mentioned: 15
# of MEN by this name: 5

1) A descendant of Noah through his son Ham.

First reference: Genesis 10:7 / Last reference: 1 Chronicles 1:9

2) A descendant of Noah through his son Shem.

First reference: Genesis 10:28 / Last reference: 1 Chronicles 1:22

3) A descendant of Abraham through his second wife, Keturah.

First reference: Genesis 25:3 / Last reference: 1 Chronicles 1:32

4) An Israelite who rebelled against King David.

First reference: 2 Samuel 20:1 / Last reference: 2 Samuel 20:22

5) A descendant of Abraham through Jacob's son Gad.

Only reference: 1 Chronicles 5:13

📍 SHEBA

of times mentioned: OT 17

Meaning: Seven

1) The land of the queen of Sheba who visited King Solomon of Israel to test his wisdom. Sheba's queen brought him gifts of spices, gold, and precious stones, part of the lucrative trade conducted by the caravans of her country. The prophet Isaiah predicted that one day, when the Redeemer comes to Zion, Sheba will bring gold and incense and praises to the Lord. In his prophecy foretelling the judgment of Tyre, Ezekiel spoke of Sheba as Tyre's merchants.

First reference: 1 Kings 10:1 / Last reference: Ezekiel 38:13 / Key references: 1 Kings 10:1–10; 2 Chronicles 9:1–12; Isaiah 60:6

2) A city that became part of the inheritance of Simeon when Joshua cast lots in Shiloh to provide territory for the seven tribes that had yet to receive their land.

Only reference: Joshua 19:2

📍 SHEBAH

of times mentioned: OT 1

Meaning: Seven or seventh

A well dug by Isaac's servants at the site that became the city of Beer-sheba. This city took its name from the well.

Only reference: Genesis 26:33

📍 SHEBAM

of times mentioned: OT 1

Meaning: Spice

A city east of the Jordan River that the Reubenites and Gadites requested as part of their inheritance because it had good grazing land for cattle.

Only reference: Numbers 32:3

👥 SHEBANIAH

\# of times mentioned: 7
\# of MEN by this name: 4

Meaning: God has grown

1) A priest who blew a trumpet before the ark of the covenant when David brought it to Jerusalem.

Only reference: 1 Chronicles 15:24

2) One of a group of Levites who led a revival among the Israelites in the time of Nehemiah.

First reference: Nehemiah 9:4 / Last reference: Nehemiah 10:10

3) A priest who renewed the covenant under Nehemiah.

First reference: Nehemiah 10:4 / Last reference: Nehemiah 12:14

4) A Levite who renewed the covenant under Nehemiah.

Only reference: Nehemiah 10:12

📍 SHEBARIM

\# of times mentioned: OT 1

Meaning: Ruins

A place to which the men of Ai chased the three thousand Israelite troops who attacked their city.

Only reference: Joshua 7:5

👥 SHEBER

\# of times mentioned: 1
\# of MEN by this name: 1

Meaning: Fracture

A descendant of Abraham through Jacob's son Judah.

Only reference: 1 Chronicles 2:48

👥 SHEBNA

\# of times mentioned: 9
\# of MEN by this name: 2

Meaning: Growth

1) King Hezekiah of Judah's scribe who represented Hezekiah and spoke to King Sennacherib's representative, Rab-shakeh, when the Assyrians attacked Jerusalem. Afterward, Shebna took a message to the prophet Isaiah.

First reference: 2 Kings 18:18 / Last reference: Isaiah 37:2

2) A treasurer (steward) Isaiah prophesied against for building himself a kingly tomb.

Only reference: Isaiah 22:15

👥 SHEBUEL

\# of times mentioned: 3
\# of MEN by this name: 2

Meaning: Captive of God

1) A descendant of Abraham through Jacob's son Levi and the line of Moses.

First reference: 1 Chronicles 23:16 / Last reference: 1 Chronicles 26:24

2) A son of King David's musician Heman, who was "under the hands of [his] father for song in the house of the LORD" (1 Chronicles 25:6).

Only reference: 1 Chronicles 25:4

👥 SHECANIAH

\# of times mentioned: 2
\# of MEN by this name: 2

Meaning: God has dwelt

1) One of twenty-four priests in David's time who was chosen by lot to serve in the tabernacle.

Only reference: 1 Chronicles 24:11

2) A priest in the time of King Hezekiah who helped to distribute freewill offerings to his fellow priests.

Only reference: 2 Chronicles 31:15

👥 SHECHANIAH

\# of times mentioned: 8
\# of MEN by this name: 7

Meaning: God has dwelt

1) A descendant of Abraham through Jacob's son Judah, in the line of the nation of Judah's third-to-last king, Jeconiah (also known as Jehoiachin).

First reference: 1 Chronicles 3:21 / Last reference: 1 Chronicles 3:22

2) Forefather of a Jewish exile who returned from Babylon to Judah under Ezra.

Only reference: Ezra 8:3

3) Forefather of another Jewish exile who returned from Babylon to Judah under Ezra.

Only reference: Ezra 8:5

4) An exiled Israelite who married a "strange" (foreign) woman. Shechaniah suggested to Ezra that he and his fellow offenders "make a covenant with our God to put away all the wives, and such as are born of them" (Ezra 10:3).

Only reference: Ezra 10:2

5) Father of a man who repaired Jerusalem's walls under Nehemiah.

Only reference: Nehemiah 3:29

6) Father-in-law of Tobiah (2).

Only reference: Nehemiah 6:18

7) A priest who returned to Jerusalem under Zerubbabel.

Only reference: Nehemiah 12:3

👥 SHECHEM

of times mentioned: 19
# of MEN by this name: 3

Meaning: Neck

1) Prince of the city of Shechem who raped Jacob's daughter, Dinah, then wanted to marry her. Dinah's brothers insisted that all males in Shechem be circumcised. While they recovered, Simeon and Levi attacked the city, killed Shechem, his father, and all the males of the city, and brought Dinah home.

First reference: Genesis 34:2 / Last reference: Judges 9:28 / Key references: Genesis 34:2–7, 11–12, 25–26

2) A descendant of Abraham through Jacob's son Joseph; founder of the Shechemite clan.

First reference: Numbers 26:31 / Last reference: Joshua 17:2

3) A descendant of Abraham through Joseph's son Manasseh.

Only reference: 1 Chronicles 7:19

📍 SHECHEM

of times mentioned: OT 45

Meaning: Ridge

A place in the land of Canaan where Jacob bought some land and built an altar called El-elohe-Israel. At the oak tree near Shechem, the patriarch buried all the idols in his household; then he built the altar at Bethel. Following Israel's conquest of the Promised Land, Shechem became one of the six cities of refuge established for those who had committed accidental murder. It was given to the Levites by the tribe of Ephraim. At Shechem Joshua gave his last address to the people of Israel, reminding them of their history and the faithfulness of God. He warned them of the dangers of idolatry and encouraged them to serve God.

Shechem was the home of Gideon's son Abimelech. The men of Shechem made him their king. But three years later he had to put down a rebellion there. Though the ruler of the city pushed the rebels out of Shechem, Abimelech conquered the city and sowed it with salt. The men in the tower of Shechem were killed when Abimelech led his supporters to burn the tower.

Rehoboam was supposed to be crowned king of Israel at Shechem. But Jeroboam, son of Nebat, and the people of Israel confronted the new king, asking him to lighten their burdens. When Rehoboam refused, the nation split into two kingdoms: Judah, which consisted of the tribes of Judah, Simeon, and part of Benjamin and was ruled by Rehoboam, and the northern kingdom of Israel. Jeroboam was crowned king of Israel and rebuilt Shechem. Same as Sichem and Sychem.

First reference: Genesis 33:18 / Last reference: Jeremiah 41:5 / Key references: Joshua 24; Judges 9; 1 Kings 12:1–20, 25

 SHEDEUR

\# of times mentioned: 5
\# of MEN by this name: 1

Meaning: Spreader of light

Forefather of a prince of the tribe of Reuben who helped Moses take a census.

First reference: Numbers 1:5 / Last reference: Numbers 10:18

SHEHARIAH

\# of times mentioned: 1
\# of MEN by this name: 1

Meaning: God has sought

A descendant of Abraham through Jacob's son Benjamin.

Only reference: 1 Chronicles 8:26

SHELAH

\# of times mentioned: 11
\# of MEN by this name: 2

Meaning: Request

1) Son of Jacob's son Judah. Judah refused to marry Shelah to Tamar, the widow of his first two sons.

First reference: Genesis 38:5 / Last reference: 1 Chronicles 4:21

2) A descendant of Noah through his son Shem.

First reference: 1 Chronicles 1:18 / Last reference: 1 Chronicles 1:24

SHELEMIAH

\# of times mentioned: 10
\# of MEN by this name: 9

Meaning: Thank-offering of God

1) A Levite who was chosen by lot to guard the east side of the house of the Lord.

Only reference: 1 Chronicles 26:14

2) An exiled Israelite who married a "strange" (foreign) woman.

Only reference: Ezra 10:39

3) Another exiled Israelite who married a "strange" (foreign) woman.

Only reference: Ezra 10:41

4) Father of a man who repaired Jerusalem's walls under Nehemiah.

Only reference: Nehemiah 3:30

5) A priest whom Nehemiah made a treasurer to distribute the portions of the Levites.

Only reference: Nehemiah 13:13

6) Father of Jehudi, who took a message from Judah's princes to the prophet Jeremiah's scribe.

Only reference: Jeremiah 36:14

7) A man whom King Jehoiakim ordered to imprison the prophet Jeremiah and his scribe.

Only reference: Jeremiah 36:26

8) Father of Jehucal, a messenger from King Hezekiah to the prophet Jeremiah.

First reference: Jeremiah 37:3 / Last reference: Jeremiah 38:1

9) Father of Irijah, who accused the prophet Jeremiah of siding with the Chaldeans.

Only reference: Jeremiah 37:13

SHELEPH

\# of times mentioned: 2
\# of MEN by this name: 1

Meaning: Extract

A descendant of Noah through his son Shem.

First reference: Genesis 10:26 / Last reference: 1 Chronicles 1:20

SHELESH

\# of times mentioned: 1
\# of MEN by this name: 1

Meaning: Triplet

A descendant of Abraham through Jacob's son Asher.

Only reference: 1 Chronicles 7:35

👥 SHELOMI

of times mentioned: 1
# of MEN by this name: 1

Meaning: Peaceable

Forefather of Ahihud, prince of the tribe of Asher when the Israelites entered the Promised Land.

Only reference: Numbers 34:27

👥 SHELOMITH

of times mentioned: 9
# of MEN by this name: 5
# of WOMEN by this name: 2

Meaning: Peaceableness, pacification

1) The mother of a man who was stoned for blaspheming the Lord.

Only reference: Leviticus 24:11

2) The daughter of Zerubbabel and a descendant of Abraham through Jacob's son Judah, in the line of the nation of Judah's third-to-last king, Jeconiah (also known as Jehoiachin).

Only reference: 1 Chronicles 3:19

3) A Levite chief appointed under King David.

Only reference: 1 Chronicles 23:9

4) A descendant of Abraham through Jacob's son Levi. Same as Shelomoth.

Only reference: 1 Chronicles 23:18

5) In David's reign, a Levite in charge of the treasures that were dedicated to the temple.

First reference: 1 Chronicles 26:25 / Last reference: 1 Chronicles 26:28

6) A son of Judah's king Rehoboam and a grandson of Solomon.

Only reference: 2 Chronicles 11:20

7) Forefather of a Jewish exile who returned from Babylon to Judah under Ezra.

Only reference: Ezra 8:10

👥 SHELOMOTH

of times mentioned: 1
# of MEN by this name: 1

Meaning: Pacification

A descendant of Abraham through Jacob's son Levi. Same as Shelomith (4).

Only reference: 1 Chronicles 24:22

👥 SHELUMIEL

of times mentioned: 5
# of MEN by this name: 1

Meaning: Peace of God

A man of the tribe of Simeon who helped Aaron take a census.

First reference: Numbers 1:6 / Last reference: Numbers 10:19

👥 SHEM

of times mentioned: 17
# of MEN by this name: 1

Meaning: Name

The eldest son of Noah, he joined Noah in the ark. After leaving the ark, Noah became drunk and lay unclothed in his tent. With his brother Japheth, Shem covered their father without looking at him. For this Noah blessed Shem. Same as Sem.

First reference: Genesis 5:32 / Last reference: 1 Chronicles 1:24 / Key references: Genesis 7:13; 9:18, 24–26

👥 SHEMA

of times mentioned: 5
# of MEN by this name: 4

Meaning: Heard

1) A descendant of Abraham through Jacob's son Judah.

First reference: 1 Chronicles 2:43 / Last reference: 1 Chronicles 2:44

2) A descendant of Abraham through Jacob's son Reuben.

Only reference: 1 Chronicles 5:8

3) A descendant of Abraham through Jacob's son Benjamin. Shema drove the original inhabitants out of the town of Gath.

Only reference: 1 Chronicles 8:13

4) A priest who assisted Ezra in reading the book of the law to the people of Jerusalem.

Only reference: Nehemiah 8:4

⚲ SHEMA

of times mentioned: OT 1

Meaning: A sound; a rumor; an announcement

A city that became part of the inheritance of the tribe of Judah following the conquest of the Promised Land.

Only reference: Joshua 15:26

👥 SHEMAAH

of times mentioned: 1
# of MEN by this name: 1

Meaning: Annunciation

Father of two of King David's valiant warriors.

Only reference: 1 Chronicles 12:3

👥 SHEMAIAH

of times mentioned: 41
# of MEN by this name: 25

Meaning: God has heard

1) A prophet who told King Rehoboam not to fight Israel when it revolted against him.

First reference: 1 Kings 12:22 / Last reference: 2 Chronicles 12:15

2) A descendant of Abraham through Jacob's son Judah, in the line of the nation of Judah's third-to-last king, Jeconiah (also known as Jehoiachin).

Only reference: 1 Chronicles 3:22

3) A descendant of Abraham through Jacob's son Simeon.

Only reference: 1 Chronicles 4:37

4) A descendant of Abraham through Jacob's son Reuben.

Only reference: 1 Chronicles 5:4

5) A Jewish exile, from the tribe of Levi who resettled Jerusalem.

First reference: 1 Chronicles 9:14 / Last reference: Nehemiah 11:15

6) Forefather of a Jewish exile from the tribe of Levi who resettled Jerusalem.

Only reference: 1 Chronicles 9:16

7) A descendant of Abraham through Jacob's son Levi. Shemaiah was among a group of Levites appointed by King David to bring the ark of the covenant from the house of Obed-edom to Jerusalem.

First reference: 1 Chronicles 15:8 / Last reference: 1 Chronicles 15:11

8) A Levite scribe who transcribed King David's divisions of the priests.

Only reference: 1 Chronicles 24:6

9) A Levite "porter" (doorkeeper) in the house of the Lord.

First reference: 1 Chronicles 26:4 / Last reference: 1 Chronicles 26:7

10) A Levite sent by King Jehoshaphat to teach the law of the Lord throughout the nation of Judah.

Only reference: 2 Chronicles 17:8

11) A descendant of Abraham through Jacob's son Levi. Shemaiah was among the Levites who cleansed the Jerusalem temple during the revival in King Hezekiah's reign.

Only reference: 2 Chronicles 29:14

12) A priest in the reign of King Hezekiah, Shemaiah helped to distribute the freewill offerings to his fellow priests.

Only reference: 2 Chronicles 31:15

13) A descendant of Abraham through Jacob's son Levi. Shemaiah was among those who distributed sacrificial animals to fellow Levites preparing to celebrate the Passover under King Josiah.

Only reference: 2 Chronicles 35:9

14) A Jewish exile who returned from Babylon to Judah under Ezra.

Only reference: Ezra 8:13

15) A Jewish exile charged with finding Levites and temple servants to travel to Jerusalem with Ezra.

Only reference: Ezra 8:16

16) An exiled Israelite priest who married a "strange" (foreign) woman.

Only reference: Ezra 10:21

17) Another exiled Israelite who married a "strange" (foreign) woman.

Only reference: Ezra 10:31

18) A man who repaired Jerusalem's walls under Nehemiah.

Only reference: Nehemiah 3:29

19) A false prophet who encouraged Nehemiah to flee from Jerusalem.

Only reference: Nehemiah 6:10

20) A priest who renewed the covenant under Nehemiah.

First reference: Nehemiah 10:8 / Last reference: Nehemiah 12:35

21) A priest who helped to dedicate the rebuilt walls of Jerusalem by playing a musical instrument.

Only reference: Nehemiah 12:36

22) A priest who helped to dedicate the rebuilt wall of Jerusalem by giving thanks.

Only reference: Nehemiah 12:42

23) Father of a prophet who ministered according to Jeremiah's words.

Only reference: Jeremiah 26:20

24) A false prophet who opposed the high priest Jehoiada and the prophet Jeremiah.

First reference: Jeremiah 29:24 / Last reference: Jeremiah 29:32

25) Father of a prince of Judah who heard Jeremiah's book of prophecies.

Only reference: Jeremiah 36:12

👥 SHEMARIAH

of times mentioned: 3
# of MEN by this name: 3

Meaning: God has guarded

1) A "mighty man" who supported the future king David during his conflict with Saul.

Only reference: 1 Chronicles 12:5

2) An exiled Israelite who married a "strange" (foreign) woman.

Only reference: Ezra 10:32

3) Another exiled Israelite who married a "strange" (foreign) woman.

Only reference: Ezra 10:41

👥 SHEMEBER

of times mentioned: 1
# of MEN by this name: 1

Meaning: Illustrious

The king of Zeboiim in the days of Abram.

Only reference: Genesis 14:2

👥 SHEMER

of times mentioned: 2
# of MEN by this name: 1

Meaning: Preserved

The owner of the hill of Samaria, which he sold to King Omri of Israel.

Only reference: 1 Kings 16:24

👥 SHEMIDA

of times mentioned: 2
# of MEN by this name: 1

Meaning: Name of knowing

A descendant of Abraham through Joseph's son Manasseh. Same as Shemidah.

First reference: Numbers 26:32 / Last reference: Joshua 17:2

👥 SHEMIDAH

of times mentioned: 1
# of MEN by this name: 1

Meaning: Name of knowing

A descendant of Abraham through Joseph's son Manasseh. Same as Shemida.

Only reference: 1 Chronicles 7:19

👥 SHEMIRAMOTH

of times mentioned: 4
# of MEN by this name: 2

Meaning: Name of heights

1) A Levite musician who performed in celebration when King David brought the ark of the covenant to Jerusalem.

First reference: 1 Chronicles 15:18 / Last reference: 1 Chronicles 16:5

2) A Levite sent by King Jehoshaphat to teach the law of the Lord throughout the nation of Judah.

First reference: 2 Chronicles 17:8

👥 SHEMUEL

of times mentioned: 3
# of MEN by this name: 3

Meaning: Heard of God

1) Prince of the tribe of Simeon when the Israelites entered the Promised Land.

Only reference: Numbers 34:20

2) An alternative name for the prophet Samuel.

Only reference: 1 Chronicles 6:33

3) A descendant of Abraham through Jacob's son Issachar.

Only reference: 1 Chronicles 7:2

📍 SHEN

of times mentioned: OT 1

Meaning: Crag

A place near the spot where Samuel set up a stone named Eben-ezer to commemorate a victory of Israel over the Philistines.

Only reference: 1 Samuel 7:12

👥 SHENAZAR

of times mentioned: 1
# of MEN by this name: 1

A descendant of Abraham through Jacob's son Judah, in the line of the nation of Judah's third-to-last king, Jeconiah (also known as Jehoiachin).

Only reference: 1 Chronicles 3:18

📍 SHENIR

of times mentioned: OT 2

Meaning: Peak

The Amorites' name for Mount Hermon. Same as Hermon, Senir, Sion (1), and Sirion.

First reference: Deuteronomy 3:9 / Last reference: Song of Solomon 4:8

📍 SHEPHAM

of times mentioned: OT 2

Meaning: Bare spot

A place God used to identify the borders of Israel when He first gave the land to His people.

First reference: Numbers 34:10 / Last reference: Numbers 34:11

👥 SHEPHATHIAH

of times mentioned: 1
# of MEN by this name: 1

Meaning: God has judged

Father of Meshullam, a Benjamite who resettled Jerusalem after the Babylonian captivity.

Only reference: 1 Chronicles 9:8

👥 SHEPHATIAH

of times mentioned: 12
# of MEN by this name: 9

Meaning: God has judged

1) The fifth son of David, born to his wife Abital in Hebron.

First reference: 2 Samuel 3:4 / Last reference: 1 Chronicles 3:3

2) A "mighty man" who supported the future king David during his conflict with Saul.

Only reference: 1 Chronicles 12:5

3) Leader of the tribe of Simeon in the days of King David.

Only reference: 1 Chronicles 27:16

4) A son of Judah's king Jehoshaphat, given "great gifts of silver, and of gold, and of precious things" by his father (2 Chronicles 21:3).

Only reference: 2 Chronicles 21:2

5) Forefather of an exiled family that returned to Judah under Zerubbabel.

First reference: Ezra 2:4 / Last reference: Nehemiah 7:9

6) Forefather of an exiled family—former servants of Solomon—that returned to Judah under Zerubbabel.

First reference: Ezra 2:57 / Last reference: Nehemiah 7:59

7) Forefather of exiles who returned from Babylon to Judah under Ezra.

Only reference: Ezra 8:8

8) A Jewish exile from the tribe of Judah who resettled Jerusalem.

Only reference: Nehemiah 11:4

9) A prince of Judah who sought to have King Zedekiah kill Jeremiah for his negative prophecy.

Only reference: Jeremiah 38:1

👥 SHEPHI

of times mentioned: 1
# of MEN by this name: 1

Meaning: Baldness

A descendant of Seir, who lived in Esau's "land of Edom." Same as Shepho.

Only reference: 1 Chronicles 1:40

👥 SHEPHO

of times mentioned: 1
# of MEN by this name: 1

Meaning: Baldness

A descendant of Seir, who lived in Esau's "land of Edom." Same as Shephi.

Only reference: Genesis 36:23

👥 SHEPHUPHAN

of times mentioned: 1
# of MEN by this name: 1

Meaning: Serpentlike

A descendant of Abraham through Jacob's son Benjamin.

Only reference: 1 Chronicles 8:5

👥 SHERAH

of times mentioned: 1
# of WOMEN by this name: 1

Meaning: Kindred

A descendant of Abraham through Joseph's son Ephraim. She built the city of Beth-horon.

Only reference: 1 Chronicles 7:24

👥 SHEREBIAH

of times mentioned: 8
# of MEN by this name: 2

Meaning: God has brought heat

1) A Levite whom Ezra called to serve in the temple upon his return to Jerusalem. Sherebiah was among a group of Levites who led a revival among the Israelites in the time of Nehemiah.

First reference: Ezra 8:18 / Last reference: Nehemiah 9:5

2) A Levite who renewed the covenant under Nehemiah.

First reference: Nehemiah 10:12 / Last reference: Nehemiah 12:24

👥 SHERESH

of times mentioned: 1
# of MEN by this name: 1

Meaning: Root

A descendant of Abraham through Joseph's son Manasseh.

Only reference: 1 Chronicles 7:16

👥 SHEREZER

of times mentioned: 1
# of MEN by this name: 1

A man sent by the people of Bethel to the prophet Zechariah to seek God's favor.

Only reference: Zechariah 7:2

📍 SHESHACH

of times mentioned: OT 2

A symbolic name for Babylon used by the prophet Jeremiah.

First reference: Jeremiah 25:26 / Last reference: Jeremiah 51:41

👥 SHESHAI

of times mentioned: 3
# of MEN by this name: 1

Meaning: Whitish

One of the gigantic children of Anak, who was killed after Joshua's death when Judah battled the Canaanites.

First reference: Numbers 13:22 / Last reference: Judges 1:10

👥 SHESHAN

of times mentioned: 4
# of MEN by this name: 1

Meaning: Lily

A descendant of Abraham through Jacob's son Judah. Sheshan had only daughters and gave one in marriage to his Egyptian servant, Jarha.

First reference: 1 Chronicles 2:31 / Last reference: 1 Chronicles 2:35

👥 SHESHBAZZAR

of times mentioned: 4
# of MEN by this name: 1

Another name for Zerubbabel, leader of exiles who returned from Babylon to Judah.

First reference: Ezra 1:8 / Last reference: Ezra 5:16

👥 SHETH

of times mentioned: 2
# of MEN by this name: 2

Meaning: Substituted

1) A leader of Moab mentioned in one of Balaam's prophecies.

Only reference: Numbers 24:17

2) A variant spelling of Seth, who was Adam's third son.

Only reference: 1 Chronicles 1:1

👥 SHETHAR

of times mentioned: 1
# of MEN by this name: 1

One of seven Persian princes serving under King Ahasuerus.

Only reference: Esther 1:14

👥 SHETHAR-BOZNAI

of times mentioned: 4
# of MEN by this name: 1

A Persian official who objected to the rebuilding of the Jewish temple.

First reference: Ezra 5:3 / Last reference: Ezra 6:13

👥 SHEVA

of times mentioned: 2
# of MEN by this name: 2

Meaning: False

1) A scribe serving in the government of King David.

Only reference: 2 Samuel 20:25

2) A descendant of Abraham through Jacob's son Judah.

Only reference: 1 Chronicles 2:49

📍 SHIBMAH

of times mentioned: OT 1

Meaning: Spice

A city built by the tribe of Reuben.

Only reference: Numbers 32:38

📍 SHICRON

of times mentioned: OT 1

Meaning: Drunkenness

A city that formed part of the border of the tribe of Judah's territory.

Only reference: Joshua 15:11

📍 SHIHON

of times mentioned: OT 1

Meaning: Ruin

A city that became part of the inheritance of Issachar when Joshua cast lots in Shiloh to provide territory for the seven tribes that had yet to receive their land.

Only reference: Joshua 19:19

📍 SHIHOR

of times mentioned: OT 1

Meaning: Dark (that is, turbid)

A river, perhaps the Nile or the River of Egypt (Genesis 15:18). When King David prepared to bring the ark of the covenant to Jerusalem, he called together all of Israel, from "Shihor of Egypt" to "the entering of Hemath." Same as Sihor.

Only reference: 1 Chronicles 13:5

📍 SHIHOR-LIBNATH

of times mentioned: OT 1

Meaning: Darkish whiteness

A landmark, probably a stream, that indicated the border of the inheritance of Asher. This landmark was mentioned when Joshua cast lots in Shiloh to provide territory for the seven tribes that had yet to receive an inheritance.

Only reference: Joshua 19:26

👥 SHILHI

of times mentioned: 2
# of MEN by this name: 1

Meaning: Armed

Grandfather of Judah's king Jehoshaphat.

First reference: 1 Kings 22:42 / Last reference: 2 Chronicles 20:31

📍 SHILHIM

of times mentioned: OT 1

Meaning: Javelins or sprouts

A city that became part of the inheritance of the tribe of Judah following the conquest of the Promised Land.

Only reference: Joshua 15:32

SHILLEM

of times mentioned: 2
# of MEN by this name: 1

Meaning: Requital

A descendant of Abraham through Jacob's son Naphtali.

First reference: Genesis 46:24 / Last reference: Numbers 26:49

SHILOAH

of times mentioned: OT 1

Meaning: Rill

A stream or spring in Jerusalem that was considered sacred by the Jews. Because the people of Judah rejected the stream's gentle waters and rejoiced in the Syrian king Rezin, the Lord promised to bring the king of Assyria against Judah. Same as Siloah and Siloam.

Only reference: Isaiah 8:6

SHILOH

of times mentioned: OT 32

Meaning: Tranquil

A town in the territory of Ephraim where the Israelites assembled after the battles to conquer the Promised Land. They set up the tabernacle, and at its door Joshua cast lots to give land to the seven tribes that had yet to receive any. Here, too, the Levites were allotted cities and their suburbs as God had commanded (Numbers 35:2). The tabernacle, Israel's worship center, remained at Shiloh until the time of Samuel.

When the tribes of Reuben, Gad, and Manasseh built an altar by the Jordan River, the rest of Israel met at Shiloh to go to war against these eastern tribes. The three tribes explained that they built this altar as a witness to their faith, not as a place of worship, and war was averted.

Israel fought the tribe of Benjamin over its abuse and murder of a Levite's concubine and vowed not to give their daughters as wives to the Benjaminites. When they realized that the people from Jabesh-gilead had not joined in the battle, the Israelite army attacked that town and killed all but four

hundred virgins, whom they brought to Shiloh. The Israelites agreed that the remaining Benjaminites should be given these women. Because there were not enough women for the tribe, the nation decided that during a festival in Shiloh the men who needed brides should catch the young women of Shiloh.

When Hannah, mother of the prophet Samuel, asked the Lord for a child, she went to Shiloh to pray. God answered her prayer, and she gave her son, Samuel, to the priest Eli to raise and train in the priesthood. Later God revealed himself to Samuel in Shiloh. When the Philistines attacked Israel and the battle went badly, Israel removed the ark from Shiloh; it was captured by the Philistines and never returned to Shiloh.

At Shiloh, the wife of King Jeroboam heard the prophet Ahijah's prediction of their son's death and the destruction of the northern kingdom of Israel. The prophet Jeremiah used Shiloh as an example of God's punishment of the unfaithful.

First reference: Joshua 18:1 / Last reference: Jeremiah 41:5 / Key references: Joshua 18:1–10; Judges 21:1–23; 1 Samuel 1; 1 Kings 14:1–18

SHILONI

of times mentioned: 1
# of MEN by this name: 1

Meaning: Inhabitant of Shiloh

A Jewish exile from the tribe of Judah who resettled Jerusalem.

Only reference: Nehemiah 11:5

SHILSHAH

of times mentioned: 1
# of MEN by this name: 1

Meaning: Triplication

A descendant of Abraham through Jacob's son Asher.

Only reference: 1 Chronicles 7:37

SHIMEA

of times mentioned: 4
# of MEN by this name: 4

Meaning: Annunciation

1) A brother of David. Same as Shimeah (2) and Shammah (2).

Only reference: 1 Chronicles 20:7

2) A son of King David, born in Jerusalem to Bathsheba (also known as Bath-shua).

Only reference: 2 Chronicles 3:5

3) A descendant of Abraham through Jacob's son Levi.

Only reference: 2 Chronicles 6:30

4) Another descendant of Abraham through Jacob's son Levi.

Only reference: 2 Chronicles 6:39

👥 SHIMEAH

of times mentioned: 4
# of MEN by this name: 2

Meaning: Annunciation

1) A brother of King David. Same as and Shammah (2) and Shimea (1).

First reference: 2 Samuel 13:3 / Last reference: 2 Samuel 21:21

2) A descendant of Abraham through Jacob's son Benjamin.

Only reference: 1 Chronicles 8:32

👥 SHIMEAM

of times mentioned: 1
# of MEN by this name: 1

Meaning: Annunciation

A cousin of King Saul and a descendant of Abraham through Jacob's son Benjamin.

Only reference: 1 Chronicles 9:38

👥 SHIMEATH

of times mentioned: 2
# of WOMEN by this name: 1

Meaning: Annunciation

Mother of Zabad, a royal official who conspired to kill Judah's king Joash.

First reference: 2 Kings 12:21 / Last reference: 2 Chronicles 24:26

👥 SHIMEI

of times mentioned: 42
# of MEN by this name: 18

Meaning: Famous

1) A descendant of Abraham through Jacob's son Levi. Same as Shimi.

First reference: Numbers 3:18 / Last reference: 1 Chronicles 23:10

2) A relative of King Saul who cursed King David when he fled Jerusalem. Later Shimei apologized to David, who pardoned him. But before he died, David warned Solomon about Shimei. Solomon told Shimei not to leave Jerusalem, or he would die. When two of Shimei's servants ran away, he left Jerusalem, so Solomon had him killed.

First reference: 2 Samuel 16:5 / Last reference: 1 Kings 2:44 / Key references: 2 Samuel 16:5–8; 19:18–23; 1 Kings 2:8–9, 36–46

3) An official who did not support Adonijah as king. Possibly the same as Shimei (4).

Only reference: 1 Kings 1:8

4) One of King Solomon's twelve officials over provisions.

Only reference: 1 Kings 4:18

5) A descendant of Abraham through Jacob's son Judah, in the line of the nation of Judah's third-to-last king, Jeconiah (also known as Jehoiachin).

Only reference: 1 Chronicles 3:19

6) A descendant of Abraham through Jacob's son Simeon. He fathered sixteen sons and six daughters.

First reference: 1 Chronicles 4:26 / Last reference: 1 Chronicles 4:27

7) A descendant of Abraham through Jacob's son Reuben.

Only reference: 1 Chronicles 5:4

8) A descendant of Abraham through Jacob's son Levi.

Only reference: 1 Chronicles 6:29

9) Another descendant of Abraham through Jacob's son Levi.

Only reference: 1 Chronicles 23:9

10) One of twenty-four Levite musicians who was chosen by lot to serve in the house of the Lord.

Only reference: 1 Chronicles 25:17

11) King David's official who was in charge of the vineyards.

Only reference: 1 Chronicles 27:27

12) A descendant of Abraham through Jacob's son Levi. Shimei was among the Levites who cleansed the Jerusalem temple during the revival in King Hezekiah's reign.

Only reference: 2 Chronicles 29:14

13) A Levite appointed by King Hezekiah to care for the temple contributions.

First reference: 2 Chronicles 31:12 / Last reference: 2 Chronicles 31:13

14) An exiled Levite who married a "strange" (foreign) woman.

Only reference: Ezra 10:23

15) Another exiled Israelite who married a "strange" (foreign) woman.

Only reference: Ezra 10:33

16) Another exiled Israelite who married a "strange" (foreign) woman.

First reference: Ezra 10:38

17) The grandfather of Mordecai, one of the heroes of the story of Esther.

Only reference: Esther 2:5

18) Head of a household whom Zechariah prophesied would be set apart before the day of the Lord.

Only reference: Zechariah 12:13

⚲ SHIMEON

of times mentioned: 1
# of MEN by this name: 1

Meaning: Hearing

An exiled Israelite who married a "strange" (foreign) woman.

Only reference: Ezra 10:31

👥 SHIMHI

of times mentioned: 1
# of MEN by this name: 1

Meaning: Famous

A descendant of Abraham through Jacob's son Benjamin.

Only reference: 1 Chronicles 8:21

👥 SHIMI

of times mentioned: 1
# of MEN by this name: 1

Meaning: Famous

A descendant of Abraham through Jacob's son Levi. Same as Shimei (1).

Only reference: Exodus 6:17

👥 SHIMMA

of times mentioned: 1
# of MEN by this name: 1

Meaning: Annunciation

Third son of Jesse and an older brother of David. Same as Shammah (2) and Shimeah (1).

Only reference: 1 Chronicles 2:13

👥 SHIMON

of times mentioned: 1
# of MEN by this name: 1

Meaning: Desert

A descendant of Abraham through Jacob's son Judah.

Only reference: 1 Chronicles 4:20

👥 SHIMRATH

\# of times mentioned: 1
\# of MEN by this name: 1

Meaning: Guardship

A descendant of Abraham through Jacob's son Benjamin.

Only reference: 1 Chronicles 8:21

👥 SHIMRI

\# of times mentioned: 3
\# of MEN by this name: 3

Meaning: Watchful

1) A descendant of Abraham through Jacob's son Simeon.

Only reference: 1 Chronicles 4:37

2) Father of one of King David's valiant warriors.

Only reference: 1 Chronicles 11:45

3) A descendant of Abraham through Jacob's son Levi. Shimri was among the Levites who cleansed the Jerusalem temple during the revival of King Hezekiah's day.

Only reference: 2 Chronicles 29:13

👥 SHIMRITH

\# of times mentioned: 1
\# of WOMEN by this name: 1

Meaning: Female guard

Mother of Jehozabad, a royal official who conspired to kill Judah's king Joash. Same as Shomer (1).

Only reference: 2 Chronicles 24:26

👥 SHIMROM

\# of times mentioned: 1
\# of MEN by this name: 1

Meaning: Guardianship

A descendant of Abraham through Jacob's son Issachar. Same as Shimron.

Only reference: 1 Chronicles 7:1

👥 SHIMRON

\# of times mentioned: 4
\# of MEN by this name: 1

Meaning: Guardianship

A descendant of Abraham through Jacob's son Issachar. Same as Shimrom.

First reference: Genesis 46:13 / Last reference: Joshua 19:15

📍 SHIMRON-MERON

\# of times mentioned: OT 1

Meaning: Guard of lashing

A city on the western side of the Jordan River conquered by Joshua and the Israelites.

Only reference: Joshua 12:20

👥 SHIMSHAI

\# of times mentioned: 4
\# of MEN by this name: 1

Meaning: Sunny

A scribe who wrote King Artaxerxes a letter objecting to the rebuilding of Jerusalem. As a result, the king temporarily stopped the rebuilding.

First reference: Ezra 4:8 / Last reference: Ezra 4:23

👥 SHINAB

\# of times mentioned: 1
\# of MEN by this name: 1

Meaning: Father has turned

The king of Admah in the days of Abraham.

Only reference: Genesis 14:2

SHINAR

of times mentioned: OT 7

The ancient land of Babel where Nimrod ruled, where the tower of Babel was built, and where the cities of Erech, Akkad, and Calneh were located. Shinar became one of the allies of Chedorlaomer, king of Elam, who made war with Sodom and Gomorrah. Later the land of Shinar was called Babylon (Daniel 1:2).

The prophet Isaiah promised that when Christ returns, His people of Shinar will be recovered.

First reference: Genesis 10:10 / Last reference: Zechariah 5:11

SHIPHI

of times mentioned: 1
# of MEN by this name: 1

Meaning: Copious

A descendant of Abraham through Jacob's son Simeon.

Only reference: 1 Chronicles 4:37

SHIPHRAH

of times mentioned: 1
# of WOMEN by this name: 1

Meaning: Brightness

A Hebrew midwife who did not obey the king of Egypt's command to kill all male Israelite babies.

Only reference: Exodus 1:15

SHIPHTAN

of times mentioned: 1
# of MEN by this name: 1

Meaning: Judgelike

Forefather of Kemuel, prince of the tribe of Ephraim when the Israelites entered the Promised Land.

Only reference: Numbers 34:24

SHISHA

of times mentioned: 1
# of MEN by this name: 1

Meaning: Whiteness

Father of two scribes who served King Solomon.

Only reference: 1 Kings 4:3

SHISHAK

of times mentioned: 7
# of MEN by this name: 1

The king of Egypt to whom Jeroboam fled when Solomon discovered he had been anointed king over the northern ten tribes. During the reign of Solomon's son Rehoboam, Shishak attacked Judah, captured Jerusalem, and took the treasures of the temple and palace.

First reference: 1 Kings 11:40 / Last reference: 2 Chronicles 12:9

SHITRAI

of times mentioned: 1
# of MEN by this name: 1

Meaning: Magisterial

King David's chief shepherd over herds in Sharon.

Only reference: 1 Chronicles 27:29

SHIZA

of times mentioned: 1
# of MEN by this name: 1

Father of one of King David's valiant warriors.

Only reference: 1 Chronicles 11:42

SHOBAB

of times mentioned: 4
# of MEN by this name: 2

Meaning: Rebellious

1) A son of King David, born in Jerusalem.

First reference: 2 Samuel 5:14 / Last reference: 1 Chronicles 4:14

2) A descendant of Abraham through Jacob's son Judah.

Only reference: 1 Chronicles 2:18

👥 SHOBACH

of times mentioned: 2
# of MEN by this name: 1

Meaning: Thicket

A captain in the Syrian army of King Hadarezer. Shobach was defeated in battle by King David and his Israelite warriors. Same as Shophach.

First reference: 2 Samuel 10:16 / Last reference: 2 Samuel 10:18

👥 SHOBAI

of times mentioned: 2
# of MEN by this name: 1

Meaning: Captor

Forefather of an exiled family that returned to Judah under Zerubbabel.

First reference: Ezra 2:42 / Last reference: Nehemiah 7:45

👥 SHOBAL

of times mentioned: 9
# of MEN by this name: 3

Meaning: Overflowing

1) A descendant of Seir, who lived in Esau's "land of Edom."

First reference: Genesis 36:20 / Last reference: 1 Chronicles 1:40

2) A descendant of Abraham through Jacob's son Judah.

First reference: 1 Chronicles 2:50 / Last reference: 1 Chronicles 2:52

3) Another descendant of Abraham through Jacob's son Judah.

First reference: 1 Chronicles 4:1 / Last reference: 1 Chronicles 4:2

👥 SHOBEK

of times mentioned: 1
# of MEN by this name: 1

Meaning: Forsaking

A Jewish leader who renewed the covenant under Nehemiah.

Only reference: Nehemiah 10:24

👥 SHOBI

of times mentioned: 1
# of MEN by this name: 1

Meaning: Captor

A man who brought food and supplies to King David and his soldiers as they fled from the army of David's son Absalom, who was staging a coup.

Only reference: 2 Samuel 17:27

📍 SHOCHO

of times mentioned: OT 1

During the reign of King Ahaz, Shocho was one of the cities of the southern low country of Judah that was invaded and occupied by the Philistines. Same as Shochoh and Shoco.

Only reference: 2 Chronicles 28:18

📍 SHOCHOH

of times mentioned: OT 1

A city of Judah near the spot where the Philistines camped before David fought Goliath. Same as Shocho and Shoco.

Only reference: 1 Samuel 17:1

📍 SHOCO

of times mentioned: OT 1

A city of Judah that King Rehoboam fortified to defend his nation. Same as Shocho and Shochoh.

Only reference: 2 Chronicles 11:7

👥 SHOHAM

of times mentioned: 1
# of MEN by this name: 1

Meaning: To blanch

A descendant of Abraham through Jacob's son Levi.

Only reference: 1 Chronicles 24:27

👥 SHOMER

of times mentioned: 2
# of WOMEN by this name: 1
# of MEN by this name: 2

Meaning: Keeper

1) Mother of one of two royal officials who conspired to kill Judah's king Joash. Same as Shimrith.

Only reference: 2 Kings 12:21

2) A descendant of Abraham through Jacob's son Asher.

Only reference: 1 Chronicles 7:32

👥 SHOPHACH

of times mentioned: 2
# of MEN by this name: 1

Meaning: Poured

A captain in the Syrian army of King Hadarezer. Shophach was defeated in battle by King David and his Israelite warriors. Same as Shobach.

First reference: 1 Chronicles 19:16 / Last reference: 1 Chronicles 19:18

📍 SHOPHAN

of times mentioned: OT 1

A city built by the tribe of Gad.

Only reference: Numbers 32:35

👥 SHUA

of times mentioned: 2
# of WOMEN by this name: 2

Meaning: A cry

1) Mother-in-law of Judah, the son of Jacob. Same as Shuah (2).

Only reference: 1 Chronicles 2:3

Meaning: Wealth

2) Daughter of Heber and a descendant of Abraham through Jacob's son Asher.

Only reference: 1 Chronicles 7:32

👥 SHUAH

of times mentioned: 5
# of MEN by this name: 3

Meaning: Dell

1) A son of Abraham by his second wife, Keturah.

First reference: Genesis 25:2 / Last reference: 1 Chronicles 1:32

2) Mother-in-law of Judah, the son of Jacob. Same as Shua (1).

First reference: Genesis 38:2 / Last reference: Genesis 38:12

3) A descendant of Abraham through Jacob's son Judah.

Only reference: 1 Chronicles 4:11

👥 SHUAL

of times mentioned: 1
# of MEN by this name: 1

Meaning: Jackal

A descendant of Abraham through Jacob's son Asher.

Only reference: 1 Chronicles 7:36

● SHUAL

of times mentioned: OT 1

Meaning: A jackal (as a burrower)

A land near Ophrah. During King Saul's reign, the Philistine army camped near Michmash and sent out a company in this direction.

Only reference: 1 Samuel 13:17

●● SHUBAEL

of times mentioned: 3
# of MEN by this name: 2

Meaning: God has favored

1) A descendant of Abraham through Jacob's son Levi.

Only reference: 1 Chronicles 24:20

2) One of twenty-four Levite musicians who was chosen by lot to serve in the house of the Lord.

Only reference: 1 Chronicles 25:20

●● SHUHAM

of times mentioned: 1
# of MEN by this name: 1

Meaning: Humbly

A descendant of Abraham through Jacob's son Dan.

Only reference: Numbers 26:42

● SHUNEM

of times mentioned: OT 3

Meaning: Quietly

A city that became part of the inheritance of Issachar when Joshua cast lots in Shiloh to provide territory for the seven tribes that had yet to receive their land. The Philistine army camped at Shunem when it opposed King Saul's army at Gilboa. A woman of Shunem provided the prophet Elisha with food and lodging when he passed through the city. In return for her help, the prophet told her that she would bear a son. When the boy became ill and died, the prophet brought him back to life.

First reference: Joshua 19:18 / Last reference: 2 Kings 4:8

●● SHUNI

of times mentioned: 2
# of MEN by this name: 1

Meaning: Rest

A descendant of Abraham through Jacob's son Gad.

First reference: Genesis 46:16 / Last reference: Numbers 26:15

●● SHUPHAM

of times mentioned: 1
# of MEN by this name: 1

Meaning: Serpent-like

A descendant of Abraham through Jacob's son Benjamin.

Only reference: Numbers 26:39

●● SHUPPIM

of times mentioned: 3
# of MEN by this name: 2

Meaning: Serpents

1) A descendant of Abraham through Jacob's son Benjamin.

First reference: 1 Chronicles 7:12 / Last reference: 1 Chronicles 7:15

2) A Levite who was chosen by lot to guard the west side of the house of the Lord.

Only reference: 1 Chronicles 26:16

● SHUR

of times mentioned: OT 6

Meaning: A wall (as going about)

A wilderness area of the northern Sinai Peninsula. Following Hagar's expulsion from Abraham's camp, the angel of the Lord found her "by the fountain in the way to Shur" (Genesis 16:7). The people of Ishmael, Hagar's son, would live "from Havilah unto Shur" (Genesis 25:18). After the destruction of Sodom and Gomorrah, Abraham lived between Kadesh and Shur.

King Saul fought the Amalekites from Havilah to Shur. When David served King Achish of Gath, he battled the Geshurites, Gezrites, and Amalekites. These people lived in the land from Shur to Egypt.

First reference: Genesis 16:7 / Last reference: 1 Samuel 27:8

📍 SHUSHAN

of times mentioned: OT 21

Meaning: A lily or a straight trumpet

The Persian capital, in the province of Elam. King Ahasuerus (also called Xerxes) reigned in Shushan. Here he held the feast at which Queen Vashti refused to appear. Esther was brought to the palace in Shushan, along with the other women from whom Ahasuerus planned to choose a wife. Esther's cousin Mordecai came to her at the palace to tell her of Haman's plan to destroy the Jews. The brave queen confronted Ahasuerus while all the Jews of the city prayed for her. She succeeded in her case with the king, and a commandment was made in the city that the Jews could protect themselves from the attack Haman had planned against them. In Shusan, the Jews killed eight hundred men and Haman's ten sons, whose bodies were hanged.

After Ahasuerus, King Artaxerxes ruled at the palace of Shushan; Nehemiah served this king. Daniel also was in this palace when he had a vision of a ram and a goat.

First reference: Nehemiah 1:1 / Last reference: Daniel 8:2 / Key references: Esther 4:8; 9:6–15

👥 SHUTHELAH

of times mentioned: 4
# of MEN by this name: 2

Meaning: Crash or breakage

1) A descendant of Abraham through Joseph's son Ephraim.

First reference: Numbers 26:35 / Last reference: 1 Chronicles 7:20

2) Another descendant of Abraham through Joseph's son Ephraim.

Only reference: 1 Chronicles 7:21

👥 SIA

of times mentioned: 1
# of MEN by this name: 1

Meaning: Converse

Forefather of an exiled family that returned to Judah under Zerubbabel. Same as Siaha.

Only reference: Nehemiah 7:47

👥 SIAHA

of times mentioned: 1
# of MEN by this name: 1

Meaning: Converse

Forefather of an exiled family that returned to Judah under Zerubbabel. Same as Sia.

Only reference: Ezra 2:44

👥 SIBBECAI

of times mentioned: 2
# of MEN by this name: 1

Meaning: Corpselike

A commander in King David's army overseeing twenty-four thousand men in the eighth month of each year. Same as Sibbechai.

First reference: 1 Chronicles 11:29 / Last reference: 1 Chronicles 27:11

👥 SIBBECHAI

of times mentioned: 2
# of MEN by this name: 1

Meaning: Meaning

One of King David's valiant warriors, Sibbechai killed Sippai, "that was of the children of the giant" (1 Chronicles 20:4). Same as Sibbecai.

First reference: 2 Samuel 21:18 / Last reference: 1 Chronicles 20:4

📍 SIBMAH

of times mentioned: OT 4

Meaning: Spice

A Moabite town that became part of the inheritance of the tribe of Reuben. In his oracle about Moab, Isaiah foretold that the harvest of Sibmah's vineyards would fail.

First reference: Joshua 13:19 / Last reference: Jeremiah 48:32

📍 SIBRAIM

of times mentioned: OT 1

Meaning: Double hope

A landmark mentioned in the book of Ezekiel as the northern boundary of Palestine. It lay between Hamath and Damascus.

Only reference: Ezekiel 47:16

📍 SICHEM

of times mentioned: OT 1

Meaning: Ridge

The place to which Abram first went when he traveled to Canaan at God's command. Here God promised He would give the land to Abram's heirs. Abram built an altar to God at Sichem. Same as Shechem and Sychem.

Only reference: Genesis 12:6

📍 SIDDIM

of times mentioned: OT 3

Meaning: Flats

A vale near the Dead Sea where Chedorlaomer, king of Elam, and his Mesopotamian allies fought with the kings of Sodom and Gomorrah and their allies. The vale was full of slime pits.

First reference: Genesis 14:3 / Last reference: Genesis 14:10

👥 SIDON

of times mentioned: 1
# of MEN by this name: 1

Meaning: Fishery

A descendant of Noah though his son Ham.

Only reference: Genesis 10:15

📍 SIDON

of times mentioned: OT 1 / NT 12

Meaning: Fishery

An ancient city of the Phoenicians that lay north of Tyre and sometimes gave its name to the people of this land (see Luke 4:26).

People from the area of Sidon followed Jesus when they heard of the things He had done. When Jesus received little response from people in the cities of Israel where He had done many miracles, He cried out that Tyre and Sidon would have humbly repented had they seen these things. When Jesus visited the area of Tyre and Sidon, the Syro-Phoenician woman called on Him to cast a devil from her daughter.

The apostle Paul stopped briefly in Sidon on his way to Rome. Same as Zidon.

First reference: Genesis 10:19 / Last reference: Acts 27:3 / Key references: Matthew 11:21–22; Mark 7:24–31

👥 SIHON

of times mentioned: 37
# of MEN by this name: 1

Meaning: Tempestuous

An Amorite king whom the Israelites defeated when he would not let them pass through his land as they turned back before the Promised Land. Israel conquered Sihon's capital, Heshbon, and all his cities. After killing all his people, they settled there, taking their livestock for themselves. Their success in the conquest of Sihon and his land became a repeated reminder of God's leading as Israel moved into the Promised Land. Rahab and the Gibeonites feared Israel because of their victory.

First reference: Numbers 21:21 / Last reference: Jeremiah 48:45 / Key references: Numbers 21:21–

25; Deuteronomy 2:26–35; Joshua 2:10; Psalm 135:10–11

⚲ SIHOR

of times mentioned: OT 3

Meaning: Dark (that is, turbid)

A river that some have identified as the Nile, others as the Brook (or River) of Egypt. It was identified as yet-unconquered land at the end of Joshua's life. Same as Shihor.

First reference: Joshua 13:3 / Last reference: Jeremiah 2:18

👥 SILAS

of times mentioned: 13
# of MEN by this name: 1

Meaning: Sylvan

A prophet chosen by the Jerusalem Council to accompany Paul and Barnabas to the Gentiles. After Barnabas and Paul separated, Paul took Silas on a new journey. Together they were imprisoned in Philippi after Paul freed a slave girl of an evil spirit. They led the jailer and his family to Christ and continued their mission in Greece. Same as Silvanus (1).

First reference: Acts 15:22 / Last reference: Acts 18:5 / Key references: Acts 15:38–41; 16:16–40

⚲ SILLA

of times mentioned: OT 1

Meaning: An embankment

An unidentifiable place near Beth-millo where King Joash of Judah was murdered by his servants.

Only reference: 2 Kings 12:20

⚲ SILOAH

of times mentioned: OT 1

Meaning: Rill

A pool in Jerusalem that was restored by Shallum during Nehemiah's repairs to the city. Same as Shiloah and Siloam.

Only reference: Nehemiah 3:15

⚲ SILOAM

of times mentioned: NT 3

Meaning: Rill

Jesus spoke of a tower of Siloam that fell, killing eighteen people. Though there is no clear identification of the tower's location, the pool of Siloam was in the southern part of King David's Jerusalem. Same as Shiloah and Siloah.

First reference: Luke 13:4 / Last reference: John 9:11

👥 SILVANUS

of times mentioned: 4
# of MEN by this name: 2

Meaning: Sylvan

1) Latin name for Silas, who accompanied Paul on his missionary journeys. Paul included Silvanus's name in his greetings to the churches at Corinth and Thessalonica.

First reference: 2 Corinthians 1:19 / Last reference: 1 Thessalonians 1:1

2) A "faithful brother" by whom Peter wrote the epistle of 1 Peter. Possibly the same as Silvanus (1).

Only reference: 1 Peter 5:12

👥 SIMEON

of times mentioned: 18
# of MEN by this name: 5

Meaning: Hearing

1) The second son of Jacob and Leah. With his full brother Levi, Simeon killed the men of Shechem because the prince of that city raped their sister, Dinah. In Egypt, Joseph held Simeon ransom until their nine brothers brought Benjamin to Egypt with them. When Jacob blessed his sons, he remembered Simeon's and Levi's anger at Shechem and cursed them for it.

First reference: Genesis 29:33 / Last reference: Exodus 6:15 / Key references: Genesis 29:32–33; 34:25; 42:18–20, 24; 49:5–7

2) A devout man at the Jerusalem temple who held

the eight-day-old Jesus and prophesied, "This child is set for the fall and rising again of many in Israel" (Luke 2:34). Simeon, who had been "waiting for the consolation of Israel" (Luke 2:25), said he could die in peace after having seen God's salvation.

First reference: Luke 2:25 / Last reference: Luke 2:34

3) A descendant of Abraham through Isaac; forebear of Jesus' earthly father, Joseph.

Only reference: Luke 3:30

Genealogy of Jesus: Yes

4) A prophet and teacher in the church at Antioch during the apostle Paul's ministry. Also called Niger.

Only reference: Acts 13:1

5) Variant name for the apostle Simon Peter.

Only reference: Acts 15:14

👥 SIMON

of times mentioned: 76
# of MEN by this name: 9

Meaning: Hearing

1) The disciple whom Jesus surnamed Peter, also called Simon Bar-jona.

First reference: Matthew 4:18 / Last reference: 2 Peter 1:1 / Key references: Matthew 16:16–17; Mark 3:16

2) One of Jesus' twelve disciples, called "the Canaanite" and "Zelotes" (the Zealot).

First reference: Matthew 10:4 / Last reference: Acts 1:13

3) One of four brothers of Jesus, as recorded by Matthew's and Mark's Gospels.

First reference: Matthew 13:55 / Last reference: Mark 6:3

4) Called Simon the Leper, he lived in Bethany. In his home a woman anointed Jesus before His crucifixion.

First reference: Matthew 26:6 / Last reference: Mark 14:3

5) A man from Cyrene, whom the Romans forced to carry Jesus' cross to the crucifixion site.

First reference: Matthew 27:32 / Last reference: Luke 23:26

6) A Pharisee who invited Jesus to eat in his home and thought Jesus should have known that the woman who anointed him with oil was a sinner.

First reference: Luke 7:40 / Last reference: Luke 7:44

7) Father of Judas Iscariot, the disciple who betrayed Jesus.

First reference: John 6:71 / Last reference: John 13:26

8) A sorcerer who became a Christian. Simon offered the apostles money to be able to use the laying on of hands to fill people with the Holy Spirit.

First reference: Acts 8:9 / Last reference: Acts 8:24

9) A tanner of Joppa who lived by the sea and lodged Peter.

First reference: Acts 9:43 / Last reference: Acts 10:32

👥 SIMRI

of times mentioned: 1
# of MEN by this name: 1

Meaning: Watchful

A Levite "porter" (doorkeeper) in the house of the Lord.

Only reference: 1 Chronicles 26:10

📍 SIN

of times mentioned: OT 6

1) An Egyptian city on which the prophet Ezekiel predicted God would pour out His wrath.

First reference: Ezekiel 30:15 / Last reference: Ezekiel 30:16

2) A wilderness south of the Negev that the Israelites crossed and camped in during the Exodus.

First reference: Exodus 16:1 / Last reference: Numbers 33:12

SINA

of times mentioned: NT 2

Meaning: Greek form of Sinai

The mountain where God appeared to Moses in a burning bush. Same as Sinai.

First reference: Acts 7:30 / Last reference: Acts 7:38

SINAI

of times mentioned: OT 33 / NT 4

The wilderness peninsula that lies between Egypt and the Promised Land through which the Israelites traveled during the Exodus. The mountain that bears this name is in the south-central part of the peninsula, in a range of mountains often called Horeb in the scriptures. God called Moses to Mount Sinai and told him to sanctify the people. At the base of the mountain, God spoke to Moses and called him up, alone, to receive the Law. Because Moses was gone for many days, his people became impatient and pressured Aaron to build them an idol in the shape of a calf. Enraged at their unfaithfulness, Moses broke the first covenant tablets when he returned. After the idol was destroyed, God called Moses back to Mount Sinai to receive a new copy.

In Sinai's wilderness Moses arranged a census of the Israelites. Then God had Moses take a census of the Levites and established their role in worship. Finally God established the celebration of Passover, and the Israelites left the Sinai wilderness.

In the book of Galatians, Paul compares the bondage of the covenant of law made at Sinai with the freedom of the law of Jerusalem. Same as Sina.

First reference: Exodus 16:1 / Last reference: Galatians 4:25 / Key references: Exodus 19; 32:1–6; 34:1–2; Galatians 4:24–25

SION

of times mentioned: OT 2 / NT 7

Meaning: Peak

1) Another name for Mount Hermon. Same as Hermon, Senir, Shenir, and Sirion.

Only reference: Deuteronomy 4:48

2) A Greek word for the name Zion. It refers to Jerusalem, especially the temple area, focusing on it as a holy city. In the book of Revelation, John sees the Lamb on Mount Sion with 144,000 saints.

First reference: Psalm 65:1 / Last reference: Revelation 14:1

SIPHMOTH

of times mentioned: OT 1

Meaning: Bare spots

A city of Judah to which David sent some of the spoils from his warfare with the Amalekites.

Only reference: 1 Samuel 30:28

SIPPAI

of times mentioned: 1
# of MEN by this name: 1

Meaning: Basinlike

A Philistine warrior, "of the children of the giant," killed by one of King David's soldiers.

Only reference: 1 Chronicles 20:4

SIRAH

of times mentioned: OT 1

Meaning: Departure

A well near Hebron. Joab called Abner back from Sirah to Hebron, where Joab killed him.

Only reference: 2 Samuel 3:26

SIRION

of times mentioned: OT 2

Meaning: God has prevailed

The Sidonian name for Mount Hermon. Same as Hermon, Senir, Sion (1), and Shenir.

First reference: Deuteronomy 3:9 / Last reference: Psalm 29:6

👥 SISAMAI

of times mentioned: 2
# of MEN by this name: 1

A descendant of Abraham through Jacob's son Judah. Sisamai descended from the line of an unnamed Israelite woman and her Egyptian husband, Jarha.

Only reference: 1 Chronicles 2:40

👥 SISERA

of times mentioned: 21
# of MEN by this name: 2

1) Captain under Jabin, king of Canaan. He fought with Barak, Israel's captain, and lost. Sisera fled on foot to the tent of Jael, the wife of Heber the Kenite. She encouraged him to come in then killed him by nailing a tent peg into his temple.

First reference: Judges 4:2 / Last reference: Psalm 83:9 / Key reference: Judges 4:13–21

2) Forefather of an exiled family that returned to Judah under Zerubbabel.

First reference: Ezra 2:53 / Last reference: Nehemiah 7:55

📍 SITNAH

of times mentioned: OT 1

Meaning: Opposition

A well dug by Isaac's servants that they had to defend against the local people, who laid claim to it. Eventually Isaac left the well to them.

Only reference: Genesis 26:21

📍 SMYRNA

of times mentioned: NT 2

Meaning: Myrrh

A city of Asia Minor north of Ephesus. It is only mentioned in Revelation, in the letter to the seven churches of Asia Minor. Christ assured these believers that He knew their works and tribulations and encouraged them to remain faithful to Him.

First reference: Revelation 1:11 / Last reference: Revelation 2:8

👥 SO

of times mentioned: 1
# of MEN by this name: 1

A king of Egypt approached by Israel's last king, Hoshea, for aid against the Assyrian Empire. News of the attempted alliance caused Assyria to overrun Israel and carry its people into captivity.

Only reference: 2 Kings 17:4

👥 SOCHO

of times mentioned: 1
# of MEN by this name: 1

Meaning: Entwine

A descendant of Abraham through Jacob's son Judah.

Only reference: 1 Chronicles 4:18

📍 SOCHOH

of times mentioned: OT 1

Meaning: To entwine (that is, to shut in)

Under King Solomon's governmental organization, a place responsible for supplying provisions for the king. Same as Socoh.

Only reference: 1 Kings 4:10

📍 SOCOH

of times mentioned: OT 1

Meaning: To entwine (that is, to shut in)

A city that became part of the inheritance of the tribe of Judah following the conquest of the Promised Land. Same as Sochoh.

Only reference: Joshua 15:35

👥 SODI

of times mentioned: 1
# of MEN by this name: 1

Meaning: Confidant

Father of one of the twelve spies sent by Moses to spy out the land of Canaan.

Only reference: Numbers 13:10

SODOM

of times mentioned: OT 39 / NT 9

Meaning: Burnt

One of five Canaanite "cities of the plain" that may have been at the southern end of the Dead Sea. Abram's nephew Lot chose this land when Abram offered him whatever area he preferred. Though the men of Sodom "were wicked and sinners before the Lord" (Genesis 13:13), Lot pitched his tents near the city. When the king of Sodom fought King Chedorlaomer of Elam and his Mesopotamian allies, Sodom lost. The city was plundered, and Lot, his goods, and some of his household were taken. Abram rescued Lot, his people, and his goods. Abram refused to take anything from Sodom's king in return for his effective raid.

When Abram learned that God planned to destroy Sodom and the other plain cities, he bargained with Him. The Lord agreed that if ten righteous people could be found within Sodom's walls, He would not destroy the city. When Abram's part of the bargain could not be fulfilled, and Sodom's men wanted to have sex with the angels who warned Lot to leave the city, the Lord took Lot's family out of Sodom and destroyed it with fire and brimstone.

The major prophets repeatedly point to Sodom and Gomorrah's extreme wickedness and God's destruction of these cities as warnings to God's people of the punishment that follows ungodliness.

Jesus told His disciples that it would be more tolerable for Sodom and Gomorrah than for a city that would not receive them. He also warned Capernaum, that if his deeds had been done in Sodom, that city would have been saved. Jesus warned that the day in which He returns will be as unexpected as the day when Sodom was destroyed. Same as Sodoma.

First reference: Genesis 10:19 / Last reference: Revelation 11:8 / Key references: Genesis 13:12–13; 14; 18:16–33; 19:1–29

📍 SODOMA

of times mentioned: NT 1

Meaning: Greek form of Sodom

Paul quotes Isaiah ("Esaias" in the KJV), saying that unless the Lord of hosts had left the Israelites descendants, they would have been like Sodoma. Same as Sodom.

Only reference: Romans 9:29

👥 SOLOMON

of times mentioned: 306
# of MEN by this name: 1

Genealogy of Jesus: Yes (Matthew 1:6–7)

Meaning: Peaceful

Son of King David and Bath-sheba, Solomon was loved by God. Despite the efforts of his half brother Adonijah to take the throne, Solomon became king over Israel with the support of his father, David.

When God came to Solomon in a vision and asked what he wanted, the king requested "an understanding heart" to rule His people (1 Kings 3:9). Because Solomon asked wisely, God gave him wisdom, understanding, and the wealth and honor he had not requested. The queen of Sheba heard of Solomon and came to ask him hard questions, and he proved his wisdom before her.

Solomon built the Lord's temple with the aid of Hiram, Tyre's king. In the high point of his reign, Solomon dedicated the temple with a prayer and benediction.

Though Solomon loved God, he also worshiped at pagan altars and married many "strange" (foreign) women, including the daughter of Pharaoh. Solomon had seven hundred wives and three hundred concubines. When he was old, his wives turned his heart away from God and he did evil, building pagan altars and worshiping there. So God promised that the throne of all Israel would be taken from his son, who would only rule over Judah.

First reference: 2 Samuel 5:14 / Last reference: Acts 7:47 / Key references: 2 Samuel 12:24; 1 Kings 3:1–14; 5:1–6; 6:1; 8:22–61; 10:1–3; 11:1–8, 11–13

👥 SOPATER

of times mentioned: 1
# of MEN by this name: 1

Meaning: Of a safe father

A man from Berea and a traveling companion of the apostle Paul.

Only reference: Acts 20:4

👥 SOPHERETH

of times mentioned: 2
# of MEN by this name: 1

Meaning: Scribe

Forefather of an exiled family—former servants of Solomon—that returned to Judah under Zerubbabel.

First reference: Ezra 2:55 / Last reference: Nehemiah 7:57

📍 SOREK

of times mentioned: OT 1

Meaning: A vine

The valley in which Samson's beloved, Delilah, lived.

Only reference: Judges 16:4

👥 SOSIPATER

of times mentioned: 1
# of MEN by this name: 1

Meaning: Of a safe father

A relative of Paul who lived in Rome. He was greeted in the apostle's letter to the Romans.

Only reference: Romans 16:21

👥 SOSTHENES

of times mentioned: 2
# of MEN by this name: 2

Meaning: Of safe strength

1) Chief ruler of the synagogue at Corinth. Sosthenes was beaten by a mob stirred up by Jewish leaders who opposed the apostle Paul.

Only reference: Acts 18:17

2) A coworker of Paul, named in the greeting of the apostle's first letter to the Corinthians.

Only reference: 1 Corinthians 1:1

👥 SOTAI

of times mentioned: 2
# of MEN by this name: 1

Meaning: Roving

Forefather of an exiled family—former servants of Solomon—that returned to Judah under Zerubbabel.

First reference: Ezra 2:55 / Last reference: Nehemiah 7:57

📍 SPAIN

of times mentioned: NT 2

Although there is no record of his making the trip, Paul told the Romans that he planned to go to Spain after he visited them.

First reference: Romans 15:24 / Last reference: Romans 15:28

👥 STACHYS

of times mentioned: 1
# of MEN by this name: 1

Meaning: Head of grain

A Christian acquaintance of the apostle Paul in Rome, called "my beloved."

Only reference: Romans 16:9

👥 STEPHANAS

of times mentioned: 3
# of MEN by this name: 1

A Corinthian Christian whose household, the first converts in Achaia, was baptized by Paul. The apostle commended the family for their ministry to believers.

First reference: 1 Corinthians 1:16 / Last reference: 1 Corinthians 16:17

👥 STEPHEN

\# of times mentioned: 7
\# of MEN by this name: 1

Meaning: Wreathe

A man of the Jewish church, "full of faith and of the Holy Ghost," Stephen was ordained to care for the physical needs of church members. He became involved in a disagreement with Jews who accused him of blasphemy. After witnessing to the Jewish council, Stephen was stoned by an angry mob that included Saul (3).

First reference: Acts 6:5 / Last reference: Acts 22:20

👥 SUAH

\# of times mentioned: 1
\# of MEN by this name: 1

Meaning: Wipe away

A descendant of Abraham through Jacob's son Asher.

Only reference: 1 Chronicles 7:36

📍 SUCCOTH

\# of times mentioned: OT 18

Meaning: Booths

1) A city where Jacob built a house and booths for his cattle. Moses made Succoth part of the inheritance of Gad. When the princes of Succoth refused to feed Gideon's men, he promised a harsh retribution. He returned there and tore the flesh of the elders of the city with thorns and briers. In the valley of Succoth, Solomon established a foundry to make the brass fittings of the temple.

First reference: Genesis 33:17 / Last reference: Psalm 108:7

2) A campsite of the Israelites on their way to the Promised Land.

First reference: Exodus 12:37 / Last reference: Numbers 33:6

📍 SUR

\# of times mentioned: OT 1

Meaning: Turned off (that is, deteriorated)

A gate in Jerusalem's temple where Jehoiada stationed a guard of soldiers for protection when he crowned Joash king of Israel. Also called "the gate of the foundation" (2 Chronicles 23:5).

Only reference: 2 Kings 11:6

👥 SUSANNA

\# of times mentioned: 1
\# of WOMEN by this name: 1

Meaning: Lily

A woman who followed Jesus and provided for his financial needs.

Only reference: Luke 8:3

👥 SUSI

\# of times mentioned: 1
\# of MEN by this name: 1

Meaning: Horselike

Father of one of the twelve spies sent by Moses to spy out the land of Canaan.

Only reference: Numbers 13:11

📍 SYCHAR

\# of times mentioned: NT 1

A place in Samaria where Jacob dug a well. In the first-century city of Sychar, Jesus met the Samaritan woman, discussed spiritual issues with her, and told her that He was the Messiah she was looking for.

Only reference: John 4:5

📍 SYCHEM

\# of times mentioned: NT 1

Meaning: Shechem

Defending himself before the Sanhedrin, Stephen spoke of Abraham's burial place in Sychem at the cave of Machpelah. Same as Shechem and Sichem.

Only reference: Acts 7:16

📍 SYENE

of times mentioned: OT 2

A town of southern Egypt, on the Nile's first cataract, at modern-day Aswan. Both references to it in scripture refer to Syene's tower and Egypt's destruction.

First reference: Ezekiel 29:10 / Last reference: Ezekiel 30:6

👥 SYNTYCHE

of times mentioned: 1
# of WOMEN by this name: 1

Meaning: Accident

A Christian woman of Philippi who had "laboured with me [Paul] in the gospel," but who had conflict with another church member, Euodias. Paul begged them to "be of the same mind in the Lord."

Only reference: Philippians 4:2

📍 SYRACUSE

of times mentioned: NT 1

A Sicilian city where Paul stayed for three days on his way to Rome.

Only reference: Acts 28:12

📍 SYRIA

of times mentioned: OT 67 / NT 8

Meaning: The highland

A nation northeast of Israel that included the biblical cities of Antioch and Damascus. During the era of the judges, Israel began to follow the gods of Syria, so God allowed His people to be oppressed by their enemies.

When the Syrians of Damascus supported Hadadezer, king of Zobah, King David conquered them and made them his tributaries. Geshur, a Syrian city that David ruled, became Absalom's home when he fled from Israel after killing his half brother Amnon. During Solomon's rule, Rezon became king of Syria and a persistent enemy of Israel.

Asa, king of Judah, paid the Syrian king Ben-hadad to break his alliance with Baasha, king of Israel, and attack Israel's cities. But Hanai the seer told Asa that because he relied on Syria, not God, he would have wars with that nation throughout his reign.

Another king named Ben-hadad brought his troops against Israel's king Ahab at Samaria. But when Israel's troops went out against Syria, the Syrians fled. However, the prophet who had foretold the victory warned Ahab that the Syrians would return in the spring. Ahab followed the prophet's plans for defense of Israel. Though Israel won the battle with the Syrians, Ahab made a covenant with Ben-hadad and let him go. Because Ahab did not obey the Lord in destroying his enemy, the prophet predicted that Ahab would die in Ben-hadad's place. Though Ahab disguised himself, he died in battle with Syria at Ramoth-gilead (2 Chronicles 18:28–34).

Naaman, commander of the Syrian army, came to the prophet Elisha to be healed of leprosy. Though he objected to washing in the Jordan River, preferring the rivers of his own nation, Naaman's servants convinced him to follow the prophet's directions, and he was healed. When Syria again fought with Israel, Elisha repeatedly warned Israel's king where the Syrians would be. Hearing that Elisha did this, the king of Syria sent an army to Dothan to capture the prophet. But instead, at Elisha's prayer, God struck the enemy with blindness, and Elisha led them to the city of Samaria, where the prophet made a temporary peace between the two nations. But King Ben-hadad (probably Ben-hadad II) besieged Samaria until there was famine in the city. When the situation became desperate, God made Israel's enemy hear the sound of a great army's chariots and horses, and the Syrians fled.

The prophet Elisha foretold the death of King Ben-hadad and the accession to the throne by King Hazael, who would make war on Israel. Jehoash, king of Judah, paid Hazael not to attack Jerusalem (2 Kings 12:17–18). Instead, Hazael and his son Ben-hadad opposed King Jehoahaz of Israel. Just before he died, the prophet Elisha foretold that Israel would strike down Syria three times (2 Kings 13:19).

King Ahaz of Judah was besieged by King Rezin of Syria and King Pekah of Israel, who captured many of the people of Judah. So Ahaz called on King Tiglath-pileser of Assyria and paid him tribte to rescue his nation. As a result, Judah became subservient to Assyria.

The prophet Amos foretold that Syria would go into captivity in Kir.

Jesus' fame went "throughout all Syria" (Matthew 4:24). When the council of Jerusalem wrote a letter declaring that Gentiles need not be circumcised, they addressed it to the believers of Syria. Paul, Barnabas, Judas, and Silas visited Antioch and delivered the letter. Then Paul and Silas visited the churches of Syria to encourage them in their faith. After leaving Corinth, Paul brought Priscilla and Aquila with him to Syria. On his final visit to Jerusalem, Paul landed in the Syrian city of Tyre and visited the church there for a week. Same as Aram.

First reference: Judges 10:6 / Last reference: Galatians 1:21 / Key references: 2 Samuel 15:7–10; 1 Kings 20; 2 Kings 5:1–14; 6:8–7:20

⚑ SYRIA-DAMASCUS

of times mentioned: OT 1

A Syrian city that King David garrisoned after he had overthrown Hadar-ezer, king of Zobah. Same as Damascus.

Only reference: 1 Chronicles 18:6

⚑ SYRIA-MAACHAH

of times mentioned: OT 1

Meaning: Aram of the two rivers

A Syrian kingdom that provided troops to the Ammonites when they had offended King David and prepared to fight with Israel.

Only reference: 1 Chronicles 19:6

⚑ TAANACH

of times mentioned: OT 6

A city on the western side of the Jordan River that was conquered by Joshua and the Israelites. This city southeast of Megiddo became a Levitical city of Manasseh, but the tribe did not drive the original inhabitants out of the city. Deborah and Barak's song, following the victory over Sisera, mentions fighting that went on between Taanach and the waters of Megiddo (Judges 5:19). Under King Solomon's governmental organization, Baana was the officer in charge of supplying the king with provisions from Taanach. Same as Tanach.

First reference: Joshua 12:21 / Last reference: 1 Chronicles 7:29

⚑ TAANATH-SHILOH

of times mentioned: OT 1

Meaning: Approach of Shiloh

A city on the border of the tribe of Ephraim's territory.

Only reference: Joshua 16:6

👥 TABBAOTH

of times mentioned: 2
# of MEN by this name: 1

Meaning: Rings

Forefather of an exiled family that returned to Judah under Zerubbabel.

First reference: Ezra 2:43 / Last reference: Nehemiah 7:46

⚑ TABBATH

of times mentioned: OT 1

A place to which the Midianites and their allies fled after Gideon and his men overcame them.

Only reference: Judges 7:22

👥 TABEAL

of times mentioned: 1
# of MEN by this name: 1

Meaning: Pleasing to God

Father of a man whom Syria and Israel wanted to make king over Judah in Ahaz's place.
Only reference: Isaiah 7:6

👥 TABEEL

of times mentioned: 1
# of MEN by this name: 1

Meaning: Pleasing to God

A man who tried to stop the rebuilding of Jerusalem's wall.

Only reference: Ezra 4:7

📍 TABERAH

of times mentioned: OT 2

Meaning: Burning

A place in the wilderness of Paran where the Israelites complained and the fire of the Lord burned the edges of the campground. When Moses prayed, the fire died down.

First reference: Numbers 11:3 / Last reference: Deuteronomy 9:22

👥 TABITHA

of times mentioned: 2
# of WOMEN by this name: 1

Meaning: The gazelle

A Christian of Joppa who did many good works. When she died, her friends called Peter, who raised her back to life. Same as Dorcas.

First reference: Acts 9:36 / Last reference: Acts 9:40

📍 TABOR

of times mentioned: OT 10

Meaning: Broken region

1) A mountain that became a landmark on the border of the tribe of Issachar's territory. This landmark was mentioned when Joshua cast lots in Shiloh to provide territory for the seven tribes that had yet to receive an inheritance. Through Deborah, God commanded Barak to draw up to Mount Tabor before engaging in battle with Sisera, commander of the Canaanites.

First reference: Joshua 19:22 / Last reference: Hosea 5:1

2) A plain (also translated "the oak of Tabor" [ESV] or the "great tree of Tabor" [NIV]) where Samuel told Saul he would meet three men who would give

him two loaves of bread following Saul's anointing as king of Israel.

Only reference: 1 Samuel 10:3

3) One of the forty-eight cities given to the Levites as God had commanded. Tabor was given to them by the tribe of Zebulun.

Only reference: 1 Chronicles 6:77

👥 TABRIMON

of times mentioned: 1
# of MEN by this name: 1

Meaning: Pleasing to Rimmon

Father of Ben-Hadad, king of Syria in the time of Judah's king Asa.

Only reference: 1 Kings 15:18

📍 TADMOR

of times mentioned: OT 2

Meaning: Palm city

A city in the wilderness, called Tamar in some translations, that King Solomon fortified.

First reference: 1 Kings 9:18 / Last reference: 2 Chronicles 8:4

👥 TAHAN

of times mentioned: 2
# of MEN by this name: 2

Meaning: Station

1) A descendant of Abraham through Joseph's son Ephraim.

Only reference: Numbers 26:35

2) Another descendant of Abraham through Joseph's son Ephraim.

Only reference: 1 Chronicles 7:25

📍 TAHAPANES

of times mentioned: OT 1

An Egyptian city that, according to Jeremiah, had "shaved the crown of [Israel's] head" because Israel had forsaken the Lord. By this, God meant that Egypt had humbled the Israelites. Same as Tahpanhes and Tehaphnehes.

Only reference: Jeremiah 2:16

TAHATH

of times mentioned: 4
# of MEN by this name: 3

Meaning: Bottom

1) A descendant of Abraham through Jacob's son Levi.

First reference: 1 Chronicles 6:24 / Last reference: 1 Chronicles 6:37

2) A descendant of Abraham through Joseph's son Ephraim.

Only reference: 1 Chronicles 7:20

3) Another descendant of Abraham through Joseph's son Ephraim.

Only reference: 1 Chronicles 7:20

♀ TAHATH

of times mentioned: OT 2

Meaning: The bottom (as depressed)

A campsite of the Israelites on their way to the Promised Land.

First reference: Numbers 33:26 / Last reference: Numbers 33:27

♀ TAHPANHES

of times mentioned: OT 5

An Egyptian city to which the Jews of Judah fled to escape the rule of the Chaldean (Babylonian) Empire. Jeremiah foretold that his people would not escape Babylon by their flight to Tahpanhes, because the Babylonian king Nebuchadnezzar would also attack and destroy Egypt. Same as Tahapanes and Tehaphnehes.

First reference: Jeremiah 43:7 / Last reference: Jeremiah 46:14

👥 TAHPENES

of times mentioned: 3
# of WOMEN by this name: 1

Queen of Egypt during the rule of Solomon and sister-in-law of Solomon's adversary Hadad the Edomite.

First reference: 1 Kings 11:19 / Last reference: 1 Kings 11:20

👥 TAHREA

of times mentioned: 1
# of MEN by this name: 1

Meaning: Earth

Great-grandson of Jonathan (2).

Only reference: 1 Chronicles 9:41

♀ TAHTIM-HODSHI

of times mentioned: OT 1

Meaning: Lower ones monthly

After he went to Gilead, Joab, King David's battle commander, visited this land when he took a census of the Israelites.

Only reference: 2 Samuel 24:6

👥 TALMAI

of times mentioned: 6
# of MEN by this name: 2

Meaning: Ridged

1) One of the gigantic children of Anak who was killed after Joshua's death when Judah battled the Canaanites.

First reference: Numbers 13:22 / Last reference: Judges 1:10

2) King of Geshur and grandfather of King David's son Absalom.

First reference: 2 Samuel 3:3 / Last reference: 1 Chronicles 3:2

👥 TALMON

of times mentioned: 5
# of MEN by this name: 1

Meaning: Oppressive

A Jewish exile from the tribe of Levi who resettled Jerusalem.

First reference: 1 Chronicles 9:17 / Last reference: Nehemiah 12:25

👥 TAMAH

of times mentioned: 1
# of MEN by this name: 1

Forefather of an exiled family that returned to Judah under Nehemiah.

Only reference: Nehemiah 7:55

👥 TAMAR

of times mentioned: 22
# of WOMEN by this name: 3

Meaning: Palm tree

1) The daughter-in-law of Jacob's son Judah. She married Judah's eldest two sons, whom God killed for wickedness. Judah refused to marry her to his third son, so she pretended to be a harlot, lay with Judah, and had twins by him. Same as Thamar.

First reference: Genesis 38:6 / Last reference: 1 Chronicles 2:4

2) The daughter of King David and the half sister of Amnon. Amnon fell in love with her and pretended to be sick so David would send Tamar to him. He raped Tamar and threw her out of his house. Her full brother Absalom heard of this and later had his servants kill Amnon.

First reference: 2 Samuel 13:1 / Last reference: 1 Chronicles 3:9

3) The beautiful only daughter of the very handsome Absalom, son of King David.

Only reference: 2 Samuel 14:27

📍 TAMAR

of times mentioned: OT 2

Meaning: A palm tree

A city identifying the boundary of the tribe of Gad in Ezekiel's vision of the land of Israel.

First reference: Ezekiel 47:19 / Last reference: Ezekiel 48:28

📍 TANACH

of times mentioned: OT 1

One of the forty-eight cities given to the Levites as God had commanded. Tanach was given to them by the tribe of Manasseh. Same as Taanach.

Only reference: Joshua 21:25

👥 TANHUMETH

of times mentioned: 2
# of MEN by this name: 1

Meaning: Compassion

Father of one of Judah's captains at the time of the Babylonian Exile.

First reference: 2 Kings 25:23 / Last reference: Jeremiah 40:8

👥 TAPHATH

of times mentioned: 1
# of WOMEN by this name: 1

Meaning: Drop of ointment

A daughter of Solomon and the wife of one of the king's commissary officers.

Only reference: 1 Kings 4:11

👥 TAPPUAH

of times mentioned: 1
# of MEN by this name: 1

Meaning: Apple

A descendant of Abraham through Jacob's son Judah.

📍 TAPPUAH

of times mentioned: OT 5

Meaning: An apple

1) A kingdom on the western side of the Jordan River that Joshua and his troops conquered. This city became part of the inheritance of the tribe of Judah following the conquest of the Promised Land.

First reference: Joshua 12:17 / Last reference: Joshua 15:34

2) A land on the border of the territory of the tribes of Manasseh and Ephraim. Though the land of Tappuah belonged to Manasseh, the town of the same name belonged to Ephraim.

First reference: Joshua 16:8 / Last reference: Joshua 17:8

📍 TARAH

of times mentioned: OT 2

A campsite of the Israelites on their way to the Promised Land.

First reference: Numbers 33:27 / Last reference: Numbers 33:28

📍 TARALAH

of times mentioned: OT 1

Meaning: A reeling

A city that was part of the inheritance of the tribe of Benjamin.

Only reference: Joshua 18:27

👥 TAREA

of times mentioned: 1
# of MEN by this name: 1

Meaning: Earth

A descendant of Abraham through Jacob's son Benjamin, through the line of King Saul and his son Jonathan.

👥 TARSHISH

of times mentioned: 3
# of MEN by this name: 2

Meaning: Topaz

1) A descendant of Noah through his son Japheth.

First reference: Genesis 10:4 / Last reference: 1 Chronicles 1:7

2) One of seven Persian princes serving under King Ahasuerus.

Only reference: Esther 1:14

📍 TARSHISH

of times mentioned: OT 21

Meaning: A gem, perhaps the topaz (as the region of the stone)

A Phoenician seaport in southern Spain that traded in silver, iron, tin, and lead and formed the western limit of the world with which the Jews were familiar. The phrase "ships of Tarshish" became synonymous with large trading vessels such as those Solomon used in his trade with King Hiram of Tyre. The psalmist envisioned the kings of Tarshish bringing King Solomon gifts (Psalm 72:10).

Jehoshaphat, king of Judah, joined with the wicked King Ahaziah of Israel to trade with Tarshish, but the ships they built in Ezion-gaber were broken and never made the voyage.

In the Psalms and the prophecy of Isaiah, the power of these vessels bows down before God. Their impressive strength cannot compare to His. Isaiah promises that when God gathers people of "all nations and tongues" to see His glory, the ships of Tarshish will bring God's people from afar (Isaiah 66:18).

When Jonah tried to flee from God's command to preach to Nineveh, he headed for Tarshish. But as the ship he boarded at Joppa was about to be shipwrecked, the sailors threw the prophet overboard at his own command. Same as Tharshish.

First reference: 2 Chronicles 9:21 / Last reference: Jonah 4:2 / Key references: 2 Chronicles 9:21; 20:35–37; Isaiah 66:19; Jonah 1:3

📍 TARSUS

of times mentioned: NT 5

Meaning: A flat basket

The main city of the Roman province of Cilicia, Tarsus was the hometown of Saul (later Paul). It was also one of the first places the apostle visited with Barnabas. When Barnabas was sent to Antioch following Peter's vision about God's acceptance of Gentiles, he stopped in Tarsus to collect Saul and bring him along. When Paul was accused of bringing a Gentile into the temple, he spoke to the crowd and proudly declared that he was born in Tarsus.

First reference: Acts 9:11 / Last reference: Acts 22:3

👥 TARTAN

of times mentioned: 2
# of MEN by this name: 1

An Assyrian military commander who conquered the city of Ashdod and participated in King Sennacherib's failed attempt to take Jerusalem in the days of King Hezekiah and the prophet Isaiah.

First reference: 2 Kings 18:17 / Last reference: Isaiah 20:1

👥 TATNAI

of times mentioned: 4
# of MEN by this name: 1

A governor who objected to the rebuilding of Jerusalem's temple and wrote the Persian king Darius. Darius commanded Tatnai to let the work continue.

First reference: Ezra 5:3 / Last reference: Ezra 6:13

👥 TEBAH

of times mentioned: 1
# of MEN by this name: 1

Meaning: Massacre

A nephew of Abraham, born to his brother Nahor's concubine, Reumah.

Only reference: Genesis 22:24

👥 TEBALIAH

of times mentioned: 1
# of MEN by this name: 1

Meaning: God has dipped

A Levite "porter" (doorkeeper) in the house of the Lord.

Only reference: 1 Chronicles 26:11

📍 TEHAPHNEHES

of times mentioned: OT 1

An Egyptian city that the prophet Ezekiel said would see God "break. . .the yokes of Egypt" as its people went into captivity. Same as Tahapanes and Tahpanhes.

Only reference: Ezekiel 30:18

👥 TEHINNAH

of times mentioned: 1
# of MEN by this name: 1

Meaning: Graciousness

A descendant of Abraham through Jacob's son Judah.

Only reference: 1 Chronicles 4:12

👥 TEKOA

of times mentioned: 2
# of MEN by this name: 1

Meaning: Trumpet

A descendant of Abraham through Jacob's son Judah.

First reference: 1 Chronicles 2:24 / Last reference: 1 Chronicles 4:5

📍 TEKOA

of times mentioned: OT 4

Meaning: A trumpet

A city of Judah that King Rehoboam fortified in order to defend his nation. King Jehoshaphat of Judah led his troops into the wilderness of Tekoa. The day before they set out, all Judah had participated in a prayer meeting to praise and petition God because the nation was about to be attacked by the Ammonites, the Moabites, and the people of Mount Seir. Following Jehoshaphat's public prayer, Jahaziel foretold that God would deliver the nation of Judah. The next morning, singers praised God while the army set out, and God turned Judah's enemies upon each other and destroyed them.

The prophet Amos was a herder of Tekoa. Same as Tekoah.

First reference: 2 Chronicles 11:6 / Last reference: Amos 1:1

♀ TEKOAH

of times mentioned: OT 3

Meaning: A trumpet

King David's battle commander Joab called on a wise woman from Tekoah to show the mourning king that he should allow his son Absalom to come back to Jerusalem. Absalom had murdered his half brother Amnon for raping their sister Tamar; then he had fled Israel. Same as Tekoa.

First reference: 2 Samuel 14:2 / Last reference: 2 Samuel 14:9

♀ TEL-ABIB

of times mentioned: OT 1

Meaning: Mound of green growth

A town on the Chebar River where the prophet Ezekiel visited some exiles from Judah. After he had been there seven days, the Lord told him he was a watchman for Israel.

Only reference: Ezekiel 3:15

👥 TELAH

of times mentioned: 1
# of MEN by this name: 1

Meaning: Breach

A descendant of Abraham through Joseph's son Ephraim.

Only reference: 1 Chronicles 7:25

♀ TELAIM

of times mentioned: OT 1

Meaning: Lambs

A place where King Saul numbered his troops before a battle with the Amalekites.

Only reference: 1 Samuel 15:4

♀ TELASSAR

of times mentioned: OT 1

When Rabshakeh threatened the people of Judah with destruction, he used the Mesopotamian city of Telassar as an example of a city that had been destroyed by his nation. Same as Thelasar.

Only reference: Isaiah 37:12

👥 TELEM

of times mentioned: 1
# of MEN by this name: 1

Meaning: Oppression

An exiled Levite who married a "strange" (foreign) woman.

Only reference: Ezra 10:24

♀ TELEM

of times mentioned: OT 1

Meaning: Oppression

A city that became part of the inheritance of the tribe of Judah following the conquest of the Promised Land.

Only reference: Joshua 15:24

♀ TEL-HARESHA

of times mentioned: OT 1

Meaning: Mound of workmanship

A city in Judah to which captives returned after the Babylonian Exile. These people could not prove they were Israelites. Same as Tel-harsa.

Only reference: Nehemiah 7:61

📍 TEL-HARSA

of times mentioned: OT 1

Meaning: Mound of workmanship

A city in Judah to which captives returned after the Babylonian Exile. These people could not prove they were Israelites. Same as Tel-haresha.

Only reference: Ezra 2:59

📍 TEL-MELAH

of times mentioned: OT 2

Meaning: Mound of salt

A city in Judah to which captives returned after the Babylonian Exile. These people could not prove they were Israelites.

First reference: Ezra 2:59 / Last reference: Nehemiah 7:61

👥 TEMA

of times mentioned: 4
# of MEN by this name: 1

A descendant of Abraham through Ishmael, Abraham's son with his surrogate wife, Hagar.

First reference: Genesis 25:15 / Last reference: Jeremiah 25:23

📍 TEMA

of times mentioned: OT 1

A place in Arabia named for one of Ishmael's sons who settled there. Job compares his grief over the lack of support he received from friends to a caravan from Tema that searched for water but did not find it.

Only reference: Job 6:19

👥 TEMAN

of times mentioned: 5
# of MEN by this name: 1

Meaning: South

A "duke of Edom," a leader in the family line of Esau.

First reference: Genesis 36:11 / Last reference: 1 Chronicles 1:53

📍 TEMAN

of times mentioned: OT 5

Meaning: The south (as being on the right hand of a person facing east)

An area of Edom that the prophets foresaw being destroyed. Ezekiel said it would be made desolate, and Amos declared God would send a fire that would "devour the palaces of Bozrah" (Amos 1:12). Habakkuk saw God coming from Teman in all His glory.

First reference: Jeremiah 49:7 / Last reference: Habakkuk 3:3

👥 TEMENI

of times mentioned: 1
# of MEN by this name: 1

Meaning: South

A descendant of Abraham through Jacob's son Judah.

Only reference: 1 Chronicles 4:6

👥 TERAH

of times mentioned: 11
# of MEN by this name: 1

Father of Abram (Abraham), Nahor, and Haran. With Abram and Nahor and their families, he left Ur of the Chaldees and headed for Canaan. But when they came to Haran, they stayed there. Terah died in Haran.

First reference: Genesis 11:24 / Last reference: 1 Chronicles 1:26

👥 TERESH

of times mentioned: 2
# of MEN by this name: 1

One of two palace doorkeepers who conspired to kill their king, Ahasuerus of Persia. Their plot was uncovered by Mordecai, and both were hanged.

First reference: Esther 2:21 / Last reference: Esther 6:2

👥 TERTIUS

of times mentioned: 1
# of MEN by this name: 1

Meaning: Third

An assistant of Paul who wrote down the apostle's message to the Romans.

Only reference: Romans 16:22

👥 TERTULLUS

of times mentioned: 2
# of MEN by this name: 1

An orator from Jerusalem who accused the apostle Paul before the Roman governor in Caesarea. Tertullus called Paul "a pestilent fellow," charging him with profaning God's temple as "a ringleader in the sect of the Nazarenes" (Acts 24:5).

First reference: Acts 24:1 / Last reference: Acts 24:2

👥 THADDAEUS

of times mentioned: 2
# of MEN by this name: 1

One of Jesus' twelve disciples, as listed by Matthew and Mark. Matthew mentions that Thaddaeus's surname was Lebbaeus. Apparently called "Judas, the brother of James" in Luke's Gospel and the book of Acts. Same as Judas (3) and Jude.

First reference: Matthew 10:3 / Last reference: Mark 3:18

👥 THAHASH

of times mentioned: 1
# of MEN by this name: 1

Meaning: Antelope

A nephew of Abraham, born to his brother Nahor's concubine, Reumah.

Only reference: Genesis 22:24

👥 THAMAH

of times mentioned: 1
# of MEN by this name: 1

Forefather of an exiled family that returned to Judah under Zerubbabel.

Only reference: Ezra 2:53

👥 THAMAR

of times mentioned: 1
# of WOMEN by this name: 1

Genealogy of Jesus: Yes (Matthew 1:3)

Meaning: Palm tree

Greek form of the name Tamar, used in the New Testament. Same as Tamar (1).

Only reference: Matthew 1:3

👥 THARA

of times mentioned: 1
# of MEN by this name: 1

Greek form of the name Terah, used in the New Testament.

Only reference: Luke 3:34

👥 THARSHISH

of times mentioned: 1
# of MEN by this name: 1

Meaning: Topaz

A descendant of Abraham through Jacob's son Benjamin.

Only reference: 1 Chronicles 7:10

THARSHISH

of times mentioned: OT 3

Meaning: A gem, perhaps a topaz (as the region of the stone)

A Phoenician seaport in southern Spain that traded in silver, iron, tin, and lead and formed the western limit of the world with which the Jews were familiar. Its ships were large trading vessels such as those Solomon used in his trade with King Hiram of Tyre. Same as Tarshish.

First reference: 1 Kings 10:22 / Last reference: 1 Kings 22:48

THEBEZ

of times mentioned: OT 3

Meaning: Whiteness

Gideon's son Abimelech conquered this city, but the people of Thebez continued to defend a tower. When Abimelech began to burn the tower, a woman dropped a piece of a millstone on his head, breaking his skull. He called his armor bearer to kill him so it would not be said that he was killed by a woman.

First reference: Judges 9:50 / Last reference: 2 Samuel 11:21

THELASAR

of times mentioned: OT 1

When Rabshakeh threatened the people of Judah with destruction, he used the Mesopotamian city of Thelasar as an example of a city that had been destroyed by his nation. Same as Telassar.

Only reference: 2 Kings 19:12

THEOPHILUS

of times mentioned: 2
# of MEN by this name: 1

Meaning: Friend of God

An otherwise unknown person for whom Luke wrote his Gospel and the book of Acts, "that thou

mightest know the certainty of those things, wherein thou hast been instructed" (Luke 1:4).

First reference: Luke 1:3 / Last reference: Acts 1:1

THESSALONICA

of times mentioned: NT 6

Meaning: Thessalos conquest

A Macedonian city where Paul preached in the synagogue. Though some people of the city believed, others accused Christians of believing in a king other than Caesar. The Christians of the city sent Paul and Silas away to Berea. Thessalonica was the hometown of Aristarchus, who sailed with Paul as he was on his way to Rome. While Paul was in Thessalonica, the Colossians helped to meet his ministry needs.

First reference: Acts 17:1 / Last reference: 2 Timothy 4:10

THEUDAS

of times mentioned: 1
# of MEN by this name: 1

A false Jewish messiah who attracted four hundred people. They scattered when he was killed.

Only reference: Acts 5:36

THIMNATHAH

of times mentioned: OT 1

Meaning: A portion assigned

A town that became part of the inheritance of Dan when Joshua cast lots in Shiloh to provide territory for the seven tribes that had yet to receive their land.

Only reference: Joshua 19:43

THOMAS

of times mentioned: 12
# of MEN by this name: 1

Meaning: The twin

Jesus' disciple whom people often call "Doubting Thomas." When Jesus wanted to go to Lazarus courageous Thomas said, "Let us also go, that we may die with him" (John 11:16). But when Jesus appeared to the others, Thomas doubted their story until he saw the Master Himself.

First reference: Matthew 10:3 / Last reference: Acts 1:13 / Key references: John 11:16; 20:24–29

THREE TAVERNS

of times mentioned: NT 1

A place between the Forum of Appius and Rome where some Christians met Paul as he traveled to Rome.

Only reference: Acts 28:15

THYATIRA

of times mentioned: NT 4

A city of Asia Minor, in the Roman province of Asia, where Lydia was converted to Christ. Here Paul was followed by a slave girl possessed with a spirit of divination. After Paul cast out the spirit, her owners brought him and Silas in front of the magistrates. Paul and Silas were beaten and imprisoned, but an earthquake opened the prison doors for them. They remained in their cell and preached to their jailor, who was converted.

Thyatira was one of the seven churches of Asia Minor addressed in the book of Revelation. Though the church in that city was faithful in many ways, it did not restrain a false prophet. She misled believers into practicing fornication and eating meat that had been sacrificed to idols. The Lord called the Christians of Thyatira to repent.

First reference: Acts 16:14 / Last reference: Revelation 2:24

TIBERIUS

of times mentioned: 1
# of MEN by this name: 1

Meaning: Pertaining to the Tiber River

The Roman emperor who was ruling when John the Baptist and Jesus began their ministries.

Only reference: Luke 3:1

TIBERIAS

of times mentioned: NT 3

Meaning: Pertaining to the river Tiberis or Tiber

The Sea of Tiberias is another name for the Sea of Galilee. The city of Tiberias, on the west shore of the sea, was named to honor the emperor Tiberius.

First reference: John 6:1 / Last reference: John 21:1

TIBHATH

of times mentioned: OT 1

Meaning: Slaughter

A city of Hadadezer, king of Zobah. After defeating Hadadezer in battle, King David brought bronze from Tibhath to Israel. When Solomon built the temple, he made various bronze temple implements from the metal his father, David, had collected there.

Only reference: 1 Chronicles 18:8

TIBNI

of times mentioned: 3
# of MEN by this name: 1

Meaning: Strawlike

The losing contender for the throne of Israel after Zimri killed King Elah.

First reference: 1 Kings 16:21 / Last reference: 1 Kings 16:22

TIDAL

of times mentioned: 2
# of MEN by this name: 1

Meaning: Fearfulness

The "king of nations" in the days of Abraham. Tidal was part of a battle alliance that kidnapped Abram's nephew Lot.

First reference: Genesis 14:1 / Last reference: Genesis 14:9

👥 TIGLATH-PILESER

of times mentioned: 3
# of MEN by this name: 1

The king of Assyria who conquered the land of Naphtali and Galilee and took the Israelites captive. When Syria and Israel attacked Judah, King Ahaz sought Tiglath-pileser's help. Same as Tilgath-pilneser and possibly Pul.

First reference: 2 Kings 15:29 / Last reference: 2 Kings 16:10

👥 TIKVAH

of times mentioned: 2
# of MEN by this name: 2

Meaning: Cord

1) Father-in-law of the prophetess Huldah, who served during the reign of Judah's king Josiah. Same as Tikvath.

Only reference: 2 Kings 22:14

2) Forefather of a man who encouraged the Israelites to give up their "strange" (foreign) wives.

Only reference: Ezra 10:15

👥 TIKVATH

of times mentioned: 1
# of MEN by this name: 1

Meaning: Cord

Father-in-law of the prophetess Huldah, who served during the reign of Judah's king Josiah. Same as Tikvah (1).

Only reference: 2 Chronicles 34:22

👥 TILGATH-PILNESER

of times mentioned: 3
# of MEN by this name: 1

A variant spelling of the name of the Assyrian king Tiglath-pileser.

First reference: 1 Chronicles 5:6 / Last reference: 2 Chronicles 28:20

👥 TILON

of times mentioned: 1
# of MEN by this name: 1

Meaning: Suspension

A descendant of Abraham through Jacob's son Judah.

Only reference: 1 Chronicles 4:20

👥 TIMAEUS

of times mentioned: 1
# of MEN by this name: 1

Meaning: Foul

Father of a blind man of Jericho who was healed by Jesus.

Only reference: Mark 10:46

👥 TIMNA

of times mentioned: 4
# of MEN by this name: 1
# of WOMEN by this name: 2

Meaning: Restraint

1) Concubine of Esau's son Eliphaz.

Only reference: Genesis 36:12

2) A daughter of Seir, who lived in Esau's "land of Edom."

First reference: Genesis 36:22 / Last reference: 1 Chronicles 1:39

3) A descendant of Abraham's grandson Esau.

Only reference: 1 Chronicles 1:36

👥 TIMNAH

of times mentioned: 2
# of MEN by this name: 1

Meaning: Restraint

A "duke of Edom," a leader in the family line of Esau.

First reference: Genesis 36:40 / Last reference: 1 Chronicles 1:51

📍 TIMNAH

of times mentioned: OT 3

Meaning: A portion assigned

1) A city that became part of the inheritance of the tribe of Judah following the conquest of the Promised Land. Same as Timnath (1).

Only reference: Joshua 15:57

2) A town that formed part of the border of the tribe of Judah's territory. During the reign of King Ahaz, it was one of the cities of the southern low country of Judah that was invaded and occupied by the Philistines. The invasion caused Ahaz to call on the Assyrians for help. Same as Timnath (2).

First reference: Joshua 15:10 / Last reference: 2 Chronicles 28:18

📍 TIMNATH

of times mentioned: OT 8

Meaning: A portion assigned

1) A city where Tamar lay in wait for her father-in-law, Judah, and seduced him, because he had not given his son Shelah to her as a husband. Same as Timnah (1).

First reference: Genesis 38:12 / Last reference: Genesis 38:14

2) Hometown of Samson's Philistine wife. Here Samson also tore apart a lion. When he returned later, there was a swarm of bees and honey in the carcass. Same as Timnah (2).

First reference: Judges 14:1 / Last reference: Judges 14:5

📍 TIMNATH-HERES

of times mentioned: OT 1

Meaning: Portion of the sun

A city in Mount Ephraim, on the north side of the hill Gaash, Timnath-heres was part of Joshua's inheritance and was the place where he was buried.

Same as Timnath-serah.

Only reference: Judges 2:9

📍 TIMNATH-SERAH

of times mentioned: OT 2

Meaning: Portion of the sun

A city in Mount Ephraim that Israel gave as an inheritance to Joshua. Same as Timnath-heres.

First reference: Joshua 19:50 / Last reference: Joshua 24:30

👥 TIMON

of times mentioned: 1
# of MEN by this name: 1

Meaning: Valuable

One of seven men, "full of the Holy Ghost and wisdom," selected to serve needy Christians in Jerusalem while the twelve disciples devoted themselves "to prayer, and to the ministry of the word" (Acts 6:3–4).

Only reference: Acts 6:5

👥 TIMOTHEUS

of times mentioned: 18
# of MEN by this name: 1

Meaning: Dear to God

An alternative name for Timothy, the apostle Paul's coworker and "son in the faith" (1 Timothy 1:2).

First reference: Acts 16:1 / Last reference: Thessalonians 1:1 / Key reference: 1 Corinthians 4:17

👥 TIMOTHY

of times mentioned: 8
# of MEN by this name: 1

Meaning: Dear to God

Coworker of the apostle Paul, his name is joined with Paul's in the introductory greetings of 2 Corinthians and Philemon. Paul also wrote two epistles of guidance to this young pastor who was like a son to him. Same as Timotheus.

First reference: 2 Corinthians 1:1 / Last reference: Hebrews 13:23 / Key references: 1 Timothy 1:2; 6:20–21

◉ TIPHSAH

of times mentioned: OT 1

Meaning: Ford

1) A ford on the Euphrates River that marked a boundary of Solomon's kingdom.

Only reference: 1 Kings 4:24

2) A town of Israel that refused to support Menahem as king. Menahem attacked Tiphsah and slaughtered all its pregnant women when he won the city.

Only reference: 2 Kings 15:16

👥 TIRAS

of times mentioned: 2
# of MEN by this name: 1

Meaning: Fearful

A descendant of Noah through his son Japheth.

First reference: Genesis 10:2 / Last reference: 1 Chronicles 1:5

👥 TIRHAKAH

of times mentioned: 2
# of MEN by this name: 1

The king of Ethiopia in the time of Judah's king Hezekiah.

First reference: 2 Kings 19:9 / Last reference: Isaiah 37:9

👥 TIRHANAH

of times mentioned: 1
# of MEN by this name: 1

A descendant of Abraham through Jacob's son Judah.

Only reference: 1 Chronicles 2:48

👥 TIRIA

of times mentioned: 1
# of MEN by this name: 1

Meaning: Fearful

A descendant of Abraham through Jacob's son Judah.

Only reference: 1 Chronicles 4:16

👥 TIRSHATHA

of times mentioned: 5
# of MEN by this name: 1

Title of the governor of Judea, used to describe Nehemiah.

First reference: Ezra 2:63 / Last reference: Nehemiah 10:1

👥 TIRZAH

of times mentioned: 4
# of WOMEN by this name: 1

Meaning: Delightsomeness

One of five daughters of Zelophehad, an Israelite who died during the wilderness wanderings. The women asked Moses if they could inherit their father's property in the Promised Land (a right normally reserved for sons) and God ruled that they should, Since Zelophehad had no sons.

First reference: Numbers 26:33 / Last reference: Joshua 17:3

◉ TIRZAH

of times mentioned: OT 14

Meaning: Delightsomeness

A Canaanite city on the western side of the Jordan River that was conquered by Joshua and the Israelites. During the divided kingdom, Tirzah became the capital of Israel.

When Jeroboam's son became sick, his wife went to the prophet Ahijah to ask if he would be healed. The prophet told her that as soon as she entered

Tirzah, her son would die. Though Baasha, king of Israel, began to build Ramah, when King Benhadad of Syria attacked his nation, Baasha returned to Tirzah, which remained the capital for the rest of his reign. Omri besieged the city, and King Zimri burned his own palace and died in it. Omri became king of Israel and kept the capital in Tirzah for six years, then moved it to Samaria.

First reference: Joshua 12:24 / Last reference: Song of Solomon 6:4 / Key references: 1 Kings 15:20–21; 16:15–18

♀ TISHBE

of times mentioned: OT 6

Meaning: Recourse

Referred to only in the description of "Elijah the Tishbite," this town in Gilead was the prophet's home.

First reference: 1 Kings 17:1 / Last reference: 2 Kings 9:36

👥 TITUS

of times mentioned: 14
# of MEN by this name: 1

The apostle Paul's highly trusted Greek coworker who traveled with him and whom Paul sent to Corinth with a letter of rebuke for the church. Titus had a successful mission, so Paul sent him again to the Corinthians. When Titus was in Crete, Paul wrote him an epistle on church leadership.

First reference: 2 Corinthians 2:13 / Last reference: Titus 1:4 / Key references: 2 Corinthians 7:6–9, 13–15; Galatians 2:1, 3

👥 TOAH

of times mentioned: 1
# of MEN by this name: 1

Meaning: To depress

An ancestor of the prophet Samuel. Same as Tohu.

Only reference: 1 Chronicles 6:34

♀ TOB

of times mentioned: OT 2

Meaning: Good

The land to which Jephthah fled after his half brothers pushed him out of Gilead. He gathered adventurers around him in Tob and ended up becoming Gilead's battle commander.

First reference: Judges 11:3 / Last reference: Judges 11:5

👥 TOB-ADONIJAH

of times mentioned: 1
# of MEN by this name: 1

Meaning: Pleasing to Adonijah

A Levite sent by King Jehoshaphat to teach the law of the Lord throughout the nation of Judah.

Only reference: 2 Chronicles 17:8

👥 TOBIAH

of times mentioned: 15
# of MEN by this name: 2

Meaning: Goodness of Jehovah

1) Forefather of an exiled family that returned to Judah under Zerubbabel.

First reference: Ezra 2:60 / Last reference: Nehemiah 7:62

2) An Ammonite who resisted the rebuilding of Jerusalem under Governor Nehemiah. With Sanballat the Horonite he interfered and tried to distract Nehemiah from his work. The two hired a man to warn Nehemiah that he would be killed, and Tobiah sent threatening letters to scare Nehemiah.

First reference: Nehemiah 2:10 / Last reference: Nehemiah 13:8 / Key references: Nehemiah 4:3, 7–8; 6:10–12, 17–19

👥 TOBIJAH

of times mentioned: 3
# of MEN by this name: 2

Meaning: Goodness of Jehovah

1) A Levite sent by King Jehoshaphat to teach the law of the Lord throughout the nation of Judah.

Only reference: 2 Chronicles 17:8

2) Forefather of a family of Jewish exiles in Babylon who participated in a symbolic crowning of the Messiah by the prophet Zechariah.

First reference: Zechariah 6:10 / Last reference: Zechariah 6:14

♀ TOCHEN

of times mentioned: OT 1

Meaning: A fixed quantity

A city that was part of the land of the tribe of Simeon.

Only reference: 1 Chronicles 4:32

👥 TOGARMAH

of times mentioned: 4
# of MEN by this name: 1

A descendant of Noah through his son Japheth.

First reference: Genesis 10:3 / Last reference: Ezekiel 38:6

👥 TOHU

of times mentioned: 1
# of MEN by this name: 1

Meaning: Abasement

An ancestor of the prophet Samuel. Same as Toah.

Only reference: 1 Samuel 1:1

👥 TOI

of times mentioned: 3
# of MEN by this name: 1

Meaning: Error

The king of Hamath who sent congratulations and gifts to King David for defeating Toi's enemy Hadadezer. Same as Tou.

First reference: 2 Samuel 8:9 / Last reference: 2 Samuel 8:10

👥 TOLA

of times mentioned: 6
# of MEN by this name: 2

Meaning: Worm

1) A descendant of Abraham through Jacob's son Issachar.

First reference: Genesis 46:13 / Last reference: 1 Chronicles 7:2

2) The seventh judge of Israel who led the nation for twenty-three years.

Only reference: Judges 10:1

♀ TOLAD

of times mentioned: OT 1

Meaning: Posterity

A city that was part of the land of the tribe of Simeon.

Only reference: 1 Chronicles 4:29

♀ TOPHEL

of times mentioned: OT 1

Meaning: Quagmire

A place in the wilderness through which the Israelites traveled on their way to the Promised Land. Near here Moses spoke the teachings of the book of Deuteronomy to Israel.

Only reference: Deuteronomy 1:1

♀ TOPHET

of times mentioned: OT 9

Meaning: A smiting (figuratively, contempt)

A place in the Valley of Hinnom, southwest of Jerusalem, where children were sacrificed to the Ammonite god Moloch. Jeremiah foretold that because of the evil Judah had done, the valley would be filled with the dead and Judah would become desolate. Same as Topheth.

First reference: Isaiah 30:33 / Last reference: Jeremiah 19:14

♀ TOPHETH

of times mentioned: OT 1

Meaning: A smiting (figuratively, contempt)

When Josiah was king of Judah, he desecrated this place in the Valley of Hinnom where children had been sacrificed to the Ammonite god Moloch. Same as Tophet.

Only reference: 2 Kings 23:10

TOU

of times mentioned: 2
# of MEN by this name: 1

Meaning: Error

A variant spelling of the name of the Assyrian king Toi, who sent congratulations and gifts to King David for defeating Toi's enemy, Hadadezer.

First reference: 1 Chronicles 18:9 / Last reference: 1 Chronicles 18:10

♀ TRACHONITIS

of times mentioned: NT 1

Meaning: Rough district

A Roman province ruled by Philip, brother of Herod Antipas.

Only reference: Luke 3:1

♀ TROAS

of times mentioned: NT 6

Meaning: A Trojan or the plain of Troy

A Roman colony and seaport that lay ten miles from ancient Troy. Here Paul received the vision of a man of Macedonia who asked the apostle to come there and help. Immediately Paul and his companions left Troas and set out for Macedonia. As Paul headed toward Jerusalem, he and seven companions traveled to Troas and stayed there for a week. The night before their departure, Paul preached until midnight. Eutychus, a young man who was seated in a window, fell asleep and tumbled to the ground. The believers took him up, dead, but through a miracle, Paul brought him back to life.

First reference: Acts 16:8 / Last reference: 2 Timothy 4:13

♀ TROGYLLIUM

of times mentioned: NT 1

A town of Asia Minor, opposite the island of Samos, where Paul stayed as he headed toward Jerusalem. Here he stayed for a while during his journey between Samos and Miletus.

Only reference: Acts 20:15

👥 TROPHIMUS

of times mentioned: 3
# of MEN by this name: 1

Meaning: Nutritive

A Gentile believer and coworker of the apostle Paul. Trophimus was falsely accused of defiling the Jewish temple, which caused an uproar in Jerusalem. He traveled with Paul on his missionary journeys but was left ill in the city of Miletum near Ephesus.

First reference: Acts 20:4 / Last reference: 2 Timothy 4:20

👥 TRYPHENA

of times mentioned: 1
# of WOMEN by this name: 1

Meaning: Luxurious

A Christian woman in Rome commended by the apostle Paul for her "labour in the Lord."

Only reference: Romans 16:12

👥 TRYPHOSA

of times mentioned: 1
# of WOMEN by this name: 1

Meaning: Luxuriating

A Christian woman in Rome commended by the apostle Paul for her "labour in the Lord."

Only reference: Romans 16:12

TUBAL

of times mentioned: 2
# of MEN by this name: 1

A descendant of Noah through his son Japheth.

First reference: Genesis 10:2 / Last reference:
1 Chronicles 1:5

TUBAL-CAIN

of times mentioned: 2
# of MEN by this name: 1

Meaning: Offspring of Cain

A descendant of Cain through Lamech and his
wife Zillah. Tubal-cain was the first recorded metal-
worker in the Bible.

Only reference: Genesis 4:22

TYCHICUS

of times mentioned: 7
# of MEN by this name: 1

Meaning: Fortunate

An Asian coworker of Paul who accompanied him
into Macedonia. Paul also sent him on missions to
the Ephesians and Colossians and perhaps to Crete.

First reference: Acts 20:4 / Last reference: Titus
3:12

TYRANNUS

of times mentioned: 1
# of MEN by this name: 1

Meaning: Tyrant

An Ephesian teacher who allowed the apostle Paul
to debate Christianity in his school "daily" for two
years.

Only reference: Acts 19:9

TYRE

of times mentioned: OT 25 / NT 12

Meaning: A stone (by implication, a knife)

A fortified Phoenician port and center of trade, Tyre
had two harbors and consisted of both an island and
a city on the mainland. King Hiram of Tyre built
a causeway to connect the two parts of the city.
Tyre became part of the inheritance of Asher when
Joshua cast lots in Shiloh to provide territory for
the seven tribes that had yet to receive their land.
But it remained in the hands of the Phoenicians,
whose trade in valuable goods such as gold, precious
stones, and almug wood extended throughout the
Mediterranean and as far as Ophir (1 Kings 9:28,
10:11). A joint trading venture between Israel and
Tyre brought King Solomon "gold, and silver, ivory,
and apes, and peacocks" (1 Kings 10:22).

King David developed a trade relationship with
Tyre and its king, Hiram (Huram), who provided
trees, carpenters, and masons to build David's palace. Before his death, David had begun to gather
cedar logs through trade with Tyre; they were to
be used by his son Solomon to build the temple
in Jerusalem. When Solomon took the throne, he
expanded the trade and labor relationship between
the countries, sending to Hiram for cedar and fir
trees, gold, and skilled carpenters to build the temple. In return, Solomon gave Hiram food for his
royal household. The two kings made a peace treaty
with each other.

After Israel built a fleet of ships, Hiram sent
Solomon sailors. From Tyre Solomon also hired the
workman Huram to do metalwork, carpentry, and
stonework for the temple (2 Chronicles 2:13–14).
After twenty years, Solomon gave Hiram twenty
towns in Galilee as thanks for his help, but the king
of Tyre was not pleased with them.

When Nehemiah rebuked the Israelites for
trading on the sabbath, men of Tyre who lived in
Jerusalem were bringing in fish and other goods to
sell on the day of worship.

In his oracle about Tyre, the prophet Isaiah foresaw the city's destruction because of its pride. Joel
rebuked Tyre for sending the people of Judah into
slavery with the Greeks (Joel 3:4–6).

People in Tyre heard of the miracles of Jesus and
came to follow Him. Because a huge crowd gathered around Him, Jesus preached to them from
a boat. When Jesus took to task Israel's cities of
Chorazin and Bethsaida, where He had done many
miracles, He told them that if these works had been
done in Tyre and its sister city, Sidon, the people
would have repented. On judgment day, He declared, it would be more bearable for those Gentile
cities than for the cities of Israel that denied Him.

When Jesus traveled to Tyre and Sidon, a Syro-
Phoenician woman insisted that He help her
daughter, who had an unclean spirit. Jesus pointed

out that He was sent to Israel and compared the woman to a dog. Instead of taking offense, she reminded Him that crumbs fell from the master's table to the dogs. Commending her great faith, Jesus healed her daughter.

King Herod Agrippa, who ruled Judea, had a dispute with Tyre and its sister city, Sidon. The cities relied on food from Judea. Because their need was great, they gained the support of the king's chamberlain (an official who cared for his sleeping quarters) and tried to make peace with Herod (Acts 12:20). When they met with the king, he made a speech. "This is the voice of a god, not of a man," they declared. Because Herod Agrippa did not correct them, an angel of God struck the king down; he was eaten by worms and died (Acts 12:22–23 NIV).

On his way to Jerusalem, Paul stayed in Tyre for a week with the believers in the city, who warned him not to go to Jerusalem. Same as Tyrus.

First reference: Joshua 19:29 / Last reference: Acts 21:7 / Key references: 1 Kings 5:1–12; 9:10–13; 1 Chronicles 22:4; Matthew 11:21–24

♀ TYRUS

of times mentioned: OT 22

Meaning: A rock

Another name for Tyre, used in the King James Version exclusively in the Prophets. Jeremiah listed Tyrus with the kingdoms on which God would bring disaster through the expansion of the Chaldean (Babylonian) Empire under Nebuchadnezzar. God told the prophet to send this message to Tyrus through the envoys who came to Jerusalem.

Ezekiel foretold Tyrus's complete destruction with God's words: "Therefore thus saith the LORD God; Behold, I am against thee, O Tyrus, and will cause many nations to come up against thee, as the sea causeth his waves to come up. And they shall destroy the walls of Tyrus, and break down her towers: I will also scrape her dust from her, and make her like the top of a rock. It shall be a place for the spreading of nets in the midst of the sea" (Ezekiel 26:3–5).

Despite its trade that spanned much of the known world and the ships that carried diverse goods, mourning would fall upon the nations Tyrus traded with. The city's destruction came because her heart grew proud (Ezekiel 28:5).

Though Nebuchadnezzar, king of Babylon, besieged Tyrus for thirteen years, he could not conquer the island portion of the city. Instead of Tyrus,

God gave Egypt to Babylon.

The prophet Amos declared that God would not turn back His wrath because Tyrus broke a treaty and delivered captives to Edom. For this God would bring down fire on Tyrus's walls (Amos 1:9–10).

Zechariah foretold that though Tyrus had built a stronghold and achieved power on the sea, neither would avail. She would lose her possessions and power. Under the attack of Alexander the Great, all this came true. Same as Tyre.

First reference: Jeremiah 25:22 / Last reference: Zechariah 9:3 / Key reference: Ezekiel 26:2–28:19

👥 UCAL

of times mentioned: 1
# of MEN by this name: 1

Meaning: Devoured

A man to whom Agur spoke the words of Proverbs 30.

Only reference: Proverbs 30:1

👥 UEL

of times mentioned: 1
# of MEN by this name: 1

Meaning: Wish of God

An exiled Israelite who married a "strange" (foreign) woman.

Only reference: Ezra 10:34

♀ ULAI

of times mentioned: OT 2

A river (or canal) near Susa, in the Elam province. Here Daniel had his vision of the ram and the goat, which symbolized the Median, Persian, and Greek empires. After he had seen the vision, a man's voice came from between the riverbanks, telling Gabriel to make the meaning of the vision clear to Daniel. The prophet saw a man who explained that the vision had to do with the "time of the end" (Daniel 8:19 NIV) and identified the vision with each of those empires.

First reference: Daniel 8:2 / Last reference: Daniel 8:16

👥 ULAM

of times mentioned: 4
# of MEN by this name: 2

Meaning: Solitary

1) A descendant of Abraham through Joseph's son Manasseh.

First reference: 1 Chronicles 7:16 / Last reference: 1 Chronicles 7:17

2) A descendant of Abraham through Jacob's son Benjamin, through the line of King Saul and his son Jonathan.

First reference: 1 Chronicles 8:39 / Last reference: 1 Chronicles 8:40

👥 ULLA

of times mentioned: 1
# of MEN by this name: 1

Meaning: Burden

A descendant of Abraham through Jacob's son Asher.

Only reference: 1 Chronicles 7:39

📍 UMMAH

of times mentioned: OT 1

Meaning: Association

A city that became part of the inheritance of Asher when Joshua cast lots in Shiloh to provide territory for the seven tribes that had yet to receive their land.

Only reference: Joshua 19:30

👥 UNNI

of times mentioned: 3
# of MEN by this name: 2

Meaning: Afflicted

1) A Levite musician who performed in celebration when King David brought the ark of the covenant to Jerusalem.

First reference: 1 Chronicles 15:18 / Last reference: 1 Chronicles 15:20

2) A Jewish exile from the tribe of Levi who returned from Babylon to Judah under Zerubbabel.

Only reference: Nehemiah 12:9

📍 UPHAZ

of times mentioned: OT 2

A place from which gold was brought to create idols. In Daniel's vision, a man wore a belt of gold from Uphaz. Possibly the same as Ophir.

First reference: Jeremiah 10:9 / Last reference: Daniel 10:5

👥 UR

of times mentioned: 1
# of MEN by this name: 1

Meaning: Flame

Father of one of King David's valiant warriors.

Only reference: 1 Chronicles 11:35

📍 UR

of times mentioned: OT 4

Meaning: Flame; hence the east (being the region of light)

A Mesopotamian place, probably a city, where Abram's father, Terah, and his family lived. Terah's third son, Haran, died in Ur. Then the family left Ur to travel to Canaan. Genesis 15:7 and Nehemiah 9:7 identify God as the force behind their move and the One who called them to found a new nation.

First reference: Genesis 11:28 / Last reference: Nehemiah 9:7

👥 URBANE

of times mentioned: 1
# of MEN by this name: 1

Meaning: Of the city

A Christian acquaintance of the apostle Paul in Rome who was called "our helper in Christ."

Only reference: Romans 16:9

URI

# of times mentioned: 8
# of MEN by this name: 3

Meaning: Fiery

1) Father of Bezaleel, a craftsman in the construction of the tabernacle.

First reference: Exodus 31:2 / Last reference: 2 Chronicles 1:5

2) Father of one of King Solomon's officials over provisions.

Only reference: 1 Kings 4:19

3) An exiled Levite who married a "strange" (foreign) woman.

Only reference: Ezra 10:24

URIAH

of times mentioned: 28
# of MEN by this name: 3

Meaning: Flame of God

1) Called Uriah the Hittite, he was Bath-sheba's first husband and a warrior in King David's army. When Bath-sheba discovered she was pregnant by the king, David called Uriah home and tried to make him go to his wife, but the faithful soldier would not do so while his fellow soldiers were in the field. So David ordered his commander, Joab, to put Uriah in the heaviest fighting so he would be killed.

After Uriah's death, the prophet Nathan confronted David with this murder and prophesied that Israel would not live in peace during David's reign. Same as Urias.

First reference: 2 Samuel 11:3 / Last reference: 1 Chronicles 11:41 / Key references: 2 Samuel 11:6–17; 12:9–10

2) Father of a man who weighed the temple vessels after the Babylonian Exile.

Only reference: Ezra 8:33

3) A priest who witnessed Isaiah's prophecy about Maher-shalal-hash-baz.

Only reference: Isaiah 8:2

URIAS

of times mentioned: 1
# of MEN by this name: 1

Meaning: Flame of God

Greek form of the name Uriah, used in the New Testament. See Uriah (1).

Only reference: Matthew 1:6

URIEL

of times mentioned: 4
# of MEN by this name: 2

Meaning: Flame of God

1) A descendant of Abraham through Jacob's son Levi. Uriel was among a group of Levites appointed by King David to bring the ark of the covenant from the house of Obed-edom to Jerusalem.

First reference: 1 Chronicles 6:24 / Last reference: 1 Chronicles 15:11

2) Grandfather of Judah's second king, Abijah. Uriel was the father of Abijah's mother, Michaiah.

Only reference: 2 Chronicles 13:2

URIJAH

of times mentioned: 11
# of MEN by this name: 4

Meaning: Flame of God

1) The priest who followed King Ahaz's command to build a pagan altar as a place of worship. When Ahaz moved the Jewish temple altars and told Urijah how to worship, the priest obeyed him.

First reference: 2 Kings 16:10 / Last reference: 2 Kings 16:16

2) Father of a man who repaired Jerusalem's walls under Nehemiah.

First reference: Nehemiah 3:4 / Last reference: Nehemiah 3:21

3) A priest who assisted Ezra in reading the book of the law to the people of Jerusalem.

Only reference: Nehemiah 8:4

4) A faithful prophet executed by King Jehoiakim of Judah.

First reference: Jeremiah 26:20 / Last reference: Jeremiah 26:23

👥 UTHAI

\# of times mentioned: 2
\# of MEN by this name: 2

Meaning: Succoring

1) A descendant of Judah who returned to Jerusalem after the Babylonian Exile.

Only reference: 1 Chronicles 9:4

2) A leader of Judah who returned from exile with Ezra.

Only reference: Ezra 8:14

👥 UZ

\# of times mentioned: 4
\# of MEN by this name: 2

Meaning: Consultation

1) A descendant of Noah through his son Shem. He possibly lent his name to Job's home territory, "the land of Uz" (Job 1:1).

First reference: Genesis 10:23 / Last reference: 1 Chronicles 1:17

2) A descendant of Seir, who lived in Esau's "land of Edom."

First reference: Genesis 36:28 / Last reference: 1 Chronicles 1:42

📍 UZ

\# of times mentioned: OT 3

Meaning: Consultation

A land east of Judah where Job lived. In Jeremiah's prophecies, Uz is listed among the lands on which God's wrath would fall through the conquest of the Chaldean king Nebuchadnezzar.

First reference: Job 1:1 / Last reference: Lamentations 4:21

👥 UZAI

\# of times mentioned: 1
\# of MEN by this name: 1

Meaning: Strong

Father of a man who repaired Jerusalem's walls under Nehemiah.

Only reference: Nehemiah 3:25

👥 UZAL

\# of times mentioned: 2
\# of MEN by this name: 1

A descendant of Noah through his son Shem.

First reference: Genesis 10:27 / Last reference: 1 Chronicles 1:21

👥 UZZA

\# of times mentioned: 8
\# of MEN by this name: 4

Meaning: Strength

1) A descendant of Abraham through Jacob's son Levi.

Only reference: 1 Chronicles 6:29

2) A descendant of Abraham through Jacob's son Benjamin.

Only reference: 1 Chronicles 8:7

3) A man who drove the cart in which the ark of the covenant was transported from Kirjath-jearim. When the oxen stumbled, Uzza reached out to steady the ark. God killed him for daring to touch the holy object. Same as Uzzah.

First reference: 1 Chronicles 13:7 / Last reference: 1 Chronicles 13:11

4) Forefather of an exiled family that returned to Judah under Zerubbabel.

First reference: Ezra 2:49 / Last reference: Nehemiah 7:51

📍 UZZA

of times mentioned: OT 2

Meaning: Strength

A garden where King Amon of Israel was buried after he was murdered by his own servants.

First reference: 2 Kings 21:18 / Last reference: 2 Kings 21:26

👥 UZZAH

of times mentioned: 4
# of MEN by this name: 1

Meaning: Strength

A variant spelling for Uzza. Same as Uzza (3).

First reference: 2 Samuel 6:3 / Last reference: 2 Samuel 6:8

📍 UZZEN-SHERAH

of times mentioned: OT 1

Meaning: Plat of Sheerah

A town built by Sherah, the daughter of Ephraim.

Only reference: 1 Chronicles 7:24

👥 UZZI

of times mentioned: 11
# of MEN by this name: 6

Meaning: Forceful

1) A descendant of Abraham through Jacob's son Levi, and a priest through the line of Aaron.

First reference: 1 Chronicles 6:5 / Last reference: Ezra 7:4

2) A descendant of Abraham through Jacob's son Issachar.

First reference: 1 Chronicles 7:2 / Last reference: 1 Chronicles 7:3

3) A descendant of Abraham through Jacob's son Benjamin.

Only reference: 1 Chronicles 7:7

4) A Jewish exile from the tribe of Benjamin who resettled Jerusalem.

Only reference: 1 Chronicles 9:8

5) Overseer of the Levites after their return from exile.

Only reference: Nehemiah 11:22

6) A priest who helped to dedicate the rebuilt wall of Jerusalem by giving thanks.

First reference: Nehemiah 12:19 / Last reference: Nehemiah 12:42

👥 UZZIA

of times mentioned: 1
# of MEN by this name: 1

Meaning: Strength of God

One of King David's valiant warriors.

Only reference: 1 Chronicles 11:44

👥 UZZIAH

of times mentioned: 27
# of MEN by this name: 5

Meaning: Strength of God

1) Son of Amaziah, king of Judah. Uzziah obeyed God, and the Lord helped him fight the Philistines and other enemies. The king fortified Jerusalem and built a powerful army. But in his power, Uzziah became proud and wrongly burned incense on the temple's incense altar. Confronted by the priests, he became angry. God immediately made him a leper. Thereafter Uzziah was cut off from the temple, and his son Jotham ruled in his name. Same as Azariah (3).

First reference: 2 Kings 15:13 / Last reference: Zechariah 14:5 / Key references: 2 Chronicles 26:1–23

2) A descendant of Abraham through Jacob's son Levi.

Only reference: 1 Chronicles 6:24

3) Father of Jehonathan, who was in charge of King David's storehouses.

Only reference: 1 Chronicles 27:25

4) An exiled Israelite priest who married a "strange" (foreign) woman.

Only reference: Ezra 10:21

5) A Jewish exile from the tribe of Judah who re-settled Jerusalem.

Only reference: Nehemiah 11:4

👥 UZZIEL

of times mentioned: 16
# of MEN by this name: 6

Meaning: Strength of God

1) A descendant of Abraham through Jacob's son Levi.

First reference: Exodus 6:18 / Last reference: 1 Chronicles 24:24

2) An army captain under King Hezekiah of Judah.

Only reference: 1 Chronicles 4:42

3) A descendant of Abraham through Jacob's son Benjamin.

Only reference: 1 Chronicles 7:7

4) A son of King David's musician Heman, who was "under the hands of [his] father for song in the house of the LORD" (1 1 Chronicles 25:6).

Only reference: 1 Chronicles 25:4

5) A descendant of Abraham through Jacob's son Levi. Uzziel was among the Levites who cleansed the Jerusalem temple during the revival of King Hezekiah's reign.

Only reference: 2 Chronicles 29:14

6) Son of a goldsmith and a repairer of Jerusalem's walls under Nehemiah.

Only reference: Nehemiah 3:8

👥 VAJEZATHA

of times mentioned: 1
# of MEN by this name: 1

One of ten sons of Haman, the villain of the story of Esther.

Only reference: Esther 9:9

👥 VANIAH

of times mentioned: 1
# of MEN by this name: 1

Meaning: God has answered

An exiled Israelite who married a "strange" (foreign) woman.

Only reference: Ezra 10:36

👥 VASHNI

of times mentioned: 1
# of MEN by this name: 1

Meaning: Weak

The firstborn son of the prophet Samuel. Vashni and his brother, Abiah, served as judges in Beersheba, but their poor character caused Israel's leaders to ask Samuel for a king to rule over them. Same as Joel (1).

Only reference: 1 Chronicles 6:28

👥 VASHTI

of times mentioned: 10
# of WOMEN by this name: 1

Queen of the Persian king Ahasuerus, Vashti refused to appear at his banquet. The king revoked her position and had no more to do with her.

First reference: Esther 1:9 / Last reference: Esther 2:17

👥 VOPHSI

of times mentioned: 1
# of MEN by this name: 1

Meaning: Additional
Father of one of the twelve spies sent by Moses to spy out the land of Canaan.

Only reference: Numbers 13:14

ZAANAIM

of times mentioned: OT 1

Meaning: Removals

Though translated "the plain of Zaanaim" in the King James Version, modern translations seem agreed that it is some kind of tree: for example, "the great tree" (NIV), "the terebinth tree" (NKJV), or "the oak" (ESV) in Zaanaim (or Zaananim). Here Heber the Kenite pitched his tent before the battle between Sisera and Barak. Sisera came to the tent of Heber's wife, Jael, and was killed by her. Same as Zaanannim.

Only reference: Judges 4:11

♀ ZAANAN

of times mentioned: OT 1

Meaning: Sheep pasture

A town of Judah that Micah foresaw would cower behind its doors when the Assyrians attacked.

Only reference: Micah 1:11

♀ ZAANANNIM

of times mentioned: OT 1

Meaning: Removals

A town that became part of the inheritance of Naphtali when Joshua cast lots in Shiloh to provide territory for the seven tribes that had yet to receive their land. Same as Zaanaim.

Only reference: Joshua 19:33

👥 ZAAVAN

of times mentioned: 1
# of MEN by this name: 1

Meaning: Disquiet

A descendant of Seir, who lived in Esau's "land of Edom."

Only reference: Genesis 36:27

👥 ZABAD

of times mentioned: 8
# of MEN by this name: 7

Meaning: Giver

1) A descendant of Abraham through Jacob's son Judah. Zabad descended from the line of an un-named Israelite woman and her Egyptian husband, Jarha.

First reference: 1 Chronicles 2:36 / Last reference: 1 Chronicles 2:37

2) A descendant of Abraham through Joseph's son Ephraim.

Only reference: 1 Chronicles 7:21

3) One of King David's valiant warriors.

Only reference: 1 Chronicles 11:41

4) One of two royal officials who conspired to kill Judah's king Joash.

Only reference: 2 Chronicles 24:26

5) An exiled Israelite who married a "strange" (foreign) woman.

Only reference: Ezra 10:27

6) Another exiled Israelite who married a "strange" (foreign) woman.

Only reference: Ezra 10:33

7) Yet another exiled Israelite who married a "strange" (foreign) woman.

Only reference: Ezra 10:43

👥 ZABBAI

of times mentioned: 2
# of MEN by this name: 2

Meaning: Pure

1) An exiled Israelite who married a "strange" (foreign) woman.

Only reference: Ezra 10:28

2) Father of a man who repaired Jerusalem's walls under Nehemiah.

Only reference: Nehemiah 3:20

👥 ZABBUD

of times mentioned: 1
# of MEN by this name: 1

Meaning: Given

An exiled Israelite who returned to Judah with Ezra.

Only reference: Ezra 8:14

👥 ZABDI

of times mentioned: 6
# of MEN by this name: 4

Meaning: Giving

1) The father of Achan. Achan disobeyed Joshua and took goods from Jericho when Israel conquered the city.

First reference: Joshua 7:1 / Last reference: Joshua 7:18

2) A descendant of Abraham through Jacob's son Benjamin.

Only reference: 1 Chronicles 8:19

3) A man in charge of the grapes for King David's wine cellars.

Only reference: 1 Chronicles 27:27

4) Forefather of a Levite who resettled Jerusalem after the Babylonian Exile.

Only reference: Nehemiah 11:17

👥 ZABDIEL

of times mentioned: 2
# of MEN by this name: 2

Meaning: Gift of God

1) Forefather of a captain of thousands under King David.

Only reference: 1 Chronicles 27:2

2) An overseer of the priests who served following the exiles' return to Jerusalem.

Only reference: Nehemiah 11:14

👥 ZABUD

of times mentioned: 1
# of MEN by this name: 1

Meaning: Given

A principal officer of King Solomon's court and a friend of the king.

Only reference: 1 Kings 4:5

📍 ZABULON

of times mentioned: NT 3

Meaning: Greek form of Zebulun

The land inherited by the tribe of Zebulun. Matthew places the city of Capernaum within its borders and points out that by living there, Jesus fulfilled the prophecy in Isaiah 9:1–2 that this tribe would see a great light.

First reference: Matthew 4:13 / Last reference: Revelation 7:8

👥 ZACCAI

of times mentioned: 2
# of MEN by this name: 1

Meaning: Pure

Forefather of an exiled family that returned to Judah under Zerubbabel.

First reference: Ezra 2:9 / Last reference: Nehemiah 7:14

👥 ZACCHAEUS

of times mentioned: 3
# of MEN by this name: 1

Meaning: Pure

A wealthy chief tax collector. Zacchaeus climbed a tree so he could see Jesus. The Master called him down, saying He would stay with him. Zacchaeus repented and promised Jesus he would give half his goods to the poor and repay fourfold anyone he had wronged.

First reference: Luke 19:2 / Last reference: Luke 19:8

👥 ZACCHUR

of times mentioned: 1
# of MEN by this name: 1

Meaning: Mindful

A descendant of Abraham through Jacob's son Simeon.

Only reference: 1 Chronicles 4:26

👥 ZACCUR

of times mentioned: 8
# of MEN by this name: 6

Meaning: Mindful

1) Father of one of the twelve spies sent by Moses to spy out the land of Canaan.

Only reference: Numbers 13:4

2) A descendant of Abraham through Jacob's son Levi.

Only reference: 1 Chronicles 24:27

3) A son of King David's musician Asaph, "which prophesied according to the order of the king" (1 Chronicles 25:2).

First reference: 1 Chronicles 25:2 / Last reference: Nehemiah 12:35

4) A rebuilder of the walls of Jerusalem under Nehemiah.

Only reference: Nehemiah 3:2

5) A Levite who renewed the covenant under Nehemiah.

Only reference: Nehemiah 10:12

6) One of the temple treasurers appointed by Nehemiah.

Only reference: Nehemiah 13:13

👥 ZACHARIAH

of times mentioned: 4
# of MEN by this name: 2

Meaning: God has remembered

1) Son of King Jeroboam of Israel, Zachariah reigned over Israel for six months before he was killed by the conspirator Shallum.

First reference: 2 Kings 14:29 / Last reference: 2 Kings 15:11

2) Grandfather of Hoshea, king of Israel.

Only reference: 2 Kings 18:2

👥 ZACHARIAS

of times mentioned: 11
# of MEN by this name: 2

Meaning: God has remembered

1) A man, possibly a prophet, mentioned by Jesus. Zacharias was killed between the sanctuary and the altar.

First reference: Matthew 23:35 / Last reference: Luke 11:51

2) A priest who received a vision that his barren wife would bear a child who would be great before the Lord. Because Zacharias doubted, God struck him dumb until the birth of the child. When he agreed with his wife to name the child John, Zacharias could suddenly speak. His son was John the Baptist.

First reference: Luke 1:5 / Last reference: Luke 3:2

👥 ZACHER

of times mentioned: 1
# of MEN by this name: 1

Meaning: Memento

A chief of the tribe of Benjamin who lived in Jerusalem.

Only reference: 1 Chronicles 8:31

👥 ZADOK

of times mentioned: 53
# of MEN by this name: 9

Meaning: Just

1) A priest during King David's reign. Zadok and the priest Abiathar consecrated Levites to bring the ark of the covenant into Jerusalem. With Zadok's help, David reorganized the priesthood. As David fled Jerusalem, attacked by his son Absalom, Zadok brought out the ark, planning to go with him. Instead, David left him behind to support him in

the city. Following Absalom's death, Zadok helped to persuade Judah to take David back as king.

When David was old, his son Adonijah tried to set himself up as king. But Zadok would not support him. Instead, at David's command, he anointed Solomon king. Solomon later made Zadok high priest.

First reference: 2 Samuel 8:17 / Last reference: Ezekiel 48:11 / Key references: 2 Samuel 15:24–29; 19:11; 1 Kings 1:8, 32–39; 2:35; 1 Chronicles 15:11–12; 24:3

2) Grandfather of King Jotham of Judah.

First reference: 2 Kings 15:33 / Last reference: 2 Chronicles 27:1

3) A descendant of Abraham through Jacob's son Levi, and a priest through the line of Aaron.

First reference: 1 Chronicles 6:12 / Last reference: 1 Chronicles 9:11

4) A young soldier, "mighty of valour," who helped to crown David king of Judah in Hebron.

Only reference: 1 Chronicles 12:28

5) A man who repaired Jerusalem's walls under Nehemiah.

Only reference: Nehemiah 3:4

6) Another man who repaired Jerusalem's walls under Nehemiah.

Only reference: Nehemiah 3:29

7) A Jewish leader who renewed the covenant under Nehemiah.

Only reference: Nehemiah 10:21

8) A priest who resettled Jerusalem following the Babylonian Exile.

Only reference: Nehemiah 11:11

9) One of the temple treasurers appointed by Nehemiah.

Only reference: Nehemiah 13:13

👥 ZAHAM

of times mentioned: 1
# of MEN by this name: 1

Meaning: Loathing

A son of Judah's king Rehoboam and a grandson of Solomon.

Only reference: 2 Chronicles 11:19

📍 ZAIR

of times mentioned: OT 1

Meaning: Little; few; young; ignoble

When Edom revolted against Judah's rule, Joram (Jehoram), king of Judah, attacked this place in Edom then fled without fully subduing the Edomites.

Only reference: 2 Kings 8:21

👥 ZALAPH

of times mentioned: 1
# of MEN by this name: 1

Father of a man who repaired Jerusalem's walls under Nehemiah.

Only reference: Nehemiah 3:30

👥 ZALMON

of times mentioned: 1
# of MEN by this name: 1

Meaning: Shady

One of King David's mightiest warriors known as "the thirty."

Only reference: 2 Samuel 23:28

📍 ZALMON

of times mentioned: OT 1

Meaning: Shady

After Abimelech and his men razed the city of Shechem, they went to Mount Zalmon to get wood to burn its remaining tower. Same as Salmon.

Only reference: Judges 9:48

📍 ZALMONAH

of times mentioned: OT 2

Meaning: Shadiness

A campsite of the Israelites on their way to the Promised Land.

First reference: Numbers 33:41 / Last reference: Numbers 33:42

👥 ZALMUNNA

of times mentioned: 12
# of MEN by this name: 1

Meaning: Shade has been denied

A Midianite king whom Gideon pursued after Zalmunna killed Gideon's brothers at Tabor. Gideon killed Zalmunna.

First reference: Judges 8:5 / Last reference: Psalm 83:11

👥 ZANOAH

of times mentioned: 1
# of MEN by this name: 1

Meaning: Rejected

A descendant of Abraham through Jacob's son Judah.

Only reference: 1 Chronicles 4:18

📍 ZANOAH

of times mentioned: OT 4

Meaning: Rejected

1) A city that became part of the inheritance of the tribe of Judah following the conquest of the Promised Land. Hanun and the inhabitants of Zanoah worked on Jerusalem's Valley Gate during the repairs under Nehemiah. Zanoah was resettled by the Jews after the Babylonian Exile.

First reference: Joshua 15:34 / Last reference: Nehemiah 11:30

2) Another city that became part of the inheritance of the tribe of Judah following the conquest of the

Promised Land.
Only reference: Joshua 15:56

👥 ZAPHNATH-PAANEAH

of times mentioned: 1
# of MEN by this name: 1

A name the Egyptian pharaoh gave to Joseph, the revealer of dreams.

Only reference: Genesis 41:45

📍 ZAPHON

of times mentioned: OT 1

Meaning: Boreal

A city east of the Jordan River that Moses made part of the inheritance of Gad.

Only reference: Joshua 13:27

👥 ZARA

of times mentioned: 1
# of MEN by this name: 1

Genealogy of Jesus: Yes (Matthew 1:3)

Meaning: Rising

Greek form of the name Zarah, used in the New Testament.

Only reference: Matthew 1:3

👥 ZARAH

of times mentioned: 2
# of MEN by this name: 1

Meaning: Rising

A twin born to Jacob's son Judah and his daughter-in-law Tamar.

First reference: Genesis 38:30 / Last reference: Genesis 46:12

📍 ZAREAH

of times mentioned: OT 1

Meaning: A wasp (as stinging)
A city of Judah resettled by the Jews after the Babylonian Exile.

Only reference: Nehemiah 11:29

♀ ZARED

of times mentioned: OT 1

Meaning: Lined with shrubbery

A valley between Moab and Edom where the Israelites camped before they fought with the Amorite king Sihon. Same as Zered.

Only reference: Numbers 21:12

♀ ZAREPHATH

of times mentioned: OT 3

Meaning: Refinement

A Phoenician city north of Tyre. During a drought he had predicted, the prophet Elijah hid from King Ahab of Israel in the Cerith ravine. When the Cerith Brook dried up, God sent Elijah to Zarephath. He asked a widow there for water and food, and she told him she was making a last meal for herself and her son. Through the prophet, God promised that her meager provisions would not run out until the Lord sent rain on the land. Later Elijah brought the son back to life, proving to the woman that he was a man of God and that the word of the Lord was true.

Obadiah foretold that Israelite exiles would possess the land as far north as Zarephath. Same as Sarepta.

First reference: 1 Kings 17:9 / Last reference: Obadiah 1:20

♀ ZARETAN

of times mentioned: OT 1

Meaning: To pierce; to puncture

This town was near Adam, where the Israelites crossed the Jordan River on their way to the Promised Land and the water stood up in a heap so they could cross on dry ground. Called Zarethan in some translations. Same as Zarthan.

Only reference: Joshua 3:16

♀ ZARETH-SHAHAR

of times mentioned: OT 1

Meaning: Splendor of the dawn

A city east of the Jordan River that was part of the inheritance of the tribe of Reuben. Zareth-shahar was "in the mount of the valley."

Only reference: Joshua 13:19

♀ ZARTANAH

of times mentioned: OT 1

Meaning: To pierce; to puncture

Under King Solomon's governmental organization, a place responsible for supplying provisions for the king.

Only reference: 1 Kings 4:12

♀ ZARTHAN

of times mentioned: OT 1

Meaning: To pierce; to puncture

In the plain of the Jordan River, between Succoth and Zarthan, workers cast the brass pieces for King Solomon's temple. Same as Zaretan.

Only reference: 1 Kings 7:46

👥 ZATTHU

of times mentioned: 1
# of MEN by this name: 1

A Jewish leader who renewed the covenant under Nehemiah.

Only reference: Nehemiah 10:14

👥 ZATTU

of times mentioned: 3
# of MEN by this name: 1

Forefather of an exiled family that returned to Judah under Zerubbabel.

First reference: Ezra 2:8 / Last reference: Nehemiah 7:13

ZAVAN

of times mentioned: 1
# of MEN by this name: 1

Meaning: Disquiet

A descendant of Seir, who lived in Esau's "land of Edom."

Only reference: 1 Chronicles 1:42

ZAZA

of times mentioned: 1
# of MEN by this name: 1

Meaning: Prominent

A descendant of Abraham through Jacob's son Judah.

Only reference: 1 Chronicles 2:33

ZEBADIAH

of times mentioned: 9
# of MEN by this name: 9

Meaning: God has given

1) A descendant of Abraham through Jacob's son Benjamin.

Only reference: 1 Chronicles 8:15

2) Another descendant of Abraham through Jacob's son Benjamin.

Only reference: 1 Chronicles 8:17

3) A "mighty man" who supported the future king David during his conflict with Saul.

Only reference: 1 Chronicles 12:7

4) A Levite "porter" (doorkeeper) in the house of the Lord.

Only reference: 1 Chronicles 26:2

5) One of King David's captains of thousands.

Only reference: 1 Chronicles 27:7

6) A Levite sent by King Jehoshaphat to teach the law of the Lord throughout the nation of Judah.

Only reference: 2 Chronicles 17:8

7) "Ruler of the house of Judah" who was in charge of King Jehoshaphat's household.

Only reference: 2 Chronicles 19:11

8) A Jewish exile who returned from Babylon to Judah under Ezra.

Only reference: Ezra 8:8

9) An exiled Israelite priest who married a "strange" (foreign) woman.

Only reference: Ezra 10:20

ZEBAH

of times mentioned: 12
# of MEN by this name: 1

Meaning: Sacrifice

A Midianite king whom Gideon pursued with three hundred men after Zebah killed Gideon's brothers at Tabor. Gideon killed Zebah.

First reference: Judges 8:5 / Last reference: Psalm 83:11

ZEBAIM

of times mentioned: OT 2

Meaning: Gazelles

A city in Judah to which captives returned after the Babylonian Exile.

First reference: Ezra 2:57 / Last reference: Nehemiah 7:59

ZEBEDEE

of times mentioned: 12
# of MEN by this name: 1

Meaning: Giving

Father of Jesus' disciples James and John and a fisherman on the Sea of Galilee. Zebedee's sons worked with him until they left to follow Jesus. James and John are frequently referred to as "the sons of Zebedee."

First reference: Matthew 4:21 / Last reference: John 21:2

👥 ZEBINA

of times mentioned: 1
# of MEN by this name: 1

Meaning: Gainfulness

An exiled Israelite who married a "strange" (foreign) woman.

Only reference: Ezra 10:43

📍 ZEBOIIM

of times mentioned: OT 2

Meaning: Gazelles

A Canaanite kingdom that, along with some Canaanite allies, made war with Chedorlaomer, king of Elam, and his Mesopotamian allies. After serving Chedorlaomer for twelve years, Zeboiim and the other Canaanites rebelled without success against the Mesopotamians. Same as Zeboim (1).

First reference: Genesis 14:2 / Last reference: Genesis 14:8

📍 ZEBOIM

of times mentioned: OT 5

Meaning: Gazelles

1) One of the five Canaanite cities of the plain that probably lay south of the Dead Sea. Along with Sodom and Gomorrah, Zeboim was destroyed by fire and brimstone. In the book of Hosea, God considers overthrowing Ephraim as he did Zeboim, but His heart changes and He doesn't do it. Same as Zeboiim.

First reference: Genesis 10:19 / Last reference: Hosea 11:8

2) A valley in the land of the tribe of Benjamin. When the Philistines camped at Michmash, they sent raiding parties "toward the borderland overlooking the Valley of Zeboim facing the desert" (1 Samuel 13:18 NIV). The Benjaminites resettled Zeboim after the Babylonian Exile.

First reference: 1 Samuel 13:18 / Last reference: Nehemiah 11:34

👥 ZEBUDAH

of times mentioned: 1
# of WOMEN by this name: 1

Meaning: Gainfulness

Mother of the evil Jehoiakim, the third-to-last king of Judah.

Only reference: 2 Kings 23:36

👥 ZEBUL

of times mentioned: 6
# of MEN by this name: 1

Meaning: Dwelling

Ruler of the city of Shechem under King Abimelech. He encouraged the conspirator Gaal to fight Abimelech's army and pushed him and his men out of the city.

First reference: Judges 9:28 / Last reference: Judges 9:41

👥 ZEBULUN

of times mentioned: 6
# of MEN by this name: 1

Meaning: Habitation

The sixth and last son of Jacob and Leah. Jacob foretold that Zebulun would dwell "at the haven of the sea" (Genesis 49:13), bordering on Zidon.

First reference: Genesis 30:20 / Last reference: 1 Chronicles 2:1

📍 ZEBULUN

of times mentioned: OT 17

Meaning: Habitation

Of the forty-four references in scripture to the word *Zebulun*, fewer than half refer specifically to the land of that name. More often, details about this territory are connected to references to the tribe.

In his blessing on Zebulun, Jacob declared,

"Zebulun shall dwell at the haven of the sea; and he shall be for an haven of ships; and his border shall be unto Zidon" (Genesis 49:13). Though Zebulun received a landlocked territory, after the conquest of the Promised Land, it was just east of the coastal lands of Asher, ten miles from the sea (Joshua 19:10–16). Zebulun never extended as far as Zidon, but it did encompass land of the Phoenicians, for whom Zidon was an important city.

Zebulun gave four towns to the Levites: Jokneam, Kartah, Dimnah, and Nahalal (Joshua 21:34–35). First Chronicles 6:77 adds Rimmon (1) and Tabor (3) to the tally, but it's possible Rimmon and Dimnah were the same town.

The judge Elon the Zebulonite died and was buried in Aijalon (2), a city of Zebulun.

The tribe of Zebulun never drove the Canaanites out of Kitron and Nahalon. Instead these pagan people lived with the tribe. Their influence undoubtedly led the tribe into idolatry. When King Hezekiah of Judah sent letters to Zebulun, inviting the people to celebrate Passover in Jerusalem, many scorned his message, but a few humbled themselves and came. However, the king noticed that many of these well-meaning people failed to follow the law by not purifying themselves beforehand.

Though Isaiah spoke of the gloom brought to Zebulun and Naphtali when those lands were invaded by the Assyrians, he also promised they would see a great light, and joy would be their harvest (Isaiah 9:1–3). The prophecy was fulfilled in Matthew 4:13–15 when Jesus moved to Capernaum and began preaching His Gospel message. Same as Zabulon.

First reference: Genesis 49:13 / Last reference: Ezekiel 48:33

👥 ZECHARIAH

of times mentioned: 39
# of MEN by this name: 27

Meaning: God has remembered

1) A descendant of Abraham through Jacob's son Reuben.

Only reference: 1 Chronicles 5:7

2) A Levite, known as "a wise counsellor," who was chosen by lot to guard the west side of the house of the Lord.

First reference: 1 Chronicles 9:21 / Last reference: 1 Chronicles 29:1

3) A descendant of Jehiel, the founder of the land of Gibeon.

Only reference: 1 Chronicles 9:37

4) A Levite musician who performed in celebration when King David brought the ark of the covenant to Jerusalem.

First reference: 1 Chronicles 15:18 / Last reference: 1 Chronicles 16:5

5) A priest who blew a trumpet before the ark of the covenant when David brought it to Jerusalem.

Only reference: 1 Chronicles 15:24

6) A Levite worship leader during David's reign. Lots were cast to determine his duties.

Only reference: 1 Chronicles 24:25

7) A Levite "porter" (doorkeeper) in the house of the Lord.

Only reference: 1 Chronicles 26:11

8) Father of a ruler of the half tribe of Manasseh under King David.

Only reference: 1 Chronicles 27:21

9) A prince of Judah sent by King Jehoshaphat to teach the law of the Lord throughout the nation.

Only reference: 2 Chronicles 17:7

10) Father of Jahaziel, a Levite worship leader of the order of the sons of Asaph.

Only reference: 2 Chronicles 20:14

11) A son of Judah's king Jehoshaphat, given "great gifts of silver, and of gold, and of precious things" by his father (2 Chronicles 21:3).

Only reference: 2 Chronicles 21:2

12) Son of Jehoiada the priest who was killed for telling Judah's people they had forsaken God.

Only reference: 2 Chronicles 24:20

13) A prophet who influenced King Uzziah of Judah and "had understanding in the visions of God."

Only reference: 2 Chronicles 26:5

14) A descendant of Abraham through Jacob's son Levi. Zechariah was among the Levites who

cleansed the Jerusalem temple during the revival of King Hezekiah's day.

Only reference: 2 Chronicles 29:13

15) An overseer of temple repairs under King Josiah of Judah.

Only reference: 2 Chronicles 34:12

16) A temple ruler during the reign of King Josiah of Judah.

Only reference: 2 Chronicles 35:8

17) An Old Testament minor prophet who ministered in Jerusalem following the return from exile. Judah prospered under his ministry as they rebuilt the temple.

First reference: Ezra 5:1 / Last reference: Zechariah 7:8

18) A Jewish exile who returned from Babylon to Judah under Ezra.

Only reference: Ezra 8:3

19) A Jewish exile charged with finding Levites and temple servants to travel to Jerusalem with Ezra.

First reference: Ezra 8:11 / Last reference: Ezra 8:16

20) An exiled Israelite who married a "strange" (foreign) woman.

Only reference: Ezra 10:26

21) A priest who assisted Ezra in reading the book of the law to the people of Jerusalem.

Only reference: Nehemiah 8:4

22) A Jewish exile from the tribe of Judah who re-settled Jerusalem.

Only reference: Nehemiah 11:4

23) Another Jewish exile from the tribe of Judah who resettled Jerusalem.

Only reference: Nehemiah 11:5

24) Forefather of an exiled family that resettled Jerusalem.

Only reference: Nehemiah 11:12

25) Forefather of a priest who returned to Jerusalem under Zerubbabel.

Only reference: Nehemiah 12:16

26) A priest who helped to dedicate the rebuilt walls of Jerusalem by playing a musical instrument.

First reference: Nehemiah 12:35 / Last reference: Nehemiah 12:41

27) A witness of Isaiah to his prophecy about Maher-shalal-hash-baz.

Only reference: Isaiah 8:2

📍 ZEDAD

of times mentioned: OT 2

Meaning: A siding

A landmark of Israel's northern border between Lebo-hamath and Ziphron. Zedad appears in God's description of the boundaries that He gave to Moses and the vision of the restored Israel that He gave to Ezekiel.

First reference: Numbers 34:8 / Last reference: Ezekiel 47:15

👥 ZEDEKIAH

of times mentioned: 62
# of MEN by this name: 5

Meaning: Right of God

1) A false prophet who predicted that King Jehoshaphat of Judah would win over the Syrians. Zedekiah struck and mocked the faithful prophet Micaiah.

First reference: 1 Kings 22:11 / Last reference: 2 Chronicles 18:23

2) Originally named Mattaniah, Zedekiah was a brother of King Jehoiachin of Judah. Nebuchadnezzar, king of Babylon, conquered Judah, deposed Jehoiachin, renamed Mattaniah as Zedekiah, and made him king. Like his brother, Zedekiah rebelled against Babylon. Zedekiah did not heed the prophet Jeremiah and imprisoned him. Nebuchadnezzar besieged Jerusalem. When the city no longer had food, Zedekiah and his troops sought to escape. The Chaldean army caught Zedekiah, killed his sons before him, and put out his eyes. They bound him and carried him to Babylon.

First reference: 2 Kings 24:17 / Last reference: Jeremiah 52:11 / Key references: 2 Kings 24:17–

20; Jeremiah 39:4–7

3) A son of King Jehoiakim of Judah.

Only reference: 1 Chronicles 3:16

4) A false prophet whom Jeremiah spoke against after Judah went into captivity.

First reference: Jeremiah 29:21 / Last reference: Jeremiah 29:22

5) A prince of Judah who heard Jeremiah's prophecy from Micaiah (5).

Only reference: Jeremiah 36:12

👥 ZEEB

of times mentioned: 6
# of MEN by this name: 1

Meaning: Wolf

A Midianite prince captured and killed by the men of Ephraim under Gideon's command.

First reference: Judges 7:25 / Last reference: Psalm 83:11

📍 ZELAH

of times mentioned: OT 2

Meaning: A limping or full

A city that became part of the inheritance of Benjamin when Joshua cast lots in Shiloh to provide territory for the seven tribes that had yet to receive their land. Here the bones of King Saul and his son Jonathan were buried in the tomb of Saul's father, Kish. After the Philistines had recovered their bodies from the battlefield and hanged them in Beth-shan, the men of Jabesh-gilead stole back their bones. King David took the bones from the men of Jabesh-gilead and saw that they were interred in Kish's tomb.

First reference: Joshua 18:28 / Last reference: 2 Samuel 21:14

👥 ZELEK

of times mentioned: 2
# of MEN by this name: 1

Meaning: Fissure

One of King David's valiant warriors.

First reference: 2 Samuel 23:37 / Last reference: 1 Chronicles 11:39

👥 ZELOPHEHAD

of times mentioned: 11
# of MEN by this name: 1

Meaning: United

A descendant of Joseph, through Manasseh, who died during the wilderness wanderings. Zelophehad's five daughters asked Moses if they could inherit their father's property in the Promised Land (a right normally reserved for sons). God ruled that they should, since Zelophehad had no sons.

First reference: Numbers 26:33 / Last reference: 1 Chronicles 7:15

👥 ZELOTES

of times mentioned: 2
# of MEN by this name: 1

Meaning: Zealot

Surname of Simon, one of Jesus' twelve disciples.

First reference: Luke 6:15 / Last reference: Acts 1:13

📍 ZELZAH

of times mentioned: OT 1

Meaning: Clear shade

A city of Benjamin where Samuel foretold that Saul would meet two men who would tell him the donkeys he was searching for had been found.

Only reference: 1 Samuel 10:2

📍 ZEMARAIM

of times mentioned: OT 2

Meaning: Double fleece

1) A city that became part of the inheritance of Benjamin when Joshua cast lots in Shiloh to provide territory for the seven tribes that had yet to receive their land.

Only reference: Joshua 18:22

2) A mountain in Ephraim's hill country where Abijah, king of Judah, spoke to King Jeroboam of Israel and his men. Abijah told Jeroboam that their golden idols and multitude of warriors did not guarantee they would win the battle. He begged them not to fight against the Lord. Though Jeroboam surrounded the troops of Judah, God defeated Israel when His people cried out to Him and gave a battle shout.

Only reference: 2 Chronicles 13:4

👥 ZEMIRA

of times mentioned: 1
# of MEN by this name: 1

Meaning: Song

A descendant of Abraham through Jacob's son Benjamin.

Only reference: 1 Chronicles 7:8

📍 ZENAN

of times mentioned: OT 1

Meaning: Sheep pasture

A city that became part of the inheritance of the tribe of Judah following the conquest of the Promised Land.

Only reference: Joshua 15:37

👥 ZENAS

of times mentioned: 1
# of MEN by this name: 1

Meaning: Jove-given

A lawyer whom the apostle Paul encouraged Titus to help on a journey.

Only reference: Titus 3:13

👥 ZEPHANIAH

of times mentioned: 10
# of MEN by this name: 4

Meaning: God has secreted

1) The second priest in the temple whom King Zedekiah sent to the prophet Jeremiah, asking him to pray for Israel. When King Nebuchadnezzar of Babylon captured Jerusalem, Zephaniah was taken to Riblah, where Nebuchadnezzar killed him.

First reference: 2 Kings 25:18 / Last reference: Jeremiah 52:24

2) Forefather of a Levite worship leader who served in the tabernacle during David's reign.

Only reference: 1 Chronicles 6:36

3) A descendant of Abraham through Jacob's son Levi.

Only reference: Zephaniah 1:1

4) Forefather of Josiah (2), in whose house the high priest Joshua received a prophecy from Zechariah.

First reference: Zechariah 6:10 / Last reference: Zechariah 6:14

📍 ZEPHATH

of times mentioned: OT 1

Meaning: Watchtower

A city taken by the tribes of Judah and Simeon. They killed the people of the town, destroyed it, and renamed it Hormah. Same as Hormah.

Only reference: Judges 1:17

📍 ZEPHATHAH

of times mentioned: OT 1

Meaning: Watchtower

Asa, king of Judah, fought Zerah the Ethiopian at this valley in Judah. God struck the enemy before Asa, and the Ethiopians were overthrown.

Only reference: 2 Chronicles 14:10

👥 ZEPHI

of times mentioned: 1
# of MEN by this name: 1

Meaning: Observant

A descendant of Abraham's grandson Esau.

Only reference: 1 Chronicles 1:36

ZEPHO

of times mentioned: 2
# of MEN by this name: 1

Meaning: Observant

A grandson of Isaac's son Esau.

First reference: Genesis 36:11 / Last reference: Genesis 36:15

ZEPHON

of times mentioned: 1
# of MEN by this name: 1

Meaning: Watchtower

A descendant of Abraham through Jacob's son Gad.

Only reference: Numbers 26:15

ZER

of times mentioned: OT 1

Meaning: Rock

A fortified or walled city that became part of the inheritance of Naphtali when Joshua cast lots in Shiloh to provide territory for the seven tribes that had yet to receive their land.
Only reference: Joshua 19:35

ZERAH

of times mentioned: 19
# of MEN by this name: 7

Meaning: Rising

1) A descendant of Abraham's grandson Esau.

First reference: Genesis 36:13 / Last reference: 1 Chronicles 1:37

2) Father of a king of Edom, "before there reigned any king over the children of Israel" (Genesis 36:31).

First reference: Genesis 36:33 / Last reference: 1 Chronicles 1:44

3) A grandson of Jacob, born to Jacob's son Judah and Judah's daughter-in-law, Tamar.

First reference: Numbers 26:20 / Last reference: Nehemiah 11:24

4) A descendant of Abraham through Jacob's son Simeon.

First reference: Numbers 26:13 / Last reference: 1 Chronicles 4:24

5) A descendant of Abraham through Jacob's son Levi.

Only reference: 1 Chronicles 6:21

6) Another descendant of Abraham through Jacob's son Levi.

Only reference: 1 Chronicles 6:41

7) An Ethiopian commander whose army fled before King Asa of Judah.

Only reference: 2 Chronicles 14:9

ZERAHIAH

of times mentioned: 5
# of MEN by this name: 2

Meaning: God has risen

1) A descendant of Abraham through Jacob's son Levi, and a priest through the line of Aaron.

First reference: 1 Chronicles 6:6 / Last reference: Ezra 7:4

2) Forefather of a Jewish exile who returned from Babylon to Judah under Ezra.

Only reference: Ezra 8:4

ZERED

of times mentioned: OT 2

Meaning: Lined with shrubbery

A brook running into the southwest corner of the Dead Sea, Zered lay between Edom and Moab. God commanded Israel to cross this brook, thus ending their years of wandering in the desert. Same as Zared.

First reference: Deuteronomy 2:13 / Last reference: Deuteronomy 2:14

📍 ZEREDA

of times mentioned: OT 1

Meaning: Puncture

Hometown of Jeroboam, son of Nebat, who became king of Israel when King Rehoboam offended his people.

Only reference: 1 Kings 11:26

📍 ZEREDATHAH

of times mentioned: OT 1

Meaning: Puncture

A place in the plain of the Jordan River near which the brass implements for the temple were cast.

Only reference: 2 Chronicles 4:17

📍 ZERERATH

of times mentioned: OT 1

Meaning: Puncture

A place to which the Midianite army fled when Gideon and his three hundred troops attacked them at Phurah.

Only reference: Judges 7:22

👥 ZERESH

of times mentioned: 4
# of WOMEN by this name: 1

Wife of Haman, the villain of the story of Esther. Zeresh, along with friends, encouraged Haman to build a gallows on which to hang Esther's cousin Mordecai—the gallows that Haman himself would later die on.

First reference: Esther 5:10 / Last reference: Esther 6:13

👥 ZERETH

of times mentioned: 1
# of MEN by this name: 1

Meaning: Splendor

A descendant of Abraham through Jacob's son Judah.

Only reference: 1 Chronicles 4:7

👥 ZERI

of times mentioned: 1
# of MEN by this name: 1

Meaning: Distillation

A son of King David's musician Jeduthun, "who prophesied with a harp, to give thanks and to praise the LORD" (1 Chronicles 25:3).

Only reference: 1 Chronicles 25:3

👥 ZEROR

of times mentioned: 1
# of MEN by this name: 1

Meaning: Parcel

An ancestor of Israel's first king, Saul.

Only reference: 1 Samuel 9:1

👥 ZERUAH

of times mentioned: 1
# of WOMEN by this name: 1

A widow and the mother of Jeroboam, who became the first king of the northern Jewish nation of Israel.

Only reference: 1 Kings 11:26

👥 ZERUBBABEL

of times mentioned: 22
# of MEN by this name: 1

Meaning: Descended of Babylon

Governor of Judah, Zerubbabel returned from the Babylonian Exile with many Israelites in his train. He began by rebuilding an altar so Judah could worship for the feast of tabernacles. When God spoke through the prophet Haggai, Zerubbabel and the high priest Jeshua obeyed, organizing workers to rebuild the temple. When Israel's enemies came to offer their help, Zerubbabel refused and tried to forestall trouble by telling them that Israel was following the Persian king Cyrus's command. God told the prophet Zechariah that Zerubbabel would finish his task.

First reference: 1 Chronicles 3:19 / Last reference: Zechariah 4:10 / Key references: Ezra 3:2–5; 3:8; 4:1–3; 5:2; Haggai 1:1–2, 12; Zechariah 4:9

👥 ZERUIAH

of times mentioned: 26
# of WOMEN by this name: 1

Meaning: Wounded

Sister of King David and mother of David's battle commander, Joab, and his brothers, Abishai and Asahel.

First reference: 1 Samuel 26:6 / Last reference: 1 Chronicles 27:24 / Key references: 2 Samuel 2:18; 1 Chronicles 2:15–16

👥 ZETHAM

of times mentioned: 2
# of MEN by this name: 1

Meaning: Olive

A chief Levite during King David's reign, Zetham was in charge of the temple treasures.

First reference: 1 Chronicles 23:8 / Last reference: 1 Chronicles 26:22

👥 ZETHAN

of times mentioned: 1
# of MEN by this name: 1

Meaning: Olive

A descendant of Abraham through Jacob's son Benjamin.

Only reference: 1 Chronicles 7:10

👥 ZETHAR

of times mentioned: 1
# of MEN by this name: 1

A eunuch serving the Persian king Ahasuerus in Esther's time.

Only reference: Esther 1:10

👥 ZIA

of times mentioned: 1
# of MEN by this name: 1

Meaning: Agitation

A descendant of Abraham through Jacob's son Gad.

Only reference: 1 Chronicles 5:13

👥 ZIBA

of times mentioned: 16
# of MEN by this name: 1

Meaning: Station

A servant of King Saul who told King David where Mephibosheth lived after David took the throne. When David fled Jerusalem, Ziba brought him food and the news that his master sought to take David's throne. David gave him everything Mephibosheth owned. When David returned to Jerusalem as king, Mephibosheth claimed his servant had lied.

First reference: 2 Samuel 9:2 / Last reference: 2 Samuel 19:29 / Key references: 2 Samuel 9:2–3; 16:1–4; 19:24–30

👥 ZIBEON

of times mentioned: 8
# of MEN by this name: 2

Meaning: Variegated

1) Grandfather of Anah, a wife of Esau.

First reference: Genesis 36:2 / Last reference: Genesis 36:14

2) A descendant of Seir, who lived in Esau's "land of Edom."

First reference: Genesis 36:20 / Last reference: 1 Chronicles 1:40

📍 ZIBIA

of times mentioned: 1
# of MEN by this name: 1

Meaning: Gazelle

A descendant of Abraham through Jacob's son Benjamin.

Only reference: 1 Chronicles 8:9

👥 ZIBIAH

of times mentioned: 2
# of WOMEN by this name: 1

Meaning: Gazelle

Mother of Joash, one of the good kings of Judah.

First reference: 2 Kings 12:1 / Last reference: 2 Chronicles 24:1

👥 ZICHRI

of times mentioned: 12
# of MEN by this name: 12

Meaning: Memorable

1) A brother of Korah (3), who rebelled against Moses and was killed by God.

Only reference: Exodus 6:21

2) A descendant of Abraham through Jacob's son Benjamin.

Only reference: 1 Chronicles 8:19

3) Another descendant of Abraham through Jacob's son Benjamin.

Only reference: 1 Chronicles 8:23

4) A chief of the tribe of Benjamin who lived in Jerusalem.

Only reference: 1 Chronicles 8:27

5) Forefather of a chief Levite, and a son of Asaph (2).

Only reference: 1 Chronicles 9:15

6) A Levite worship leader who was part of King David's reorganization of the Levites.

Only reference: 1 Chronicles 26:25

7) Forefather of a ruler over the Reubenites under King David.

Only reference: 1 Chronicles 27:16

8) A mighty man of valor who served King Jehoshaphat of Judah.

Only reference: 2 Chronicles 17:16

9) A captain of hundreds who made a covenant with the priest Jehoiada.

Only reference: 2 Chronicles 23:1

10) "A mighty man of Ephraim" who killed a son of King Ahaz and two of his officers.

Only reference: 2 Chronicles 28:7

11) Father of a Benjamite who was chosen by lot to resettle Jerusalem after returning from the Babylonian Exile.

Only reference: Nehemiah 11:9

12) Forefather of a priest who returned to Jerusalem under Zerubbabel.

Only reference: Nehemiah 12:17

👥 ZIDKIJAH

of times mentioned: 1
# of MEN by this name: 1

Meaning: Right of God

An Israelite who renewed the covenant under Nehemiah.

Only reference: Nehemiah 10:1

👥 ZIDON

of times mentioned: 1
# of MEN by this name: 1

Meaning: Fishery

A descendant of Noah through his son Ham.

Only reference: 1 Chronicles 1:13

📍 ZIDON

of times mentioned: OT 20

Meaning: Lie alongside (as in catching fish)

A Phoenician seaport north of Tyre, sometimes

called "great Zidon" because of its power and influence. Though the tribe of Asher received Zidon as part of its territory, they never drove out the Zidonians. Instead the pagan worship of Zidon began to influence Israel and led to Israel's oppression by pagan peoples.

To Zarephath, a town belonging to Zidon, God sent the prophet Elijah after he prophesied a time of drought. Under Ezra's direction, men of Zidon brought cedar trees to Jerusalem for the rebuilding of the temple.

Against Tyre and Zidon, Phoenicia's major cities—whose names are often connected in the Prophets—Isaiah spoke an oracle of Tyre's destruction. With Tyre's destruction, Zidon, too, would be brought low. Jeremiah included Zidon in the list of places that would drink the cup of God's wrath, and the prophet warned the people of Zidon that God had given their lands into the hands of the Chaldean king Nebuchadnezzar. Before Pharaoh attacked and overwhelmed Gaza, Jeremiah foresaw that Zidon and Tyre would be cut off from all help. He foretold that God's glory would be made clear in Zidon, and His judgments would be executed there.

Through the prophet Joel, God accused Zidon of taking His silver and gold and other treasures into its temples. Zidon's inhabitants had sold the people of Judah and Jerusalem to the Greeks. God would pay them back, selling their children into Judah's hands, and they, too, would be sold to the Sabeans. Same as Sidon.

First reference: Genesis 49:13 / Last reference: Zechariah 9:2 / Key references: Judges 1:31; Isaiah 23:1–4, 12; Ezekiel 28:21–23

👥 ZIHA

of times mentioned: 3
# of MEN by this name: 2

Meaning: Drought

1) Forefather of a family of temple servants who returned from exile.

First reference: Ezra 2:43 / Last reference: Nehemiah 7:46
2) An official over the temple servants after the Babylonian Exile. Possibly the same as Ziha (1).

Only reference: Nehemiah 11:21

📍 ZIKLAG

of times mentioned: OT 15

A town that became part of the inheritance of the tribe of Judah following the conquest of the Promised Land. Ziklag became part of the inheritance of Simeon when Joshua cast lots in Shiloh to provide territory for the seven tribes that had yet to receive their land. But it did not remain in Israel's control. When David served Achish, king of Gath, the king gave him Ziklag to live in. There many mighty men of valor came to David from Saul's own tribe of Benjamin and from Gad, Judah, and Manasseh.

The Amalekites invaded Ziklag and carried off the Israelites' wives and children, including David's wives Ahinoam and Abigail. A deserted Egyptian servant of an Amalekite brought David and his men to the Amalekites so they could rescue their families. In Ziklag David heard the news that Saul was dead, and he killed the messenger, who thought he had brought good news and expected a reward. Even after David's death, Ziklag remained in Judah's hands.

Ziklag was resettled by the Jews after the Babylonian Exile.

First reference: Joshua 15:31 / Last reference: Nehemiah 11:28 / Key references: 1 Samuel 27:3–6; 30; 1 Chronicles 12:1–22

👥 ZILLAH

of times mentioned: 3
# of WOMEN by this name: 1

Meaning: Shade

Second wife of Lamech, a descendant of Cain. Her son was Tubal-cain.

First reference: Genesis 4:19 / Last reference: Genesis 4:23

👥 ZILPAH

of times mentioned: 7
# of WOMEN by this name: 1

Meaning: Trickle

Servant of Leah. Leah gave Zilpah to her husband, Jacob, as a wife because she thought her own childbearing days were ended. Zilpah had two sons,

Gad and Asher.

First reference: Genesis 29:24 / Last reference: Genesis 46:18

👥 ZILTHAI

of times mentioned: 2
# of MEN by this name: 2

Meaning: Shady

1) A descendant of Abraham through Jacob's son Benjamin.

Only reference: 1 Chronicles 8:20

2) One of a group of "mighty men of valour" who fought for King David.

Only reference: 1 Chronicles 12:20

👥 ZIMMAH

of times mentioned: 3
# of MEN by this name: 3

Meaning: Lewdness

1) A descendant of Abraham through Jacob's son Levi.

Only reference: 1 Chronicles 6:20

2) A descendant of Abraham through Jacob's son Levi.

Only reference: 1 Chronicles 6:42

3) Forefather of a Levite worship leader who helped to consecrate the temple during King Hezekiah's reign.

Only reference: 2 Chronicles 29:12

👥 ZIMRAN

of times mentioned: 2
# of MEN by this name: 1

Meaning: Musical

A son of Abraham by his second wife, Keturah.

First reference: Genesis 25:2 / Last reference: 1 Chronicles 1:32

👥 ZIMRI

of times mentioned: 14
# of MEN by this name: 4

Meaning: Musical

1) A man killed by Phinehas (1) for blatant sexual sin.

Only reference: Numbers 25:14

2) The king of Israel who conspired against King Elah and killed him. After usurping Elah's throne, Zimri killed Elah's male relatives, fulfilling the prophecy of Jehu (1). Zimri reigned for seven days before Israel made Omri king in his place. When the capital was taken, Zimri burned down the king's house with himself inside it.

First reference: 1 Kings 16:9 / Last reference: 2 Kings 9:31

3) A descendant of Abraham through Jacob's son Judah.

Only reference: 1 Chronicles 2:6

4) A descendant of Abraham through Jacob's son Benjamin, through the line of King Saul and his son Jonathan.

First reference: 1 Chronicles 8:36 / Last reference: 1 Chronicles 9:42

📍 ZIMRI

of times mentioned: OT 1

Meaning: Musical

One of many nations that would drink the cup of God's wrath, according to the Lord's revelation to Jeremiah. Though Zimri is listed with Elam and Media, nothing is known about this country.

Only reference: Jeremiah 25:25

📍 ZIN

of times mentioned: OT 10

Meaning: A crag

A desert explored by the twelve spies whom Joshua sent to view the Promised Land. Kadesh, where Moses' sister, Miriam, died and the Israelites quarreled with God, was in the wilderness (or desert) of Zin. The Israelites camped here after they left Ezion-geber and made their way toward Mount Hor. When the Promised Land was divided between the tribes, the desert of Zin was on the southern border of the tribe of Judah's territory.

First reference: Numbers 13:21 / Last reference: Joshua 15:3

👥 ZINA

of times mentioned: 1
# of MEN by this name: 1

Meaning: Well fed

A Levite who was part of David's reorganization of the Levites. Same as Zizah.

Only reference: 1 Chronicles 23:10

📍 ZION

of times mentioned: OT 152

Meaning: Conspicuousness

Originally the name for a fortified mound on one of Jerusalem's southern hills, Zion, or Mount Zion, became the name for the temple mount, then the city of Jerusalem, and was even sometimes applied to the whole nation of Israel. It is often used in a poetic sense that glorifies God and Israel's role in bringing about His purposes.

Though the tribe of Judah had previously conquered Jerusalem, David reconquered the city, which was then held by the Jebusites. The new king promised that whoever first struck the Jebusites would be his battle commander, a position that Joab won. David lived in the fortress at first; then he built the city's fortifications while Joab restored the rest of the city.

Solomon brought the ark of the covenant to Zion, where it was placed in the temple on the spot claimed by tradition as Mount Moriah. The temple was dedicated with sacrifices and a prayer by King Solomon (2 Chronicles 5–6).

The psalms speak of Zion in connection with God's glory and salvation, and the "daughter of Zion" personifies Jerusalem and its people. God is spoken of as living in Zion (Psalms 76:2; 135:21) and having chosen Zion as His dwelling place (Psalm 132:13). During the Babylonian Exile, the people of Judah wept when they thought of their destroyed city (Psalm 137:1).

Isaiah made frequent use of the word Zion. Though Judah faced destruction, the prophet foresaw a day when all nations would flow to Zion, and the law would go out of the city as God judged the nations and swords were beaten into plowshares. The prophet also encouraged the people of Zion to take heart, for God's anger would turn from them and He would punish the Assyrians, who threatened their safety. Though Judah stubbornly sought protection in Egypt, against God's command, the prophet foresaw a day when the people of Judah would again live in Zion and no longer weep. God's ransomed people would return to the city singing and would experience everlasting joy.

Because Assyria despised Jerusalem, God promised King Hezekiah of Judah that He would turn the enemy back and Assyria would never enter Jerusalem. This took place when God killed 185,000 Assyrians in their camp overnight. The rest returned home. Repeatedly Isaiah's prophecy encouraged God's people to trust in His salvation. Though Zion doubted, He could no more forget His people than a mother could forget her child, and He would comfort them. A day would come when unbelievers would not enter the city and God would return to Zion. A Redeemer would come there and Israel would turn from sin.

Jeremiah also called the people of Judah to return to God, who would bring them to Zion even as the Chaldeans (Babylonians) came from the north. When Zion would seek to repent, God would not relent for a time. But as others called her an outcast, God's compassion would turn again to Zion. Again His people would sing on Zion's heights. The prophet promised the destruction of Babylon for its mistreatment of Zion.

The prophet Joel foretold a day of the Lord in which God's wrath would fall first on His own people in Zion, then on their enemies. Obadiah added that during this day, some in Mount Zion would escape, and it would be made holy. "Deliverers will go up on Mount Zion to govern the mountains of Esau. And the kingdom will be the Lord's" (Obadiah 1:21 NIV).

Micah took the leaders of Israel to task for their dishonest rule and promised that Zion would be destroyed. He repeated Isaiah's promise that the law would go forth from Zion, swords would be beaten into plowshares, and all people would live in peace. Though Zion left the city and was sent to Babylon, she would be rescued by God.

Zephaniah encouraged Zion, telling the city she would rejoice when the Lord took away His judgments against her and came into Zion's midst and rejoiced over her. Zechariah promised that the Lord's cities would "overflow with prosperity" (Zechariah 1:17 ESV), and Zion would be comforted. Again, Zion would be the apple of God's eye, and He would make the nations that plundered her become plunder. Zion, he declared, would rejoice when her king came to her, mounted on a donkey. This prophecy was fulfilled in Jesus' earthly ministry and will again be fulfilled in His messianic kingdom. Same as Jebus, Jebusi, Jerusalem, and Salem.

First reference: 2 Samuel 5:7 / Last reference: Zechariah 9:13 / Key references: 2 Samuel 5:7–9; 1 Chronicles 11:4–9; Isaiah 2:1–4; Micah 4; Zechariah 9:9

♀ ZIOR

of times mentioned: OT 1

Meaning: Small

A city that became part of the inheritance of the tribe of Judah following the conquest of the Promised Land.

Only reference: Joshua 15:54

👥 ZIPH

of times mentioned: 2
# of MEN by this name: 2

Meaning: Flowing
1) A descendant of Abraham through Jacob's son Judah.

Only reference: 1 Chronicles 2:42

2) Another descendant of Abraham through Jacob's son Judah.

Only reference: 1 Chronicles 4:16

♀ ZIPH

of times mentioned: OT 8

Meaning: Flowing

1) A city that became part of the inheritance of the tribe of Judah following the conquest of the Promised Land.
    When King Saul pursued him, David stayed in the wilderness of Ziph. At Horesh, in this wilderness, David made a covenant with Saul's son

Jonathan. When the people of Ziph planned to hand David over to Saul, David heard about it and remained in the wilderness of Maon. Later the Ziphites came to Saul at Gibeah and told him where David was hiding. Saul brought his warriors to the wilderness of Ziph. David slipped into their camp at night and took a spear and water jug from beside the king. In the morning, he stood a distance away and confronted Saul's battle commander Abner with his failure to protect the king. David spoke with Saul and showed him the spear, proving that he would not take advantage of the king's vulnerability and kill him during the night.
    King Rehoboam of Judah fortified Ziph to defend his nation.

First reference: Joshua 15:24 / Last reference: 2 Chronicles 11:8

2) A city that became part of the inheritance of the tribe of Judah following the conquest of the Promised Land.

Only reference: Joshua 15:55

👥 ZIPHAH

of times mentioned: 1
# of MEN by this name: 1

Meaning: Flowing

A descendant of Abraham through Jacob's son Judah.

Only reference: 1 Chronicles 4:16

👥 ZIPHION

of times mentioned: 1
# of MEN by this name: 1

Meaning: Watchtower

A descendant of Abraham through Jacob's son Gad.

Only reference: Genesis 46:16

♀ ZIPHRON

of times mentioned: OT 1

Meaning: To be fragrant
A place that God used to identify the borders of Israel when He first gave it to His people.

Only reference: Numbers 34:9

ZIPPOR

of times mentioned: 7
# of MEN by this name: 1

Meaning: Little bird

Father of the Moabite king Balak, who consulted the false prophet Balaam.

First reference: Numbers 22:2 / Last reference: Judges 11:25

ZIPPORAH

of times mentioned: 3
# of WOMEN by this name: 1

Meaning: Bird

Daughter of the Midianite priest Reuel (also known as Jethro) and wife of Moses. She had a disagreement with her husband over the circumcision of their firstborn son.

First reference: Exodus 2:21 / Last reference: Exodus 18:2

ZITHRI

of times mentioned: 1
# of MEN by this name: 1

Meaning: Protective

A descendant of Abraham through Jacob's son Levi.

Only reference: Exodus 6:22

⚲ ZIZ

of times mentioned: OT 1

Meaning: Bloom

A cliff near which the Moabites and Ammonites camped when they planned to attack King Jehoshaphat of Judah. God told the king to go to Ziz, and "at the end of the brook, before the wilderness of Jeruel," he would find his enemies. The Lord promised to fight for Judah. When Judah obeyed God, the Ammonites, the Moabites, and the inhabitants of Seir fought among themselves, and Judah picked up the spoil.

Only reference: 2 Chronicles 20:16

ZIZA

of times mentioned: 2
# of MEN by this name: 2

Meaning: Prominence

1) A descendant of Abraham through Jacob's son Simeon.

Only reference: 1 Chronicles 4:37

2) A son of Judah's king Rehoboam and a grandson of Solomon.

Only reference: 2 Chronicles 11:20

ZIZAH

of times mentioned: 1
# of MEN by this name: 1

Meaning: Prominence

A Levite who was part of David's reorganization of the Levites. Same as Zina.

Only reference: 1 Chronicles 23:11

⚲ ZOAN

of times mentioned: OT 7

An Egyptian city in the northeastern portion of the Nile River delta, Zoan became the capital of northern Egypt during that nation's twenty-fifth dynasty. Taking the unfaithful northern kingdom to task, the psalmist Asaph pointed out that when Israel was in Egypt, at Zoan, God did miracles before the people of Ephraim. Despite Egypt's reputation for its wise men, in his oracle concerning that nation, Isaiah called the officials of Zoan fools. Ezekiel prophesied that God would set Zoan on fire.

First reference: Numbers 13:22 / Last reference: Ezekiel 30:14

⚲ ZOAR

of times mentioned: OT 10

Meaning: Little

A Canaanite city of the plain that Lot looked toward when he chose the plain of the Jordan River as his land. Zoar joined in the Canaanite war against King Chedorlaomer of Elam and his Mesopotamian allies. When destruction was about to fall on Sodom, Lot asked the angels who came to warn him if instead of fleeing to the mountains, he could go to Zoar. The city was not destroyed as a result of Lot's request. He and his family left at dawn, and all except his wife, who was turned into a pillar of salt for looking back, reached the city after sunrise. Afraid to stay in Zoar, Lot and his daughters fled to a cave in the mountains.

When God showed Moses the Promised Land from Mount Nebo, he could see as far as Zoar. The prophet Isaiah foretold that Moab's fugitives would go as far as Zoar when they tried to escape their own nation's destruction. Same as Bela.

First reference: Genesis 13:10 / Last reference: Jeremiah 48:34

ZOBA

of times mentioned: OT 2

Meaning: A station

After their king, Hanun, offended King David, the Ammonites hired men from Zoba to fight against Israel. Same as Zobah.

First reference: 2 Samuel 10:6 / Last reference: 2 Samuel 10:8

ZOBAH

of times mentioned: OT 11

Meaning: A station

A Syrian kingdom with which King Saul battled as he fought the enemies surrounding Israel. When King David sought to control land by the Euphrates River, he fought Hadadezer, son of Zobah's king Rehob, as far as Hamath. David dedicated the plunder from his conflict with Zobah to the Lord. Later Zobah supported the Ammonites as, having offended David, they went to battle with him. Nevertheless, one man of Zobah came to serve David; one of his brave warriors was "Igal the son of Nathan of Zobah" (2 Samuel 23:36).

When David conquered Zobah, Rezon gathered rebels around him and took control of Damascus. During Solomon's lifetime, Rezon was his enemy. Same as Zoba.

First reference: 1 Samuel 14:47 / Last reference: 1 Chronicles 19:6

ZOBEBAH

of times mentioned: 1
# of WOMEN by this name: 1

Meaning: Canopy

Daughter of Coz, a descendant of Abraham through Jacob's son Judah.

Only reference: 1 Chronicles 4:8

ZOHAR

of times mentioned: 4
# of MEN by this name: 2

Meaning: Whiteness

1) Father of Ephron, who sold Abraham a burial place.

First reference: Genesis 23:8 / Last reference: Genesis 25:9

2) Grandson of Jacob through his son Simeon.

First reference: Genesis 46:10 / Last reference: Exodus 6:15

ZOHELETH

of times mentioned: OT 1

Meaning: Crawling (that is, serpent)

A stone south of Jerusalem, near the spring of En-rogel, where King David's son Adonijah sacrificed sheep, oxen, and cattle. Adonijah also invited to this place the royal officials and his brothers—except Solomon—as he attempted to become king of Israel.

Only reference: 1 Kings 1:9

ZOHETH

of times mentioned: 1
# of MEN by this name: 1

A descendant of Abraham through Jacob's son Judah.

Only reference: 1 Chronicles 4:20

ZOPHAH

\# of times mentioned: 2
\# of MEN by this name: 1

Meaning: Breadth

A descendant of Abraham through Jacob's son Asher.

First reference: 1 Chronicles 7:35 / Last reference: 1 Chronicles 7:36

ZOPHAI

\# of times mentioned: 1
\# of MEN by this name: 1

Meaning: Honeycomb

A descendant of Abraham through Jacob's son Levi.

Only reference: 1 Chronicles 6:26

ZOPHAR

\# of times mentioned: 4
\# of MEN by this name: 1

Meaning: Departing

One of three friends of Job who mourned his losses for a week and then accused him of wrongdoing. God ultimately chastised the three for their criticism of Job, commanding them to sacrifice burnt offerings while Job prayed for them.

First reference: Job 2:11 / Last reference: Job 42:9

ZOPHIM

\# of times mentioned: OT 1

Meaning: Watchers

A field near the top of Mount Pisgah where King Balak of Moab built seven altars and burned a bull and a ram on each. He tried to convince Balaam to curse the Israelites, who were about to invade the Promised Land.

Only reference: Numbers 23:14

ZORAH

\# of times mentioned: OT 8

Meaning: Wasp (as stinging)

A town that became part of the inheritance of Dan when Joshua cast lots in Shiloh to provide territory for the seven tribes that had yet to receive their land. Samson's parents lived in Zorah when the angel of the Lord came to them to tell them they would have a son. Samson was buried between Zoar and Eshtaol in the tomb of his father, Manoah. When the Danites were seeking their own land, they sent spies from Zoar and Eshtaol to scout out the land.

First reference: Joshua 19:41 / Last reference: 2 Chronicles 11:10

ZOREAH

\# of times mentioned: OT 1

Meaning: A wasp (as stinging)

A city that became part of the inheritance of the tribe of Judah following the conquest of the Promised Land.

Only reference: Joshua 15:33

ZOROBABEL

\# of times mentioned: 3
\# of MEN by this name: 1

Genealogy of Jesus: Yes (Matthew 1:12)

Meaning: Descended of Babylon

A descendant of Abraham through Isaac; forebear of Jesus' earthly father, Joseph.

First reference: Matthew 1:12 / Last reference: Luke 3:27

ZUAR

\# of times mentioned: 5
\# of MEN by this name: 1

Meaning: Small

Father of a prince of the tribe of Issachar in Moses' day.

First reference: Numbers 1:8 / Last reference: Numbers 10:15

👥 ZUPH

of times mentioned: 2
# of MEN by this name: 1

Meaning: Honeycomb

An ancestor of the prophet Samuel.

First reference: 1 Samuel 1:1 / Last reference: 1 Chronicles 6:35

📍 ZUPH

of times mentioned: OT 1

Meaning: Honeycomb

A district through which Saul passed as he searched for his father's lost donkeys. Saul's servant advised him to seek out Samuel the prophet and ask where they should search. Samuel told them the donkeys had been found and then anointed Saul king of Israel.

Only reference: 1 Samuel 9:5

👥 ZUR

of times mentioned: 5
# of MEN by this name: 2

Meaning: Rock

1) A Midianite king killed by the Israelites at God's command.

First reference: Numbers 25:15 / Last reference: Joshua 13:21

2) A descendant of Abraham through Jacob's son Benjamin, and a relative of King Saul.

First reference: 1 Chronicles 8:30 / Last reference: 1 Chronicles 9:36

👥 ZURIEL

of times mentioned: 1
# of MEN by this name: 1

Meaning: Rock of God

A chief of the Levites under Eleazar (1).

Only reference: Numbers 3:35

👥 ZURISHADDAI

of times mentioned: 5
# of MEN by this name: 1

Meaning: Rock of the Almighty

Father of a prince of Simeon in Moses' day.

First reference: Numbers 1:6 / Last reference: Numbers 10:19

MAPS

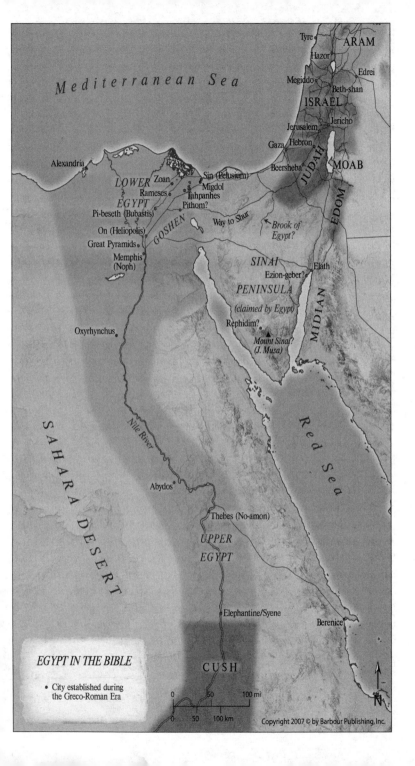

EGYPT IN THE BIBLE

• City established during the Greco-Roman Era

Copyright 2007 © by Barbour Publishing, Inc.

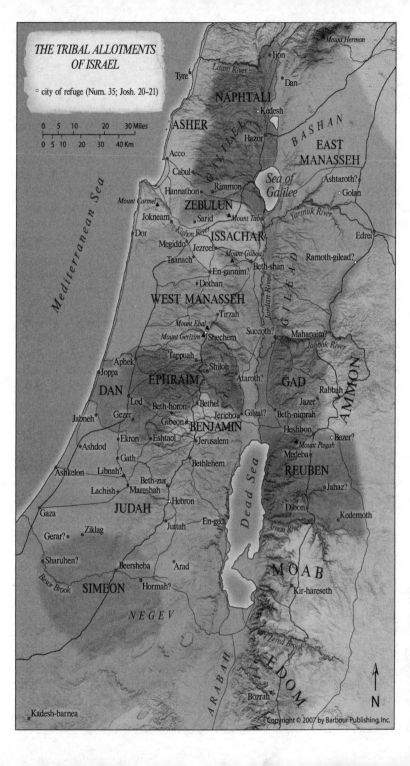

THE TRIBAL ALLOTMENTS
OF ISRAEL

° city of refuge (Num. 35; Josh. 20–21)

0   5   10   20   30 Miles
0 5 10   20   30   40 Km

Mediterranean Sea

Mount Hermon

Tyre
Litani River
Ijon
Dan

NAPHTALI
ASHER
Kedesh
Hazor
Acco
Cabul
Rimmon
Hannathon
Sea of Galilee

BASHAN
EAST MANASSEH
Ashtaroth?
Golan

Mount Carmel
ZEBULUN
Sarid
Mount Tabor
Yarmuk River
Jokneam
Dor
Megiddo
Kishon River
ISSACHAR
Jezreel
Mount Gilboa
Beth-shan
Edrei
Taanach
En-gannim?
Dothan
Ramoth-gilead?

WEST MANASSEH
Tirzah
Mount Ebal
Mount Gerizim
Shechem
Succoth?
Mahanaim?
Jabbok River
Tappuah
Shiloh
Ataroth?
GAD
AMMON
Aphek
EPHRAIM
Joppa
Rabbah
Lod
Beth-horon
Bethel
Jazer
Gezer
Gibeon
Jericho
Gilgal?
Beth-nimrah
Jabneh
BENJAMIN
Heshbon
Ekron
Eshtaol
Jerusalem
Bezer?
Ashdod
Mount Pisgah
Gath
Medeba
Ashkelon
Libnah?
Bethlehem
REUBEN
Lachish
Beth-zur
Mareshah
Jahaz?
Gaza
Hebron
Dibon
Kedemoth
JUDAH
En-gedi
Dead Sea
Gerar?
Ziklag
Juttah
Sharuhen?
Beersheba
Arad
MOAB
SIMEON
Hormah?
Kir-hareseth
Bezor Brook
NEGEV
Arnon River

ARABAH
Zered Brook
EDOM
Bozrah

Kadesh-barnea

N

Copyright © 2007 by Barbour Publishing, Inc.

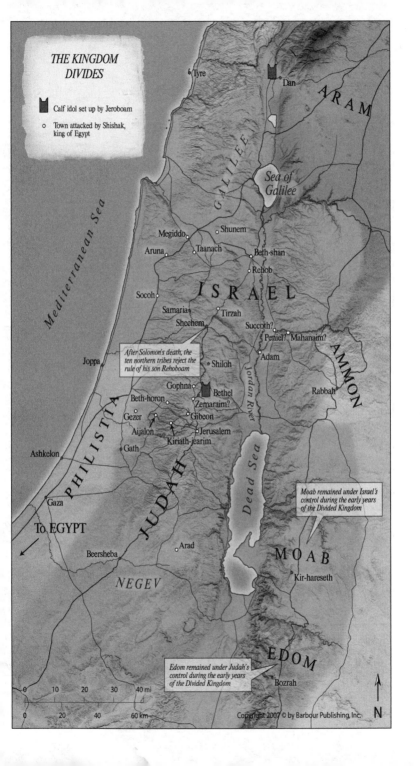

THE KINGDOM DIVIDES

Calf idol set up by Jeroboam

o Town attacked by Shishak, king of Egypt

Mediterranean Sea

Tyre

Dan

ARAM

GALILEE

Sea of Galilee

Megiddo

Shunem

Aruna

Taanach

Beth-shan

Rehob

ISRAEL

Socoh

Samaria

Tirzah

Shechem

Succoth?

Peniel?

Mahanaim?

AMMON

After Solomon's death, the ten northern tribes reject the rule of his son Rehoboam

Shiloh

Adam

Jordan River

Gophna

Bethel

Rabbah

Beth-horon

Zemaraim?

Gezer

Gibeon

Aijalon

Jerusalem

Kiriath-jearim

Joppa

PHILISTIA

Gath

Ashkelon

JUDAH

Moab remained under Israel's control during the early years of the Divided Kingdom

Gaza

TO EGYPT

Beersheba

Arad

Dead Sea

MOAB

NEGEV

Kir-hareseth

Edom remained under Judah's control during the early years of the Divided Kingdom

EDOM

Bozrah

0 10 20 30 40 mi

0 20 40 60 km

Copyright 2007 © by Barbour Publishing, Inc.

N

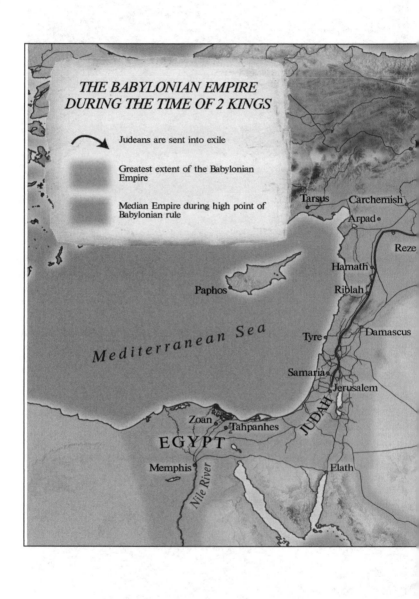

THE BABYLONIAN EMPIRE
DURING THE TIME OF 2 KINGS

Judeans are sent into exile

Greatest extent of the Babylonian
Empire

Median Empire during high point of
Babylonian rule

Tarsus   Carchemish

Arpad

Reze

Hamath

Riblah

Paphos

Mediterranean Sea

Tyre   Damascus

Samaria

Jerusalem

JUDAH

Zoan   Tahpanhes

EGYPT

Memphis   Nile River   Elath

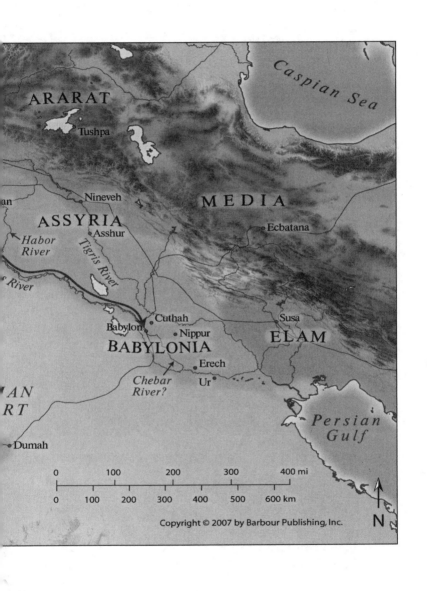

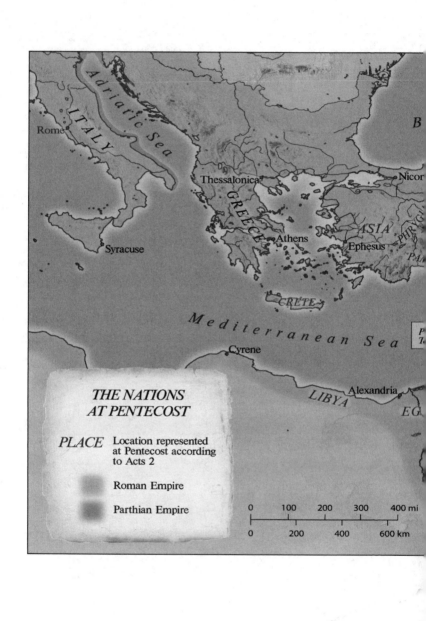

THE NATIONS
AT PENTECOST

PLACE   Location represented
at Pentecost according
to Acts 2

Roman Empire

Parthian Empire

Caspian Sea

PONTUS

Artaxata

CAPPADOCIA

Melitene

MEDIA

PARTHIA

Antioch

Ecbatana

Dura-Europas

MESOPOTAMIA

SYRIA

Ctesiphon

Susa

ELAM

Jerusalem

DEAD

ARABIA

Persian
Gulf

ARABIAN
DESERT

Tema

Red
Sea

N

PAUL'S VOYAGE
TO ROME

Black Sea

BITHYNIA & PONTUS

Adramyttium

A S I A

Ephesus

GALATIA

CAPPADOCIA

idus

LYCIA

PAMPHYLIA

CILICIA

Antioch (Syria)

RHODES

Myra

CYPRUS

S Y R I A

Mediterranean Sea

100   50 mi

200   75 km

Sidon

Caesarea

PALESTINE

Jerusalem

E

T E

Gortyna

a

Alexandria

E G Y P T

N

AVENS

Copyright © 2007 by Barbour Publishing, Inc.

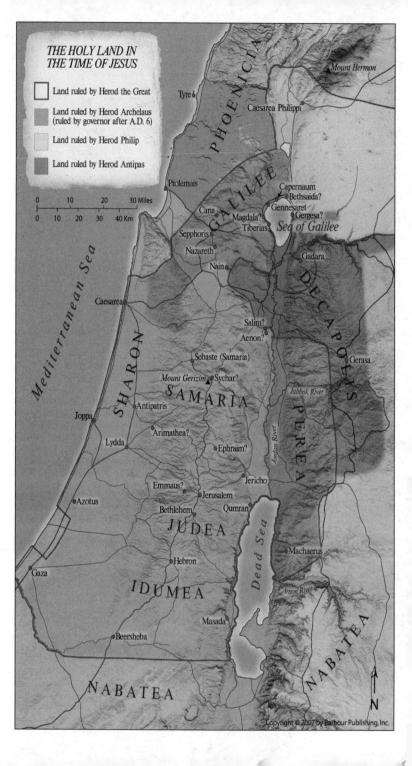

THE HOLY LAND IN
THE TIME OF JESUS

Land ruled by Herod the Great

Land ruled by Herod Archelaus
(ruled by governor after A.D. 6)

Land ruled by Herod Philip

Land ruled by Herod Antipas

| 0 | 10 | 20 | 30 Miles |
| 0 | 10 | 20 | 30 | 40 Km |

Mount Hermon

Tyre

PHOENICIA

Caesarea Philippi

Ptolemais

GALILEE

Capernaum
Bethsaida?
Cana
Gennesaret
Magdala?
Gergesa?
Tiberias
Sea of Galilee

Sepphoris

Nazareth

Gadara

Nain

DECAPOLIS

Caesarea

Mediterranean Sea

SHARON

Salim?
Aenon?

Sebaste (Samaria)

Mount Gerizim Sychar?

SAMARIA

Gerasa

Jabbok River

Antipatris

Joppa

Arimathea?

Lydda

PEREA

Ephraim?

Jordan River

Emmaus?

Jericho

Azotus

Jerusalem

Qumran

Bethlehem

JUDEA

Dead Sea

Gaza

Hebron

Machaerus

IDUMEA

Arnon River

Masada

NABATEA

Beersheba

NABATEA

N

Copyright © 2007 by Barbour Publishing, Inc.